Church and Revolution

Church

and

Revolution

Catholics in the Struggle
for Democracy
and Social
Justice

THOMAS
BOKENKOTTER

IMAGE BOOKS
DOUBLEDAY
New York   London   Toronto   Sydney   Auckland

AN IMAGE BOOK
PUBLISHED BY DOUBLEDAY
a division of Bantam Doubleday Dell Publishing Group, Inc.
1540 Broadway, New York, New York 10036

IMAGE, DOUBLEDAY, and the portrayal of a deer drinking from
a stream are trademarks of Doubleday, a division of
Bantam Doubleday Dell Publishing Group, Inc.

Library of Congress Cataloging-in-Publication Data

Bokenkotter, Thomas S.
Church and revolution : Catholics in the struggle for democracy and
social justice / by Thomas Bokenkotter.
p.   cm.
Includes bibliographical references and index.
1. Christianity and justice—Catholic Church—History—19th
century.   2. Christianity and justice—Catholic Church—
History—20th century.   3. Democracy—Religious aspects—Catholic
Church—History—19th century.   4. Democracy—Religious aspects—
Catholic Church—History—20th century.   5. Catholic Church—
History—19th century.   6. Catholic Church—History—20th century.
I. Title.
BX1795.J87B65   1998
261.8'088'22—dc21   97-49429
CIP

ISBN 0-385-48754-1

1   3   5   7   9   10   8   6   4   2

Contents

Contents

Introduction

THIS BOOK deals with an interesting historical question: How did the Catholic Church—which, on the morrow of the French Revolution, was one of the most conservative and even reactionary of the world powers—become, by the mid-twentieth century, a very progressive force in world affairs? As the well-known journalist Murray Kempton said in 1996, the Catholic Church is today the leading defender of human rights in the world. In its famous document "The Church in the Modern World" *(Gaudium et Spes),* the Second Vatican Council ranged over the whole gamut of contemporary social issues and put itself on record as totally committed to the struggle for greater social justice in every sector of human life. The council transformed the Church into a principled supporter of the institutions, practices, and principles of the free society. The Catholic Church was, in fact, the only institution behind the Iron Curtain that consistently opposed Communist oppression. In consequence, historians credit it with a major role in bringing down the totalitarian system. Moreover, in his many journeys the present pope hardly allows an occasion to pass during which he does not insist on the need for greater equality and respect for human rights, and the need to alleviate endemic poverty.

The history of the gradual awakening of the Catholic social conscience has been studied by numerous scholars, and the overall lines of development are pretty well agreed on. One of the latest studies, *Social Catholicism in Europe (From the Onset of Industrialization to the First World War)* by Paul Misner,[1] covers a good part of the ground very well. I don't intend to repeat his fine analysis. What I am trying to do here is tell the story from a different angle—mainly through the lives of those Catholics I regard as prime movers in raising the Catholic social consciousness.

I've assembled therefore a number of remarkable personalities, "Social Catholics" whose dramatic lives span the two centuries that have elapsed since the French Revolution. They are spread across the spectrum of religious, intellectual, national, and social categories. They include the convert English cardinal Henry Manning; two French priests, Felicité de Lamennais and Henri Lacordaire; the devout French academician Frederick Ozanam; as well as two other French laymen, Count Montalembert and Albert de Mun. Also included are the Italian priest Don Sturzo, foe of Mussolini; the great Irish emancipator Daniel O'Connell; plus the two Irish Catholic revolutionaries Michael Collins and Eamon de Valera. There are also chapters on two brilliant converts: Jacques Maritain, who was French, and the American Dorothy Day. Finally, the last section focuses on the French journalist Emmanuel Mounier, the German chancellor Konrad Adenauer, the Salvadoran archbishop Oscar Romero, and the Polish factory worker and electrician Lech Walesa. I thought Karl Marx should be included because of his impact on the Social Catholics. I've also devoted a chapter to the arch reactionary and curial associate of Pope Pius X, Monsignor Umberto Benigni, to convey some idea of the incredible resistance encountered by the Social Catholics as they struggled to bring the Church into the modern world.

I have called this book *Church and Revolution* because these Catholics were often intimately involved in the revolutions that have shaken Western society over the past two centuries and helped to fashion the Church's response to them, especially to the French Revolution and the Marxist revolutions. The Catholics I've focused on here were, I believe, illustrative of Political and Social Catholicism at its best. I believe they were people of formidable courage and social imagination, and I feel they should be a perpetual inspiration to all of us who pray for the continual advancement of Christ's kingdom of justice and peace in the world.

[1] New York: Crossroad, 1991.

Church and Revolution

ONE

The French
Revolution
(1789–1914)

EATH, near and seemingly inescapable, threatened the Catholic Church but God took pity . . . He opened the treasury of His mercy and sent the Revolution. People saw only its horrible side; they still had to see its salutary consequences. Without it where would it be? Nothing less than this storm could have swept away the deadly fog which covered a stagnant and polluted society. The Revolution was for France the pangs of birth; for the Catholic Church it was a rebirth." These were the words of Félicité de Lamennais. Ironically, he later concluded that the Church's refusal to come to terms with the Revolution spelled its doom.[1]

The French Revolution was indeed a watershed of Church history. The Catholic Church in France was torn apart by the Revolution. Clergy and faithful lay people were massacred, thirty thousand of France's priests were deported, and the Church's property was confiscated, its commanding station in French society radically diminished. Few historical events, in fact, have had such damaging consequences for the Catholic Church. Nor was the damage confined to France; thanks to the expansionist policy of its

---

[1] Henri Girard, *Un Catholique Romantique: Frédéric Ozanam* (Paris: Éditions de la Nouvelle Revue Critique), pp. 18–19.

leaders, the "benefits" of the Revolution were extended to the many areas of Europe later conquered by the revolutionary army under Napoleon. Indeed the European Church's experience of the Revolution was so profoundly negative that, for more than a hundred years afterward, most Catholics, European ones at least, instinctively rejected the liberal political and social ideas associated with the Revolution.

And yet few would have predicted the Revolution would have such a disastrous outcome for the Catholic Church.

France's Fiscal Crisis

In the late 1780s, France was plunged into a revolutionary situation by a fiscal crisis that greatly weakened the monarchy. The expense of France's part in the American War of Independence created a deficit of 20 percent, with interest on the public debt consuming 318 million livres or more than half the total expenditure. This fiscal crisis was used by the aristocracy to challenge the authority of the king while carrying on a policy of obstructionism through the Parlements, judicial bodies with a veto over legislation. As a solution, the king's finance minister Charles Alexandre de Calonne offered a direct tax on all landowners. It would have remedied many of the most glaring inequities of the system, not least the burdensome feudal duties still imposed on the peasants. But he failed to get his reforms through the Assembly of Notables. When his successor, the Archbishop Loménie de Brienne, failed also to get a reform through the Parlement of Paris, he tried stripping the Parlements of their power to block reform—a move that caused civil disturbances around the country.

The only alternative was to call a general assembly of clergy, aristocracy, and people—the States General. But before they could be gathered, Loménie de Brienne himself was replaced by Jacques Necker, a Swiss-born financier and the only man thought capable of averting total financial chaos. Unfortunately he was not the one suited to guide the country through its perilous passage from absolute to constitutional monarchy.

The election of the deputies to the States General underscored the privileged status of the nobles and clergy. Each male member of the nobility over the age of twenty-five could vote, as could each bishop and parish priest. On the other hand, the members of the third estate who were at least twenty-five could vote only indirectly; that is, the voting was in stages so that those elected at the first stage had to convene again to elect a percentage of their number. This process was repeated at a third and sometimes even a fourth stage, depending on the locale.

The parochial clergy for the most part welcomed the meeting of the estates, and showed their democratic tendencies and also their suspicion of the bishops. They elected mostly pastors of parishes and only forty-six bishops out of the total of 301 clergy.

The deputies took with them to Versailles lists of the reforms desired by their constituents. These "cahiers" still remain in the archives and paint a fascinating picture of the economic, social, and political condition of France in the spring of 1789. As the cahiers show, there was much agreement between the orders over such urgent tasks of reform as the need for a constitution, for individual liberty and liberty of the press, for decentralization, and for an end to royal despotism. They also show that the privileged classes were not ready to surrender their privileges and accept equality whether political, social, or fiscal.

The cahiers indicate that the Revolution began with hardly any trace of the anticlericalism that would later do so much damage. "The evidence of the *cahiers de doléance* suggests that religion was not a major issue in 1789; only 10% called for abolition of the tithe, only 4% for abolition of the great monastic houses and only 2% for the sale of all ecclesiastical land."[2] What was particularly of concern was a better distribution of the Church's wealth, with less going to the higher and more to the lower clergy, who were often very poor.

The cahiers of the first estate suggest that many of the parish clergy were sympathetic to these proposals, especially those concerned about the maldistribution of the Church's revenues. They also shared some of the political aspirations found in the other cahiers.

The Gathering Storm

Amid growing tension the States General were formally opened by Louis XVI after a stately ceremonial procession at Versailles on May 5, 1789. The deputies immediately clashed over the issue of how to verify their credentials. The third estate insisted they should be verified in common, but the

[2]T.C.W. Blanning, "The Role of Religion in European Counter-revolution," in *History, Society and the Churches,* D. Beales and G. Best, eds., (Cambridge, England: University Press, 1985), p. 199.

nobles and the clergy demurred because they believed this would lead to voting in common too.

The third estate went ahead anyway and verified the credentials. Soon after, the clergy began to align themselves with the third estate. The first to do so were three priest-deputies from the province of Poitevin. In "crossing over," they declared: "We come, Messieurs, preceded by the torch of reason, moved by love of the commonweal, to take our places at the side of our fellow citizens, or our brothers."[3] On June 22 the archbishop of Vienne led 150 clerical deputies (out of a total of 295) to join the commons.

The moderates might have worked out a compromise but were unable to prevail against radicals like the Abbé Emmanuel Sieyès, Bishop Henri Grégoire, and Issac René Guy le Chapelier on the one side and, on the other, reactionaries like Jean Cardinal Maury and Jean-Jacques d'Éprémesnil, a leading *parlementaire,* who were opposed to all compromise.[4] The latter were able to stymie Necker, who saw that the king could save his authority only by seizing the initiative—meeting with the deputies and himself proposing some liberal reforms. But the hard-liners prevailed with the king and a royal séance was delayed until June 23.

The royal session on June 23 proved to be a turning point. The king made it perfectly clear that there were to be no fundamental alterations in the feudal order. The estates were to preserve their ancient distinction by meeting separately, except where they might agree to decide together some issues of common concern. Certain reforms, such as an end to arbitrary arrest and press censorship, were deemed acceptable but there was to be no derogation of the fiscal immunities of the first two orders except those they might surrender voluntarily. "The throne thereby committed itself to preservation of the traditional social hierarchy and aristocratic preeminence. As a result of this decision the Revolution was to mean the conquest of equality of rights."[5]

After dismissing the assembly, the king left. The third estate remained, however, and when an emissary of the king reminded them of the king's orders, Honoré Comte de Mirabeau thundered out their defiance: "Sir,

[3] Quoted in review of Norman Ravitch, "The Catholic Church and the French Nation, 1589–1989," *Commonweal* (July 12, 1991), p. 442.

[4] Norman Hampson, *A Social History of the French Revolution* (London: Routledge and Kegan Paul, 1963), p. 65.

[5] Georges Lefebvre, *The French Revolution From Its Origins to 1793* (New York: Columbia University Press, 1962), p. 113.

. . . you have no right to speak here . . . Go tell the king we shall not stir . . . save at the point of the bayonet."[6]

Here again the clergy played a decisive role in forcing the hand of the king when, on June 24, they once again joined the defiant commons. The king appeared to yield on June 27 when he ordered the privileged orders to fuse with the third estate. His concentration of troops in the vicinity of Paris, however, sent a different signal.

There is no doubt that the lethargic king, by his weak and vacillating response to the crisis, bore great responsibility for the disasters that were to follow. A strong king would have seized the opportunity to mediate between the two sides and not have let events overtake him as Louis did. Thus "the transition to a limited monarchy might have been achieved without resort to counter-revolution on the one hand or appeal to mass violence on the other."[7]

When June turned into July the mood of Paris became increasingly anxious as the king's German and Swiss mercenaries moved to surround the capital. Public opinion became increasingly radical, and sporadic outbreaks of mob violence and riots over bread-rationing occurred daily. Hunger mobilized the people. The Revolution, in fact, began in conjunction with a rise in prices that was starving the masses. Cereals represented the main item in the budget of the lower classes; it is most significant that the year 1789 saw a total increase of 127 percent in the price of wheat and 136 percent in the price of rye, while wages lagged far behind.

Aggravating the rise in prices was a rise in the population. Catastrophes no longer erased whole age groups, while the average life expectancy at birth had risen to twenty-nine years by the time of the Revolution. France's population had reached twenty-five million. Unemployment may well have reached 50 percent in the towns while the cost of living increased by about 15 to 20 percent. It was, therefore, surely no coincidence that the uprising began in July when the prices of wheat and rye reached the highest point of the entire eighteenth century.

The potential for insurrection built up to a critical mass when news reached Paris on Sunday, July 12, that Necker had been dismissed. The city exploded in fury. Crowds of people gathered around orators who harangued them and urged them to take up arms. One of the obvious places to find

[6]Quoted in Albert Goodwin, *The French Revolution* (New York: Harper & Brothers, 1962), p. 70.

[7]Goodwin, *The French Revolution,* p. 71.

arms was the Bastille, a towering ancient fortress in the east end of Paris. It was also a target because of its menacing cannon that was pointed at the populace. A crowd of Parisians and members of a recently formed urban militia surrounded the massive structure. The Bastille's commander Governor de Launay seemed willing to negotiate and agreed not to fire on the attackers while negotiating. But a misunderstanding occurred when the drawbridge fell and the mob pressed into the inner court, where they were sprayed with bullets by the garrison's mercenaries. Not knowing that two of their own had dropped the drawbridge, the attackers thought they had been booby-trapped by de Launay. Furious and no longer willing to accept the commander's offer to surrender they successfully stormed the citadel, sliced off de Launay's head, and carried it through the street on a pike.

The Bonfire of Privilege

The fall of the Bastille was hailed around the world as a great victory for human freedom. It told the court in unmistakable terms that the third estate was now in charge. Bowing to necessity, the king recalled his troops that were ringed around the capital. The victory of the people was further underscored by the king's personal visit to the capital on July 17, the adoption of the tricolor as the national flag, and the formation of the new municipal Commune of Paris.

The fall of the Bastille also sent a message to those in the towns and cities who were only too ready to seize the chance to overturn the old oppressive order. Spontaneously, peaceably in some places but violently in others, the bourgeoisie along with the starving poor wrested control from the central government and halted the collection of taxes. The first tenuous forms of democracy and popular power began to appear.

Nor was the lesson of the Bastille lost on the peasants who were already angered by the failure of the National Assembly to show any concern for their plight as they staggered under the disastrous effects of the bad harvests of 1789—the worst of the century. Brandishing pitchforks and muskets they besieged the chateaux, burned many of them down, and destroyed the papers that contained the hated titles to feudal dues.

The peasant uprising frightened even the deputies at Versailles, who were not alarmed by the municipal revolts that were controlled by and served the interests of the middle class. The peasant revolts were a different matter: The work of a dispossessed rural proletariat, they constituted a grave threat to order and to the sacred principle of private property.

The deputies were caught in a painful dilemma. They could hardly do without the support of the peasants but to suppress them they would need the king and his army, thus giving Louis the chance to recover much of his lost authority. The solution crafted by members of the Breton Club[8] was to appease the peasants by inducing the liberal aristocrats to make a voluntary renunciation of their feudal rights and privileges. Their example, it was hoped, would prove contagious and persuade the more conservative nobility to follow suit.

The plan worked beyond the expectations of its authors. The first to act was one of the wealthiest nobles, who stood up and renounced feudal dues that were worth an enormous sum. His example proved contagious. Nobles rose in rapid succession to divest themselves of some of their privileges, such as seigneurial justice and exclusive hunting rights.

This voluntary sacrifice was remarkable but actually much less complete than appeared at first. Second thoughts in the following week led them to backslide and they made the most onerous feudal dues redeemable in cash. The clergy, for their part, were concerned about their tithes and even questioned the validity of the whole affair—a move that boomeranged when the anticlerical majority retaliated by deciding for total abolition of tithes.

Whereas the middle class benefited the most from the sacrifice of privilege, the peasants did make some real gains. The end of their personal servitude and the termination of seigneurial justice were not insignificant reforms.

"The Rights of Man"

Fiscal and ecclesiastical reform had also begun and a constitution was in the making. The need was now felt to step back and analyze the basic principles that would guide the deputies in drawing up a constitution. They wanted to proclaim to the world the meaning of their revolution, to set forth their political creed, and to set up a clear standard by which future acts of the government might be measured. Their great Declaration of the Rights of Man was approved by the Constituent Assembly on August 26, 1789.

It was not to be a mere list of abstract ideals but a statement of principles rooted in and reflective of actual human experience. It would reflect the insights of the Enlightenment as well as Christian belief in the dignity of the

---

[8] Founded by Breton deputies, it evolved into the Jacobin Club.

individual. There was also the felt need to improve upon both the English and the American Bill of Rights. In enunciating these rights of man it is also noteworthy that the deputies paid homage to the "Supreme Being" and invoked His blessing on their endeavor.

The rights they proclaimed were those of man as a citizen sharing in both the rights and duties flowing from membership in society. They were thought of as natural rights and were enumerated as liberty, property, security, and resistance to oppression. Liberty was defined as "the power of doing whatever does not injure another" and was further specified as the right to speak, write, and publish freely one's opinions, even the religious ones, as long as there was no abusive use of this power. Liberty also entailed freedom from arbitrary arrest.

While the concept of natural rights formed one pillar of the Declaration, the other was formed by its doctrine of national sovereignty: Authority stemmed not from the king but from the will of the people (embodied in the state).

In spite of its great contribution to the world's dialogue on freedom, the Declaration was no doubt seriously flawed. Critics have scored it as individualistic and totalitarian, defects that put serious limits on the exercise of freedom. It is individualistic inasmuch as its concept of human freedom does not include the freedom of citizens to organize in the pursuit of common goals. Religious freedom is interpreted as "freedom of opinion," not as the freedom of corporate worship, mission, and teaching by a confessional body. Economic freedom consists of the right to own property, not the right to form workers' unions. Intellectual freedom emerges as the right to express one's beliefs, not the right to operate schools. "This atomistic individualism guided the subsequent Jacobin persecution of the church, the abolition of the corporation and the weakening of the family in the name of individual freedom."[9]

It is also totalitarian inasmuch as it ascribes all authority to the state without sanctioning the network of intermediate social bodies (family, church, economic association) that traditionally exercised corporate rights not thought to be derived from the state. Against this total power of the state the individual is left naked and powerless to resist. "God emerges less as the source of the rights of the inviolate person than as the soul of the nation-state whose decisions now carry divine authority."[10]

---

[9] John Conley, "The Bicentennial of a Political Idea," *America* (June 24, 1989), p. 575.
[10] Ibid., p. 594.

Lord Acton's judgment is still worth noting: "The errors that ruined their enterprise may be reduced to one. Having put the nation in the place of the Crown, they invested it with the same unlicensed power, raising no security and no remedy against oppression from below, assuming, or believing, that a government truly representing the people could do no wrong. They acted as if authority, duly constituted, requires no check, and as if no barriers are needed against the nation."[11]

The king refused to sanction the Declaration and once again decided to use force to put down the Revolution. The Flemish troops he called in showed utter contempt for the Revolution and trampled on its symbol, the national cockade. Word of this soon reached Paris and the city exploded. A shortage of food had already caused great distress and a mob of hungry women set out for Versailles, followed by Lafayette and the National Guard. Intimidated by the riotous mob that nearly murdered the queen, the king yielded to their demand to return with them to Paris.

The assembly followed the king to Paris and there continued to meet the challenge of reform. Its achievements were no doubt remarkable. As Acton says, "The States General of 1789 are the most memorable of all political assemblies. They cleared away the history of France and with 2500 decrees they laid down the plan of a new world for men who were reared in the old."[12] Many of its administrative and judicial reforms endure to the present day, not least the division of France into eighty-three departments to replace the old provinces.

Conflict with the Church

Up to this point an alliance of the Church and the Revolution seemed possible. The virulent anticlericalism that would later surface was minimal, as we have seen, while the lower clergy manifested democratic tendencies and appeared generally sympathetic to the liberal direction of the Revolution—most notably when they voted to join with the third estate on June 19 and helped to stiffen its resistance to the king at the time of the Tennis Court Oath. In fact, conflict between the Revolution and the Church did not erupt until the deputies unilaterally took it upon themselves to reform the Church, an institution that was older than the three estates, older than the

[11]John E. D. Acton, *Lectures on the French Revolution* (New York: The Noonday Press, 1959), p. 199.
[12]Ibid., p. 198.

feudal system, older than the Crown. The quarrel that ensued would retard the reconciliation of the Church and liberalism for over a century.

There was indeed a need for reform. The Church was by no means a "perfect society." It was immensely rich, possessing as much as 10 percent of the land surface of France. Its ills, moreover, were apparent to any observer with a sharp eye: Many of its monasteries were half empty and yet very rich, and in the eyes of critics were occupied by idle men who led lives unredeemed by any social utility. Voltaire's sharp tongue expressed the feelings of many when he called the monks useless men who took inviolable oaths to be slaves and fools and live at the expense of other people. On the other hand, orders such as the Capuchins and Carthusians and the numerous teaching and charitable orders of nuns were highly respected for their zeal and labors.

One of the few but spectacular church scandals of the time involved Cardinal de Rohan, the prince bishop of Strasbourg. Madly in love with Marie Antoinette, he intended to seduce her with a magnificent diamond necklace he planned to give her at night in the royal park. But he was tricked when one of his creditors sent a decoy, disguised as the queen, who grabbed the necklace and ran. The de Rohan scandal pointed up a glaring weakness of the system of appointments in the Church: the monopoly over them held by the aristocratic families. Their sons were often installed in episcopal palaces before they were dry behind the ears—as had been the case with de Rohan. Although most of them led lives untouched by scandal, they were often more interested in worldly affairs and the gossip of the court than in spiritual matters.

Another of the scandalous inequities of the system was the distribution of the Church's wealth. At the top, luxury abounded in the episcopal palaces and even in the houses of many of the religious orders whose abbots and abbesses lived and traveled around in princely style. At the same time, the hard-working "lower" clergy and parish priests often had to eke out a living in their humble abodes while leading lives of service.

How much alienation from the Church was there before the Revolution? Recent studies have indicated that the Church was losing ground during the last half of the eighteenth century. According to Ralph Gibson, much of this decline can be explained by the attempt of the clergy to impose a model of Catholicism that was no longer viable for the mass of Catholics. The model they used was still basically the one bequeathed to them by the Council of Trent (although its roots reached well back into the Middle Ages): a severely authoritarian, strictly hierarchical form of religion, "an intellectual's religion, hostile to popular culture; [one that] rejected the world as a vale of tears and a den of iniquity; it emphasized morality, and particularly a repressive sexual morality, rather than spiritual values; it was dominated by clerics who combated all forms of spontaneous religious expression by laymen; and it relied heavily on the threat of damnation to keep the faithful in line."[13] Thus while calling for reforms the clergy still hoped to reinforce this model, a model increasingly rejected by the third estate.[14] This basic disharmony of views helps to explain much of the later conflict of the clergy with the third estate.

A certain incompatibility between Catholicism and rising capitalism may well have contributed to the estrangement of the elite. The bourgeoisie saw the world as something to be manipulated and transformed; Catholicism saw it as resting in the hands of God, who intervened constantly in its operations. The bourgeoisie tended to be optimistic about the possibility of progress, which seemed to be negated by the Church's emphasis on original sin. The Church preached charity to the poor while the bourgeoisie saw them as shiftless. The bourgeoisie regarded lending at interest as a vital part of the economy while the Church condemned it as the sin of usury. And the bourgeois tried to make as much money as he could while the Church frowned on this attitude.

But in spite of people's growing disaffection with it, the pervasive presence of the Church was simply a fact of life in France. Nor was there initially much thought in the National Assembly of trying to change this situation. The cahiers called for correction of the various abuses and such reforms as a more just allocation of revenue and a restructuring of dioceses and parishes. Something also had to be done about such things as the excessive number of holy days, the system of tithes and clerical fees, and the decayed state of many of the religious orders. Ecclesiastical tithes were abolished in the great bonfire of privileges that took place on August 4. The next step was taken with a proposal to expropriate the immense property of the Church in order to save the country from bankruptcy. The government obligated itself in turn to pay the salaries of the clergy and to take over the costs of poor relief, public education, and public worship formerly defrayed by the Church. Though opposition from the clergy was substantial, the bill passed by 568 to 346.

[13] Ralph Gibson, *A Social History of French Catholicism 1789–1914* (New York: Routledge, 1989), p. 15.
[14] Ibid., p. 33.

Even more clerical opposition was aroused by the National Assembly's espousal of religious toleration and its refusal to recognize the Catholic Church as the state religion with exclusive rights over public worship. But the move that proved fatal for the future of the Revolution was one that seemed logical to many deputies. Since they were now in charge of the Church's finances, they felt they had the right to determine how the money would be spent; that is, they wanted the Church reorganized along more rational and more national lines. Like the country, the church was to be regenerated by the Revolution—if necessary, in spite of itself. These deputies' view of the omnipotent authority of the state led them to believe they could reorganize the Church without consulting either the pope or the bishops. This was the kind of reasoning behind the creation of the Civil Constitution of the Clergy of July 12, 1790, which precipitated a decisive rupture.

The constitution made a number of radical changes in church procedures: Bishops and pastors were to be elected by the people and were made subject to the disciplinary control of the state; all jurisdictional links with the pope were severed while communion with him as head of the Church was retained. The dioceses were reduced in number from 135 to 83 (to make their boundaries correspond to the departments) and the parishes were reorganized on more rational lines.

In themselves these changes were not obviously as absurd as reactionaries thought. The long Gallican tradition in the French Church had always stood for a large degree of independence from Rome. Nor was election of bishops unheard of in the history of the Church. And the disciplinary control over the clergy that was granted to the laity might be beneficial in dealing with such obvious abuses as nonresidence of the clergy. There was definitely a need to correct the gross inequities in clerical salaries, and finally the deputies made no claim to authority over doctrinal questions. But the upshot of the reforms was that the Church would no longer be an independent corporation in the hands of the clergy but would be based firmly on the sovereignty of the French people—hence the right of all active citizens to vote in elections to Church office.

That the clergy would ever accept popular sovereignty applied to the Church was a dubious proposition. But their immediate response was only partially negative. For instance, they strenuously objected to elections that would allow anticlericals, heretics, and even atheists to vote for parish priests and bishops. Where the assembly disastrously miscalculated, however, was in its unilateral way of instituting these reforms. In the eyes of many of the clergy this was a violation of the Church's spiritual authority.

Some leaders of the hierarchy thought the issue could be resolved if the Church were at least given the opportunity to confirm the reforms. This could have been done at either an episcopal synod or national council or by the pope. These possibilities failed, however. The deputies rejected a synod or council for fear of it becoming a forum for counterrevolutionary propaganda. Moreover, their totalitarian idea of popular sovereignty did not really allow for negotiation with the Church. They did tacitly allow the bishops to appeal to the pope for authorization, but Pius VI, a rather weak and ineffectual man, dillydallied instead of replying.

Losing patience, the assembly crossed the Rubicon on November 27, 1790, and required all priests holding office to swear an oath to uphold the constitution or be dismissed. They felt the clergy would grumble but ultimately go along with it; they couldn't imagine that the clergy would be willing to sacrifice their livelihood over a theological subtlety. Assembly members were in for a rude awakening: nearly half the clergy and all but seven bishops refused to take the oath.

The sticking point was over the ultimate source of authority. For the deputies, national sovereignty was indivisible and absolute and all bodies within the society were subject to it, including the Church. For many of the clergy, on the other hand—especially those deeply committed to the Tridentine (from Trent) hierarchical model—the idea of the clergy being subjected to lay control was simply unacceptable. Still, a large majority of the clergy might have taken the oath had it included some kind of clause like "excepting in spiritual matters."

Scenes of pathos were enacted in the assembly as the clerical deputies rose to take or refuse the oath. The bishop of Agen tried to speak but the deputies of the Left shouted him down. He tried again: "It is with a heart torn by grief . . ." ("Hear, hear," from the Right); but he was again shouted down. Finally, after further interruptions, the bishop finished his speech, the gist of which was that he would not take the oath.

Emotion also ran high in the parishes on the Sunday designated for pastors to take the oath. At the packed church of Saint Sulpice the curé gave a fiery sermon on hell, then began to attack the National Assembly. Cries of "Order!" filled the air as the organist drowned out the curé's remarks with the revolutionary song *Ça Ira*. In villages and towns all over France, pitched battles occurred when an elected constitutional priest arrived to take over a parish.

As one might surmise, all sorts of reasons entered into the decision to take or refuse the oath. Devout men who took the oath, nearly half of the clergy, were persuaded by the fact that the pope himself had not spoken, due to the long tradition of Gallicanism in France and to all sorts of pastoral, social, and political pressures as well. Group solidarity often played a role too, as studies show. In some areas 80 percent or more of the clergy took the oath and in other areas it was vice versa.

The outcome was two churches that now stood angrily facing each other in France: the constitutional, led by the clergy who took the oath, versus the so-called non-juring church led by the clergy who rejected the oath. The schism was formalized when in February 1791 Talleyrand, bishop of Autun, and Bishop Gobel, future constitutional bishop of Paris, both consecrated bishops newly elected by the people to lead the constitutional church.

The refractory non-juring priests were ousted but not yet otherwise persecuted and they often stayed in the vicinity, hoping to reoccupy their posts in time. Those in Luçon, for example, were advised by their deposed bishop to find a barn or other building in which to say mass with whatever vessels and vestments they could procure. He urged them to maintain a foothold while encouraging resistance to the revolutionary government.

The pope finally broke his silence in March 1791. He officially condemned the principles of both the Revolution and the Civil Constitution (March 11 and April 13, 1791). The rupture between the Holy See and France was not repaired until Napoleon signed a concordat with the papacy in 1801.

The consequences of this schism were incalculable. Until this point the Revolution had the support of the overwhelming majority of the population. But now the harsh treatment of their priests turned many if not the majority of faithful Catholics against the Revolution. Eventually those persecuted for religious reasons allied with those persecuted for political reasons, causing Roman Catholicism to become the religion of the counter-revolution.

Flight of the King

The king found the Civil Constitution of the Clergy most repugnant, and after the pope condemned it his conscience was tortured by the sanction he had given it. Moreover, he had never sincerely accepted the Revolution and only play-acted the part of a patriotic and paternal ruler. He bided his time, entertaining all sorts of schemes that might enable him to escape and then return at the head of an army to restore his absolute authority. His decision to escape was finally triggered by an incident in Holy Week of 1791. Unable in conscience to take Holy Communion from a constitutional priest, he planned to take it from a non-juring priest at St. Cloud, his palace on the outskirts of Paris. But he was caught leaving by a mob of Parisians who saw the trip as a ruse and surrounded his carriage to keep him from leaving.

This insult to his dignity and his conscience proved to be the last straw. Two months later on June 20, under cloak of darkness, he and the royal family fled. The fate of the Revolution hung in the balance as Louis and Marie Antoinette, in disguise and with their two children, trundled along in a huge berliner coach heading for the frontier to reach an escort of loyal Austrian troops. Bad luck, however, foiled their plan. As they neared their rendezvous with the troops, the couple was recognized by a vigilant posting master who was able to alert the townsfolk at the border town of Varennes and barricade the road to stop the king and his family—ironically only a few hundred yards away from their armed escort. A dozen mischances had doomed them: if the posting master had not returned at that precise moment, if the king and queen had not shown themselves at that moment, if the fresh relay of horses supposed to meet them at Varennes had not been moved from the prearranged spot, if one of the escorts had not lost his way. But the divinity that shapes our ends had other plans for the Bourbons.

After the break with the Church and the flight of the king, events moved constantly in a more radical direction. War with the other European countries soon loomed as the flight of the king aroused the hitherto unalarmed monarchs of Europe. Conscious now of the danger threatening their thrones, they began to rally around the beleaguered Louis. The emperor of Austria and the king of Prussia issued a declaration calling for all the powers of Europe to unite to restore Louis' rightful authority. Great Britain too showed similar concern as she looked for an excuse to revenge herself for French interference in the Americans' War of Independence.

At the same time (June 1791), a sense of impending chaos had already convinced most of the original revolutionary leaders (such as Sieyès, Lafayette, and Talleyrand) that it was time to bring an end to the Revolution and to work out a compromise with the king, even though the streets rang with cries to oust him. These moderates, therefore, tried to work out a solution to the crisis that would preserve the monarchy. The radicals at the Cordelier Club, however, had other thoughts. They posted a petition on the Champs de Mars calling for the king's ouster and punishment. Thousands—the humble, the poor, the illiterate—signed it. But a tumult ensued. In attempting to restore order, soldiers of the National Guard under Lafayette shot and killed some fifty of the petitioners. The massacre widened the breach between conservatives in favor of retaining the monarchy and those calling for a republic, between those fearful of a general assault on property and privilege and those who preached social equality and wanted measures to alleviate the poverty of the masses.

The Dogs of War Unleashed

The schism within the Church and the flight of the aristocracy severely strained the unity of the nation but it was the outbreak of war—declared against the emperor of Austria on April 20, 1792—that constituted the real watershed of the Revolution. The war completely destroyed what unity remained after the break with the Church and ignited the ferocious tendencies that would be so common to twentieth-century revolutions. The war was to last almost without interruption for twenty-three years. It was favored by almost all of the parties. The royal family hoped it would lead to their restoration to full power by invading foreign armies; the monarchist party in the assembly hoped to use it to impose a strong monarchy, while the Girondins thought it would enable them to bend the king to their wishes.

But once the dogs of war were loosed, the descent into chaos and blood madness was swift. Families, friends, and colleagues turned against each other and tore the nation apart. The most violent quarrels occurred between parties of the Left, whose leaders began by questioning each other's loyalty and ended by murdering one another.

The war also enabled the sans-culottes henceforth to have a major influence on the course of events. As their name indicates, they preferred trousers to the knee breeches of the upper classes. Not being a distinct economic class they are not easily definable. They occupied a social stratum roughly between the well-to-do bourgeoisie and the very poor proletariat. Urbanites, artisans, shopkeepers, and clerical workers, with little formal education, they tended to see things in black and white, were easily moved by slogans, and believed in taking the bull by the horns.

They showed this attitude when they took the lead in overthrowing the monarchy in August 1792 after the flight and capture of the king. They were able to gain political control of the forty-eight sections of Paris and arm themselves with pikes while welcoming the *fédérés,* armed volunteers from the provinces who joined them. The invading Prussian Duke of Brunswick played into their hands when he issued a manifesto promising to restore the French king to his rightful authority and wreak frightful vengeance on all who dared raise a hand against the royal couple. In response, the sans-culottes formed an insurrectional commune and bypassed the assembly they now regarded with contempt. They marched on the Tuileries and forced the king to flee to the assembly for protection. But the assembly, bowing to pressure from the sans-culottes, incarcerated the royal couple in the grim baronial tower of the temple under the watchful eye of sans-culotte guards.

Many of the sans-culottes were ferociously anticlerical. As the Prussians continued their march on the city the sans-culottes turned savagely on the clergy, whom they regarded as traitors jeopardizing the Revolution. A band of sans-culottes converged on an open cart that was taking some priests to prison. After dragging them from the cart they murdered them on the spot. Then they broke into the Carmelite monastery and butchered dozens more. Finally they made the rounds of the prisons, massacring not only the many priests confined there but also—as their blood-lust boiled over—any other prisoners they could lay their hands on. Besides the 220 to 260 priests, the victims also included about 170 boys and girls and thirty-five prostitutes as well as some two hundred thieves and debtors.

Very little was done on the part of the responsible authorities to stop the massacres. Jean Paul Marat, the fire-eating rabble-rouser, had in fact called for the massacre of the enemies of the Revolution while Georges Jacques Danton himself did nothing to stop it, although it is true that he was preoccupied with the effort of organizing a last-ditch defense of Paris. But hardly a public body or a political leader in Paris could honestly have said, "I am innocent of the blood of this just person."[15]

On September 21, 1792, the members of the newly elected National Convention met and officially declared France a republic. Elected by universal male suffrage they were given a mandate to endow France with a republican constitution. The elections showed that by and large the populace was satisfied with the Revolution. The peasants in particular were happy to be free of their feudal obligations and simply wanted to be left alone to make use of their new access to the land.

---

[15]J. M. Thompson, *The French Revolution* (Oxford, Basil Blackwell, 1943), p. 306.

A New Age

By a grand coincidence the convention met to elect its officers on the day the national army won its first victory. At Valmy on September 20, 1792, the half-trained French volunteers forced the Duke of Brunswick's Prussian regulars to retreat. "A new age in the history of the world!" exclaimed Goethe from his vantage point with the Prussian troops.

The good news reached the convention as it faced its first big decision— what to do with the dethroned king. Once the vote was taken to put him on trial for treason, a verdict of guilty was a foregone conclusion as the evidence of his commerce with the enemy was plentiful. In fact he was declared guilty by a nearly unanimous vote. But whether to punish him by exile, imprisonment, or death was hotly debated, and the final vote in favor of death was 380 to 310.

The sentence was carried out on January 21, 1793. After receiving Communion from a non-juring priest of Irish birth, Louis was taken by closed carriage to the Place de la Révolution. Along the two-and-a-half-mile route, armed citizens stood two deep while the constant tattoo of the drums drowned out any cries of sympathy. After five minutes of prayer the king mounted the scaffold while an immense throng—some on the rooftops, some on piles of debris, some holding children—waited in suspense. As he looked out over them, the drums fell silent and he said, *"Peuple, je meurs innocent"* (My people, I die an innocent man). A moment later the executioner held up the king's severed head. While some dipped their handkerchiefs in his blood, others danced around the scaffold singing the *Marseillaise*.[16]

The king was dead. The question now was, Could France govern itself? Indications were not reassuring. The Revolution now took on a radical character leading to dictatorship and terror. The fear of foreign intervention and internal subversion now aroused the extremists, who would for almost two years dominate France. One of their first moves was to embark on a policy of expansion of the Revolution that would put them at war with the rest of Europe and compromise their efforts to stabilize their gains. Turning their revolution into a European crusade they issued a decree on November 19, 1793, that promised assistance to all peoples who wanted to recover their freedom. It was a memorable decree for "it proclaimed the solidarity of

[16]Ibid., p. 334.

all revolutionaries throughout the world, and consequently threatened all previously existing thrones and organs of government."[17] It risked provoking a universal war, which would be a social war based on the new gospel of liberation for all the oppressed.

Radical vs. Radical

Most unwise was their decree of December 15 which announced that the "liberated" lands would pay their own way. It called for the confiscation of ecclesiastical and noble property and made the unstable French assignats the legal tender. Predictably these policies served only to alienate the "liberated" peoples.

Moreover the two leading parties, the Girondins and the Montagnards, worked ceaselessly against each other. Although both were of the Left, both anticlerical, and both in agreement on the need to combine economic liberalism with programs of social welfare, they fought each other viciously. Personal rivalries and a difference of opinion about the relative importance of the capital versus the provinces fueled their mutual enmity. Their quarrels played into the hands of the sans-culottes, with whom the Montagnards had to ally themselves in order to overcome the Girondins. The main source of the sans-culottes' power was their dominance of the insurrectionary Commune of Paris, which controlled the police and the National Guard and therefore had control over the capital.

As Girondin vied with Montagnard for control of the assembly, several disasters befell the infant republic in March. The strongly Catholic people of the Vendée rose in rebellion. Incensed by the draft of their young men into the revolutionary army and deeply disturbed by the anticlericalism of the regime, they began a guerrilla campaign that posed a serious challenge to the regime. A few days later the French troops in the Netherlands were forced to retreat, and France once more faced an invasion. In addition, the ever-tightening blockade imposed by Great Britain, now at war with France, exacerbated France's intractable social and economic problems.

As an atmosphere of crisis enveloped the country, emergency measures were taken to reinforce the power of the central government and put down the counterrevolutionaries. A revolutionary tribunal was set up to provide summary trials for those accused of treason. Eighty deputies armed with full

[17]Albert Mathiez, *The French Revolution* (New York: Russell & Russell, Inc., 1962), p. 284.

powers were dispatched to the provinces to crush the growing opposition. And finally, on April 6, a nine-member Committee of Public Safety was established to bring some kind of system into running the government.

In the meantime the ruling Girondins had totally alienated the sans-culottes by their efforts to save the king, their obvious distrust of the masses, their refusal to institute price controls, and a number of other unpopular measures. Allied with the Montagnards, the sans-culottes formed an Insurrectional Committee, took over the National Guard, surrounded the National Convention on June 2, and demanded the expulsion of the Girondins. Deeply chagrined, the convention tamely submitted to the pressure of the mob and ordered twenty-nine of the Girondins put under house arrest.

The Girondins were not finished yet. They had many sympathizers in the provinces and their expulsion was the signal for a widespread uprising in the name of federalism. The provincial bourgeoisie were also fearful of a Jacobin onslaught on private property. But the Girondin rebels were hurt by their association with royalist intriguers and were no match for the fiery enthusiasts of the revolutionary communes in the provinces. Neither were the Girondins able to win over the peasants, whose loyalty to the Revolution was generally retained by the convention's social reforms. The aristocrats' estates were broken up into small lots for acquisition by the peasants and the common land was divided among them. Finally those feudal dues that still remained were abolished without compensation, thus completing the dismantling of the feudal regime that had begun on August 5, 1789.

The Girondins' revolt soon began to sputter out. But the general situation in the summer of 1793 was still very alarming for the true believers. A series of military reverses on the frontier allowed the Prussian and Austrian armies to threaten the capital once more, while the troops needed for its defense had to be diverted to the rebellious Vendée and to other provinces where the federalists still posed a threat. To deal with the crisis the nine-member Committee of Public Safety was replaced by a twelve-member committee of more radical Montagnards, including the formidable Robespierre.

These twelve men governed during the critical and chaotic period from September 1793 to the following July 27 (or 9 Thermidor of the year Two of the Revolution). They held their sessions at night in secret. They were mostly men with small minds but big egos and little political experience, nobodies destined for humdrum careers until chance lifted them for a brief spell to the heights. Authoritarian and short-tempered, often exhausted and with nerves on edge, stirred by revolutionary passions, they quarreled readily while managing to project a picture of unity. They ruled a nation in terrible turmoil: Half the country rejected their authority while the political clubs and revolutionary committees often got the upper hand over them. Meanwhile all sorts of enemies mingled in the streets—counterrevolutionaries, secret agents of other governments, deserters from the army, and half-crazed self-appointed saviors.

What had turned these affluent professionals into radical revolutionaries? They were all relatively young (only Robert Lindet was over forty); eight of them were lawyers and all were intellectuals greatly devoted to the idea of progress. With Rousseau they would say society was artificial and only had to be made more natural. Change seemed an easy matter to them. Theirs was a faith in social planning that was naive to say the least. As followers of Rousseau, like most of the intelligentsia, they were devoted to beautiful abstractions, ideas such as "the people," "the nation," "the sovereign general will." Such ideas were simple, clear, and attractive. In their minds there could be only two sides—those who were devoted to the public interest and justice, like themselves, and those devoted to private interests—a selfish, sinister, and evil brood. There was no need to compromise, therefore, nor even to tolerate free discussion when disagreement arose.

Écrasez L'Infame

Like many French intellectuals, these men no longer looked to the Church for moral and intellectual leadership. They were happy with the damage inflicted on the Church by the Revolution for they felt it had owned too much property, was too powerful as an organized force in politics, and had ceased to perform its functions with rational efficiency. Moreover they felt scorn for much of the church ceremonial, the pompous vestments, the religious processions, the clang of bells, and the consecration of wafers. In fact virtually all the members of the convention were followers of natural religion; they believed in a Supreme Being conveniently distant, they "dwelt on man's abundant capacity for natural virtue and regarded priests as charlatans and revealed mysteries as a delusion. Revealed religion, they would say, was in its death throes, soon to expire before the searching eye of reason."[18]

Jacques Nicolas Billaud-Varenne was perhaps the most anticlerical of the lot. He believed that the Catholic Church was a fraud pure and simple. "However painful an amputation may be," he wrote in his discussion of the

[18]R. R. Palmer, *Twelve Who Ruled* (Princeton, N.J.: Princeton University Press, 1941).

Church, "when a member is gangrened it must be sacrificed if we wish to save the body." He advocated radical reforms: confiscation of all church property, control of clergy by the state, abolition of the office of bishop, if possible, and reduction of dogmas to one—the immortality of the soul. He wanted the ritual simplified so that the most ignorant peasant could understand it. He felt that the clergy should be allowed to marry and should be treated like any other citizens. He would do away with all mystifications introduced by "cunning priests" who had corrupted the simple religion of Jesus.

The military crisis that had brought these men to power reached its maximum intensity in September 1793 and marked a decisive turning point in the Revolution. Extremists among the Montagnards and the sans-culottes were able to exploit the atmosphere of suspicion and distrust and whip up the fury of the populace against the "enemies of the Revolution"—the clergy, food hoarders, corrupt war contractors, overly ambitious generals. They believed there was only one remedy: the Terror. As Louis Antoine de Saint-Just put it, "You must punish not merely traitors but the indifferent as well; you must punish whoever is passive in the Republic . . . we must rule by iron those who cannot be ruled by justice."[19] This spirit was embodied in the draconian Law of Suspects of September 17 that mandated swift execution after a summary trial of anyone denounced as a traitor. The processions to the guillotine increased in length and included Marie Antoinette, the twenty-one Girondin leaders, Madame Roland, and Madame du Barry.

It is sometimes thought that the aristocracy provided the majority of victims. But the most superficial analysis of the names given in the register of the Paris municipality shows that the number of ex-nobles executed by the Revolutionary Tribunal from November 1793 to March 1794 was always less than the number of priests and members of religious orders. The large number of priests, monks, and nuns who came before the tribunal shows that there were still men and women who put religion before life, and attempted to carry on the work of the "refractory" church while intriguing against the government that persecuted it. Their influence can be discerned behind every counterrevolutionary movement, especially in the west and north.[20]

[19]Hampson, *A Social History of the French Revolution,* p. 198.
[20]Thompson, *The French Revolution,* p. 437.

Down with Christ!

The Terror soon combined with de-Christianization to ravage the clergy, both constitutional and non-juring. Jacques Hébert, the ex-religious Joseph Fouché, and their friends started the campaign to de-Christianize the republic by means of specifically antireligious terror. Editor of a newspaper called *Père Duchesne,* Hébert wrote in the rough-and-ready, black-and-white style of the sans-culottes whose leader he was. His coarse, inimitable language mingled broad humor, down-to-earth common sense, wisdom, and violent attacks on the clergy and the rich as well as the corrupt politicians. His juiciest four-letter words he reserved for priests—"power-mad hypocrites who betrayed Jesus, *'le bon sans-culotte'*—the best Jacobin who ever lived." By September 1793 Hébert had achieved a dominant influence over the Jacobins and the Commune, and used it to pressure the convention into accepting his radical social program: the incarceration of suspects, the application of price controls, and the establishment of a revolutionary army.

The first move toward de-Christianization was made in September in the provinces by the representative Fouché. His campaign against the Church set the pattern of de-Christianization for the rest of the country. The French people, he proclaimed, recognized no dogma except their own sovereignty. He banned religious ceremonies outside churches, ordered the destruction of calvaries and crosses, stripped the cemeteries of religious emblems, and posted notices that "Death is an eternal sleep." In one of the towns he visited he unveiled a bust of Brutus, "god of the festival," and preached against religious sophistry. A few days later he denounced celibacy, ordering all priests to marry and to adopt a child or support an elderly person.

The movement was the culmination of an anticlericalism and anti-Christian attitude already manifest in various ways. For example, some localities with religious names were renamed, and newborn citizens were given non-Christian names. In fact the Revolution itself began to take on the character of a religious cult with such things as its own sacred oaths, sacred trees of liberty, and altars of the fatherland. Moreover, the constitutional clergy were suspected of being royalists and their reluctance to approve the execution of the king reinforced this suspicion.

The spark lit by the fanatics Hébert, Fouché, and others caught fire, and de-Christianization swept across the land. The convention gave it impetus by a profoundly anti-Christian act. On October 5, 1793, it promulgated a new calendar based on a new era that began with the abolition of the monarchy on September 22, 1792. The old calendar was abolished, the calendar that made the birth of Christ the supreme event of history and constantly reminded people of the Christian religion by its Sundays, its saints days, its cycles of Christmas and Easter. The new calendar dropped all reference to Christianity and rearranged the months and weeks along supposedly more rational lines, with each of the twelve months divided into three weeks of ten days each, leaving five supplementary holidays at the end of the year.

In Paris, altar linens from the Sainte Chapelle were made into shirts for soldiers, church books were sold to grocers for wrapping paper, images of the saints were mutilated, and relics were burned. One of the first great triumphs of the de-Christianizers was the resignation of Gobel, the constitutional bishop of Paris, who was shaken out of his slumber in the middle of the night by armed sans-culottes who invited him to resign. Which the poor man did, pronto. Churches were closed or turned into "temples of reason." A young lady garbed in white was enthroned on the altar of Notre Dame Cathedral as the Goddess of Reason, attended by a throng of citizens including members of the convention.

Some historians have tried to explain de-Christianization as the work of patriots concerned about the danger to national defense posed by the Church. But many of these "patriots," especially among the sans-culottes, were also driven by a kind of visceral hatred of the clergy and the Church and a wild joy in smashing it to pieces. As Ralph Gibson says, "The origin of this mentality has not been researched into, and we don't really know why Paris was—and would remain—such a hotbed of anticlericalism."[21]

No doubt one of the most potent roots of the fury had to do with sex. The Tridentine model with its severe repression of sexuality met with great resistance, especially among the male population. The effort to force priests to marry was in part an attack on the sexually repressive nature of Tridentine Catholicism by forcing them to admit their own sexuality. Also, as Richard Cobb argues, there was resentment toward priests because of the power the confessional supposedly gave them over women—a power that belonged by

---

[21] Gibson, *A Social History of French Catholicism 1789–1914*, p. 45. The sexual ethic of the Church was always strict in theory while in practice the medieval Church's discipline in the matter tended to be mild. But the Council of Trent's emphasis on church authority and its encouragement of frequent confession helped to emphasize the seriousness of sexual sins, so that sin became almost synonymous with sex in the popular mind.

right to the husband but that, in popular folklore, was used by priests to debauch innocent females.[22]

The clergy, of course, bore the brunt of the campaign. In some areas they resigned en masse and more than a few took wives as a proof of their break with orthodox Catholicism. At Beauvais about fifteen priests, including the bishop, married, and by 1803 a total of fifty of the 480 priests in the Department of the Oise had done so. All told, about six thousand priests married during the Revolution. Their motivations, as one would suspect, were mixed. Many were only temporizing until better times and simply married their housekeepers *pro forma*. Others used de-Christianization as an excuse for doing something they had always wanted to do. Some justified themselves by pointing out that celibacy was merely an ecclesiastical law. The total number of priests who put aside the cloth would, it seems, number around 20,000—most of them constitutionals (the non-jurors had emigrated or were hiding—or dead). But although they were acting under compulsion, their "apostasy" had the effect of wrecking and discrediting the constitutional Church. By the spring of 1794 there were only around 150 parishes where mass was still celebrated.

In their attempts to destroy Catholicism, the de-Christianizers did not intend to leave a religious vacuum, for they still shared the old regime's principle that no state could survive without a public religion. The new French religion, they decided, would be philanthropic Deism. The provinces followed the example of Paris and its Goddess of Reason. Innumerable young girls decked out as Reason or Liberty or Nature led processions through innumerable towns to altars erected to the new religion.

The provincial town of Strasbourg, like other provincial towns, saw its Feast of Reason on 30 Brumaire, November 20. A great procession formed at nine o'clock in the morning, made up of Propagandists, girls dressed in white, local Jacobins, public officials, and a miscellany of citizens. Bearing a bust of Marat, the crowd marched to the Temple of Reason, the erstwhile cathedral over whose portals were placed a large tricolor and a placard reading "Light after darkness." More flags draped the interior, and in the nave stood the usual symbolic mountain with statues of Nature and Liberty at the summit. On the mountainside were portrayed "monsters with human face, reptiles half buried in fragments of rock," symbolizing the frustrated powers of superstition. An orchestra

[22]Ibid., p. 45.

played and the gathering (alleged to number ten thousand) sang a "Hymn to Nature":

> Mother of the Universe, eternal Nature,
> The People acknowledges your power eternal;
> On the pompous wreckage of ancient imposture
> its hands raise your altar . . .

Monet, the mayor of Strasbourg, then made a speech in praise of reason. The surgeon-general of the Army of the Rhine denounced priests, tyrants, rascals, aristocrats, intriguers, and moderates. Euloge Schneider abdicated his priesthood; many other clergy renounced their errors. A fire on the altar consumed "the remains of saints beatified by the court of Rome and a few Gothic parchments," and outside in the street fifteen cartloads of legal and historical documents from the archives of the diocese went up in flames.[23]

But converting the populace to a new religion would take more than mounting such displays. The religion of Reason or of Nature or of Liberty or even of the Supreme Being proved too vague and abstract for the ordinary people. They might take momentary delight in a "Republican Lord's Prayer" with its petition: "Give us this day our daily bread, in spite of the vain attempts of Pitt, the Cobourgs, and all the tyrants of the Coalition to starve us out," but the novelty soon wore off and the homilies of the local politicians proved a stifling bore. The abolition of Sundays and religious festivals especially met with widespread resistance. And "the new emancipation was sometimes only skin-deep. When a sudden hailstorm threatened the crops at Coulanges-la-Vineuse in the Yonne, for instance, the frightened peasants dispersed the local Jacobin Club, reopened the church, and spent the night ringing the church bells, singing hymns and imploring divine mercy."[24]

While religion survived among the masses it was generally rejected by the revolutionary leaders. At the same time, with the exception of Bishop Grégoire and a few others, Church dignitaries no longer gave any support to the Revolution. Thus a new source of division was inserted in the life of France—anticlerical versus clerical—that would remain for more than a hundred years.

---

[23] Palmer, *Twelve Who Ruled*, p. 188.
[24] Hampson, *A Social History of the French Revolution*, p. 206.

Robespierre vs. Danton

Robespierre and his colleagues realized that the majority of Frenchmen still remained loyal to the forms of Roman Catholicism, and they felt that the religious Terror would only demoralize and confuse the people. Besides, the blasphemous crudity of the de-Christianizers offended Robespierre's religious sensibilities. Moreover, his suspicious mind linked de-Christianization with the so-called foreign plot—a supposed effort by British secret agents to undermine the Revolution by sowing discord in the ranks of the leaders. De-Christianization, he decided, must be terminated at all costs. Joining him in this effort was Danton—for his own reasons. He and his associates were increasingly appalled by the bloodshed as the Terror continued to claim victims. Moreover, some of these "indulgents," as the Dantonists were called, were themselves in danger of ending up on the scaffold by reason of their corrupt financial practices. Nor were Danton's own financial practices above reproach. The Dantonists therefore called for a policy of clemency in part to save their own necks.

They hoped Robespierre's attacks on Hebert and the de-Christianizers would split the Committee of Public Safety and enable Danton to re-enter the committee and substitute a policy of clemency for the Terror. But the scheme didn't work. Hebert and his minions were quickly dispatched when they attempted a coup, while Robespierre sniffed out Danton's plot and attacked Danton and his policy of clemency in two important speeches.

The one he delivered on February 5, 1794—"Principles of Political Morality"—has been called "one of the most noble utterances in the history of democracy."[25] In describing the aim of the Revolution, Robespierre showed himself a true child of the Enlightenment as he painted a vision of a humanity regenerated, a society based on equality where low and cruel passions would be restrained by laws and all generous feelings awakened; where justice reigned and would secure the welfare of each individual; where commerce would become the source of public wealth instead of monstrous riches for the few; where truth would be honored instead of show, merit instead of intrigue, reason instead of the tyranny of custom—and above all where a people would flourish, magnanimous, powerful, and happy. As the chosen instrument of this regeneration, France would be the

[25]Palmer, *Twelve Who Ruled*, p. 275.

glory of all free peoples, the terror of oppressors . . . and on and on in the same poetic, utopian vein.

Only democracy could bring about such a society, Robespierre insisted. The principle of democracy is virtue, the love of the law and of one's country, which, in a democracy, means the love of democracy and equality. However, in time of revolution virtue must be buttressed by terror. For though the people can be governed by reason, its enemies can be controlled only by terror. Therefore "If the basis of popular government in time of peace is virtue, the basis of popular government in time of revolution is both virtue and terror: virtue without which terror is murderous, terror without which virtue is powerless."[26] The republic was to be identified with the reign of virtue. As Saint-Just expressed it: "Monarchy is not a question of kingship, it is crime; the republic does not lie in a senate, it is virtue." Naturally such a viewpoint excluded compromise with the unrighteous: "The republic unites us against all vicious men . . . One rules the people by reason and its enemies by Terror" (an anticipation, in moral terms, of the Marxist "democratic dictatorship of the proletariat").

The ferocity that Robespierre and Saint-Just showed toward the enemies of virtue was the inevitable corollary of their sincere, if fanatical, vision of a coming utopia in which the repressive state has "withered away," leaving a free society of disinterested citizens to live in harmony and peace. As Norman Hampson points out: "They may have aimed at re-creating the Roman republic, what they produced was a blue-print for twentieth-century totalitarianism, and their ideas have a strangely modern look."[27] Ominously also, the bond between war and democracy was forged. The revolutionary government was necessary to win the war; but if war ended it would mean the end of the revolutionary government, which was necessary to found the democratic and constitutional state and put down internal factions.

When evidence accumulated of the financial corruption of a number of the Dantonists, Robespierre and the Committee of Public Safety decided to act. They arrested these men and drew up charges that were flimsy in the extreme: Danton had consorted with persons now in discredit, had praised dubious patriots, and on and on. The picture Robespierre painted was a travesty and makes one wonder how much he was motivated by malice and envy. In the trial—a terrible preview of twentieth-century political trials— Danton confronted the tribunal like a lion at bay. As he roared out his

[26]Ibid., p. 275.
[27]Hampson, *A Social History of the French Revolution,* pp. 222–223.

defiance and his contempt for the committee his words ricocheted off the walls and could even be heard by the crowds gathered outside. Enormous pressures were put on the revolutionary tribunal to guarantee a verdict of guilty, but even so Danton had to be silenced and the trial shortened as popular sentiment in his favor threatened to get out of hand.

Once Danton was safely dispatched to Valhalla, the committee no longer had to contend with an organized opposition and it was free to concentrate on the war effort. The conduct of the war, in fact, was one of the great successes of the revolutionary government. French armies invaded Spain and the Palatinate and won a great victory over the Austrians at Fleurus on June 26, which made possible the reconquest of Belgium. It was the first chapter in the saga of the revolutionary army that Napoleon would take over and lead across Europe, spreading the gospel of equality if not of liberty across the land.

Robespierre's Turn

But at the very moment when the gods of war were smiling on it, the Committee of Public Safety began to disintegrate. Differences over social and economic policy surfaced when Saint-Just, Robespierre, and Couthon identified themselves with a plan to distribute among the poor the estates of "proven" suspects. They also espoused other social reforms repugnant to their more conservative colleagues. Differences of personality also played a large part, as did the natural wear and tear on the nerves of men working so closely together under incredible pressures.

There is no doubt also that Robespierre was chiefly responsible for the disintegration. Cold, suspicious, aloof, uncompromising, and seldom able to smile, he was not the one to smooth the ruffled feathers of colleagues who found his ascendancy irritating. Moreover he alienated a number of the cynics, skeptics, and de-Christianizers among them with his Rousseauian religion of the Supreme Being, which could be taken as a gesture of peace to the Catholics. And these colleagues were greatly incensed when his "Supreme Being" was worshiped at a huge outdoor rally attended by hundreds of thousands and pontificated over by Robespierre himself in splendid robes.

Even more disturbing to many in the convention was the law of 22 Prairial he put through. It speeded up the procedures of the Revolutionary Tribunal and failed to mention any grant of immunity to members of the convention—a very frightening omission to those who felt Robespierre had marked them out for the same fate as Danton.

Finally, besides the natural enemies of the government—such as refractory priests, royalists, and the like—there were also many in the convention, as well as in France itself, who were simply fed up with the revolutionary government; they were disgusted with its sanguinary Terror and convinced that, with France's frontiers now safe, the committee and Robespierre's "dictatorship" were no longer tolerable.

With hatred, disgust, and anger toward the government building up on all sides, and with the split in the Committee of Public Safety weakening his position, Robespierre proved unable to fend off his enemies in the convention. After spending day and night garnering support from the Plain (the moderates in the convention who had hitherto backed Robespierre), they managed in a chaotic debate on 9 Thermidor to get the upper hand. After preventing Saint-Just and Robespierre from seizing the podium, they passed a motion by an obscure Dantonist to have the pair arrested.

The sans-culottes were too divided to save them, and Robespierre and Saint-Just seemed unable to act decisively, perhaps feeling they had lost the moral ground of their authority—their claim to represent the nation. When the jailers refused to incarcerate him, Robespierre took refuge in the Hôtel de Ville; and when guardsmen came to arrest him he turned a pistol on himself but only shattered his jaw. Taken unconscious to the antechamber of the Committee of Public Safety, he was laid on a table, and as he regained consciousness tried to wipe away the blood from his mouth while some of the bystanders jeered him. He was guillotined the next day with Saint-Just and Couthon; and in the days that followed, eighty-seven members of the Commune shared their fate.

Two opposing versions of the denouement of Thermidor exist. One side sees it as the victory of patriots over a fanatic on his way to being a dictator who would have tried to establish a rigorously regulated and puritanical society. For the other side it was a great tragedy, ending for a long time the possibility of establishing a democracy founded on a high idea of morality.

Napoleon vs. the Clergy

The revolutionary government did not survive the fall of the Robespierrists. A now solidly bourgeois convention used the newly reorganized army and National Guard to get the upper hand over the sans-culottes. On May 22, 1795, the newly purged army surrounded the Faubourg St. Antoine, the last outpost of the sans-culottes. Starved and unarmed, they surrendered without a fight. The people's hope for an egalitarian republic was dashed. The Revolution was over. The ascendancy of the bourgeoisie had begun.

But within a few years the irreconcilable Jacobins and counterrevolutionaries made France ungovernable. Dictatorship seemed the only solution. Napoleon gladly agreed.

Only twenty-six years old, this strange genius vaulted into power over France by a series of amazing military feats. Invading Italy in 1796, he dismantled the feudal regimes and set up a series of satellite republics. It was all, in his mind, a crusade to spread the benefits of the Revolution to the rest of Europe. Goethe believed that Napoleon stood for all that was reasonable, legitimate, and European in the revolutionary movement.[28]

Resuming the war of conquest, Napoleon pursued it beyond all discretion. His potentially most dangerous foes, he realized, were the Catholic clergy and he tried to secure their cooperation. Contemporary accounts show, however, that the clergy were often in the vanguard of the guerrilla activities that harassed Napoleon's troops. With crucifix and daggers in hand, priests would lead the attacks on his troops. When they were caught he had them executed without compunction. He burned down the house of one rebel priest who was the Duke of Modena's confessor, and erected on the rubble a pyramid inscribed: "Punishment of a raving priest who abused his ministry and preached revolt and murder."[29]

Recent works on Switzerland, the Tyrol, Tuscany, and the Rhineland written by specialists all note the counterrevolutionary role of the priests and how effective priests were in organizing resistance to Napoleon and the French.[30] Various reasons explain their hostility. For some it was their experience of the pillaging, undisciplined French armies, as recorded in this account by the parish priest of Haaren near Aachen in his register for January 1793:

I shall pass over the irksome, grievous and hideous assaults perpetrated against my person. It would also take too long to describe how and in what fashion these atheists tormented, plundered and ill-treated the people, especially those living in isolated houses . . . or how they blasphemed against God, the Blessed Virgin Mary, and our dear saints, re-

[28]Georg Brandes, *Goethe* (New York: Frank-Maurice, Inc., 1925), Vol. 2, p. 260.

[29]Owen Chadwick, *The Popes and the European Revolution* (New York: Oxford University Press, 1981), p. 452.

[30]Blanning, "The Role of Religion in European Counter-revolution," p. 206.

viled the clergy, abused and disrupted church services and all other forms of Christian worship.[31]

Some priests had other grievances against the revolutionary regimes, in particular their loss of status as the result of the secularization of education, censorship, and marriage, and the prohibition of public religious ceremonies. Napoleon continued his effort to convert Catholics to the doctrines of the Revolution and to persuade them that its ideals of liberty, equality, and fraternity were found in the Gospel; but his words were belied by the spectacle of his troops plundering property and taking hostages.

However, some of the bishops and priests—for the most part in southern Italy—took Napoleon's new order in stride and some even spoke well of it. One of these was no less than Cardinal Chiaramonti, bishop of Imola and later Pope Pius VII. In a 1797 Christmas sermon widely disseminated by Napoleon, the pope said: "Christian virtue makes men good democrats . . . Equality is not an idea of philosophers but of Christ . . . and do not believe that the Catholic religion is against democracy."[32]

While occupying a good part of the papal territories, Napoleon originally intended to spare Rome itself. But when a young French general was shot and killed in a fracas with papal troops in December 1797, the incensed Napoleon occupied Rome and set up a republic. At a ceremony on the Capitoline around the equestrian statue of Marcus Aurelius, a tree of liberty was planted and the people were solemnly proclaimed Sovereign of Rome. Everyone was ordered to use the new French calendar, which few Romans understood. The legal obligation to be present at mass was abolished. The pope himself was removed to a convent at Siena while not a voice was raised in protest—a fact that shows how little loved the pope was in his role as a political sovereign. The Vatican was stripped of treasures including four wagonloads of silver from St. Peter's.

In Belgium the persecution of the Church was more thorough than anywhere else except France. Priests who refused to take an oath to hate monarchy and be faithful to the republic—a majority of the clergy—were driven out of their parishes, imprisoned, and deported. When their congregations tried to carry on with "white masses" (that is, without consecration), their churches were closed. One priest managed to live in his own parish through the troubles of 1798–1799 but had to change his clothes up

---

[31]Ibid., p. 205.
[32]Chadwick, *The Popes and the European Revolution*, pp. 455–456.

to four times a day. All told, some 865 priests were imprisoned or deported while others went underground in disguise as factory workers or farm laborers. Belgian Catholics later looked back to those days as a time of heroic sacrifice and saw a link between the Church's sufferings and the struggle for national freedom. As Owen Chadwick says, this link "made possible the contribution of Belgians during the nineteenth century to the idea of a Liberal Catholicism."[33]

The experience of French, Italian, and Belgian Catholics was repeated elsewhere when French troops arrived. In fact, in many parts of Europe, popular religiosity was greatly intensified by the struggle against the French invader. Many miracles occurred, for example, which appeared to show whose side the Almighty was on. In Lecce in Puglia, for instance, the local republicans planted a liberty tree but word soon spread that the town patron St. Oronzo turned his head away in disgust and indicated by a gesture that he might leave town for good. The populace hearing the news rushed to tear up the tree and then paraded through the streets with an image of the saint, crying "Long live St. Oronzo! Long live the King!" Afterward they vented their wrath on the imprudent republicans. As one author says, "All over the peninsula—and indeed all over Catholic Europe—the French learned to their cost that talking, weeping, blinking Madonnas, or whatever, were usually the prelude to riots."[34]

A Conciliatory Pope

In 1799, with much of Catholic Europe in tatters under the French boot and with the central government of the Church dispersed and the pope in exile on his deathbed, many observers thought the poor old man would be the last pope. But at his death, thirty-five cardinals managed to assemble in Venice on the island of San Giorgio in December 1799 to elect a new pope. It took them three months to do so, however, since conservatives wanted a man clearly identified with the counterrevolution while moderates sought a more pliable prelate. The latter finally prevailed in electing Cardinal Chiaramonti—an unhappy choice for those who remembered his Christmas sermon baptizing democracy, and a dangerous choice in the minds of those who saw him as a mere youth of fifty-eight.

At the same time, on the eve of becoming sole ruler of France, Napoleon

---

[33] Ibid., p. 480.
[34] Blanning, "The Role of Religion in European Counter-revolution," p. 209.

showed that he was seeking some kind of accommodation with the Church. He is supposed to have told a gathering of priests in Milan that "without religion we walk in the dark; the Catholic religion is the only one to give man unfailing light on his origin and his latter end . . . France has had her eyes opened through suffering, and has seen the Catholic religion to be the single anchor amid storm."[35] One thing is certain: Napoleon respected the power of religion over the average person's mind. As a good child of the Enlightenment he spoke very skeptically at times of religion and the Church, while as the child of a devout Corsican woman he spoke at other times like a believing Catholic. But there is no doubt that his real god was power. His interest in the Church was to use it as a means of controlling the people. He knew that it was absolutely necessary for the peace of France to reconcile the Church with the Revolution, or at least with his version of it. And in fact the Napoleonic Code did embody the essential elements of the Revolution by its affirmation of the equality of all citizens before the law, the right of the individual to choose his profession, the supremacy of the lay state, and a regime of tolerance for all religious beliefs.

Religious peace being important for the success of his regime, he had to find a way to heal the now deeply rooted and bitter division between constitutional and non-juring clergy. This could only be accomplished by winning over the non-jurors, who were much more numerous and influential than the constitutionals. He wanted them to accept a settlement along the lines of the earlier Civil Constitution, a maneuver he knew would be impossible without the aid of the pope. So he told the archbishop of Vercelli, Cardinal Martiniana: "Go to Rome and tell the Holy Father that the First Consul wishes to make him a gift of thirty million Frenchmen."[36] His very arduous negotiations with Consalvi, the brilliant emissary of the pope, finally terminated in the Concordat of 1801—the prototype of subsequent nineteenth-century papal concordats. Its signing was celebrated with fitting pomp at Notre Dame Cathedral at Easter of 1802. The First Consul was met at the great western door—like any Bourbon king—by the archbishop, and at the elevation the troops presented arms for the thirty-two-year-old Corsican general. The Roman Catholic religion was recognized as "the religion of the great majority of Frenchmen," the agonizing schism between the constitutional and non-juring clergy was ended, and Napoleon

---

[35] Chadwick, *The Popes and the European Revolution,* p. 484.

[36] J. McManners, *The French Revolution and the Church.* (London: S.P.C.K., 1969), p. 143.

had solved one of the most vexing problems he inherited from the Revolution.

The chief points of the concordat were five: All bishops, both constitutional and non-juring, had to hand in their resignations to the pope, who could accept them if he so desired; the first Consul had the right to nominate the bishops who would then be canonically instituted by the pope; the Church would not seek to recover its alienated property; the clergy would be paid by the state; and finally, the practice of the Catholic religion would be regulated by the police in areas that might affect public order. While some of this was a bitter pill for the pope to swallow (for example, state payment of the clergy, loss of the Church's total control over marriage, the family, and education), on the whole the concordat gave the pope power over the Church that had been undreamed of before. No previous pope would have dared to require the resignation of the entire French episcopate. This subordination of the bishops was neither planned nor foreseen, but the genius of Napoleon accidentally confirmed the popes in a power that seventeen centuries of Vatican politics had been unable to achieve. Gallicanism was dealt a mighty blow.

Was the papacy now reconciled with the Revolution, at least in part? It may have seemed so at the time. But history writes with very crooked lines.

In 1804 the pope made the extraordinary gesture of coming to Paris at Napoleon's behest to preside at the little emperor's self-crowning. Although Pius was acclaimed by reverent and kneeling crowds along the way, he was also denounced by intellectuals for acting as chaplain to a despot. But it was a price he was willing to pay to secure greater freedom for the Church. Moreover, as Owen Chadwick says, "That the Pope should be *needed* to sanction this transfer of revolutionary power was an astounding recognition of his utility as a symbol of conscience and duty, because he represented the Catholic ideal which still, in spite of all that had happened, was the faith of most of the French people."[37]

Within a few years, however, pope and emperor were locked in a conflict that began when Napoleon insisted that the pope join his continental blockade against England. When the pope refused he was taken prisoner and hustled off to France, where he spent six years in lonely exile, unwilling to accept a large annual income offered by Napoleon to keep him in a gilded cage.

After Napoleon's defeat at Waterloo, the victors—England, Prussia, and

[37] Chadwick, *The Popes and the European Revolution,* pp. 493–494.

Russia—met at the Congress of Vienna to build a new world order on the ruins of Napoleon's empire. For them the word "revolution" conjured up twenty-five years of turmoil and violence, disorder, and even anarchy. For them only monarchs firmly seated on their thrones, ruling by divine right, could keep Europe from falling back into chaos. Therefore they put the Bourbons back on their thrones and perched Napoleon on a rock two thousand watery miles away. They also restored the pope as the absolute monarch of the Papal States. But try as they might they could not undo the work of the Revolution—the magnitude of social and political transformation was too extensive. France and the rest of Europe could never return permanently to a hierarchical society, held together by an alliance of throne and altar, in which status was determined by birth and monarchs ruled by divine right.

Impact of the Revolution

Modern European politics began with the French Revolution, "the profound social convulsion from which modern Europe was born."[38] The terms Right and Left, coined during the Revolution and used generally thereafter, show how the French Revolution became a litmus test of political viewpoints. Likewise the subsequent use of the terms "liberal" and "conservative"—popularized by the Revolution—betray the Revolution's dominant influence on European politics. The polarization it brought about showed that the very idea of revolution had changed. It was no longer seen as a transference of power from one group to another while an essential continuity was maintained. Now it was viewed as a radical, comprehensive break with the past. No institution was left untouched. Even family and private property were put at risk. People began to speak of *the* Revolution as a kind of permanent force waiting in the wings to totally subvert and transform society.

"In fact the Revolution did to the Roman Catholic Church what the Reformation failed to do. It appeared to have destroyed its structure if not its being."[39]

The impact of the Revolution on the Church was indeed tremendous. The tragic schism between a considerable body of Frenchmen and the Church was final; de-Christianization as a program failed, but anticlerical-

[38]Hampson, *A Social History of the French Revolution,* p. 265.
[39]Chadwick, *The Popes and the European Revolution,* p. 481.

ism remained as its permanent vestige. One would no longer be Catholic simply by virtue of being French, for the Revolution put an end to the quasi-universal practice of religion in France. It achieved this in many ways, but two were probably more crucial than others: The Revolution decimated the clergy, and it presided over the childhood of a generation that grew up outside the influence of the Church. The Church lost its control over the daily life of the people. The process of secularization introduced by the laws of 1794 opened a new chapter, and the secular spirit continued to spread. Civil divorce, civil marriage, and the secular school system were its most visible expressions.

Outside of France, the Catholic Church was transformed nowhere more dramatically than in Germany. There the Catholic prince bishoprics—including the three great elector archbishops of Mainz, Trier, and Cologne as well as many other bishoprics, abbeys, and collegiate churches—were dismantled. Although the rule of the bishops was benign, it was now seen to be archaic in the light of the reforming ideas associated especially with the Enlightenment and the Revolution. Moreover, with the threat from the French revolutionary armies, this patchwork of bishoprics was seen as an obstacle to the defense of Germany. Prussia, Austria, and Bavaria took the lead in secularizing and absorbing them. Many Catholics now found themselves under Protestant rulers. Church property was taken over and monasteries dismantled. The Church was reduced to an agency of the state, its schools and clergy supported by the state.

The most severe impact of the Revolution throughout Europe was felt by the old religious orders. The Benedictines alone lost more than a thousand abbeys and priories. By 1815 almost no monks existed in Western Europe except in Spain, where Joseph Bonaparte's suppression was relatively mild. Many of the monks driven out settled down to a different kind of life and had no desire to return. The monasteries slowly revived but never attained their prerevolution numbers. This disruption of monasticism and the dispersal of its great libraries had a very damaging effect on Catholic scholarship. Fewer eminent monk scholars meant fewer scholars among the clergy in general.

The situation of the bishop was significantly changed by the Revolution. His diocese was no longer dominated by monks and he therefore had less need to appeal to Rome in any squabbles with them. Nor did he any longer have to fear oppressive actions by the local squire or baron, who had been stripped of power. One of the bishop's main concerns was the condition of the churches whose windows, walls, and roofs were in grave need of repair.

The bishop of Campagna was horrified by "the indecency and ruin of the worship of God" in a church he visited, where he was forced to remove the reserved sacrament because there was no lamp, no wax, and no incense, and where the floors were wet and the priests unwilling to say mass while the people had no place to kneel.[40]

Priests were few since the seminaries had been closed for many years and vocations had fallen off catastrophically. Bishops complained they had to tolerate priests in lay clothes, priests who failed to say mass, priests who were nonresident. Some saw the requirement of celibacy as the biggest obstacle to increasing the number of clergy and spoke out against it. But the revolutionaries had made it difficult to argue against celibacy. In forcing priests to get married they had linked clerical marriage, in the minds of Catholics, with the vilest acts of tyranny. In south Germany, nevertheless, the debate over celibacy waxed very strong. Twenty-three Catholic laymen led by professors from Freiburg im Breisgau petitioned the lower house of the Baden Parliament, the grand-duke, and the archbishop to abolish celibacy. When the petition was signed by fifty ordinands, the archbishop refused to ordain them unless they retracted. In Württemberg some women protested against celibacy as a slight on their sex.

Without doubt the quarrel of the Church with the Revolution also had a profoundly negative influence on the development of the Church's social conscience. As Georges Lefebvre says, "The revolutionary bourgeoisie came to think that the principles of 1789 and Catholicism were irreconcilable while the Church reached the same conclusion. The Church's abhorrence of republican forms in the nineteenth century derived in large part from its experience of the Revolution."[41]

---

[40]Ibid., p. 583.

[41]Georges Lefebvre, *The French Revolution from 1793 to 1799* (New York: Columbia University Press, 1964), p. 277.

TWO

Three Who Failed: Lamennais (1782–1854), Lacordaire (1802–1861), and Montalembert (1810–1870), Pioneers of Liberal Catholicism

MEETING at the Congress of Vienna (1814–1815), Napoleon's victors hoped to extinguish the flames of revolution still smoldering in the ruins of his empire. They would eradicate the heresies of liberalism and nationalism and restore the old order. However, once spread abroad by the French Revolution, these ideas were too powerful, too intimately in touch with the deep yearnings of humanity, to be stamped out by fiat. The cry *"Liberté, égalité, fraternité"* would continue to echo and re-echo in the halls and streets of Europe and stir the hearts of millions. An era of revolution opened up in spite of Metternich, the Austrian statesman and architect of the conservative order as defined at the Congress of Vienna. Revolutionaries proliferated, conspiring and plotting to overthrow Metternich's system.

The Church was a natural ally of Metternich because of its totally negative experience of the Revolution. But a small number of Catholics felt that counterrevolution was a hopeless option and began a movement to reconcile the Church with the Revolution—liberal Catholicism. It was to fail for many reasons, and not until Vatican II (1962–1965) would the Church finally lay to rest its antiliberal position and officially endorse the liberal

doctrines on such issues as separation of church and state, freedom of conscience, freedom of speech, and freedom of the press.

Three Frenchmen were intimately identified with the ill-starred movement of liberal Catholicism: Félicité de Lamennais, Charles Count de
Montalembert, and Henri Lacordaire. The fascinating drama of their inter-
secting lives throws much light on a key chapter in the history of Church
and Revolution.

Although a pragmatic kind of liberal Catholicism had already evolved in
Belgium and in Ireland, not to mention the United States, it was in France
with Lamennais that liberal Catholicism first appeared as a consistent doctrine. Liberal Catholics summed up their doctrine in three basic formulas:

a) *God and liberty*. In opposition to the liberalism of the anticlerical
Voltairians they called for freedom for all.

b) *A free Church in a free state:* a very ambiguous formula that could later
cover Leo XIII's doctrine in the encyclical *Libertas* as well as the most
absolute and most hostile separation of Church and State.

c) *Renunciation of privileges:* The Church should no longer claim special
privileges but only the rights proper to any other association (that is, the
régime of "le droit commun").

When the French Revolution overthrew the old order that privileged the
Church it proclaimed the neutrality of the State toward all religions and
instituted liberty of conscience for all. Then it imposed a radical reform on
the Church, which was modified by Napoleon when he finally signed the
Concordat of 1801 with Pope Pius VII. In practice, this concordat led to a
subordination of the Church to the state. Napoleon, however, was over-
thrown and the Congress of Vienna (1814) restored as far as possible the
prerevolutionary old order *(ancien régime)*. But Napoleon's concordat was
retained and the Church was kept under the control of the state.

This situation was labeled "enslavement of the Church" by the diminu-
tive French priest, Félicité Robert de La Mennais (in ordinary usage,
Lamennais) who began a campaign to restore its freedom. Eventually his
effort to win freedom for the Church enlarged his understanding of human
freedom itself and changed him from a despiser of the Revolution into an
ardent champion of revolution and freedom.

Young Lamennais

Lamennais was born at St. Malo in Brittany in 1782 (a few steps away from
the house where his great romantic precursor Chateaubriand was born

fourteen years before). Only seven years old when the Revolution erupted, Lamennais grew up in a country torn apart by it. His original hostile attitude toward the Revolution was no doubt colored by his own family's experience with it. His father was a prosperous shipowner who at first welcomed the Revolution. As a leading member of the local bourgeoisie he felt, like his peers, that it was high time to overhaul the obsolete machinery of government and do away with the outdated privileges of the aristocracy and the clergy.

Lamennais' uncle Des Saudrais was also initially an enthusiast for the Revolution, and as a town councilor he took a leading part in the exciting events that brought the Revolution to St. Malo. He took part in enforcing the Civil Constitution of the Clergy, which involved dismissing the local non-juring pastor and installing a constitutional curé. But the two brothers' enthusiasm cooled considerably when the Terror arrived in December 1793 in the person of Le Carpentier, a Jacobin emissary from Paris who de-Christianized the town with a vengeance and extorted such great sums of money from the rich merchants that Lamennais' father was all but ruined.

Félicité Robert de La Mennais (Lamennais)

Meanwhile the willful and intractable young Lamennais was fortunate in getting the type of education that exactly suited him. After his mother's death when he was only five or six, and with his father preoccupied with business, his tutoring was taken over by his uncle Des Saudrais, a man of no small intellectual curiosity. A devotee of Rousseau, Des Saudrais believed in letting children freely follow their bent. At first little Féli showed hardly any interest in books, but under his uncle's gentle encouragement he soon began to roam freely through Des Saudrais' well-stocked library. He became an omnivorous reader and eventually learned a number of languages including Latin, Greek, and Hebrew. Unlike his brother Jean, who manifested at an early age a robust simple faith, Féli had a long struggle overcoming the doubts engendered by his wide reading in Rousseau and other skeptical philosophers. However, shortly after Jean himself was ordained priest in 1800, it seems, Féli made his first confession and Communion.

Unwilling to enter his father's business, unable to settle on a career, and suffering from a failed romance, Féli finally found a focus for his life in religion. Guided by Jean he began an intense study of the Bible and the Fathers of the Church while ranging widely over medieval, modern, and contemporary philosophers and theologians. Much of his study was carried on in a beautiful retreat belonging to his grandmother—La Chesnaie, a small secluded country house near Dinan. Situated on the edge of a little lake surrounded by tall trees and deep woods, it was an oasis of solitude wonderfully suited for calming his restless temperament and enabling him to plunge deeply into the world of ideas. This in fact was to be his only world for the rest of his life. His life was to be the life of the mind, his mission an intellectual one.

His intense study of theology and the Church bore fruit in two works: *Réflexions* (1809), a program for renewal of the Church; and *Tradition* (1814), a three-volume study of Church history reflecting his recent conversion to ultramontanism, a theology of the Church that emphasizes the authority of the pope.[1] One of the main factors in making him a fervent ultramontane was Pius VII's heroic resistance to Napoleon's attempt to make the Church a tool of French policy. While the French bishops spinelessly capitulated, Pius alone stood firm and prevented a disgraceful surrender of the Church to the unscrupulous tyrant. For Lamennais, nothing was better calculated to prove the need for a strong papacy.

---

[1] It was ultimately affirmed at the first Vatican Council (1869–1870).

A Book That Stirs a Nation

On March 9, 1816, after much soul-searching and procrastination, Féli took the step that many think a terrible mistake for a man of restless and independent nature. He was ordained a priest. A year after his ordination he published a book that catapulted him onto the public stage of France, and won him a role as a kind of chaplain to the romantic movement just coming into its own. One can hardly imagine how a book called *An Essay on Indifference* could have created such a sensation, but there were several reasons. The book confronted questions that were on many people's minds. One such question, causing much anxiety, was whether there might be some connection between the horrors of the Revolution and France's rejection of religion. The book was also in harmony with the growing feeling that the Voltairian rationalism of the eighteenth century entailed an arid, myopic view of reality. Finally, the book's engaging style caught the eye of persons who would otherwise never have glanced twice at a book by a priest.

The first volume of the *Essay* argued the proposition that religion is absolutely necessary for the existence of society (a conviction that was to survive Lamennais' eventual rupture with institutional religion). He contended that religion raises people above the level of naked self-interest and inculcates a concern for the common good. It promotes harmony by giving people a sense of shared beliefs and it guarantees true liberty by reminding those in power of power's limits. In contrast, he excoriated the idea that society could have originated in a social contract between separate, independent individuals—the philosophy popularized by Locke and the eighteenth-century philosophers. Self-contained, isolated, and arbitrarily willed individuals would never be able to rise above selfish interests for the sake of the common good, Lamennais argued. And religion as a matter of fact was the essential cement of every society known to history.

In the second volume Lamennais launched an all-out attack on autonomous reason. In its place he postulated *general reason,* that is, the truths that all people have held at all times. It is this general reason that makes known the basic truths that are needful for life—such truths as the existence of God, the immortality of the soul, the prospect of eternal reward and punishment, the necessity of prayer and worship, the moral law, the fall of man, and the need for a redeemer. These truths, he argued, were revealed to mankind in a primal revelation and were communicated from generation to generation by tradition or by the testimony of the human race—what he called the *sensus communis.* This common testimony of mankind explains the certainty people have about these truths. Left on its own, individual human reason would only stumble around in darkness, certain of nothing but its lack of certainty.

In this view, the truths delivered in the primal revelation are shared with more or less clarity by all the religions. However, they had to be revealed a second time to Israel in the Mosaic religion because of the spread of idolatry among the nations. It was this revelation that was finally fulfilled in the third revelation, brought by Jesus Christ and thenceforward conveyed faithfully only in the tradition of the Catholic Church. Lamennais develops these arguments at great length with a marvelous variety of illustrations and historical data.

Two aspects of his thought foreshadowed his later decision to leave the Church. First, Lamennais' primary concern was not with Catholicism as such but with the social effects of Catholicism, its "sociological relevance," as it were. The Church's value for him was solely dependent on how well it carried forward the movement for social regeneration. Once he became convinced that it would not and could not fulfill this mission, he had no alternative but to leave it. The second aspect dovetailed with the first. For his concept of the *sensus communis* furnished him with a means of reaching certitude independently of the Church, and thus provided him with an alternative authority to the Church.[2]

Lamennais' onslaught on individual reason was a bold undertaking at a time when Cartesianism, with its emphasis on individual reason, still reigned in the schools and seminaries of the Church; it earned him many enemies, the Jesuits in particular. But his powerful apologia for ultramontanism won him favor with the pope, Leo XII, who received him most cordially in Rome on his visit in 1824.

Liberal Catholicism, Voilà!

Much encouraged from that visit, Lamennais returned to France to take up his work for a regeneration of society by and through a regeneration of the Church. He had three basic items on his agenda: to lead an intellectual renewal of the Church along the lines already sketched out in his *Essay;* to call for complete liberty for the Church, which he saw as the indispensable condition for its renewal; and to work for the triumph of ultramontanism.

Lamennais felt very strongly about the Church's lack of liberty. The

[2]Peter Stearns, *Priest and Revolutionary* (New York: Harper & Row, 1967), p. 42.

restored Bourbon monarchy used the Church to stave off the forces of revolution, and in return granted it various favors such as reestablishing its control over the secondary schools and providing it with much-needed material support. But the monarchy kept a firm grip on the Church, prohibiting national or provincial synods, dictating the curriculum in its seminaries, censoring the pastoral letters of the bishops, and even restricting their communications with the pope. This was Gallicanism with a vengeance—an intolerable situation, in Lamennais' eyes. But worst of all, unlike prerevolutionary Gallicanism, the state no longer based its authority on Christian principles. Neutral in regard to religion, it acknowledged neither God and his commandments nor the existence of objective truth and moral obligations.

This bondage of the Church to a religiously neutral state, whose main concern was to use the Church for its purely secular purposes, was a terrible scandal for Lamennais and, he believed, the principal cause of the Church's decadent state. Moreover he saw that the Bourbons' effort to turn back the clock was stupid. By 1825 he was already predicting their doom and warning that the Church would be dragged down with them in their destruction. The only solution he saw was the separation of church and state—one of the main goals of the liberals, who derived their political agenda largely from the French Revolution. He was still loath to accept the whole program of the liberals, whose hostility to the Church committed them to nullifying its influence. Moreover he saw their penchant for revolution as an invitation to social chaos.

Two developments eventually moved him to accept the liberal doctrine in toto. The first occurred in Belgium where, in 1828, Catholics united with the liberals to throw off the yoke of the Dutch sovereign whose arbitrary rule had managed to infuriate both liberals and Catholics. To seal their union with the liberals, the Belgian Catholics agreed to accept the liberal doctrines of separation of church and state, complete freedom of the press and of speech, and the like. Belgium thus provided Lamennais with an exciting model of the kind of regime he was beginning to envisage for France. The deciding event occurred at home, where on April 21, 1828, the French minister of education took away the bishops' control over the primary schools. This tightening of the screws confirmed Lamennais in his opinion that the ultimate objective of the government was the nationalization and subjugation of the Church. He concluded it was high time to break with the state and call for the kind of freedom the Catholics in Belgium and the United States enjoyed.

This he did in his next book, *The Progress of the Revolution and the War Against the Church* (1829). The Church, he said, should ask only one thing from the state—freedom. By freedom he meant the Belgian model of liberty of conscience, liberty of the press, liberty of education, and separation from the state. He also implored the clergy to rally around their chief pastor in Rome. The spirit of revolution, he now saw, was inextinguishable, and the Church must prepare itself for a long period of violence and turmoil before it could bring to birth a new Christian social order out of the ashes. Liberal Catholicism, *voilà!*

He began with the help of a priest friend, Philippe-Olympe Gerbet, to gather around him at La Chesnaie a group of youths whom he hoped to imbue with his vision of a regenerated society and a regenerated Church. They would form a community of scholars devoted to research in many fields—philosophy, theology, ancient languages, natural science—a sort of Catholic institute of research to renew the Catholic mind. Their publica-

Jean Baptiste Henri Lacordaire

tions would reflect the seriousness of liberal Catholicism and would constitute the Church's answer to Denis Diderot's great infidel encyclopedia, that
landmark of the Enlightenment. Dozens of France's most gifted youths
found their way to La Chesnaie during the short period between 1828 and
1833. Some of them left vivid recollections of their stay there. Others chose
not to join the community but greeted Lamennais' program for a liberal
Catholicism with great enthusiasm. Among them were a number of future
celebrities such as Victor Hugo, Lamartine, Alfred de Vigny, and Saint-
Beuve. Lamennais' two closest disciples were Henri Lacordaire and Comte
Charles de Montalembert.

Lacordaire Finds a Kindred Spirit

Jean Baptiste Henri Lacordaire was born at Recey-sur-Ource, a village near
Dijon, on May 12, 1802. His father, a surgeon, died when Henri was only
four, and his mother had to scrape together the money to put Henri and his
three brothers through school. At the age of ten he entered Dijon's Lycée
Impérial where his brilliance was soon recognized. At twelve he made his
First Communion, but he called it his "last religious joy" before losing his
faith. In 1819 he entered law school at Dijon. Its technical approach to law
he found dry and uninspiring but he was able to find a number of like-
minded friends with whom he formed a club, the Société d'Études. Hungry
seekers after truth, they discussed the great issues of politics, philosophy,
history, and literature in late-night sessions that left a lasting impression on
him.

After his studies at Dijon he left for Paris to train for the bar. His obvious
talent was soon noticed. A celebrated advocate predicted a brilliant career
for him but urged him to gain mastery over his great verbal facility. Nonetheless, Lacordaire reported, "I lived poor and solitary, without exterior
enjoyment or agreeable ties in society, without attraction for the world, or
enthusiasm for the theatre; in fact without any passion of which I was
conscious, unless it were a vague tormenting desire of renown."[3] At the
same time he experienced religious yearnings which he somehow sensed
would eventually overcome his "very incredulous mind." One evening he
read St. Matthew's Gospel and began weeping. As he himself said: "When a

[3]Lancelot Sheppard, *Lacordaire* (London: Burns and Oates, 1964), p. 12.

man weeps he will soon believe."[4] He went to confession and made his Communion at the Cathedral of Notre Dame.

Within six months he entered the seminary. Not at all used to the kind of docility expected of a seminarian, he raised eyebrows by his provocative questions and independence of mind. He further incurred suspicion by forming "particular friendships" (friendships between two members of a religious community that were on a more intimate level than custom allowed). An "untamed horse," they called him, who had to be broken. And he soon learned the difference between the Société d'Études and a seminary. The latter's repressive atmosphere was a great trial for one so much devoted to the play of ideas and so imbued with enthusiasm for the world's movement toward greater freedom. But in spite of many difficulties he remained convinced of his vocation; though held back from ordination with his class, he persevered.

He certainly nurtured no illusions about the mediocrity of the clergy. Ordained in 1827, he found himself completely out of sympathy with his fellow priests who had little experience of the world and were happy with the union of throne and altar under the restored Bourbon monarchy. As he said in a letter to Foisset, "What do the priests in the parish do? . . . Shut up within their sanctuary, where they watch over the stones which still remain to them, they are incapable of defending it from the attacks from outside."[5] He looked around at the people and saw how hated the Church was for its complicity with a monarch trying to revive the old regime. He also knew that the monarchy was doomed and that the Church would pay a steep price for its blindness.

Assigned to teach at a secondary school, the Collège Henri Quatre, he was confirmed in his pessimism by the behavior of the students. The boys made a mockery of the sacraments they were compelled to receive; some even took the host at Communion and used it to seal their letters to their parents. Totally discouraged, he made plans to leave for New York to do missionary work in a country where he believed the Church was free and uncontaminated by gross hypocrisy, and where the clergy were liberal as well as orthodox. But before leaving he paid a visit to Lamennais, whose system of thought he had once regarded as unsound but whose recent conversion to liberalism intrigued him. He wanted to meet this priest, "the only great man in the Church of France," who shared his belief that the

---

[4] Ibid., p. 16.
[5] Ibid., p. 20.

Church should befriend the brave new world being born and bless its commitment to greater liberty. He was somewhat taken aback to find the great man physically unimpressive, slight of stature and carelessly dressed; in fact, a rather drab-looking human being, who might be taken for a sacristan. But he also found him—in words that might later cause him to wince— "simple, good and devoid of pretence." Shortly after this meeting, the July Revolution of 1830 overthrew the reactionary Bourbon monarchy. As Lamennais had predicted, the Church became as much a target as the monarchy. Priests were afraid to appear in the streets and the archbishop's palace was sacked.

When Lacordaire heard that Lamennais was starting a daily newspaper to advance the cause of liberal Catholicism he abandoned his plans for New York and joined in the venture. They called the paper *L'Avenir*—The Future—and gave it the motto "God and Liberty." Published from October 16, 1830, to November 15, 1831, it claimed to be the first daily paper founded in Europe to defend the interests of Catholicism.

Charles de Montalembert

Count Montalembert Signs On

The two partners were soon joined by a young aristocrat, Charles Count de Montalembert, then twenty years old. He was the scion of a family whose aristocratic lineage stretched back into the dim medieval past. Two of his ancestors had fought beside St. Louis at the capture of Damietta in 1249. The thought of these illustrious forebears who had fought for causes not always successful inflamed his romantic imagination. "I am the first of my blood," he wrote in 1860, "to have warred exclusively with my pen. But my pen itself has become a sword which serves honorably in the harsh and holy struggle of conscience, of truth, of right majestic and unarmed against the triumphant oppression of falsehood and evil."[6]

Charles spent his boyhood in England where his father, le Comte Marc-René, had landed in 1792 in flight from the Revolution. When Marc-René returned to France with Louis XVIII in 1814 he left his four-year-old son in England with his grandfather, James Forbes, a devout Protestant. It was Forbes who instilled in the young Charles a love of prayer and a zest for learning. Called back to the continent by his father in 1819, Charles continued his studies at the College Ste. Barbe where he won first place and where his piety astonished his typically unbelieving schoolfellows. It also surprised his father who was at most a nominal Catholic tinged with the rationalism of the eighteenth century. A sojourn in Sweden with his father, who served as the French Minister there, ended on a note of tragedy when the sister young Montalembert loved dearly fell ill and died on the way home. He was devastated by the loss, much as John Henry Newman had been by the death of his sister a year before.

The death of Charles' sister confirmed his dark view of life. Like so many romantic intellectuals of the time, he spoke of the ennui that filled his heart as he contemplated a bleak universe. A romantic indeed to the marrow, he despised the "shabby and degrading" rationalism of the eighteenth century: "My philosophy is not of this world, I detest deduction, reasoning and all the silliness of the professionals."[7] He remained a romantic to the end. Although he carried himself with the aloof air of an aristocrat—his long frock coat always buttoned to the collar, pince-nez cocked—those who

---

[6] Quoted in Marvin O'Connell, "Montalembert at Mechlin: A Reprise of 1830," *Journal of Church and State* (Autumn, 1984), p. 517.

[7] Ibid., p. 518.

were his intimates, and they were few, knew him as a man full of fire and passionate in his enthusiasms. Most passionate was his love of the Church, a burning love that weathered all the suffering the institution inflicted on him. At the end of his life, battered and bruised by her, he could still say: "There is no one alive who loved the glory of the Church more than I."[8]

When the July Revolution of 1830 broke out, the young Montalembert hurried home from England only to be sent packing by his father, who had no desire to see a son on the barricades. Charles traveled instead to Ireland and made a pilgrimage to Derrynane to meet the great Daniel O'Connell who, to his disappointment, acted and talked just like a good-natured farmer. This letdown, however, dampened none of his enthusiasm for the Catholics of Ireland. He returned from Ireland enthusiastic about its Catholics, who had just won a great victory for freedom by using parliamentary methods to secure the Emancipation Act of 1829. Ireland seemed to fulfill Montalembert's dream of a reconciliation of liberalism and Catholicism, a dream to which he had already alluded three years earlier in his diary: "God and Liberty—these are the two principal motive-powers of my existence. To reconcile these two shall be the aim of all my life."[9]

It was in Ireland that he heard about the start of a French Catholic daily newspaper called *L'Avenir* whose slogan was "God and Liberty." The first few issues filled him with enthusiasm. "At last," he wrote to a friend, "a splendid destiny now opens for Catholicism. Disengaged forever from its alliance with political power, it is going to recover its force, its liberty, and its primal energy."[10] Hurrying back to France, he sought out Lamennais who invited him to join the staff. Soon afterward he met Lacordaire and later recalled his first impression of this priest—"of slender form, delicate and religious features, glittering black eyes, sculptured brow and a voice, vibrant, vigorous and infinitely sweet. Born for struggle and for love, he bore already the seal of the double royalty of spirit and talents. He appeared to me charming and terrible."[11] Lamennais, Montalembert, and Lacordaire soon formed a closely knit trio determined to shake the old Church out of its doldrums and confer on it the blessings of liberty, unwelcome though they might be. Mutual personal magnetism explains much of their relation-

---

[8]Jose Cabanis, *Lacordaire et Quelques Autres: Politique et Religion* (Paris, Gallimard, 1982), p. 15.

[9]James Finlay, *The Liberal Who Failed* (Washington: Corpus, 1968), p. 26.

[10]Quoted in Alec Vidler, *Prophecy and Papacy* (New York: Charles Scribner's Sons, 1954), p. 175.

[11]O'Connell, "Montalembert at Mechlin," p. 527.

ship. Montalembert spoke of Lamennais with deepest affection: "I have won an admirable friend and a master. I have moreover found a mission, a set of attitudes which must direct and vivify my whole life. I swear I shall be faithful."

The Battle for a Liberal Church Begins

For thirteen months they waged their battle for liberal Catholicism. Their newspaper soon won international acclaim. *L'Avenir* claimed to be integrally Catholic and sincerely liberal: integrally Catholic in its unswerving loyalty to Rome and sincerely liberal in its determination to champion the liberties of all individuals and communities within the state. Whereas the editors believed that the Catholic faith was best suited to promote the well-being and stability of society, they also believed it should no longer claim special consideration from the state. The French Revolution had so changed the climate of opinion that this would now be counterproductive. The government should merely make it possible for rival beliefs to contend with each other so that, in the end, truth might prevail. *L'Avenir* hoped to rally all those who wanted a genuinely liberal regime, whatever their creed or party.

Lamennais summarized their program under six heads: 1) *Complete religious liberty:* The Church must be completely separated from the state. It must sunder the golden chains that fettered it to the state. 2) *Freedom of education*—because without it, true religious freedom and freedom of thought could not be safeguarded. 3) *Freedom of the press*—since a Christian must believe in the power of truth rather than trusting in censorship, which never succeeded anyway in stamping out error. 4) *Freedom of association*—which is a natural right and essential for a democratic society. Individuals must be able to organize to voice their opinions and protect their interests in the great debate that constitutes the very essence of democracy. Otherwise, despots will take over. 5) *Decentralization*—as one of the enemies of freedom is concentration of power in unresponsive bureaucracies. To avoid this, there must be provision for affairs to be handled at the lowest level feasible, letting each locality as far as possible handle its problems in its own way and in accord with its own conditions and traditions. 6) Finally, *universal male suffrage:* Lamennais here moved a half century ahead of his time—even beyond most liberals—by espousing near-complete democracy as the only way of achieving these freedoms. This was in accord with his doctrine of the universal consensus of mankind as the basis of religious certainty. Casting off its age-old alliance with the monarchy, the Church must now put its trust in the people.

Separation of church and state was a very radical idea for Europeans at a time when every major religion on the continent still received government support, and every major European country possessed an official or semi-official church. But Lamennais could not understand how, after the experience of the Revolution, any intelligent Catholic could not see the harm done to the Church by its union with the state.

Lamennais' idea of uniting all liberals in a common cause was based on his belief that ultimately liberalism would find its best ally in the Catholic Church. This accorded with his political philosophy that a just society could not be based on the theory of classical liberalism. The atomized individuals it postulated could never reach agreement on the basic principles needed to form a just society. Without agreement on the true principles of justice, the outcome would be predictable: The strong would simply prevail over the weak. True liberty could be guaranteed only by the Catholic Church since it alone could guarantee spiritual unity and inculcate the true principles of justice. "Let us not tremble before liberalism," he urged his readers, "let us Catholicize it."

Not content to remain in the world of theory, the three wanted to demonstrate liberal Catholicism in action. For this purpose they established the General Agency for the Defense of Religious Freedom. The Agency dealt with cases involving infringement of freedom, usually religious but also in other areas. They also encouraged the formation of similar associations at the local level, and soon a number of these were functioning in provincial towns. This was one of Lamennais' most constructive ideas, and, like a number of his ideas, destined for a bright future. It was an original idea at a time when most Catholics thought the interests of the Church should be safeguarded by negotiations between clergy and government. Accustomed as we are today to all sorts of lay organizations dedicated to furthering the Church's mission, it is hard for us to appreciate the novelty of the Agency.

One of its noteworthy battles with the government was over its attempt to open a free school for poor children in Paris. Notified of the Agency's intentions, the police soon appeared and ordered the forty or so children and their two masters out of the building. Lacordaire refused to budge. Declaring that freedom of education was now a reality, he told the puzzled children to stay put. But the police were adamant and led them out. Lacordaire stuck to his guns until he, too, was finally forced to leave.

Montalembert and Lacordaire were arrested and put on trial. At that point Montalembert's father died, leaving his title to his son. The trial therefore had to be moved to the House of Peers where both Montalembert and Lacordaire were able to display their impressive oratorical skills. They lost the case, but the fine of a hundred francs seemed a small price to pay for the invaluable publicity their cause received.

There is no doubt that *L'Avenir* struck a resonant chord among a select number of Catholics, especially the younger clergy. The word "freedom" has a magic of its own, and numerous letters were received from supporters who applauded the newspaper's efforts. But its enemies far outnumbered its friends. The still precarious government resented the newspaper's constant criticism of its church policies, and looked on its call for democracy as dangerously subversive. Even most liberals did not share Lamennais' fervor for democracy and thought the very idea of a liberal–Catholic alliance some kind of trick. However, it was the great number of enemies within the Church itself that decided the fate of *L'Avenir*. The bishops and the majority of Catholics found a number of reasons for rejecting Lamennais' novel ideas. They were conservatives who remembered the horrors of the great Revolution and were not eager for a replay. What good could possibly come from a union with the liberals who were sworn enemies of God and the church? They also worried about the spread of unbelief and irreligion but did not see separation from the state as the answer. They agreed that the Church could use more freedom but not at the price of giving license to error and impiety. Moreover, separation would reduce the Church to beggary as there was no tradition of free-will offerings by the people. Very disturbing to the bishops was the spirit of insubordination that seemed so much a part of the movement. *L'Avenir* regularly, in fact, denounced the bishops as blind, worldly, and cowardly, while inciting the laity to take actions on their own. If this situation were allowed to continue, the bishops felt, it would mean the breakdown of proper order in the Church. Finally, the bishops were Gallicans and had no sympathy with Lamennais' ultramontanism.

By 1831 these opponents had turned on the heat. Some denounced *L'Avenir* in their pastorals. The archbishop of Toulouse warned against "these bizarre systems and absurd errors." Others forbade their priests and seminarists to read the paper. Many of them petitioned the pope to censure these revolutionaries who were creating havoc in the Church. Noise over the controversy reached a crescendo as some other Catholic papers stooped to slander and rumor-mongering to discredit Lamennais. They pulled his words about regeneration of the Church out of context to prove that he was another Martin Luther, and they accused him of secretly urging priests to unite to destroy the episcopate. While these nasty charges were false, the full truth was that Lamennais was not unequivocally committed to the Church as were his associates. He was, in fact, constantly torn between his commitment to social reform and his commitment to the Church. While he publicly proclaimed his orthodoxy, he privately wavered as he saw the gap widen between his dream of a democratic Catholicism and the actual Catholicism he experienced.

Appeal to Rome

As episcopal pressure increased, subscriptions began to fall off and *L'Avenir* was soon in desperate financial straits. The editors' first thought was to simply shut down and wait for a better day. But Lacordaire, it seems, came up with the idea of going to Rome and presenting their case to the Holy Father. An approving word from Pope Gregory XVI, he argued, would silence their enemies. Even no word at all would be in their favor, showing that they were at least not in error. Finally, the worst case—a condemnation—would at least satisfy their need to know where they really stood with the pope and would be better than a cowardly surrender to their vile opponents. Lamennais agreed, although privately he was increasingly skeptical about the possibility of the pope assuming the role *L'Avenir* had assigned to him of guiding the political liberation of mankind. He was not encouraged, to say the least, by the papacy's alliance with the Hapsburgs and by its repressive policies in the Papal States. But Lamennais could not easily give up his dream and hoped against hope that he could win Gregory over to his vision.

Having publicly announced their intention to appeal to the pope, the three pilgrims of "God and Liberty" set out in November 1831. Once arrived in the Papal States they were distressed by some of the scenes that greeted their eyes. Lamennais tells of meeting the papal police leading some wretched prisoners in chains who cried out to the three Frenchmen for alms. Rome itself was a great trial for Lamennais, who despised the city he called a "moral desert . . . a great tomb where there are nothing but worms and bones." As it turned out, the trio was unable at first to secure an audience with the pope, and as the weeks dragged on Lamennais became severely depressed and near despair. Finally on February 25, 1832, after they had submitted a long memorandum pleading their cause, they were told by Cardinal Pacca that the pope's judgment would take time and that they would do best to return to France. Pacca also told them of the pope's displeasure with their political activities. But Lamennais would not take the hint and insisted on an audience, which the pope finally granted them. Ushered into the pope's small office they knelt, kissed his feet, and stood while he chatted pleasantly about French Catholics and then dismissed them without a word about their main concern.

At this point Lacordaire saw the handwriting on the wall and left Rome. But Lamennais and Montalembert prolonged their stay until July. Meditating on the sad state of the Church, Lamennais deplored the silence of the papacy: "Immense questions have been raised in the world, they . . . have produced a ferment in society and are inflaming it like a burning fever; what has she [Rome] said? Nothing." Unfortunately for Lamennais, however, Rome was going to speak, and soon.

Lamennais and Montalembert made their way in leisurely fashion to Munich, which they reached in the middle of August. There by chance they met Lacordaire, who was on a visit. In spite of the growing tension between Lacordaire and Lamennais, they went together to a banquet in their honor given by some distinguished Catholic intellectuals. A Bavarian folk song was being sung when Lamennais was called from the table. He returned shortly with unchanged demeanor and simply asked the singers to repeat the part of the song he had missed. Then he leaned over and whispered to Lacordaire, "I have just received an encyclical of the pope against us; we must not hesitate to make our submission."[12]

Lamennais Defiant

The encyclical was *Mirari Vos,* a document that condemned liberal Catholicism. The Church, the encyclical declared, did not need regeneration; granting freedom of conscience would be sheer madness, separation of church and state a bad idea, liberty of the press an abomination. The encyclical also stressed the duty of obedience to the authority of princes.

Lamennais' version of the affair—echoed by many historians—saw the pope as simply a tool of Metternich and the reactionary European powers. Recent research, however, has altered this view. It is true that Metternich was deeply concerned about Lamennais' visit to Rome. If the pope were to show any sign of approval of Lamennais' ideas, it would deal a tremendous blow to the conservative cause. The weight of the Church's immense moral authority thrown behind the revolutionary movement might tilt the balance

[12]Vidler, *Prophecy and Papacy,* p. 212.

in favor of revolution in countries now embroiled in the struggle. This was already the case in Belgium, where victorious liberalism owed so much to Catholic support. While Metternich felt sure that the new pope would offer no encouragement to liberalism, he was taking no chances.

Metternich therefore did all in his power to make sure that the pope would not be taken in by the pilgrims. For instance, he sent a memorandum to the pope emphasizing the dangers involved in their ideas. But as a recent scholar, Alan Reinerman, says, the pope didn't need Metternich's prompting in order to take a negative view of the pilgrims of "God and Liberty." A Camaldolese monk for most of his life, with little experience outside the cloister, Gregory had been faced with a revolution on his doorstep only two days after his election on February 2, 1831. The uprising had spread rapidly from the part of his realm called the Legations, enveloping his whole domain and nearly chasing him from Rome. Only the intervention of the Austrians had saved the day, and the menace of a new outbreak was always present.[13]

One can imagine Gregory's state of mind, therefore, when in December 1831 he heard about that firebrand French priest and his two young disciples coming to ask his support for liberalism and revolution. Perhaps he recalled his predecessor Leo's remark characterizing Lamennais as one of those "lovers of perfection who, if one let them have their way, would turn the world upside down."[14] The likelihood of his endorsing Lamennais' program was, in fact, nil. Gregory was so conservative that he had tenaciously resisted heavy pressure from Metternich to introduce even relatively minor reforms in the administration of the Papal States. What chance was there of his accepting the drastic changes in political and social attitudes advocated by Lamennais?

Still, the Lamennais affair required careful handling. Lamennais' outspoken attitude toward the French hierarchy placed the pope in an unhappy and potentially compromising situation. If he spoke out against Lamennais he would alienate the latter's numerous supporters in France; and if he did not, he would greatly disturb the French bishops. In any case the pope was not eager to publicly condemn Lamennais. He was willing to believe in his good motives and he appreciated the great services Lamennais had rendered to the Holy See, and might still render. He was especially reluctant to alienate one

[13] Alan J. Reinerman, *Austria and the Papacy in the Age of Metternich* (Washington, D.C.: The Catholic University of America, 1989), Vol. 2, p. 251.

[14] Vidler, *Prophecy and Papacy,* p. 96.

of the few intellectual giants the Church could boast of at the time, even though he considered his ideas "dangerous aberrations." Gregory's advisers recommended that he simply ignore Lamennais' presence in Rome until he got the message and left—a policy the pope in fact followed, despite great pressure from Metternich and the Russian and French governments. Lamennais himself finally forced the pope to speak by submitting to him the February 1832 memorandum on his religious ideas, formally requesting that judgment be passed on them.

Even then the pope was reluctant to speak out. Had Lamennais been willing to abandon his political activities, the pope would probably have allowed the matter to rest without further action. But he was shown letters written by Lamennais and intercepted by Metternich's postal service that were most critical of the pope. They also showed that Lamennais intended to continue his political activities and that he interpreted the pope's silence as approval. The papal consultants now agreed that a public statement of disapproval was necessary. Hence *Mirari Vos*. The trio's first reaction to the encyclical was complete submission. They could hardly have acted otherwise in view of their extreme ultramontanism and their previous declarations that they would abide by the decision of the Holy Father. The pope was satisfied that the affair was now over.

Lamennais returned to the peace and quiet of La Chesnaie to reassess his whole position. He was joined by Lacordaire, who stayed with him for a time; but a fundamental disagreement had now come between them. Lacordaire's commitment to the Church was absolute; life without the Church was unthinkable for him. Lamennais' commitment, on the other hand, had never been this deep and now he was convinced that the future lay with humanity, whose cause the Church had deserted. Long silences between the two kept growing. At last, when Lamennais let go with one of his biting remarks, Lacordaire left the table, packed his bag, and took off without even a goodbye. He later recalled looking back and seeing his onetime "master and father" silhouetted against the darkening sky at sunset. The two never spoke to each other again.

By the middle of 1833, Lamennais had altogether given up hope that the papacy would be able to fulfill the mission he had assigned it. "Providence," he said, "has sent Gregory XVI to close a long period of crimes and ignominy, to show the world just how low the human part of the divine institution can sink . . . the old hierarchies, both political and ecclesiastical, are disappearing together; they are no more than two spectres that embrace one another in a tomb."[15] Not surprisingly his relations with the pope deteriorated at a rapid pace.

Lamennais' enemies kept up a vicious campaign of rumors and denunciations to Rome demanding that the Mennaissians (the followers of Lamennais) be compelled to sign an explicit renunciation of their errors (fifty-six of them, according to an indictment drawn up by the archbishop of Toulouse and signed by most of the French bishops). Metternich shared the French bishops' concerns, especially since he had evidence that the Belgian Catholics still adhered to the doctrines of liberal Catholicism while they maintained a prudent silence. The Austrian chancellor was able to keep the pressure on by sending the pope a number of Lamennais' intercepted letters revealing the alleged insincerity of the priest's submission. Finally d'Astros, the archbishop of Toulouse, published a letter he had received from the pope in May 1833 registering the pope's worries about the sincerity of Lamennais' submission. An incensed Lamennais wrote immediately to the pope, declaring his submission to papal judgment in matters of faith, morals, and discipline. Period.

But what about political issues? Since Lamennais left this out, the pope demanded a further clarification. In reply Lamennais asserted that while he fully accepted papal authority in religious questions he remained "entirely free in the purely temporal order." On November 28 the pope indignantly demanded "a simple, absolute, and unlimited" declaration of submission to the doctrine of the encyclical *Mirari Vos*. Totally exhausted, Lamennais caved in. On December 11 he signed the asked-for simple and unqualified act of submission.

It was an impulsive act on the part of a man who had been in the storm center of controversy for years, denounced by the highest authorities in church and state and targeted by relentless enemies on all sides. Surely, also, Lamennais hesitated before the fearful prospect of being cut off from the Church for which he had spent his life. He later described himself as so worn down by the struggle that he would have signed even if he had been asked to state that the pope was God and alone to be worshiped. In a moment of near nervous collapse, he had finally decided for peace at any price. His real thoughts, however, were soon to come pouring out. He wrote to Montalembert a month later, saying he had violated his conscience in signing the submission and was now suffering some fundamental doubts about the truth of Catholicism itself. His greatest torment, however, was the

[15] Ibid., p. 226.

thought that people might accuse him of conniving with the degenerate despots who were trampling down the people everywhere. To rebut such accusations he decided finally to publish a manuscript that had been burning in his pocket for some time, *Paroles d'un Croyant* (Words of a Believer), a paean to revolution.

Published in April 1834, the book sold out almost immediately and created a sensation all over Europe. People lined up in queues to read it in reading rooms; students gathered to hear it read. The authorities were extremely alarmed. (Montalembert, who was traveling in Austria at the time, said he never opened a newspaper without seeing Lamennais' name on the front page.) The book was written in the style of an Old Testament prophet. As Alec Vidler says, "There is no book quite like it—no book that has caught to the same extent the spirit and style of the prophetic and apocalyptic writings of the Bible, together with the simplicity of the evangelical parables."[16] Lamennais astonished his contemporaries by relating the Bible to the political realities of the time and identifying the liberation of the oppressed with the cause of Christ. Lamennais prophesied the overthrow of the existing social order and the inevitable victory of the people over the corrupt political and ecclesiastical rulers who oppressed them. The new order would draw on Christian principles of liberty and equality but would owe nothing to the Church, which had forfeited its role by its connivance with the rich and the powerful. God would now act directly through the people.

The pope called it a product of hell and wasted no time in response. Within a month his reply was drafted, and on June 24 *Singulari Nos* appeared, condemning the book by name as a "book small in size but immense in perversity." Lamennais affected to regard the encyclical with contempt. "The word that once moved the world would not today move a school of little boys," he wrote to Montalembert.[17] It was merely a political document, he said, the personal opinion of Mauro Capellari (the pope's given name) and nothing more. Lamennais was now, having cleansed his conscience, at peace with himself; he would have resumed saying mass if it could have been arranged. In the meantime he was content to await the necessary transformation of the Church that he was sure would come, even though he had no idea what form it would take.

[16] Ibid., p. 248.
[17] Ibid., p. 253.

Montalembert Agonistes

Montalembert tried to persuade his friend and master to submit, citing the scandal he would cause to all those he had brought back to the Church, and the loneliness he would face in taking a road away from all his friends. He compared his friend to Luther, who like Lamennais had claimed to prefer conscience to the pope. But, Montalembert reminded Lamennais, Luther had not spent twenty years exalting the infallibility of the pope; nor had he betrayed the confidence and expectations of as many souls as Lamennais would in leaving the Church. Montalembert himself remained in an agony of indecision for some months, torn between his devotion to liberty and his passionate devotion to the Church "whose glory," as he said later, "he loved more than any person alive."[18] Finally he was horrified to learn that Lamennais, who had been the greatest champion of the papacy, was not only speaking against it in the most scornful terms but was also predicting the proximate demise of the Church itself. The awful truth finally sank in: Lamennais was losing, if he had not already lost, his faith. Lamennais had been like a father to him. "It is not only your genius that I admire," he wrote to Lamennais at the time, "it is your heart above all that I have loved; your heart so tender, so loving, so good, so cruelly wounded and pierced. I put my entire life at your disposal."[19] Leaving Lamennais would mean leaving one who had taken the place of his own father, who had always been too busy for him.

Lacordaire, for his part, pleaded passionately with Montalembert not to give up on the Church: "You cannot imagine the immensity of my pain, nor of my friendship. Alas, whom have I loved if not you. Without you and without the Church, why would anything matter . . . My whole life belongs to you. It is you whom I search and whom I ask for from God. You are my self, you are my friend, my brother, my sister; I have loved you too much to be able to be happy without you" (February 3, 1834). But where Lacordaire exuded affection, Montalembert saw the seeds of extremism. Montalembert told Lamennais that Lacordaire was the same inflexible extremist he had been before but that now he worshiped "Rome" as he had once worshiped "freedom." And he went on: "Oh, what I wouldn't give to

[18] Cabanis, *Lacordaire et Quelques Autres,* p. 15.
[19] Ibid., p. 19.

be able to sacrifice the Church to freedom like you or freedom to the Church like him. But I can't do either. I'm a miserable wretch."[20]

Finally Montalembert could no longer put off his decision. He realized he could not bear separation from the Church, which was more a mother to him than his real mother who, like his father, had shown him little affection. The Church alone could console him for "those intimate sufferings that no political or intellectual activity could relieve."[21] He took to heart the words he had once directed to Lamennais: "I see you with terror going down a road that will lead you step by step away from all your Catholic friends into a frightful solitude among men who have neither your heart, nor your conscience, nor your God. Have pity on yourself."[22] On December 8, 1834, Montalembert made an unqualified submission to both encyclicals. However, the break with Lamennais was only gradual. They continued to write affectionately to each other for a year or two until the strain became too much. By the middle of 1836 their relations had altogether ceased.

Lamennais was never formally excommunicated and no definite date can be given for his actual break with the Church. But in his *Affaires de Rome* (1836) he registers the rupture. Catholicism, he said, is bound to die. But real Christianity, which has inspired all that is best in European history and culture, will live on.

Lacordaire Reigns in the Pulpit

After splitting with Lamennais, Lacordaire was received back by the archbishop of Paris, de Quelen, and once more appointed chaplain to the Visitation convent. At this point he formed a close friendship with Mme. Swetchine, a Russian emigré and convert to Catholicism whose salon in Paris was frequented by influential members of the politico-religious establishment. She took the solitary and inexperienced priest under her wing and became his guide and spiritual counselor. "From that time," he said, "I took no decisive step without discussing it with her and to her I owe that in many dangers I never came to grief."[23]

It was upon her advice that he renewed his submission to *Mirari Vos* and also that, on the appearance of *Paroles d'un Croyant,* he issued his *Considér-*

---

[20]Louis Le Guillou, *L'Évolution de la Pensée Religieuse de Félicité Lamennais* (Librairie Armand Colin, 1966), p. 222.

[21]Vidler, *Prophecy and Papacy,* p. 255.

[22]Le Guillou, *L'Évolution de la Pensée Religieuse de Félicité Lamennais,* p. 227.

[23]Sheppard, *Lacordaire,* pp. 41–42.

ations sur le Système Philosophique de M. de Lamennais. A negative assessment, it consummated his break with Lamennais. But Lamennais' shadow continued to hover over Lacordaire for the rest of his life and to complicate his relations with Church authorities, for many of whom he remained a potentially dangerous innovator.

A new opportunity to use his great talents opened up for him in 1834. A group of young intellectuals led by Frederick Ozanam were seeking a priest who could speak to the rising generation of intellectuals and show how Christianity was in harmony with the aptitudes and needs of modern society. Their choice fell on Lacordaire, whom they wanted for the traditional Lenten Conferences at Notre Dame in 1834. But when the Archbishop Henri de Quelen turned thumbs down they offered Lacordaire the pulpit of Collège Stanislas instead. His lectures proved an overwhelming success, attracting such eminent luminaries as Victor Hugo and Chateaubriand. In the meantime, Archbishop de Quelen had second thoughts about Lacordaire's speaking at Notre Dame. An imposing personality, a Catholic royalist of the old school with little knowledge of theology, de Quelen had no sympathy with Lacordaire's democratic egalitarianism. But he had to face the fact that his own series of Lenten sermons had failed miserably. The priests he chose for the job were the best he had, but the pews remained empty. During a chance visit of Lacordaire, de Quelen decided apparently on the spur of the moment to make his move. "I propose to entrust to you the pulpit of Notre Dame. Will you accept it?"

Lacordaire realized his moment of destiny had arrived. This was his opportunity to reach the elite of Parisian society with his passionate message—that the Church was open to all that was good and true in the ideas and aspirations of the times. If he failed he might not have the chance again, and he had only a few weeks to prepare.

The time for the first sermon was set for 2 P.M. on Sunday, March 1. As the archbishop entered in procession, he was startled by the sea of faces. A crowd of at least five thousand filled the great church, waiting for the man they had heard so much about. With rapid stride Lacordaire mounted the pulpit, a slim handsome figure with flashing black eyes, closely cropped hair, and a high brow. Nervously gripping the edge of the pulpit he looked down on the archbishop, as pale and visibly tense as he was. The worldly-wise and skeptical audience, most of them more or less Deists, looked up at him like spectators before a show. But with a sudden loud cry he jolted and visibly moved them: "Assembly! Assembly! What do you seek? The truth? Then you don't have it yourselves?" The archbishop, he recalled, "raised his head and cast on me a look of astonishment."[24] He felt at that moment that he had won the battle.

And indeed he had. As the weeks went by the crowds continued to swell until police barriers had to be put up. People came as early as five in the morning to get a seat. The audience included some of France's most famous literary and political personalities. Lacordaire was the man of the hour, besieged by people in search of spiritual guidance.

He dominated his huge audience, using every stop of his fine voice from a barely audible whisper to a roaring crescendo; he moved slowly back and forth, flinging his arms out to make a cross or to trace a broad curve; at times he tore his listeners out of their seats by the sheer force of his eloquence. He was Chateaubriand in the pulpit, some said. Today the rhetoric seems over-blown, the language stilted, the history no longer convincing. But he was fully in harmony with the flowery, sentimental Romantic idiom of the time and he was in fact a master of the idiom.

Unlike the typical priest of his time, preaching outdated sermons larded with theological and doctrinal abstractions, Lacordaire knew how to find common ground with his audience. He began his first sermon with a point they could all agree on—namely, the Church as a fact: that no matter how you looked on the Church, it was indeed an enormous fact of human history. With this as a starting point he then dealt successively with the necessity of the Church, its constitution and authority; its founding, and the teaching of mankind before it was founded. Being one who loved the Church intensely, he could preach his theme with burning sincerity. And the church he preached was a church sure of itself, open and in touch with the life around it, sharing its aspirations and not lost in dreams of a glorious past.

In his hands the sermon also became a vehicle of self-revelation. Having adopted the experimental method by starting with the fact of the Church, he continued in this vein by often putting himself forward as one sharing the same aspirations and enthusiasms as his audience, fully involved in the strug-gle and turmoil of their times, passionately concerned like them with the same questions. Hearing him, they could say: "So he has felt this way too, he has thought about this too? . . ." He too believed in human freedom; he too was enthusiastic about the horizons opened up by the Revolution. His argument for conversion was not so much logical as emotional. The

---

[24]Philip Spencer, *The Politics of Belief in Nineteenth-Century France: Lacordaire, Michon, Veuillot* (London: Faber and Faber, 1951), p. 62.

individual listening would say to himself: If this man suffered from the same sense of futility and hopelessness as myself and was able to find hope and healing in the Church, maybe it might work for me too. They wanted to believe but had found it impossible. Lacordaire often moved them to belief in spite of themselves. Lacordaire's Notre Dame Conferences turned out to be one of the most dramatic events of nineteenth-century Church history.

At the very peak of his popularity, however, he sprung a surprise on his hearers. Concluding his series in 1836, he announced his decision to resign and "to retire into solitude with my own weakness and with God." The truth was that, in spite of the approval of the archbishop and the positive effects of his preaching on the French public, he felt discouraged by the relentless attacks of his enemies and wondered whether he should remain in the public eye, if doing so would be a problem for the Church. He decided to spend some time in Rome, a stay that he prolonged for over a year. During that time he published his *Lettre sur le Saint-Siège,* an answer to Lamennais' book, *Les Affaires de Rome.* Lacordaire's *Lettre* helped much in allaying Rome's fears that he too would prove a renegade like Lamennais. But it did not appease his die-hard Gallican and legitimist enemies, including such worthies as Metternich and Cardinal Lambruschini. They could never forgive him his association with Lamennais. The intrigues and plots they mounted against him continued for the rest of his life and cost him much grief.

During this period of quiet prayer and study in Rome, Lacordaire felt a call to join a community of priests. But which order to join? Many of them were still in great disarray and under ban in various countries, including France. After much thought he decided on the Dominicans, even though they too had fallen on hard times. He had to overcome formidable opposition from those in the Church who thought he was simply trying to establish a rallying-point for Lamennais' former disciples. But in 1843 at Nancy he managed to establish the first Dominican house in France since the revolutionary suppression of the order in 1790. That year he also resumed his sermons in Notre Dame, garbed now in the black-and-white robe of a Dominican. His next nine years were years of great activity as a preacher, not only in Paris but throughout France.

Montalembert Soldiers On

While Lacordaire continued his work in the pulpit, Montalembert pursued a brilliant career in the upper house of the assembly (the Chamber of Peers), where he devoted his great oratorical talent to the defense of the Church. His eloquent speeches won him the admiration if not the agreement of his colleagues. Blessed with a sonorous voice as "penetrating as a sword," he spoke extemporaneously with great power. One of his colleagues said, "I have never seen the human voice have such an effect on an assembly."[25] Even his skeptical colleagues, though unsympathetic to his aims, were impressed by his obvious sincerity.

Like Lacordaire he continued to remain faithful to the basic convictions of his *L'Avenir* days. His guiding principle was his belief in what he called the two paramount truths of the times: that freedom can establish nothing without religion, and that religion can reconquer nothing without freedom. His liberalism also included belief in constitutional government, a parliamentary system on the British model, and limiting the central government to the protection of property at home and the national interest abroad; and a conviction that the individual should enjoy as much freedom under law as was possible without detriment to the good of society and the rights of his neighbor.

His main complaint against his fellow Catholics was their fear of freedom and their tendency to identify the Church with an outdated political system. He felt that it was imperative for them to accept modern liberties and to give up any idea of securing a privileged position in the state. Catholics, he argued, should ask for no more and no less than the freedoms granted to all by the law. In fact, he never tired of stating his belief that each and every one of the modern civil rights were most useful to the Church, whether it was universal suffrage, equality before the law, or freedom of teaching, of association, of the press, or of conscience. In fact, these rights were actually more useful to the Church, he insisted, than to her opponents.

But instead of the old divisive tactics of *L'Avenir* he was determined to use a cautious, pragmatic approach to wean Catholics away from their outmoded political ideas. He set about organizing a political party of Catholics to use the political rights granted them by the liberal constitution that was then in force. Their experience of the modern freedoms, he believed, would teach them to appreciate the value of those freedoms. The central issue around which he organized his Catholic party was freedom of education—the right to have one's own schools. The highly centralized French system was at the time under the control of the state university whose secularist and Voltairian professors imposed on the students their anti-Cath-

[25]Cabanis, *Lacordaire et Quelques Autres,* pp. 23–24.

olic prejudices and treated the "ancient faith and the Church of France like
an orphan child."[26] The only remedy Montalembert saw was for Catholics
to win the right to open their own schools. With this objective in mind he
was able to organize the Catholic vote and deliver it to candidates who
favored freedom of education. As a result, in 1846 Montalembert's Catholic
"party" elected 140 deputies pledged to support Catholic schools.

A Liberal Pope?

In the same year liberal Catholicism got a real boost when Giovanni Maria
Mastai-Ferretti was elected to the throne of Peter as Pius IX. As he was
reputed to be a liberal, his election astonished the world and discombobulated the reactionaries. Metternich exclaimed: "I was prepared for everything but the election of a liberal Pope."

Lacordaire managed to meet with the new pope in 1847 and saw that he
was sincerely committed to political reform. But he had no illusions about
the staggering difficulties that faced the pope. A revolutionary faction was
on the loose in the Papal States, while on the opposing front Pius's revision
of papal policy met with enormous reactionary opposition, especially from
the Jesuits. "They were persuaded," Lacordaire said, "that modern society
was an unrealizable fancy and that inevitably, sooner or later, Europe would
come once more under the government of an absolute power. All their
plans since 1814 were drawn up with this fundamental idea in mind . . ."[27]
Nevertheless Pius forged ahead, granting his subjects a constitution that
established a bicameral government and provided for elections by indirect
suffrage.

Filled with hope for the future of liberal Catholicism, Lacordaire returned from Rome to Paris and on February 10 preached a panegyric of
Daniel O'Connell, who had recently died. In his eulogy of O'Connell he
praised Pius IX as the great reformist successor to the Irish leader:
"O'Connell could die, Pius IX was alive. O'Connell could be silent, Pius
IX spoke. O'Connell could descend into the tomb, Pius IX was seated on
the chair of St. Peter."[28]

Two weeks later the streets of Paris were alive with the sounds of revolution. The hour of the Second Republic had dawned and Louis Philippe

[26]Finlay, *The Liberal Who Failed*, p. 167.
[27]Quoted in Sheppard, *Lacordaire*, p. 100.
[28]Cabanis, *Lacordaire et Quelques Autres*, p. 310.

took his leave in haste. But unlike the revolution of 1830, this time the Church was not one of the targets. The liberal Catholics had done their work well to the extent that at least the Church was not looked on as an enemy of freedom.

A New Era?

At first Lacordaire welcomed this revolution and the Second Republic as an act of Providence. In the first flush of enthusiasm he decided to join his two friends Frederick Ozanam and the Abbé Maret in publishing a newspaper to be called *L'Ère Nouvelle* (The New Era). They wanted to rally Catholic support for the revolution: "Liberty, equality, fraternity is the very Gospel itself," Ozanam wrote to his brother.[29] They also wanted to educate the people, especially their Catholic brethren, on the need for social reform. Sensitive to the deplorable state of the workers, they were anxious to promote legislation that would provide remedies. "This revolution," they said, "must be not only political but social." They had their work cut out for them, since few Catholics acknowledged even the existence of a social problem. The clergy, coming from either the aristocracy or the peasantry, had little or no experience of conditions in the factories and the slums. They accepted the prevailing laissez-faire philosophy of the liberals and saw poverty and starvation merely as a regrettable aspect of the mysterious laws by which the social order functions.

L'Ère Nouvelle caught on quickly and soon had over 20,000 subscribers, an extraordinarily high figure for the time. But its earnest proposals for social legislation fell largely on deaf ears in the Catholic community. And it caused a falling-out between Lacordaire and Montalembert, who thought the revolution a disaster. He castigated Lacordaire as "a golden-tongued demagogue."[30] "Lacordaire," he said, "is one of those who pretend that the Republic is the fruit of Calvary; confuse socialism with democracy and democracy with Christianity; and who defend such errors as the progressive income tax, paper money, and the right to work."[31] For Montalembert the revolution meant the end of the constitutional monarchy, which he thought the best possible political system. Moreover, the dissolution of the Chamber

---

[29]Cabanis, *Lacordaire et Quelques Autres,* p. 266.

[30]Spencer, *The Politics of Belief in Nineteenth-Century France,* p. 125.

[31]Cabanis, *Lacordaire et Quelques Autres,* p. 324.

of Peers meant that he would now have to campaign for election in a world turned upside down by the advent of democracy.

As it turned out, all three of *L'Avenir*'s old team were elected to the Constituent Assembly in April 1848.

Friends Divided

In the interval since his break with the Church, Lamennais had settled in Paris and had endeared himself to the poor by his writings and active charity in their behalf. In the pages of *L'Avenir* he had already drawn attention to the plight of the poor. And in his later writings one finds some very moving descriptions of their horrible condition, their damp hovels, the rags that could not keep them warm, the little piles of straw they had to sleep on with hardly any cover, their lack of sufficient food. If people would only listen, he said in an 1839 article, they could hear the anguished cry of the poor. And it was this cry that sounded out the great and fundamental question facing Europe: The question raised by the impoverished masses.

Lamennais predicted the end of the existing social order, whose laws had been written by a conservative well-to-do class to preserve their own interests. But their world was doomed to disappear, he said, since it was opposed to human progress and to the ideas of justice so deeply rooted in the human heart. His support of radical causes landed him in prison for a year in 1840, for writing works advocating defensive violence in the cause of revolution. While in prison he worked on his *Esquisse d'une Philosophie* (An Outline of Philosophy), which Kenneth Rexroth says surpasses Trotsky's theory of the Permanent Revolution because it puts revolution at the center of ontology.[32] But although he espoused a kind of vague socialism he never identified with any of the various brands of socialism that were bandied about at that time. Friedrich Engels thought Lamennais inclined toward communism, and Marx invited him to join in a journalistic venture—an invitation he turned down. For good reason, since Lamennais' "socialism" had little in common with Marx's so-called scientific socialism. Lamennais rejected the idea of class warfare and defended the right of private property. Give the state control of all property, he said, and you will make the citizen more a slave than the Negro on the plantation. While emphatic about the rights of the people, he also spoke of their duties. "Rights without duties is anarchy,"

[32]Kenneth Rexroth, "Lamennais," *Continuum* 7 (Winter/Spring 1969–1970), p. 169–183.

he said. Moreover he remained profoundly religious in outlook, and insisted on the importance of faith in God and on the need for personal spiritual renewal as the basis for the renewal of society.

While Lamennais fought for the poor in his writings, Lacordaire had been an advocate of social justice in the pages of *L'Ère Nouvelle*. He won his seat in the Constituent Assembly, after a heated campaign during which he was called everything from a communist to a monarchist to a Jesuit. On the opening day of the assembly he dared to come garbed in his black-and-white robes, a sight that would have touched off a riot only a few years before. But instead he was given a tremendous ovation by a crowd of well-wishers who bore him in triumph to the door of the chamber. He took his seat on the extreme left only a few rows below Lamennais.

In a sad commentary on the way politics divides, the three former friends and partners were no longer on speaking terms. When Montalembert got up to speak, Lamennais would leave the room. And Victor Hugo recalled how he saw Lamennais, who was usually somber and silent, chatting, gesturing, and laughing while a bishop was speaking. Dressed in a green blazer, bow tie, and light vest, as noted by de Tocqueville, Lamennais still carried himself like a priest, slipping through the crowd with modest gait, looking neither right nor left, with a look on his face of one who might walk over the heads of kings.

Lacordaire's enthusiasm for the republic was soon spent. A mob of Parisians, fearing the worst from the newly elected conservative assembly, tried to intimidate the deputies by invading the chamber and threatening them with violence. They targeted Montalembert for special vengeance because of a speech he made against the radicals. One of the mob even singled out Lacordaire. "See that vulture over there," he said (with his long bony neck and hood Lacordaire did resemble one), "I'd like to wring his neck." The mob dispersed when the bugles of the troops were heard, but the whole business unsettled Lacordaire's faith in the republic, which was never very strong in the first place. He thought constitutional monarchy actually the best form of government; moreover he soon realized he wasn't cut out for the kind of deal-making and maneuvering that is so much a part of politics. He submitted his resignation after only a month in office. "I'm no Richelieu. I'm just a poor little monk who loves peace and a quiet space."[33] He returned to the task he loved—preaching.

[33] Cabanis, *Lacordaire et Quelques Autres*, p. 320.

Montalembert Turns to the Right

As a leader of 250 deputies pledged to the Catholic program, Montalembert wielded considerable power and was able to put his stamp on some of the most important measures passed by the assembly of 900 men. Unfortunately for the future of the Church, Montalembert failed to take the side of the angels in the great debate over the lot of the poor. Their demand for jobs and decent wages was supported by the socialists and radicals who moved the provisional government to respond by setting up the so-called work-shops. But as the cost of maintaining this program skyrocketed, the middle-class deputies, including Montalembert, resolved to turn off the spigot as soon as they got the chance. Their chance came when the elections in June 1848 returned a very conservative assembly. They promptly closed the workshops, precipitating extremely violent riots that lasted for days. Work-ers clashed with the middle class, tearing Paris apart and taking some 1,500 lives. The victory of the middle class was followed by a harsh and cruel repression.

One of the victims of the riots was the archbishop of Paris, Monsignor Affre, who stopped a bullet in front of a barricade as he was trying to mediate between the combatants. He was seen as a martyr and his funeral turned into a triumph for the Church. Seven hundred priests took part as his body was borne uncovered. People pushed and shoved forward to touch the casket, and the white gloves and stockings of the military became quite black in the melee. The intense feelings aroused by the archbishop's sacrifice disposed people more favorably toward the Church than they had been for a long time. In fact the Church emerged from these June days as one of the two powers in place in the country, along with the Party of Order, a coalition of the bourgeoisie and the nobility that came together to "save France." An alliance between the two powers was easily arranged by Mon-talembert; the bourgeoisie and nobility were now anxious to have the Church on their side, while the Catholics were just as anxious to uphold law and order.

In the negotiations between the Catholics and the Party of Order, Mon-talembert showed both the narrow limits of his liberalism and his inability to rise above his middle-class prejudices. Tragically unprepared to deal sympa-thetically with the plight of the workers, he saw their just demands as a dangerous assault on the rights of private property and social order. But as recently as 1839 he had written feelingly of the terrible lot of the workers he had seen in England. The greedy capitalists, he had said, exploited the life and energy of an enormous mass of men, women, and children and gave nothing in return—neither religious consolation, nor security for old age or sickness, not even air to breathe in their disgusting factories. He saw children of seven or eight condemned to fifteen hours of work with their legs encased in iron boots to keep them standing when sleep overcame them.[34] Even earlier, in the pages of L'Avenir, Montalembert had called for improvement of the lot of the working class and for laws to protect the worker. The goods given by our Heavenly Father to all his children must be made accessible to all, he had exclaimed. How did he forget all this only ten years later?

Marx provided the reason. In his *Communist Manifesto* (1848) he declared that the specter of communism was haunting Europe; and now Montalembert, like so many of his class terrified by the violence of the prospect, no longer spoke about social justice or the miserable condition of the worker. Instead he berated them for their vices. "Some talk about the polluted air the workers have to breathe," he said. "What about the hearts (among them) that are profoundly polluted by unbelief and immorality?"[35] Having now become the great defender of the sacred rights of property, his only word to the workers was to be resigned to their poverty and to look for their reward in the hereafter. "There is no middle term," he said. "Today we must choose between Catholicism and Socialism."[36] By reason of his power and prestige, his interpretation of the revolution was accepted by the majority of the clergy and lay Catholics. After all, they were the very sections of society—peasantry, bourgeoisie, nobility—which stood to lose the most in what Montalembert feared was the threat of a general assault on property. The political success of Montalembert in this regard fixed French Catholics in a political and social conservatism that characterized them for a long time. And it opened up a chasm between the French Church and the workers that remains to this day.

The Catholics' reward for their alliance with the Party of Order was the Falloux Law, a bill that provided for a Superior Council of Public Instruction that would include bishops and subject the state university to control by the predominant interests of French society. It also sanctioned the opening of "free schools," which in practice meant schools run by religious associa-

---

[34] Ibid., pp. 42–43.
[35] Ibid.
[36] Spencer, *The Politics of Belief in Nineteenth-Century France*, p. 127.

tions. In the course of the debate over the Falloux Law, Montalembert showed how reactionary he had become when he proposed even educational reform as a way of combating socialism. The secularist education then in vogue, he believed, disposed the student to socialism. Moreover, in his opinion, the system of universal public education erred in giving education to the children of workers and peasants, thereby developing expectations that could not be fulfilled.

Worst of all, Montalembert played a leading role in 1848 in securing the presidency of Louis Napoleon, nephew of the first Napoleon and an adventurer involved in various conspiracies and revolts. Having settled in London, Louis returned to France at the outbreak of the 1848 revolution and was elected a deputy. Montalembert supported his bid for the presidency in return for Louis' support for freedom of education and his promise to rescue Pope Pius IX, who had just been chased out of Rome by the revolution. Louis delivered on his promises and for several years Montalembert was one of his most dependable supporters in the Chamber of Deputies.

Louis had hardly an ounce of religion in him. Temperamentally of the Left but opposed by the republicans, he turned for support to the Right. His main supporters were the middle class, which was frightened by socialism; the army, which was ready to impose order; and the Church, which was willing to teach respect for authority. Moved by fear of anarchy and pressured by the Catholic hierarchy, Montalembert even supported the 1851 coup d'état that established Louis as a virtual dictator. Within a few weeks, however, Montalembert realized the enormity of the mistake he had made, "the greatest of my life." He saw that his fear of socialism had led him into this trap. Greatly repentant, he became a bitter and courageous foe of the dictatorship. In fact, he became the only declared opponent sitting in the legislative body. As Chateaubriand remarked, he was one of those still standing when others were on their knees.[37]

Unlike Montalembert, the other two members of the old *L'Avenir* team did not hesitate in condemning the coup. Lacordaire saw it as an irreparable disaster: "The violation of a country's constitution by military force," he said, "is always a great public calamity preparing fresh troubles in the future and the progressive decline of the civil order." Lamennais' revulsion, of course, knew no bounds. He compared France to a "black, damp, cold cave where in the silence and darkness venomous reptiles crawl and make your skin creep; this is the kind of dwelling they have given us . . . [a regime

[37]Cabanis, *Lacordaire et Quelques Autres*, p. 102.

based on] the priest, the soldier and the spy . . . France today is a country more sealed off than China . . ."[38] Catholicism, he declared, was incompatible with freedom.

An Unrepentant Liberal

Lacordaire found it extremely depressing to see his fellow Catholics in tow to a shameless dictator. No longer loyal to Montalembert, the Catholic party found a new leader in Louis Veuillot, the brilliant and crafty convert journalist whose daily newspaper *L'Univers* waged an unremitting campaign against liberal Catholicism. Veuillot despised parliamentary government, and preached day in and day out his gospel of intolerance, proclaiming his watchword: "Error has no rights." In such a climate Lacordaire saw the futility of continuing his sermons at Notre Dame. How could he try to show that the Church was relevant to the times when the opposite message was trumpeted every day from Veuillot's newspaper pulpit, and enthusiastically accepted by the body of Catholic clergy and people.

Lacordaire decided to retire and devote his time to writing. He returned to the pulpit in Paris only once, when the archbishop begged him to preach for a charity benefit in Saint Roch Church; he would interrupt his silence for a moment to show that he did not share in the general adulation for the emperor. His allusions to Louis in his sermon, in fact, were so pointed that his auditors were astonished. "It would require no army here to close my mouth," he exclaimed, "a single soldier would be sufficient. But God has given me for the defence of my speech and of the truth which is in it, something which can withstand all the empires of the earth." He somehow escaped punishment but was never allowed to preach in Paris again.

When Bishop de Salinis, a former friend and Mennaisian, praised Louis' regime in a pastoral, Lacordaire could not contain himself. He was glad, he wrote, that he could live as a solitary and "protest by his silence and from time to time by his words against the greatest insolence ever authorized in the name of Jesus Christ." Nor would he be one of those, he said at the same time, who "having claimed 'liberty for all'—civil, political and religious liberty—now unfurl the standard of the Inquisition, and hail Caesar with acclamations that would have excited the scorn of Tiberius."[39] In spite

[38]Louis Le Guillou, ed., *Correspondance Générale* (Librairie Armand Colin, 1981), Vol. VIII, pp. 799–800.

[39]Sheppard, *Lacordaire*, p. 122.

of his groveling confreres, Lacordaire remained convinced that the Church alone could still provide a space between the despotism of the strongman and the despotism of the masses. It would not be able to do so, however, until after a great struggle.

One great joy he did have was being reconciled with the repentant Montalembert. The two met by chance at the Gare de Lyon and spent eight hours together on the train. "It was something like eighteen years since that had happened to us. I found him thinking as I do about a whole host of matters. It seemed to me we were back in 1832 when twenty years ago we were returning together from Munich to Paris."[40]

Out of the public eye now, Lacordaire devoted the rest of his life to building up the Dominican order, serving as provincial, writing occasionally, and running a secondary school for boys at Sorèze in the south of France. His work with youth was the source of his greatest delight. The school prospered under his benevolent, intelligent guidance, and, as one might expect, the religious formation was based on respect for the boys' freedom. No one was coerced to attend services, and as a result, he said, "Religion has gained an empire in this school which it never again will lose . . . an empire established not by constraint, or by the mere pomp of external worship, but by the sincere and unanimous conviction of the pupils, by duties fulfilled in private, by aspirations known to God alone . . . by those solemnities in which all hearts meet together."[41]

At last his long-time addiction to overwork caught up with him and illness began to sap his strength. He was able to journey to Paris for his solemn reception into the Académie Française in 1860, but by June of 1861 he took a turn for the worse. When Montalembert came to see him at the end of September, Lacordaire was only able to hobble forward to meet him on the lawn. One of his last letters, written on November 2, was to the historian and one-time prime minister François Guizot to thank him for his book *L'Église et la Société Chrétienne en 1861*. "I share your thoughts," wrote Lacordaire, "about . . . the necessity of religious freedom sincerely practiced for the good of the State and of all Christian communities, about the distinction between the liberal spirit and the revolutionary spirit, which alone can save the world and the Church."[42] A few days later he was

[40] Ibid., p. 133.
[41] Ibid., p. 161.
[42] Ibid., p. 175.

anointed and after three days' agony died on November 20, in his sixtieth year. The funeral in Toulouse was attended by some 20,000 people.

Lamennais' death had occurred four years earlier, when he was stricken by a fatal illness while putting the finishing touches on his translation of the *Divine Comedy*. Refusing to be reconciled with the Church, he had said, "I wish to be buried in the middle of the poor and like the poor, with nothing to mark my grave, not even the simplest stone. Carry my body straight to the cemetery and do not bring it to any church."[43] Afraid of a demonstration the government insisted the burial take place before dawn. But as the handful of mourners started their procession to the cemetery, word spread through the slums: "Lamennais is being carried to his grave." The tiny band soon became an immense throng that pushed its way through the police into the cemetery. There were no speeches as the body was lowered into the grave and a stick thrust into the ground with a paper marked "Félicité Robert de La Mennais." Someone said, "That is all. Go home."

The Lonely Liberal Catholic

Montalembert fought on for their common cause in the pages of *Le Correspondant*, a journal which he edited. But he was unable to woo Catholics away from their alliance with Louis Napoleon. They exulted in "the restoration of the Christian monarchy personified by the Napoleons." The bishop of Rennes saluted Louis at the door of his cathedral as "the bulwark of the nineteenth-century papacy, the most devoted to the Church of all the French kings since Saint Louis."[44]

Most Catholics now hearkened to their new oracle, Louis Veuillot, who despised the bourgeois magnates of the Party of Order for their narrow self-interest, their prejudices, and above all their religious indifference. He called Montalembert's alliance with this irreligious Party "an unholy" one. By harping constantly on this point in the pages of *L'Univers,* he was able to draw most of the clergy and laity away from the liberal Catholic nucleus around Montalembert. "France will reject parliamentary government the way it rejected Protestantism or it will perish in its efforts to vomit it up . . ." Veuillot declared.[45] A writer with a genius for invective, Veuillot delighted in reviling modern science, philosophy, progress, and liberty

---

[43] Rexroth, "Lamennais," p. 182.
[44] Cabanis, *Lacordaire et Quelques Autres,* p. 107.
[45] Finlay, *The Liberal Who Failed,* p. 126.

while singing the praises of the Inquisition. In 1861 Lacordaire excoriated him: *"L'Univers,"* he said, "is in my eyes the complete negation of the Christian spirit and of human common sense. I don't think the Church has ever been defended by such depressing people."[46]

Veuillot called liberal Catholics "men of little pride and weak faith, with Esau's appetite for the mess of pottage." Montalembert called Veuillot and his writers "a band of calumniators and public defamers." The two men lived side by side on the rue du Bac and sometimes they could be seen refusing to look at each other as they entered the nearby St. Thomas Aquinas Church for Vespers.[47] The ultramontane party led by Veuillot did not attract the same amount of talent as Montalembert's liberal Catholic party, although Veuillot himself was easily a match for anyone on the other side. Veuillot also had powerful allies—the lower clergy, the great majority of the laity, and Rome. With his political position in ruins, Montalembert now appeared to his critics as a kind of pitiable Don Quixote, his drooping banner "God and Freedom" mocked and scorned by his fellow Catholics. Veuillot was the one who spoke for them, the man who said: "The word liberty is not used in Christian countries." As someone said at the time, Catholics loved the use of force as long as it was used on others and loved intolerance as long as it was directed at the ideas of others. Montalembert, by contrast, exclaimed, "To want freedom for the Church and 'servitude' for everyone else in the times in which we live is to ask for what is impossible."

While his words fell on deaf ears in France, they were heeded in Belgium, whose constitution was created by a union of liberals and Catholics. The cardinal-primate, Englebert Sterckx, a large-minded man, decided to hold a universal congress of Belgian Catholics in 1863 in Malines and to invite Montalembert to give the keynote address. Though in bad health and prematurely aged, Montalembert seized the chance to pronounce his political testament and his ideal of a free church in a free state. His telegram to the cardinal was dramatic: "I shall come if I am alive."

Greeted by the three thousand present with "an explosion of applause the likes of which I never heard before," he began his speech with a salute to Belgium, "Catholic and liberal."[48] It was, he said, the only country where Catholics were not at a disadvantage in public life. He went on to unfold his

---

[46] Cabanis, *Lacordaire et Quelques Autres,* p. 108.
[47] Ibid., p. 110.
[48] O'Connell, "Montalembert at Mechlin," p. 534.

thoughts on the Church's need to deal realistically with the spread of freedom and democracy, fruits of the great revolution that had given birth to contemporary society. Democracy is here to stay, he argued. It is already triumphant in half of Europe and tomorrow will triumph in the other half. The old alliance between throne and altar is doomed and the efforts to renew it have only weakened the Church. But there is no reason to fear. There is not a single modern freedom that in the future would not be necessary or at least very useful to the Church. He took each one in turn and spelled out their advantages: universal suffrage, equality before the law, and freedom of teaching, of association, of the press, and of conscience.

Freedom of conscience, the one that caused Catholics the most trouble, he called the most precious, the most sacred, the most legitimate, and the most necessary of all the freedoms. Here he knew he was on dangerous ground for his Catholic opponents considered this freedom above all to be anti-Christian in origin and the preferred weapon of the Church's enemies. To accept it, he insisted, did not mean subscribing to the absurd idea that one religion is as good as another. Actually, he claimed, Catholics needed it more than any others since they were the only ones who alarmed oppressors of the religious conscience. Look, he said, at the deplorable state of the Church in countries still wedded to the old system of coercion—Italy, Portugal, Spain. It is the best demonstration of the system's futility. "The Spanish Inquisitor saying to a heretic, 'The truth or death!' is as odious to me as the French terrorist saying to my father, 'Liberty, fraternity or death!' The human conscience has the right to demand that it never again have imposed upon it these hideous alternatives."[49] When Montalembert was finished, Cardinal Sterckx rose and shook his hand warmly while the old man smiled down at the applauding crowd.

Montalembert warned his audience that the immediate prospects of liberal Catholicism were not good. The beleaguered Pius IX had absolutely no tolerance for liberalism. On one occasion, it was reported, the pope had exclaimed to a group of French tourists with his eyes blazing: "I have always condemned liberal Catholicism," and shaking his upraised hands, had added with force, "I will condemn them forty more times if I have to."[50] In fact, Montalembert was quickly reprimanded by the Vatican and threatened with a public censure. His two speeches at Malines moved Pius IX to take a step he had been contemplating for some time: the issuance of a general con-

[49] Ibid., p. 536.
[50] Cabanis, *Lacordaire et Quelques Autres,* p. 113.

demnation of modern errors, including those associated with liberalism. And so the famous Syllabus of Errors appeared on December 8, 1864. People around the world were startled to hear that among the eighty errors condemned were freedom of religion, the doctrine of progress, and liberalism.

It was a most unfortunate document, betraying the impulsive nature of the pope and creating the maximum amount of misunderstanding. It consisted largely of verbatim extracts lifted out of their original context in previous papal documents—extracts properly understood only if put back in that context. The masterly corrective feat of putting them back into context was accomplished in a few weeks by the liberal French bishop Félix Dupanloup. By making a subtle distinction between thesis and hypothesis he was able to show that Rome did not mean to condemn or repudiate the liberal constitutions actually in force in such countries as Belgium, England, Latin America, and the United States. Letters from 600 of Dupanloup's fellow bishops poured in, thanking him for rescuing them from a most embarrassing situation.

But Pius himself favored an intransigent interpretation from Veuillot's pen and, in spite of Dupanloup's subtle gloss, the popular impression was that the pope had indeed condemned ideas that were the basic currency of the modern state. Montalembert cried out in horror and shame to his friend Falloux. "How our enemies will use it as their war cry! . . . At the end of my career," he said, "I find myself disavowed, blamed, humiliated, sacrificed and at the mercy of fanatics."[51] He reread Lamennais' *Affairs of Rome* in order to learn how to avoid his old master's mistake of trying to explain himself to Rome and then having to explain his explanations. He resolved instead to maintain absolute silence.

He now spent most of his time traveling and writing. For a political being like himself, condemnation to inaction was a depressing fate. As his health declined he spent long periods at his chateau, La Roche in Burgundy, with its large rooms hung with tapestries, and his great library. He wrote to one friend, "Suffering and weakness are my daily bread," and to another, "There are many days when I can't even get out of my bed . . . pray that I may carry this heavy cross."[52] Before the end came, however, he had to bear another heavy cross. News broke that a council was in the offing and that a movement had been started to proclaim the infallibility of the pope. It was

[51]Ibid., p. 115.
[52]Ibid., p. 122.

the supreme irony of his life that he who had done so much to promote ultramontanism now stood horrified to see it taken to its logical conclusion: the definition of papal infallibility—a definition that would set the seal on the pope's condemnation of liberal Catholicism.

Critics were not slow to label Montalembert's opposition to the definition as inconsistent with his previous fervent ultramontanism. But he replied in a letter to the *Gazette de France* of March 7, 1870, that he had always opposed the idea of the personal, separate infallibility of the pope, and he stigmatized the move as an outrageous attempt to impose a dictatorship on the Church. Absolute monarchy in the Church, he declared, was to him as repugnant as it was in the state. And, he said, those who would impose it on the Church were prepared "to sacrifice justice, truth, reason and history to the idol they have erected in the Vatican." Montalembert had always fought against idolatry of whatever stripe—idolatry of privilege, idolatry of the Bourbons, of Louis Napoleon, of universal suffrage, and of revolution. No human regime, he held, should ever be idolized. For him, "the human spirit must always be free to question, to criticize and to be convinced through intellectual persuasion; force must never be applied."[53]

He now had but a few days to live. He had not left his house since February when he had dragged himself to St. Thomas Aquinas to receive Communion. But on the eve of his death, friends found the emaciated white-haired old man more full of life, more brilliant than ever. The next morning he felt a sharp pain near his heart. His last words were *"Pardon, mon Dieu."*

Lamennais, Lacordaire, and Montalembert's dream of a liberal Catholicism, dealt a mighty blow by Gregory and Pius, seemed to expire with the three of them. Their efforts, however, were not in vain. Again and again their tattered old banner would be raised in the Church. In fact, many parts of the Catholic Church kept the dream alive in spite of the Syllabus. A long list of Catholic scholars, intellectuals, and statesmen would be fervently liberal: Lord Acton, Ludwig Windthorst, Don Sturzo, Marc Sangnier, and Jacques Maritain, among the most noteworthy. But the official Church remained committed to its medieval worldview and continued to hold that the principle of freedom of religion should only be tolerated as a necessary evil. Even the brilliant English convert Ronald Knox could dare to say that when you are in power we demand freedom on the basis of your principles;

---

[53]Bernard Aspinwall, "Montalembert and 'Idolatry,' " *The Downside Review* 89:162.

when we're in power we deny you freedom on the basis of our principles.[54] And up to the eve of Vatican II the modern world was regularly reminded, by such intransigents as Cardinal Ottaviani or the Spanish cardinal Segura, that the Roman Catholic Church was and always would be radically intolerant. It was only at Vatican II that their mouths were finally shut. For those who wonder why it took so long for this to happen, perhaps the story of Lamennais and his two colleagues may offer the hint of an explanation.

[54]Ronald Knox, *The Belief of Catholics* (New York: Sheed and Ward, 1940), pp. 203–204.

THREE

Daniel O'Connell
(1775–1847):
Liberal Catholic Leader
of a Bloodless Revolution

O NE OF THE FIRST SIGHTS to greet the eyes of a visitor to Dublin is the towering column crowned by an enormous image of Daniel O'Connell. He gazes down over O'Connell Street, the city's main thoroughfare, reminding all who pass of Ireland's greatest son. He found the Irish Catholic masses a people still under the boot, a nation of serfs, beaten into the mud by their English Protestant conquerors. He lifted them up, straightened their backs, organized them into a potent political force, and set them on the path to independence and freedom—introducing them to French-Revolutionary ideas of liberty and democracy but without the violence that marred the French experiment.

The story goes that before he died at Genoa in May 1847 while on the way to Rome, O'Connell committed his soul to its Creator, his heart to Rome, and his body to Ireland. When his heart was delivered to the pope, Pius IX called him "the great champion of the Church, the father of his country, the glory of the Christian world." In Paris in Notre Dame Cathedral on February 10, 1848, Lacordaire at the height of his fame preached a memorable panegyric of Daniel O'Connell.

"Your glory," Montalembert said of O'Connell, "is not only Irish, it is Catholic. Wherever Catholics begin anew to practice civic virtues, and

Daniel O'Connell

devote themselves to the conquest of their legislative rights under God, it is your work. Wherever religion tends to emancipate itself from the thraldom in which several generations of sophists and lawyers have placed it, to you, after God, it is indebted."[1]

The French Revolution taught O'Connell the futility of violence; he would rationalize the world, not revolutionize it. But he detested much of 1789, especially its persecution of the Church and its aggressive Jacobin secularism, though he favored its separation of church and state. The example of the American Revolution was much more important for him than was the French. His egalitarian and libertarian ideas, for example, were traceable to the American Revolution.

A People Beaten Down

To understand Daniel O'Connell one must realize the roots of Ireland's tragic relationship with England, going back to the twelfth century when King Henry II established direct rule over the area around Dublin and was accepted by the Irish kings as lord of Ireland. The pope himself, Alexander

[1] Oliver MacDonagh, *The Emancipist: Daniel O'Connell, 1830–47* (New York: St. Martin's Press, 1989), p. 316.

III, extended full recognition to this extension of Anglo-Norman rule over Ireland. The English hegemony was challenged, however, when powerful Gaelic kings asserted their control over many parts of Ireland. By the time of the Reformation the English royal power was confined to a small area around Dublin. When Henry VIII broke with the pope he tried to take Ireland with him, but with no success. Irish Catholic reverence for the pope and loyalty to the Holy See was too deeply rooted in its history. The Irish Church was able to resist the imposition of Protestantism and to maintain its independence from the English monarchy.

To gain control, the English sent over Protestants to colonize Ireland. This policy continued under the Stuarts, during whose reign power passed from the old English and Irish upper classes to the new colonists and landowners who were able to secure confiscated property. In the English civil war (1641–1645) between Parliament and King Charles, the Irish Catholics sided with the king and paid a heavy price when Cromwell proved victorious. Those involved were either executed or deported, and even the innocent were allowed to hold land in only one of the provinces (Connaught). No tolerance was extended to the clergy. Mass was forbidden. The organization of the Church was severely crippled. When the Stuarts were restored in 1660 some alleviation took place. But holding little land and no political power, Catholics remained reduced to insignificance. When the Catholic James II took over in 1685, Catholics were granted many favors. In the Glorious Revolution (1688), James took his army to Ireland where he was joined by the Catholics but failed to win over more than a handful of Irish Anglicans. These joined the forces of the new king of England, William III of Orange, and helped defeat James at the Battle of the Boyne. Once again the defeated Catholics felt the full measure of Protestant wrath. A penal code was enacted which, if put fully into effect, would have extinguished the Catholic Church in Ireland. Its basic concern, however, was not with religion but with property as the key to political power. Under its aegis Catholic ownership of land was reduced to 5 percent during the eighteenth century.

Although Catholics had in practice been barred from Parliament since 1660, they were now legally excluded by the imposition of an oath that no Catholic could take. Acts were passed designed to complete the extinction of the clergy. All regular clergy and all clergy exercising jurisdiction were banished. A particularly stringent oath abjuring the Jacobite cause was imposed on the clergy in 1709. Most of the clergy refused to take it and were subject to severe penalties if caught. "Priest-catchers" were paid a sum for turning in priests. But catching priests was a risky occupation, for, if caught in the act, the catcher could find himself facing a mob of angry Catholics.

Eventually the Catholics were able to reorganize and set up their diocesan and parish system. If they were discreet they could find ways to worship—in their mass houses or at their mass rocks. Devotion to the mass was in fact the hallmark of the persecuted Irish faithful. Bishop MacMahon of Clogher in 1714 told of the stratagems used to conceal the identity of the priest, so those questioned could truthfully say they did not know who the priest was; the priest would say mass with his face veiled or in a closed room with the congregation on the outside.[2] In Dublin especially they had to maintain a low profile, but their sheer numbers made it difficult for the government to greatly restrict their activities. In outlying counties where there were few Protestants there was a sense of "live and let live." Records in Galway, for instance, show that a search of three friaries and three nunneries was made in 1731. It states that no religious could be found, but the records of the Augustinians and the Dominicans for the same year notes the amount of money spent on "claret to treat the sheriffs in their search."

Finally in 1792, with winds from the French Revolution blowing strongly across Europe, and with the prospect of an imminent war with France, the British prime minister William Pitt induced the Irish Parliament to make some concessions to the increasingly restless Catholics. Several Catholic relief bills were passed in 1792 and 1793. The last one granted Catholics access to civil and military office but effectively barred them from parliament because of the required oath of loyalty to the king as supreme head of the Church.

Up from the Bog

News of the relief bill reached the seventeen-year-old Catholic Irishman Daniel O'Connell, then studying at the Jesuit College in Douai, France, and opened a new world of possibility for him.

The son of Morgan O'Connell and Catherine O'Mullane, Daniel stemmed from a long line of hardy Catholic natives of the coast of Kerry, isolated by mountains from the rest of Ireland. The Ireland he grew up in still labored under the penal laws. Living conditions for many in the rural areas were primitive. While the Catholic merchant class in the towns was

---

[2]Patrick Corish, *The Irish Catholic Experience* (Wilmington, Del.: Michael Glazier, 1985), p. 132.

accumulating considerable wealth, and the number of Catholic landowners was increasing, the rural poor lived in constant fear of starvation.

It was customary for parents of large families to ease the crowding in their homes by fostering out their infant children. Shortly after birth, Daniel was put out this way to a herdsman's family with whom he spent his first four years. His abode was typical of the peasantry, a cabin with no window and no chimney and with a floor of mountain rock polished by the hooves of the sheep who at night were let in to share the cabin with its inhabitants. A smoldering piece of bog-wood filled the room with smoke and gave off only a little heat. At the age of four Daniel was adopted by his uncle Maurice, better known as "Hunting Cap," and moved to Darrynane, his uncle's spacious house. Hunting Cap was one of the Irish Catholics who were able to prosper in spite of the penal laws. Many of them made their living as merchants dealing mainly in foreign trade. Hunting Cap shipped meat, hides, and salt, which he manufactured himself, to England and France while bringing back silks, laces, and textiles, wines and spirits, tobacco, sugar, and tea. A bit of smuggling was thrown in for good measure.

Darrynane stood in a ruggedly beautiful valley where purple mountains loomed over a wide expanse of the Atlantic. Here Daniel grew up learning to read and write under the tutor his uncle secured for him. When he reached the age of fifteen his uncle sent him and his brother Maurice to France for their education. They enrolled first in college at St. Omer in 1791 and then went on to Douai in 1792, where Daniel showed his mettle by winning many honors. In the meantime the revolution convulsing France swept close to the boys at Douai, when, while they were on a walk one day, some soldiers shouted insults at them. They heard daily reports of the carnage by guillotine and war. The unsettled conditions soon forced the college to close, and Daniel and his brother took off for London in haste, even leaving behind Daniel's violin. But Daniel took along a lasting impression of bloodshed as the ultimate evil.

He began serious preparation for his career in law, entering Lincoln's Inn in London in January 1794. Daniel already showed the liberal tendencies that were to mark his political career. In the journal he kept at the time he registered his opposition to the widespread use of capital punishment for a large assortment of crimes; he also espoused the cause of feminine equality. His journal shows that during this period he systematically applied himself to a regimen of reading that touched on many fields of knowledge. Tom Paine's *Age of Reason* and *The Rights of Man* were particularly influential. Paine's *Rights* and William Godwin's very radical tract *Political Justice* were the most ardent expressions of the sympathies aroused by the French Revolution. Godwin's profound belief in human perfectibility was most congenial to Daniel. Godwin was also convinced of the eventual disappearance of such traditional institutions as marriage, religion, private property, and monarchy. Two of Godwin's ideas were to constitute the very core of O'Connell's political philosophy: his opposition to violence and revolution, and his belief in the absolute importance of enlisting public opinion in order to promote social change. "All government," O'Connell wrote at the time, "is founded in opinion . . . Make men wise, and . . . you make them free."[3]

Paine's *Age of Reason* was a deistic, antidogmatic, anti-ecclesiastical, anti-Christian tract even though it did pay homage to Jesus as a great philanthropist. It gave O'Connell, he said, "a great deal of pleasure," and at least momentarily made a deist of him. Reading other freethinkers such as Voltaire, Rousseau, and Hume moved him in the same direction. The change was not lasting, for he returned to Catholic faith and practice within a few years and eventually became a very devout Catholic. All students of O'Connell, however, would agree that his education greatly opened his mind and imbued him with a very accepting attitude toward those of other religious beliefs.

When O'Connell returned to Dublin in the fall of 1796 to continue his legal studies, he found the country at fever pitch. Revolution was in the air. The United Irishmen were formed to secure the complete separation of Ireland from England. To give them assistance in throwing off the English yoke, an expeditionary force of French troops arrived off the coast, but the attempt was abortive. Nevertheless the excitement continued. O'Connell—who, in the meantime, had been admitted to the bar—had little faith in revolution as the solution to Ireland's problems; but, swayed by patriotic passions, he joined the United Irishmen and was even put under surveillance by the authorities. When the rebellion broke out in May 1798 he was far from the bloodletting, having prudently left Dublin for his father's house in Kerry. From his distant post he could watch the development of the Irish Revolution philosophically, and from it he learned two lessons that were to guide him all his life. One was how easily revolutions are corrupted by treachery and cowardice. The other was an abiding distrust (and pity as well)

---

[3] Quoted in Oliver MacDonagh, *The Hereditary Bondsman* (New York: St. Martin's Press, 1987), p. 41.

of the masses, once they are released from "rational" control. "Oh, Liberty, what horrors are perpetrated in thy name!"[4]

Emancipation—Yes! Union—No!

In the aftermath of the Irish Revolution, O'Connell was faced with the first critical test of his political acumen. William Pitt, still the prime minister of England, had wanted for years to destroy the independence of the Irish Parliament by uniting it with the English Parliament, and he now saw his chance. In the eyes of many, the Irish Parliament had discredited itself by its behavior during the rebellion when, unable to deal with the insurrection its own policies had provoked, it had to call for help from England. But in order to dissolve the Irish Parliament, Pitt needed the support of the Catholics. As bait he held out to them the promise of full emancipation, which would remove all the remaining disabilities they suffered from. Feeling no love anyway for the oppressive Protestant parliament, the bishops fell for Pitt's offer and helped to mobilize Catholic support for the Union.

O'Connell was of a different mind. Why, he thought, should the Catholics trust Pitt, who had betrayed them in the past? Would it not be better to rely upon their own organization and their own leaders, who had brought down the whole penal code over the last forty years? And how could they desert their old Protestant ally Henry Grattan, the man who had already done so much for them and who was now fighting so desperately to save the Irish Parliament—which he, more than any other, had created? When a mass meeting of Catholics was organized in Dublin in 1800 to protest against the union of the two parliaments, O'Connell was chosen to propose the principal resolution.

To take a stand on such an explosive issue was a real risk for O'Connell, who was just beginning his career. He dared to oppose the Irish Catholic leaders and the bishops. At the same time he chanced being arrested as a traitor under the martial law still in effect, with habeas corpus suspended. In these tense circumstances, any speech against the Union on the part of a Catholic could easily be construed as treason. This, his first public speech, contained the substance of what he would preach as an Irish agitator for the rest of his life. O'Connell insisted that in spite of reports to the contrary, Catholics were not in favor of the Union. In fact, he said, no inducement could get them to favor the Union. They would not favor the Union even if

[4]Ibid., p. 65.

they were in turn to be rewarded by the benefits of emancipation. O'Connell realized that emancipation with the Union would be a hollow victory. Ireland could never attain prosperity as long as its vital interests were in the hands of an English parliament.

We must keep in mind that the Catholic case for emancipation rested on the belief shared by Englishmen and Irishmen alike in the basic human rights of civil and religious liberty. But the exclusion of Catholics from political life was also a basic feature of the great settlement of the Glorious Revolution of 1688. To call it into question would be to challenge the whole British way of life, the union of church and state, and the very definition of citizenship. Besides, admitting Catholics to the polity would hardly be the end of the matter; what of the other groups excluded from the political life of the nation—the Protestant dissenters as well as the disenfranchised masses?

O'Connell had all along predicted that the bargain struck between the Catholics and William Pitt would not be honored. And he was soon proven right. The bishops and other Catholic leaders had been hoodwinked. Pitt was unable to deliver on his promise of emancipation for the Catholics. The bigoted King George and the bigots in Pitt's own cabinet were too much for him, and he himself was forced from office.

In the next years O'Connell's energies were absorbed by his profession and his marriage to Mary O'Connell (her maiden name also). By the end of 1804 his great success at the bar had increased his income considerably and his second son was born. Both situations gave him food for thought. Were he not a Catholic, his professional attainments would have assured him of a glorious career. Moreover he bitterly realized that the future of his sons would soon be shackled by the restrictions against their religion. The only remedy, he realized, was to secure full recognition of the right of Catholics to full participation in the life of Ireland. Above all they must be accorded the right to serve in public office—the primary object of emancipation.

Increasingly O'Connell devoted his time to the work of the Catholic Committee, an association mostly of upper-class and rather conservative Catholic laymen organized to defend the interests of the Catholic community. In order to secure emancipation they were still willing to accept the union of the two parliaments and to allow the British government a veto power over the appointment of Catholic bishops. O'Connell, however, rejected this timid policy. For him emancipation would be a fraud unless the Irish got control over their affairs by having their own parliament; furthermore the veto would emasculate the Irish episcopate. O'Connell was determined to keep the heat on the government by constant agitation, using two weapons: English common law and Irish public opinion. He would exploit the traditional English rights of petition and assembly to the full, while making as much noise in the process as possible.

Later, in 1814 when it appeared that Pope Pius VII was ready to yield the veto in return for restoration of the Papal States, O'Connell organized a meeting in a Carmelite church in Dublin where he proclaimed his absolute and undying opposition to the veto and repudiated the right of the pope to bind the consciences of Irish Catholics in any particular without the Irish bishops' assent. "I am sincerely a Catholic but I am not a papist," he exclaimed.[5]

The government tried to squelch O'Connell and the Catholic Committee by appealing to a law that forbade the formation of any organization of Catholics that had a representative character. But each time the magistrates closed down a meeting, O'Connell would challenge the decision in court and thus raise the public's awareness of the issue. Thus when the Catholic Committee was threatened with suppression, O'Connell replaced it with a new organization, the Catholic Board, that was less open to challenge.

As part of his general strategy, O'Connell felt it was important to manifest a bold defiant attitude in place of the servile and timorous approach of the old guard on the Catholic Committee. He wanted to teach the Irish Catholics not to crouch, not to fear, and to regard themselves as the equals of the Protestants. But O'Connell insisted, in the course of this defiance, that they eschew all violence and even illegality. He wanted nothing more nor less than fair and full treatment under the British Constitution. It was an "extraordinary doctrine and recipe for a demagogue to offer the masses whom he intended to 'create.' But, albeit inert and hidden for at least a decade, it contained the dynamite which would eventually blow apart the old Protestant ascendancy in Ireland."[6]

The mantle of Catholic leadership was now indisputably fixed around O'Connell's huge frame. He was greeted with tumultuous enthusiasm whenever he appeared at a public meeting. On his morning walk between his home on Merrion Square and the courts he resembled a highland chieftain as he lifted his legs in the military step he had picked up as a trainee and shouldered his umbrella like a pike while followed by his train of admirers.

His career at the bar had proven most successful. His shrewd insight into

[5] MacDonagh, *The Hereditary Bondsman*, p. 130.
[6] Ibid., p. 115.

the workings of the average Irishman's mind made him a master at cross-examination. No other barrister could approach him in talent and vigor. His income had risen commensurately. And he was now the father of a large family in a marriage that brought him great personal happiness. Nevertheless he was willing to jeopardize much of this by leading the agitation for Catholic rights.

The Magee Trial

The measure of O'Connell's defiant willingness to take on the English establishment can be gauged by an episode that took place in 1813. Robert Peel ("Orange Peel" as O'Connell immediately labeled him), the new chief secretary, had arrived to manage affairs in Ireland in 1812. He was only twenty-four but already a rising star in the British government and he came to Ireland determined to suppress the agitation organized by O'Connell. He and his attorney general William Saurin watched closely therefore for any chance to destroy or intimidate the opposition press and teach the Catholic agitators a lesson. They saw their opportunity when the editor of the *Dublin Evening Post,* John Magee (incidentally a Protestant but a friend of the Catholics and active in the Catholic agitation), published a tirade accusing the English governors of Ireland, past and present, of oppression and corruption. Peel and Saurin pounced on Magee and put him on trial for libel. Then they packed the jury with hostile Protestants.

The whole affair was a blatant maneuver by Peel to muzzle the press and cow the opposition. O'Connell knew that Magee, his client, didn't stand a chance. Nevertheless, he decided to use the trial to expose the nefarious practices of Saurin and the British administration in Ireland, and to plead the Catholic cause with every ounce of energy he possessed.

There was a general sense of history in the making on July 27, 1813, as O'Connell rose to face not only the judges of the bench but also Saurin in wig and gown, the commander-in-chief of the forces, other high officials, and Peel himself. Knowing the jury was implacably hostile to him, O'Connell made no effort to ingratiate himself. Instead he began defiantly by admitting it was a hopeless and cheerless task to try to get a fair verdict from them. Avowing that open discussion of the conduct of public officials is a duty and not a crime, he launched into a blistering attack on Saurin, whose opening address he called a "farrago of helpless absurdity." In a thundering voice he lambasted the attorney general with all the might of his power of invective, characterizing Saurin as a man devoid of taste and genius, with a soul lost in twilight murkiness. Reviewing the whole dark history of Saurin's tenure, he hurled charge after charge against him. Saurin, he roared, "may insult, may calumniate, may prosecute but the Catholic cause is on its majestic march . . . its success is just as certain as the return of tomorrow's eve." For four hours he continued his inflammatory harangue; those in the courtroom were so spellbound and even intimidated by the performance that the chief justice himself could not bring himself to intervene, though it was obvious that O'Connell's oration had little to do with Magee's own case.

It would be almost impossible to realize what this single speech meant to the downtrodden Catholics of Ireland. The proof that one of their own could dare to chastise the chief law officer of the Crown in a scathing torrent of words galvanized them, made them aware of their own potential, and renewed their courage for what had begun to seem a hopeless struggle. O'Connell's four-hour speech—beautifully structured, fertile in invention, and rich in allusions—was the forensic masterpiece of his career and marked the real beginning of the Catholic emancipation movement.

A Duelist in Spite of Himself

Some time after the Magee affair, an incident occurred that would haunt O'Connell for the rest of his life. In the course of a speech he referred to the aldermen of Dublin as a "beggarly corporation." One of them, named D'Esterre, heard about it and asked O'Connell whether he had in fact made such a remark. O'Connell replied tartly that no remark he made could begin to express the contempt he felt for that group of gentlemen. The series of heated exchanges that then took place soon became public knowledge. Suspense built up, together with the anticipation of a violent outcome.

D'Esterre was a pugnacious little man and he let it be known that he was going to horsewhip O'Connell in the public square. But he was unable to carry out this threat when crowds of supporters on both sides gathered and created a melee. The next day he challenged O'Connell to a duel. Though the Church forbade dueling and O'Connell was committed to nonviolence, as the champion of the Catholics he could hardly refuse a challenge from a Protestant. A site was chosen outside the city, and that evening O'Connell set out to meet his opponent with a sharp sense of foreboding. The Catholics of Ireland waited with trepidation—surely a huge man like O'Connell would make an easy target for D'Esterre, who was known as a crack shot.

Daylight was beginning to fail as O'Connell reached the site, which was already filled with crowds of excited peasants from the nearby farms. An hour passed before D'Esterre arrived. O'Connell spent the time nervously pacing up and down, praying to St. Brigid. No priest could be present but O'Connell was able to soothe his conscience by reminding himself that the duel had been unavoidable. And he knew that a priest was hiding nearby to assist him if he were to fall mortally wounded. Dusk had almost fallen when the signal was given and the two men started heading toward each other. As the handkerchief fell, both men fired. D'Esterre's gun exploded and the bullet merely dropped at O'Connell's feet, but D'Esterre fell mortally wounded as O'Connell's shot hit its mark.

Word soon spread and the Catholics could hardly believe the news. It was surely a miracle, they thought, for few had expected O'Connell to come out of the ordeal alive. Bonfires blazed out across the land; and, though muted out of respect for the fallen D'Esterre, rejoicing went on throughout the night. O'Connell, however, was filled with terrible remorse. He had not only killed a man but left his widow and two small children nearly destitute. He tried to get the woman to share his income but she refused. She did, however, accept for her daughter an annuity that O'Connell faithfully paid for the rest of his life.

Another challenge to a duel came in 1815 from no less a dignitary than Robert Peel himself, after an exchange in which O'Connell accused Peel of a "paltry trick." Both men seemed ready to let the thing blow over, but a series of misunderstandings led Peel to challenge and O'Connell to accept a duel. O'Connell's wife, however, was determined not to let it happen. She had the police put her husband under house arrest. Her intervention delighted O'Connell's enemies, who now taunted him with using his wife to keep out of combat.

But a second chapter occurred when both antagonists agreed to fight outside the country in Ostend, Belgium. O'Connell managed to get away without his wife's knowledge. But on his way through England he was arrested and detained, while Peel, thanks to the connivance of the government, was able to reach Ostend. There he entertained the press with his bravado while spending his time in target practice. Trapped in London, poor O'Connell cut a rather sorry figure and was blamed for the fact that the duel of the century had failed to happen. The whole affair slightly tarnished O'Connell's image as the dauntless champion of his oppressed countrymen.

The Warrior Undaunted

The period from 1815 to 1823 saw the chances of securing emancipation in steep decline. With Napoleon defeated and France no longer a threat, the need to conciliate the Catholics disappeared. The fight was anything but fair. O'Connell was up against a government that had no scruples about using the libel law, packing juries, and appointing subservient judges to quell any opposition. The Catholics themselves were more concerned about surviving in a depressed economy than worrying about emancipation, which in any case would not add a farthing to their incomes. But O'Connell continued throughout this dreary season to carry on the struggle. His petitions to enact Catholic emancipation were regularly sent to Parliament and were as regularly disregarded or voted down. He was also forced to contend with the division within the Catholic ranks between the vetoists, who were willing to accept a royal power of veto over the appointment of Catholic bishops in return for emancipation, and those who refused any such compromise.

At the same time, he was increasingly beset by financial difficulties. Undoubtedly the most talented lawyer in Ireland, he had no trouble making plenty of money. But he was totally devoid of common sense when it came to managing it. His financial irresponsibility kept his large and still growing family hovering constantly on the brink of ruin. His letters are filled with references to his messy finances and the artful stratagems he was always devising to meet the latest crisis. Part of the problem was his inability to say no to friends who begged him for loans. Moreover he maintained a lavish lifestyle that went beyond even his ample means. His prodigious earnings demanded prodigious labor. By 1822, O'Connell was working a sixteen- or seventeen-hour day. On May 14 of that year he wrote to Mary, "My trade goes on flourishingly. All the rest of the Bar are complaining but I was never doing so much. In your absence I have nothing to take up a moment of my time but law. I rise at half after four, breakfast at a quarter after eight, dine at a quarter after five and go to bed between nine and ten."[7]

During this discouraging period, O'Connell employed a new conciliatory tack, emphasizing the loyalty of Catholics to the Crown while constantly searching for common ground for Irish Catholics and Protestants. In 1821 when George IV made the first visit of an English monarch to Ireland

[7] Ibid., p. 187.

since 1399, O'Connell pulled out all the stops in his speech of welcome and presented the king with a laurel crown. But none of this advanced the cause of Catholic emancipation an inch. An observer noted, "The entire body seemed to have relapsed into their ancient sluggishness and to have surrendered their cause to the arbitration of blind chance, or the choice and convenience of their enemies."[8] The Irish Tories took the policy of conciliation as a confession of weakness.

Emancipation at Last

In 1822, having established his reputation as an able administrator, Peel returned to England to become home secretary. Thanks to his skill and the restrictive laws he had obtained from Parliament, agitation by the Catholics and O'Connell had been kept to a minimum. He had even managed to embarrass O'Connell personally in the affair of the abortive duel. But whereas most Catholics had given up hope for change, O'Connell remained undaunted. In fact, he was on the verge of unveiling an entirely new strategy. He was going to attempt nothing less than the organization of the whole populace—a feat never before contemplated, whether in Ireland or any other country. At a meeting of influential Catholics in Dublin in May 1823, O'Connell got the endorsement of leading Catholics for a proposed Association of Catholics to watch over Catholic interests and redress Catholic grievances.

O'Connell was able to dramatize the Catholic cause by making the most of various incidents. For example, when the sexton of the Anglican St. Kevin's churchyard refused to turn the usual blind eye and allow a priest to recite prayers over the grave at a Catholic funeral, O'Connell exploited the incident to remind tens of thousands of Irish Catholics of their inferior status and turned the affair into an indictment of the entire system of Anglican discrimination. Progress was slow at first. Meetings had to be abandoned for lack of a quorum of ten, and O'Connell himself did most of the work. But the considerable attention given to the association's activities by the press greatly magnified its influence.

Thanks to the work of the association, the Catholic population became increasingly politicized and the groundwork was laid for a mass movement. To get it underway O'Connell next proposed collecting a penny a month from the head of each Catholic household in Ireland, to be used for legal aid

[8]Ibid., p. 181.

for Catholics, for the press, and also for a variety of other needs including the building of churches and schools. Eventually O'Connell saw that the clergy could play a key role, especially in the countryside. It would be their job to collect the "rent" each month from their parishioners. Their response at first was rather cool, but when the youngest and ablest of the bishops, Dr. Doyle, a former soldier and a professor of theology, joined the association things began to happen. Priests who had held back from the association felt encouraged and enlisted in large numbers. They soon became the driving force of the movement outside the cities, and in consequence their influence over the people rapidly increased.

The association grew by leaps and bounds. Meetings were held across the country with demonstrations surpassing any ever held before. By October 1824 a great network of hundreds of thousands of Catholics was in place under the command of O'Connell, who at last reaped the reward for twenty years of dreary labor. The Irish Catholic movement had now taken shape and O'Connell's popularity knew no bounds. Peel was frightened by the political monster he saw taking form before his eyes. In fact it proved to be the most powerful political machine that British history had ever witnessed.

The big breakthrough occurred in 1826 in Waterford when Thomas Wyse, a Catholic merchant, and J. Sheehan, one of a new breed of political priests, brought about a local revolution. They mounted a campaign to oust the anti-emancipationist Lord George Beresford from his seat in Parliament and elect the Protestant but pro-emancipationist Villiers Stuart. Their campaign became a model for political Catholics. The Beresfords had long held a monopoly on the seat, assuring their tenants' votes by means of bribery and intimidation. Sheehan and Wyse countered with a number of effective tactics: promising financial help to those evicted, appealing to the conscience of those who might perjure themselves by accepting bribes (an act stigmatized as a mortal sin), keeping a checklist of each voter and how he would probably vote, transporting voters to the polling places, and the like. They won by an overwhelming majority. O'Connell, who had played a leading part in the triumph, was overjoyed. He now saw that the connection between the Protestant landlords and the Catholic tenants could be broken. To indemnify those tenants who voted against the wishes of their landlords and were evicted, a new "rent" was proposed by O'Connell that once again was very successful and showed the unity of the Catholics. The cause of these victims of injustice was especially dear to the priests, whose political education took another leap forward. Scenting victory, O'Connell felt it was time to leave behind "temperateness, moderation and conciliation . . .

we must call things by their proper names . . . and rouse in Ireland a spirit of *action.*"[9] Four years (1822–1826) had transformed the political temper of O'Connell and his country.

O'Connell used the example of Beresford to pressure Irish members of Parliament to support emancipation but the votes needed still fell short. In the meantime he further refined the association's methods. A system of churchwardens was instituted in each parish to oversee the business of the association, which now included taking a census, keeping the electoral registers, making reports on evictions, and monitoring the proselytizing by Protestant evangelicals and the oppressive practices of the established church. On Sunday, January 13, 1828, meetings in conjunction with mass were held simultaneously in nearly 1,600 of the 2,500 parishes in Ireland. The total attendance of a million and a half was an impressive demonstration of Catholic force and the effectiveness of its organizing methods. O'Connell commented: "The combination of national action—all Catholic Ireland acting as one man—must necessarily have a powerful effect on the minds of the ministry and of the entire British nation. A people who can be thus brought to act together and by one impulse are too powerful to be neglected and too formidable to be long opposed."[10]

When an election was set for County Clare for the summer of 1828, the association pledged to bring forth their own candidate to oppose Vesey Fitzgerald, a member of the hated Duke of Wellington's cabinet. But when no one else could be found to run, O'Connell, with some misgivings, announced his own candidacy. He didn't mince his words:

> The oath (for a member of Parliament) at present required by law is, "That the sacrifice of the mass and the invocation of the Blessed Virgin Mary and other Saints, as now practiced in the Church of Rome, are impious and idolatrous." . . . Mr. Fitzgerald . . . has often taken that horrible oath . . . I would rather be torn limb from limb than take it.[11]

Although his opponents were hoping otherwise, the Church closed ranks behind O'Connell. At Sunday mass, priests would exhort their flocks to get behind O'Connell. Later they even trudged alongside them as they journeyed to the voting site in Ennis. By contrast, the lord of the manor arrived in his carriage with his tenants trailing behind him. On arrival he cautioned

[9] Ibid., p. 231.
[10] Ibid., p. 247.
[11] Ibid., p. 250.

them on how to vote while shaking his fist and waving his hat. But with shaking limbs they typically proceeded to the booth and voted instead for O'Connell, praying that it wouldn't mean eviction from their little cabins.

It was apparent to most observers in Ireland as well as England, and even in Paris and Vienna, that the fate of emancipation hung in the balance. This feeling certainly created a sense of high drama in the scene during the week of polling in the busy little market town of Ennis with its gray skies and limestone buildings. The 3,000 voters were accompanied by a host of supporters, relatives, and friends. A hundred and fifty priests took care of the logistics involved in handling the tens of thousands of visitors. No drinking was allowed and a remarkable spirit of discipline kept things peaceful. When a priest announced that a 40-shilling freeholder who had voted against O'Connell had dropped dead, the people fell to their knees in silence. O'Connell won by 2,057 to 982, the kind of margin he needed to make a telling point with England's rulers. As O'Connell now put it: "They must either crush us or conciliate us. There is no going on as we are." O'Connell left Ennis in a triumphal car. Emblazoned on it in gold letters was his own favorite epigraph:

> Hereditary bondsmen! Know ye not,
> Who would be free themselves must strike the blow.

In the view of Peel and the Duke of Wellington, the Irish landlords, both Whig and Tory, were losing political control over their tenantry. It was obvious that O'Connell and the association would take the first opportunity to repeat their victory and in due time there would be many Catholics elected who would not be able legally to take their seats in Parliament. By undermining the political influence of property, the triumph of the tenantry over the gentry would mark the beginning of a social revolution. Public order and the structure of society itself would be endangered if there was a long delay in conceding emancipation. Though Peel and Wellington read the handwriting on the wall, the reactionaries in Ireland and England, including King George IV, were fiercely determined to "preserve the integrity of our Protestant Constitution." While waiting for the next session of Parliament, O'Connell for his part had to steer a cautious course—keeping up the momentum while controlling the enthusiasm of his followers lest his enemies be given a pretext to suppress the movement. One helpful development in this interim was the accession to the cause of the Irish Protestant liberals, who took a stand in favor of emancipation.

O'Connell left for London in February 1829 and waited in suspense while Parliament again considered the question of Catholic emancipation. At first he was going to attempt to take his seat before a bill to enact it was passed, but prudence prevailed and he waited while the bill wound its way through the House of Commons and the House of Lords. Ironically, it was Peel himself who stood up in the Commons and moved for a committee of the whole to reconsider the laws imposing disabilities on Roman Catholics. Peel delivered an outstanding speech of over four hours favoring emancipation. Frequently interrupted by cheers so loud as to be heard outside in Westminster Hall, he insisted on the need to end the interminable and fruitless contests that bedeviled Ireland.

On April 13 the king signed the bill and O'Connell exulted in a letter to his wife, Mary, noting the very "minute" of liberation—"about twenty minutes after four by the Dublin clocks."[12] To a friend he wrote, "It is one of the greatest triumphs recorded in history—a bloodless revolution more extensive in its operation than any other political change that could take place."[13] As the history of the struggle made clear, O'Connell belonged to the second of the two great camps of nineteenth-century radicalism. Unlike those who preached the necessity of violence, he believed in the efficacy of moral rather than physical force and was most happy that not a drop of blood had been shed to secure emancipation.

Catholic emancipation was a great personal triumph for O'Connell but it was also momentous in its consequences for British politics. It spelled the end of the old Tory party and undermined the belief of many Englishmen, particularly the ultra-Protestant Tories, in the system, which had surrendered to the Catholics and further capitulated to the Protestant dissenters by repeal of the Test and Corporation Acts in 1828. All of this gave real encouragement to the Whigs and Radicals who were bent on reform. Moreover, O'Connell's Catholic Association provided a direct model for the British political unions that were to play a large role in the crises over the Reform Bills of 1831 and 1832.

A New Campaign—Repeal

Repeal of the Union was always the primary goal for O'Connell. To obtain it he would have been willing to sacrifice Catholic emancipation. He had realized, however, that Catholic emancipation could be used to organize

[12]Ibid., p. 268.
[13]Ibid., p. 269.

and mobilize the Irish people into a disciplined body ready to demand the restoration of the Irish Parliament. By 1829, with the success of emancipation, this objective had been accomplished: He had created an organized, passionate, and disciplined Irish Catholic opinion. The Association of Catholics was, in fact, the most powerful political machine British history had ever witnessed. It was based on the willingness of poverty-racked farmers and workers to sacrifice their liquor and tobacco to pay their dues. Their great sacrifice committed them to the cause. "Modern Irish nationalism emerged as a badge of dignity and a promise of hope for a people who, in the century before O'Connell, had lost those human qualities."[14] "O'Connell's campaign was a great demonstration for all of Europe "of the power of organized public opinion under the direction of a political genius."[15]

When in 1835 the Whigs finally showed a willingness to fight for substantial reforms, O'Connell signed a pact with them, engaging himself to support them and abandon his agitation for repeal. O'Connell remained loyal to his commitment until 1840, by which time it was obvious that meaningful reform would not occur. After ten years of arduous labor, O'Connell had little to show. Ireland was still captive to the same vested interests, a prey to the same deeply rooted evils. It was time to revive the agitation.

O'Connell held the first public meeting of the National Association of Ireland in April 1840; it was rechristened the Loyal National Repeal Association in 1841. As in the Catholic Association, a national network of repeal wardens was set up to collect the monthly dues, keep members in touch with the activities in Dublin, and provide repeal reading rooms furnished with nationalist newspapers and other material. However, O'Connell ran into difficulty attracting recruits. His old allies were now established in their careers and not willing to jeopardize them for a very uncertain cause. The hierarchy seemed indifferent. The unfriendly noted the small size of O'Connell's meetings and scoffed at him as an old has-been.

But their scoffing was premature. He found the issue he was looking for in 1842 when the Government passed a poor law that was ill adapted to the Irish situation and met with determined resistance from the masses. He immediately used this in his campaign for repeal by citing the law as an

[14]Lawrence J. McCaffrey, *Daniel O'Connell and the Repeal Year* (Lexington, Ky.: University of Kentucky Press, 1966), p. 6.
[15]Ibid., p. 8.

example of the kind of inept legislation with which the British Parliament regularly saddled the Irish. He was also able to hitch his repeal movement onto Father Mathew's Temperance movement that was sweeping the country. His agents recruited members at the vast outdoor meetings where the completely apolitical Capuchin priest preached total abstinence. O'Connell's enemies accused him of unfairly co-opting Mathew's movement, but O'Connell was determined to unite the two causes and flattered Father Mathew, insisting, "It is the temperance that will give us the repeal." O'Connell felt that the two issues fused beautifully. The anti–poor law campaign engendered enthusiasm, while temperance fostered the discipline necessary to keep the enthusiasm under control.

Another powerful weapon was handed to O'Connell in the fight for repeal when three remarkably talented young journalists—Thomas Davis, John Dillon, and Charles Gavan Duffy—joined his Repeal Association. Imbued with a great love of Ireland's history and culture, they wanted to make the Irish people proud of their rich heritage. For this purpose they founded the *Nation,* a newspaper intended to create a cultural nationalist opinion in Ireland, and filled its pages with some of the finest writing produced at the time. Many of the ballads still favored among the Irish in America and the Commonwealth first appeared in its pages. The editors were especially anxious to loosen the repeal movement's association with Catholicism by stressing the common grievances shared by the Irish of all faiths, and the mutual profit they would gain from the liberation of their country. "They gave Irish nationalism its most powerful newspaper voice, and traditions and doctrines that were permanently to shape its character."[16] But their passionate cultural nationalism found little resonance in the soul of the profoundly pragmatic O'Connell, who even at times ridiculed their literary efforts. His focus was on getting Ireland full civil, political, and religious rights as well as the requisite economic advantages. Repeal, he believed, was necessary to obtain them, but if the Union could guarantee them he was ready to accept the Union.

O'Connell's argument was essentially the same as the one the Americans had used in seeking independence from England. The social contract between government and the people involved mutual duties as well as rights. The English, O'Connell claimed, had broken the contract by using bribery and fraud to bring about the Union.

In line with his philosophy of nonviolence, O'Connell believed firmly

[16]Ibid., p. 24.

that the sheer moral force of Irish opinion would ultimately secure repeal as it had emancipation. However, he failed to note one tremendous difference between the two struggles. The agitation for emancipation was able to count on a divided English public, as the liberal section of opinion sided with O'Connell's struggle. But British parliamentary as well as public opinion was unanimously opposed to repeal. Nevertheless O'Connell felt that 1843 was the repeal year. In January he issued a manifesto that listed the main reforms that Ireland needed and repeal would bring: the abolition of tithes and an end to the poor law, fixity of tenure for tenants, help for manufacturers, and democratic suffrage by secret ballot. In a later manifesto he included the separation of church and state in a free Ireland.

He organized a series of massive outdoor meetings in April with the ostensible purpose of drawing up petitions for repeal, but with the primary purpose of making a powerful impact on British public opinion. Hundreds of thousands turned out for these "monster meetings," as *The Times* dubbed them. Many came with torches the night before and when dawn broke they could be seen spread out across the hillsides hearing mass said by the priests or eating their simple breakfasts. A colorful parade of dignitaries in coaches or on horseback escorted O'Connell to the platform already crowded with Catholic priests. In his finest form he would pull out all the stops, going on for hours about the greatness of Ireland, the nobility and strength of its people, the benefits that repeal would bring, while his hearers wept and laughed and cheered. He renewed his commitment to nonviolence but recognized the possibility of war. Irishmen, he declared, may have to make the choice of living as slaves or dying as freemen, and he promised that if Peel's troops trampled Ireland it would be his dead body they would trample on first.[17]

More than half of the bishops and a great majority of the priests came out as staunch supporters of repeal, a situation the Vatican found worrisome; it smacked of the Revolution, which throughout the whole period had been a constant threat to the Vatican. Fransoni, the Cardinal Prefect of Propaganda, told the Irish clergy to ignore politics and concentrate their energies on spiritual matters. But one of the most ardent agitators, Bishop Higgins, vowed to die for the cause if necessary, and through a third party warned the Vatican not to interfere in Irish politics.

O'Connell made a great effort to attach the Protestant clergy, aristocracy, and middle class to the repeal movement. He assured them that the disestab-

[17] Ibid., p. 57.

lishment of their church would not be followed by a Catholic establishment and ascendancy. But all to no avail. Ensconced in their position of privilege, they were not likely to trade it for an uncertain status in a new order.

By the summer of 1843 O'Connell had duplicated his feat of 1829, having mobilized and disciplined the forces of Irish nationalist opinion. If repeal proved unattainable he hoped at least to force some substantial concessions from Peel, and failing that, the overthrow of the Peel ministry and its replacement by the Whigs. Peel's strategy was to ignore the repeal movement until O'Connell's frustrated followers abandoned their leader in disgust or resorted to physical force. If the latter occurred, Peel would have the legal justification to crush the nationalist movement and leave O'Connell's life work in a shambles. While still pretending to ignore O'Connell, Peel began gathering evidence to convict the Irish leader of sedition. In the meantime, however, O'Connell's success in mobilizing millions made Peel realize how profoundly alienated the Irish Catholics were from the government. He saw that continuing British rule within the framework of the constitution would be impossible. The responsibility for the sad state of affairs, he saw, rested with the British government whose policies were so frightfully out of touch with the convictions and needs of the Catholic populace.

To conciliate the alienated Catholics, Peel realized, far-reaching changes were needed. One of the most important was the need to wean the clergy from their alliance with the radical nationalists. In this regard, "Ireland indeed presented a unique situation in the Age of Metternich—a revolutionary Catholic hierarchy and clergy encouraging agitations threatening existing political institutions and traditional property rights."[18] As Alexis de Tocqueville noted after dining with a number of bishops and priests:

> The feelings expressed were extremely democratic. Distrust and hatred of the great landlords; love of the people, and confidence in them. Bitter memories of past oppression. An air of exaltation at present or approaching victory . . . Clearly as much the leaders of a Party as the representatives of the Church.[19]

Peel and his colleagues believed that this connection could be broke—if something could be done about the poverty of the Church and the low level

---

[18] Ibid., p. 156.
[19] Quoted in Angus Macintyre, *The Liberator* (New York: The Macmillan Company, 1965), p. 115.

of clerical education. Priests who were well trained, with a cosmopolitan outlook, and not dependent on the pennies of their flock, would not be so ready to embrace the nationalist ideas of their anti-British laity.

Although outright financial aid to the Catholic Church was out of the question, considering the depth of British anti-Catholic sentiment, Peel planned to begin by increasing the subsidy to Maynooth Seminary which had been originally set up and endowed by the government to keep future priests from having to study abroad where they might be exposed to radical ideas. But in the meantime some of the clergy spoke of their readiness to die for "old Ireland." As one priest told his audience, the Catholic clergy of Ireland lived with and for their people and "with the people and for the people every good priest is ever prepared to die."[20] O'Connell worried about this kind of militant enthusiasm and began to speak of the long struggle ahead. He "would consent," he said, "to the shedding of no man's blood, save his own."[21]

As the year wore on, the monster meetings continued to draw huge crowds. A German traveler describes a meeting he witnessed in June at Dundalk:

> Never did I see anything like it. I have seen princes make their solemn entry into Cologne. All was child's play to this. There was no walking in the streets; all were either borne or pushed. I looked down and I saw nothing but heads—not even shoulders were visible. Never did I hear anything like that prolonged, that never-ending *Hurrah* for O'Connell. He descended from his carriage and instantly a large broad path opened for him, and as instantly closed when he had passed. It was the passage of Moses through the Red Sea to the very life.

In August at Tara, the ancient capital of Ireland, a crowd of over a million assembled to hear their captain. Finally, the last meeting of the year was announced. It would be held on Sunday, October 8, at historic Clontarf in the outskirts of Dublin. The number expected was supposed to make Tara look like a caucus. It was the opportunity Peel was waiting for to call "the old demagogue's bluff." He had already filled Dublin with troops; he had warships stationed within easy reach of Dublin Bay. He gave orders to ban the meeting, but the ban was not published until late Saturday afternoon, by which time many were already en route to the spot.

[20] Ibid., p. 177.
[21] Ibid., p. 181.

The young hotheads among the organizers wanted to pick up the gauntlet and fight for their freedom. But the great gambler drew the line; he
would not send thousands of his pike-armed followers into a senseless
slaughter. The meeting was called off and emissaries were dispatched to the
highways to turn back the host of repeal pilgrims making their way to
Clontarf. After being welcomed with tremendous cheering by the Repeal
Association the next day, O'Connell told them that a disorganized, untrained throng was no match for a trained army. He lifted their morale by
reaffirming his determination to "carry the repeal of the Union without
one drop of blood . . . in such a way that I can face my Redeemer . . .
and have no sin upon me."[22]

Peel's next move was to arrest O'Connell, his son, and some colleagues
and charge them with conspiracy to undermine the constitution and spread
disaffection in the army. The government rigged the proceedings in the
most outrageous fashion. Not one Catholic in a predominantly Catholic
country was allowed on the jury. O'Connell's performance during the trial
revealed a shocking decline in his condition. The tremendous strain of the
monster meetings and the continual tension of avoiding the slaughter of his
people had taken its toll. He could muster only a half-hearted speech in his
own defense. He spoke of his "utter abhorrence of violence and bloodshed," but the verdict was a foregone conclusion. The repeal leaders were all
found guilty and sentenced to prison.

A successful appeal to the British High Court rescued O'Connell from
what had turned out to be a rather comfortable confinement in the prison
governor's residence. In overturning the guilty verdict the court said that if
the practices found in this trial were to continue, then trial by jury in
Ireland would be "a mockery, a delusion, and a snare." While Peel was
reeling from the blow, O'Connell was greeted at the gates of the prison by
a frenzied throng. Waving flags and banners, they helped him onto a huge
triumphal chariot and escorted him to the old Parliament House on College Green. There they halted while O'Connell, lifting his green cap,
pointed with a sweeping dramatic gesture to the home of the old Irish
Parliament. The mighty roar that poured from the crowd could be heard
for miles around.

Peel pursued his efforts to conciliate the Irish Catholics and to weaken
the hold that O'Connell had on them by policies that would improve the
Church's finances, better the education of its clergy, and advance the status

---

[22]Ibid., p. 201.

of the Catholic middle class. He also got the Vatican to repeat its instruction to the clergy to avoid involvement in politics. Cardinal Fransoni advised the hierarchy "to cherish among the people quiet, tranquility, and peace . . . and constantly teach by example, precept or deed, submission to the temporal power in those matters which pertain to civil affairs."[23] The response of the hierarchy was politely to ignore Rome's recommendation. Peel worked away at the bishops nonetheless. He was able to put through a charitable-bequests act eliminating the legal barriers that restricted the Catholic Church from inheriting property. By handing this plum to the bishops, Peel and his allies felt they had made a big step toward their goal of breaking O'Connell's hold on the clergy and their alliance with the nationalists.

But O'Connell was once again able to offset Peel's victory by exposing negotiations between the British government and the Vatican over a concordat that would give the former control over the political allegiances of Irish bishops and priests. The news created a storm in Ireland. The Irish nationalists were furious at the possibility of any alliance between Rome and Westminster that would deprive them of their most valuable allies, the priests. They simply would not accept any interference of the Vatican in Irish politics. The issue was not laid to rest until 1845, when Archbishop Murray received word from an authoritative Roman source that the reports about such a concordat were "quite unfounded."

Peel's next move, to obtain a substantial increase in the government subsidy to Maynooth Seminary, was well received by all sectors of Irish Catholic opinion. Following on this success, his Irish Colleges bill was intended to break the hold of the clergy and mass opinion on the members of the Catholic middle class by offering them an education that set them on an equal cultural footing with Protestants of the same class. The bishops rejected the program as a snare that would alienate young Catholics from their faith, and forced Catholics to boycott the excellent colleges that were established. As a result, nineteenth-century Irish Catholicism lost a great opportunity to raise its intellectual level. However, one can only speculate about what harm Peel's policy might have caused the Church by dividing the Catholic body.

In the meantime O'Connell's deterioration, so apparent at his trial, only accelerated. A yet-unrecognized fatal illness sapped his strength. Having lost his wife nearly ten years before, he fell crazily in love with a young Protes-

---

[23]McCaffrey, *Daniel O'Connell and the Repeal Year*, p. 218.

tant girl who felt only admiration for him, while his embarrassed family tried to shield the lovesick old fool from the scoffers. No longer the commanding orator and prince of Conciliation Hall, he offered his repealers only half-baked ideas about what they should do next. Worked up at times to a blind rage, he spared neither friend nor enemy in his lashing out. His lackluster son John tried to fill his shoes but proved to be a religious bigot and a total disaster. The Young Irelanders of the *Nation* finally took their leave, sundering their always tenuous relationship with the O'Connellites.

But in the end, the competing visions of O'Connell and Peel were both shattered by an event outside the realm of politics. In 1845 a fungus attacked the Irish potato crop. The ensuing famine took the lives of a million and a half Irish, and drove another million to leave the island. Though Peel took swift relief measures, including the purchase of Indian corn and meal in America to prevent food prices from rising, his assistant secretary of the treasury, Charles Trevelyan, did not believe in the principle of government aid. Laissez-faire ideas dominated the Whig government that took over in 1846 under Lord John Russell and it refused to buy any more food. The inadequate measures taken further embittered the populace toward the British government. And the traditional hostility between landlord and tenant was intensified, for many landlords did little to succor their starving tenants and some even engaged in large-scale evictions. The chance, if ever there was one, of forging a spiritual bond between Ireland and Great Britain was buried forever in those stench-filled potato fields.

Feeble and bowed, O'Connell traveled around Ireland and gasped at the horror, the skeletons of the dead and the agonies of the dying. He made one last stand in the House of Commons begging for mercy for his dear poor. Disraeli called it "a strange and touching spectacle to those who remembered the colossal energy and clear and thrilling tones with which he once startled, disturbed and controlled senates" to behold the great O'Connell reduced to "a feeble old man muttering before a table."[24] His plea was of no avail. But O'Connell did not depart before savoring a final victory over Peel, whom in alliance with the Whigs he helped to overthrow.

Now in the last stages of his disease, he was advised to travel south and decided to make his journey a pilgrimage to the Holy Father. Accompanied

---

[24]Benjamin Disraeli, *Lord George Bentinck: A Political Biography* (London: Constable, 1905), pp. 159–160.

by his priest and getting weaker at every stage, he began suffering fits of delirium in Genoa. Shouting defiance at Peel he struggled to get up, yelling, "I have it . . . the repeal. I have it here in a box." Finally on May 15, 1847, he died murmuring "Jesus! . . . Jesus! . . . Jesus!"

O'Connell indeed became a legend within his lifetime in spite of many detractors. Who, for instance, would expect the English to look kindly on a papist and a rebel? For them he was "scum condensed of Irish bog, ruffian, coward, demagogue."

However, some of the most vitriolic debunkers of the O'Connell legend were Irish patriots who accused him of leading his people astray. Two of them in particular—his contemporaries, the Young Irelanders John Mitchel and Charles Gavan Duffy—devoted much of their time, energy, and wit to desecrating his memory. They could not forgive him for calling off the Clontarf monster meeting in October 1843 for fear of a massacre. Irish liberty, they believed, could be won only by the sword, whereas O'Connell's doctrine of nonviolence caused a needless detour and fatally postponed the inevitable bloodshed on the day of reckoning.

For nearly a century after his death, from 1848 to 1922, his memory was besmirched by all the frustrated patriots in Ireland who needed a scapegoat. For the militant nationalists he was the worst enemy Ireland ever had; for the doctrinaire idealists of the 1922 Civil War he was a vulgar pragmatist. Only after the trauma of the Civil War, fought over the policy (between supporters and opponents) of compromise with the British, did many see O'Connell's political realism in a more favorable light. Likewise, as the bloody drama in Northern Ireland continues to unfold today, there is more sympathy with O'Connell's belief in nonviolence and his conviction that a live patriot is worth a graveyard of dead ones.

What was his legacy for Social Catholicism? First, O'Connell made a signal contribution to the cause of liberal Catholicism. He was the first Catholic political leader in Europe and perhaps the first in any major Christian denomination to advocate the ideas of the French Revolution, especially religious freedom and separation of church and state. The advent of O'Connell, like that of his American contemporary Andrew Jackson, set in motion the forces of democracy and the beginning of the end of rule by the elites. He influenced the French liberal Catholics—Lacordaire, Lamennais, and Montalembert—who regarded his campaigns for emancipation as models for political action in Europe. One thing he would not countenance was any use of violence, which he felt only alienated moderate opinion by identifying reform with revolution. In fact, O'Connell was, as Donal Mc-Cartney says, "the nearest thing to a convinced pacifist that Irish history ever produced."[25]

Second, the core of his social philosophy was based on his belief in the liberty of the individual. His liberal convictions were formed by his reading of Paine, Voltaire, Gibbon, Rousseau, Adam Smith, Bentham, and Godwin. He consistently denounced discrimination on the grounds of creed, color, and even gender.

Third, O'Connell and his followers always tended to subordinate economic to political issues and can scarcely be said to have evolved a coherent policy of social reform. As landlords and landholders, they had little interest in a radical reconstruction of Irish society. Certainly they were never principally concerned with the vital and increasingly urgent problems of the land system. O'Connell was simply not positioned well to be a conductor for the economic passions pent up in Ireland. His sympathy with the philosophical radicals and free traders posed an absolute hindrance to Irish social and agrarian reform.

Fourth, his approach to the trade union question was governed by his emphasis on individual liberty. He has been accused of hostility to unions but he did not condemn trade unions in principle. What he targeted were those restrictive practices that he felt only made matters worse for workers as well as employers. The closed shop, for instance, he thought caused the decline of Dublin's industry by increasing the cost of labor. Certainly this was an understandable but wrongheaded concept of the nature of unions.

Fifth, on social issues in general he was not much ahead of the Church of his day, which preached the importance of charity and focused on family ethics. Moreover, in accord with the Church, he tended to think in unchanging moral terms that prevented him from a proper appreciation of socioeconomic factors and changing conditions of the economy.

Sixth, his only long-term solution to the problem of Irish poverty was industrialization. But he recognized its high human cost and joined the London Workingmen's Association, which sought to improve the condition of the working class through education.

The moral standards he imposed on himself as a politician were uncommonly demanding. Although a most agile political tactician, he would not

---

[25]Donal McCartney, *Daniel O'Connell* (New York: Fordham University Press, 1985), p. 28.

compromise his basic principles. Gladstone called him the greatest popular leader the world had ever seen.[26] As one of his biographers said: "He inculcated in the masses of his country political awareness and expertise to a degree perhaps unparalleled in the Europe of his day."[27]

[26] Macintyre, *The Liberator,* p. 297.
[27] Oliver MacDonagh, *Ireland: The Union and Its Aftermath* (London: George Allen & Unwin, Ltd., 1977), p. 55.

FOUR

Frederick Ozanam (1813–1853): A "Yes" to the Revolution

AS WE'VE ALREADY NOTED, Lamennais once said, "The Revolution was for France the pangs of birth; for the Catholic Church it was a rebirth." Although Lamennais later forswore these sentiments they aptly sum up Frederick Ozanam's providential view of the Revolution and provide the key to his whole life and thought.

Ozanam was one of the first liberal Catholics, the relatively small group within the Church who felt that the great need of the nineteenth century was the reconciliation of church and revolution, liberty and authority, science and faith, democracy and Christianity. Their hope was that the Catholic Church would play a key role in this work. At the same time, Ozanam was also a pioneer of Social Catholicism in his awareness of the need for social justice for the working classes. He was the founder of the St. Vincent de Paul Society and deeply committed to its works of charity, but he also felt strongly that charity was not enough; justice was also necessary, and he advocated social reforms that later found expression in Pope Leo's encylical *Rerum Novarum*.

Frederick Ozanam

Early Life

Frederick's father, Jean-Antoine, had served in the army during the French Revolution and later under Napoleon. By all accounts he was a brave and daring soldier who was wounded five times and earned the approving notice of Napoleon himself. One of Jean-Antoine's most daring exploits was the rescue of his own father, Bénédict (Frederick's grandfather), from agents of the Committee of Public Safety as they were about to put Bénédict to death. After a wild cross-country ride to Bourg, where his father was held captive, he forced the committee members at gunpoint to hand Bénédict over. Then he managed to elude the gendarmes sent to pursue him and returned the old man safely to his wife. Young Frederick loved to hear his father tell this story over and over.

After leaving the army, Captain Ozanam went to Lyons where he met the twenty-seven-year-old Marie Nantas. They married on April 22, 1800, when he was only nineteen. She too had experienced the horrors of revolutionary terror when Lyons was put under siege. She was forced to hide in cellars while her beloved elder brother was executed when the city fell.

Jean-Antoine and Marie started a silk business in Lyons but lost everything when it failed. After moving to Milan (at that time part of Napoleon's empire), the brilliant Captain Ozanam was able to start over in a new career as a physician, completing his medical studies in two years. The valor he showed on the battlefield was again displayed during an epidemic of typhus that broke out in Milan in 1813. Remaining at his post, he tended the dying while his colleagues fell stricken around him. In the same year Frederick, his fifth son, was born and baptized in the Church of the Servites—later St. Charles Borromeo Church. When Milan fell to the Austrians after Napoleon's defeat at Waterloo, Doctor Ozanam and the family resettled in Lyons, where he secured the coveted post of physician at the municipal hospital.

The Ozanam family was a happy one. In a letter to his mother, Frederick recollected the many happy days he spent near her bosom, her "caresses and spoiling, [and] gentle words while I worked at the table beside you, . . . the counsels, and, sometimes, the good-natured growls of Papa, my long walks with him and his stories."[1] Jean-Antoine and Marie were staunch Catholics and they would gather their children at evening for prayer and study of the Bible. Jean-Antoine often gave public witness to his faith by marching, candle in hand, in the processions honoring the Blessed Sacrament. Both parents also gave constant proof of their Christian charity and compassion. Some of Doctor Ozanam's patients were destitute but he was always ready to rush to their bedside in emergencies, while his wife often left hearth and home to visit their miserable tenements and comfort the sick and dying with her prayers.

Young Frederick was described by one of his teachers at the Royal College as "cheerful, even gay . . . He loved a joke dearly, and was sure to be in the midst of any fun going, for there was never a boy more popular with other boys."[2] But like the young Lamennais he began to roam intellectually through the gloomy forest of the Voltairian skeptics, and, like him, was shaken to the roots by what he read. He described his crisis of faith as a time of extreme desolation; he felt suspended over an abyss of despair while the "noises of a world which believed not assaulted his ears." Through the loving care of a priest philosopher, M. Noirot, he eventually overcame his doubts, but the searing experience left him with a deep feeling of sympathy for unbelievers. And he promised God that he would devote his days to the service of the truth, which gave him such joy and peace.

After brilliant studies at the Royal College of Lyons he had to choose a profession—a matter already decided for him by his father, who intended

[1] Albert Paul Schimberg, *Frederick Ozanam* (Milwaukee: The Bruce Publishing Company, 1946), p. 27.
[2] Ibid.

him for the law. Doctor Ozanam felt sure his brilliant son would some day be a judge in the Royal Court of Justice. This preconceived paternal notion went totally against Frederick's grain and caused him much grief. His real interests lay in literature and the study of languages, but he forced himself to pore over the arid legal texts. Nonetheless, he found time to read widely and prepare himself for the great task he felt lay ahead—a defense of the Catholic faith that would be based on the most comprehensive linguistic, historical, and anthropological research. He studied English and Hebrew as well as Italian, Latin, and Greek, and even dipped into Sanskrit deeply enough to serve his future scholarly work. He was seventeen when the Revolution of 1830 overthrew the Bourbons and starkly posed the question of what the new order would mean for the Church. The victorious middle class, repeating Voltaire's aphorism *"Écrasez l'infame,"* believed the Church would perish with the Bourbon regime to which it had been so intimately tied. Ozanam, however, remained unshaken in his faith that some kind of alliance was possible between the Church and the Revolution.

His first excursion into apologetics, a one-hundred-page refutation of Saint Simonianism, was occasioned by the arrival in Lyons of devotees of this utopian quasi-religious philosophy. The Saint Simonians had a peculiar answer to the burning question about the form religion would take in the new order. Having a more positive view than the Voltairians, they believed Christianity would be metamorphosed into a humanitarian and socialist religion that would guide humanity into a new age. Ozanam's *Réflexions sur la Doctrine de Saint-Simon* received the plaudits of a number of leading French intellectuals including Lamartine and Chateaubriand, and a favorable review in Lamennais' paper *L'Avenir*.

Frederick continued his legal studies and at his father's behest left Lyons for Paris in 1831 to study at the university. He was depicted at the time as "of slender build, pale, with an oval face and a nose slightly larger than the average, eyes set wide apart and a forehead both high and broad. His hair was long, black, rather unkempt. Altogether not a handsome or stylish youth." (Later in life he wore a moustache and a beard.) He could be seen walking through the streets of Paris with a book in his hands, reading and occasionally absent-mindedly bumping into people as he went. A shy, terribly homesick, and melancholy student, he didn't take to the atmosphere of Paris. But fortune smiled on him. On a chance visit to the eminent scientist André-Marie Ampère, he made such a favorable impression that André-Marie invited him to live with the Ampères. The two years he spent with

Ampère—the "Newton of electricity," a great scientist, and a pious Catholic—influenced him profoundly. Ampère's deep and radiant faith especially made a great impression on the youth. One day, feeling discouraged and depressed by the generally irreligious attitudes of Parisians, Frederick wandered into the Church of St. Étienne du Mont to say a prayer. While kneeling there he happened to notice a gentleman over in the far corner of the church rapt in prayer and completely oblivious to his surroundings. Then he realized it was his host, Monsieur Ampère, and the sight of that great genius completely absorbed in prayer gave him such a lift that he walked out into the sunlight of Paris like a new man.

The "City of Light" presented an enormous challenge to the faith of a Catholic. Arriving at Paris in the immediate aftermath of the 1830 revolution, Frederick was appalled by the hostility to the Church. "Paris displeases me," he said, "because there is no life, no faith, no love." Undaunted, he determined to mount a spiritual counter-revolution and soon made his presence felt at the university. Drawing together a band of like-minded Catholic friends, he led them in challenging the materialistic and irreligious professors who gratuitously attacked the Church in the course of their lectures. One of his major battles was with Théodore Jouffroy, one of the brightest lights on the Sorbonne faculty and a constant mud-slinger. On one occasion Jouffroy lashed out at the Church as the enemy of science and liberty, and then ignored a reply that Ozanam asked him to read to the class. Refusing to let up, Ozanam submitted a joint protest with the signatures of fifteen students. Jouffroy capitulated. He read the statement and then promised that he would be more careful in the future about his treatment of the students' religious beliefs.

But in view of the massive forces of unbelief and skepticism in Paris, Ozanam and his friends felt the need to address the widest possible audience for the Church's message. The thought struck them of securing Notre Dame Cathedral and putting in its pulpit the most dynamic preacher they could find. They decided on Père Lacordaire, well known by reason of his association with Lamennais' ill-fated *L'Avenir,* and someone they knew could speak to their generation. The archbishop, Henri de Quelen, initially opposed the choice of Lacordaire but eventually acquiesced. Launched with incredible success by Lacordaire, the Conferences of Notre Dame became a permanent feature of French Catholic life and were of utmost importance in the intellectual history of French Catholicism.

As a liberal Catholic, Ozanam believed passionately in free and open dialogue with the Church's opponents. Unlike many Catholics of his day he radiated tolerance and confidence in the power of truth to overcome error. In his mind there was no place for force, personal condemnation, or invective in religious controversy. In order to encourage an exchange of ideas with those of other faiths or no faith, he and his friends started a kind of debating club that they called a "conference of history." They met in the Latin Quarter flat of Monsieur Bailly, a professor of philosophy who presided benignly over their logomachies. Then as always Paris was a cauldron of conflicting philosophies and religions, and Ozanam's club soon became a battleground in the war of ideas. Ozanam and his Catholic friends were usually able to give as good as they got from the freethinkers and Voltairians, with Frederick's considerable knowledge of history standing them in good stead.

Founding of St. Vincent de Paul Society

At a certain point Ozanam and his friends began to wonder what they were accomplishing with all this sound and fury. They had little to show in terms of their main objective, which was gaining souls for God and the Church. As they wrestled with the problem, a remark by one of the unbelievers provided the answer. While arguing about the Church's history and its record of ministering to the needy, the young man exclaimed: "Don't talk about what the Church has done for the poor in the past—show us what it is doing for the poor now!" The remark stung Ozanam to the quick and he realized immediately what needed to be done. *"Allons aux pauvres,"* he exclaimed. That very night Ozanam and his friend Le Taillandier carried a load of coal and wood up the rickety stairs of a Paris tenement. Inside a frigid room they found several poor, shivering people without enough clothing or bedding to keep them warm. The two students lit a fire at the empty hearth and felt the sudden gust of warmth as they watched the flames flicker and spread.

The fire enkindled by Frederick Ozanam and his friend that night aptly symbolized the fire of charity that he and his friends would enkindle in the hearts of many Catholics around the world. For soon after that nocturnal visit, Ozanam and Le Taillandier gathered a number of their friends together to form a society dedicated to visiting and helping the poor. They called it the St. Vincent de Paul Society, and it is still found today in over 300,000 parishes in the Catholic world.

Paul Lamache, the last survivor of the original group of seven members, remembered the "flame burning in Ozanam's eyes" and the way his voice trembled as he proposed the formation of a charitable Catholic association. A meeting to launch the project was held one evening in May 1833 at the office of Monsieur Bailly. All present pledged themselves to carry out humble and unselfish works of charity. In time they chose as their society's patron St. Vincent de Paul, whom they had already begun to invoke. They also turned for advice to Sr. Rosalie, a Vincentian sister, whose love of the poor gained her the title "Mother of the Poor."

One of the first visits Ozanam made was to a family in which the alcoholic father beat the mother regularly. The poor woman had to "work herself to the bone" for the sake of the five children and was in constant despair. Frederick eventually was able to get her and the children away from the father by locating her and two of the children in Brittany and finding employment for the other children in Paris.

The work of the society was balm for Frederick's soul and a remedy for the depression caused by homesickness and the unbelieving atmosphere of Paris. He began to recapture the love of fun and the spirit of gaiety that was once so much a part of him. In a letter he told his mother of a walk he and his confreres had taken to nearby Nanterre to celebrate the Feast of Corpus Christi. There they happened on and took part in a charming religious procession moving along flower-strewn paths. Later they stopped at an inn where they had a merry old time with the help of some wine, twice "baptized" by the host, and afterward made their way home by the light of a full moon.

The little group began to expand as word got around the Latin Quarter and elsewhere of what was afoot. The eminent literary critic Saint Beuve called the growth of the society "a memorable spectacle . . . amid so much unbelief" and thought it a hopeful sign of a coming renewal of the Christian spirit. By the end of 1834 they counted over a hundred members—exuberant young men full of enthusiasm and ideas and quite articulate. But as their growing numbers made it difficult to carry on the meetings in their accustomed personal style, Ozanam felt it was time to divide the society into separate chapters. Others were dismayed at a move they thought might jeopardize their esprit de corps and sever bonds of friendship they highly valued. Ozanam himself felt the pull of these arguments and he, too, dreaded the separation from dear friends; but convinced that it was God's will, he was able to get his proposal accepted after a stormy debate. At the same time, other such societies were established elsewhere as the flame began to spread.

While actively involved in the society, Ozanam still managed to obtain a doctor of laws degree in 1836. Any joy he felt was overshadowed by the thought of having to return to Lyons and be confined "within the narrow limits of a court." His instinctive antipathy was soon justified. He found the atmosphere of the courtroom most uncongenial; deep-dyed idealist that he was, he was sorely tried by the hassles, the compromises, and the conflicts of the courtroom. He longed to return to his real love, literature.

His years back at Lyons were depressing ones for other reasons also. While on a trip to Paris he received word of his father's sudden death. The poor man had fallen down the rickety steps of a tenement while visiting one of his impoverished patients. The loss was totally devastating for Frederick, who had idolized him—a man, he said, whose nature "through revolutions, adversities, and in the soldiers' camp . . . remained noble; he maintained his sense of justice unimpaired, his charity to the poor unwearied."[3] In going over his father's accounts after the funeral, Frederick found that one third of the visits his father had made to patients were done without remuneration.

Two years later his mother, whom he had taken care of during a long illness, died. His only consolation was the peaceful manner of her death as she slipped serenely into a deep sleep and gently breathed her last. As in the case of his father, the void he felt was overwhelming. But in time he came to feel that he was not alone for he felt her presence as he prayed, "just as we used to pray together at the foot of the crucifix."

Matrimony at Last

With the care of his mother no longer demanding a good part of his energy, he now faced a decision that he had long pondered without resolving— should he become a priest or a religious, or should he stay in the world either as a celibate or a married man? In view of his unblemished life, his devotion to the Church, and his special talents, many thought he was destined for the priesthood. And he was much impressed by the example of Lacordaire, who had given up his glorious pulpit at Notre Dame to join the Dominicans in a life of prayer, mortification, and poverty. The two had become close friends and Lacordaire gave him a glowing description of life in the novitiate where he had been joined by eight young Frenchmen, one

[3]Ibid., p. 122.

more gifted than the other. He gave Frederick a nudge, telling him how ardent was his desire "of one day addressing you as Brother and Father."[4]

However, there was another priest, Frederick's early mentor Father Noirot, whose advice carried even greater weight and who did not think him suited for the cloister. And there was another consideration: As the driving force behind the Society of St. Vincent de Paul, he felt he was needed to preside over its continued expansion and prosperity. After months of uncertainty, he finally concluded that he should stay in the world but still left open the question of marriage. Noirot, who read his heart like a book, advised him to get married. But Frederick was terrified by the thought of being bound permanently to another "weak, miserable human creature, however perfect she may be." He even admitted to an "incredible repugnance" for marriage. But now he began to feel "a void growing within me which neither friendship nor intellectual work fills."

While in this quandary he happened to pay a visit to the rector of the university, Monsieur Soulacroix, and in a moment it was all decided. Passing through the drawing room into the rector's study, he noticed a young girl tending to her invalid brother, too preoccupied to pay much attention to the stranger. But he was quite impressed. As he continued a discussion with his host, his eye kept wandering through the open door to the bright, fair face bending over her little ward, gently caressing and amusing him. "How sweet it would be," he thought, "to have a sister like that to love me."[5] His incredible repugnance suddenly vanished.

The problem of how to take the first step was solved when Father Noirot took it on his own to speak to Monsieur Soulacroix about the possibility of marriage between Frederick and Amélie. Though Noirot had acted on his own, Frederick was delighted and henceforth used all sorts of pretexts to visit Monsieur Soulacroix in order to get at least a glimpse of the young lady. He soon won her affections and the two decided to announce their engagement when Frederick returned from Paris, where he had some highly important business to attend to. This was an exam in September of that year (1840) to qualify for the chair of foreign literature at the Sorbonne.

The exam was an incredibly grueling affair demanding a virtually encyclopedic knowledge of literature—three days of examinations on Greek, Latin, and French texts followed by a full day given to German, English, Italian, and Spanish works. In addition there was a defense of two theses in

[4]Ibid., p. 136.
[5]Ibid., p. 142.

two eight-hour sessions. Finally the candidate had to discourse on a subject picked by lot; Frederick's was the history of the Latin and Greek scholiasts—the worst possible topic. However, Frederick finished first—an amazing triumph considering that the other competitors were all well-known professors at the Collège de France.

His success meant that he would have to begin his lectures on foreign literature at the Sorbonne in January of 1841. He would therefore be separated for six months from Amélie whom he had now betrothed and "whose smile was the first ray of happiness . . . in my life since the loss of my poor father." But all went well, and on June 23, 1841, at ten o'clock in the Church of St. Nizier near Lyons the two were joined in holy matrimony. The church was packed with family and friends including Frederick's fellow members of the St. Vincent de Paul Society. As he said, "I could scarcely keep sweet tears from falling . . . I did not indeed know where I was."

Their honeymoon took them to Italy and to Rome where Pope Gregory XVI welcomed them and, leaving formalities aside, conversed privately and amiably with the two, showing special interest in Ozanam's work on Dante. Then he extended his hand to bless them and their families. In December 1840 they arrived in Paris and settled eventually in an apartment on the Rue de Fleurus with a lovely view of the Luxembourg gardens.

A Catholic Scholar at the Sorbonne

When the morning of his first lecture arrived on the first Saturday in January 1841, Frederick was—as always on such occasions—nervous and shy. As he began his lecture on Dante he felt exhausted and dull and the words came haltingly to his lips. But with a mighty act of the will he overcame his inhibitions and was soon in total command. Later many of those present crowded around him and expressed their admiration of his performance, while even the press took notice of the brilliant new professor. But he attributed it all to the prayers of his family and friends.

It was of no small importance for the Church in France that a young man of such faith and talent now occupied a post at the Sorbonne. No Catholic had done so for half a century, while the Voltairians and rationalists had been having a field day. They systematically denigrated the Church and its history and were constantly on the lookout for ways of embarassing Catholics. But Ozanam soon showed the difference a dedicated scholar could make. As he said in a letter, "While Mm. Michelet and Quinet are attacking Christianity itself under the name of Jesuitism, I tried in three consecutive lectures to defend the Papacy, monks and monastic obedience. I did this in the presence of a very large audience."[6]

He was quick to lend his support to Montalembert's campaign for freedom of education, and spoke publicly of his pride at the count's efforts. "I hear," he said, "the accents of St. Gregory VII, of St. Anselm, of St. Bernard in that defense of the liberties of the Church, at once the oldest and the youngest and most imperishable of all liberties."[7] On another occasion he faced down a gang of unruly students who were hissing and booing Charles Lenormant while he was lecturing. Lenormant's recent conversion to the Christian faith had earned him the enmity of Michelet, the renowned historian and popular lecturer who instigated the demonstration. Ozanam simply got up and motioned for silence, and then excoriated the troublemakers for depriving the lecturer of the liberty to which they were supposedly so dedicated. His words struck home and they settled down.

According to one of his students, the first impression he made was rather negative. They saw a nearsighted man with little grace or elegance and a plain face topped by a tangled mass of hair. But they were soon captivated by the flashes of wit and intelligence that transformed his plain features. He was indeed a born teacher whom his students soon learned to love. He knew how to arouse their interest in a subject and he was always willing to spend time with them individually over their problems and concerns. He was particularly devoted to their spiritual interests and was able to draw many of them back to the faith. One student wrote to him: "What a great number of sermons failed to do for me, you have done: You have made me a Christian. Accept this expression of my joy and gratitude."[8] One of the familiar sights near the Sorbonne was of Ozanam being escorted home through the Luxembourg gardens by a group of his students.

The demands Ozanam made on himself were strenuous to the extreme. Besides the labors of teaching and writing he kept up his work with the St. Vincent de Paul conferences and his visits to the poor. His devoted wife Amélie worried constantly as she watched him overworking himself, and tried to get him to slow down. But all to little avail; his health finally snapped and he was stricken by a malignant fever in 1846.

This was the beginning of the slow martyrdom that lasted until his death in 1854. With his faithful Amélie and little Marie, his adored daughter, he

[6] Ibid., p. 165.
[7] Ibid., p. 160.
[8] Ibid., p. 157.

embarked in December 1846 on the first of many journeys in search of health. A government research grant enabled him and his family to travel to Italy, where they first visited Florence and then Rome. There a glimpse of the Holy Father, Pius IX, at a ceremony brought tears to Ozanam's eyes. Later the three were received by the pope who graciously insisted that Marie be seated. Frederick was happy to report that "Little Marie behaved like an angel." He was also happy to hear the pope praise the good work being accomplished by the Society of St. Vincent de Paul. Later he joined a huge crowd in front of the papal palace as they wildly applauded the pontiff who appeared on the balcony and blessed them. The pope had just introduced some liberal reforms and his popularity was enormous. (Word went around that even the pope's cat was liberal.) Watching the scene, Ozanam was ecstatic, believing he was watching a dream come true: the lamb lying down with the lion—the Church and the Revolution finally at peace.

After Rome came Assisi and it was here that his work *The Franciscan Poets* was conceived. It established his reputation as the preeminent authority in this field. It has been said that the poetic and mystical soul of Frederick himself is mirrored in this work, which captures so well the spirit of Francis and his troubadors. One of the poets Ozanam drew from undeserved obscurity was the mad genius Jacopone da Todi, a herald of Dante and, like Dante, a fierce adversary of Pope Boniface VIII.

On an earlier visit to the Vatican in 1833, Ozanam had been greatly touched by Raphael's fresco depicting Dante crowned with a laurel wreath. Henceforth he devoted much time and energy to the study of the great Florentine, and not the least of Ozanam's scholarly achievements was to rescue Dante from the hands of detractors like Voltaire. Some of them saw Dante as a neurotic genius, a sinister witness to the darkness of the Dark Ages, while others saw him as a forerunner of Protestantism and a member of an anti-papal sect. But Ozanam, deeply versed in the theology and philosophy of Aquinas, was able to show how profoundly Catholic Dante was and to reveal the intimate bond that united his masterpiece with Aquinas's *Summa*.

A Social Catholic Ahead of His Church

Though his scholarly achievements were of a high order, it is his contribution to Catholic political and social thought that is of greatest interest. He was one of the first Catholics to face the problem of social justice in the new industrial mass society. As factories began to proliferate, spewing their smoke and grime into the air, the cities began to bulge with the poor who serviced them. Many were drawn to the city by the promise of work but they often failed to find it, or were laid off when the economy faltered, thus swelling the ranks of the unemployed. They lived in abominable conditions, in shacks and hovels if they were lucky and in caves and under bridges if they were not. Disease, violence, and crime were rampant.

Ozanam described the kind of scenes he witnessed on his visits to the poor:

> Half of these districts . . . are made up of narrow, twisting streets where the sun never penetrates, where a carriage cannot move without danger, where a man in a dress coat cannot pass without causing excitement and bringing to the doors groups of naked children and women in rags. On both sides of a foul gutter are some five-story houses, several of which contain fifty families . . . At the back in a sort of cave lives a family without any other bed than a little straw upon the bare earth . . . [they] hang their bread in a linen rag in order to keep it away from the rats.[9]

The condition of the poor was worsened by the nature of the government. From 1830 to 1848 France was ruled by the so-called July Monarchy of Louis-Philippe, a middle-class, liberal government that restricted political rights to the wealthy and espoused a laissez-faire economic philosophy. When the poor complained, Guizot, the leading minister, responded: "Get rich yourselves."

There was indeed little evidence of concern for the poor in the materialistic bourgeois atmosphere of the July Monarchy. The fortunate were too busy chasing after riches or spending their time in the idle pleasures of the gaming room or the dance hall. The poor and the unemployed grew increasingly desperate and started down the path of violence; some of the street disturbances began to resemble civil war. In Lyons during a vacation Ozanam saw silk-workers battling the army and he wrote: "It is the battle of those who have nothing and those who have too much; it is the violent collision of opulence and poverty which makes the earth tremble under our feet."

Nevertheless his basically Christian optimistic outlook made him feel that social reform was possible; and in a course on commercial law he gave at Lyons in 1840 he presented the only formal exposition of his social thought

[9]Thomas E. Auge, *Frederick Ozanam and His World* (Milwaukee: The Bruce Publishing Company, 1966), p. 33.

that later found echoes in the papal encyclicals. Ozanam analyzed the conditions of production and of work without condemning freedom of exchange or profit, but cautioned against its dangers and potential abuses. Laissez-faire liberalism he condemned for its reduction of the worker to just another piece of machinery whose wage was kept at the minimum needed for subsistence. Only a living wage met the demands of justice, he believed, and he predicted future violent conflict otherwise. Charity, he said, was not the answer to the social question; only justice can establish a true human relationship between employer and laborer. He was wary of government intervention that could cripple business, but at the same time he condemned any extreme of free-market theory that put the worker at the mercy of the employer. He believed that some form of worker organization was needed, and that government intervention was necessary in extraordinary circumstances.

The idea of social reform was relatively new and had first surfaced during the Enlightenment. For many conservative Catholics it was a chimera. The most influential of these, Joseph De Maistre (1753–1821), saw poverty, disease, and earthly misfortune as inevitable and as punishments for the sins of an individual, a family, or a nation. Coming from an entirely different background was the brilliant reactionary Louis Veuillot (1813–1883), who as editor of the Catholic daily *L'Univers* did more than any other French Catholic to swing the Church in France over to the conservative side.

For one shining moment, however, it seemed that the French Church was ready to follow Ozanam's lead. The efforts of men like Ozanam, Lacordaire, Montalembert, and the archbishop of Paris, Monsignor Affre, seemed to align the Church with the liberal, socially conscious forces of France. By 1848 a revival of Catholicism was much in evidence; many returned to the practice of the faith.

That year Europe was swept with an enormous burst of revolutionary fervor. France again led the way. The February Revolution overthrew the bourgeois monarchy of Louis Philippe and installed a democratic regime. Ozanam threw his support wholeheartedly behind the new republic and urged his fellow Catholics to do the same. He welcomed the Second Republic as an act of providence. "My knowledge of history," he said, "forces me to the conclusion that democracy is the natural final stage of the development of political progress, and that God leads the world thither."[10] His erudite study of the Church in the fifth century showed how the Church

---

[10]Schimberg, *Frederick Ozanam*, p. 215.

had turned to the barbarians when they overran the Roman empire, civilizing them and leading them eventually to the high level attained by medieval culture. He saw a similar role for the Church of his time because the masses needed her saving, elevating care as much as—if not more than—the barbarians. "Turn to the mass of the people to whom we are unknown . . . Help them not with alms which humiliate, but with social and ameliorative measures which will free and elevate them . . . Let us go over to the barbarians *(Passons aux barbares)* and follow Pius IX."[11]

The word "democracy" was anathema to most Catholics, for whom it evoked the bloody Terror of the Revolution and the horrors visited upon the Church. But undaunted, Ozanam joined with Lacordaire and Abbé Henri Maret, a liberal Catholic priest, in publishing *L'Ère Nouvelle,* a newspaper that would try to rally Catholics to the cause of Christian democracy and social reform. Throughout the tense months of 1848, Ozanam in his articles stood behind the forces struggling for a new order in France. Like Marx and de Tocqueville he saw the real issue of the Revolution as a social one—the question of unemployment and wages. He tried to convince the upper classes that they could not ignore these vital issues of social justice. *L'Ère Nouvelle* spoke of a Christian socialism and advocated a policy that seemed revolutionary to most Catholics, calling for legislation to protect children, to provide for sickness in old age, for comanagement of industry, and for compulsory arbitration as well as profit-sharing for workers.

His Hope for Christian Democracy Expires with the 1848 Revolution

But events soon smothered their call for a Christian democracy.

The rich and the powerful in France were terribly frightened by what they saw as a revolt of the poor. Elections in April returned a Constituent Assembly with a majority opposed to republicanism and social reform. After dispersing a mob that tried to overthrow the Convention, the assembly on May 24 dismantled the National Workshops, a program for relief of the unemployed. The hungry, jobless workers exploded with rage and grabbed whatever weapons they could. Paris became the theater of pitched battles between the workers and the National Guard. Gradually, street by street, barricade by barricade, the soldiers cordoned off the less-well-armed work-

[11]Ibid.

ers. A hundred thousand men were involved in class war in its purest form—
the workers of Paris against the rest of France.

On guard duty himself, Ozanam patrolled the boulevards and thanked
God he didn't have to use his rifle though he heard "shots fired in the
neighboring streets." He and his friends searched their minds desperately for
some way to end the fighting. Finally they thought of seeking the help of
Archbishop Affre. Unlike what happened in the Revolution of 1830, when
many bishops had to go into hiding, the events of 1848 showed how much
better disposed the workers had become to the Church. Even though Catholics in general lacked any meaningful contact with the workers, Ozanam
and Catholics like him had done much to end their hostility to the Church.
Thus the idea of Archbishop Affre acting as a mediator between the two
sides seemed quite reasonable.

The archbishop agreed, though with a sense of impending doom he first
made his confession. Accompanied by Ozanam and his two friends, and
dressed in the full regalia of his office, he set out for the Place de la Bastille,
the center of the conflict. The officers there pleaded with Affre not to go
ahead, but, preceded by a young man carrying a white flag, he approached
the barricades and began to parley with several men who had come out
from behind the barricades. But suddenly a drumroll commenced and was
taken by both sides as a signal to resume firing. As the shots rang out the
archbishop slumped to the ground with a bullet in his chest. He was carried
to the house of a priest nearby and died the next day. His last words were,
"At least let my blood be the last you shed."

The rebellion of the workers was finally crushed with remorseless vengeance by the upper classes as many of the hapless defeated workers were
massacred by the victors. Heartbroken by the outcome of the revolution and
feeling some responsibility for the death of Affre, Ozanam nevertheless
refused to despair. "I believed, I still believe, in the possibility of Christian
democracy; in fact I believe in nothing else as far as politics are concerned."
And while not omitting his visits to the poor for even a day, he continued to
pour out articles in *L'Ere Nouvelle* to arouse the conscience of the *gens de bien*
(the well-to-do).

"You have crushed the insurrection," he told them, "you have now to
deal with an enemy with which you are not acquainted, which you dislike
hearing spoken . . . *misery* . . . in Paris alone the number of individuals
out of work amounts to two hundred and sixty-seven thousand." He then
went on to describe the conditions of the slums he visited. "Low, damp and

noxious rooms . . . no paper, often not a single piece of furniture . . .
In a house on the rue des Lyonnais we ourselves saw married couples
without even a bed. One family lived in the depths of a cellar, with nothing
but a handful of straw on the earthen floor, and a rope fastened from wall to
wall, from which the poor creatures hung their bread in a rag to keep it out
of the reach of the rats . . . [nor is there] room for that ready excuse of the
hardhearted, that the poor are wretched by their own fault . . . In these
foul cellars and garrets, sometimes next door to sloth and vice, we have
often come upon the loveliest domestic virtues, of a refinement and intelligence that one does not always meet with under gilded ceilings."

At this time he addressed a meeting of the Vincentians (St. Vincent de
Paul Society) about the work of relief that the government assigned to them,
urging them to be messengers of reconciliation with the embittered workmen. When a terrible cholera epidemic broke out the next year, Ozanam
organized the Vincentians into teams to nurse the stricken and bury the
dead. In two months some two thousand sick received their ministrations
and three-fourths recovered. "The rest," he reported, "died a happy death
fortified with the rites of the Church."

The year 1848 was a great watershed for French Catholicism. It meant
the end of the attempt to reconcile the Church and modern society on the
basis of a democratic socialism. Great numbers of workers now joined the
camp of the socialists, having been disappointed in their hopes in Catholicism.

Most Catholics in France were now prepared to follow Veuillot, the talented
but reactionary editor of the widely circulated journal *L'Univers*. Veuillot
had discovered, so he thought, a basic incompatibility between Catholicism
and democracy. He called the defeated June insurgents "reptiles and street
vermin" suffering from "pride, not hunger." Even Montalembert himself
pilloried schemes to nationalize the railways as creeping socialism. "The
poor would be always with us and should be grateful for charity," he
expostulated.

The Catholic democrats were drowned in the flood of reactionary verbiage. As we've already seen, most Catholics eagerly threw their weight behind Louis Napoleon, who overthrew the republic in 1852 and installed his
authoritarian regime. The roots of the ferocious anticlericalism of the socialists and republicans can be traced to this period. As Martin Nadaud, who

was one of them, said, he would die happy "to the sounds of the churches crumbling under the hammers of the people."[12]

The demise of the Christian democratic movement was a chastening experience for Ozanam. Thanks to his historical sense and his profound faith, however, he did not abandon hope for the eventual triumph of Christian democracy. After these days of chaos and blood, he continued to write as an advocate for the poor and to devote himself to his ministry to them. Ozanam was dedicated heart and soul to this ministry. He saw work among the poor as an expression of love and he showed this love in many ways. Christ in the persons of His poor was not an empty phrase for him. He treated them with the same respect he showed toward people of prominence and with even an extra measure of courtesy, never failing to take off his hat when visiting them, for instance.

His concern for those in need sometimes stretched his wife's patience. On one occasion he learned that one of the families he visited was forced to pawn their belongings in order to pay their rent. Among the items pawned was a commode that was a family heirloom they cherished and needed. Their sad plight weighed on Frederick's mind, and though it was the Christmas season and his family was celebrating he thought he ought to go at once and redeem the item. But Amélie demurred and tried to divert his thoughts. All to no avail, for Frederick persisted in his unhappy mood and didn't even show his usual delight as his daughter played with her toys. Finally he got up, went to the pawnshop, redeemed the commode, and returned it to the family in question. Then he returned home and joined happily in the celebration.

Illness and Death

All the while, Ozanam continued to wrestle with grave illness. Finally work was totally out of the question and the last year of his long martyrdom began. Leaving Paris in July 1852 with Amélie and Marie, he began the last of his journeys in search of health—crossing southern France, the Pyrenees, to Burgos in Spain, then back to France and a stay in Marseilles. Finally he set out for Italy once more to visit Pisa and Florence. As with all his travels it was a pilgrimage of faith, and he sought out shrines to Our Lady where he

[12]Roger Magraw, *France 1815–1914: The Bourgeois Century* (New York: Oxford University Press, 1983), p. 139.

would kneel in fervent prayer. At Burgos, Ozanam's mystical love of the Virgin flamed out in these words:

Ah, holy Virgin, my Mother, what a powerful woman you are. In exchange for the poor house of Nazareth where you lodged his son, God has built you such magnificent abodes . . . Some of them I know well. There is Notre Dame of Cologne and Notre Dame of Milan and of Pisa, Notre Dame of Paris, of Amiens and of Chartres, Saint Mary Major and Saint Mary of Florence . . . The very thought of thee gives grace and beauty to the works of man![13]

He made it a point to visit with the Vincentians along the way wherever he found a branch of the society in existence. At a meeting of the Vincentians in Florence on January 30, 1853, he reminded them that the society stood not for the cold charity of philanthropy but the kind of "love that mixes with the tears of the unfortunate whom it cannot otherwise console; . . . caresses and cares for the naked, forsaken child, gives shy youth a friendly counsel, sits with benevolent sympathy beside the sickbed and listens without the slightest sign of weariness to the long, pitiful stories of the poor . . . a love, O my friends, [that] can come only from God."

He believed that the crucial issue of his times was the terrible gulf between the haves and the have-nots, between opulence and poverty. He was convinced that the "world had grown cold" and that "it is for us Catholics to rekindle the vital fire which has been extinguished." It was therefore a great joy for him to witness the amazing spread of the Society of St. Vincent de Paul around the world. During his lifetime, branches were established in Italy, England, Scotland, Ireland, Germany, the United States, French Canada, Poland, Mexico, and Spain. After his death the society continued to grow by leaps and bounds.

By the spring of 1853 his health had declined to the point that little hope was left. In Pisa on April 23, his fortieth birthday, he cried out sorrowfully with Isaiah:

I said in the midst of my years: I shall go to the gates of death . . . my life is swept from me and is rolled away as a shepherd's tent . . . My eyes are weakened with looking upwards. Lord, I . . . will recount to thee all my years in the bitterness of my soul." (Is. 38:11–15)

---

[13] Kathleen O'Meara, *Frederick Ozanam* (New York: The Catholic Publication Society, 1883), p. 286.

As he meditates on this text he cannot hold back his tears, and from the depths of his sorrow he pleads with God to spare his life. "Only forty years!" he cries, "and I have so much to live for—my dear Amélie, and the work that is doing so much good . . . Will you spare me, if I sell one half of my books and give the proceeds to the poor, if I confine my activities to the duties of my official position and devote the rest of my life to visiting the poor, teaching apprentices and soldiers?" But then he pulls himself together: "Perhaps my God, Thou dost not will that . . . it is written at the commencement of the Book that I am to do Thy Will! I said: I come, Lord! . . . If thou wert to chain me to a bed of suffering for the rest of my days, it would not suffice to thank Thee for the days which I have lived."

In July the little family went to the village of Antignano on the seashore. By August his condition was so far gone that he had to spend most of his time on a couch at the end of a little garden. However, on August 15, the Feast of the Assumption, he resolved to attend mass and receive Communion at the little church nearby. Declining to use a carriage he said, "It may be my last walk in this world, and I wish to make it a visit to my God and his blessed mother." With a supreme effort, leaning on Amélie's arm, he was able to make it to the church for mass—his last one.

His two brothers—Charles, a physician, and Alphonse, a priest—had come to assist him in his last hours. Knowing his desire to die in his beloved country, they were able to get him aboard a ship, which after a gentle crossing landed in Marseilles. There they found a bed for him in the home of relatives. In his beautiful panegyric, Lacordaire wrote:

When he had reached the land of his ancestors and of his works, he appeared to suffer no more. All traces of apprehension had disappeared; his figure exhibited a calm, which belonged neither to life nor to death; nothing could equal the serenity of his mind and of his features. He spoke little, but he had a pressure of the hand, a smile for those whom he loved.

The priest who gave him the last sacraments told him to trust in God's mercy and not be afraid. Frederick whispered, "Ah, why should I fear him, I love him so!" On the evening of September 8, with his breathing labored and painful, he opened his eyes, raised his arms, and cried out: *"Mon Dieu, mon Dieu, ayez pitié de moi!"*—his last words before succumbing moments later.[14] He was eventually buried in the crypt of the Carmelite Church in Paris, which has remained a shrine for pilgrims from around the world.

[14]Schimberg, *Frederick Ozanam*, pp. 295–296.

Lacordaire preached a beautiful eulogy at a memorial service, and those who sent condolences to Amélie included the Holy Father, Pius IX. Montalembert wrote to Amélie "as an old soldier in the same cause who will forget neither his instruction nor his example."[15]

His Legacy for Social Catholicism?

Pope John Paul II beatified Frederick Ozanam during his trip to Paris in August, 1997, in recognition of his outstanding holiness and dedication to the ministry to the poor. Ozanam's St. Vincent de Paul Society was the first organized effort of Catholics to deal in more than an episodic way with the problems caused by industrial capitalism. There are now nearly 50,000 local societies, with an estimated million members serving the poor and elderly all over the world.

He lived in a time when most Catholics still shrank away in horror from the new world opened up by the French Revolution. Like the Bourbons, they "had learned nothing and forgotten nothing." But Ozanam was of that small band of Catholics who meditated deeply on the meaning of the great cataclysm that had so devastated the Church. He saw the Revolution as humanity's cry for greater freedom, and as a key figure in the short-lived Christian democracy of 1848 he tried to move the Church to hear that cry and join the struggle.

The workers' revolution in Lyons when he was a young man opened his eyes to social injustice, and he was henceforth scathing in his criticism of the prevailing indifference to the lot of the poor. He emphasized the role of poverty and social injustice in causing revolutions. "It is a social question; do away with misery, Christianize the people, and you will make an end of revolutions."[16]

His St. Vincent de Paul Society functioned as a seedbed of concerned Catholics who were challenged to analyze and correct the problems of gross social inequality. One such leader in social ministry was Don Bosco, who introduced the society into Turin. Another noteworthy member was Giuseppe Toniolo, professor of political economy and the recognized master of Catholic social teaching in Italy. Toniolo was consulted by Leo XIII when the latter drew up his epoch-making encyclical *Rerum Novarum*. Ozanam's

---

[15] Ibid., p. 325.
[16] O'Meara, *Frederick Ozanam*, p. 226.

influence has continued to spread through the Church as recognition of his prophetic role has grown.

For many Catholics, however, he is probably remembered best as the founder of the St. Vincent de Paul Society that has done so much to awaken the average Catholic to the needs of the poor.

FIVE

Karl Marx's (1818–1883) Call for a Workers' Revolution

THE REVOLUTION in Paris that ended Ozanam's dream of a Catholic social movement was part of the wave of liberal, nationalist revolutions that swept Europe in 1848. Rulers were forced to accept various liberal reforms; Prince Metternich, the Austrian architect of repression and its chief symbol, saved his skin only by taking flight; a similar ordeal faced Pope Pius IX, who had to flee Rome in disguise. But the revolutionaries proved unequal to the task of holding on to their gains and soon fell under the onslaught of the troops of Czar Nicholas I and his Prussian and Russian allies. The Prussian, Austrian, and Russian monarchs recaptured their absolute power, and the pope was restored to Rome in April 1850 by a French army. The leaders of the counterrevolution were merciless in crushing the hopes of a revolutionary generation.

One of those who refused to despair was Karl Marx, a young man of twenty-nine and the main author of the *Communist Manifesto,* published on the eve of the revolution. Although Marx hailed the uprising as the dawn of worker liberation and spent his inheritance buying arms for the workers, he was not greatly downcast by the defeat of the liberals. Holding no faith in their goal of free elections, he looked forward instead to an armed revolutionary dictatorship of the proletariat.

Karl Marx

The author of a recent study of Marxism argues that the encounter with Marxism—our age's dominant form of secularism—has been the defining event for twentieth-century Christianity.[1] Certainly Marx deserves attention in any history of Social Catholicism since it originated to some extent in response to Marx's ideas. Moreover, Catholic liberation theology, a recent development, shows some influence of Marx.

Marx did not invent socialism but he claimed to be the first to give it a scientific foundation. Socialism can be traced back to Plato, while Thomas More and a few other philosophers toyed with communist ideas. However, hardly a trace of socialism in the modern sense can be found in either thought or practice previous to the nineteenth century. No socialistic books, for instance, can be found on the lists of censored literature before the nineteenth century. There were no well-defined communists among the participants in the French Revolution, and if communists like to trace

[1] Denis R. Janz, *World Christianity and Marxism* (New York: Oxford University Press, 1997).

themselves back to the French Revolution it is to the ideal of equality rather than to any specific economic proposals carried out at that time. It was not until the early nineteenth century that a number of thinkers appeared who espoused the idea of socialism as a practical alternative. Without question, the most important was Karl Marx.

Early Years

Marx was born at two o'clock in the morning of May 5, 1818, in Trier, near the Porta Nigra in Rhenish Prussia. His father Heinrich, who stemmed from a family with a long line of rabbis, had been baptized a Protestant a year or two before Karl's birth. It was a step taken for purely worldly motives because a Jew had no chance of advancement in the Prussia of that day. For similar nonreligious reasons, Karl too was baptized a Protestant at the age of six. The man who later denounced all religion as "the opiate of the people" grew up in a town that was 93% Catholic and filled with churches and ecclesiastical buildings.

Though Karl himself was raised in comfort, Trier was a town where unemployment and poverty were endemic and soup kitchens a necessity. The future founder of so-called "scientific socialism" and dreaded enemy of capitalism observed daily, as he grew up, the ravages of poverty and misery that confronted him as he walked the streets of Trier. In spite of his brilliance Karl did not stand out as a student in the local Gymnasium or high school. His overall average was a little below B plus. After graduating in 1835 he moved on to the University at Bonn where he began studies in law and literature. But they failed to hold his interest and he spent most of his time enjoying the boisterous life of student society.

Two men had a singular influence on Marx's early development: One was his father, Heinrich, conscious of his son's great intellectual talents, who tried to guide him into a productive career in law and provided him with generous financial help. The other was a neighbor, Freiherr von Westphalen, a distinguished Prussian government official who was attracted by Karl's striking ability and spent long hours in conversation with him. Von Westphalen treated young Marx as an intellectual equal and encouraged him to read deeply in the great classics of literature, including Shakespeare and Cervantes. It was no doubt their influence and example to which Karl owed much of the enormous self-confidence that carried him through many dark years of poverty, illness, and persecution.

Karl was also extremely lucky in love. Though by all accounts a rather

ugly young man, described by an acquaintance as "nearly the most unattrac-
tive man on whom the sun ever shone," he very early won the heart of
Freiherr's daughter, Jenny—a pretty, witty, and strong-willed young lady
who after their engagement had to wait seven years to become his wife. She
proved to be the greatest blessing of his life, steadfast in her loyalty to Karl
through many years of terrible hardship and misery.

Papa Heinrich doted on Karl and manifested enormous patience with his
son's spendthrift ways and inability to settle down to an ordinary career.
Eventually, however, he could no longer contain himself and he poured out
his wrath in a long letter to Karl, whom he accused of being a "slovenly
barbarian, an antisocial person, a wretched son, an indifferent brother, a
selfish lover, an irresponsible student, and a reckless spendthrift"—a description that later found an echo in the criticisms of Marx's enemies.

In 1836 Karl left Bonn and entered the University of Berlin. Though
founded only in 1810, it was already an illustrious institution thanks to its
leading professors, among them Georg Wilhelm Friedrich Hegel, Johann
Gottlieb Fichte, Friedrich Daniel Schleiermacher, and Friedrich Carl von
Savigny. Karl followed the lectures of von Savigny, who emphasized the
historical approach to law. He also attended lectures on such subjects as
geography, art history, and the Book of Isaiah. But most of the time he
worked on his own, devouring books with incredible energy and filling
notebooks, always seeking to fit his knowledge into a coherent system.

For a while Marx found Hegel helpful in this regard. Hegel sought to
identify universal laws governing all of history, which he interpreted as a
constantly ascending movement of the human spirit. Conflict, tension, and
struggle was a necessary part of this "dialectical" process: Rival systems of
ideas confronted each other and in this clash of opposites a higher level of
consciousness—a "synthesis"—was reached, in which the opposing views
were reconciled through mutual transformation. History, according to Hegel, shows a constant growth of self-awareness in humanity as a whole,
which finds its greatest clarity in the most intellectual and cultivated, sensitive and inquiring spirits of any given period—the thinkers, artists, scientists,
and philosophers, who are necessarily most conscious of the progress of
human development. Marx later took his distance from Hegel on a number
of important points but always remained basically a Hegelian, viewing history as human progress achieved through the scientifically identifiable and
predictable clash and resolution of opposing (albeit material) forces.

A profound influence on Marx's view of religion at the time was Ludwig
Feuerbach's *The Essence of Christianity (Wesen des Christentums),* published in

1841. Marx eagerly assimilated Feuerbach's main arguments for atheism: First, God was created by man when two purely human concepts were joined: the concept of infinity, derived from man's consciousness of infinity, and the concept of a universal human nature. Second, God was a projection of human needs to assuage human suffering. And third, so-called "divine revelations" were now revealed by historical criticism to be tissues of fables and fairy tales. Convinced, Marx soon decided that religion was passé and hardly worthy of serious discussion.

He also was deeply influenced by Feuerbach's critique of Hegel. Hegel, Feuerbach said, attributed all the interwoven acts and thoughts of an age to the spirit of the age. But, as Feuerbach said, the spirit of the age is only the sum total of the phenomena of the age. Therefore, to say that these phenomena are determined by the Spirit of the Age is to say that they were determined by the totality of themselves, which is a mere tautology. In fact, Feuerbach insisted, Hegel actually retreated into the swamps of mysticism, for the Hegelian "Idea" is actually just another name for God.

To really explain what happens in history, Feuerbach says, we must investigate the actual material conditions of people. For it is their material relationships that determine how men think and what they do. These relationships explain, for instance, why people invented a God and why they practice religion. The illusions of religion and its promise of eternal happiness are created (albeit unconsciously) to provide solace for the miseries caused by the lack of the material means of happiness. This book, though "badly written, unhistorical and naive," as the historian Isaiah Berlin says, hit Marx just at the time he was growing increasingly dissatisfied with Hegel's abstractions.[2]

While at the University of Berlin, Marx joined the Young Hegelians and became a friend of Bruno Bauer, an instructor in the theological faculty and intellectual leader of the club. It was the fashion of many disgruntled radicals of the day to attack Christianity, which they saw as one of the main pillars of political reaction. David Strauss's book *The Life of Jesus (Das Leben Jesu,* 1835) relegated much of the Gospel to the realm of myth and provided ammunition for the skeptics. But Bauer found even Strauss too timid and published his own studies, *History of John (Geschichte des Johannes,* 1840) and *Critique of the Evangelical History of the Synoptics (Kritik der evangelischen Geschichte der Synoptiker,* 3 vols., 1841–1842). These went beyond Strauss in attributing the Gospel story to the imagination—not, like Strauss, that of

[2] Isaiah Berlin, *Karl Marx* (Oxford University Press, 1963), p. 79.

the Christian community, but that of a single mind. Pilloried as godless and subversive, Bauer lost his hope of a professorship and so did Marx, judged guilty by association.

With his hopes for an academic career in shreds, Marx turned to that refuge of many disappointed academics—journalism. In May 1842 he became a contributor to the *Rheinische Zeitung* and in October was chosen to be its editor. Marx was, as always, polemical, disputatious, a courageous critic of social injustice, and determined to move the paper in a leftward direction. Still, at this point he was not a communist nor even a social radical; he knew and cared little about economics or communism and was basically a liberal humanist, concerned about human rights in the tradition of the Enlightenment and the French Revolution. He was soon in hot water with a series of articles denouncing the Russian government, which, in the minds of all Western liberals, represented the most ghastly embodiment possible of obscurantism and oppression. The Prussian government couldn't ignore this attack on its chief ally, and Marx was soon out on the road again.

His destination this time was Paris, where he and Jenny, having just been married in a Protestant church (they were registered as of the Evangelical faith), settled in 1843. In the first article he wrote after his arrival he adumbrated the philosophy that he would spend his life articulating. He denounced religion as a delusion, the sigh of the distressed creature in a heartless world, "the opium of the people." To abolish religion, he went on, one must abolish the conditions that require such illusions. Using the Hegelian dialectics of negations and syntheses, he then assigned the historic task of emancipation to the proletariat. Only the proletariat could overcome the division of society into classes and could produce, through a Hegelian synthesis, the new classless society. The revolution that would establish the proletarian classless society would, he believed, take place in Germany. Thorough-minded Germans could not make a revolution without making a fundamental revolution.

Marx and Engels Join Forces

The years 1843 to 1845 that he spent in Paris were crucial years for Marx. Paris was the home of European revolution and radical ferment. The great Revolution of 1789 was a living tradition and inspired both the triumphant middle class, now holding the levers of power, as well as the discontented workers who were seething with radical idealism. And it was there that

Marx, the theorist of the proletariat, began to associate with real proletarians and to witness the class struggle at first hand.

During his stay there he got to know some of the foremost radicals of his time. One of these, the Russian aristocrat Mikhail Bakunin, a giant in stature, was both admired and feared by Marx. They formed a wary friendship that eventually soured into a lasting enmity. Another was Pierre-Joseph Proudhon whose book, *What Is Property* (Paris, 1840), became one of the staples of radical literature. Marx also cultivated an intimate friendship with the German poet Heinrich Heine, like himself an expatriate who had found the German political and spiritual climate uncongenial. Heine also was deeply influenced by Hegel and was, like Marx, a baptized German Jew. Heine later returned to religion and came to despise Marx and his radical friends as "godless, self-appointed gods." They reminded him of the Babylonian king Nebuchadnezzar who fell from God's grace and was condemned to eat grass like an animal in the field.[3]

In Paris Marx also had the encounter that decisively influenced the future course of his life when Frederick Engels stopped to meet him in August 1844. Engels was on his way home to Barmen, Germany, where his father owned a small factory. Like Marx, Engels was deeply read and conversant with all the natural sciences. An astonishing linguist, he once learned Persian in three weeks and called it "child's play." Marx and Engels were two of a kind—both were witty, arrogant, vulgar, and especially crude and nasty in their polemics with the capitalists. The two enthusiastic young Germans soon sealed a friendship that was to last until death. They had met before and Marx was already deeply impressed by an article Engels had written, "Outlines of a Critique of Political Economy." But this time they were able to spend ten days together, exploring each other's ideas ranging over the whole spectrum of current issues. They found themselves in remarkable agreement. Engels, reared in a Lutheran Pietistic family, was bitterly hostile to religion and shared Marx's view of it as the drug of the downtrodden. Like Marx he found the philosophy of materialism most congenial. Finally, he too was totally opposed to the status quo and ready to work unceasingly to bring down the whole established social, political, and religious order.

Engels played an important role in the conversion of Marx to communism. Marx had already evinced interest in the communist movement and had familiarized himself with the writings of the French theorists and utopians such as Fourier and Cabet. Moreover he had also taken a great interest in

[3] Saul Padover, *Karl Marx* (New York: New American Library, c. 1980), p. 89.

the problems of the Parisian workers, and had already attended some of the meetings of the German and French communists. But his contact with Engels fixed his resolve to commit himself totally to the communist movement.

Engels also stimulated his interest in economics, which Marx had only begun to take up but which soon became the dominant focus of his thought. In time he became thoroughly conversant with the works of the classic English economists James Mill, David Ricardo, and Adam Smith. They had a deep and lasting impression on him. In an essay at the time, based on his readings, he explored the concept of alienation—later a key term in the Marxist ideology. In the modern industrial economy, he held, man was alienated from nature, from his fellow human beings, from his work, and from himself.

In 1845 the authorities moved against him for an article he penned in 1844 for *Vorwarts,* a semi-weekly German-language paper. Marx argued there for the necessity of a revolution in order to establish socialism in Prussia. On the morning of January 25, his wife Jenny says in her *Reminiscences,* "The police commissioner came to our house and showed us an order of expulsion . . . Karl Marx must leave Paris within 24 hours." Arriving in Brussels a week later (he was given a week's grace) he found free lodging with a tavern owner who was kind to German refugees. Jenny and their first child followed him a few weeks later and they began their three-year sojourn in the Belgian city, moving from one slummy quarter to another, always on the verge of financial disaster that was staved off only by Karl's endless borrowing. The second of his seven children, Laura, was born there several months after their arrival. Though under the constant watch of Prussian police spies, Karl was still free enough to plot and plan, to organize the communists in preparation for the great communist revolution.

Engels soon joined him, having quit his job in his father's factory; he described his old position as an abomination that had forced him to act as "a bourgeois active against the proletariat." He especially despised his father's pietistic religion with its "trite vision of hell" and what he called its "Christian malice . . . enough to drive one nuts."[4] Eight years later, unable to make a living in journalism, he joined his father's textile firm in Manchester. This implacable foe of capitalism did so well that he was able to retire at fifty with enough capital to provide a comfortable life for himself

[4] Ibid., p. 108.

and the Marx family. Like a very good capitalist Engels even rode to hounds with the local gentry, whom he despised but found most amusing.

Marx and Engels then began their second book, *The German Ideology,* which—like their earlier effort, *The Holy Family*—attacked the German writers and radicals of the Hegel-Feuerbach school. Here's how they described the role assigned to the proletariat in the communist philosophy:

> For the proletarians, on the other hand, the condition of their own existence, labor, and with all the conditions of existence governing modern society, has become something accidental, something over which they, as separate individuals, have no control, and over which no social organization can give them control . . . The proletarians, if they are to assert themselves as individuals, will have to abolish the very condition of their existence (which has, moreover, been that of all society up to the present), namely, labor. Thus they find themselves directly opposed to the form in which, hitherto, the individuals, of which society consists, have given themselves collective expression, that is, the State, and must overthrow the State in order to assert their own personality.[5]

In the summer of 1845 the pair made their first visit to the center of world capitalism to meet with a number of the foreign communists and English radicals who lived in London. "Communism," a term popularized by the utopians Fourier and Saint-Simon, was not yet very well defined. London communists were in general opposed to revolutionary violence and secret conspiracies and felt that any revolution would have to be postponed until the workers were well prepared and educated for their role. Before leaving London, Marx and Engels helped to organize a Communist Correspondence Committee in order to exchange information about revolutionary activities in other countries. (It was to be replaced in 1847 by the Communist League, with Marx as president of its Brussels branch.)

Back in Brussels, Marx's group of communist co-workers at this time numbered only twenty or so. The members of the Communist Correspondence Committee were not of the proletariat but mainly intellectuals including physicians, journalists, and writers. Marx dominated their meetings, radiating energy, will power, and unshakable conviction. A description by a noncommunist guest at the time offers a remarkable portrait of Marx:

[5] Ibid., p. 111.

A man of thick black hair, hairy hands, his coat buttoned crookedly, he nevertheless looked like a man who had the right and the power to command respect, even though his appearance and behavior might seem peculiar enough. His movements were clumsy, but bold and self-assured; his manner defied all the usual social conventions. But they were proud, with a tinge of contempt, and his sharp, metallic voice was remarkably suited to the radical judgments he delivered on men and things. He spoke in nothing but imperatives, the words tolerating no opposition, penetrating everything he said with a harsh tone that jarred me almost painfully. The tone expressed his firm conviction of his mission to dominate men's minds and to prescribe laws for them. Before my eyes stood the personification of a democratic dictator.[6]

Marx showed how dictatorial he could be in dealing with Wilhelm Weitling, a famous agitator and utopian communist, who has been described as the last and most eloquent descendant of the men who raised peasant revolts in the late Middle Ages. Weitling preached a message of class war and terrorism to the disaffected and alienated elements of society, especially the most deeply wronged and desperate who had nothing to lose by bringing down the existing society. His fervent belief in the solidarity of all workers, his personal stoicism, and the many years he had spent in prison had conferred on him an authority of European magnitude. Marx recognized his importance and his sincerity. He was much impressed by Weitling's call for class warfare, by his understanding of economic reality, and by his understanding of the way political parties masked their real aims behind deceptive façades. Moreover he respected Weitling's achievement in creating the nucleus of an international communist party. However, Marx also saw him as muddled, hysterical, and a source of confusion, and was determined to destroy him.

At the meeting of the Communist Correspondence Committee in Brussels on March 30, 1846, Marx came down with full force on Weitling whose itinerant organizing efforts had resulted in several failed worker uprisings. Marx abhorred such—in his mind—irresponsible actions. "Tell us, Weitling," he demanded in his rasping voice, "you who have made so much noise with your communist preaching . . . have won over so many workers that they thereby lost their work and their bread . . . [how] do you

[6]Ibid., p. 118–119.

justify your social-revolutionary actions?"[7] When the shaken Weitling noted in his reply, with obvious allusion to Marx, that unlike certain ivory tower theorists he (Weitling) could speak from personal experience of the suffering workers, the enraged Marx brought his fist down on the table, shouting "Ignorance has never yet helped anyone!" The meeting broke up in disarray, and later one participant, blaming Marx, said the whole affair made him vomit. Cast into the outer darkness by Marx, poor Weitling finally managed to secure passage to America where his utopian communism receded into obscurity.

Pierre-Joseph Proudhon, social theorist and anarchist, author of the saying "Property is theft," was another target of Marx's merciless invective. Born in 1809 in Besancon of poor parents, Proudhon tended cows as a boy while reading intensively. Forced to leave college by his father, who insisted he earn his living, he found work in printing. At the same time he used the occupation to further his education, and in 1840 published his pamphlet *What Is Property?* His answer? In one word: "theft." Proudhon had two main targets: the accumulation of wealth and the use made of it to control government and dominate the poor. In other words, political control was based on economic control. He rejected God, and God's personification in Christ, as totally evil, and believed Christianity would disintegrate with the progress of scientific knowledge.

For Proudhon, competition was the greatest of all evils as it fostered an acquisitive and unjust society that forced men to outwit, defeat, and exterminate each other. The remedy for Proudhon was the establishment of a "mutualist" cooperative system that allowed the acquisition of a small amount of private property but not the accumulation of capital. The agents of such a transformation had to be the real victims of the system—the small farmers, the small bourgeoisie, and the urban proletariat. In his view, opposition from the rich would be certain since their generous instincts had long ago atrophied. The workers could succeed only by a slow peaceful process through which they would impose their own pattern on the rest of society by economic pressure. One thing they must avoid above all: organizing themselves politically, since if victorious they would reproduce the same authoritarian forms of control from which they had tried to escape.

On one occasion Proudhon had counseled Marx to beware of intolerance and to eschew all dogmatism, and had aroused Marx's ire by warning him not "to offer the proletarians only blood to drink." When Proudhon sent

[7]Ibid., p. 119.

Marx a copy of his work, *Philosophy of Poverty,* in 1846, Marx thought Proudhon's gradualist ideas dangerous and wanted to annihilate his doctrine and influence with one immense blow. He excoriated the book as shapeless, ridiculous, philosophic poison, feeble Hegelianism, ignorant of the real movement of history, a dialectical phantasmagoria. Marx, however, overreached himself; the sheer brutality of his onslaught created sympathy for his victim, and Proudhon's influence continued to increase in the following years. He was a writer who knew how to crystalize the radical ideas of his time in arresting epigrams that traveled well. His advocacy of political nonparticipation, industrial action, and of decentralized federalism had a long-lasting influence on French radicals and socialists. Proudhonism is the direct ancestor of modern syndicalism, whose main weapon has been the general strike aimed at destabilizing society by stopping all vital services.

The Manifesto

Engels urged Marx to attend the second congress of the Communist League that was to be held in London in November 1847. To provide focus for his partner, Engels prepared a kind of catechism of the communist faith, which is of historic interest. Thus:

1. Q. What is communism?
   A. Communism is the doctrine of the conditions for the liberation of the proletariat.
2. Q. What is the proletariat?
   A. The proletariat is the only social class which derives its livelihood solely from the sale of its labor and not from the profit of capital . . .
3. Q. How did the proletariat arise?
   A. It arose through the Industrial Revolution.
4. Q. Under what conditions does the proletariat's sale of its labor to the bourgeoisie take place?
   A. Labor is a commodity like any other, and its price is determined by precisely the same laws as any other commodity . . .

Question 10 envisaged a dictatorship of the proletariat similar to the one Lenin was to establish seventy years later in Russia.

A ten-day debate about methods and principles occupied the communists attending the second congress. Unlike some of their more windy confreres, Marx and Engels had very precise ideas of where they ought to be going.

This is reflected in Article 1 of the new statutes of the Communist League, which stated as its objective: "The overthrow of the bourgeoisie, the rule of the proletariat, the annihilation of the old bourgeois society based on class contradictions, and the establishment of a new society without classes and without private property."

On the same day that the members adopted the statutes they authorized Marx to draft "a detailed theoretical and practical party program" to serve as a manifesto of the communist party. Marx returned to Brussels, where at that time his wife gave birth to their third child, and he began work with Engels on the *Manifesto*. It was published anonymously at the beginning of 1848. It begins memorably:

> A spectre is haunting Europe—the spectre of Communism. All the powers of old Europe have united in a holy alliance to exorcise this spectre. The Pope and the Czar, Metternich and Guizot, the radicals of France, and the police-spies of Germany.

The *Manifesto* insists at the outset that all history is a history of class struggles. Wherever we look, the pages of history reveal this fact—the patricians, knights, plebeians, slaves in Rome, feudal lords, vassals, guildmasters, apprentices, and serfs pitted against each other. In modern times two great hostile classes have gradually emerged from the wreck of feudal society: the bourgeoisie and the proletariat. The bourgeoisie is the class that harnessed modern industry in its own interests and developed the great world markets that generated incredible wealth. With pitiless energy it ruptured all the relationships that bound man to man according to feudal codes of honor, and reduced all social ties to "naked self-interest and callous cash payments." Even relations within the family are reduced to mere money relations.

The *Manifesto* does pay tribute to the tremendous productive forces unleashed by the bourgeoisie. It dwells on the array of inventions—railways, steamships, machinery of all kinds, and the like—by which it has subdued nature and cleared whole continents, canalized rivers. But it has proven unable to cope with a lethal threat to its existence—the recurring crises that bring to a standstill its mills and its factories. The cause is to be found in the epidemics of overproduction, which are intrinsic to the system.

Moreover, the bourgeoisie, the *Manifesto* says, has also produced the class that is destined to destroy it—the proletarians. The workers have been turned into mere appendages of machines; their labor, monotonous and without attraction, has been turned into a mere commodity so that wages are kept at a bare subsistence level in accord with the laws of supply and demand. But the bourgeoisie has provided the workers with the means of their own salvation. Concentrating them in the great factories it unites them, making them more aware of their common interests and preparing them for the final critical battle between their class and the bourgeoisie.

The proletariat is the only truly revolutionary class. The other classes that are falling victim to the greed of the bourgeoisie—the lower middle class, the small manufacturer, the small shopkeeper, the peasant proprietor—all struggle only to save their position in the middle class. They are therefore not revolutionary but conservative. In the words of the *Manifesto:* "All previous historical movements were movements of minorities, or in the interest of minorities. The proletarian movement is the conscious movement of the immense majority in the interest of the immense majority."

"The communists," it further declares, "are, practically, the most progressive and resolute section of the working class of all countries; they have, theoretically, the advantage over the great mass of the proletariat of understanding the conditions and general results of the proletarian movement. The immediate aim of the communists is the same as that of all other proletarian parties: organization of the proletariat on a class basis; overthrow of the supremacy of the bourgeois; conquest of political power by the proletariat." Communist principles, it says, are not derived from speculative or philosophical theorizing but are simply a "general expression of actual conditions of an existing class struggle, of a historical movement going on under our own eyes."

The *Manifesto* declares that the proletariat will wrest all capital from the bourgeoisie and centralize all instruments of production in the hands of the state—that is, of the proletariat organized as the ruling class. Moreover, the *Manifesto* claims that the communist call for abolition of hitherto existing property relations is not a distinctive feature of communism, as the ongoing struggle between the classes has continually involved the abolition of previous existing property relations. The *Manifesto* also deals with various charges made against the communists—for example, that they would abolish the family and do away with marriage, and that they were opposed to patriotism. To the charge that communists would abolish religion and morality, the *Manifesto* sets forth the radical materialistic view that philosophical, moral, and religious ideas are by-products of the prevailing economic system: The radical change in property relations envisaged by communism would inevitably mean radical changes in society's basic ideas.

The *Manifesto* then calls for:

1. Abolition of property in land and confiscation of ground rents to the state.
2. A heavily progressive income tax.
3. Abolition of inheritance.
4. Centralization of credit in the hands of the state by means of a national bank with state capital and an exclusive monopoly.
5. Centralization of the means of transport in the hands of the state.
6. National factories and instruments of production; cultivation of the land in accordance with a general social plan.
7. Obligation of all to labor; organization of industrial armies, especially for agriculture.
8. Free public education for all children and abolition of child factory labor.

In closing, the *Manifesto* says the communists refuse to conceal their aims. They call boldly for the coming of the communist revolution. The workers have nothing to lose but their chains. It urges workers of all lands to unite. As Saul Padover says, the *Manifesto* introduced a new and foreboding note into the revolutionary movement by appealing to the passions of class conflict and hate. Up to this time socialists had spoken in terms of universal brotherhood and peace; Marx spoke of the classes as enemies of one another and fomented an attitude of hatred and violence. In so doing he sharply distinguished socialists from communists. Socialists believed in humanitarianism and democracy, whereas communists—in Marx's view—were committed to an apocalyptic class war against the rest of society. Their ultimate victory was assured since they were the chosen instruments of the only god they recognized—the historical process.

The *Manifesto* had no influence on the revolutions that broke out in the major capitals of Europe in 1848, but its call to revolution eventually resounded from pole to pole. It was probably the greatest masterpiece of propaganda the modern world has seen.

The Hard Life of a Revolutionary

In February 1848 revolution broke out in Paris, the capital of European revolutions, and led to the provisional republic. Marx hailed it as the great dawn of worker liberation and spent most of the 6,000 francs from his father's estate to buy arms for the Brussels workers. Tipped off, the police arrested Marx as well as his wife Jenny, who was thrown in jail on the charge of vagrancy and locked up with prostitutes and derelicts. After spending eighteen hours in jail, Jenny went back to her "three poor little children." When Marx got home they were all ordered to leave Brussels without delay.

Arriving in Paris, they found it still wearing the scars of the recent revolution: windows broken, trees chopped down, and stones piled up for the barricades. Welcome news came from Germany that the placid Germans had caught the fever and frightened King Friedrich Wilhelm IV into granting their demands. The democratic upsurge was not destined to last, however. Within a few months Wilhelm recovered his nerve and sent his Prussian troops to close down the Diet in Berlin. The parliament in Frankfurt suffered the same fate after a year of futility. In spite of Marx's conviction that the time was not ripe for the German workers to revolt, he and Engels felt it necessary to go to Germany to fight for communism, which had become a "scare word." Leaving the Marx family with Jenny's mother in Trier, the two men headed for Cologne. They found the communists in a pitiable state, lacking the numbers or the experience to have much of an impact. Marx insisted that they should join democratic societies and carry on their propaganda from inside them. In his newly founded communist newspaper, the *Neue Rheinische Zeitung,* Marx poured scorn on the fumbling liberals and democrats who had failed to put a parliamentary democracy together. Marx, of course, shed no tears over the failure of their experiment since his goal was the total overthrow of the social order.

A young German revolutionary who later became a U.S. citizen and Republican statesman met him at this time and described him later:

> I have never seen a man whose bearing was so provoking and intolerable. To no opinion, which differed from his, he accorded the honor of even a condescending consideration. Everyone who contradicted him he treated with abject contempt: every argument he did not like he answered either with biting scorn at the unfathomable ignorance that had prompted it, or with opprobrious aspersions upon the motives of him who had advanced it. I remember most distinctly the cutting disdain with which he pronounced the word bourgeois—that is, as a detestable example of the deepest mental and moral degeneracy—he denounced everyone that dared to oppose his opinion.[8]

In Cologne the authorities, who were waiting for an opportune moment to deal with Marx, finally found it when Marx penned a furious indictment

---

[8] Ibid., p. 141.

of the Hohenzollern dynasty whose whole history, he declared, was a monstrous series of "breaches of faith and perfidies." An order was signed for his expulsion. Marx went into hiding and issued the last number of the newspaper in red print. "We are ruthless," he proclaimed defiantly in his editorial, "we ask no consideration from you. When our turn comes, we will not conceal our terrorism."[9] Then he and Engels traveled around Germany trying to stir up revolution, but with no success.

His next move was back to Paris where he and Jenny, the three children, and Lenchen, their devoted maid, squeezed into a tiny apartment. But within a few weeks the police caught up with him. He was to be banished to a remote province in Brittany noted for its unhealthy climate. Marx saw it as an attempt to finish him off and decided he preferred the fogs of London to the bogs of Brittany. Engels soon joined him there. Expecting another wave of revolution to hit Europe soon, they thought it would be a short stay. But their forecast was wrong. The nineteenth century produced no more revolutions except the brief Paris Commune (1871) that was so murderously suppressed. Marx was to spend his remaining thirty-four years in London, a man without a country.

His first years in London were marked by terrible poverty and misery. Unable to pay the rent for their sleazy room, he and his family were brutally evicted on a cold and rainy day, their beds placed in the street while a crowd gaped at the children who were weeping to see their little toys repossessed. Marx next found two tiny rooms in Soho where they stayed for six years.

A Prussian spy described the rooms:

> Marx lives in one of the worst, and thus cheapest, quarters in London. He lives in two rooms, the one with a view on the street is the living room, the one in the back is the bedroom. In the whole lodging not a single piece of good furniture is to be found; everything is broken, ragged and tattered; everything is covered with finger-thick dust; everywhere the greatest disorder. In the middle of the living room there is a big old table covered with oilcloth. On it lie manuscripts, books, newspapers, the children's toys, the scraps of his wife's sewing, tea cups with broken rims, dirty spoons, knives, forks, candlesticks, inkwell, drinking glasses, Dutch clay pipes, tobacco ashes—in a word, everything piled up helter-skelter on the same table.[10]

[9] Ibid., p. 147.
[10] Ibid., p. 11.

While living in this squalor Marx sired a baby by their faithful maid Lenchen—a matter that was kept secret from Jenny and the family. He also lost three children—Guy, one year old, who died in 1850; Franziska, a little over one year old, in 1852; and in 1855, seven-year-old Edgar, the chubby jolly favorite nicknamed Musch. When Franziska died, Jenny had to beg the money to buy her a coffin. When little Musch fell sick, Marx, ill himself, stayed up night after night to nurse him and was inconsolable when he died. His hair turned white overnight and the family had to move to get away from the tragic atmosphere of the tiny rooms that Musch had so enlivened. Marx wrote to a friend four months after Musch's death:

> Bacon says that really important people have so many relationships to nature and the world, so many objects of interest that they easily get over any loss. I do not belong to these important people. The death of my child has deeply shattered my heart and brain, and I feel the loss as freshly as on the first day.[11]

In the squalor of his London homes Marx received numerous fellow radicals and refugees including Louis Blanc, Giuseppe Mazzini, Ferdinand Lassalle, and Mikhail Bakunin. The radicals and communists in England were relatively free to propagate their ideas and carry on their intrigues and squabbles. In sharp contrast with the continent, where the police were always on the lookout for their type, the English atmosphere was tolerant and permissive.

From 1851 to 1861 Marx worked as a foreign correspondent for the *New York Daily Tribune,* which he proudly called the "foremost English-language American newspaper." Its founder-publisher Horace Greeley was a radical himself, absolutely courageous and outspoken in espousing his advanced and egalitarian social views. Acquiring Marx was a notable coup for Greeley since a half million refugees from the failure of the revolutions of 1848 to 1849 had come to New York and naturally retained an interest in the Old World.

Engels proved himself indispensable, as he so often had. While Marx learned to write English, Engels acted as his ghost-writer and later his translator. But Marx soon mastered the language, and over the ten years he contributed at least 321 articles to the paper. He was shabbily treated by editors who recklessly altered and cut his work, sometimes using his articles without acknowledgment or accepting and then failing to print them.

[11]Ibid., p. 162.

Moreover, the meager income he derived from his articles was not enough to pay the bills. He and the family lived constantly on the brink of starvation. But he was still able to keep up a rigorous schedule of writing and research for his studies of political economy, which had begun in 1850 and preoccupied him at intervals for the rest of his life. Using the spacious reading room of the British Library, away from the "nagging and misery" of his tenement, he could concentrate on his research. He pored over books and articles on demography, mining, agriculture, agronomy, credit, banking and finance, rent theory, and economic history. He worked his way through major authors in English, German, French, Italian, Greek, and Latin. His studies, he always claimed, convinced him that class struggle was the basic pattern of all history. It was not something he invented, he said, but had to be obvious to anyone deeply read. He considered Benjamin Franklin an original thinker and applauded him for formulating the basic law of modern political economy.

He found extremely useful the official "Reports of English Factory Inspectors," which impressed him greatly by their honesty. Here was the evidence he needed to demonstrate the horrors of the capitalist system and what the factory machines were doing to their helpless operators. "We read of a young woman who lost her right arm . . . of a man who had his leg sawed off . . . of a youth who had both arms torn from their sockets, the abdomen ripped open, and head crushed."[12] War bulletins from the Crimea were less horrifying, he concluded.

The fruit of his research, *A Critique of Political Economy,* was a work based on his key idea: economic determinism, the theory that economic relationships totally condition all other human activities—cultural, religious, political, and so on. The structure of their property relations determines what kind of God people worship, and what kind of political system they will devise. When economic conditions start to change, a whole way of life is called into question, a struggle that begins to transform the political, legal, religious superstructure to correspond with the new economic conditions. Marx claimed to be scientific in his analysis because he described actual and verifiable states of affairs. Previous socialist thinkers, ignorant of economics and political history, could only construct unreal, unworkable utopias.

The *Critique of Political Economy,* finally published in June of 1859, was a monumental flop that brought no reward of any kind. Even the socialists found it disappointing with its page after page of dry economic facts. Marx

[12]Ibid., p. 175.

remarked on the irony of writing a book about money when he had none himself. But worse was to come when, in 1861, the loss of his job with the *Daily Tribune* made his already desperate financial affairs impossible.

At just this time he almost forfeited the precious friendship of Engels, who had so often come to his rescue. Engels' Irish mistress, Mary Burns, died suddenly in 1863, leaving him totally prostrate with grief. Instead of words of sympathy from Marx he got a letter filled with lamentations about Marx's own financial worries and just a few curt words about Mary. Engels, completely furious at Marx's icy response, was ready to call it quits. But Marx was able to salvage their friendship by an apology and a plea for forgiveness, explaining that his seeming coldness was not due to a lack of sympathy for Engels in his grief but to his own family's extremely dire circumstances: He could no longer pay the rent or buy food or coal, and his children could not attend school because there was no money for tuition and their clothes were not presentable. In fact, at that very moment he was on the point of taking his wife to a charity lodging house and sending out his oldest daughters to work as governesses. Engels was himself in very tight circumstances; only by borrowing money himself was he able to save Marx's family from a sad fate. When in 1869 Engels, by that time an eminently successful businessman, was able to retire and sell his share in the Manchester business of Engels and Ermen, he provided Marx with a generous annuity. Thus Marx was finally guaranteed security for the rest of his days, but not before his own health and that of his wife and surviving daughters had been permanently marred by their years of poverty.

Marx and the International

On September 28, 1864, Marx attended a meeting to found the International Working Men's Association at St. Martin's Hall. It was the beginning of a new phase in his career, as he had remained politically inactive in England after the failure of the 1848 revolutions and was not well known in English radical and laborite circles. The hall was crowded with radicals and laborites of numerous nationalities, each with his own theory and his own axe to grind. The English were against special privilege, the Germans against capitalism, the Irish against the British, the Poles against the Russians, and the Italians against the Austrians.

Marx was put on a subcommittee to draw up a program and statutes for an international organization. The group met in Marx's home, and his domineering personality and superior intellect made him the obvious choice for the job. In a week he had the program and statutes ready and both were adopted by the governing body, the General Council. For the next eight years, until internal squabbles caused the International's demise, Marx used it to further his long-range vision of revolution. Thanks to Marx, as Padover says, the International became a major chapter in the history of revolution.[13]

Marx's inaugural address in 1864 became the charter of the movement. Here was a sober, moderate neo-Marx, not the flaming prophet of the *Manifesto*. The address was a product of his maturity, reflecting his wide reading in nondoctrinaire literature and his positive impressions of English society. Having observed their parliamentary system at work, he had come to appreciate the fairness and decency of the English, their respect for individual liberty, and their tolerance of diverse viewpoints. Police brutality and political persecution were practically unknown. And though great inequality and poverty persisted, the basic stability of English society suggested the possibility of nonviolent social change through the mechanisms of political democracy.

In his inaugural Marx recognized the leadership of England in the realms of investment, wage policies, labor relations, and other basic capitalist tools. He noted that, in spite of the general accumulation of wealth after the revolutions of 1848, little had trickled down to the workers. Pauperism and misery were rife. Nevertheless, Marx observed, between 1848 and 1864 two important steps forward had been taken: the ten-hour day had become law and the cooperative movement was greatly strengthened. For Marx the cooperative movement had the potential to liberate the worker from the exploitation inherent in the wage system. By becoming a part owner, the worker would feel satisfaction and even joy in his work, conscious that the profits were fairly distributed to all the partners.

In closing, Marx insisted on the need for solidarity of workers around the world if they were to put an end to the criminal policies of the capitalists who squandered the blood and treasure of the people in their piratical wars. He pointed to Russia as the most horrendous example of this barbarity. However, he said nothing about communism per se or the need for revolution. The message was moderate and calculated to appeal to the typical English trade union member.

Marx believed strongly in the importance of the press in getting the word out. The first journal to print the documents and reports of the Interna-

[13] Ibid., p. 224.

tional was a London weekly, the *Bee-Hive*. In its heyday the International had some eighteen affiliated publications across Europe that disseminated its radical ideas: among them, universal male suffrage, direct taxation, a shorter workweek, expansion of cooperatives, and nationalization of land. Moreover, in spite of his abhorrence of the bourgeoisie, Marx made every effort to get the attention of the bourgeois press. The day the London *Times* published one of their documents was a memorable one in the headquarters of the International.

The International was run democratically along the lines of a federal system. At the top was a policy-making body, the General Council, which met regularly in London. Under it were federal councils set up in each country. At the base were sections that were organized in many towns of England and Western Europe. Annual congresses were held, which drew sixty to seventy or so delegates from the various countries. The decisions and resolutions of the congress were supposed to bind the whole membership but they were hard to enforce. One of the most vexing tasks of the General Council, in fact, was arbitrating the disputes and squabbles among fractious members, many of whom delighted in hairsplitting altercations over dogma. Expulsion was used as a last resort with members who defied arbitration; but in time the repeated use of this sanction led to the disintegration of the International.

From the beginning the other members of the General Council were glad to have Marx, the most articulate and determined of them all, assume the main responsibility. He found the work burdensome and time-consuming but believed it gave him a unique opportunity to exert real influence on the world proletariat.

One of the questions much debated among radicals had to do with the proper site for the headquarters of the International. Some of them thought it should be in Paris or somewhere on the continent where revolutionary ferment was strong. But not Marx; he insisted on England as the ideal location. This accorded with his view that certain preconditions were necessary for revolution. Technological and economic developments had to reach a certain point; the workers had to acquire the necessary technical and organizing skills; they also had to reach a certain stage of class-consciousness. England, he believed, was the country most favorable to the fulfillment of these conditions. It was destined therefore to play the starring role in the great drama of world revolution.

Das Kapital

Marx finished the first volume of *Das Kapital* in the spring of 1867 and took it to Germany himself to get it published. While waiting for its publication he spent a very enjoyable interlude with his friend Dr. Ludwig Kugelmann in Hanover. Kugelmann, a participant in the 1848 revolutions, was a communist zealot and a fanatical admirer of Marx. Kugelmann's wife expected to meet a seedy hate-spewing revolutionary but was surprised to find an elegant cavalier who charmed them all. They were much impressed by his encyclopedic knowledge and easy familiarity with the great European literary classics—Cervantes, Shakespeare, Goethe, Heine, and Schiller, as well as the philosophers. Even Bismarck, soon to become chancellor of a united Germany in 1871, heard about Marx and sent an emissary to win him over to his side by offering him a job. Strangely enough, on his way home Marx ran into Bismarck's niece when he overheard a young lady at the station in London wondering out loud how she would manage all her luggage with so few porters available. He gallantly offered his services and ended up escorting Bismarck's aristocratic and arch-conservative niece around Hyde Park and to the "ice shops" in the interval before her train left.

Das Kapital appeared on September 14, 1867. In this, as in his other numerous works, his general aim was to discover the laws of the social economy of "free and associated labor"—an ideal he believed attainable through socialism. At the same time he would expose the errors of the bourgeois political economists who spoke as though the laws of the capitalist economy were natural and eternal, when, in fact, they were historical and contingent. He would thereby unmask capitalism's pretension to be the natural or eternal mode of production. Once armed with knowledge and the requisite organization, the workers could "then destroy the ruinous effects of the natural laws of capitalist production and replace them with the spontaneous action of the laws of the social economy of "free and associated labor." In short, the workers could change the historical laws of their own behavior. This was consistent with Marx's overall view that "the aim of science . . . was not just to explain the world but also to change it."[14]

To this end he traced the rise of capitalism out of feudalism and analyzed the property system of capitalism, the capitalist mode of production, the

[14]James Farr, "Science: Realism, Criticism, History," in *The Cambridge Companion to Marx* (New York: Cambridge University Press, 1991), pp. 119–120.

workings of the competitive market, and the economic and social implications of these features of the capitalist economy. He also described the conditions of the life and work of the working class, documented with material from the official reports of the British inspectors—an appalling picture that left the capitalist with no excuse. In sum, Marx argued that capitalism produces an exploitative, inhumane system in which workers become mere appendages to machines.

A number of the key concepts he set forth in *Kapital* became common currency wherever people discussed issues of workers' rights, poverty, and oppression.

Surplus value: The value a worker adds to a product which is expropriated by the capitalist.

Immiseration: Marx's theory that the misery of the working class would continue to increase in a capitalist society. With not enough jobs to go around, the bourgeois "coupon clippers"—who do not work—enjoy a comfortable, affluent lifestyle. Their children are well cared for while the children of unemployed workers go hungry and have to beg in the streets or dig in garbage cans for scraps of food.

Repression: A necessary part of a capitalist society as a standard response to capitalist crises. His point was underlined by the twentieth century's rise of fascism with its rejection of due process, outlawing of political opposition and of trade unions, combined with nationalist propaganda.

Alienation: The theory that workers are, in the capitalist system, alienated from the products of their labor, from each other, and from their own distinctly human capacity to create and enjoy beautiful things.

Ideology: Denotes the need of the ruling class to convince the other members of society that the ruling class's interest is also the common interest. Thus the reigning ideas, ideals, and beliefs of a society serve only the interests of the ruling class, but this fact is artfully concealed. Hence a "false consciousness" is created in the working class, which does not realize it has been duped.

Base and Superstructure: The material means of production or the "base" which conditioned the so-called "superstructure" consisting of the culture and laws of a society.

War and Imperialism: Marx's perception of war as intrinsic to capitalism: The insatiable drive for profits, he argued, led the more powerful bourgeois countries to exploit the weaker societies. As an example he pointed to the imperialist expansion of the British Empire that fueled the first large-scale capitalist enterprises. Such expansion could not be limited to commercial competition between the imperialist nations, but inevitably led to competition on the battlefield.

Marx gave a number of reasons why he believed that capitalism would inevitably collapse and be replaced by a socialist system. First, it was doomed by its own internal contradictions: Overproduction was inevitable in the capitalist economy as each firm was under constant pressure to expand to keep up with its competition. And as inventories increased, the rate of profit would decrease, causing layoffs that in turn decreased consumption—thus leading to a downward spiral as unemployment increased and businesses failed. Second, capitalism was necessarily exploitative since it required that workers be paid only a fraction of the true value of their labor: his so-called "surplus value" theory of wages. Third, modern industry's congregating workers together gave them the means of joining together in a struggle against their oppressors.

"The mixture of abstract economic theory and concrete illustration from actuality, all bound together by the materialist conception of history and a religious view of historical inevitability, made what Cromwell would have called a 'fulminous compound.' "[15] Marx warned in his preface to *Das Kapital* that the work would stir up "the furies of private interest." But actually it fell flat in its first edition despite a publicity campaign well organized by Engels and himself. Marx naively complained that even the workers had let him down. But how could he have imagined that poorly educated workers would flock to buy such a ponderous and expensive tome? The general indifference nearly drove him mad as he anxiously scanned the press for signs of any mention. Only a few serious reviews—which were in Germany—appeared during the first several years after the book's publication, and Marx regarded two of these as mere piffle or, as he put it, "philosophic twaddle . . . smart-assing peevish, know-it-all, nit-picking." The world was slow to take notice until 1872, when new editions and translations appeared.

[15]J. Hampden Jackson, *Marx, Proudhon, and European Socialism* (New York: Collier Books, 1962), p. 141.

His Nemesis: Bakunin

Toward the end of 1868, the International's fourth year, disruptive tendencies had begun to threaten it. The greatest threat arrived in the person of the giant Russian nobleman Mikhail Bakunin, an anarchist, whose theory of revolution was very much opposed to that of Marx.

Anarchism was not a new idea. Some highly utopian anarchist works had appeared in the sixteenth and seventeenth centuries in France and England. During the late eighteenth century, William Godwin's work *Enquiry Concerning Political Justice* (1793) provided a more practical view of anarchism. It was followed by Proudhon's anarchistic *What Is Property?* (1840). Both men reflected the demands of the radical side of the bourgeoisie, which gained power in the French Revolution at the expense of the aristocracy and the crown. Unfortunately the bourgeoisie soon assumed the role of an aristocracy and left the humble masses to shift for themselves. The radicals then turned toward Chartism and the super-radicals toward anarchism. As one scholar, David Apter, wrote, "The virtue of anarchism as a doctrine is that it employs a socialist critique of capitalism and a liberal critique of socialism."[16]

To fully understand Bakunin we have to understand the tormented soul of the Russian intelligentsia in the nineteenth century, afflicted as its members were with an acute sense of rootlessness and lack of identity. Russia's remarkable history had left its people with a feeling of belonging neither to the East nor to the West. The ideas and principles imported into Russian culture from the West proved to possess little creative force once divorced from the traditions in which they had developed. Although educated Russians had assimilated the values of the Enlightenment and the French Revolution, they were unable to reconcile them with the crude despotism of the czarist regime. The failure of the Decembrist uprising in 1825 had closed off all hopes for reform and made only more evident the embarrassing backwardness of their country. With no field for their energies and ambitions in their static and authoritarian society, and driven by an acute sense of alienation, the Russian intelligentsia took refuge in German Idealistic philosophy. Johann Fichte and Friedrich Schelling proved especially attractive.

---

[16] Quoted in Anthony Masters, *Bakunin* (New York: Saturday Review Press/E. P. Dutton & Co., Inc., 1974), p. xviii.

Mikhail Bakunin, one of these tormented Russian souls, was born in 1814, the son of a wealthy noble landowner. He grew up on a remote estate surrounded by the beauties of nature in the midst of a large and loving family. Tutored by a liberal and humanist father, he lived a life, as he put it, of feeling and imagination. A sojourn in the military brought him, at the age of nineteen, to St. Petersburg and to a crisis in his spiritual development when he discovered Schelling and Fichte. He was especially impressed by Fichte, especially Fichte's belief that love, not rational reflection, was the root of existence—as in St. John: "Who dwells in love dwells in God and God in him." Or again, as Fichte put it, that the realization of the Absolute is achieved from the self-realization of finite wills; that man's striving for freedom is at the same time a longing to commune with all other individual consciousnesses in an identical affirmation of the Absolute. Fichte's philosophy offered Bakunin a way of resolving the inner conflict caused by his yearning for self-realization versus his urge for self-surrender. Bakunin at that time spoke repeatedly of his desire to "destroy" his personality by "dissolving into the Absolute," as had Christ.

In 1837, with great joy Bakunin discovered Hegel who offered a solution to Bakunin's search for wholeness and self-realization even more compelling than that of either Fichte or Schelling. Hegel saw all history as the evolution of the Idea or the Spirit. Through his dialectical process, Christianity emerged as a higher synthesis of the principles of Jewish and Greek religion. With the reformation it reached a final stage in which the world would become freely reconciled with religious faith in a rational state. This idea of a dialectic logic of history came as a welcome insight to Bakunin, who applied it to his own intense inner struggle, for it seemed to show how the two conflicting elements of his personality could be integrated in an eventual synthesis. His optimism was unbounded: "I have a long and difficult path ahead before I reach my reality but this I do not fear—the more the negations, the fiercer the struggle, the deeper will be the harmony and reconciliation."[17] We find here the source of a paradox he cherished: the urge for destruction versus the urge to create. As Aileen Kelly says: "In his eagerness to reach the goal of wholeness Bakunin had stripped the dialectic of its historical dimension, in which Spirit gradually appropriates the eternal world through the advance of rationality in institutions, and had telescoped it into the present as a process taking place within his own personality."[18]

---

[17] Aileen Kelly, *Mikhail Bakunin* (Oxford: Clarendon Press, 1982), p. 60.
[18] Ibid., p. 55.

What did Hegel have to do with Bakunin's conversion to revolution? It must be seen within the context of a left-wing Hegelian movement that had arisen. Up to this point Hegel's interpretation of history provided support for a right-wing reactionary political stance. His dialectical view of history posited the Prussian regime as the outcome of a synthesis that made it the highest expression of Absolute Reason. At the same time, Hegel saw the Christianity of his day as a synthesis that reconciled reason and Spirit. But the foundations of right-wing Hegelianism were undermined by several developments. First, certain devastating attacks on Christianity appeared in the 1830s: David Strauss's *Life of Jesus* reduced Jesus to a myth, while Bruno Bauer and Ludwig Feuerbach published works arguing that religion itself was merely the projection of human aspirations. Secondly, Hegel's dialectical view of history was revised by a Polish philosopher, August von Cieszkowski, to support a leftist political stance. For Hegel's three periods of history, von Cieszkowski substituted three moments of consciousness: the first moment, "instinctive perception," followed by the second moment, "rational thought," culminating in nineteenth-century philosophy (specifically Hegel's) which prepared for the third moment (or third age), "praxis," in which the divisions of consciousness would be resolved not in thought but in action—that is, a synthesis of thought and action.

Girded with this antireligious and proactive philosophy, the leftist Hegelians declared war on the status quo. As the political situation deteriorated, "the leftist Hegelians insisted that there could be no compromise between past and incoming forms of Truth: all traditions, institutions and dogmas which had outlived their time must be negated, swept away in the headlong progress of Reason."[19] In this interpretation they overlooked the fact that, in Hegel's account of the progress of reason, the lower forms of the "Idea" were not destroyed but transcended and preserved in the higher synthesis.

In 1842 Bakunin published a famous article, *Die Reaktion in Deutschland,* that announced his arrival in the leftist Hegelian camp. He observed that German literature and thought were saturated with that spirit of negation which the French Revolution had ushered onto the historical stage. As examples he cited the work of Strauss, Feuerbach, and Bruno Bauer. A deep sadness, he said, envelops culture. No one believes in anything anymore; the political and religious institutions are a mass of contradictions. He went on to argue that a dialectic was at work pitting a positive (the old order) against a negative (the democratic party); the latter sought freedom, though at

19 Ibid., p. 878.

present only through negation. He predicted that both sides would be swallowed up in the "new affirmative, organic reality."

Another important influence on Bakunin at this time was Lamennais' book *Politique à l'usage du peuple*. As we have seen, the priest's mystical faith in the infallibility of the masses caused him to desert a pope who had proved his fallibility by failing to understand the mission Lamennais had assigned him (the pope), namely, to take the lead in the liberation of the masses. Like some utopian socialists, Lamennais preached a Christianity of earthly regeneration that would lead inexorably to the brotherhood of man. Bakunin was much taken with Lamennais' idea that, in the providence of God, nothing could stop progress toward the goal of universal brotherhood. "What was novel for him was the conception of the conquering 'whole' as the popular masses, with their earthly aspirations."[20] And his heart beat fast as he envisioned a great role for himself in the coming drama on the grand world historical stage that Lamennais painted in vivid colors.

"Open your eyes and hearts," Bakunin wrote in *Die Reaktion,* "to the trembling expectation of mankind. Even in Russia, in that boundless snow-covered kingdom . . . the air . . . is fraught with storms! . . . Repent . . . the Kingdom of God is at hand . . . Let us trust to the Eternal Spirit which only . . . destroys because it is the inexhaustible and eternally creating source of all life. The urge to destroy is also a creative urge."[21]

This famous sentence launched Bakunin's revolutionary career. With it he moved from the Hegelian Right to the Left, from preaching love to his little circle of family and friends to preaching revolution on the European stage.

Also very influential on the development of Bakunin's anarchism at this time was Pierre-Joseph Proudhon, whom he met in Paris in the mid-forties. The two men spent much time together as Bakunin introduced Proudhon to Hegel and Proudhon impressed Bakunin with his attacks on the state, on God, and on private property. As Bakunin said later, "Proudhon, when not obsessed with metaphysical doctrine, was a revolutionary by instinct; he adored Satan and proclaimed Anarchy."[22]

A very significant key to Bakunin's activity was always his intense need to achieve integration and self-realization. Left Hegelianism met this need by giving him a way of integrating the inner and the outer worlds. Bakunin

[20] Ibid., p. 92.
[21] Ibid., p. 94.
[22] Anthony Masters, *Proudhon* (New York: E.P. Dutton & Co., 1974), p. 74.

freely generalized from his own need for wholeness to see it as the goal of all humanity. Mankind would achieve inner harmony or integration by a transformation of the world through revolution. In other words, Bakunin's urge for self-assertion found expression in idealizing the act of revolution as the moment when man becomes himself, his inner duality resolved.

As Aileen Kelly points out, these "illusions" of Bakunin have deep roots in the human psyche. And she notes that this "pursuit of wholeness, in all [its] ideological forms . . . is the pursuit not of the natural and immediate but of the ideal, of a philosophical chimera as far removed from recorded human experience, past or present, as the Kingdom of God on earth . . . Bakunin's vision of the unified human personality of the distant future may differ from the Marxist one in its rhetoric and the immediacy of its appeal but it comes from the same philosophical stable and imposes the same constraints on the choice of means."[23] Since force proves to be the only means of eliminating the tension between the individual and the whole, in this view, the pursuit of unity inevitably leads to a dictatorship. It is seen at first only as a means to a goal, but as the goal recedes to a distant future, the despotism which was to "lead to paradise becomes instead a desperate simulation of paradise itself."[24]

The revolution, Bakunin believed, would be the work of the peasant masses, for only they would act instinctively and with the spontaneity essential, in his mind, to revolution. In fact, the opposition between the theorizing of the intelligentsia and the spontaneity of the masses formed the core of his political ideology. This direction of his thought was no doubt accelerated by his reading of Lamennais, who held that the instincts of the people were the highest reflection of divine wisdom in the world.

The opposition Bakunin posited between theory and life is one reason for his hatred of Marx. Marx's so-called "scientific socialism" was for him just a mass of dry, lifeless, and sterile abstractions—the way of thinking typical of the regimented German soul. He met Marx for the first time in 1848 in Paris. He spoke also of meeting Lamennais there; and later, in Brussels, he became acquainted with Montalembert and some Jesuits who tried to convert him.

In the meantime he watched, as he said, in expectation of the revolution that was sure to come. For him, revolution would be the miraculous moment in which the divine was actualized in man: "I await my fiancée,

---

[23]Kelly, *Mikhail Bakunin,* p. 291.
[24]Ibid.

revolution. We will be really happy—that is, we will become ourselves, only when the whole world is engulfed in fire."[25] Bakunin was ecstatic when news broke of the revolution in Paris in February 1848, and predicted that it would engulf Europe. He felt that soon all of Europe, not excluding Russia, would become a federated democratic republic. Moving around Europe with the idea of uniting German and Slav democrats in a common revolutionary party, he took part in an insurrection in Dresden in 1849 that was sparked by the Saxon king's rejection of a constitution approved by the Saxon Diet. Bakunin was arrested and interned by Saxon authorities in Konigstein. Courageously he paid the steep price his chosen vocation demanded: brutal mistreatment in prison, chains, loathsome food, scurvy that caused the loss of his teeth. A wrecked giant, he was sentenced to death several times but each time it was postponed. The two years he spent in the Saxon and Austrian prisons would have broken anyone who lacked his iron constitution. Immersed in total silence, he retreated into a completely interior life, hardly aware of what was going on around him—in an ironic travesty of his former Fichtean philosophy with its distinction between the interior (or only real) life and the outside (or unreal) life. Eventually he was handed over by the Austrians to the Russians, who locked him in the grim fortresses of Petropavlosk and Schluesselberg and kept him in solitary confinement for five years. He was then sent to Siberia. After four years he managed to escape and make his way to London by a circuitous route through Japan and California. In October of 1865 he moved to Naples where his material existence was vastly improved thanks to his friendship with Princess Obolensky, a young woman connected with two of Russia's most ancient aristocratic families. She had gathered around her a circle of alienated intellectuals who lived off her generosity. These radicals provided him with his first recruits for his secret society, the International Brotherhood.

In 1864 he had renewed his acquaintance with Marx and was soon locked into a power struggle with him. Their personalities were total opposites. Marx was an authoritarian, Bakunin a libertarian. Marx believed in political action by the workers to conquer the state; Bakunin opposed political action and wanted to destroy the state. Bakunin accepted the risk of temporary chaos at the demise of the state, but felt chaos was less dangerous than the evils from which no form of government could escape. He especially feared any organization set up by Germans, whom he considered natural lackeys;

[25]Ibid., p. 112.

any organization they created was bound to become despotic. To under-mine Marx's International Working Men's Association, therefore, Bakunin set up his *Alliance Internationale de la Democratie Socialiste* in 1868. It declared for absolute equality and the abolition of the State—ideas that Marx labeled "shit." Marx and the General Council outlawed the Alliance but this did not slow down the crafty Bakunin, who was able to keep his loyal following. Standing before them in his peasant blouse and wreathed in cigarette smoke, the giant Russian could whip them to a fury as he fulminated against tyranny.

A Catholic Response

One opponent that Marx might have taken more seriously, if he had been able to foresee the future, was Wilhelm von Ketteler (1811–1877), Bishop of Mainz, who strove mightily to awaken the Church to the plight of the workers. Scion of an aristocratic Westphalian family, Ketteler burst onto the public stage in Germany when he was elected to the Frankfurt National Assembly in 1848. He gave a series of sermons in the Mainz Cathedral which are considered the beginning of German Social Catholicism. "The social question," he declared, "looms larger than ever demanding solutions more harshly than ever."[26] Ketteler's later study, *The Labor Problem and Christianity* (1868), and his 1869 writings constitute "the most important step forward between 1848 and 1891 in terms of Social Catholics coming to terms with industrialization on the European scene."[27] Ketteler's focus was on social realism and practical measures. He called attention to the main problem: the misery of the poor. He was even accused of communism—for Marx a bad joke. In fact, Marx said: "The rogues (for instance Bishop Ketteler) . . . are flirting with workers' problems."[28]

Ketteler was in fact very wary of capitalism but thought its horrible effects could be mitigated through social measures. To this end, Ketteler exhorted Catholics to overcome their romantic preference for bygone eras and to recognize the legitimate currents of the time. By this, he did not mean an abandonment of the tradition, but quite the contrary—a true

---

[26]Joseph N. Moody, ed., *Church and Society: Catholic Social and Political Thought and Movements* (New York: Arts, Inc., 1953) p. 408.

[27]Paul Misner, *Social Catholicism in Europe (From the Onset of Industrialization to the First World War)* (New York: Crossroad, 1991), p. 138.

[28]Karl Marx, *Collected Works* (New York: International Publishers, 1988), Vol. 43, p. 354.

reclaiming of it. While eschewing sentimental "high medieval" notions of charity, he found Thomas Aquinas's teaching on the common good and the relative nature of property rights most helpful in devising a Catholic position that avoided the extremes of communism and liberal capitalism. His interpretation of Aquinas contained the germ of the whole later Catholic social doctrine. But basically Ketteler was not a theorist. He asked the socialist Ferdinand Lasalle for advice, and even read Engels' "The Condition of the Working Classes in England in 1844."

By 1865 Ketteler had come to realize the need for state intervention to humanize conditions in the factories, and by 1869 he overcame his previous reservations and endorsed the British trade-union model. Workers, he believed, would have to organize in their own associations to assert their claims on society. Rules of fair play had to be established by law, including measures dealing with child labor, hours of work, hygienic conditions, Sunday rest, accident insurance, right of unions, and inspections. Without the state's involvement, he declared, there could be no solution. He also underlined the importance of the Church's role and its obligation to condemn the practice of treating labor as just a commodity—an attitude that actually made the condition of the worker worse than slavery. He emphasized the help that Christianity could bring through its institutions for the sick and the poor, its support of Christian marriage and family life, its education in culture and values, and its associations of all kinds.

In 1869 he issued his great memorandum on the pastoral and social ministry for the German Bishops' Conference at Fulda: Called "Welfare Work of the Church for the Factory Workers," it reviewed comprehensively the state of the social question in Germany. It called for an expansion of social mediation services between employer and employees, and stressed the need to stimulate the clergy's interest in the social question. Some priests, he said, should be assigned to study economics and be trained in welfare services. He followed this up with special efforts in his own seminary to train socially aware priests, who eventually played an important role in the growing German Catholic social movement.

Several young priests of Aachen, inspired by Ketteler, organized a Christian labor movement—the Paulusverein—for workers in 1869. Marx, who visited the area at the time, thought it ominous. But its rapid rise was followed by a rapid decline in the 1870s as Bismarck's *Kulturkampf,* a full-scale persecution of the Catholic Church, got into full swing. In this situation Ludwig Windthorst, the leader of the Catholic Center party, thought social initiatives a luxury. Even so, a motion proposed during this period by

Count Ferdinand von Galen (a Catholic and a nephew of Ketteler) was the first effort at social policy put forward in the Reichstag. Bismarck's Socialist Law outlawed any labor agitation, effectively squelching German Social Catholicism until 1890.

The Paris Commune

On July 19, 1870, the Franco-Prussian war broke out and caused further disintegration of Marx's International Working Men's Association. Marx saw the war as both imperialist and nationalist, and urged the workers on both sides not to support the war. His words had little effect, however, as the war proved extremely popular with the common people. It fomented nationalist pride; in particular it fomented anti-German sentiments in France, which played into Bakunin's hand. His people were able to spread the lie that the International was a tool of the Prussians.

The International was also gravely weakened by its connection with the Paris Commune, which was organized in 1870. After the French surrender at Sedan and the capture of Napoleon III, Adolphe Thiers, France's chief executive, signed a treaty whose harsh terms included the cession of Alsace-Lorraine to Germany and an indemnity of five billion francs. Radicals in Paris refused to accept the treaty, rebelled, and set up their own government, the Commune. The term meant only a township but it became confused with communism, in part due to Marx. The communards espoused a philosophy of government that would change France into a federation of democratic autonomous communes. Actually the majority of the members were not communists but a highly heterogeneous collection of individuals—followers of Blanqui, Proudhon, and Bakunin, with a sprinkling of new-Jacobins—who proclaimed death to all tyrants, priests, and Prussians. Workmen, soldiers, writers, painters, bohemians, and adventurers, they were all swept up in a common revolutionary wave. After throwing off the Empire and withstanding the siege they now saw all the specters of the past about to return: the generals, the financiers, the priests. Revulsion at the prospect was almost the only bond that united the communards. As hysteria took over, they began to slaughter indiscriminately all suspected opponents. Among those executed was the archbishop of Paris who had been held as a hostage. Europe watched the bloodbath with growing indignation and disgust. People even on the left saw the communards as social incendiaries and lunatics bent on the destruction of all religion and morality. Bakunin, however, was ecstatic at seeing a large part of Paris going up in flames. The "fire seemed to him a symbol of his own life, and a magnificent realization of his favourite paradox: 'The passion for destruction, too, is a creative passion.' "[29]

Pitted against a professional army, the insurgents fought bravely, especially the revolutionary workers who displayed incredible bravery. The struggle reached a horrible climax when Thiers' troops overwhelmed the communards, and in the full fury of class hatred wreaked bloody vengeance on a scale not seen again until the days of Hitler and Franco. Estimates of the number of those butchered vary from 20,000 to 36,000; and in the ensuing reign of terror, another 20,000 of the working class were court-martialed and many of them deported to penal colonies.

Marx originally saw the struggle as a new stage in the world revolution, but believed it was not ruthless and radical enough. He regarded it as a political blunder, but in his pamphlet *The Civil War in France* he hailed the massacred workers as the first martyrs of international socialism. By paying them homage he helped to create the heroic legend of socialism that Lenin, thirty years later, would allude to in pointing out "the emotional and symbolic value of a great heroic outburst, however ill conceived, however damaging in its immediate results."[30]

Marx was heaped with public odium as he and the International were charged with responsibility for the events. He couldn't care less: "I snap my fingers at the canaille!" he said.[31] But permanent damage was done to the International as it was associated with the outrages of the Commune. In particular it dealt a blow to the International's alliance with the English trade union leaders. The unionists sought only to raise the standard of living of skilled workers, and had no desire to be associated with a notorious revolutionary conspiracy. At the 1872 meeting of the International in London, the trade unionists won the right to form a separate local organization instead of being represented by the International's General Council. Also at this meeting a resolution was carried by the English delegates to form a separate political party to represent the interests of the workers. The new political party was not set up during Marx's lifetime, but the English Labor Party was born at this meeting, and may be regarded as Marx's greatest single contribution to the internal history of his adopted land.

In an interview Marx gave to reporters from the *New York World* and the

[29]Berlin, *Karl Marx,* p. 161.
[30]Ibid., p. 259.
[31]Ibid.

New York Herald in 1871, he insisted on the inevitability of the workers' conquest of political power. But he argued that this did not have to be by violence: in some countries it might occur through a peaceful process. However, he felt that the aristocracy and moneyed men would use violence in any case to keep a shift in power from happening. In one instance, at least, his views were prophetic: He predicted the coming revolution of the workers in Russia—"when the first weak Czar succeeded to the throne."[32]

Das Kapital *Catches On*

When the first edition of *Das Kapital* finally sold out, Marx had the opportunity to revise the book as well as to publish it in a more accessible and cheaper form. In the United States, the bastion for Marx of the modern bourgeois society, a real comedy occurred when a publisher saw in the table of contents the heading "The Accumulation of Capital" and in 1890 sent out advertising circulars for a deep tome by a learned German scholar showing one "how to accumulate capital." The response was immediate and the edition was completely sold out.

Its first authentic success was registered in Russia, where the first foreign translation was made (no English translation appeared in his lifetime). The Russian censors thought it too "scientific" to make sense to the ignorant common people. But Russian intellectuals discussed it widely and it was already being quoted by rioting radical Russian students as early as 1873. Lenin, only a child at the time, was soon to become Marx's most powerful disciple; it was mainly through him that Marx would exert an enormous influence on our century.

Marx was most anxious to have the book do well in France for in his mind it was the historic land of revolutions and the intellectual pacesetter of Europe. Finally in 1875 a French translation was published and sold well. By this time Marx's ideas had taken hold also in Germany. He summarized them in the "Gotha Programme," his address to a joint congress of the two main German labor parties held at Gotha in 1875. The Gotha Programme formed the ideology of the Social-Democratic Party, which within two decades after Marx's death was Germany's largest single political party. By the First World War it was the most powerful socialist party in Europe, though by then its Marxist socialism was much watered down.

How to explain the amazing success of a book whose theories virtually all

[32]Padover, *Karl Marx*, p. 258.

economists now regard as obsolete? As Saul Padover says in his biography: "The qualities of style, irony, moral judgment, vision and social relevance have made *Das Kapital* a world classic."[33] Marx naturally claimed that his theories had universal validity because they were "scientific" and based on "objective" analyses of the capitalist economy. But it seems closer to the truth to see his appeal as rooted in the image of the angry prophet denouncing the age-old sins of greed, oppression, and injustice while using the "tools and data of political economy to propound his vision."[34]

The battle to preserve the International allowed Marx little time to complete the revision he wanted to make of *Kapital*. Mountains of papers and correspondence covered his desk while a typical meeting of the General Council (often at his home) could run until one in the morning. In 1872 he decided the time had come to step down.

One of his major concerns was the threat posed by Bakunin to the worker solidarity and unity that were absolutely essential to avoid another debacle like 1848. Bakuninism meant a return to utopianism and the negation of the idea of the single, carefully concerted revolution organized to begin at the right moment, directed from a common source and to a common end. "Bakuninism led to the dissipation of the revolutionary impulse, to the old romantic, noble, futile heroism, rich in saints and martyrs, but crushed only too easily by the more realistic enemy, and necessarily followed by a period of weakness and disillusionment likely to set the movement back for many decades."[35]

Marx decided it was time to have it out with Bakunin at the next congress set for the Hague in September of that year. This congress proved to be one of the largest and most representative in the history of the International. Sixty-five delegates came from fifteen European countries, the largest contingents from France and Germany. Since it was only one year after the Paris Commune, the authorities were naturally concerned and determined to prevent any such recurrence by the "scoundrels of the Paris Commune." They deployed troops, doubled the sentries, and used police spies to keep a close surveillance on the proceedings. Bakunin was himself conspicuously absent, while Marx—with his swarthy complexion, black suit, and monocle—dominated the debates. It was a struggle for the soul of the radical movement. Specifically, the Bakuninists, in keeping with their anarchist

[33] Ibid., p. 209.
[34] Ibid., p. 221.
[35] Berlin, *Karl Marx*, p. 235.

philosophy, wanted to deprive the General Council of its authority to dictate to or suspend anyone. Convinced that Bakunin's Alliance was trying to destroy the International, the congress voted overwhelmingly to expel Bakunin. But Marx knew how infected the Latin and Swiss workers were with the Bakuninist doctrine of direct violence without any revolutionary theory. For safety's sake, therefore, he proposed that the headquarters of the International be moved to New York. The motion created a furor but it passed by a small margin.

At a meeting later in Amsterdam, Marx spoke to a group of pro-Bakuninists, and arguing against anarchist doctrine he insisted on the need for organized political action on the part of the workers. The time was coming, he said, when the workers would have to seize power and build new organizations of labor. Moreover, although in some countries such as America and Britain the takeover of power might be accomplished by democratic means, in autocratic countries—that is, most countries on the continent—the workers would have to use violence. The question of whether nonviolent revolution was ever feasible soon became a burning issue among Marxists. Marx's idea of relocating the International in the New World proved unworkable as it fell prey to the usual bickerings and squabblings. The International was formally dissolved by the General Council at a meeting in Philadelphia in 1876.[36]

Bakunin made his last stand as a revolutionist between October 1872 and September 1873 but could not arrest the deterioration of the Bakuninist movement. He was now sixty, broken, perpetually short of funds, disillusioned, and desiring only peace. He was tired of "rolling Sisyphus's stone against the triumphant forces of reaction."[37] In October 1874 he settled down in Lugano with his long-suffering wife, Antonia. He kept in touch with developments but had no wish to plunge again into the active political scene. Hoping for a substantial sum from the sale of the family estate, he purchased a beautiful villa near Lugano. He sent a warm and loving letter, redolent with nostalgia, to his brothers to come and enjoy his "little king-

---

[36] The International was reborn in 1889 as the Second International, representing the Social-Democratic parties. Its demise occurred when World War I broke out but the debate over nonviolent revolution continued among Marxists. Finally the Third International, or Comintern, was founded in March 1919 espousing Lenin's belief that Marxism demanded violent revolution and dictatorship. A split occurred. Socialists who followed Lenin's view took the name "communists" while those in favor of democracy kept the name "socialists" or "social democrats."

[37] Masters, *Bakunin*, p. 243.

dom of heaven." But his time and money were running out and creditors seized his villa. In June, seeking help for his rapidly deteriorating health, he entered a hospital at Berne where he died at midday on July 1, 1876.

Bakuninism did not die but spread to many countries. Its doctrine of total destruction of the existing social order made sense to a certain number of radicals who, like Bakunin, feared that Marxism would only replace the old tyranny with a new one. The revolution they called for would tear down all existing institutions—the government, the church, the courts, the army, the banks, and the schools. The rebuilt society would be made up of autonomous communes that were loosely linked in a federation.

With the demise of the International in 1872, Marx hoped to continue his work on Volume II of *Das Kapital* but it proved impossible. He was neither physically nor psychologically capable any longer of sustained creative work. He spent the last decade of his life mainly in a desperate search for health. He embarked on many trips to take the mineral waters at Karlsbad, using the name Carl Marx to avoid trouble with the police.

In spite of his poor health Marx kept up with everything going on in the world and often received visits from continental radicals and socialists. One of these was Jules Guesde, a French radical Marxist who came to get his and Engels' assistance in founding a socialist labor party in France. They helped him draft a program that called for a number of progressive labor measures including the eight-hour day, prohibition of child labor, a minimum wage tied to the cost of living, equal pay for women, worker participation, public education, and the progressive income tax as the only tax.

Marx's beloved wife, Jenny, died on December 5, 1881, and was buried in unconsecrated ground in Highgate Cemetery in London. Marx was so ill he couldn't attend, and Engels gave a short speech at the grave. The loss devastated Marx, who lasted only fifteen months more—time he spent in restless travel to resort after resort in search of health. By March of 1883 his cough was continuous, his throat strangled with mucus, and his breathing labored. In addition a lung tumor began to bleed. On March 14, 1883, Engels happened to visit and went upstairs to find Marx stretched out on his bed with the fixed stare of the corpse. His burial in Highgate Cemetery next to his wife took place in the presence of a small group of family, friends, and communist colleagues. In his obituary Engels adverted to the millions of followers that Marx already could claim in the mines of Siberia as well as in the workshops of Europe and America. "His name will live on through the centuries, and so will his work," Engels said.

What also lived on in Marx's disciples was the attitude of intolerance and authoritarianism so characteristic of the master. The vindictive hatred with which Marx pursued those who did not submit to his dominance was copied by legions of communist party and government officials. Proudhon predicted as much in this definition of communism that he penned in 1864:

> A compact democracy having the appearance of being founded on the dictatorship of the masses, but in which the masses have no more power than is necessary to ensure a general serfdom in accordance with the following precepts and principles borrowed from the old-absolutism: indivisibility of public power, all-consuming centralization, systematic destruction of all individual, co-operative and regional thought (regarded as disruptive), inquisitorial police.[38]

Marx taught his communist followers that history was on their side—an idea that for a hundred years carried a certain degree of credibility. Instead of creating a workers' paradise, however, his disciples set up an army of faceless bureaucrats run by a clique of autocrats incapable of producing the shared abundance dreamed of by Marx. What they did produce was a generation of democratic revolutionaries who, in a few startling months in the fall of 1989, rose up and destroyed the communist regimes of Eastern Europe and installed governments based on the "liberal freedoms" so despised by Marx.

The demise of communism has given rise to a new quest for the historical Marx. A number of questions are now being hotly debated among Marxist and other scholars. Was Marx basically a humanist whose ideal form of government would have been participatory democracy? Or, in other words, was Leninism-Stalinism based on a distorted version of Marxism? Did Marx really believe in the inevitability of communism or was his vision of humanity's future open-ended? Should Marxism be equated with dogmatism and totalitarianism? Whatever may be said of attempts to separate Marx from the failed regimes that claimed him as their master, he remains one of the pivotal figures in the history of socialism—one who certainly cast a giant shadow over the Western capitalist world for a hundred years.

---

[38]Jackson, *Marx, Proudhon, and European Socialism*, p. 147.

SIX

A Bishop Who Heard What Marx Was Saying: Henry Edward Manning (1808–1892)

ENRY EDWARD MANNING, a high-ranking member of the Anglican clergy, converted to the Roman Catholic Church in mid-life and rose quickly in the hierarchy to be made a cardinal in 1875. Blessed with many talents, he left an enduring mark on the English Catholic Church. In the area of social justice he was one of the small band of Social Catholics who were alive to the growing problems of the factory workers. Like them he found it ominous that so few of his fellow Catholics were concerned about the plight of exploited and alienated workers. Like them also he was terribly concerned about the progress of atheistic socialism under Karl Marx, whose thunderous call for a workers' revolution resounded throughout Britain and Europe.

Early Years

Manning was born in 1808 at Copped Hall, Totteridge, a few miles from London. His grandfather, William Coventry Manning, established a family business based on the sugar trade. Henry Edward's father, William, took over the business in time and it prospered while he also engaged in politics as a member of Parliament and Governor of the Bank of England. When the

War of 1812 gave British ships a virtual monopoly of trade with the West Indies, the lucrative profits apparently enabled William Manning to purchase an estate at Combes Bank. In this idyllic setting Henry Edward spent his youth.

His father's first wife had been a cousin of William Wilberforce, the abolitionist and a leader of the Evangelical movement. Through him William Manning too played a leading role in the movement. After she died William married his second wife, Henry Edward's mother, who was also fervently Evangelical and inculcated this spirit, or tried to, in her son. She insisted on absolute truthfulness and he later remembered her ordering him down on his knees to beg God's forgiveness for telling a fib. He also remembered how his father read prayers and a sermon on Sunday nights and how the whole family went to church together.

He spent his teenage years at Harrow, a public school noted for its brutal discipline, where little attention was given to religion and much to sports, at which he proved to be quite adept. The same talent no doubt showed up in his accuracy at stone-throwing in the pitched battles the boys fought with

Henry Edward Manning

the local townsfolk. His schoolmates remembered him as quite a fop and a great devotee of Lord Byron, a graduate of Harrow some years before. Manning called these years "my greatest danger . . . and the least religious time of my life."[1] "I had faith, a great fear of hell, and said my prayers; beyond, all was a blank."[2] However, the qualities that were later to be so prominent in his character soon became apparent: a steely determination to achieve a goal, self-confidence and self-control, and the ability to make the most of his talents and opportunities. Although not reckoned a really good scholar he decided to aim for a First Class in the classics at Oxford, a prize that seemed considerably beyond his grasp. At that point, he says, he "ceased to vegetate," and once enrolled at Oxford's Balliol College he began to ready himself for the great ordeal. There would be no failure of nerve such as John Henry Newman had suffered nine years before when he barely managed to scrape by the examiners with only a passing grade.[3] As Manning said, "If I fail, I will fail in Livy not in steadiness of principle."[4]

He did not fail. Six names were on the list for First Classes that term and Manning's name was among them. He also won laurels at the Union debating society where his very first speech was a memorable occasion. In the very hotbed of Toryism he dared to take on a formidable Tory, Sir John Hammer, over the issue of free trade, which Manning supported. Next to making a maiden speech in Parliament, making one at the Oxford Union was the most daunting challenge a would-be speaker could face. Manning later recalled how a momentary panic seized him as he first heard the sound of his voice. But he was able to recover quickly and he spoke with such logic, grace, and feeling that his audience was amazed. Next morning his name was on everyone's lips in Oxford.

He soon showed that he could speak extemporaneously and impressively on any subject, ignorance of the topic notwithstanding. As his biographer Edmund Purcell says, "He spoke at every meeting, on all subjects, at length, with unfailing fluency and propriety of expression."[5] Unrivaled in debate, he found the experience intoxicating, and though destined by his father for a church career he began to dream of a future in politics. He paid regular

---

[1] Robert Gray, *Cardinal Manning* (New York: St. Martin's Press, 1985), p. 16.

[2] Edmund Sheridan Purcell, *Life of Cardinal Manning* (New York: Macmillan and Co., 1896), p. 19.

[3] Newman was later an outstanding religious thinker and convert to the Catholic Church, made a cardinal in 1879.

[4] Gray, *Cardinal Manning*, p. 26.

[5] Purcell, *Life of Cardinal Manning*, p. 35.

visits to the House of Commons where he imagined himself fighting for some great cause. He formed a close friendship with William Gladstone, who was leaning toward the ministry. "Who knows how different the Victorian Age might have been if Gladstone had stuck to his original ambition of becoming a clergyman and Manning had achieved a seat in parliament."[6]

Just then his father's bankruptcy changed Manning's prospects unalterably. The British trade monopoly ended with the return of peace in 1815, and the less favorable economic circumstances gradually brought down his father's business. For Henry it meant the ruin of his hopes for a career in the House of Commons since this required either a great deal of money or a rich patron to secure a seat. For a time he refused to accept his fate and took a job as a clerk in the Colonial Office to bide his time—work that he found boring to the extreme. A bid for marriage to a young lady with connections failed when her father rejected him because of his lack of prospects.

A Career in the Church

Some unfriendly biographers have interpreted Manning's next move—a decision to seek Holy Orders in the Church of England—as a worldly act by one who saw it as the best field in which to use his great talents now that his dream of eminence in political life was ruined. His biographer Purcell, on the other hand, notes that Manning in old age insisted on the sacrifice he had made in taking orders. Whereas there is no clear evidence from the earlier period about his motives, there is indication that he was wrestling with religious issues and did experience a kind of religious conversion. In any case he managed to secure a fellowship at Merton College which allowed him to begin his preparation for the ministry. He had few illusions about the church he was preparing to serve. He would later recall that even as a young man he found it secular, pedantic, and unspiritual. "I remember the disgust with which I saw a dignitary in Cockspur Street in his shovel and gaiters."[7]

The ills afflicting the Anglican Church are well documented. Money was one—too much in the hands of some and not enough in the hands of others. Some bishops commanded incomes that in today's figures would amount to a million dollars or more, while many parsons could barely feed

[6] Gray, *Cardinal Manning,* p. 25.
[7] Ibid., p. 35.

their families and managed only by holding down more than one parish. Some squires holding title to the revenues of a parish paid curates only subsistence wages.

Many of the Evangelicals, who were inclined to a more ardent type of religion, were former Anglicans who had followed John Wesley out of the Anglican Church. Those who remained had a very attenuated idea of their Church. Their essential doctrine was that the Holy Ghost acted directly on each individual soul, effectively dispensing with the need for the Church and its sacraments except as a sign of fellowship. The Communion service, for instance, was regarded as just a commemorative rite and infrequently celebrated. Spiritually the Church was not exactly a glowing witness to the Gospel it preached (or was supposed to preach). One message it did convey clearly—the importance of gentlemanliness. As the saying went: "And there remain these three, faith, hope and gentlemanliness, and the greatest of these is gentlemanliness."

One of the clearest signs of the Anglican Church's decay was its failure to deal with the shift of populations caused by the industrial revolution. A report of Parliament in 1824 indicated that there were some four million souls in the cities without a place of worship. But proposals for reform were looked on unkindly by the clergy, and the Reform Bill of 1831 was opposed by twenty-one out of twenty-three bishops. Many Englishmen turned against the Anglican Church as a bastion of reaction, and many observers predicted its imminent disestablishment if not demise. The as-yet still Anglican John Henry Newman and his friends had accused their country-men of "national apostasy" and in 1833 launched the Oxford Movement to save the Church.

Manning meanwhile settled in at the Merton College library reading "acres of Anglican writers," from the High Church Caroline divines with their great sense of Catholic tradition to divines like Bishop Tillotson who preached an ethical Protestantism. Manning was personally confronting for the first time the doctrinal chaos in Anglicanism. Merton was near New-man's college, Oriel, and Newman's diary in 1832 indicated that he and Manning dined together several times. "Perhaps," as Robert Gray says, "at these meetings Manning began to glimpse the possibility of grounding his faith more securely on dogma enunciated by a divinely appointed Church."[8] The following year was a momentous one for Manning. He was ordained in June, installed as Rector of Lavington, and in November took a

[8] Ibid., p. 42.

bride—Caroline Sargent, the daughter of the previous Rector of Lavington, who had died prematurely.

Under Newman's Influence

Like a number of the Evangelicals in his circle of relatives and friends, Manning at this point began to feel the limitations of the Evangelical approach. The Evangelical revival had produced men of great spiritual power but their descendants were not able to reach the same level. They used the same words and phrases that had once electrified sinners and moved them to tears of repentance, but these often seemed empty formulae now, parroted with little effect. There was a need, Manning and many others felt, for more substance than Evangelicalism could provide. Above all Manning was concerned with the issue of authority. "By what authority," he asked himself, "do you lift the latch of a poor man's door and enter and sit down and begin to instruct or correct him?"[9] He found the answer in Newman's first *Tract for the Times,* the series of pamphlets emanating from the group of Anglican scholars at Oxford. They were engaged in a campaign to revive Catholic tradition in the Church of England. As Newman said in this tract: "I fear we have neglected the real ground on which our authority is built—our APOS-TOLICAL DESCENT."[10]

Within two months Manning himself was distributing the *Tracts* around the parishes of West Sussex. Newman, the theologian of the Oxford Movement, had worked out a system that Manning found irresistible. Its starting point was the idea that faith is not something one reasons oneself to. One comes to faith and matures in faith by being faithful to one's conscience. God, as Newman liked to repeat, does not save his people with the help of syllogisms, or as St. Ambrose supposedly put it, *"Non in dialectica placuit Deo salvum facere populum suum."*

Human reason is inherently skeptical. It is only by obedience that one grabs and holds on to faith. But obedience to whom or to what? Conscience, yes, but conscience must be instructed. And who or what has the authority to instruct conscience? Scripture, some would say. But Scripture by itself, Newman argued, is not equal to the task, for like faith itself it is vulnerable to the all-corrosive force of the human intellect. The Protestant reliance on private interpretation of Scripture leads to confusion and chaos.

[9] Ibid., p. 49.
[10] Ibid., p. 50.

Only a living body—the Church—can stand up to this all-dissolving force and guide the soul through the welter of subjective interpretations of Scripture. Only the divinely appointed Church has the authority to instruct the conscience and lead it to the holiness that is the sure ground of faith.

The task that Newman and the Oxford dons took on then was to convince their fellow Englishmen that the rickety, rotten old Church of England was the one, holy, catholic, and apostolic Church, the divinely appointed oracle of God's revelation and the guide of the conscience. Study of the Fathers of the Church was imperative in Newman's scheme. They were witnesses to the pure fount of Christian doctrine and the surest guide in determining the true Catholic faith. For Newman and his colleagues who wanted to revive Catholic doctrine in the Church of England, the teachings of the Fathers were to be the norm of what Catholic doctrine was.

But the Fathers did not always agree and sometimes even contradicted each other. The solution of the Tractarians was to use the test proposed by St. Vincent of Lerins (d. before 450) to determine what was truly Catholic; namely, whatever was believed "everywhere, always, by all." Manning contributed a study of St. Vincent to one of Newman's tracts and continued to move toward the Tractarian position. In 1834 he was converted to belief in the real presence of Jesus in the consecrated bread and wine, and established daily Matins and Evensong in his parish. In 1835, at the tender age of twenty-seven, he preached before the assembled clergy of Chichester on the Apostolic Succession and lectured the reverend elders on the awesome responsibilities of their office. The fact that he was prematurely bald must have helped him pull it off. "I'm glad about Manning," was Newman's comment.

His sermon on the "Rule of Faith" preached in Chichester Cathedral betrayed his growing debt to Newman in its insistence on the need for an objective standard of truth. This was to be found, Manning argued, not primarily in Scripture but in the creeds of the primitive Church, which enabled the Church to choose rightly among the different interpretations of Scripture. His questioning of the supreme authority of Scripture and the exaltation of church authority infuriated the Evangelicals but won him further praise from Newman.

There was already in Manning's thought an implied recognition of the infallibility of the Church insofar as it had been given a divine mission to teach revealed doctrine. But at this point the future champion of papal infallibility had no sympathy for such a doctrine and blamed it for the tendency of the Roman Church to pronounce doctrines which, he felt, had no basis in the primitive Church.

His scholarly and theological interests did not keep Manning from carrying out his duties to his flock as a Sussex country clergyman. One parishioner, however, later recollected how "he was an out-of-the-way serious man. Always reading and walking up and down in front a-reading as if seemingly he could find no rest . . . [He] always drove a pair of greys. Old John Tribe he used to have to stop 'em half an hour together while he got out and sat down somewhere and took no notice of no one."[11] At the same time Manning tried to be a good sport, jousting on ponies with his nieces and playing a good game of cricket. But he was not the kind of priest who could convincingly let his hair down, and as one parishioner recalled, "People said he was cold . . . but he were a wonderful churchman. He looked like an archangel when he prayed."[12]

Tragedy struck suddenly when his wife Caroline died in 1837 at the age of twenty-five after a brief illness. It was a devastating loss and his only solace was his work. "All I can do now is keep at work," he told Newman a month or so after Caroline's death. "There is a sort of rush into my mind when unoccupied I can hardly bear."[13]

Manning did not at this point, unlike Newman, believe in the superiority of celibacy for those called to the priesthood, but for him there was to be no replacement for Caroline. Looking back forty-three years later he recalled that he had lived as a widower "without ever wavering in the purpose of living and dying as I now am."[14] In April of 1838 he made the first of his eventual twenty-two trips to Rome. It was not a good time to be favorably impressed by papal spiritual claims. Gregory XVI was holding on to his temporal power, but precariously and with the help of a network of police spies and Metternich's Austrian troops. Manning found the Roman Catholic services and devotions repulsive but he found the interior of St. Peter's "beyond anything one can imagine." He met Dr. Wiseman, the rector of the English college, and later recalled that Wiseman was not even a bishop at the time. "How little we thought that he and I should have the first two palliums in the hierarchy of England."[15]

At home Manning's extraordinary talents were increasingly recognized in

[11] Ibid., p. 59.
[12] Ibid., p. 58.
[13] Ibid., p. 64.
[14] Ibid., p. 65.
[15] Ibid., p. 76.

wider social circles. Appointed Archdeacon of Chichester in 1840, he reiterated in his inaugural sermon his confidence in the English Church as a "regenerator of the Christendom that seems now dissolving and the centre of a new Catholic world."[16] While a student he had formed a close friendship with William Gladstone, who was now swiftly climbing the political ladder in London. Gladstone gave him an entree into spheres of influence that assured him of success. But even without Gladstone, Manning was bound to make a mark. As his biographer says, an "easy flow of anecdote was perfectly offset by the clear steady gaze emanating from a countenance that suggested, in its handsome but taut features, the most rigorous mortification." The poet Aubrey de Vere thought he looked like a saint in a picture by Raphael. "No power on earth," Bishop Phillpotts exclaimed, "can keep Manning from the Bench [of bishops]."[17] But pace Phillpotts Tractarianism was not the golden key to the episcopacy. Any connection with Newman or Pusey was poison to such ambitions.

Newman himself was increasingly unsure of his position. Whereas his effort to revive the Catholic tradition had evoked considerable sympathy within the clerical and lay elite, the mass of Englishmen remained indifferent to Newman and all his works. And he had to admit to himself that his was a "paper religion" having little contact with the reality of the English Church. Moreover, he saw in early Church history ominous parallels with the present situation. The Monophysites, for instance, who broke with the rest of the Church at the time of the Council of Chalcedon reminded him of the current situation of the Church of England. In 1841 he published his final tract, *Tract XC,* which argued that the Thirty-Nine Articles were open to a Catholic interpretation. The bishops would have none of it and rebuked him publicly. The whole affair proved the futility of trying to pour new wine into old wineskins, and henceforth Newman was on his "deathbed" as an Anglican.

Manning was alarmed when Newman, having resigned from his office in the Church, wrote to him: "I think the Church of Rome the Catholic Church, and ours not part of the Catholic Church because not in communion with Rome."[18] Manning forwarded the letter to Gladstone, who reacted violently. "I stagger to and fro like a drunken man and am at my wits' end," he replied. He nevertheless felt that his "good angel" (as he

[16] Ibid., p. 82.
[17] Ibid., p. 76.
[18] Ibid., p. 93.

called Manning) would be able to expose the weakness in Newman's argument. Manning instead invited Newman to visit Lavington where he might see the evidence of God's presence in Anglican parish life. Newman declined.

Badly shaken by Newman's argument, Manning went ahead anyway and delivered a Guy Fawkes Day sermon that contained the obligatory denunciations of the pope, though not as venomous as was customary. Some saw in it a Machiavellian move to keep his options open; it actually, however, reflected a desperate need to be convinced of the validity of Anglicanism. The prospect of switching allegiance to Rome was, after all, no easy thing to contemplate. Anti-Catholic prejudice in England at this time was as vicious as ever, if not more so because of Newman's agitation. (A Catholic priest, Newman later said, was apt to be treated by the average Englishman as if he were some "hideous baboon, or sloth or rattlesnake, or toad which strove to make itself agreeable."[19]) But Manning's doubts multiplied, and when in 1845 Newman submitted to Rome, they crystallized. Upon being informed by Newman of his move, Manning replied in a burst of feeling: "Only believe always that I love you. If we may never meet again in life at the same altar, may our intercessions for each other, day by day, meet in the court of Heaven."[20]

Before leaving the English Church, Newman wrote an *Essay on Development* that convinced himself, if no one else, that the additions the Roman Church had made to the ancient faith—such as papal primacy, veneration of relics, and the concept of purgatory—were not the corruptions he had previously denounced but were actually legitimate developments. Manning, in contrast, liked to think of church doctrine as a fixed deposit; doctrines subject to "evolution" might well evolve themselves out of existence. Manning naturally found the approach of the *Essay* uncongenial, but he judged it a work of genius nonetheless.

On the Road to Rome

Manning's impression of Newman as somehow slippery and skeptical originated at this time, and it would later weigh heavily on their relationship. But

[19]John Henry Newman, *The Present Position of Catholics in England* (New York: Longmans, Green, and Co., 1899), p. 265.
[20]Gray, *Cardinal Manning,* p. 106.

Newman's *Essay* did "open his eyes" to one fact: namely, the need for a living voice divinely commissioned to safeguard the revelation.

Manning henceforth found his own position almost unbearable: "Not therefore Roman, I cease to be Anglican."[21] And yet he was looked up to as a leader. He was haunted by the idea that he would end up in the Roman Church, drawn there by the way Rome "satisfied the WHOLE of my intellect, sympathy, sentiment, and nature, in a way proper, and solely belonging to itself."[22] The strain of wearing a mask began to tell and his health broke down. The illness led him to deep self-scrutiny and an awareness of deeply rooted sinfulness: "I am capable of all evil, nothing but the hand of God has kept me from being the vilest of creatures." He made a formal confession and called it the "greatest conscious act of his life."[23] The disregard of auricular confession in the Church of England, he felt, greatly weakened its claim to be Catholic.

In 1847, after recovering, he headed a second time for Rome in a mood much more receptive than that of his previous visit. Passing through Belgium, Germany, and Switzerland en route, he was greatly impressed by the Catholic services he attended, by the throngs in attendance, by the attentiveness and devoutness of the people. The Protestant services by comparison he found dull, dreary, cold, abstract, and not very well attended.

The first Englishman he met in Rome was John Henry himself, now just a student at the Collegio di Propanda. Newman hardly recognized Manning, so altered was his appearance by the illness. Always fascinated by politics, Manning spent time with the radicals who were riding high in Rome at the time. He also saw a lot of Gioacchino Ventura, a disciple of Lamennais and a priest who still believed in an alliance of the Church with the people. That thought seems to have struck a sympathetic chord with Manning, who later echoed it in an 1848 charge that the Church needed to be with the "poor of Christ, the multitude which have been this long time with us and now faint by the way; with the masses in mines and factories."[24]

Manning's stay in Rome coincided with a grave crisis for Pope Pius IX, who had mounted the papal throne in 1846. His initial encouragement of the Italian liberal and nationalist movements had gained him enormous popularity. But, as Ventura noted, the pope's popularity waned rapidly

[21] Ibid., p. 112.
[22] Ibid., pp. 112–113.
[23] Ibid., pp. 116–117.
[24] Ibid., p. 123.

when he found himself unable to satisfy the expectations he had aroused. When on April 29, 1848, the pope delivered an Allocution in which he categorically denied any sympathy with republican ideals or with any schemes to make him the head of an Italian federation, he lost all popular favor. Manning's response to Pius was strictly personal: When the pope passed by and blessed him, Manning fell to his knees. Pius never forgot the sight of the English archdeacon on his knees in the Piazza di Spagna. Manning thought it impossible not to love Pius IX: "His is the most English countenance I have seen in Italy."[25]

Stopping off at Milan on his return he prayed at the tomb of Charles Borromeo that the saint might help him decide whether the Council of Trent was right and the English Church wrong. Back again in England, he entered the final stage of his agony. Newman thought he would never convert, and complained to Henry Wilberforce: "What does Manning mean by telling you there is "a deep gulf' between him and me while he tells all Catholics that he is already quite one with us?"[26]

Intellectually convinced of Rome's claims, he still lingered and continued to put on a brave face while his influence within the Anglican Church remained enormous. As F. D. Maurice, a leading cleric of the time, remarked: "His power with the clergy is very great, greater certainly than that of any man living."[27] Manning feared that somehow he might be suffering from delusion: "If it was a delusion perhaps she [Caroline] would have saved me." A little later he said he felt that Caroline was guiding him from another world.[28]

In his correspondence he bemoaned the sad state of the English Church. It had no real authority and was spiritually sterile, unable to produce any of the higher forms of devotion: "We cannot form one Sister of Mercy."[29] Anglicanism, he said, is in essence the same as Protestantism: "a chaos, a wreck of fragments without idea, principle, or life. It is to me flesh, blood, unbelief, and the will of man." And again: "I am ready to say—I do not say that the Church of England teaches the doctrine of the Real Presence, but I must say that either those that deny it or I ought not to be priests of the same Church."[30]

[25] Ibid., p. 125.
[26] Ibid., p. 128.
[27] Ibid., p. 129.
[28] Ibid., p. 134.
[29] Ibid., p. 130.
[30] Purcell, *Life of Cardinal Manning*, Vol. I, pp. 514–515.

The Gorham Case Ends All Doubt

Manning still hesitated to make the move that would tear him from his comfortable niche and the church he loved, strip him of most of his friends, and utterly destroy the worldly prospects that he sometimes confessed he still cherished. But any doubts he still had were finally quenched by the affair of one Reverend George Cornelius Gorham, an Anglican clergyman. Gorham had run afoul of a High Church bishop, Henry Phillpotts, because of his (Gorham's) denial of the doctrine of baptismal regeneration—that through baptism a person is cleansed from sin, sanctified with the Holy Ghost, and incorporated into the body of Christ. The good bishop, described by his enemies as a quarrelsome old tyrant with a dreadful countenance, had refused to install Gorham as vicar of the village of Brampford Speke near Exeter. Gorham's appeal finally reached the highest Anglican court, the Judicial Committee of the Privy Council, composed mainly of lay lawyers. It decided in favor of Gorham.

For Manning the battle for Catholic doctrine in the Church of England was now lost forever. Especially depressing for him was the reaction of the Anglican clergy, who showed hardly any interest at all in the outcome of a case he regarded as a matter of life and death. What more proof did one need of the doctrinal vacuity of the Anglican Church and its subservience to civil authority? He was now absolutely certain that he would have to bid farewell to the Anglican Church. As he said to Robert Wilberforce in a letter written on August 5, 1850: "If I stay I shall end a simple mystic, like Leighton. God is a spirit, and has no visible kingdom, church, or sacraments. Nothing will ever entangle me again in Protestantism, Anglican or otherwise."[31]

Though there was no longer in his view a shred of rational argument left to keep him, Manning still forebore to make the final break. He no longer spoke of his perplexities but only of his suffering. Gladstone made a desperate effort to restrain him during long hours of discussion, while Newman, in Birmingham, wondered whether the gossip about Manning's imminent conversion could be true. At last, on March 25, 1851, Manning went into the city and legally resigned his archdeaconry; then he entered the Catholic Cathedral, knelt before the Blessed Sacrament, and said his first "Hail Mary." Here he describes his last act of worship in the English Church:

[31] Ibid., p. 559.

. . . that little chapel off the Buckingham Palace Road. I was kneeling by the side of Mr. Gladstone. Just before the Communion Service commenced, I said to him, "I can no longer take the Communion in the Church of England." I rose up—"St. Paul is standing by his side"—and laying my hand on Mr. Gladstone's shoulder, said, "Come." It was the parting of the ways. Mr. Gladstone remained; and I went my way. Mr. Gladstone still remains where I left him.[32]

On April 6, Passion Sunday, he was received into the Roman Church in the Jesuit church on Farm Street. Gladstone exclaimed in a state of shock: "I felt as if he had murdered my mother by mistake." Newman was filled with "inexpressible joy."[33]

The English Catholic Church he entered was still an insignificant sect. In 1851 it numbered some 700,000 souls; this was a great increase, however, from the 60,000 estimated by Edmund Burke seventy years before, and an increase due not to any English Catholic revival but to Irish immigration.

Cardinal Wiseman, the archbishop of Westminster, was ecstatic at the conversion of such a distinguished clergyman, and in his fanciful way thought it a harbinger of the conversion of England itself. He ordained Manning after a couple of months, and (anxious to further his Romanization) sent him to Rome for further study. On the journey, Manning's bag was stolen and with it his wife Caroline's letters. He was devastated, lost for hours in silent grief. Finally he remarked: "The loss was probably necessary—necessary to sever all bonds to earth."[34] One of Manning's companions on his journey to Rome was another converted Anglican priest, George Talbot, Wiseman's personal representative in Rome and a schemer of the first rank who had already managed to seal a close friendship with the pope. The friendship Manning formed with Talbot was to play a most important role in his rise to power.

Assigned to study at the Academia Ecclesiastica (a nursery of cardinals), the former archdeacon of Chichester was not exactly thrilled to be back in the classroom. But he was soon able to skip the lectures and study instead under the direction of the celebrated theologians Giovanni Perrone and Passagilia. He was also honored by regular invitations from Pius IX who, as he recalled in his journal, "he saw nearly every month, and . . . spoke with him . . . freely on many things. It was the beginning of the confi-

---

[32]Ibid., p. 617.
[33]Gray, *Cardinal Manning,* p. 140.
[34]Ibid., p. 151.

dence which was never broken . . . I owe to Cardinal Wiseman and to Pius IX all that has befallen me in my Catholic life . . . [which] has come upon me without any seeking."[35]

Trouble with Dr. Errington and the Old Catholics

Although invited to stay in the pope's entourage, Manning wanted only to do the work of a simple priest. He returned to London and plunged into pastoral work with the same energy and efficiency he had shown as a parson. He was soon sought after as a preacher and was especially successful in making converts among the elite of London society, one of them being the lawyer Edward Badeley, who had represented the bishop of Exeter in the Gorham case.

Manning also proved to be just the kind of able and efficient administrator that Wiseman needed. One of Wiseman's concerns was the plight of the miserable London Irish poor who were neglected by the Church. He tried to find a religious order that would agree to work among them but none of the five he consulted found it a feasible mission. With Manning back from Rome, Wiseman now had the man to take on this difficult assignment and to found the order of priests that Wiseman wanted. Modeling the order on one founded by Charles Borromeo two hundred and fifty years before, Manning called these priests the Oblates of St. Charles. On arrival at Bayswater, Manning found a church without a roof, the relic of a previous attempt to establish a Catholic presence. Within a year Manning had readied the church—whose Gothic style had been Italianized—for an opening in July 1857 attended by a host of the Catholic aristocratic and clerical elite. His progress was incredible. By 1865 he had established three more churches and eight schools serving some 790 children. His oblates now numbered over twenty members. His biographer Purcell refers to the almost infinite variety of works large and small in which he was engaged.[36]

While Wiseman and the pope looked on in admiration, there was considerably less enthusiasm in other quarters of the Church, especially among the "old Catholics." These were members of families that had lived under the penal laws for generations and had survived by minding their own business and keeping to themselves. They were conservative with little taste for the

Roman practices and devotions that Wiseman and Manning were trying to introduce. Their piety was undemonstrative. They liked a sober mass with little ceremony and little music and were suspicious of such things as the rosary or the invocations of the saints. They felt little personal loyalty to the pope although they respected his authority in an abstract way.

Converts such as Newman and Manning who came barging into the Church at full tilt were at odds with this mentality in many ways, and the old Catholics resented their attitude of intellectual superiority, their enthusiasm for things Roman, and their ostentatious piety. "Where old English priests had eschewed even black coats, convert priests gloried in sporting Roman collars and in parading in cassocks and birettas."[37]

The leader of the old Catholics was a formidable prelate, Dr. George Errington, a conscientious, uncompromising, straightforward cleric whose family tree boasted numerous martyrs. His huge stature and hawk-like countenance bespoke a man who relished combat. He soon found in Manning an opponent worthy of his steel. Their differences arose over the kind of training that should be given in the seminary, specifically in St. Edmund's, the local seminary. The tradition of the place was best described as gentlemanly.

Manning predictably wanted a much sterner kind of model; or as he put it, he wished to instill the "ascendancy of Rome over every other kind of spirit." The basic reforms he favored would, he believed, produce a more learned, more disciplined, and more ascetic type of priest, one who could hold his own against the priests of the religious orders. As things stood, the educated laity found their needs unmet by the typical secular priest and were seeking out the religious priests. With Wiseman's help, Manning was able to get some of his oblates on the staff of St. Edmunds. But things did not improve. Manning wrote to his friend Talbot in August 1860 about "the smoking (and drinking) that goes on . . . that the Oblates are hated as 'sneaks,' because they enforce rules; that if a student makes a visit to the Blessed Sacrament he is an Oblate; at which I say *Deo Gratias.*"[38]

Errington realized that the oblates intended to Romanize the institution along Manning's lines. His response was typically unequivocal. The two men locked horns and for two years the tempest raged. Errington had allies among the canons of the Cathedral Chapter, upon whose dislike of Manning he could rely. (One of them, in a characteristic burst of tut-tuttery,

[37] Gray, *Cardinal Manning*, p. 146.
[38] Purcell, *Life of Cardinal Manning*, Vol. II, pp. 124–125.

labeled Manning "a forward piece.") But Manning's influence in Rome was his ace. His friend George Talbot, the confidante of the pope, called the old English Catholics "one of the greatest evils in England," while Manning reported to Talbot that "we have two great antagonists, the Protestant Association of Bayswater [founded to counteract Manning's success there] and the Chapter of Westminster."[39] When Wiseman was accused of letting Manning run his diocese he rebutted the charge but said there was no way that he could keep such a priest at a distance, for "in all England there is not a priest who, in double the time, has done what Dr. Manning has for the advantage of the Catholic Church."[40]

Errington's stand had pitted him against Wiseman, who soon realized that he was in an impossible situation. If the division was to be healed, Errington would have to go. The pope agreed and in two audiences begged Errington to go gracefully. But Errington was not one to back down and refused the offer of another diocese. Finally he was stripped of his post and his right of succession and ended up doing parish work, happy to be out of church politics for good. Ironically, Rome upheld his side of the issue when they ordered the oblates out of St. Edmunds.

An Ultra Roman on the Throne of Westminster

At this point, however, the pope was preoccupied with much weightier matters than the oblates. In a deal with Cavour, the prime minister of Sardinia-Piedmont, Napoleon III betrayed the pope and let Cavour's troops march in to take over the Papal States and then massacre the papal army at Castelfidardo in September 1860. Within two months, all that remained of the thousand-year-old papal kingdom was Rome and a small piece of territory around it. Using his spiritual weapons, the only ones left, in his famous Syllabus of Errors of 1864, Pius condemned Cavour's ideology of "Progress, Liberalism, and Modern Civilization."

Most Englishmen were horrified to hear the pope condemn progress (the ultimate blasphemy, as Robert Gray says), but Manning thought the syllabus was inspired, infallible, and one of the "greatest acts of his pontificate."[41] For him the temporal power of the pope was divinely guaranteed and the effort to destroy it a sign of the advent of the anti-Christ. His passionate

[39] Gray, *Cardinal Manning,* pp. 166, 168.
[40] Ibid., p. 171.
[41] Ibid., p. 175.

conviction on this score strained his relations with Gladstone, which were resumed only after a ten-year gap. Even Rome found some of Manning's statements on the subject extreme. In regard to his friendship with Newman, which he had always professed to value deeply, the issue of temporal power caused a split that was never healed. Newman with his deep historical sense could never believe, as Manning seemed to, in temporal power as a datum of revelation. It was remarkable that the friendship of the two lasted as long as it did, considering Newman's personal touchiness and his lack of sympathy with Manning's type of ultra ultramontanism.[42] Newman instead leaned toward Lord Acton's type of open Catholicism (Acton later believed that Newman himself was an ultramontane at heart).[43] But for Manning, Newman was simply not Roman enough. Manning was quite fearful of a resurgence of the old Anglican and Gallican spirit in the English Church in spite of what Wiseman had done to scotch it. Wiseman's suffragan bishops, for instance, were in Manning's opinion still contaminated with it. For their part the bishops found Manning "extreme, exaggerated, contentious."[44]

Newman now complained of the "dull tyranny of Manning" and began to suspect Manning as the cause of certain troubles he began having with the Roman authorities. He thought his suspicions confirmed when his plan to establish an Oratory at Oxford fell afoul of Rome and the bishops. Manning, he believed, was behind it all. But he was wrong. It was true that Manning had very strong opinions about the dangers to the faith of young Catholics attending Oxford, and that he opposed Newman's presence there as likely to attract Catholic students. But Manning's anti-Oxford view was standard Catholic policy at the time, and he was innocent of any personal vendetta against the Oratorian in the matter. Unfortunately for Manning's reputation, however, his part in keeping Newman out of Oxford established him as "the demon figure in that powerful and insinuating Newmanite lore which has dominated the history of nineteenth-century English Catholicism."[45]

Another supposed blot on Manning's escutcheon was the charge that he wormed his way into the chair of Westminster by unworthy schemes—supposedly through his contacts with Talbot in Rome. In fact it was the canons of Westminster (Manning called them the incompetents) who set the

---

[42]See p. 42.
[43]John Edward Dalbert Acton, liberal Catholic and prominent historian.
[44]Gray, *Cardinal Manning*, p. 185.
[45]Ibid., p. 193.

stage for Manning's appointment when they sent in Errington's name as their choice for the seat. The pope was outraged and began a month of devotions to the Holy Spirit for guidance. Manning himself urged Talbot to work for the choice of Bishop Ullathorne or another priest, a Dr. Cornthwaite, for the job. That he himself would be chosen he thought unimaginable, for "I have consciously offended Protestants, Anglicans, Gallican Catholics, national Catholics and worldly Catholics and the Government and public opinion in England which is running down the Church and the Holy See in all ways and all day long."[46]

But the pope did choose him for the post, after, he said, hearing the voice of the Holy Spirit himself telling him to choose Manning. On May 8, 1865, Manning received the official notice of his appointment as archbishop of Westminster. Although Manning's numerous enemies accepted the blow with magnanimity, Newman was scarcely overjoyed and thought it would be a great trial to the old Catholics in the priesthood. Manning prepared himself for his awesome task by making a retreat during which he recognized some truth in his critics' charges that he was imperious, presumptive, sharp. But he saw this as unavoidable: "When I was in a system of compromise I tried to mediate, reconcile and unite together those who differed. When I entered a system which, being divine, is definite and uncompromising, I threw myself with my whole soul and strength into its mind, will and action . . . Less definite, positive, uncompromising, aggressive, I can never be."[47]

Manning as an archbishop was as indefatigable as ever and even more so. As one of his canons said: "He was always ready to listen to everyone and to help everyone, and to take part in every good work."[48] One undertaking that called forth his amazing energy was his part in securing the definition of papal infallibility. The movement to define the infallibility of the pope at an ecumenical council gained great headway in the 1860s. There were many reasons for this development, not least of which was the feeling that the authority of the Church, assailed on all sides, needed reinforcement. Manning was in total agreement with this view. After all, he had left the Anglican Church at great personal cost because he finally realized its total lack of authority, and he was convinced that the papacy was the only bulwark against the faith-destroying forces of rationalism and atheism.

[46]Ibid., p. 199.
[47]Ibid., p. 204.
[48]Ibid., p. 206.

He poured all his energy into the movement and soon earned Newman's barbs as part of "the insolent and aggressive faction" that was pushing for a definition of infallibility. The council opened on December 8, 1869, and Manning soon emerged as the chief whip of the infallibilist party. He managed to get himself nominated to the all-important *Deputatio de Fide,* which drafted the definition of infallibility, and he was behind the maneuvers that excluded opponents from this committee. When he heard that Gladstone, at the behest of Lord Acton, might induce the European powers to foreclose the council, Manning sent Gladstone a solemn warning against such an action. Through his private access to the pope he was able to exert great influence on the proceedings, earning himself the nickname "the devil of the council."

The definition was promulgated on July 18, 1870, amid the crash of thunder and lightning that flashed through the aula and rained shards of glass down around the papal throne. For Manning the scene evoked images of Mt. Sinai and the ten commandments. Even though the definition was much more qualified than he wished, he was overjoyed. He immediately issued an extreme interpretation that extended infallibility to a whole range of church teachings beyond obvious dogmas. His erstwhile associates in the Anglican Church looked on in anger and amazement at a former archdeacon who was more papal than the pope. Newman looked on only in sadness and bowed before "adorable, inscrutable Providence."

Champion of the Poor and the Workers

Manning saw as one of his primary tasks the need to raise the social awareness of the Catholic community. In fact, his impact on the Catholic social conscience was profound. Until he arrived on the scene, British Social Catholicism was decidedly paternalistic. Like Lacordaire he insisted that the Church must actively ally itself with the people if Christianity was to survive. To further this effort in the Catholic Church, he recommended recruiting priests from the middle class and from the Irish instead of relying solely on the old upper-class English families. Manning abjured the social lethargy of able Catholics, noting that the greatest works of social betterment in England—the temperance movement, the warfare against traffic in young girls, and social legislation on behalf of the working class—had all begun outside the Church.

Manning got to work immediately on concrete institutional needs. One of his most pressing concerns was to provide some Catholic education for the poor of his diocese, and also to establish orphanages and reformatories for children who would otherwise be put in surroundings inimical to their faith. Putting aside plans to build a metropolitan cathedral at Westminster ("Could I leave 20,000 children without education, and drain my friends and my flock to pile up stones and bricks?"), he threw himself into fund-raising with great success. By the spring of 1867, over twenty new schools had been opened.[49]

Manning's impact on the Catholic social conscience was profound. However, it is important to realize that Manning did not create out of nothing. A number of initiatives already taken by both priests and lay people had prepared the ground. When Manning arrived on the scene the Catholic Church in England was a church of the poor—mainly Irish immigrants, an Irish proletariat seemingly rootless and densely packed in slums. The Church's ability to connect with these people, to sustain their faith, and to win their devotion attracted a number of educated socially sensitive spirits devoted to their welfare. This was especially true in Scotland. Not that there was much radicalism. As outsiders Irish Catholics remained conservative; and many of them having suffered from the petty discrimination of official-dom in prisons and workhouses, they were deeply suspicious of govern-ment.

Manning's social consciousness had developed early, in his days as Anglican vicar of Lavington where he had observed the lot of the poor agricultural laborers. As archdeacon of Chichester he retained this concern for the poor, and, for example, devoted one of his pastoral charges to the need of the farmworkers for longer holidays. After his conversion he spent eight years in Bayswater, London, an area with large numbers of Irish Catholics and therefore one of London's poorest sections. The church he served here, St. Mary of the Angels, still stands gaunt and bare among the jumble of flats, coalyards, and warehouses. He called the years spent here his happiest. He gained first-hand experience of the miserable state of the Irish poor and grew to love their rich brogue and honest sincerity. Later he would say, "My politics are social politics . . . my radicalism [goes] down to the roots of the sufferings of the people."[50]

Manning saw that the Anglican Church had lost its hold on the people by being too closely identified with the government, the ruling aristocracy, and

[49] Purcell, *Life of Cardinal Manning,* Vol. II, p. 355.

[50] Vincent Alan McClelland, *Cardinal Manning* (New York: Oxford University Press, 1962), p. 19.

the landlords. He saw a similar insensitivity at work within the higher ranks of his adopted Church, and he had little sympathy with priests like Newman who seemed so little conscious of the need for social reform. For Manning, social reform and Christian doctrine were inseparable and his sermons rarely lacked a social theme.

He remained throughout his career a great champion of the underdog, believing that Christianity must be practical and attentive to the needs of the poor. He made no bones about excoriating the wealthier members of his flock for their self-indulgent and wasteful luxuries, their jewels, the ornaments and baubles bought with money that could have been spent on orphans and poor families. Nor was it enough to give generously to charity. In fact, he insisted, this was the coldest form of charity. He urged Catholics to gain firsthand knowledge of the problems of the poor by actually feeding the hungry, tending the sick, and clothing the naked with their own hands, and even sharing their lives. Manning's judgments on British society were fearless and severe. He felt that its besetting sins were pride, arrogance, and presumptiousness. He also felt that the upper classes were increasingly corrupt, and he predicted a calamity if the capitalist system did not reform itself.

Manning's views on the rights and duties of labor were most emphatic. "There is no justice, mercy or compassion in the Plutocracy. There is my creed." In 1874 he told an audience at the Leeds Mechanics' Institute: "I claim for Labour, and the skill which is always acquired by Labour, the rights of Capital. It is Capital in its truest sense."

On domestic economic issues he held very decided opinions. He realized that Britain was losing its industrial supremacy as its work force fell increasingly behind in the technical skills needed to compete in a changing world.

He had strong forebodings of a coming great social upheaval. In 1886 a severe recession crippled the economy and he could see the ravages of hunger and starvation all around him. While exhausting his own resources in almsgiving, he continued to insist that individual charity was not enough. As part of a deputation to Downing Street, he decried the theorists whose laissez-faire economics falsely justified the exploitation of the weak and enabled these theorists to tolerate conditions that they were not called on to suffer. He criticized the powerful for their sheer indifference to the suffering they caused. Society existed for man, not man for society, he asserted. The duty of government to assist the destitute must come before its duty to maintain an open market.

When his critics called him a socialist he was unperturbed. "I would call it Christianity," was his retort. Socialism was just a label, he said on another occasion, used by reactionaries against advocates of change. Anyone who protests against "free contracts" or "starvation wages" was called a socialist. Anyone who could not stomach the dogmas of economic liberalism was labeled a radical. While quick to repudiate such associations, he was happy to be called a Mosaic radical—that is, one who tried to get down to the roots of the suffering of his people. Sometimes he could sound like Marx but he made a firm distinction between state intervention and state control. In Manning's view, the government should facilitate works of public utility but should never be the actual employer, lest the arrangement devolve toward a dangerous centralization. He noted on another occasion that socialism "identifies social evils with society itself, and kills the patient to cure his maladies."

Although a strong defender of the right of private property, Manning did not subscribe to speculative social theories. The real source of his ideas was the New Testament. When Thomas Huxley chided him for talking about the worker's right to a job, he firmly replied, "I am very sure what Our Lord and his Apostles would do if they were in London."[51] Manning's actions were also informed by a deep sense of compassion. One friend, Lady Dilke, noted that when he spoke of the misery of the poor his countenance reflected acute anguish, and she went on to say that it was not only "his brilliant understanding . . . [but] his passionate capacity for feeling that made him one of the most striking personalities I have known."[52]

Manning's passion for social justice only increased with the years. He was especially insistent on the need of the Church to stand on the side of the people. It was imperative in his mind if the Church was ever to win back the masses. He was most anxious to have the Church identify itself with the cause of Labor and wanted the Holy See to support every movement to broaden the rights and liberties of the working classes. In his lecture on "The Rights and Dignity of Labour," which he revised in 1887, he declared that he was neither a communist nor a revolutionary but he insisted that a worker's labor was his capital, that it should have the rights of capital, and that both forms of capital—the capital of strength and skill and the capital of money—need each other. "Whatever rights capital possesses, labour possesses."[53] Against the dogma of the political economists of his day, he argued in favor of some form of regulation in the labor market. "If the hours

[51] Gray, *Cardinal Manning*, p. 305.
[52] Ibid.
[53] Purcell, *Life of Cardinal Manning*, Vol. II, p. 644.

of labour resulting from the unregulated sale of a man's strength and skill shall lead to the destruction of domestic life, to the neglect of children, to turning wives and mothers into living machines, and of fathers and husbands into—what shall I say, creatures of burden?—I will not use any other word—who rise up before the sun, and come back . . . wearied and able only to take food and to lie down to rest; the domestic life of men exists no longer . . . [and at the same time] a piling-up of wealth like mountains in the possession of classes or of individuals . . . we dare not go on in this path."[54]

As his strong views became widely known, social reformers of all stripes made their way to Archbishop's House to get his blessing on their causes. John Ruskin, the English man of letters who called for radical social change and espoused a form of Christian communism, found Manning a kindred spirit. Even though Ruskin found Manning's narrow Catholicism uncongenial, the two became fast friends. Another visitor was Henry George, the American whose views were much more radical than Manning's. He managed to tone them down for the benefit of his host and later was able to claim Manning as a friend.

The Great Dock Strike of 1889

The event that positively immortalized Manning in the annals of labor history was his decisive intervention in the great dock strike in the autumn of 1889. The strike was a new development that caught the world by surprise as it demonstrated the power of even unskilled labor when organized. By 1889 conditions on the wharves had deteriorated and unrest was on the rise. Ben Tillett, who had previously organized the Gas-workers' Union and gotten them an eight-hour day, was now the leader of the dock laborers. Tillett presented several demands to the dock directors including a raise of one pence per hour. The raise proposal was rejected and the men struck on August 14. Soon the stevedores, watermen, sailors, firemen, porters, riggers, scrapers, engineers, ballast heavers, and shipwrights all joined in the strike and the huge London port was paralyzed.

Manning, always fearful of impending chaos, was acutely aware of the dangers of the situation. He watched the tens of thousands marching through the streets under the eye of the police and saw the possibility at any moment of a bloody and disastrous confrontation. He knew very well that

[54]Gray, *Cardinal Manning*, pp. 646–647.

any fanatic, drunkard, or fool with a match could at once have turned the whole port into a blazing inferno with incalculable losses. Now eighty-two, he decided nonetheless that he could not stand by. He had links with both parties to the dispute: His father and brother had been dock company directors, and he also had close contacts with the trade union leadership through his friendship with Ben Tillett. Manning had previously encouraged Tillett during his work organizing the Gas-workers' Union. His intervention was an act of great courage, given the potential for catastrophe and the risk of public censure to himself. The next several weeks would test to the limit his great qualities of force of will and tenacity of purpose.

The story was told at the time that Manning went to see Ben Tillett, who was not home. He sat down to wait, and when Tillett finally returned his landlady told him that a priest had been waiting for him all afternoon. Tillett found him reading the latest adventures of Sherlock Holmes in the *Strand* magazine. Manning asked him if the strikers could hold out much longer and if they were in the state of grace. "I don't know about that but they're certainly in the state of hunger," Tillett replied.

Manning's first sortie—a meeting with the joint committee of dock company directors—was not encouraging. They were as unmoved by his plea to forego importing scab labor from Holland as they were unimpressed by his predictions of revolution. "Never in my life," he said, "have I preached to so impenitent a congregation."

A Committee of Conciliation was then formed consisting of Manning, the bishop of London, and several other prominent figures. They proposed a compromise that would fix the hourly wage at sixpence starting on January 1. Both sides accepted this proposal after much wrangling. But when Tillett and Burns, the other strike leader, brought it back to their colleagues they rejected it, insisting on September 4 as the starting date—to which a few of the companies had already agreed. At this point the bishop of London deserted the committee. Of those remaining, Manning alone continued to make a serious effort to keep the two sides negotiating.

On Sunday, September 8, he met Tillett who had just returned from a rally in Hyde Park Square; Tillett told Manning the workers were ready to accept October 1 as the starting date. But it was clear that the workers were in no mood to make any further concessions. Besides the natural pride that drives adversaries in a heated quarrel and the feeling that victory was imminent, their morale was also greatly strengthened by the support they were getting from the press and by the large infusion of funds coming in from sympathizers, especially in Australia.

Manning decided his only chance to break the stalemate would be to meet with the entire strike committee. The meeting was held in the classroom of a school on Kirby Street. Manning urged the men to accept November 4 as a compromise starting date but they resisted strenuously. The heated debate went on for hours. Finally, in the last great speech of his career, Manning made a tremendous emotional appeal reminding the men of the sufferings of the women and children and of the great public issues involved. The hour was now late and at last a vote was taken. Manning's compromise carried.

"The Cardinal's peace," one newspaper proclaimed, as congratulations— among them those of the pope and even Cardinal Newman—poured into the Archbishop's House. Manning was called the primate of all England.[55] In the next May Day procession the workers carried his picture alongside that of Karl Marx. There were of course the snide remarks of those who had no love for the cardinal, not least among them the *Times,* his enemy. Even within the Church there were grumblings. Many of the old Catholics thought his whole performance unseemly; some of them attributed his actions to senility. One of these was Cardinal Vaughan, Manning's close assistant and successor. But Manning's witness to the efficacy of social Catholicism was an inspiration to Catholics around the world and his name was revered in workmen's clubs in France, Germany, and Belgium no less than by the Irish dockers of the East End.

While he had tried to preserve an attitude of neutrality during the strike, Manning confessed afterward that the more he thought about it the more he sided with labor. As ruinous for all sides as strikes could be, he still saw them as sometimes labor's only resort when all else failed. He noted the growing disproportion between the enormous profits of the capitalists and the scanty wages of the workers and he knew the exploiters would not give in without a struggle.[56] "Brutal" was his word for an article in the *Times* which "claims for Capital the absolute dictatorship of labour."[57]

Apostle of Social Catholicism

Prevented now by advanced age from accepting an invitation to the famous Social Congress at Liege in 1890, he addressed the delegates in a letter that

---

[55]Manning was made a cardinal in 1875; Newman in 1879.

[56]Gray, *Cardinal Manning,* p. 311.

[57]McClelland, *Cardinal Manning,* p. 148.

set forth the regulatory measures he deemed essential, including Sunday rest, freedom of association and arbitration, limits on children's and women's labor, and an eight-hour day. He even proposed some regulation of profits and salary as a guide for free contracts between labor and capital. "I do not believe," he said, "it ever to be possible to establish pacific relations between employers and workers without acknowledging, setting and establishing by public act a right and proper measure to regulate profits and wages, a measure by which all free contracts between capital and labor would be governed."

Manning and Church–Labor Relations in the U.S.

Manning was heavily involved in the outcome of other affairs with great significance for the future of Social Catholicism. One involved an American priest, Father Edward McGlynn, pastor of St. Stephen's Church in New York City, who regularly appeared on public platforms with Henry George who called for nationalizing the land. McGlynn was able to fend off his enemies in the Roman Curia with the help of his boss Cardinal McClosky, a friend of labor. But when Michael Corrigan succeeded McClosky, a new song was heard in the land—a dirge for labor, as Corrigan's social conscience was Neanderthalian. Corrigan ordered McGlynn to cease his advocacy for George and when McGlynn refused, Corrigan suspended him. When McGlynn was summoned to Rome and refused to go, Corrigan ousted him from his parish. At this point Cardinal Gibbons of Baltimore stepped into the fray. Like Manning, Gibbons believed strongly in the need of the Church to ally itself with the cause of the people and the trade unions. He urged McGlynn to take his case to Rome and present it as a matter of principle. Gibbons then learned that McGlynn was due to be excommunicated and George's *Progress and Poverty* to be put on the Index of forbidden books. He appealed for help to Manning, who in his role as a member of the Congregation of the Index saw to it that George's work was not condemned. The rest of the matter was cleared up a few years later when the excommunication of McGlynn was lifted and he was restored to his parish.

The other American affair that heavily involved Manning was the fracas over the Knights of Labor, a union founded in 1869 which began to grow rapidly after 1878. In 1886 it was headed by a devout Catholic, Terrence

Powderly, and had received the benediction of Cardinal Gibbons who declared that "any and every movement consistent with justice and fair dealing toward their employer and having for its end the amelioration of the conditions of the labouring class deserved encouragement."[58] As the union neared the height of its influence, antagonistic prelates in Canada and the United States called for its condemnation, suggesting that it be banned under Rome's prohibition of secret societies for employing some of the same rituals—secret handshake, password, oath, and initiation ceremony—as the Masons.

Gibbons saw clearly the enormous rift such a condemnation would mean for church–labor relations, and set sail for Rome to wage the crucial battle himself. Manning apprised the Curia of the state of affairs while he simultaneously plied Gibbons with valuable inside information—whose opinions counted, who could be won over, and the like. In his Memorial (or report) to the Curia, Gibbons took care to quote Manning about the need for the Church henceforth to deal with the masses rather than with parliaments and princes, and on the danger of alienating the working classes. Manning kept up his own efforts by writing a letter to the *Tablet* openly praising the Knights. The piece was picked up and widely reproduced in Catholic journals around Europe: "The Knights of Labour," wrote Manning, "and the English trade unions represent the right of labour and the rights of association for its defence."[59]

The dual efforts of Gibbons and Manning wrought a success. The Knights were not condemned and a grave setback for Social Catholicism was averted. Gibbons was so grateful for Manning's help that he journeyed to London to thank him personally. Many years later Gibbons saluted his "indomitable courage and perserverance" in bringing about a happy end to an affair in which the Church faced the choice of either antagonizing the wealthy and the powerful or letting down the working classes. Thanks largely to Manning, she made the right decision.

Support for Irish Home Rule

No account of Manning is complete without taking note of his insistence on justice for Ireland. His appointment as archbishop coincided with the return of the Irish question to the forefront of English politics. Manning left

[58] Ibid., p. 155.
[59] Ibid., p. 157.

no doubt about where he stood. His "Letter to Lord Grey" was a denunciation of centuries of English misrule over that tragic land. He blamed the
policies of England for the rise of Fenian terrorists. What else reasonably
could be expected, he exclaimed, from a people who saw nearly every acre
of their land confiscated? "If poverty was ever afflicted by one nation on
another, it has been inflicted on Ireland by England,"[60] he once said. He
also said, "It's fortunate for my neck that I was not born in Ireland. Had the
Land of the Saints given me my birth I would have been hung long ago."[61]

He often lectured his old friend Gladstone on the evils of English policy
in Ireland, and in particular called for the abolition of the Protestant supremacy in Ireland. He was therefore delighted when Gladstone, now the
British prime minister, successfully passed the Irish Church bill disestablish-
ing the Anglican Church in Ireland, "for Manning the heaviest blow the
Reformation and the Royal Supremacy have ever received."[62] Gladstone,
in turn, thanked Manning for his "firm, constant, and discriminating support" during the battle over the bill.

In 1889 Manning was delighted when the English electorate appeared
ready to support Gladstone's alliance with Parnell's Irish nationalists in the
effort to carry home rule for Ireland. But this opportunity was lost when
Parnell was named by Captain William Henry O'Shea as the corespondent
in a divorce suit he brought against his wife. O'Shea conferred with Manning before making a public announcement of his intentions, and Manning
tried to stave off the disaster by insisting on the need for more evidence of
O'Shea's wife's infidelity. But when the scandal finally broke in November
1890, Manning warned the Irish hierarchy to break with Parnell and not to
put politics before faith and morals. He was equally emphatic in urging
Gladstone to demand the removal of Parnell from the head of the Irish
nationalists. As Robert Gray says, "The tone of Manning's letters suggested
that he was addressing a political novice rather than the greatest Prime
Minister of the nineteenth century."[63]

His advocacy of home rule for Ireland was always tempered by the need
to have Irish Catholic MPs in the English Parliament to safeguard the
interests of English Catholics. One solution he favored would have arrogated

[60]Gray, *Cardinal Manning*, p. 223.

[61]Ibid., p. 314.

[62]Purcell, *Life of Cardinal Manning*, Vol II, p. 393.

[63]Gray, *Cardinal Manning*, p. 313.

extensive authority to local Irish government while maintaining national representation in Westminster, but this failed to win support.

Last Days

Manning lived long enough to see his labors on behalf of Social Catholicism vindicated by the monumental encyclical *Rerum Novarum*, in which Leo XIII set down authoritatively many of the ideas Manning had long espoused—ideas that he shared with other leaders of Social Catholicism throughout the Catholic world. In a letter Leo sent to Manning with a copy of the encyclical, the pope expressed his gratitude for the "important communication" Manning had sent him. At Leo's request, Manning translated the encyclical into English. He presented the encyclical together with a commentary on it that constituted his "testament on the social question." Published in the *Dublin Review* of July 1891, it declared: "All of a sudden they [the civil powers] find that the millions of the world sympathise with the Church, which has compassion on the multitude, rather than with the State or plutocracy which has weighed so heavily upon them."[64] Noting in particular that the pontiff condemned socialism yet admitted the need for the intervention of the state, Manning buttressed the argument by pointing to social legislation such as the abolition of slavery or the mining and factory inspection laws, legislation that had already more than proven its worth. In support of the pope's call for the protection of women and children, Manning argued that if the relations of labor and capital were just, women would not be forced to work outside as well as inside the home.

Manning's physical decline in his last years was very gradual and he was blessed with full control of his faculties to the very end. Death came swiftly when a bout with bronchial pneumonia took him to his bed on Saturday, January 9, 1892. By Wednesday his deterioration was evident and he was barely able to whisper, as, clothed in rochet and mitre, he received the last solemn rite for a prelate from the assembled canons. After reciting the definitions of the Vatican Council he murmured: "It is pleasant to have been able to do everything." Before losing consciousness he fumbled under his pillow, pulled out a little dog-eared book, and gave it to Bishop Vaughan, saying, "Into this little book my dearest wife wrote her prayers and meditations. Not a day has passed since her death on which I have not prayed and meditated from this book. All the good I may have done, all the good I may

---

[64] *Dublin Review,* (July 1891), p. 167.

have been, I owe to her." His last coherent words were in Latin: *"Deposui jugum, opus meum consummatum est"* (I have laid down the yoke, my work is done).

The funeral of Henry Edward Manning took place on January 21, 1892. It was an eloquent witness to the unique place he held in the hearts of Englishmen that, although the eldest son of the Prince of Wales and heir to the throne died on the same day as Manning, it was Manning's funeral that drew the largest number of people into the streets of London. As he lay in state from Saturday to Tuesday, traffic in the neighborhood of Victoria was brought to a halt. On Sunday afternoon a queue of mourners four abreast stretched for more than half a mile in spite of police efforts to keep the line moving. And on Wednesday, when his coffin was borne in procession, the pavements along the four-mile route were jammed not only with Irish but with English of every class and creed. All in all it was the most impressive demonstration of mass emotion of the late Victorian period.[65]

How has Manning been remembered? His fate in this regard was indeed unfortunate. His huge popularity with the working classes and the poor could not outbalance the influence of opinion-makers in and out of the church who had little fondness for his memory. His controversial stands and hard-hitting criticism of the rich had made him enemies. Intellectuals in general saw his ultramontanism as the mark of some strain of mental deficiency. Political conservatives saw him tinged with extreme socialist and radical views.

The discord between Newman and himself was perhaps Manning's heaviest cross. He lamented the fact that though he had always tried to speak and act in union with the Holy See, Newman's name was used against him to sow ill-will and dissension. If only the two could have spoken and acted together instead of at cross-purposes, had they but worked in unison, "the unity of Catholic truth would have been irresistible."[66] Now that Manning was gone, adherents of Newman accused him unfairly of pursuing a personal vendetta against their hero.

Most savage of all was the portrait of Manning sketched by Lytton Strachey in his widely read *Eminent Victorians*. Building on the tendentious biography by Edmund Purcell, Strachey portrayed Manning as an unscrupulous careerist schemer "whose appetite for supreme dominion had been whetted by long years of enforced abstinence and the hated simulations of

[65] Gray, *Cardinal Manning,* pp. 1–3.
[66] Ibid., p. 282.

submission." His relations with Newman are described by Strachey as "the meeting of the eagle and the dove; there was a hovering, a swoop, and then the quick beak and the relentless talons did their work."[67] Nonsense like this helped to fix the image of Manning, even among many Catholics, as on the whole a rather unsavory ecclesiastic, redeemed only to some extent by his progressive views on social reform. Robert Gray's recent biography goes far to rehabilitate him. Gray's conclusion is worth quoting: "When the last sneer has been sneered at his careerist instincts, and the last *frisson* of intellectual superiority extracted from consideration of his theological extravagances, consider the bare fact that remains. A man of rare ability, ruthless will, dominating temperament and high ambition began his life as the slave of secular glory and ended it as the hero of the poor, the weak, the outcast, and the despised."[68]

Manning's Legacy for Social Catholicism

1. Manning carried on the work of Ozanam and Ketteler in furtherance of social reform. He associated the concern for social justice with the message of the Gospel so emphatically that this association remained a permanent part of the English Church's witness in spite of its generally conservative character.

2. His intervention in the great London dock strike was crucial to bringing about a settlement. It sealed his alliance with labor and won him the affection of the workers who formed a great cortege at his funeral, once more carrying his picture along with that of Karl Marx. The fact that a cardinal carried such weight with the workers dramatized for the whole world the progress of Social Catholicism.

3. His success in dissuading Rome from condemning the Knights of Labor was a signal contribution to the cause of Social Catholicism. Such a move by Rome would have alienated many members of the working class and played into the hands of the communists.

4. He played a key role in the preparation of Pope Leo XIII's encyclical *Rerum Novarum*, which laid the groundwork for Catholic social teaching even to the present day.

[67] New York: Modern Library, 1933, p. 85.
[68] Gray, *Cardinal Manning*, p. 327.

SEVEN

Albert de Mun (1841–1914): Knight of the Syllabus, from Royalist to Reformer

B Y THE TIME Count Albert de Mun had finished his maiden speech in the French Chamber of Deputies in March 1876, the anticlericals grasped one thing—a new champion of the Church had arrived on the scene. Within a few weeks they discovered something more: Unlike the typical well-bred, charming but empty-headed aristocrat, de Mun was a man to be reckoned with, a gifted orator and a strong personality. Léon Michel Gambetta, the anticlerical lion of the chamber, saluted him as another Montalembert. De Mun's political career would last nearly forty years and eventually win him universal respect as one of the great figures of the Third Republic.

He is also remembered as a champion of lost causes who devoted the first part of his career to the restoration of the monarchy and the restoration of the Church to a privileged position—two equally chimerical goals. When later he took up the cause of social reform, putting forward the most advanced ideas of his day, he was rejected by his fellow Catholics. The span of his career throws much light on the obstacles faced by Social Catholics under the pontificate of Pius X.

A Born Soldier

Albert de Mun was born at Lumigny near the Seine and the Marne in a chateau that still stands there. His family boasted an aristocratic pedigree extending well back to the Middle Ages. Through the centuries they had remained loyal to king and church. Albert's grandfather, an exception to the family rule, was a liberal, a lover of Madame de Staël, and a skeptic like many of his eighteenth-century peers. Nonetheless his son Adrien, the father of Albert, ran true to form as both an intense legitimist and a devout ultramontane Catholic.

The estate revenues of the de Muns were considerable and Albert grew up in a secure and comfortable family whose military tradition he intended to carry on. As he later admitted in his memoirs, he loved his horses and games more than his books, a preference he greatly regretted later on when he tried to make up for the lacunae in his education. He graduated from the military academy of St. Cyr, two-hundredth in a class of 249. An aristocrat to the marrow, he was, like his father, an intense and devout Catholic,

Albert de Mun

fervently ultramontane and fervently royalist. He was also a devoted friend of the Jesuits who had played an important part in his education.

The young cavalry officer's first assignment landed him in Algeria, the scene of frequent native uprisings. His romantic imagination had conjured up visions of the adventure and glory he would find in Africa but he found the reality quite different. The era of conquest was over and the job of the army was merely to secure the conquered territory while warding off occasional raids from wandering tribes. On one occasion his unit was attacked by Arabs at night, and the men did fight fiercely for their lives until help arrived at dawn. But most of their time was spent at tedious duties.

The four years he spent there were nevertheless an education for de Mun. He spent many hours in solitude, studying the desert flora and fauna while taking copious notes and developing a habit of close, accurate observation that stood him well throughout his life. He developed a keen interest in history that would become a passion. He found himself deeply impressed by the Islamic religion, which challenged him to a deeper appreciation of his own Catholic faith. And he was enthralled by the mystery of the desert with its infinite horizons and fantastic shapes constantly shifting with the wind under the pitiless sun. He recalled at times being swept into ecstasy while contemplating this landscape, his soul soaring above the material world—mystical moments when he felt within himself the unity of creation with the creator and a great sense of being at peace with the merciful Lord. Other times he felt just as deeply his identity as a sinner far from God. These experiences fortified his faith for the battles ahead with the enemies of the Church.

Algeria also fortified him in his love of France. At times he would be overcome by nostalgia for his *patrie* and he felt in the most searing way the bonds of blood, heart, and culture that tied him to his native land. "France!" he would cry out, not "la France" but rather "France" as though he were addressing a living person. Already he was beginning to sense a political destiny and a desire for glory in the nation's service in the war with Prussia that he knew was soon to come.

Origin of the Cercles

Come it did in July 1870. The young de Mun was assigned to a general's staff and by his heroism earned the Cross of the Legion of Merit. But following the shameful French defeat in 1871, de Mun ended up as a prisoner of war with a lot of time to think over the debacle and its cause. He was thus in a receptive mood when a Jesuit priest placed in his hands a copy of the royalist Émile Keller's *L'Encyclique du 8 Décembre et les Principes de 1789,* a study of the Syllabus of Errors (1864) and Pope Pius IX's condemnation of liberalism. Written five years before the war, the pamphlet deplored what Keller felt was the widespread moral decay in France and traced it to the French Revolution. The Revolution, he believed, removed the restraints of family, king, and church, and proclaimed the moral autonomy of the individual with its cry of *"Liberté, égalité, fraternité."* This extreme individualism destroyed the ancient guild system that united owner and worker together through bonds of mutual obligation. In the new capitalistic society the defenseless worker was handed over to the indifferent mercies of owners who enforced long hours for low wages. Keller saw the Syllabus of Errors as a protest against this inhuman situation. It opposed the spirit of economic individualism by proclaiming that men were not solitary beasts doomed to unending struggle with one another, but brothers bound together in the fellowship of Christ. But the pope's cry had gone unheard and Keller predicted that the workers would soon rebel and tear the country apart.

De Mun and his friend and fellow officer René de La Tour du Pin were startled by what they believed was the accuracy of Keller's insights. As Catholic aristocrats they had always despised the Revolution, its egalitarianism and its anticlericalism. Hence they were naturally receptive to Keller's linking of France's moral decay with the Revolution, and they had just seen evidence of it in the humiliating rout of their army under Prussian fire.

Shortly after de Mun's release from Prussian captivity, he was sent to take part in putting down the rebellion of the workers who on March 18, 1871, had set up the short-lived Paris Commune. The savagery on both sides appalled him. A fierce curse leveled at him by a dying prisoner shocked him profoundly and made him realize the terrible chasm that had opened up in France between the workers and the rest of the country. The upper classes, he was convinced, were totally ignorant of the conditions of the poor, and were content in their ignorance.

He and La Tour du Pin had hardly started puzzling over the key to this newly revealed problem of class conflict when de Mun came into contact with Maurice Maignen, a religious brother of the Congregation of the Brothers of St. Vincent de Paul. Maignen had been inspired to a ministry among the poor of Paris by Jean-Léon Le Prévost who had himself been drawn to works of charity among the poor by Frederick Ozanam. Maignen had helped Prévost found the Congregation of St. Vincent de Paul in 1845. They were convinced that there was a need for a new type of religious order that would join priests and laity in a common ministry to the poor.

In his memoirs, *Ma Vocation Sociale,* de Mun recalled how he had met Maignen who was then seeking funds for his young workers' club in the slums, and how impressed he was by Maignen: "Standing before me in plain laymen's clothes, gray-haired, gray-bearded with a slight smile and thoughtful face expressing both tenderness and strength." A natural aristocrat, de Mun thought, and detected under Maignen's controlled features the soul of a poet and the imagination of an artist.

Pointing out the window to the Tuileries, which had been left in ruins after the fighting, Maignen said to de Mun: "You yourselves are really responsible for this, the rich, the great, the successful who amused yourselves so lightheartedly within those ruined walls, who passed by the people without knowing them . . . their needs, their sufferings. I live with the people, and I tell you that for their part they do not hate you. They simply have no contact with you or you with them. Go to them with your heart open . . . and you will see that they will understand you."[1] These words made a deep impression on de Mun and he promised Maignen to do anything necessary to build a bridge with the workers.

A few days later the young men at Maignen's club, many of them sons of the massacred insurgents, were surprised to see before them a uniformed young officer with a bluff moustache. As they regarded him quizzically de Mun began to speak with great earnestness, urging them to be soldiers of Christ and to work for the renewal of France. Touched by his words they listened with increasing interest and at the end warmly applauded him. After the meeting was over he walked through the snowy streets for hours, savoring his experience with the sense that his life's work was opening up before him. He believed he had found a way of repairing the torn social fabric and recovering the workers for the Church: by establishing Maignen's clubs (Cercles) everywhere. They would be centers where workers could gather to relax, to get counseling and material help. They would be equipped with reading rooms and gymnasiums and would provide games of all kinds, even concerts. He was acutely aware of the Church's failure in regard to the poor. It had nothing to offer them besides occasional alms and charity and exhortations to accept their lot and look for their reward in the next life. What

[1]Benjamin Martin, *Count Albert de Mun* (Chapel Hill: The University of North Carolina Press, 1978), p. 13.

was terribly needed, de Mun saw, was an organized social effort, which the Cercles could provide. Most important, the Cercles as he envisaged them would involve participation by the members of the upper classes and especially the factory owners. They would be encouraged to meet with the workers and by mutual discussion come to a better understanding of each other's problems.

De Mun's overt loyalty to the pope stood him in good stead when he met with typical opposition from conservative bishops fearful of lay independence, and from factory owners who smelled a union rat. Pius IX blessed the Cercles in a note to de Mun in January 1872, and on April 7, 1872, they consecrated the first club—located in Belleville, where some of the worst excesses of the war with the Commune had taken place. Factory owners, army officers, and aristocrats mingled with the workers, who looked a little uneasy. De Mun hopped onto a chair and gave a brief speech that touched them all with its message of hope. Exhilarated by the cordial atmosphere, de Mun and La Tour du Pin left the meeting "drunk with victory."[2]

Unfortunately but perhaps inevitably de Mun's plan for the Cercles had built-in limitations that would diminish its potential. Bound by the prejudices of his class and his inbred sense of noblesse oblige, he made no provision for any real control by the workers themselves. His concept was hierarchical and paternalistic, with authority remaining in the hands of the *classes dirigeantes* (the upper classes). All activities both recreational and cultural as well as the programs for material assistance were to be controlled by the chaplain (usually a Jesuit) and the "sponsors" who were drawn from the owner class. Finally there were religious requirements: attendance at mass on certain occasions, even the wearing of a medal proclaiming the Immaculate Conception. As time went on, de Mun would see that benefaction was not enough: Universal social reforms must be brought to bear.

Even so, the growth of the Cercles was spectacular. By 1875 there were some 150 clubs nationwide with some 18,000 members—a success largely due to de Mun's outstanding talents as a speaker and organizer and his message of hope for people who were dispirited and divided. His hearers saw a tall, broad-shouldered officer in uniform, sporting a moustache, "his youthful handsome face . . . rugged and crinkled, [with] its high cheekbones . . . broad forehead and brown receding hair. He bore himself martially, but not stiffly, and in conversation his large gentle eyes belied the

[2]Ibid., p. 17.

sternness of his face."[3] The effect of his words was often electric and greeted with outbursts of applause and cheers. At one gathering a young worker ran up and planted a kiss on his cheek, exclaiming *"Mon capitaine,* you are the honor of your uniform." Back at the barracks de Mun could regularly be seen sitting at the corner of a table, busy at his correspondence while an orderly polished his boots and helped him with a change of uniform.

For the next twenty years the history of French Social Catholicism is largely the story of de Mun and the Cercles. As his movement picked up momentum it was eyed with hope by the conservatives who thought it might help the monarchists and clericals gain control over the working classes. The republicans rejected out of hand any movement led by royalists like de Mun and La Tour du Pin. As the republicans stepped up their attacks on the Church, the leading Catholic journalist Louis Veuillot urged de Mun to unleash his rhetoric and let them have it. De Mun readily complied, with a series of fiery speeches damning the Revolution and tracing the country's decay to its principles.

This activism was finally too much for the army, which needed to maintain at least the appearance of nonpolitical neutrality. An order was issued forbidding Paris-based officers to speak before any but military assemblies. De Mun was now faced with one of the gravest decisions of his life. If he wanted to continue his work with the Cercles he would have to leave the army—a terrible sacrifice *("très dur, plus dur que je ne l'avais pensé tout d'abord"*—"harder than I at first realized")[4] for a dedicated soldier like himself. But there was no way out. In October 1875 he placed his letter of resignation on his prie-dieu and offered his strength to the cause of God.

His Counterrevolution

Now out of uniform, de Mun reasoned that a political career offered the best prospect for promoting the agenda of the Cercles. With the help of the Church in 1876 he was able to win a seat in the National Assembly from the district of Pontivy in Brittany, a royalist, clerical stronghold. When the assembly's republican majority invalidated his election in February 1876 on the basis of clerical interference, he ran again and won a decisive victory. The Catholic press hailed him as the "Knight of the Syllabus," henceforth a popular tag.

[3] Ibid., p. 19.
[4] Letter quoted in Charles Molette, *Albert de Mun* (Paris: Beauchesne, 1970), p. 164.

Much of de Mun's political life would be spent in contest with the republicans, whose conception of life was fundamentally hostile to Catholicism. Liberal Protestantism, Kantian ethics, and Spencer and Darwin were some of the major influences on the republicans' world view. The cornerstone of their political creed was an almost religious faith in the French Revolution, which they felt had liberated Frenchmen from clerical domination. They believed they had fulfilled the promise of the Revolution in part by achieving universal male suffrage. Belief in progress was in fact essential to their faith and this was coupled with belief in the unlimited possibilities of human reason and science. Catholicism, on the other hand, they called a religion for idiots, and for many of them all forms of religion were suspect. One of their leaders, Jules Ferry, said their aim was to "organize humanity without God and without kings."[5]

The radical republican program was summed up in Gambetta's slogan *"Cléricalisme, voilà l'ennemi!"* ("Clericalism is the enemy"). It championed an extremely individualistic philosophy aimed at depriving the Church insofar as possible of all influence over the life of France, especially in the areas of marriage and education. It stood for separation of church and state, liberty of the press and of assembly, free and compulsory lay public education, and the removal of the laws against trade unions.

De Mun took a strong messianic view of his role in what he saw as a great drama pitting the forces of Good, embodied in the Church, against the forces of Evil, embodied in the republic. It was an approach certainly not calculated to lessen the antagonism between the Church and the republic. When he spoke in the chamber it was often in the tone of one exorcising evil spirits. But by his own admission he was a deeply divided soul, torn by conflicting thoughts and emotions. Naturally indolent, he was driven to a life of action by a strong sense of duty, a tension made manifest in regular and excruciating headaches. He had a great need to believe but was constantly afflicted by doubt. And no doubt his tendency to authoritarianism was the obverse of his doubts. He could be coldly lucid one moment and carried away by emotion the next. He could pursue his enemies without mercy while admiring them at the same time. Likewise in his faith, he was at once zealous and complacent, serious and frivolous, proud and humble. "Never master of myself," he confided in letters to his spiritual director,

---

[5]Adrien Dansette, *Religious History of Modern France* (London: Nelson, 1961), Vol. II, p. 32.

Father du Lac, "I can be so sharp, hard and personally offensive . . . and yet I pray and take communion." [6]

To represent his political creed, de Mun used the term "counterrevolution"; some on the right found this too inflammatory but de Mun felt it best expressed his philosophy. De Mun's parting shot on leaving the chamber, following the temporary nullification of his election, defined as sharply as possible the chasm between himself and the Left: "You are the Revolution," he said. "That is sufficient to explain why we are the Counterrevolution! What was this Revolution of yours? . . . the overthrow of kings, the unchaining of popular passions and bloody riots, a doctrine. . . . that pretends to found society not on the will of God but on that of man."[7] In de Mun's words, the duty of the counterrevolution was:

> To oppose to the Declaration of the Rights of Man, which has served as the basis of the Revolution, the proclamation of the Rights of God, which must be the foundation of the Counterrevolution, and the ignorance of which is the true cause of the evil that leads our society to ruin. To aspire to an absolute obedience to the principles of the Catholic church and to the infallible teaching of the pope, and to carry through all the consequences that naturally are the result in the social order of the full exercise of the law of God on societies.[8]

His thought derived from his study of the classic Catholic conservatives Joseph de Maistre, Juan Donoso Cortés and Louis de Bonald, and from the Syllabus itself. He neither sought nor gave quarter: "The Church and the Revolution are irreconcilable, either the Church must kill the Revolution, or the Revolution will kill the Church."[9] The true conservative, de Mun claimed, stood behind the Church and therefore called for a monarchy submissive to its laws. Louis Veuillot was thrilled to jump on de Mun's bandwagon.

De Mun did not want to return to the *ancien régime* with its materialistic Enlightenment and its oppression of the poor. He called instead for "a Christian society." But as Paul Misner says, though Donoso Cortés and Ketteler might, at mid-century, still plausibly think of the reChristianization of Western Europe from the ruins of failed liberalism, restorationist dreams

---

[6]Philippe Levillain, *Albert de Mun* (Rome: École Française de Rome, 1983), pp. 185–187.

[7]Martin, *Count Albert de Mun*, p. 37.

[8]Dansette, *Religious History of Modern France,* Vol. II, p. 33.

[9]Ibid., p. 36.

were futile after the "modern schism" of 1870. Nearly a century after the radical watershed, no neat line divided the "Revolution" from the tradition. French Catholics were left with the task of distinguishing the good from the bad, the valid from the harmful, the living from the dead elements in the two traditions—"the religious one of Catholicism and the modern national one of revolution and counterrevolution." Albert de Mun blocked this process of common Catholic discernment to the best of his ability by his insistence on interlocking Catholicism with his "counterrevolutionary pathos."[10]

In the elections of 1879 de Mun ran for office again in Pontivy but lost to the republican Le Maguet. The republicans, now comfortably in the majority, stepped up their attacks on the Church and their efforts to secularize France. They focused particularly on education (nearly half of all French schoolchildren were in Catholic schools). A decree was issued in 1880 that banned those religious congregations most engaged in teaching (including the Jesuits) and forced nearly 10,000 religious to exit the country. In 1882 all religious instruction in state primary schools was prohibited. In 1884 divorce (illegal since 1816) was restored to the Civil Code.

Public prayers were now forbidden. Compulsory Sunday rest was abolished and not reinstituted until a quarter of a century later to prevent the exploitation of labor. Space in cemeteries could no longer be arranged to keep the graves of non-Catholics or suicides separate from consecrated Catholic ones. The office of military chaplain was abolished. Nuns were supposed to be disallowed as nurses in the hospitals, although this measure was never widely implemented. And with the intention of reducing the number of priests, seminarians were no longer to be exempted from military service. (This measure actually proved advantageous because it provided the seminarians with a valuable experience of real life.)

Outraged at this ceaseless assault on their religion, beleaguered conservatives began to talk of insurrection and hoped to win over de Mun to the idea. His Cercles now counted around 50,000 workers who might be formidable allies in the event of a putsch. But in spite of some inflammatory speeches calling for a restoration of the monarchy, de Mun continued to insist that the Cercles movement was not a political party and would serve only as a model of what a Christian society could be.

[10]Paul Misner, *Social Catholicism in Europe*, pp. 166–167.

A Shaken Monarchist

Like most French Catholics at the time, de Mun was a passionate believer in monarchy as the answer to France's problems. His most forthright declaration in favor of the monarchy occurred at Vannes on March 8, 1881. He spoke at a monarchist gathering held under an immense tent in the court of a grand chateau. Some two thousand guests including clergy and army officers were seated facing a vast platform decorated with the coats of arms of the king and a huge tapestry with the *fleur-de-lis*—the arms of Brittany. Seated on the platform were the royalist committees, many of the nobility, and the press. For the first time de Mun committed himself unmistakably to the Bourbon pretender, the Count de Chambord. De Mun denounced the republic, its vices, its dictatorship, its terrorism. He called the republic the heir of the Commune of 1870, which for him marked the great divide between the Revolution and the counterrevolution. The Commune of 1870, he said, hurled defiance at God, a defiance perpetuated by the republic. In destroying authority the Revolution had opened the road to despotism and anarchy, whereas the monarchy, based on Catholicism, could solve the social question. We need, he said, a king, not any king but a Christian prince fully conscious of his Christian duties.

The political repercussions of this speech were universally bruising for de Mun. The secular press excoriated him as the leader of the clerical intransigents while some Catholic journals accused him of opposing Leo XIII. Cardinal Guibert declared de Mun's intervention inopportune, while the nuncio, Msgr. Czacki, accused him of undermining the policy of the Holy See. Nevertheless the vision of a "Christian king" who could reunite France and restore the Church to its rightful position continued to haunt him. De Mun therefore suffered a cruel blow when Chambord died unexpectedly on August 24, 1883. Standing at his casket de Mun felt crushed, "the past, the hopes of the future all fleeting." Chambord, an upright and honorable man, had been gripped by a mystical belief in not only the divinity of royalty, but also in his own position as the savior of France. In this respect he was so completely medieval that he had been little able to understand the turn of events since the French Revolution. The new pretender, the Count of Paris, on the other hand, de Mun saw as a "modern" who did not fit his picture of a Christian prince. One never dared to approach Chambord without kissing his hand, de Mun would lament, and never dined with him except in white tie, whereas the Count of Paris freely shook your hand and customarily dined with you in black tie. De Mun's aristocratic soul shrunk back from Chambord's successor; from this point on, his hope for the monarchy began to fade.

Social Reformer

Fortunately for de Mun, he had never regarded the restoration as an end in itself, but simply as a condition of reestablishing a social order capable of saving France. As he worked out a new political philosophy, the Syllabus remained his guide, "the light which illuminates our way." At the same time, however, he was profoundly convinced of the need for social reform. A million inhabitants of Paris had hardly enough air to breathe and lived in hovels without running water or light. The revolutionary syndicalist Fernand Pelloutier described in many articles how underemployed workers lived in places like Goutte'd'or and Montmartre. In dark and sordid alleys they engaged in "endless quarrels and cheerless fornications amid the stench of sweat and excrement issuing from windowless rooms and open latrines." They resorted to drink as a form of anesthesia, bringing upon themselves illness and early death. How could anyone witness all this, Pelloutier asked, and not see the need for revolution?[11] Those who managed to find work lived from day to day without the slightest security for the future, constantly threatened by illness, accidents, and layoffs. They had no holidays or days off, no chance of saving. Wages lagged far behind profits. With a base number of 100, wages for miners in 1890 stood at 161 while profits rose to 236. Nor were wage scales in line with the harshness of working conditions in the mines where men fell victim to explosion, suffocation, anemia, and tuberculosis. Although some foreign industrialists had already introduced the eight-hour day, Pelloutier saw no chance of its introduction into France.

Through unions and strikes the workers sought to improve their condition and to win for their families at least a modicum of security. As their determination and discontent grew, so did the number of strikes; these strikes were by no means all successful, or even partially so, but in some instances the workers won concessions that, in the context of the times, seem fairly impressive.

In spite of the act of 1884 the employers denied the very right of unionization and were determined to prevent the establishment of unions. The

---

[11]Bede K. Lackner and Kenneth Roy Philp, eds., *Essays on Modern European Revolutionary History* (Austin, Texas: University of Texas Press, 1977), p. 46.

direction of the labor movement changed accordingly, as workers found themselves forced to strike often to protect even the existence of their unions. These conflicts taught them that they could use their numbers to wrest from their employers' hands the reins of political power. This development caused the bourgeoisie to fear that their own bold contribution, universal male suffrage, might well turn into their undoing. The fear was justified, for the socialists were making gains denouncing a political order in which "the power of money paralyzes or corrupts parliaments, intimidates and dupes the masses."

The owners' idea of industrial organization was rooted in paternalism, and in their minds political activity by the workers reflected a dangerous insubordination that must be effectively restrained. Owners would harass politically conscious workers, curtail their activities, and even fire them, while workers protested their right to organize politically and challenged the conservative parties at the polls. Thus some of the bitterest strikes of the period were essentially political. The issue was whether workers could freely participate in politics.

Although de Mun had orginally advocated mixed unions of employers and workers as more akin to the spirit of the Cercles, he now supported separate unions as championed by Léon Harmel, the Catholic manufacturer and social activist who argued that the presence of employers put undue pressure upon the workers. Even de Mun's conservative Catholic friends called him a socialist. But he received dramatic encouragement in Rome when, in several private audiences, Pope Leo sought his advice for an encyclical he was preparing on social reform—the epochal *Rerum Novarum*.

A Strange Monarchist Interlude

So far de Mun had little to show for his efforts in the political arena. He was unable to convert his friends on the Right to his program of social reform, while his romantic visionary approach had proven ineffectual in his struggle with the anticlericals. The public position of the Church was, if anything, more at risk than ever. The Knight of the Syllabus was in need of a new horse. Unfortunately, instead he found a man on a black horse—a curious episode in his career that highlights his characteristic lack of political judgment.

He thus got involved in a scheme of the conservatives to overthrow the Third Republic and to put the Count of Paris on the throne. The man they intended to lead this effort was a popular, flamboyant young French general.

Georges Ernest Jean Marie Boulanger, who came from a Catholic conservative background. He had transferred his allegiance to the radicals and been appointed minister of war. When he incurred disgrace by certain maladroit actions that almost precipitated a war with Bismarck, he was exiled to the provincial garrison of Clermont Ferrand. The general was induced by the conservatives to run for election as the candidate of all those disaffected by the political corruption of the Third Republic. France seemed ripe for a dictatorship. Sensing the impotence of Parliament, Boulanger called for the dissolution of the chamber and the convocation of a constituent assembly to revise the constitution. The strategy of the monarchists was to exploit the success of Boulanger in order to hold a plebiscite (to restore the monarchy), after which he could safely be discarded.

De Mun was drawn into the plan in spite of grave misgivings about the character of Boulanger, whom he considered a renegade general and a disgrace, a man "without strength of character, purpose, or even political skill." He was willing to suppress those feelings in the hope of turning out the scoundrels who were persecuting the Church. He endorsed Boulangism at a "countercentenary" organized to offset the centenary celebrations of the Revolution of 1789. But Boulangism collapsed in a single stroke on April 1, 1889, when, upon hearing that he might be put on trial for plotting the overthrow of the regime, the cowardly general took flight to Brussels with his mistress. Convicted of treason in absentia, he eventually committed suicide. The Boulangists were defeated at the ballot box by the republicans. De Mun found himself more boxed in than ever—*persona non grata* to the conservatives for his lukewarmness on monarchy, and to the republicans for his part in the Boulangist conspiracy.

Rallies to the Republic

As the restoration of monarchy appeared more and more a lost cause, de Mun and a significant number of conservatives began to seek some way of uniting with the moderate republicans (the so-called "opportunists") to form a parliamentary majority. They finally found their leader in Jacques Piou, a barrister from Toulouse, and they formed the Constitutional Union of the Right with a program that included economic policies pleasing to moderate republicans and religious policies attractive to conservatives.

The Opportunists reacted favorably to Piou's platform, but before he could finalize a deal with them he needed more support within his own conservative ranks. Help came from an unexpected quarter. On November

12, 1890, at a banquet in honor of the French Mediterranean fleet (most of whose officers were monarchists), the prestigious Charles Cardinal Lavigerie, primate of North Africa and archbishop of Algiers, amazed those present when he offered a toast to the republic! The guest of honor, Victor Duperre, a Bonapartist and vice-admiral, was so discombobulated that he barely managed a reply: "I drink to his Eminence the Cardinal and to the clergy of Algeria."[12]

The cardinal's bold act was prompted by Pope Leo's choice of Lavigerie to prepare French Catholics for a change in papal policy toward the republic. The pope had already laid the groundwork in his 1885 encyclical *Immortale Dei,* which declared that the Church would bless any legitimate form of government provided it acknowledged God as the source of all authority.

Although it was obvious that the pope himself must be behind Lavigerie's move, some Catholics could not bring themselves to admit it. Others, including de Mun, took refuge in the false hope that the pope only wanted them to cooperate with the republic, not to become republicans. To embrace the republic without qualification was too painful a prospect for a class whose forebears had held for centuries to the conviction that to die for the king was the highest form of honor. For them the republic was a whore; they were not at home to republicans.

The bishops pussyfooted while Lavigerie called them "mitred rabbits." At last the pope cut off the debate by issuing his 1892 encyclical *Inter Innumeras (Au Milieu des Sollicitudes)* which called on Catholics to give their allegiance to the republic *"sans arrière-pensées"* ("without second thoughts"). Catholics, it declared in effect, must cease identifying their cause with that of the monarchy. Rather they should unite with the moderate republicans to form a large conservative party that could bring about a stable government and an end to religious strife. The pope also discouraged them from forming the kind of solely Catholic parties found in Germany, Austria, and Belgium, an idea which de Mun himself had favored.

Leo's idea of joining Catholics and unbelievers had revolutionary implications. It represented a drastic revision of the Church's teaching on religious freedom as expressed in Pius IX's Syllabus of Errors. In an unprecedented interview with *Le Petit Journal,* Leo praised the kind of liberty practiced in the United States as the foundation of relations between the civil authority and the religious conscience.

Many Catholic monarchists retired from active politics rather than re-

---

[12]Dansette, *Religious History of Modern France,* Vol. II, p. 79.

nounce monarchism and their king. Even de Mun, though ready to obey, as always, tried to find some room to maneuver. But finally he traveled to Rome to assure the pope personally of his intention to "rally to the republic." Overjoyed, the aged pontiff embraced him and begged him to serve as an emblem of the Ralliement, even as he had for Social Catholicism.

De Mun was resolved not to allow the new party of Catholic "Rallies" (those heeding Leo's call to rally to the republic) to be the mere "gendarmes of bourgeois society." He called on Catholics to side with the lower classes and to seek laws protecting workers as much as capital. His enemies accused him of fomenting class war. Even the majority of the Rallies were not in sympathy with his Social Catholicism. Undaunted, he continued stressing the need for experimentation and change and stunned even his Social Catholic colleagues by insisting that it was time to change the Cercles themselves by encouraging the workers to stand up for themselves. It was evident that his two main objectives—defense of the church against the anticlericals and promotion of social reform—were proving to be incompatible, and the stress began to tell on his nerves. Finally his health broke and he had to retire from the fray to his estate at Lumigny for a long period of rest.

Leading the Charge Against Dreyfus

Eventually de Mun was able to return to public life, but his next controversy would cast a long shadow over his career. De Mun's personal involvement began when a stranger came to his door in May 1897. Matthieu Dreyfus came to ask his help in reversing the court-martial in 1894 of his brother Alfred—a Jewish officer accused of selling secrets about French artillery to the Germans. The main piece of evidence against Alfred was a memorandum *(bordereau)* taken from the wastebasket of the German Embassy and passed on to a Major Hubert Joseph Henry of French Intelligence. It appears probable that Henry recognized the handwriting as that of a friend, the shady character Count Marie Charles Ferdinand Walsin Esterhazy. Unable to destroy the document because it had already been seen by others, he attributed it instead to Dreyfus, whose handwriting unhappily bore a certain similarity to that on the document.

Dreyfus was an unlikely candidate for suspicion, being financially well off, but several factors conspired to victimize him. He was unpopular among his fellow officers because of some disagreeable traits of character. Moreover, anti-Semitism was at a fever pitch precisely at this moment. In his book *La France Juive* (1886) and his newspaper the *Libre Parole,* the anti-Jewish agitator Édouard Drumont had carried on a campaign against Jewish officers in the army. Then, prejudice against the Jews as unscrupulous financiers had recently been stirred up by the collapse of the Union Générale bank, a Catholic rival of the Rothschilds, and by Jewish involvement in the Panama scandals.

Dreyfus's trial was held in secret, and in addition to the *bordereau,* a dossier of trumped-up documents was adduced as evidence. The jurors took little time in convicting him of treason in spite of his protestations of innocence. He was publicly degraded on January 5, 1894, and sentenced to solitary confinement for life on the infamous Devil's Island off the coast of French Guiana.

While Dreyfus languished there under the blazing sun, Colonel Georges Picquart found evidence pointing to Major Esterhazy as the actual culprit. Resisting incredible pressures to silence him, Picquart refused to hold his peace and dedicated himself totally to the rehabilitation of a stranger. In the meantime Matthieu Dreyfus had already mounted a campaign for a new trial to clear his brother. The army exiled Picquart to Tunis and stonewalled the whole business. Knowing de Mun's reputation as a champion of the oppressed, Matthieu Dreyfus called on him hoping to secure his help in the fight. But he hadn't taken into account de Mun's devotion to the army and his zeal for its honor. De Mun gave him a brief, chilly reception and had his valet show him out.

As agitation in favor of Dreyfus mounted, the opposition grew more determined to refuse a retrial. An enormous proportion of the army came from reactionary families; clericals and anti-Semites joined hands. The chief of staff himself, General de Boisdeffre, was counseled by a prominent Jesuit, Père Du Lac, who was also de Mun's spiritual director. By calling the Dreyfus agitation an attack on the honor of the army, they were able to win over jingoist sentiment in an alliance of "the sword and the aspergillum." For Georges Clemenceau, the fiery republican, the "essence of the Dreyfus affair was the struggle of the French Revolutionary tradition against the blind authoritarianism of caste."[13] The Dreyfus case split France apart like a ripe melon. Everyone had an opinion for or against; duels were fought over it, whole families were divided. A famous cartoon showed in one panel a large family gathered around the table with the father speaking, and the caption "No one is to speak of it." The next panel showed table and chairs

[13]Harvey Goldberg, *The Life of Jean Jaurès* (Madison, Wisc.: The University of Wisconsin Press, 1962), p. 217.

overturned, forks and knives flying through the air, dishes broken, and the caption "They spoke of it."

De Mun took the lead in the chamber in defending the army. Pounding on the rostrum, his voice soaring with emotion, he called the Dreyfusards partisans of treason, suggested that the Jews were behind the whole conspiracy, and implored his fellow deputies to stand up for their most precious possession, the "honor of the army."[14] Cries of "Bravo!" filled the chamber as de Mun was given tremendous applause.

Public pressure, however, finally forced the army to reopen the investigation. When Esterhazy was falsely exonerated, Émile Zola came out with his famous article *"J'Accuse!"* charging the army and the government of a cover-up. The government would have left the whole matter there, but de Mun once again stirred up the deputies with an impassioned harangue calling for Zola's head. His resolution to put Zola on trial for libel passed by an overwhelming vote, and Zola, who was found guilty, took refuge in England.

In an effort to settle the matter once and for all, the minister of war, General Cavaignac, adduced a document that was supposed to show Dreyfus's guilt beyond the shadow of a doubt. To his dismay the document turned out to be a forgery concocted by Colonel Henry. The forger fled to Brussels and committed suicide and the Dreyfusards were at last able to force a retrial. The judges, army officers imbued with the spirit of caste and fearful of their superiors, convicted him again, adding the absurd qualification "with extenuating circumstances." The government, however, immediately pardoned him. He was later completely exonerated, restored to military rank, and awarded the Legion of Honor.

The affair obviously sheds no luster on de Mun, who never showed a certain right-wing obtuseness more than in this episode. The complacency, conservatism, and prejudice he manifested unfortunately mirrored a good part of the Catholic community. Led by the virulently anti-Semitic religious of the Assumptionist Order and their mass circulation daily *La Croix,* Catholics let their ever-ready prejudice against the Jews ensnare them in the controversy and oppose a revision of the verdict. As Adrien Dansette says, "Almost all the Church's friends were opposed to Dreyfus, and almost all her enemies, the Jews, the Protestants, and the free-thinkers, were on the other side."[15] While the Vatican and the French bishops prudently held aloof from

---

[14]Martin, *Count Albert de Mun,* pp. 116–117.
[15]Dansette, *Religious History of Modern France,* Vol. II, p. 181.

the ruckus, nevertheless de Mun and the Assumptionists caused the Church to be identified with the anti-Dreyfusard, and even antirepublican, cause.

Poor Pope Leo saw his Ralliement go down the drain of the Dreyfus affair, although even without the affair it is hardly likely that the Ralliement would have succeeded. The quarrel between the republicans and the Catholics was too deeply rooted, the animosities and bitterness too inflamed for too long, to expect a true reconciliation in such a short course of time. However, the effort was not all in vain. The seeds sown by the pope, de Mun, and others would blossom later following the great war.

Action Libérale: A New Catholic Party

The alliance of "opportunists" and the right wing that had been engineered by de Mun collapsed, and a new government was formed that was now dominated by the Left. Under the new premier, René Waldeck-Rousseau, the goverment was determined to make the Church pay for its part in the Dreyfus affair by tightening the anticlerical screws—a policy that radicals, socialists, and the left-leaning opportunists could all agree on. An Associations Bill was passed in November 1899 with two parts: The first granted broader liberty to such groups as political parties, labor unions, and the like. The second made the authorization of religious teachers dependent on both chamber and senate, threatening the very existence of the Catholic schools. Either house could delay any such authorizations indefinitely and hence close the schools at will.

De Mun denounced those responsible as "Jacobins" of the Left. "The Revolution," he said, "in the name of tolerance and freedom, burned churches and guillotined priests. Its descendants have no such dark designs; they limit themselves to closing the convents and oppressing consciences." Many independent and progressive republicans also took a negative stand on the bill as an attack on basic human rights. De Mun saw them as potential allies in a coalition that might wrest power from the radicals and socialists. But with the first signs of angina appearing, de Mun turned to Jacques Piou to form a new Catholic conservative party, the Action Libérale. The aim was to consolidate the Rallies and then form an alliance with right-wing republicans (progressives and independents—formerly called "opportunists").

The Action Libérale debuted as a potentially powerful Catholic party that extended beyond liberal Catholicism. Its program was summed up in the motto: "Liberty for all, equality before the law, improvement of the workers' condition, and *droit commun* (no special privileges for the Church)."

The election campaign of 1902 was their first test, fought largely around the issues of anticlericalism and socialism. Action Libérale combined the goals of Social Catholicism (such as unionization) with the traditional ideals of liberal Catholicism—decentralization, freedom of education, and freedom of worship. The new party was attacked therefore from all sides—by the republicans who accused it of being a clerical party in disguise and by the integralist Catholics who accused it of making concessions to the government. As the campaign proceeded, the Action Libérale rhetoric became quite shrill and negative. Piou denounced "the official organization of an atheist crusade" that would abrogate the Concordat, secularize Notre Dame, and dismantle most of the churches. In Benjamin Martin's view, Abbé Pierre Dabry was essentially right in "condemning it for adopting as members elements hostile to the republic, making religious demands the basis of its platform, and presenting itself basically as a party of reaction."[16]

Eighty percent of the electorate turned out at the polls and gave the Left 51 percent to the opposition's 49 percent. In spite of the closeness of the popular vote, the electorate had ratified the anticlerical policy of the government. The Action Libérale ended up with 78 seats out of a total of 585 while their allies, the progressives and independents, secured 155. The extreme right took 13 seats. The ministry was able to get control of 321 seats to the opposition's 264.

The elections brought in a new prime minister, Émile Combes, who had his own scores to settle with the Church. Once a student of theology, he had lost his faith as the result of an arduous intellectual quest and had been dismissed from the seminary after being told he was too "proud." He now seemed bent on punishing the Church for its sins, real or imagined. As his first ruthless move he ordered three thousand Catholic schools sealed shut. When challenged by de Mun and others he replied coolly: "We will go all the way." He lived up to his word and the devastating results revolted the great poet Charles Péguy, a Dreyfusard himself, who spoke of "the great pity of the churches of France."

Fearing that violence might erupt in Brittany when the gendarmes came to close the schools, de Mun—risking a heart attack—went there and dashed from village to village urging the men to lay down their pitchforks and harpoons. A moment of high drama occurred near his summer home at Roscoff where two companies of infantry and a hundred gendarmes faced three thousand armed Roscoffites at dawn around the school. De Mun

---

[16]Martin, *Count Albert de Mun*, p. 148.

thrust himself between the two sides and got them to retreat a few critical yards, and then climbed over the wall of the barricaded school and persuaded the nuns to leave peacefully.

De Mun and Piou used the agitation over the closures to their advantage. Exploiting the indignation while preaching nonviolence they continued to build their party, which they now renamed the ALP (Action Libérale Populaire). De Mun called for mammoth protest demonstrations. He and Piou organized a march by the "Mothers of Paris." Ten thousand turned out to march behind Madame Piou and Countess de Mun down the Champs Élysées to the presidential palace. Large sums of money flowed into ALP coffers from the religious congregations—money that had to be "laundered" to conceal its origins and avoid the stigma of clericalism. This was imperative if the ALP was to be the nucleus of a large conservative opposition party embracing many besides Catholics. One great asset the ALP could use in its organizing was the support of Pope Leo XIII, who blessed it as the heir to Social Catholicism and the Ralliement, the two policies he counted on to revive the French Church.

They were able to purchase a number of regional newspapers, and—together with *La Croix*—blanketed the country with their message. The ALP's *Bulletin Action Libérale* soon expanded to become nearly a weekly review featuring editorials on the questions of the day. A reader would soon realize that the party stood for the defense of the Church's rights, fiscal restraint, and reform legislation along Social Catholic lines. The success of their effort was evident by 1904 when they could count some seven hundred local committees with 160,000 members. (The socialists by comparison numbered only 35,000 in 1905.)

But even as the ALP passed from strength to strength—it eventually garnered 2,000,000 members from 1500 local chapters—changes underway in Rome were putting its favored status increasingly at risk. In 1903 Pope Leo, under whose blessing and protection the ALP had flourished, died at the age of ninety-three. Giuseppe Sarto, now Pope Pius X, was something else entirely. Of peasant origins, Sarto was the first pope in centuries to know real poverty. He was remarkably pious, narrow-minded, and little inclined to the diplomatic approach of his predecessor. As the French socialist paper *L'Humanité* put it, he was a cross between "a village curé (priest) and an archangel with a flaming sword."[17] De Mun hastened to Rome to size up the new man and got a whiff of what lay ahead. As a favorite of Leo

[17] Goldberg, *The Life of Jean Jaurès*, p. 320.

he had been spared the elaborate etiquette compulsory in the papal court—kneeling and other formalities. But now he was compelled to observe them again. It was an unpleasant omen and a harbinger of things to come.

New Momentum for Social Catholicism

While the wealthiest Catholics prayed that *Rerum Novarum* would be shelved and forgotten, de Mun was determined to make up the ground lost for Social Catholicism as a result of the Dreyfus affair and the renewed anticlerical campaign. The 1903 ALP "social congress" called unhesitatingly for a broad *code du travail* incorporating most of de Mun's proposals of the last three decades: a living wage, improved working conditions, shorter workdays, prohibition of work on Sundays, and old-age pensions as part of a national program of sickness, accident, and unemployment insurance.

The 1905 Congress, however, opened on a tepid note. De Mun's social agenda had in the interim lost ground among the members. The fourteen hundred delegates squeezed into the Salle de la Société de Géographie responded with only polite applause when de Mun proclaimed: "We pursue . . . a social work." The next morning was devoted to a long report on unions. It approved the spread of unionization among workers as a chief instrument of education, progress, and social pacification, and called on owners to engage willingly in collective bargaining with their workers. Here the composure of some delegates snapped. One industrialist seized the floor and declared unions a pernicious influence; the only way to improve the worker's lot, he said, was by cutting taxes and closing cabarets.

De Mun and Piou were back on safer ground when they focused the attention of the delegates on the injustices perpetrated against the Church. The radical socialist Aristide Briand who had succeeded Combes in 1905, passed a bill separating church and state. Its provisions put all church property under the control of the state through lay-dominated associations, surrendered the state's part in the appointment of bishops, and discontinued the payment of priests' salaries. De Mun announced that the political score would be settled without compromise; the 341 deputies who voted for the separation would be made to understand that "no excuse can cover them."

At the closing banquet de Mun, visibly exhausted, got up to say just a few words and was greeted by a great wave of applause. Then there was a hush as the delegates leaned forward. "I remain," he said, "a Catholic above all else, resolved to subordinate all political questions to the defense of my faith." Being a Catholic, he further declared, meant not merely the practice of religion but devotion to liberty, patriotism, and social justice—virtues the ALP clearly manifested. It lacked only victory, he said, and it should seek that "in the heart of the small and humble people, where springs forth the inexhaustible source of sacrifice and devotion. There is the root of your strength. There is the supreme hope for tomorrow, toward which today, with the last effort of my voice, I cast the most profound cry of my soul." Instantly the delegates jumped to their feet clapping and cheering. It was a wonderful climax.

Foiled by Clemenceau

The ALP was by now the dominant party on the right, and with its allies among the progressives and the independents, victory in 1906 seemed a credible possibility. The idea of Piou as the next prime minister and de Mun as a power behind the throne no longer seemed far-fetched.

For a time it even seemed the government would hand the ALP the victory by its clumsy application of the separation law. Word had gotten around that even the consecrated Host and sacred relics would be examined by those taking inventory of church property. Militant Catholics barricaded the churches and there were skirmishes between the police and Breton fishermen armed with harpoons. Finally one of the demonstrators was shot dead by a policeman returning fire. The ALP then posted placards warning that the administration of the sacraments would be jeopardized if the radicals and socialists won the election.

Now in earnest fear of an ALP victory, Clemenceau deployed a two-pronged strategy. First, he suspended operation of the separation law. Then he trumped up a charge that the ALP was conspiring with the syndicalist labor union (Confédération Générale du Travail [CGT]) to embarrass the government by fomenting a series of revolutionary disturbances immediately before the election. The election was finally a disaster for the ALP. The public was unconvinced by ALP propaganda that the government was out to destroy "God, family and nation." They were more interested in maintaining stability than trying a new direction. The coalition won only 41 percent of the vote while the ALP itself dropped fourteen seats. Any hope of leading a majority was dashed. Henceforth the ALP would have to resign itself to being only a voice in the chamber. But de Mun reminded the "malevolent Jacobin" Clemenceau that "France and the church have between them a long and mysterious alliance, which, through long travails, has formed the body and fashioned the soul of our nation. That cannot be abolished."

At first Clemenceau worked on a compromise that would allow priests free use of the churches if they would present an annual declaration of intent. But when on Vatican orders Cardinal Richard rejected the proposals, Clemenceau decided to tighten the screws. He ordered the priests expelled from their rectories. In Paris the aged and infirm cardinal had to be carried out on a litter. When the Catholic people stood firm behind the clergy, the government backed down by agreeing to recognize the priests as "unofficial occupants" of the churches. This compromise brought a certain measure of peace, but the Church was left still sorting out its bewildering changes of fortune. In a material sense the Church had suffered a ruinous defeat in the confiscation of most of its property save the church buildings themselves. But by the same token it had won a spiritual victory since the vigor and fortitude manifested by the pope, the clergy, and French Catholics as a whole gained it new respect even from its enemies. This was demonstrated when more than fifty thousand people attended the funeral of Cardinal Richard less than a year after his eviction; another sign was the number of important conversions that occurred at the time, involving such outstanding figures as Charles Péguy and Ernest Psichari.

Social Catholicism in Eclipse

As the furor over the separation law died down, de Mun resolved to renew his personal campaign for Social Catholicism. He believed it to be one of the keys to national renewal. Turning to the press he spoke out in favor of the rights of the bakery apprentices and seamstresses, and called for the rights of all workers including state employees to strike. Unionization and collective action were the wave of the future, he believed; the critical question was whether this shift would be achieved through revolutionary syndicalism or the corporatism of Social Catholicism.

Jean Jaurès, the leader of the socialists, saw de Mun's move as an attempt to steal part of the socialist program. "Since the Church can no longer count simply on the faith of its followers, it is trying to trap the workers with a handful of reform proposals."[18] For his part de Mun, in his book *Ma Vocation Sociale* (1908), wondered in a tone of irony and despair how it could be that after forty years of Social Catholic effort so many Catholics still

[18]Ibid., p. 272.

regarded any form of government intervention as essentially socialist. They still believed, he lamented, that personal charity alone could alleviate the condition of the workers.

At this same time, the ALP was falling prey to divisive forces. A new enemy—the Action Française, a restorationist movement led by Charles Maurras—had infiltrated its right wing. Though an atheist, Maurras managed to recruit a Catholic following impressed by his oft-expressed esteem for Catholicism as the source of the values that he believed made the country great: above all, order and a respect for authority and tradition. Though relatively ineffectual in France before the Great War the Action had numerous sympathizers in the Curia who worked assiduously to undermine the ALP. They had to tread lightly, however, since the ALP was the most visible symbol of Leo XIII's agenda for social reform and the Ralliement. Pius was anxious to avoid a direct repudiation of either of Leo's projects even though he viewed both as failures.

Meanwhile, the official news from the Vatican was most disheartening. Le Sillon, a movement to reconcile Catholicism and democracy led by a charismatic young Catholic and dynamic speaker Marc Sangnier, came under condemnation. The main influence behind the condemnation was that of the so-called "integrists" (so named because they stood for an *integral* Catholicism that allowed no concessions to so-called modern ideas), who had managed to convince the Pope that Le Sillon was tainted with modernism.

Hearing the sad news, de Mun thought immediately of Lamennais and the pilgrims of God and liberty and wondered if Pius X was not out to revive the bleak years of Gregory XVI and Pius IX. His worst fears were confirmed when he read the charges against Le Sillon when it was banned in 1907: They attracted non-Catholics to their ranks, they denied the church's hierarchical view of society, they praised democracy as a superior political system, and more of the standard attacks. Any Social Catholic might fall under such a sweeping ban. No one was much surprised subsequently to read in *Le Temps* a headline inquiring: "The condemnation of M. de Mun next?"

De Mun's anguish and even despair were overwhelming, as one of his letters revealed:

> When I arrived back here I found the terrible papal letter. I read it through at a sitting, and I found myself greatly moved. As all the others . . . [while] quite remarkable, profound, and highly researched. But too, as in the other encyclicals, what a smashing blow, striking far beyond

those intended, attacking indirectly all who in some form or another have subscribed to Sillonist doctrines, encouraging all of those who, for reasons more or less openly avowed, struggle against the social works and philosophy inaugurated by Leo XIII . . . But for the present, what trouble, tests and uncertainty! . . . I do feel myself . . . profoundly troubled, uncertain of my way and worried what gain the eternal enemies of Catholic social action will take from this . . . I am sad at the thought of all the abuse that will be hurled at those not condemned by the encyclical but simply part of the social Catholic movement . . . especially young priests [who will be discouraged] . . . Am I also to see the social movement to which I have attached my name founder and die?[19]

The ALP's conservative coalition lost again in the election of 1910, and now realized they could never come to power without broader support. With this in mind de Mun began searching for ways to conciliate Briand, who was once more the prime minister and who might be persuaded to ally his Center with the Right instead of the Left. Pressure from Rome forced an end to the delicate probings that de Mun and Piou had made of Briand and the moderates. This final blow vanquished any hope of an ALP comeback. The decline of the party was evident at the 1911 congress where only four hundred delegates showed up and the atmosphere was shrill and negative. The party began to seem old, feeble, and defeated.

The Patriot Overshadows the Social Catholic

De Mun was by no means finished. In fact, his political star was set to reach its all-time zenith. If the avenue of social reform was closed to him for the time being, he could still employ what he saw as the other key to the renewal of French society: a revival of patriotism. The urgency of this need was reflected in things as basic as the deplorable ignorance of French history among graduates of the French schools, 50 percent of whom could not identify Jeanne d'Arc and 75 percent of whom could not explain why July 14 was a national holiday. De Mun was also frightened by the precipitous decline in the number of youths interested in the military, while antimilitarist feeling ran high in the army and the desertion rate increased each year. He had been outraged at the humiliation of France when, in 1905, German forces kept her from establishing a protectorate in Morocco. He

[19]Martin, *Count Albert de Mun*, pp. 234–235.

saw all of it as part of a pacifist trend that he abhorred and that he blamed especially on Jaurès and the socialists. He called Jaurès the "gravedigger of France" on one occasion when Jaurès and the socialists disrupted the assembly by standing on their desks and singing the *Internationale* to protest a military defense bill.

Catholics, de Mun thought, were providentially suited to lead the way in reviving the spirit of nationalism and patriotism because their respect for tradition put them in closer communion with the soul of the nation. He saw this opinion confirmed by the immense crowd attending a splendid ceremony in 1909 at Notre Dame honoring the recently beatified Jeanne d'Arc; this was a triumphant event that eclipsed anything he had ever seen. The crowds shouting *"Vive la religion! Vive la pucelle! Vive la France!"* were for him "the great cry of national revival," a sign that France was returning to its Catholic tradition.[20]

In July 1911 the German cruiser *Berliner* plowed into the Moroccan port of Agadir to show that Germany was once more determined to contest French domination of Morocco. The French had just put down a popular uprising there and occupied the town of Fez, seemingly a prelude to establishing a protectorate over Morocco. The French prime minister Caillaux, fearful of German wrath, in secret negotiations signed a convention that gave Germany part of the French territory in the Congo.

All hell broke loose when the convention was announced. France could no longer ignore the grim reality: The nation had let its armed forces deteriorate and could no longer stand up to the German bully. People said the pacifists had sapped the national will to resist. The spirit of antimilitarism had spread and France had failed to listen to the prophets like de Mun who had called for a revival of nationalism and a strong policy in Morocco.

De Mun immediately rallied resistance to the convention in the Foreign Affairs Committee and through his editorials for *L'Écho de Paris,* which had the largest circulation in Paris. Finally he surprised everyone and frightened his family when he announced that he would make a formal speech in the chamber against the treaty. He had not mounted the rostrum for nearly ten years on physicians' advice that his weak heart might not stand the strain. But with the country in grave peril he felt he had to take the chance.

As the hour approached and people began to fill the galleries, de Mun looked pallid and nervous. The spectators craned their necks to see this tall, slim figure with soldierly bearing who had overnight become the symbol of

[20]Ibid., p. 217.

French nationalism. When he started toward the rostrum, cheers and applause broke out and swelled to a mighty roar, the deputies of the Right, the Left, and the Center all joining in with cries of "Bravo!"—an outburst of feeling not witnessed in the chamber since the days of Dreyfus.

Facing the assembly, de Mun stood for a moment amazed and unbelieving but quickly regained his composure. His face glowing, his first words were halting but he was soon in total command and spoke fluently with his old mastery. Why, he demanded, was there such urgency to sign this convention? Had Germany threatened war? Every question he threw out was loudly cheered and he was forced to pause to let the echos die out. Pointing directly at Caillaux he showed no mercy: "Honor is the first of the [nation's] interests. You should thank this generous nation that may save you from yourself." A roar of approval shook the house.

The deputies, aware of France's unreadiness, were not about to offend Germany by repudiating Caillaux's convention. But they could and did repudiate Caillaux, whose ministry fell a few weeks later. Reflecting on the fall of Caillaux in an article for *L'Écho de Paris,* de Mun wrote: "I have no authority now in the councils of government and I say this not without bitterness, but I call upon France's representatives to find a strong leader. My pen and my words are at his service and I am resolved to pursue to the end the campaign that I open today."[21]

De Mun Forges an Alliance with the Moderate Radicals

With this manifesto de Mun served noticed that he was set to embark on an entirely new course in his political life. At the age of seventy, when most men are pretty well fixed in their ideas, he decided on a risky venture that was as great a shift as his conversion to the Ralliement twenty years previous. Passionately dedicated to nationalism and rearmament, de Mun felt that this issue could bring about a whole new alignment of forces in the chamber. He reasoned that the ALP might be able to forge an alliance with the moderate radicals by focusing on their common desire to rekindle the spirit of patriotism and bolster the defense of France.

In forging an alliance with the moderates, de Mun had the advantage of the many social and cultural links he had with their world. He could in the

[21] Ibid., p. 247.

same evening "debate genteelly with Germain Bapst the strategy of the battle of Rezonville in 1870, receive verses from George de Porto-Riche, consult Arthur Meyer of Le Gaulois, and then turn to greet Millerand, Briand, and particularly Paul Deschanel, handsome, dashing, empty-headed, the dandy of the moderates."[22] In 1908 when three vacancies opened in the Académie Française, Raymond T. Poincaré, a candidate, sought assistance from de Mun who was already a member with broad influence within that august body. With the help of de Mun, Poincaré's bid was successful.

But back in Rome the integrist intransigents led by Pius X and his secretary of state, Cardinal Rafael Merry del Val, were set to brook no cooperation with the enemy—that is, the radicals who were responsible for the separation law, the persecution of the religious orders, and the secularizing of the schools. As de Mun had earned the hatred of the royalists in 1892 by embracing the Ralliement, he now, by seeking rapprochement with the church's enemies, risked the wrath of the integrists and, like the Sillonists, the humiliation of a public disavowal by his church and an abrupt end to his political life.

But de Mun was convinced that the leaders of the Church were being unrealistic. It was high time to abandon the whole idea of returning to a Catholic France. De Mun was convinced by now that the Church would simply have to accept its reduced status in France and work slowly by conversion and example to improve it. Instead of working to overthrow the anticlerical laws, the best that Catholics could hope for would be to seek their liberal enforcement. This would have to be done by secret deals with the moderate radicals who could not be expected to antagonize the Left by any open changes in policy toward the Church.

His chance to begin his maneuvers came with the selection of Raymond Poincaré as premier. A colleague of de Mun in the Académie Française, Poincaré was a talented and wealthy attorney, a pragmatist with a proven ability to get along with the diverse factions in the government. Like de Mun, Poincaré saw in the face of the German threat the need to heal the division between clericals and anticlericals. Nationalism would be "the bridge to arch over the clerical line." He had responded positively to some remarks by de Mun emphasizing the need for French unity in spite of past differences over religion, and now entrusted de Mun with a delicate diplomatic mission to Belgium. Though he continued to enforce the anticlerical

[22]Ibid., p. 237.

laws (for example, closing fifty Catholic schools at that very time), he showed other signs of good will such as mentioning the need to have a national holiday honoring Jeanne D'Arc.

Gradually de Mun was able to win over the downtrodden ALP to his aim of making it a part of a conservative and moderate majority, in order to bargain for whatever concessions he could get. But uncertain now of its identity and wondering about its survival, the ALP followed a timid line on touchy issues it had previously fought for. Social Catholicism disappeared from its agenda although de Mun himself continued to carry its banner, crafting legislation in the Labor Committee and campaigning for it in the press.

Poincaré continued to show de Mun marks of his favor such as assigning him to evaluate the Greek, Bulgarian, and Serbian plenipotentiaries who were in Paris on their way to the London Peace Conference. For his part de Mun increasingly saw Poincaré as the only hope of bringing about the rearmament which he (de Mun) called for constantly in his columns. De Mun was convinced that war was inevitable and saw the fighting in the Balkans as the dawn of the apocalypse.

Poincaré had good reasons for seeking closer ties with de Mun. He was anxious to become president of France and de Mun was crucial to getting him the conservative vote he needed since the radicals were sure to block him. Indeed the radicals tried to derail the alliance of de Mun and Poincaré by making an appeal to Catholic prejudice. They spread stories about Madame Poincaré's illegitimacy, her years as Poincaré's mistress, and their civil marriage. Poincaré reacted by secretly promising de Mun to have the marriage blessed as soon as it was possible to determine that his wife's previous husband was no longer alive. He also promised to ease up on enforcement of the anticlerical laws.

Thanks largely to the pact with de Mun, in 1912 Poincaré won election as president of the republic by an overwhelming margin (483 to 287). De Mun apostrophized him in words that could apply just as well to himself: "You have the power to reorient national life."[23]

De Mun now felt that the coalition of moderates and conservatives would be able to maintain control of the government, keeping the radicals at bay while focusing on national defense. But as part of the bargain, de Mun had to convince the Catholic deputies to swallow the bitter pill of laicity, that is, the policy originally espoused by the anticlericals that denied the Church a

[23]Ibid., p. 264.

privileged status in law, especially in such matters as education and marriage. De Mun's success was evident in January 1913 when none of the Catholics opposed a vote of confidence on a pledge of "national defense, social progress, and laicity." The integrists in France and at the Vatican were predictably horrified at this "betrayal" by the "Knight of the Syllabus." De Mun was able to blunt their reaction to some extent by informing the Vatican that Poincaré had fulfilled his promise to have his marriage blessed—in secret.

On the old front Cardinal Merry del Val was unfailingly incensed by de Mun's dogged personal attempts to breathe new life into Social Catholicism—an idea that del Val had wanted buried with Leo XIII. When de Mun came out in favor of the right of workers to have their own unions, del Val warned him in an otherwise laudatory letter against flirting with such dangerous ideas as social equality, which smacked of modernism. He bemoaned the ideas of some social Catholics who spoke of experience and history affecting "natural law" as though the eternal principles of natural law could be thus mutable. Del Val had already put the clamps on Henri Lorin, an occasional collaborator of de Mun and founder of the *semaines sociales*—an annual week of study for Social Catholics. Del Val ordered Lorin to repudiate the teaching that there was "a natural right to join a union, that private property was not inviolable, and that justice bore a greater burden than charity in the solution of social problems."[24]

But a swift change of attitude toward de Mun occurred in the Curia as it became evident to Merry del Val and his colleagues that Pius X was near death. De Mun's strategy of alignment with the moderates was tacitly accepted and even received an unofficial blessing from the undersecretary of state, Cardinal Pacelli. By this time also the imminence of war preoccupied everybody. The Social Catholics, in the meantime, had to tread lightly with the condemnation of Le Sillon hanging over them. De Mun's nearly moribund Oeuvre des Cercles was tolerated, but other more vibrant movements like his ACJF (founded in 1886 to train youths in social action) had to keep a low profile.

Minister of Public Confidence

De Mun had consistently predicted a war with Germany that would begin in the Balkans, although he did not recognize the potential significance of

[24]Ibid., p. 277.

Franz Ferdinand's assassination on June 28, 1914. He left for his summer home, looking forward to his first ride in an automobile. At the end of July he hurried back to Paris, arriving shortly before Germany declared war on August 3. There was never any doubt about France's vote to fight Germany in a war of *revanche,* of which some had dreamed since 1871.

Standing before the casket of his arch opponent, the socialist Jaurès, felled by an assassin's bullet, de Mun called for an end to all division for the sake of a "sacred union." When the chamber erupted in a tumult after war was declared, de Mun was seen striding across the room to grasp the hand of Édouard Vaillant, a lieutenant of Jaurès. Vaillant, a Communard, had never spoken to the cavalry officer who had taken part in the repression of 1871. Shortly afterward Théophile Delcassé, one of those responsible for France's rupture with the Vatican, said to de Mun in a voice bereft of sarcasm: "Will God be with us too?" (referring to the alliance de Mun had just concluded with Great Britain). De Mun answered: "Yes, you may rest easy. God forgives and takes into account the sacrifices of Catholics. He will grant their prayers."[25]

Regretful that his infirmity kept him from active duty, de Mun nevertheless plunged into a round of furious activity. He organized the army chaplaincy that had been eliminated by the anticlericals but was now restored and greatly augmented with the onset of war. He also joined the war ministry as overseer of the reprovisioning of troops. But his great contribution was his daily column in the *L'Écho de Paris,* which won him the title "minister of public confidence." Each day after mass, visits to the wounded at the Red Cross, and consultation with his staff, he would sit down to compose his column. His words were infused with the spirit of hope, courage, and unbounded optimism. Even as the Germans swept through Holland and Belgium and were poised to take Paris, he remained undaunted. "Be heroes! France expects it of you!" he told the troops. He exulted when General Joffre first blunted, then halted, and finally reversed the German attack. He saw the war as a grand means of moral regeneration.

Anxious to match the sacrifices of those in battle, he drove himself to the absolute limit and had to be carried from one office to the next in a light armchair as his heart gave way. He was so preoccupied that not even a message from the newly elected pope Giacomo dell Chiesa, Benedict XV, an opponent of the integrists, seemed to make an impression. His friends and family looked on in distress as they watched him sink slowly under the

---

[25]Ibid., p. 290.

load. When he finally collapsed, the priest who arrived heard him murmur, "I did not know that I was so ill." He died shortly after receiving extreme unction.

Under an ashen gray sky on a rainy autumn day, the body of Albert de Mun was laid to rest in the cemetery of La Chartreuse in Bordeaux. The president of the republic, Poincaré himself, led the procession from the cathedral followed by many of the dignitaries of France, most of the deputies and senators, and twenty thousand mourners. The president of the chamber, Deschanel, delivered a eulogy calling de Mun "the immortal honor of France" and was embraced by Poincaré, openly weeping. His faithful associate Jacques Piou reminded the gathering that de Mun had spent forty years defending lost causes—Social Catholicism, the established church, and nationalism. During his life, Piou observed, de Mun defended unpopular causes but died the most popular man in France.[26]

Legacy

What was de Mun's legacy for Social Catholicism? His ideas on social reform were the most advanced of his day and after considerable delay were vindicated by Pope Leo in his *Rerum Novarum*. But de Mun accomplished little himself for social reform. He had no ready constituency for his ideas as the conservative Catholics were not attuned to his message and the radicals were alienated by his clericalist program. He could only watch later with frustration as the radicals and socialists took over and implemented the ideas of social reform that he had championed a decade earlier.

He met with frustration also in his efforts to restore the Church to a privileged position. France was a vastly more secular society at the end of his career than it was when he began. In time he came to realize that the Church had to settle simply for freedom. For this he was targeted by the integrists, who refused to accept the reduced public position of the Church.

It's quite clear that while blessed with great oratorical and organizing ability, de Mun was lacking in political intuition. He took up royalism at the very moment it became obviously a dead cause, letting himself be seduced by wishful thinking into taking part in a third-rate political melodrama featuring the great ham actor General Boulanger. Then, abandoning his belief that monarchy was France's only salvation, he dutifully accepted Pope

[26]Ibid., pp. 295–296.

Leo's charge to rally behind the republic. But after forming a working relationship with the moderate republicans and getting a taste of national influence, he wagered it all on the guilt of Dreyfus and took the conservatives once more into the political desert.

Only his nationalism eventually found resonance in the body politic. As a former army officer he was the most vocal patriot of his day, calling in season and out for strengthening the military. But even here he was ignored until the arrogant moves of a bellicose Germany awakened France to its danger. Finally his prophetic role was recognized and for the first time in his career he exerted real influence on the course of events. Subordinating the cause of the Church and social reform to the cause of national defense, for the time being, he and his party were able to enter the government as partners of Poincaré and the moderates.

It was only after his death that his lifelong effort to integrate Catholics into France's political life bore real fruit for the Church. In the 1920s France reestablished diplomatic relations with the Vatican, stopped the harassment of Catholic private schools, and incorporated de Mun's Social Catholic ideas into reform legislation. The French Parliament adopted everything he had called for—Sunday rest, limitation of hours of work, protection for working women and children, and insurance for workers suffering from accidents, disease, or old age. Moreover, after 1945 the Mouvement Républicain Populaire adopted de Mun's (and Sangnier's) program of Social Catholicism as its own."[27]

---

[27] Ibid., pp. 298–299.

EIGHT

Monsignor Benigni's
(1862–1934)
Counterrevolution

MONSIGNOR UMBERTO BENIGNI lacked the firebrand air of a leader of the social counterrevolution. A bespectacled, roly-poly Italian priest, he worked out of a small, poorly equipped office on the Corso Umberto I in Rome assisted only by four Polish nuns. Yet he was a dangerous and cunning man, the extent of whose activities went unfathomed by friend and foe alike. This unprepossessing cleric was the creator and controller of a worldwide network of Catholic informants devoted to doing as much damage as they could to the liberal, democratic, and modernist elements within the Church. Armed with the secret dossiers he kept on the private lives of every member of the Curia and countless others, Benigni waged a decades-long war on behalf of integralist Catholicism and in defense of the church faithful to Pius IX's Syllabus of Errors.

Social Catholicism in Italy

The Italian Catholic social movement comprised numerous organizations and forces, united ultimately by a common religious faith and obedience to the pope. It was the counterpart of the widespread Catholic social movements that developed in other countries such as Germany, Austria, and Belgium. These movements in defense of the rights of the Church were something new. In the old era, when church and state were united there was no need to call on the people to defend these rights. But this became necessary after the French Revolution and especially after the revolutions of 1848 and the rise of the threat from militant anticlericals, liberals, and socialists.

In Italy the Catholic social movement was galvanized by the confiscation of the Papal States and of church properties by the leaders of the Italian Unity Movement, who seized Rome in 1870. The pope retreated to the Vatican as a "prisoner" and henceforth followed a policy of intransigence. He refused to recognize the new liberal state, and by the decree *Non Expedit* forbade Catholics to take part in its politics. Those who followed the papal line, the intransigent Catholics, did more than rail at the liberals. They engaged in organizational work aimed to improve the living conditions of the Catholic peasant and landowner, and they began to manifest increasingly popularist and even demagogic tendencies.

By 1887 "the Catholic movement," as it was known, had registered remarkable progress in certain parts of Italy. Under the umbrella of the so-called "Opera dei Congressi" there were some 500 diocesan committees in northern Italy that fostered a large network of banks, mutual benefit societies, and recreational and cultural associations, as well as a flourishing press. In fact, among the bishops and clergy of northern and, to a lesser extent, central Italy there was a strong, lively tradition of awareness and commitment to the economic and social needs of their flocks—especially the poor peasantry—as well as the purely spiritual needs. There was also a powerful political consciousness, born of the struggles between "intransigents" and "conciliatorists": the former boycotted the liberal state in the wake of unification and the destruction of the pope's temporal power; the latter advocated compromise and cooperation.

The leaders of the Opera took their inspiration from the Syllabus in opting for the policy of "intransigence" toward the liberal ruling elite. At the same time the Opera cultivated a positive relationship with the masses by its devotion to social and charitable activities. At first the pace of the movement's expansion was slow, in part because the clergy feared conceding too much influence to the laity. But by 1887, Pope Leo was convinced of the futility of seeking "conciliation" with the Italian regime and he threw his weight behind the Opera. Those of liberal tendencies in the Catholic intelligentsia kept aloof from the Opera and its consistent hostility to all things modern. Otherwise, however, the great mass of Catholics were soon won over.

Origins and Early Career of Umberto Benigni

Umberto Benigni began life in Perugia in 1862, the oldest of five children. Not much is known about his childhood. His family's circumstances were extremely modest and he soon learned how hard money was to come by and how critical it was for family members to help each other. He entered the seminary when he was only eleven. When he was a student of sixteen, the archbishop of Perugia, Joachin Cardinal Pecci, was elected pope and took the name Leo XIII. At eighteen, Benigni was recruited to serve as secretary to Perugia's new archbishop. He was ordained at twenty-two and was sent to Rome for further study at the Seminario Pio, an institution distinguished from other Roman academies by its considerably more open attitude toward modern thought.

After completing his studies Benigni returned home to serve as a professor of history and also as chaplain to the diocesan chapter of the Catholic Association, which coordinated a variety of diocesan activities. In this latter connection he published a newsletter, *Il Piccolo Monitore,* a very modest organ but one that enabled him already to display the qualities of the mature writer—his sharp eye, his verbal facility, and his polemical spirit. It also revealed other traits—a tendency to self-aggrandizement and a weakness for inflating the significance of his own work and affairs.

While Social Catholicism was well advanced elsewhere in northern and central Italy, Perugia at this time remained an undeveloped backwater, devoid of both commerce and industry. Political power was in the hands of the anti-Catholic liberal aristocracy. Benigni's assignment to organize a regional "social action" committee met with general indifference from the bishops and the laity alike. Nevertheless, Benigni was already gaining recognition as a young man of promise. The Opera dei Congressi, now centralized under a national committee, was divided into five sections, of which the second section (Dell' Economia Sociale Cristiana) held special importance. The up-and-coming Benigni was invited to join the second section at the national level.

A Militant Papa

Pope Leo by now was in the process of revising the Church's political stance with a special focus on France and on current social movements, especially Christian democracy. A supreme realist, Leo knew that the union of altar and throne had seen its day and that the future of the Church lay henceforth in its direction toward the people. But though the main thrust of his policies would eventually lead to opening the Church wide to the modern world, this was not Leo's intent. He still dreamed of restoring Christendom and his own temporal power, but this time through popular rather than monarchist means. Benigni shared the pope's vision and swore to remain faithful to the death, according to his motto: "For the Pope always and with the Pope."

To Benigni this meant perpetual war against modern society, born of the revolution: The characteristic of the modern epoch, he wrote, is revolution. Fruit of the errors and the sins of past centuries, it is basically only an expression of the ancient battles of good and evil, truth and error, the power of hell against the work of divine redemption. The Catholic Church, he maintained, resisted and opposed the modern preoccupation with revolution, confident of ultimate victory based on her Founder's promise. Those horrified by the present evils and wanting to share in the Church's victory, he urged, should enlist as soldiers to fight under the Church's direction.[1]

Benigni divided his black-and-white world into two forces—clericals and anticlericals; in the latter category he lumped together liberals, socialists, masons, and Jews, the most dangerous being the socialists, the "reds," who aimed to destroy the clergy. They were the "enemies of freedom and humanity." But he declared war on all the anticlericals, a war without concessions or compromise that he would wage relentlessly for the rest of his career.

On July 3, 1892, there appeared the first issue of a new journal edited by Benigni. The *Rassegna Sociale* devoted its attention exclusively to social issues in the spirit of Pope Leo's encyclicals. With the rise of socialism, Benigni wrote in his pithy style:

> There is now only one choice—God or the revolver. The workers will either be seduced by the socialists into a slavery worse than the one they have endured under the liberals or return to the Church their true de-

[1] Emile Poulat, *Catholicisme, Démocratie et Socialisme* (Tournai: Casterman, 1977), p. 66.

fender . . . Let the priest go down to the factory and meet the workers and let them shake hands as sons with a good father. Only the Church can generate an order based on love; outside of her there is nothing but the disorder of egotism and hatred.

On May 1, 1893, Benigni became chief editor of one of the principal Italian Catholic dailies, the *L'Eco d'Italia,* with headquarters in Genoa. For a young priest of thirty-one the list of his distinctions was already considerable: professor at the seminary, head of both the diocesan and regional Catholic Action, director of the first Italian journal of "Catholic sociology," head of an important subcommittee of the National Catholic Opera dei Congressi and a member of its central board. One observer hailed him as "the most dynamic and vigorous champion of the clerical cause."[2] It was obvious that he was on his way up.

During his two years as editor of *L'Eco d'Italia,* he poured vitriol on his favorite enemies. One cartoon illustrates his overall style of polemics. It showed Italy as Prometheus bound and devoured by a vulture (labeled "freemasonry") but with Hercules (the Vatican) on the way to its rescue. Benigni carried the same kind of imagery over into his text: Religion was a splendid star whose brilliance overshadowed the somber and bloody comet of anarchism; capitalists were vampires sucking the blood of the people by their usury and speculation; Leo XIII was the lion of Judah destined to have a splendid victory over the infernal monster who persecuted the Church.

Like many of his Catholic contemporaries in Europe, Benigni was virulently anti-Semitic. Behind liberalism and freemasonry, behind the troubles of the Church, he always saw lurking the omnipresent Jews who were the ones ultimately responsible for keeping the pope a prisoner in the Vatican, as he asserted. He even propagated the gruesome calumny that Jews practiced ritual murder of Christian children.[3] Unquestionably, Benigni bears some responsibility for the wave of anti-Semitism that swept Italy and Europe in the 1920s.

In edition after edition of *L'Eco,* Benigni hammered away on the theme that only the spiritual reunion of pope and people would free Italy from its present chaos—a situation created by the bourgeois liberals. Their rejection of God and religion had paved the way for the godless anarchists and communists who would show no mercy should they come to power. He pointed

[2]Ibid., p. 116.
[3]Emile Poulat, *Intégrisme et Catholicisme Intégral* (Tournai: Casterman, 1969), pp. 362–364.

out that during the workers' May Day parades the good bourgeoisie already had to hide for fear of the proletariat. For Benigni this signaled the end of laissez-faire liberalism that had already been condemned by *Rerum Novarum*.

The future, Benigni believed, belonged to Catholicism, "papalism," and Christian democracy. But in the meantime there would be brutal and somber days ahead as Satan and his allies engaged in a frontal assault on the mystical spouse of Christ. The so-called liberal Catholics were dreamers in believing that any modus vivendi could be had with these enemies. At times Benigni framed the whole struggle as a titanic conflict between Lucifer and the pope and he was haunted, even terrified, by the possibility of a victory of the forces of Satan. It would be a cosmic catastrophe that would plunge the world into a barbarism beyond anyone's imagining. But Catholics, he insisted, need not despair: As Leo had reminded them in some twelve encyclicals, they had at hand an infinitely powerful weapon, the rosary—the very weapon used by St. Dominic in the twelfth century to defeat the Albigensians, an enemy every bit as insidious and terrible as the enemy of today. Above all, he insisted there must be no concessions—whether spiritual, social, or political—to modernity. Even Leo's call to rally to the republic did not imply any acceptance of the depraved democracy of the freemasons and socialists. The pope meant only that Catholics should accept the fact of the republic in order to Christianize it.

In the summer of 1895, Benigni resigned his post at *L'Eco*. He had fallen afoul, it seems, of the archbishop of Genoa, Monsignor Romaso Reggio (1818–1901). A moderate liberal and friend of the liberal Italian government, Reggio was unhappy with the democratic evolution of society but favored a don't-rock-the-boat philosophy. So Benigni ended up in Rome in the Vatican Library cataloging books and nursing his wounds. "I have found," he announced a bit pompously, "what Dante and Petrarch sought in vain, peace."

Forcibly sidelined from the fray, he shed any remaining illusions about the effectiveness of Catholic action. The world shaped by the liberals, he felt sure, was in its death throes but he doubted that Catholics were in any condition to assist the process. Leo was correct about the direction the Church ought to go, but Catholics as a whole lacked the requisite understanding and energy to implement the pope's vision. Benigni quit the trenches and retreated to a life of study. But he still believed the moribund Church was somehow destined to arise and take the lead in an immense social regeneration—a triumph of the Church that would recall its dynamic influence in the early medieval age of Charlemagne.

Climbing the Ladder During a Critical Decade for the Church (1898–1907)

Despite his banishment by the archbishop of Genoa, Benigni quickly climbed the clerical ladder. From his first humble post at the Vatican Library he was appointed political editor in 1900 and then, in 1901, director of the official Vatican newspaper, *Voce della Verità*. He received a simultaneous appointment to teach church history at the Roman Seminary and in 1902 began publishing his own scholarly journal of history, *Miscellanea*. The next year he left his position at *Voce* to teach at the Propaganda College. In 1904 he moved into the Roman Curia as a secretary in the Congregation of the Propaganda, and in 1906 he was named to the Congregation of Extraordinary Ecclesiastical Affairs as its assistant secretary.

What was Benigni's mature characer? A man of considerable intellectual acuity, he was praised by such leading Social Catholics as Henri Lorin and Léon Harmel for his broad awareness of social issues. Physically he was a rather odd-looking, fat little round ball of a priest whose eyes peered through gold-rimmed glasses and sparkled with intelligence and curiosity. A brilliant conversationalist, he would sit and ramble on nervously in a barely controlled stutter with his legs, arms, and head constantly in motion.

According to his students, Benigni based his lectures in church history on the primary sources. They also gave him credit for raising the intellectual level at the Roman Seminary. But some found his lectures disorganized and his view of history depressing. One of them, Ernesto Buonaiuti, later a well-known modernist, called him extremely skeptical, hard as steel, a deep-dyed pessimist. Buonaiuti was shocked one day, he said, when Benigni told him that history was nothing but a continual vomiting and that one should not expect anything good from human beings; the Inquisition, Benigni declared, was the only answer. What Benigni hated most in modern culture was "the new Rousseauistic religion of humanity" that he saw surfacing among the modernists and Loisyists.[4]

The crisis in the Church at this time over the rise of modernism and Christian democracy was rooted in a conflict of generations. The younger

---

[4] Alfred Loisy (1857–1940), a French biblical scholar and founder of French Modernism, who lost his faith in traditional Catholicism but remained in the Church in order to modernize her teaching. Modernism was condemned by Pope Pius X in 1907 in the encyclical *Pascendi*.

generation of Catholic intellectuals and activists wanted a total change in the Church's approach to the modern world. They had a vision of a revitalized Catholicism, a Church striving to reconcile science and faith, a Church seeking to help rebuild society on the basis of Christian social principles, a Church supportive of democracy—the kind of Church already emerging from the ashes of the liberal state in Belgium, Austria, and Germany.

Murri—Lamennais Resurrected

Italy's leading Christian democrat at this time was Romolo Murri (1870–1944), a young priest who gained a large following of young Catholics within the Opera dei Congressi due to his personal magnetism and his new ideas. He believed the movement toward democracy in Italy posed a great opportunity for the Church. Murri was ordained in 1893 and took a doctorate in theology from the Gregorian in Rome. He also attended lectures of the Marxist Antonio Labriola, who awakened his keen mind to the factors of time and history—factors completely neglected in his neo-Thomist theological studies. He spent a good part of the years 1894 to 1896 developing an argument, based in part on historical materialism, to the effect that Catholicism, not socialism, would provide the key to a sound social order. Reviving Lamennais' dream he urged the Church to put itself at the head of the democratic movement and thus turn the tables on its liberal and socialist adversaries, restoring hegemony of the Church over Italian culture.

Murri propagated his message through his journal *Cultura Sociale*. In its pages, he further developed the idea that the proletariat in partnership with the Church was destined to lead humanity to a higher stage of social awareness. But for this to take place, the Church had to forsake its paternalistic attitude toward the workers and get behind the drive to establish a democratic order. Murri wanted the Church to abandon its policy of abstention from Italian politics, and, as he said, "re-enter history." He saw the contrast between the dome of St. Peter's and the tricolors on the Quirinal, the seat of the Italian government, as a "sign of the conflict between two different and mutually antagonistic cultures,"[5] and he believed in fighting the liberal secular state to the bitter end. But Murri carried on the liberal Catholic tradition, which had begun with Lamennais, with his views on the auton-

---

[5] Hubert Jedin and John Dolan, eds., *History of the Church* (New York: Crossroad, 1981), Vol. IX, p. 93.

omy of the lay Christian in temporal matters and on the separation between the domain of the Church and that of the state.

As the leader of youth against the paternalistic old guard in the Opera, Murri called insistently for lay initiative autonomy and the expansion of Catholic programs in the area of politics, suffrage, and legislation. "The task of Christian Democracy was the awakening of the people to their rights as well as to their strengths so that they could 'conquer' their rightful place in society."[6] Leo basically admired the vital energies of the youth movement gathered around Murri and saw them as the hope of the future. But the pope also feared losing control over their initiatives. Hence his encyclical *Graves de Communi* (January 18, 1901), which insisted on the nonpolitical nature of Christian democracy and its subordination to the hierarchy.

But the differences between Murri's *giovani* (youth) and the old guard loyal to Paganuzzi were absolutely irreconcilable and a schism loomed. Leo then called on Giuseppe Toniolo for help. If anyone might have solved the rift it was this great Catholic sociologist. But the cause was hopeless, though Leo went to his grave still believing that the two parties could be reconciled.

Benigni in Debate with Murri

Murri and Benigni actually had much in common. Both were devoted to the papacy and committed to the battle against secular liberalism and socialism. Both were dedicated to social action. But Benigni wanted to import the new social spirit without altering the Church's own power structure while Murri believed a more profound change was needed—a new religious consciousness that would mean a type of Catholic less submissive to authority and more ready to take self-directed action.

The debate between Murri in the pages of *Cultura Sociale* and Benigni in those of *Voce della Verità* waxed hot and heavy during 1901. Benigni accused Murri of confusing Christian democracy with liberal Catholicism and its acceptance of the modern freedoms. Murri accused Benigni of failing to realize that the democratic movement stood at the crossroads and would become either socialist or Christian. Benigni accused Murri of violating the clearly expressed intent of Pope Leo who urged Catholics to stay out of Italian politics and to focus on social and religious action. In return one of Murri's allies, the journal *Domani d'Italia,* argued that Benigni and his ilk

[6]Sandor Agocs, *The Troubled Origins of the Italian Catholic Labor Movement, 1878–1914* (Detroit: Wayne State University Press, 1988), p. 97.

were doing a great wrong to the Church by refusing to understand the spirit of the pope's encyclicals. Leo didn't want Catholics just to parrot his words but to act on their own initiative to mobilize all Catholics and lead the Church out of its impasse vis-à-vis the modern world. What the pope really wanted, *Domani* said, was for Catholics to take over the leadership of the masses at this critical turning point.

Ominously for Murri, the big guns of the papal and integralist press—*L'Unita Cattolica, La Civiltà Cattolica,* and *L'Osservatore Romano,* rallied behind Benigni's program of a unity that denounced any compromise with bourgeois liberalism or Marxist demagoguery and called for a literal adherence to papal directives. But Murri would not back down. Altogether fed up with Benigni, Murri blasted him in *Cultura Sociale,* deriding Benigni and his ilk for stupidly complaining, yearning for a past that was gone forever. While the young Christian democrats struggled to renew the Church by opening it to modern social and cultural problems, he said, the old guard were doing their best to frustrate these efforts. And how sad, he commented bitingly, to see among them Don Umberto Benigni, who as a young priest had been a fervent democrat himself.

Vatican tolerance for Murri was now approaching its limit. He had been wrong in imagining that in spite of the plain sense of the pope's words, Leo's *Graves de Communi* favored his own views. And he complicated his problems by an ill-timed speech delivered less than a month after the election of Leo's successor. Experience, he argued, showed that freedom itself was not enough; what was needed was freedom with Christianity. Pope Leo had shown that the two were not opposed but mutually enriching. Conservatives had tried to keep the Church allied with the enemies of freedom, but this alliance was expiring under their very eyes. He then went on to say that for Catholicism to be a force for democracy, freedom, and justice, it must itself be renewed at its source, namely by an intellectual and spiritual renewal and a return to the Gospel. As an aid to the reinvigoration of the Catholic message, modern critical methods must be adopted in the teaching of biblical studies. Predictably the hierarchy proved ill-equipped to grapple with this direct challenge.[7] A month later Cardinal Respighi disavowed the speech in the name of the new pope. For Benigni the idea that the Church itself needed renewal was the final proof that Murrism was actually modernism.

[7]Roger Aubert, *The Church in a Secularised Society* (London: Darton, Longman and Todd, 1978), p. 197.

An Integralist Pope

The new pope, Giuseppe Sarto, had taken the name Pius X expressly to show his bond with the four previous Piuses who had fought against the Revolution. Like these namesakes he was intent on restoring a traditional Catholic social order in a world that had become the devil's playpen. In his first encyclical, *E Supremi Apostolatus* (1903), he voiced his alarm:

> We feel a kind of terror considering the gloomy state of humanity at the present hour. Can one ignore the extremely dangerous disease that at this moment, much more than any in the past, attacks human society? Worsening from day to day, it gnaws away at its very marrow as it is bringing about its destruction.

Unlike Leo, the new Pius was no intellectual. He was a man of the people but in the restricted traditional sense—hostile to the new forms of capitalism and concerned about the exploited workers. In immediate political matters he was a pragmatist. In regard to the Italian liberals, there was little doubt the pope would follow the path of his predecessor. As patriarch of Venice he had already worked out an alliance of the moderate parties against the radicals and socialists, and he soon showed that he was open to some arrangement with the moderate liberals in Italy's government. Thus he soon modified Leo's *Non Expedit* of 1870 to allow Catholics at least a minimal participation in the political process.

As Pius worked out this new clerico-moderate orientation, one of his biggest headaches was the Opera dei Congressi, which he called a *putiferio* (a mess). Within the Opera the polarization was now extreme between Murri's youthful, exuberant disciples on the left and the intransigent old guard on the right. The pope pinned his hopes of still salvaging the organization and the unity of the Catholic movement on the center, which was supposedly committed to the papacy's nonpolitical concept of Christian democracy. But then Giovanni Grosoli, the man Pius handpicked as president, fouled up the papal strategy by issuing a circular that seemed favorable to Murri's ideas. That was it. The pope decided the Opera was ungovernable and on July 28, 1904, dissolved it as a national organization. The participating committees in each diocese were put under the authority of their local bishops. Only the section in charge of Catholic social services and faithful to the Vatican's concept of Christian democracy was retained. Murri and his allies formed their own Lega Democratica Nazionale; but this, cold-shouldered equally by the Vatican and the socialists, failed to have any great impact. By the time Murri was excommunicated in 1909, a victim of the antimodernist crusade, most of the young Christian democrats had rejoined the Catholic mainstream.[8]

The Spider's Web

Benigni kept his peace and remained behind the scenes. Fully confident in the new pontiff, he believed that time was on the side of the Church. This conviction did not prevent him, however, from exploiting his vantage point in the Curia to devise a personal means of assisting Pius' campaign against the modernists and Christian democrats. In 1907 he was able to set up a network of spies around the world consisting of Catholics who shared his integralist vision of the Church. At the center was his *Corrispondenza di Roma,* or news bulletin, which he started on May 23, 1907; in 1909 it was renamed *The Correspondence of Rome.* Situated at the hub of the Church he was ideally located to feed the information he gathered into the newsletters, which he circulated among members and friendly journalists.

From his sparsely equipped office, Benigni directed his network of correspondents around the Catholic world. Benigni insisted on the need for secrecy: his agents were never to reveal to anyone the source of information passed on to them. When a document was marked *"sub sigillo"* (under the seal), its contents were to be kept absolutely confidential; however, if only marked "confidential," its contents could be divulged in certain cases but the document itself had to be destroyed.

In 1909 he set up an international association, the Sodalitium Pianum, blessed and financially assisted by the pope though never canonically approved by him. According to its statutes, the association was named after St. Pius V, the "valiant defender of the Church and the Catholic world against its interior and exterior enemies."[9] Its program stated that membership was open to "integral Roman Catholics who accepted integrally the doctrine, discipline, and directions of the Holy See . . . The society," it declared, "is integrally counterrevolutionary, because it is the adversary not only of the Jacobin revolution and sectarian radicalism but equally of religious and social liberalism . . . We consider as wounds on the human body of the

[8]Married in 1912, Murri would be reconciled with the papacy in 1943.

[9]Pius V (1504–1572), previously general of the Inquisition, he embodied the spirit of the Counter-Reformation in its most militant anti-Protestant form.

Church the spirit . . . of democracy . . . as well as of intellectual modernism." An official commentary on the text spoke of the "Counter
Church which prepared during the eighteenth century for its great war for
the conquest of the world and having declared this war in 1789 . . . has
now achieved this conquest by conquering the banks, the press and the
school which have delivered the rest [of the world] to it."[10]

Benigni's media empire diversified and grew, first with *Paulus,* a bulletin
for internal Vatican communications, and then in 1912 with A.I.R. or
International Agency Roma, a press bureau that issued daily and weekly
bulletins. His aim via the latter was to influence coverage of Vatican news in
the world press. Realizing the enormous power of the press as the age of
democracy dawned, he hit on an idea that now seems obvious—furnishing
the press with news releases that would reflect the Vatican's point of view.
Assiduously cultivating friendly relations with both the secular and the
Catholic press, he was able to build up a whole list of dailies around the
world that published his news releases faithfully.

One of Benigni's great ambitions was to centralize the entire Catholic
press under his own control. His success was phenomenal and it made him
for years the "most influential" member of the Curia.[11] Until then virtually
unknown abroad, he now became the man of the hour, the symbol of curial
intransigence and a champion of the Vatican's hard line. He was also a
convenient target for those who opposed the pope's policies but didn't want
to critize the pope openly.

Benigni maintained the clandestine operation of his organizations bril-
liantly. His agents worked by leading their targets into confidential talk
about acquaintances and associates while remaining noncommittal themselves. Meanwhile Benigni took elaborate steps to see that the real names of
the major players, including himself, were never used in speech or writing.
Benigni relied on a list of some 726 code words, twelve of which referred to
himself. Among them were Charles, Charlotte, Mme. Arz, Jerome, Arles,
Kent, Amie O, and Gus. *The Correspondence of Rome*—his bulletin was
"Nelly," Pope Pius was "Michel" or "la baronne Micheline" (a reference to
the archangel Michael), Cardinal Merry del Val was "la princesse George"
(for St. George, the dragon-slayer). The Jesuits were "Nasly" from a tele-
scoping of the name of their founder, Ignatius Loyola; Eugenio Pacelli, the
Vatican undersecretary of state at the time, was referred to as Pack. Christian

---

[10]Poulat, *Intégrisme et Catholicisme Intégral,* pp. 119–123.
[11]Poulat, *Catholicisme, Démocratie et Socialisme,* p. 370.

Democrats or Social Christians were called Ennais—a reference to Lamennais, who Benigni regarded as the founder of "social modernism."

Illustrative of Benigni's bizarre epistolary style is a 1912 telegram to a Belgian journalist wherein he explains why he did not shut down his bulletin *The Correspondence of Rome* as expected.

> Dear Friend,
>
> I find myself again under an avalanche of paper work which explains . . . why my correspondence is broken down. You received my letter announcing the imminent departure of Miss Nelly; then my dispatch announced that she would not leave. The reason is that at the last minute her papa Charles let Michel and George know that Nelly preferred to leave rather than just stay around doing nothing. In fact (this is strictly between us) the prudence of Monsieur George is immense; around here they call him Fear. This prudence is especially applied to poor Nelly; for fear of causing incidents, George insists she avoid taking any fresh air; as a result she has become very anemic. So her papa decided to send her away. But at the last minute Michel and George . . . insisted that they would never let Nelly leave since they hold her in such great esteem and affection.

The main task of the Sodalitium was denouncing and disseminating information about suspected modernists—some, like Cardinal Piffi, "guilty" of no more than a displeasingly "frivolous" lifestyle. One Belgian monsignor was reported for allegedly commenting that he "didn't give a damn for the pope." Others were targeted for being Christian democrats or for their connections with Action Populaire, the French Catholic party founded by Albert de Mun. The Jesuits, who were beginning to take the offensive against the integralists, were special objects of Benigni's ire. He called them "those foxes." Benigni's operation was responsible for the ruination of many careers, and no doubt took a serious toll on the lives of faithful members of the Church.

The unsavory nature of Benigni's activities is graphically illustrated in the case of two priests, Ernesto Buonaiuti and Mario Rossi. In December 1909 they were interrogated by the Holy Office on suspicion of modernism on the basis of information supplied by a fellow priest, Pietro Perciballi, one of Benigni's informers. Perciballi had sneakily obtained the incriminating information during a pretended "friendly" visit with an acquaintance of

Buonaiuti and Rossi. The pope himself had supplied the needed cash for the operation.[12]

Love as the Key to the Problems of Poverty

Pius X's views on issues of social welfare were as conservative as his theological ones. *Caritas* (love), he felt, should be the governing principle of social life. He made this point in an address he gave a few years before he became pope. Reminiscing about his youth in mid-nineteenth-century Padua, he said:

> Even then people complained about the ever increasing number of poor and beggars in this town. A learned and saintly teacher who was a young boy during the eighteenth century repeatedly told us in school that there was no reason for such complaints in those times because without the luxury of public assistance . . . charity took care of all. The substitution of official alms for private alms amounts to the destruction of Christianity, and it is an attack on the principle of property. The tie of love that alone can unite the poor and the rich is broken, poverty becomes a public function, a public office, a public occupation.[13]

However, by the turn of the century even conservatively inclined Catholics were beginning to realize the need for public welfare measures. For one thing, they saw that the rich were too likely to evade the demands of "charity." But Giuseppe Melchior Sarto, the future Pius X, remained fixed in his belief that the existence of rich and poor was divinely ordained: The poor provide an occasion for the rich to gain merit by their freely given alms, while the poor gain merit by their gratitude and their humble acceptance of their lowly lot. "The social symbiosis that united the rich and the poor within the fold apparently came to be seen by Sarto as an essential condition for a Christian community, and hence indispensable to the survival of the church as an institution."[14]

In his personal life Sarto lived out this philosophy to the letter. His acts of charity were legendary. When he was a country priest his firewood was always available to the needy and his granary almost always empty, its contents given away to those in need. Later as a prince and bishop of the

---

[12]Poulat, *Intégrisme et Catholicisme Intégral*, p. 588.
[13]Agocs, *The Troubled Origins of the Italian Catholic Labor Movement*, p. 32.
[14]Ibid., p. 33.

Church, he was generous to a fault, lived like a poor man, and supposedly even had to borrow money for the train ride that brought him to Rome and the papal throne.

In line with his extremely conservative outlook, the pope was not at all in tune with the trade union movement. In 1896, while Patriarch of Venice, he spoke to a gathering of social scientists "about the inexplicable mystery of inequality among men on earth that is as necessary as it is inevitable, and that would return the day after a generous dreamer would think of abolishing it." Even to think of class conflict was to his mind a sin altogether contrary to the true spirit of Christian charity. On these grounds he consistently condemned strikes.

Pope Leo XIII had tentatively endorsed the "simple union" *(unione semplice)* consisting exclusively of workers. His endorsement reflected his general acceptance of some experimentation in ideas. Thanks to this attitude and thanks to his encouragement of priestly involvement in social action, the Italian Catholic labor movement made considerable headway during the last years of Leo's reign. But espousal of the simple union involved many Catholic activists in strikes with overtones of class struggle, and the sight of priests on the picket line horrified Catholic conservatives. The issue of the *unione semplice* had become a major point of contention in the Catholic social movement. The profoundly conservative Pius opposed the *unione semplice* and was determined to make the "mixed union"—of workers and management—the basic organizational form of the Italian Catholic labor movement. This would also mean returning priests to their traditional role as mediators rather than disturbers of social peace.

Besides the issue of the mixed union, there was also much controversy in the Church at this time over the so-called "religiously neutral" or interconfessional unions—in other words, unions whose identity and membership were not exclusively Catholic, and hence not obliged to Rome in any way. Benigni and the integralists stigmatized these neutral unions as a form of social modernism that was rife in Italy, France, Belgium, and especially Germany. The interconfessional unions flourished largely in the industrial Rhineland around Cologne. Hence those who favored them were said to belong to the "Cologne school," while those who favored exclusively Catholic labor unions were said to belong to the "Berlin school" led by Cardinal Kopp. Benigni's attacks on the interconfessional unions greatly influenced Kopp. A big brouhaha erupted between the two schools during Pius' tenure. The German Catholics, unlike Catholics elsewhere, were not docile and mounted considerable resistance to Vatican decrees they felt were unwise. The pope finally decided compromise was the most prudent course and on September 24, 1912, issued the encyclical *Singulari Quadam* that fully approved of the Berlin type of union but accorded to the Cologne type a qualified tolerance. He allowed this exception, as he said, only to avoid greater evils.[15]

The Sacrificial Lamb

A separate issue involving the recalcitrant German Catholics had grave repercussions for Benigni personally. On September 1, 1910, the pope imposed an antimodernist oath on those holding office in the Church, including pastors and professors. The German Church, proud of its superior organization and its tradition of scholarship, did not look kindly on the idea. It was not that the bishops were at all favorable to modernism, but they felt the oath unnecessary and demeaning. The German government, too, had a significant stake in the issue because the oath represented an attempt by the Vatican to exercise direct control over the Catholic universities, which in Germany were purposely state-supported. Accordingly, the Prussian minister to the Holy See met with Merry del Val to request that the oath not be imposed on professors in the universities. When a few days later del Val issued an instruction to this effect, the German government felt it could claim some credit for the change in the Vatican's policy. But *L'Osservatore Romano,* in high dudgeon, flatly denied the existence of any outside influence.

This slap in the face roused a storm of indignation and protest by the Germans who took it as one more example of the overweening pretentions and arrogance of the Curia. At a meeting of the Landtag of Prussia on September 7, 1910, a heated debate opened up over the Roman Curia's "high-handed attitude" toward Germany. Chancellor Bethmann-Hollweg finally arose to deliver an address many considered to be the most important of his tenure. He noted the potential that the antimodernist oath had for reviving old religious quarrels in Germany, and how he had tried to explain this to the Curia. As to *L'Osservatore*'s denial that the German interventions had any effect on Rome's decision to modify the oath, he said: "This is

[15]The discrediting of the Christian labor movement in Germany by the integralists undermined its potential for growth. Figures for 1913 show 2,500,000 workers organized in the free unions while only 340,000, or 12 percent, were in the interconfessional unions. Also there were an estimated 800,000 Catholic workers organized in the socialist unions who were probably no longer practicing Catholics.

hardly the way to encourage normal diplomatic relations." While the pope assured Germany of his desire for peaceful relations, some of his actions seemed to express the opposite intent. Each page of German history, the chancellor said, "shows the responsibility of those who push the two confessions into combat."[16] Calling for Germany to stand up to the pope, one deputy insisted that no other power in the world was as skillful as the Vatican in taking advantage of the slightest sign of wavering on the part of an opponent. But Germany now stood to gain the upper hand, he explained, and in fact the Vatican had already blinked; the "one in charge of the Vatican press service" had done so. But, he went on, the good news is that the "one in charge of the Vatican press service" had been relieved of his duties.

It was true. Benigni had lost his prestigious post in the Vatican Secretariat. What had happened? There was much uninformed speculation at the time. But, as the historian Poulat shows, it all boiled down to the need for a peace offering to Germany. Benigni was chosen as the sacrificial lamb as the Germans had for some time regarded him as the chief cause of their bad relations with the Curia.

The removal did not immediately affect Benigni's wide-ranging influence. As the German minister, Muhlberg, said in 1912: "The influence of Benigni on the Catholic press is in no way diminished . . . He is not only in touch with Catholic papers in every country but his influence is felt even over prestigious secular ones . . . He still meets with the Cardinal Secretary of State and Benigni's replacement, Msgr Pacelli [later Pope Pius XII] . . . refers to him as his friend . . . The situation works well for the Vatican; officially he is a nonentity but at the same time they allow him to spread his poison without bearing the responsibility."[17] Without question, however, the tide had turned on Benigni. From all directions, opponents of Benigni and his brand of integralism now joined forces and made their pressure felt. In a letter signed by a majority of its French bishops, the French Church asked that Benigni be removed from influence altogether because of his violent and surreptitious attacks on them. Spearheading the movement against Benigni and the integralists was a Catholic journal of the Cologne school, the *Düsseldorfer Tageblatt,* which in February 1914 published an exposé of a "center of international intrigue"—Benigni's spy ring. The author was Father Hubertus Honer, a Dutch priest of the Camillian order. In Austria the Jesuits targeted the *Osterreichs Katholische Sonntagsblatt,* a

---

[16] Poulat, *Catholicisme, Démocratie et Socialisme,* pp. 426–429.
[17] Ibid., p. 435.

staunch integralist journal edited by Father Anton Mauss (1868–1917). The journal published an article in October 1913 accusing the Jesuits of joining the ranks of those who are "neither with the pope nor with the Church." The Jesuit Austrian provincial sued Mauss for libel in the diocesan court and won. In addition, the Jesuits and other Social Christians led a campaign to turn public opinion against the *Sonntagsblatt.* Letters in support of the effort were sent to the archbishop of Vienna by the heads of all the important Catholic movements in Austria as well as by 1500 priests of the Vienna diocese.

Benigni Agonistes

Of all his enemies, real and imagined, the Jesuits were the ones Benigni loathed most. As he said in a 1914 letter to his agent in Ghent, Alphonse Jonckx, the Jesuits intended to exploit their false reputation for integral Roman Catholicism to foist on the church an interconfessional and Christian democrat policy. Benigni's view of the Jesuits was corroborated from a totally different perspective by a perceptive former priest and modernist, Ernesto Rutili: "The Jesuits as the avant garde?" he said, "Some would think it a joke to call them . . . the partisans of a new direction for the bark of Peter . . . But there's no doubt they have declared war on the fanatical conservatives, the papal integral Catholics . . . this is to say they [the Jesuits] have taken a position against the directions of Pius X who loves, protects and encourages the integralists."[18] The pope indeed deplored the new orientation of the Jesuits. As Cardinal Gasparri later said, "Pius X was not sure of their orthodoxy and believed them tainted somewhat with modernism."[19] The pope's distrust caused the Jesuit general at the time, Franz Xavier Wernz (1842–1914), much distress and may have hastened his death.

The last great battle of Pius' pontificate and the first great defeat inflicted on the integralists began with an anti-union article, "Sindacalismo cristiano," in *La Civiltà Cattolica* of February 21, 1914, by Father Giulio Monetti, who was a theologian highly esteemed by the pope. He denounced the *syndicats chrétiens* (Christian trade unions) as an offspring of the detestable revolution and a contradiction in terms. He scoffed at such ideas as the "social function of property, workers' rights, and solidarity." Instead

[18] Poulat, *Intégrisme et Catholicisme Intégral,* p. 443.
[19] Ibid., p. 391.

of organizing "strikes"—defined as outrageous, demagogic usurpations—the workers would be better off striving to win the good will and affection of their employers. Charity is needed, not the exotic social justice that some try to make credible. In the final analysis, Monetti argued, intervention of the state in labor matters would only injure the just freedom of the individual.

The article was obviously a trial balloon for an upcoming papal document—an anti-union syllabus, so to speak. To understand what such a document might have meant one must realize, as Paul Misner says, that the formation of Christian labor unions with varying degrees of autonomy was "the most striking development in Social Catholicism throughout Europe in the period before 1914."[20]

On May 27 in an allocution that turned out to be a kind of last testament, Pius deliberately lent clear support to the integralists' cause as he insisted on the need to maintain an "integral" Catholic faith. To make sure that priests preserved this doctrinal integrity he urged the cardinals to see that priests avoid the company of Catholics of suspect faith, as well as books and articles not approved by the Church. Happening to meet Father Chiaudano, the editor of *La Civiltà,* he told him: "Stay the course . . . Fight against Catholic unionism . . . They're screaming because you've touched the wound."[21]

Benigni was extremely pleased by the allocution which, he said, helped to alleviate the "terrible moral and material stress" he was feeling. As he told his constituents: "Our dear Baron Michel," he said, "has just made a wonderful declaration in our favor . . . Courage!" Unfortunately, Benigni no longer enjoyed the support of the majority of the College of Cardinals. Well-organized pressure from moderate and liberal senior cardinals had so far forced the pope to delay making any definitive decree on integralism. The parties were still at a standoff when the pope's death on August 20 made moot the tantalizing question: Would Pius X have issued an anti-trade-union encyclical that would have turned the Social Catholic clock back forty years?

Benigni saw only a bleak future ahead. His forebodings can be glimpsed in a paper found in his ally Jonckx's file. Scribbled in crayon on the back of a wedding invitation, it lists Benigni's ratings of the current cardinals about to vote for the next pope, dividing them into three categories—those too old

[20]Misner, *Social Catholicism in Europe,* p. 322.
[21]Poulat, *Intégrisme et Catholicisme Intégral,* p. 490.

to have much influence, those he could count on, and the rest. The latter were described with such remarks as "liberal" or "nullity" or, in one case, "less than null." Some of them were denigrated in rather colorful terms: Cardinal Mercier, for instance, was "linked with all the traitors in the Church"; O'Connell of Boston "used money to get ahead"; Vannutelli was "the dirtiest scum one could imagine, ready for any treason"; Merry del Val was "the great Fear"; Billot was "on the right side, but blind and in tow to Merry del Val"; Rampolla was "a dreamer, a megalomaniac, the Jules Verne of ecclesiastical policy." In fact, out of all eighty-five, Benigni apparently thought well of only nine.

Before Pius died he had named fourteen more cardinals, ten of whose nominations Benigni had predicted. One that he failed to foresee, Giacomo Della Chiesa, was a former member of the Curia and no friend of Benigni's. In the conclave, Maffi and Della Chiesa split the votes for a number of rounds while the opponents of a more liberal policy tried to block both. The cardinals who were convinced that the integralists had done severe damage to the Church finally succeeded in electing Della Chiesa by thirty-eight votes against eighteen for Serafini, the candidate of the integralist cardinal De Lai.

Della Chiesa chose the name Benedict XV. In his inaugural encyclical Benedict gave the integralists a plain warning to desist from their denunciations. His antipathy toward Benigni was well known. Did he, as the story goes, offer his ring to each curial dignitary as he walked past but hold his hand back when he came to Benigni? (*"Se non è vero è ben trovato!"* as the Italians say.[22])

The new atmosphere in Rome was described by the Marquis Filippo Crispolti in a letter to his wife: "One now breathes more easily . . . the title 'scholar' no longer has negative implications . . . Msgr Duchesne [a noted historian of the church] is no longer a *bête noire* . . . Redress has been made to other victims of the fanatics . . . Benedict XV often insists on the need to respect the authority of the bishops . . . The words 'integral or papal Catholic' are taboo . . . He always speaks well of non-Catholics."[23]

[22]Ibid., pp. 601–602. The Italian expression: If it isn't true, it should be!
[23]Ibid., p. 601.

Nemesis at Benigni's Door

But Benigni's goose was only really cooked several years later when a cache of his letters and papers seized by the German military during the war were at last made public. After the war, the papers had come into the possession of Father Guerts, a Dutch priest-journalist, who invited the brilliant church historian Fernand Mourret (1854–1938) to take a look at them. Mourret immediately boarded a train in Paris on February 12, 1921, and arrived that evening at Guerts' residence in Holland. He instantly realized the importance of the cache. In a letter to his friend Maurice Blondel, he noted: "The Pope (Pius X) was convinced that a vast conspiracy of modernists, liberals, and Christian democrats threatened the church and it was urgent they be unmasked."[24]

Mourret took copious notes back with him to Paris. Wanting to keep the matter quiet until he could notify a higher authority, he showed them only to his superior and a few other priests and friends. Some of the material was so comical they couldn't help laughing. But much of it they found simply disgusting. The Jesuits were especially upset at the way they were constantly vilified by the integralists. For the great Catholic philosopher Maurice Blondel, the shock was virtually physical so horrific was the picture it revealed of the integralists' machinations in the Curia. "What foul motives or sadistic impulses would drive people to do this kind of thing?" he cried. "Was it money, power, revenge, love of intrigue . . . Were they dupes . . . of political agents?" And lurking behind it all, he wondered, was there not the Evil One? "Think what they have done: the holy men they've driven crazy, the weak destroyed, and think how they've poisoned the atmosphere, sterilized the intellectual and social movement launched by Leo XIII!"[25] It was too much!

Mourret drew up a memorandum based on his investigation and sent it to Rome. In this *Mémoire Anonyme* he described in detail the character of the Sodalitium Pianum, organized and directed by Monsignor Benigni and the network of affiliated groups that Benigni also set up. Mourret noted that the "soul of the Society" was the secrecy that Benigni emphatically insisted on. Mourret saw to it that his memorandum was confided to a high-ranking

[24] Ibid., pp. 38–44.
[25] Ibid., p. 41.

official of the Curia whom he could trust. He knew that nailing Benigni would not be easy since he had some powerful protectors in the Curia.

Replying in September 1921 to Mourret's anonymous *Mémoire,* Benigni insisted the attack was the work of a coalition organized to fight the antimodernists and antidemo-liberals. On the tenth of November, 1921, Benigni was invited to explain the nature of the Sodalitium Pianum and the reason for its clandestine operation. In reply Benigni stated that Sodalitium from its inception had the full approval of the pope, who on several occasions personally blessed the enterprise and who supplied it with a thousand lire a year. Benigni justified the use of a secret code for the same reason that governments, embassies, and banks use one, namely to conceal information that might aid one's enemy. In the service of the Holy See the Sodalitium had to carry out missions that required secrecy.

Certainly, Benigni went on, none of the Sodalitium's "secrets" were withheld from the pope, who through his secretary was kept informed on a nearly daily basis of its activities. Nor was the Sodalitium a secret to its many friends among the cardinals, bishops, and clergy, and even the laity. In an accompanying personal letter to Cardinal Sbaretti who was conducting an investigation, Benigni rejected as calumnious the allegations that he lived in high style with servants. Anyone who visited him could see that he was a poor man (as he had always been) living in the smallest apartment in his building, barely managing by picking up jobs teaching. What was going on, he said, was easy to see: The Sodalitium had been the work of Pius X, created to serve him amid risks and dangers. The hatred and rancor it generated against the pope was now turned against Benigni. With the pastor dead, the wolves now howl against the pope's faithful watchdog.

But Nemesis was at the door. On November 25, 1922, the Sodalitium was ordered disbanded. The reason given was its violation of canon law's ban against an "association of espionage."

A Born-Again Fascist

Cast into the outer darkness, Benigni now watched the world move toward the apocalypse he had long felt coming, first with the World War and then with the Russian Revolution. For him Bolshevism, "the most terrible calamity to strike humanity," was the latest stage of the one and indivisible *Revolution*—starting with the Protestant revolt in the sixteenth century and continuing through the French and on to the Russian revolution. Benigni's obsession with "Revolution" was intimately connected with his profound anti-Semitism. His prejudice in this regard was based on the delusive conviction that "world Jewry" directed the "Revolution." The Jews, he believed, were imbued with a messianic faith that the "Revolution" would revenge them on the Christians who had persecuted them for centuries. Benigni let himself believe that a hidden global network backed by immense financial power kept the pot of social disorder constantly boiling.[26] The precise way in which Benigni's own clandestine creation exactly mirrored his own paranoid fantasies would be merely pathetic were it not for the fact that he exercised real power to destroy lives and to lead on countless Catholics in their hatred for the Jewish people.

Even as his influence faded, Benigni fought on. He began collaboration with Paolo De Töth, a priest and fiery former editor of *L'Unità Cattolica,* one of the leading intransigent journals. In the pages of their new journal *Fede e Ragione,* Benigni and De Töth carried on their battle against the usual suspects: liberal Catholicism, socialism, modernism, Judaism, laicism, and the rest. A prime target of Benigni's ire was Don Sturzo's successful Popolare party. Although made up almost entirely of Catholics, the party professed to be nonconfessional. At first Benigni and De Töth were also adamantly opposed to fascism and considered Mussolini one of the rank materialists of history. Fascism's aim, they believed, was to de-Christianize Italy and to deify the state. But as the fascist noose tightened around Italy's throat and Mussolini began making friendly overtures to the Church, *Fede e Ragione* moderated its hostility. Sturzo and his liberalism, it declared, were greater evils than Mussolini and his fascism. The journal's sympathy toward fascism increased when Mussolini declared war on the freemasons and even more so when he restored the crucifix to the classrooms and religion to the schools. No doubt Benigni and De Töth were happy to see Sturzo forced into exile as the Church gave its blessing to Mussolini's regime of terror and blood.

In 1924 Benigni began to replicate, more or less, the espionage system he had created during his Vatican period. He set up a new bureau of information, Agenzia "Urbs," reporting this time not to the pope but to Mussolini's l'OVRA—the equivalent of the German Gestapo. For Benigni, fascism stood for order against the forces of disorder. In addition, Urbs published two periodicals, the biweekly *Veritàs* and the monthly *Romana,* and also various pamphlets, often anti-Jesuit ones. Benigni also formed the Intesa Romana di Difesa Sociale (Roman committee for Social Defense), an echo

[26]Poulat, *Catholicisme, Démocratie et Socialisme,* pp. 442–445.

of the Sodalitium. Members had to be Christians, of the "Aryan" race, and committed to "Religion, Family, and Country." Besides its devotion to order, fascism also appealed to Benigni because of its mystical vision of Rome as the mother of civilization. Fascism, he believed, was providentially destined to revive the universal civilizing mission of Rome in place of a faltering and divided Catholicism. In his bitter last years, Benigni's cup of vitriol brimmed over. Any Catholic viewpoint other than his own terrified and revolted him:

> Repugnant hypocrites! . . . whether they preach the word of Lenin or piously mutter pacifist paternosters . . . No more nonsense. It's time to mount a patriotic and social defense against the monsters who have put themselves outside the law.[27]

As pitiful as he was hateful, Benigni ended in an isolated, hostile desert largely of his own imaginative making. "My banner is drooping on the ground," he wrote in a becalmed moment. But his final letters more often reveal a soul in torment, overwhelmed by a sense of futility:

> After a half century of swallowing filth I have no concern about my reputation . . . life for me is vomit . . . If I were as virtuous as my philosophy I could look on the cross with confidence; but I'm counting on his infinite mercy to pardon me . . . for hating this dog's life . . . What a way of the cross . . . Here I am without a penny, reduced to poverty.[28]

At times he sounded like a skeptic. But those who knew him well testified to his "integral" faith. He died on February 27, 1934, according to the *Giornale d'Italia* retaining "full lucidity of spirit" to the end. No mention of his passing was made in the Vatican's official newspaper, *L'Osservatore Romano,* nor in *La Civiltà Cattolica* where he had long since ceased to exist. A good number of the laity attended his funeral, including several dozen members of parliament and twelve carabinieri in full-dress uniform—but only two members of the clergy, both of them former members of the Sodalitium.

[27] Ibid., p. 466.
[28] Ibid., pp. 469–471.

Benigni's Impact

The sad career of Monsignor Benigni illustrates the course of Catholic integralism at the turn of the century. Favored by the pope, Benigni and his cohorts were able to inflict considerable harm on the "modernists"—a term they applied to anyone who tried to adapt the Church's teaching to the intellectual, political, and social trends set in motion, they felt, by the French Revolution. For them the French Revolution was indeed the original sin of the modern world.

Social Catholicism was nearly destroyed by the integralists but, as Paul Misner has said, its roots were sunk so deep in some bastions of Catholicism that it could not be eradicated. The Catholic labor movement, in particular, suffered a serious setback, but it survived to prepare the ground for further progress. In contrast to the crisis of 1848, the doors of the Church were kept open for a new surge of democracy.

In spite of its decline at the death of Pius X, integralism did not disappear and probably never will. Integralism will always remain as a temptation for certain Catholics with a straightforward and oversimplified view of papal and church authority. Integralism will always have a special allure for those insecure souls who look to the Church as a refuge in a world of constantly accelerating change.

NINE

Don Sturzo (1871–1959)

vs.

Mussolini's Revolution

"We have here [referring to Mussolini] in fact, a revolution in many ways as fundamental as the French and Russian revolutions."[1]

MANY OF THE PEOPLE in Rome, upon awakening on the morning of October 28, 1922, were startled to hear the roar of thousands of voices singing "Giovanezza." A strange procession greeted their eyes—a ragged collection of men armed in the most fantastic manner with revolvers, sporting rifles, cudgels, machine guns, even hoes and table legs.[2]

At a window of the Villa Ruffo Scaletta, a priest watched as the procession marched by under black banners decorated with the skull and crossbones. He turned his face to the wall and wept—for Italy but also for the priesthood because of the priests he saw marching under the ghastly banners. The next day the leader of their "revolution," Mussolini, joined them and took over Rome.

The priest who wept at the window was Luigi Sturzo, one of the greatest statesmen of the twentieth century; he was the founder of the Italian Chris-

---

[1]J. S. Barnes, *The Universal Aspects of Fascism* (London: Williams and Norgate, 1928), pp. 14–15.

[2]G. Salvemini, *The Origins of Fascism in Italy* (New York: Harper Torchbook, 1973), p. 378.

Luigi Sturzo

tian Democratic party (originally called the Partito Popolare), a courageous foe of fascism, a prophet who never wavered in his devotion to democracy at a time when it was questioned on all sides, especially in his Church, and a priest according to the order of Melchisedech. The historian Binchy characterized him as "a radical social reformer . . . candid, fearless, brilliant, and above all else an honest man."[3]

Academic Youth, Activist Priest

Luigi Sturzo was born at Caltagirone in Sicily on November 26, 1871, into a family linked with the rural aristocracy. His father Felice, Baron of Altobrando, was a devout Catholic active in the affairs of his community. His mother, Caterina Boscarelli, was the daughter of a physician. She was well read, especially in religious literature, a woman of deep faith and solid piety who profoundly influenced Luigi's own religious development. She was a strong woman and a strict mother—one you obeyed, as Luigi's brother Mario recalled, because you knew there was no alternative. She gave Luigi a

[3]D. Binchy, *Church and State in Fascist Italy* (London: Oxford University Press, 1940), p. 65.

happy and secure childhood and encouraged his interests in music, art, and religion.

Sturzo's uncle, Emmanuel Taranto, was active in Sicilian politics and host to many of the leaders of the nascent "Catholic movement." One of Sturzo's boyhood memories was hearing Emmanuel recall in rapturous tones the great days of the Irish patriot Daniel O'Connell, of the Italian liberal Father Ventura, and of the Revolution of 1848.

Sturzo entered the seminary in 1883 and tackled his studies with zest, editing a paper named *La Saetta* and trying his hand at poetry. One poem already shows the glimmerings of a social conscience in a reference to oppressed and miserable people. However, his ambition was to become a professor of philosophy and sociology. What first turned him to Catholic action, as he recalled in his old age, was an old manual he found in his uncle's library when he was about sixteen. It was the handbook of the Opera dei Congressi, or Association of Catholic Committees, the first national organization of Italian Catholics dedicated to social action.

Luigi was engaged in advanced studies at the Jesuit-run Gregorian University in Rome when in 1894 his ambition for an academic career was overtaken by his decision to devote himself to the social apostolate. The sudden change was occasioned by his first visit to the slums of Rome. The sight of the wretched misery of the city's poor devastated him; in fact, he was so sickened that he couldn't eat for days afterward. He put aside his reading of Aquinas and Augustine and began to pore through the tomes of the socialists in search of an answer. At the same time he frequented the company of some of the leading Catholic intellectuals of the time including Father Romolo Murri and Monsignor Giacomo Radini Tedeschi, later bishop of Bergamo and mentor of Angelo Roncalli (Pope John XXIII). He was also able to attend lectures by the outstanding Catholic sociologist Giuseppe Toniolo. The latter's "Program of Catholics faced with socialism" (Programma di Milano, 1894) was for its time a forward-looking and even revolutionary program of social reform. It attributed the success of socialism to the prolonged violations of the Christian social order of justice and charity. It called for, among other things, redistribution of the land to the peasants and profit-sharing for workers.

Thus inspired, Sturzo returned to Caltagirone and plunged into a heavy round of organizing farmers' and workers' associations. He soon established a network of small banks based on the parishes and also formed a young workers' movement. At the same time he endeavored to stir up interest among the clergy in social problems.

His personal energy and effectiveness notwithstanding, young Sturzo had his work cut out for him. Social Catholicism was by this time well on its way in the northern and central regions of Italy. But apart from a few exceptional areas in Sicily and Calabria, southern Italy and the islands had little tradition of organized Catholic social action on which to build such a movement. In fact in all of Sicily there were only five diocesan committees and nine worker cooperatives; and before Don Sturzo's efforts, there were none in Caltagirone.

Moreover, in Sicily clerical ignorance was endemic and clerical indolence and immorality rife. It was not easy to create a new activist model of priesthood with men whose work since time immemorial was confined to strictly ritualistic and "churchy" activities. Nor was it easy to create a social conscience in a clergy heretofore submissive to the local squire, a clergy whose mental horizons were extremely narrow and whose concerns were typically limited to petty local quarrels over titles and honors.

It was only with the election of Leo XIII that a change in the south began to take place. His call for a social Catholicism in the encyclical *Rerum Novarum* (1891) met with a good reception in the Sicilian Church. Interest in social programs caught fire in the seminaries, and throughout the dioceses clergy and lay Catholics gathered to discuss social problems. Catholic journals began to resound with lively debates over such topics of social justice as the meaning of Christian democracy. At first the interest in social problems stayed on the level of theory. But the move from theory to social action took place after strikes broke out all over Sicily in 1892 involving labor unions (called *fasci*) of miners and agricultural laborers often under socialist leadership. The outbreaks caused panic among the Italian upper classes and brought about the fall of the government. For Catholics it was a great shock to realize that the supposed religiosity and conservatism of the rural peasantry was an illusion. It forced them to come to terms with the full import of *Rerum Novarum* and its insistence on the need for social reform.

The first bishop in Sicily to foster the Catholic social apostolate was the bishop of Agrigento, Gaetano Blandini. His episcopate, in fact, is representative of the transition in the age of Leo XIII from the conservative and traditional parish to the social, activist parish with its rural credit unions and cooperatives. Up to this time tradition confined the role of the priest to religious rituals and preaching. But Pope Leo encouraged the priest to go beyond this role when he made a casual remark to the pioneer French Social Catholic Leon Harmel in the course of an audience: "The clergy has to leave the sacristy and live with the people. The parish priest does not have to limit himself to be the minister of the cult and guardian of faith; but has to be the friend and adviser of the people in their earthly interests also." "Out of the sacristy" soon became a watchword among progressive-minded bishops and priests.[4]

Sturzo's efforts reflected the spread of a new movement within the Church called Christian Democracy which had originated in Belgium, France, and Germany. In Italy it was given great impetus by Sturzo's friend Romolo Murri who was determined to shake his fellow Catholics out of their doldrums. The Church, he insisted, could no longer afford to remain aloof from the political and social developments of the time; it must either get involved in the new world created by democracy or lose many of its youth to socialism. To combat the propaganda of the socialist journal *Critica Sociale,* Murri founded a journal he named *Cultura Sociale.* Sturzo was greatly influenced by Murri, especially by his idea that the laity's task in the world was complementary but not essentially subordinate to the Church's salvific work in the spiritual realm.

Sturzo's Vision

In Caltagirone, however, Sturzo avoided speculations or theories and simply began organizing. Flushed with enthusiasm, he addressed the bishop and members of the local branch of the Opera dei Congressi about the new age of the people that was coming upon them, and the need to have faith in the people. Determined to work within the structures of the Church, he organized in 1895 a workers' group affiliated with the central Opera. He showed his populist sympathies in attacking aristocrats, the bourgeoisie, and socialists for undermining the faith of the people. He proclaimed a counterrevolution that Catholics would wage not with arms but with the cross to win back the masses to Christ. He was resolved to observe the papal ban on participation in Italian politics until the time when the ban was lifted. In the interim, he felt, the ban would provide time for Catholics to grow in social awareness so that when the time came to enter politics they could do so without merely becoming bourgeois liberals themselves.

The government was composed of liberals not at all devoted to democracy who saw a definite threat to their hegemony in this democratic strategy and tried to cut Sturzo and his kind off at the pass. Instructions were sent out to the police to monitor clerical involvement in political activity, and in

[4]Agocs, *The Troubled Origins of the Italian Catholic Labor Movement,* p. 77.

particular to ban meetings in churches. When Sturzo held a meeting to organize a people's bank in the sacristy of the Church of St. Benedict in Militello, it was rudely terminated by the police and he was arrested. He defended himself by arguing that the sacristy was not part of the church. He escaped a penalty but was made aware that it would be dangerous to continue on this path. Undaunted, he started a bimonthly journal, *La Croce di Costantino,* to serve as an organ of the diocesan and parochial committees in Caltagirone. On the masthead were inscribed two quotations from Leo XIII: "If democracy is Christian it will give to your country a future of peace, of prosperity, and of happiness"; and "One cannot deny the existence of a universal democracy that will be, depending on our zeal, either socialist or Christian." His adversaries promptly burned a copy of *La Croce* in the piazza of Caltagirone while the crowd sang a hymn to Garibaldi.

In 1901 several addresses Sturzo gave before the Italian Catholic Association at Milan showed his comprehensive grasp of the problems of Sicilian industrial and agricultural workers. He pointed out that the small scale of these enterprises and their absence of machinery made it virtually impossible for them to compete with the large factories of the north. A lack of capital and a traditional spirit of cutthroat competition hurt everyone: The craftsmen were reduced to a sorry state and many of them had to stay constantly on the road to find the few available jobs. In spite of their desperate situation, it was hard to organize the Sicilian craftsmen into cooperatives. Part of the reason lay in their history of independence. But the root cause, Sturzo thought, was the nature of industrial capitalism itself. The large factories could spew out goods at prices the individual artisan could not match.

In these speeches Sturzo addressed the problems of the farmer in Sicily. He set forth a vivid picture of the distress of the tenant farmers, who were terribly exploited by foremen who took the place of the absentee landowners and charged the tenant farmers excessive rent. In addition, the tenant farmers were charged usurious rates on loans they took out in order to buy seed. The remedies, Sturzo said, were obvious: the farmers needed to unite and form cooperatives to eliminate the foremen; there was also a need for government regulation of the tenant contracts and for education to make farming more efficient. In 1896 Sturzo began setting up rural banks that would make loans to members at low interest rates. By 1905 there were 145 of these Catholic rural banks in the region.

In sum, by 1900 Sturzo's basic ideas had taken the shape they would retain for the rest of his life. Especially noteworthy was his belief that

ownership of small and middle-sized property was the best means of securing social stability. He also evinced a particular wariness toward industrialization, which gave rise to an alienated proletariat and tended to destroy the
family and tradition. One remedy he favored was the formation of cooperatives. He also favored regionalism as opposed to state centralism, believing
that local governments should have prior responsibility in meeting the needs
of the people. This was connected with his concept of freedom, which
demanded that people be intimately involved in the decisions that affect
their interests and that they not allow themselves to be made wards of an all-
knowing and benevolent state.

At this time both socialists and Catholics, each vying for the loyalty of the
masses, were committed to the cooperative ideal. They differed, however, in
their views of private property: The Catholics believed that the peasant
should have the right to his own piece of property, while the socialists
permitted private property as only a stage on the way to its abolition in a
collectivist state. The socialists were also more willing to use the strike as a
weapon against powerful owners. Catholics preferred less confrontational
methods. But, at least initially, the socialist case for strikes prevailed in Italy
and work stoppages proliferated throughout the country. Government statistics, in fact, show that during the fourteen years ending in 1900 there
were a total of 2,555 factory strikes with 676,669 workers participating. In
that time period there were 178 agricultural strikes with 84,022 participants,
and from 1901 to 1914 there were 2,978 agricultural strikes with 1,500,300
participants.

Although hesitant at first, Catholics finally realized that the steadily worsening condition of the working masses might necessitate the use of strikes.
The first Catholic-organized strike was led by the peasants in Palazzo Adri-
ano in 1901. Sturzo lost no time in coming out in their support and praising
the parish priest who organized the strike. Thanks to this strike, Sturzo said,
Christian Democracy had now acquired a name, a conscience, and maturity. He himself led a strike of 80,000 peasants at Caltagirone two years later
over the same issue—exorbitant rent demanded by the proprietors. Before
going out on strike the workers tried to reason with the owners and their
foremen, but to no avail. It was Sturzo's first strike action and his first
"grande agitazione di massa"; it lasted three months and ended in victory for
the strikers. But Catholic organizers had much catching up to do, for the
socialists were far ahead in organizing the peasantry. In 1913 the number of
"red" rural labor leagues was 2,151 with 286,181 members, while the number of "white" Catholic locals was 315 with a total membership of 52,220.

Sturzo soon saw the close connection between the peasant struggle and the politics of the commune, and concluded that agrarian reform could be attained only by breaking the monopoly of political power held by the landowners. In 1899 he ran successfully for mayor of Caltagirone on a populist program and won. In 1905 he was also elected deputy *pro-sindaco* and provincial counselor, posts he held until 1920. In these capacities he was able to carry out reforms that left a deep imprint on the administration of Caltagirone, one of the most important being a policy of strict financial accountability. In addition, during his fifteen years in office he carried through a number of municipal reforms and built community houses for the workmen, a municipal power plant, and a technical high school.

Hard Years for a Christian Democrat

In the meantime the Opera dei Congressi was torn between the conservatives who used the Catholic organization as a papal auxiliary committed to intransigence, and young activists inspired by *Rerum Novarum* who saw the Opera as a vehicle toward the formation of a Catholic mass party committed to Christian Democracy. Sturzo defined Christian Democracy as a "system in which the interests of the people will be guaranteed and safeguarded by the people themselves with the representation of every 'class' in Parliament." Like Lamennais nearly a hundred years earlier he looked to the day when the Church would take the lead in vindicating the rights of the "proletariat."[5]

But Pope Leo, over ninety and under pressure from reactionaries in the Curia, dissociated himself from Christian Democrats like Sturzo and Murri and in 1901 came out with an encyclical, *Graves dei Communi*. It defined Christian Democracy in a nonpolitical sense as merely beneficial works of mercy on behalf of the people. But since the pope did not explicitly condemn political Christian Democracy, the new movement continued to grow much to the distress of the old guard within the Opera. This tension exploded at the Opera's congress in Bologna in 1903. One side spoke of the rights of the papacy but the other side, much more numerous, spoke of the rights of the poor to the point that one journalist felt he was present at a "workers' " or socialist assembly.[6]

---

[5] From articles by Sturzo in *La Croce di Costantino* 1900–1901 cited in John Molony, *The Emergence of Political Catholicism in Italy* (Totowa, N. J.: Rowman and Littlefield, 1977), p. 41.
 [6] Ibid., p. 28.

★ ★ ★

Pope Pius X, who succeeded Leo in 1903, was a pious man with little understanding of the complexities of modern problems. He felt little sympathy for the Christian Democratic wing of the Opera, in part because of Murri's "modernist" tendencies, but also because of the radical nature of the Christian Democratic program. Pius resolved the problem of the split within the Opera by dissolving it as a national body and putting the diocesan and regional committees under tight control by the bishops. The pope also lent aid and comfort to the mania for orthodoxy that had taken possession of Vatican officialdom. As a result, *Le Sillon,* Christian Democracy in Italy, and Murri personally went down the tube. In all, as one author recently put it, Pius "transformed the Leonine garden of ideas into a desert and called it the kingdom of God."

Undaunted, Sturzo continued his work on the local level. He admitted that the Christian Democrats' effort to politicize the Opera was misguided, for the Opera's proper mission was essentially religious. What was needed, he felt, was a national party of Catholics that would be independent of Church authority. He outlined the nature of such a party in a speech on December 29, 1905, at Caltagirone that has been called the Magna Charta of the Christian Democratic party. This new party, he said, would have a social democratic content and would aim at the regeneration of civic life. It would be inspired by Christian principles but would not have a religious agenda. It would not enter politics as an agent of the pope but as a vehicle for citizens inspired by Christian principles to contribute to the solution of social and political problems. The party would shelve the volatile "Roman question"—the issue of the precise territorial claims of the Vatican within Italy—until the time when the nation had changed its attitude toward the Church.

The statement breathed with his passionate belief in democracy. Any other option for the new party was inconceivable for him. The superiority of democracy, he felt, no longer needed proof. Democracy was essential for the regeneration of society in Christ—the aim of Catholic political activity. Catholic conservatism, he believed, was obsolete. And if this issue must cause division within the ranks of Catholics, so be it. Fortunately, for the future of Christian Democracy in Italy, Sturzo was able to avoid Murri's sad fate.[7] The latter wanted the Church to take the lead of the nascent democratic movement and he formed the National Democratic League in 1905 to

[7]See previous chapter on Benigni.

unite Catholics committed to democracy. His opponents, the integralists, still wedded to dreams of throne and altar, were powerful in the Vatican and were able to tar him with the modernist brush and have him excommunicated. But they failed to trap Sturzo, who stayed clear of theological speculation and tended his affairs in Sicily. He knew how to bide his time.

The years that stretched from the dissolution of the Opera and Murri's demise to the First World War were especially trying for Sturzo. He was very much at odds with the Vatican, which now became directly involved in Italian politics. The Vatican virtually abandoned the *Non Expedit* and, through Gentiloni, the head of Catholic Action, was able to marshal the Catholic vote behind politicians who promised to support favorite Catholic policies such as anti-divorce laws, state-sponsored religious education, and efforts to stem the tide of socialism. This "Gentiloni Pact" sickened Sturzo who knew that these Vatican-backed candidates were not only reactionary but corrupt and violent. It was, he believed, a betrayal of the workers and the poor.

In fact Sturzo saw the whole of national politics as one vast, corrupt machine—backed by the Mafia, countenanced by the Church, and suffered by the people. Refusing to despair, he kept his eyes on the future and continued to build the foundations of a national party within the remnant of the Christian Democrat movement in Sicily. His chief concern was to preserve the social organizations—the network of banks and unions—that he hoped would one day be the basis of a great mass party. During these frustrating years he was able to register some success in local administrative politics while simultaneously holding at bay his personal enemies in the Church who came close to destroying him. Just how close was revealed to him in a 1914 audience with Pius X who greeted him affectionately with the words, "Oh, Mister Mayor, haven't they excommunicated you yet?" "No," Sturzo answered, "unless you are ready to do it." "Not I, dear Sturzo," the pope replied with a laugh, "but watch out for the others," and dismissed him with a blessing on his work.[8]

As Mayor of Caltagirone and an unswerving social reformer Sturzo lived constantly in the eye of the storm. At one point his local political enemies decided to get rid of him with a little help from the Mafia. Shots were fired on him as he was out walking with his breviary, and a letter threatening his life was sent to his brother, the bishop, who begged him to quit while he was still alive. The maneuvering of Sturzo's Vatican enemies came to a halt

[8]Gabriele De Rosa, *Don Luigi Sturzo* (Turin: Unione Tipografico-Editrice Torinese, n.d.), p. 146.

when Benedict XV ascended the papal throne in 1914. Benedict himself had been targeted by the heresy hunters, and as pope was determined to put a stop to their machinations. Sturzo was appointed to the governing board of Catholic Action, which widened his sphere of influence.

The outbreak of war in 1914 was welcomed by Sturzo, strangely enough. He saw it as bringing to light the hidden moral reserves of the people, of creating a "nation where previously there had been no more than a multitude," "the great test of our life as a young nation," an "antidote to the all-pervasive materialism and egocentricity, a sacred and tragic moment."[9] But later, in his old age, he admitted that the results had been totally otherwise. Besides the tremendous loss of life, the war left Italy divided and turbulent, leaning to the left, with a broken economy and no leader to pull the country together.

Launching the Partito Popolare

The war did, however, heighten the awareness of Italians as sharers in a national destiny. No longer would they be willing to allow a narrow elite to run their country as they had since unification. It was this change in consciousness that made it possible for Sturzo to launch his great national party, Il Partito Popolare (Populist Party). He did so with a profound faith in Parliament as the apex of democracy and he saw that the key to revival of the country lay in a parliamentary reform. It must be a reform that would free the Italian state from the bonds of the past and open the way to "a fuller more vital expression of Italian democracy."[10]

What Sturzo meant by a fuller and more vital expression of Italian democracy was soon made clear. In December 1918 he formed a provisional executive committee composed of a group of lay Catholic leaders—a remarkable body of men, idealistic, dedicated, and with a large fund of experience. With their support Sturzo drew up an appeal to "all free and strong men." This appeal called for the cooperation of all to build a just and lasting peace, bring about social justice, improve the condition of the workers, and release the spiritual and material energy of all the peoples that make up the society of nations. Thus was born the Partito Popolare Italiano. As John Molony says, it was a decisive moment in the development of the modern

---

[9] Ibid., p. 178.
[10] Molony, *The Emergence of Political Catholicism in Italy*, p. 46.

Italian state.[11] And the Italian communist Antonio Gramsci saw the new party as the most important fact in Italian history since the Risorgimento, the nineteenth-century movement that had led to the unification of Italy.

While the main thrust of its social teaching was based on *Rerum Novarum* and the principle of democratic reform, the party platform was designed to appeal to millions of voters of diverse social classes. The platform contained modern and progressive goals: condemnation of imperialism, proportional representation, the vote for women, land reform, complete separation of church and state, a firm legal respect for freedom of conscience, and an increase in local autonomy. Though organized by Catholics and inspired by Catholic social doctrine, it was not to be a Catholic party, as Sturzo and the other Christian Democratic leaders understood it. Indeed Sturzo hoped to rally many voters outside the Catholic fold to its program. Sturzo declared that the party was nonconfessional (that is, having no specific religious content) and independent of ecclesiastical authority. To show this, he rejected the label "Christian Democracy" in favor of "Partito Popolare," the party of the people. But the big question remained unanswered: Was independence from the Vatican possible for Catholics in political life?

The laicist press was skeptical. They could not believe that the Holy See had nothing to do with the formation of a party organized by Catholics. Even when the Vatican issued the most forceful denial of any association with the Partito Popolare.

Prior to launching the party, Sturzo had received the Vatican's assurance that it would not place obstacles in the way. The Vatican position was one of bare tolerance, the Holy See looking on Sturzo's party only as the least objectionable of the parties on the left. Especially bothersome to Rome was the fact that the party's platform made no mention of the Roman question as well as its espousal of religious liberty for all, which *La Civiltà Cattolica* identified as the heresy of liberalism. Still another cause of Rome's discomfort was the party's social reform proposals which seemed to smack of socialism. With the recent Russian Revolution casting its apocalyptic shadow over the world, it hardly seemed a good time to flirt with socialist ideas. At the first party congress in Bologna (1919), the call for a "Party of the Christian Proletariat" added fuel to the fire.

Actually the Popolare did much to save Italy from socialism. Its fostering of small private farms kept many small landholders, tenants, and sharecrop-

[11] Ibid., p. 48.

pers away from socialism. The socialists claimed the Popolare vaccinated Italian workers against revolution.

But more serious in the eyes of the Vatican than the PPI's socialist tendency was its capture of the loyalty of the Catholic masses. The PPI had gained "the enthusiastic, near-unanimous adherence . . . of the Catholic unions (which had themselves joined together in an autonomous confederation—the CIL—in 1918), of the press, of the peasant leagues and the bulk of the parochial clergy. Thus the hierarchy lost control over most of the old Catholic movement."[12] The Holy See would no longer have the leverage of the Catholic masses in its relations with the Italian state and particularly in its efforts to restore its privileged position in Italy. In sum, from its inception the Vatican felt no great love for the PPI and gave it no direct support. Not that Sturzo wanted such support, for in his mind it was better not to exist at all than to exist as a mere tool of the Vatican.

While the new party drew the attention of Catholics away from the Vatican, it also drew the attention of Catholics away from the aggressively secularist Italian liberalism. As John Pollard says, "The birth of the PPI was . . . a blow to the Liberal establishment: if Catholic electoral support had helped to save Giolitti's Liberal Majority in 1913 then the PPI's intransigently independent electoral policy helped to destroy it in 1919 and the Party's equally intransigent parliamentary tactics thereafter made life extremely difficult for the coalition Premiers, Nitti and Giolitti."[13] And as Richard Webster notes, "The long Catholic struggle against Liberalism had become fruitful when, during the crisis of the 1890s, it had stopped proclaiming itself as a religious crusade and had taken up the tasks of social reform. Whatever was really valuable in Liberalism, Democracy, and Socialism had been taken into the Catholic movement, sifted and purified by the Christian conscience, as Sturzo conceived it."[14]

General Catholic support for the new party was widespread, including the adhesion of twenty dailies and fifty weeklies. In fact the party proved attractive to a wide variety of Catholics and soon numbered among its adherents industrialists, professionals, old conservatives and young radicals, big capitalists and small farmers, directors of the Bank of Rome as well as small shareholders in credit unions. The unfortunate Murri, several years

[12]John Pollard, *The Vatican and Italian Fascism, 1929–1932* (New York: Cambridge University Press, 1985), p. 21.

[13]Ibid.

[14]Richard Webster, *Christian Democracy in Italy, 1860–1960* (London: Hollis & Carter, 1960), p. 54.

excommunicated and his political star well in eclipse, predicted harshly that the PPI, with its catchall base of support, would never galvanize as an effective political force. A party so diverse in its constituency, argued Murri, would fail "to take up a clear and firm position in the field of social justice because it was not a homogeneous and strong party but a gathering of men held together only by electoral interests and in it the participation of the clergy was by far the most important element."[15] But it was impossible to argue with the PPI's breathtaking success at the polls.

In 1919, as mobs marched under the red banner of revolution, Catholics went to the polls for the first time—"the most notable event of twentieth-century Italian history."[16] The result was startling and for some even awesome. The fledgling PPI won 20 percent of the vote and a hundred seats in Parliament. Only the socialists showed a similar vitality, winning 32 percent of the vote. Ominously, one loser was a "gentleman" from Verona, Benito Mussolini, whose new party didn't gain a seat.

The Partito—A Bat or a Mouse?

Sturzo's manner of life was frugal and even austere. At home in his native Sicily he rose early for mass in his small chapel. Away he would often work late into the night and then escort his followers to a nearby church for prayer and he expected them to cultivate his own spartan habits. No mixer, he much preferred seclusion, and though he wielded great power and helped to form two cabinets, he was virtually invisible on the public stage and was called the "sphinx of Italian politics." Physically his dominant feature was his great eagle's beak of a nose. With nothing of the demagogue, his honesty and fairness were recognized by even his most bitter enemies. Not a great orator, he gave speeches that were terse but very effective. Refusing to use secretaries, he wrote all his correspondence in his own distinctive longhand. Totally dedicated to work, he showed himself to be an astute politician and told another politician: "You statesmen dine too much, wine too much, trifle too much." And he advised his followers, "Be practical—that is the thing in life."

As the PPI gathered under Sturzo's leadership, the prospects for Italian democracy were most discouraging. Socialists battled fascists in the streets, while strikes crippled industry. The war had taken the lives of 670,000

[15]Molony, *The Emergence of Political Catholicism in Italy*, p. 56.
[16]Ibid., p. 67.

soldiers and many of the three million or so who returned were often unable to find work. Parliament itself was loaded with deputies lacking any real commitment to democracy, while the liberals in charge lacked a coherent vision and had no program except for strengthening the police. As for the PPI, as one of its enemies charged, it didn't know whether it was a bat or a mouse. It was more of an "organized hope" than a cohesive party. Or, as another critic said, "It was a machine in which a great number of little cogs turned in one direction and a few large cogs rotated in the opposite direction, disturbing or altogether paralyzing the working of the small ones."[17] But one historian has pointed out that "the party had two strong points: Catholic labor which in 1920 numbered 1,180,000 including 935,000 on the land, and [the support] of the lower clergy."[18]

The Partito joined the government but soon found itself in a bind. The liberal prime minister, Francesco Nitti, refused to accept the nine-point program of social reform that the Partito put forward as the price of collaboration. At the same time, the tensions between the conservative and progressive wing of the Partito grew more intense. The Left insisted upon more radical social reform while the Right wanted more focus on the interests of the Church. Sturzo was able to hold the party on its Center–Left base and obtained agreement on the principle that they could not take a responsible role in any government ministry that did not have a clear-cut progressive program of economic reform. Sturzo insisted that the PPI was unique in that it alone fought against "the centralist state, economic monopoly and communistic socialism." This mildly leftist stance would finally cost him the support of the conservatives and much of the upper clergy, both of whom eventually found their way into the fascist camp.

In the elections of 1920 the Church put tremendous pressure on Sturzo to unite with the "forces of moderation," that is, the liberals and conservatives, in order to defeat the socialists at the polls. "To the clerical mind, the only way to stop Bolshevism was the imposition of law and order and those concepts were enshrined in the old conservative forces of the right."[19] The cardinal archbishop of Genoa, Boggiani, warned his people of the danger the PPI posed to the Church by severing Catholics from ecclesiastical authority and not leading them along the "true path to follow in public

[17] Salvemini, *The Origins of Fascism in Italy,* p. 143.

[18] Richard Webster, *The Cross and the Fasces: Christian Democracy and Fascism in Italy* (Palo Alto: Stanford, 1960), p. 62.

[19] Molony, *The Emergence of Political Catholicism in Italy,* p. 86.

political life"—the path mapped out by Pius IX sixty-five years before in the Syllabus of Errors. But Sturzo maintained his stand: Catholics would no longer be used by conservatives as a pool of easily caught votes if he could help it.

In the autumn of 1920, the workers in northern Italy launched a sitdown strike at the Alfa Romeo plants in Milan and Turin. The strikes then spread throughout the peninsula. Half a million workers all over Italy occupied the factories. The strike turned out to be a debacle for its socialist organizers, who called the strike a necessary moment of the revolutionary development and of the class war and called on the workers and farmers to occupy the banks, the workshops, and the land. The factory workers attempted to operate their plants independently but soon found that without technical guidance, raw materials, and the confidence of foreign markets, occupation of the plants was useless. They finally had to agree to terms that merely allowed them some participation in management. The "revolution" collapsed when they abandoned the factories on October 1, 1920.

The strike was a moment of truth for Sturzo and the Popolari. Would they side with the workers and be accused of sharing in their Soviet dream or side with the capitalists and conservatives and lose whatever credibility they had with the workers? In the end the Popolari merely issued some vague statements affirming solidarity with the workers. Though the liberal minister had been satisfied to sit back and wait for the strike to fail, his neutral policy was a major mistake: The only profit of the uprising was reaped by the fascists who could now exploit the resentment and fear it had fostered among the propertied classes, the great landowners, and the industrialists. The fascists escalated their attacks on socialists and Popolari and continued as before with their campaign to win over the fearful members of the middle class neglected by the other parties—the small shopkeepers, civil servants, returned soldiers, and unemployed students, who were all frustrated by the constant series of strikes and the encroaching anarchy.

Mussolini—from Marxism to Fascism

Meanwhile, the man awaited his hour; his method was violence and his weapon the revolver. As he said in a remark quoted by *L'Osservatore Romano*, the Vatican newspaper: "The revolver is more beautiful than a woman. The woman talks too much, never arrives at a conclusion and betrays. The automatic speaks very little, but it makes itself understood immediately."

Benito Mussolini was born in 1883 in the muddy village of Predappio in

Romagna, situated in an expanse of arid hillsides and dirt tracks off the beaten path. His father, Allessandro, and grandfather were natural rebels who spent time in prison for their beliefs. Allessandro was a blacksmith, self-educated, often out of work, and one of the earliest socialists in Italy. He read *Das Kapital* to the family and used a heavy strap to keep them under control. Later Benito described his family life as lacking tenderness and affection and as the reason that he developed a closed personality. His mother was a devout Christian who had to put the unruly Benito in a boarding school. It was run by the Salesians, who awakened the children at five to march them to daily mass, dragging them if necessary, as it was in Mussolini's case. By all accounts he was a violent, ill-tempered boy who bullied his fellow students. He once knifed a classmate and later mentioned that he enjoyed thinking of the scars the fellow still wore. He was unwilling or unable to make any male friends but boasted of his long string of female conquests and his exploits at the local brothel. He once knifed his girlfriend and generally was not slow to use violence to get what he wanted.

He received his diploma in 1901 and began the life of an intellectual bohemian. By 1903 he was calling himself an "authoritarian communist" who despised Parliament and preached terrorism and mob violence to ex-propriate the ruling class. His mentor at the time was Marx, whom he called the greatest of all theorists of socialism, the man who had stressed the values of materialism, personal egoism, and economic determinism, and the one who had rescued socialism from the Christians and made it scientific. Mussolini despised Christianity and called Jesus an ignorant Jew and religion a sickness. He found in Nietzsche justification for his contempt for the Christian virtues of resignation and humility, and proclaimed a socialist morality that celebrated violence and rebellion. Nietzsche's doctrines of the superman, the "will to power," and "the weak to the wall" were ideas he found most congenial. After a brief period of military service, he tried teaching but this proved unsuccessful. The children at one school nicknamed him the "tyrant" though he was unable to keep order and had to bribe them with sweets. He turned to insurrectionary socialism and was arrested for leading a strike of farm workers. But, as an observer noted, he seemed to lack any real depth of conviction and to be driven only by the need to gain attention and satisfy personal feelings of revenge.

What he really believed in was violent defiance of the law and he urged his fellow socialists not to resort to the law courts but to take an eye for an eye with their own hands. He called for a bloody social revolution that would lead to the dictatorship of the proletariat. He tried his hand at journalism as the editor of various socialist papers (to one of which at Forli he gave the name *La Lotta di Classe,* The Class Struggle). He made the Church a constant target of the ferocious rhetoric he used in his columns: Priests were "black microbes," servants of capitalism, and poisoners of young minds. He condemned the Church for its authoritarianism (Ha!) and even wrote a pulp novel that featured a lecherous cardinal as its villain.

In July 1912 at a congress of socialists at Reggio he stepped into the national limelight with impressive speeches calling for revolution. Only twenty-eight at the time, he became a member of the dominant faction of the party directorate. Appointed editor of the socialist newspaper *Avanti,* a big national daily, he soon doubled its readership while filling its pages with utopian rhetoric. He excoriated the bourgeois parliament and predicted a coming revolution that would move Italy forward to the ultimate goal of communism.

In 1914, world war erupted. In socialist theory it was supposed to be the catalyst for the proletarians to rise and overthrow their masters. Accordingly, Mussolini denounced it at first as a purely capitalist affair. But he soon realized that the proletariat was not about to rise, and in a sudden about-face he confessed publicly his mistake in opposing the war. When the party balked at this turnabout, he resigned and founded a new paper, *Il Popolo d'Italia,* with French government and local industrialist funds. His excommunication by the socialists was expected but it angered him nevertheless and he swore they would live to regret it.

He now envisioned the great possibilities for Italian expansion opened up by the war, and he added his paper's voice to the chorus of those who wanted Italy to join the combatants. A noisy minority, they were able to drag Italy into the war by an adroit use of propaganda and pressure tactics, including instigating riots. Mussolini himself was conscripted and experienced the horrors of life in the trenches. Invalided out after a grenade-thrower he was operating exploded, splicing him with forty fragments, he took over *Il Popolo d'Italia* again. The rout of the Italian army at Caporetto on October 24, 1917, struck him with terrible force and hastened his passage from socialism to the authoritarian set of ideas he called fascism. Marxism he now condemned as a "heap of ruins," its obsolete doctrines of class warfare and the dictatorship of the proletariat obsolete.

On March 23, 1919, he launched the movement that two years later would become the Fascist Party. It was antidemocratic and anticlerical with a program of radical social reform that embraced many socialist ideas such as progressive taxation, expropriation of factories and land, and the vote for women. It constituted a ragtag collection of futurists, anarchists, communists, syndicalists, republicans, Catholics, nationalists, and liberals of various stripes. In Mussolini's first show of strength in the balloting of 1919, he failed to receive a single vote in his own home village of Predappio. But this did not discourage him because he intended to rely on bombs and guns rather than ballots in the great struggle ahead. And he still had *Il Popolo d'Italia* to keep his movement going. In the meantime he tried to learn as much as he could from the experience of Lenin, whom he greatly admired though he pretended to be shocked at the tyranny of the Russian's regime. At the same time, he cynically promoted the threat of a communist danger in Italy that he alone was equipped to handle. "Mussolini resolved all contradictions in the magic word 'revolution.' Those who believe in the 'revolution' must live in danger, challenge life, dare or die. Action for the victory of 'revolution' does not need to be justified either by logical rules or by moral principles."[20]

The Fascist Reign of Terror

In the summer of 1921, the Fascists began a new mode of operation. Thousands of them would converge on a town or city in motor lorries or on trains. Then they would begin a wholesale looting of union headquarters, communist clubs, popular libraries, cooperative societies, and even the homes of socialists or Popolari. Finally they would force the mayor and town counselors to resign and hand over the administration to a Fascist commissioner.

On July 1, 1921, the mayor of Roccastrada refused to obey an ultimatum from the "Italian Fighting Fasci of Tuscany." In no time about seventy Fascists descended on the town, firing revolvers into the air while burning down the woodcutters' union and cooperative stores as well as the mayor's house. A few weeks later, they returned at four-thirty in the morning and began burning and looting before the slowly awakening peasants realized what was happening. As the rogues moved on to another town, one of their number was killed by peasants firing from behind a hedge. Unable to capture the ones responsible for the killing, the Fascists tore into the town, shouting and stabbing at random and mortally wounding four persons. Fifty

[20]Salvemini, *The Origins of Fascism in Italy*, p. 344.

others were seriously wounded and seventeen houses were reduced to heaps of ashes. The thirteen police officers stationed in the town did nothing to stop the massacre and made no arrests even though the leader of the local Fascists was well known in the region. Roccastrada was a small town, but Treviso was an important city and here the target was Sturzo's Popolari who had recently taken the part of some laborers against two Fascist-affiliated landowners. On July 12, 1921, a hundred trucks preceded by a white motorcar pulled into the town with fifteen hundred men armed with rifles, grenades, machine guns, and steel helmets. They broke into and sacked the offices of the Popolari's newspaper and then took over the town, sacking and looting while again the police and soldiers stood by.

Italian Democracy in Crisis

From the spring of 1921 until the Fascist March on Rome in October 1922, the Socialists, Popolari, and democratic-liberal groups of the parliamentary Center faced a common problem—the occupation by the Fascists of key areas of Italy and the constant expansion of Fascist military rule. At this juncture the prime minister, Giolitti, made a tragic mistake that proved to be Mussolini's big break. Thinking he could play the Fascists against the socialists, he invited Mussolini's party into his national electoral bloc. This move gave the Fascists a real boost but did not weaken the Socialists. The Fascists slugged and bludgeoned their opponents during the election campaign, while the liberals and the police were unwilling to interfere. When the new Parliament returned in 1921, it included thirty-five Fascists and fifteen members of the new Italian Communist party that was formed by a split among the Socialists. His coalition in ruins, Giolitti resigned, an act that effectively spelled the end of Italian liberalism. Promptly abandoning his alliance with the liberals, Mussolini joined the extreme Right and spent much of his time organizing his squads of "Black Shirts" into a national militia. Their violence attracted youth, students in particular, who enjoyed such tactics as dosing their victims with huge quantities of castor oil. The Black Shirts in short order settled on their signature gesture: the Roman salute with raised arm.

There was soon a great influx of wealthy and conservative young men into Mussolini's Fascist Party. Sons of lawyers, doctors, and war profiteers, they took revenge on the workers. "If they met men in working clothes, they fell on them and began beating them. Their mentality was on a par with that of the Communists, who had beaten and murdered anybody who was decently dressed."[21]

Wherever a conflict broke out between employers and workers, "black-shirt squadrons" appeared and attacked the workers—killing the leaders and looting and destroying the unions. At first the Black Shirts focused on the Socialists but soon they also struck at the Popolare unions and their consumer cooperatives.

The Fascists gained strength by the day. Increasingly funded by the large financial and industrial interests, the party continued its campaign of thuggery against Catholic youth, members of Catholic associations, and the Popolari. In the Udine region they had started to proclaim, "To the gallows with the priests!" The papal mouthpiece *L'Osservatore Romano,* unsparing in its criticism of the Fascists, despaired equally of the other parties and their inability to create the "discipline, authority, freedom and justice" the country needed.

The Popolari constituted the only remaining cohesive force in the center of the spectrum and began to entertain the idea of collaborating with the Socialists. However, the Socialists in Italy were still mouthing the slogans of anticlericalism and the class struggle and were not yet ready for collaboration. Sturzo himself viewed cooperation with the Socialists as the best hope for the country because only they and the Popolari had politically viable programs. He clear-sightedly refused any connivance with violence or subversion and he rejected political alliances that had proven useless. Meanwhile relations between the Vatican and the Popolari turned colder as Sturzo continued his refusal to make the temporal problems of the Vatican a major concern of the party.

In the midst of the crisis Pope Benedict died. The press praised him as the creator with Sturzo of the Popolari and speculated about the fate of the Popolari under a new pope. The answer was not long in coming. The newly elected pontiff—Achille Ratti, who as pope was called Pius XI—was a priest who had followed a most unusual path to the papacy, having spent most of his life as a librarian and medieval scholar. Cardinal Gasparri, the Vatican secretary of state, had in previous years recognized the intellect behind Ratti's unassuming visage and had him sent to Warsaw as papal nuncio where his skillful work earned him the see of Milan in 1921. In less than a year Ratti was catapulted, with Gasparri's help, onto the throne of Peter.

[21]Ibid., p. 294.

As people speculated about the new pope's orientation the parliamentary crisis continued. Sturzo was counting on Filippo Meda to form a government and sent him a telegram at Milan asking him to "sacrifice himself." Meda came to Rome and told the King, Victor Emmanuel III, that he couldn't take the job, and then returned posthaste to Milan. "The great chance had slipped away through a failure of nerve."[22] The man who did step forward, Luigi Facta, was a fifth-rate politician whose ragtag government of liberals, reformists, and Popolari was unable to rally the nation against the fascists.

By October 1, 1922, Italian democracy had only a few weeks to go. There were still some signs of life: Parliament was functioning, the army and police were still loyal, the economy was not bankrupt, the government was still intact, the judiciary was in place. What was lacking was any sense of unity. Tragically, the man who promised to restore it was "of Cerberus and darkest midnight born." Few Italians at the time could imagine into what depths of degradation and horror he would plunge the nation. Neither could they "dream of the chords his example would strike in the diseased mind of a teutonic enormity," nor of the maelstrom of terror waiting for Europe and the world, once Italy bowed to the dictator in October 1922.[23]

As the country slipped into chaos, Mussolini played his cards with remarkable skill. He asserted his willingness to work within the parliamentary system while hinting that he might be ready for a coup. One of his main advantages was the refusal of his opponents, including Sturzo, to take him altogether seriously, as in the case of Hitler a decade later. Mussolini's opponents saw him as a mere journalist and a charlatan whom they could control. As Fascist violence accelerated, the pope publicly deplored the fratricidal warfare and urged the country to return to God, while he thwarted the PPI at every turn.

To understand the Vatican's role in the debacle we have to keep in mind Pius XI's own mentality. A friend of the great business magnates of Lombardy, he was an authoritarian with no Christian Democrat sympathies. He had even allowed the Fascists to carry their banners into the Duomo of Milan while he was archbishop there. Moreover, the idea of any alliance of Catholics with the "godless" socialists was anathema. He was therefore very susceptible to Mussolini's carrot-and-stick approach. Mussolini indulged in rhetorical praise of Catholicism, of its universality, of its greatness as the

---

[22] Webster, *The Cross and the Fasces*, p. 75.
[23] Molony, *The Emergence of Political Catholicism in Italy*, p. 127.

glory of Rome. He also spoke of the need to help finance the Church's schools, hospitals, and churches. But this was the same man who on December 12, 1919, wrote in *Il Popolo d'Italia:*

> We profoundly detest all forms of Christianism, that of Jesus as much as that of Marx. We greet with extraordinary sympathy the revival in modern life of the pagan cult of force and audacity . . . Enough, red and black theologians, of all churches. No more false and sly promises of a heaven which will never come! Enough, ridiculous saviors of the human race. The human race does not give a damn for your infallible prescriptions granting happiness. Leave the path open to the primal forces of the individual. No other human reality exists except that of the individual.

Mussolini temptingly offered a settlement of the Roman question and a privileged position for the Church—while bluntly threatening large-scale destruction of Catholic organizations and parishes if the offer was spurned.

On October 24 at Naples, Mussolini told Black Shirts from all over Italy: "Either we are allowed to govern, or we will seize power by marching on Rome." For the next several days, back in Milan, Mussolini carried on the pretense that he wanted to work within the system. He tried to soothe the fears of leading liberals by setting forth some modest reforms he promised to implement if given the reins of power. At the same time, however, his Black Shirts were occupying the telephone exchanges and government offices. At this point, Facta's weak government in Rome belatedly put its foot down. Facta asked Victor Emmanuel to sign a decree declaring a state of emergency and allowing the army to impose martial law. The king agreed and the army prepared to crush the revolt. Four hundred miles away in Milan, Mussolini barricaded himself in his office while an order for his arrest was signed. Incredibly the king then changed his mind and refused to sign the decree—a monstrous betrayal. For there is no doubt that, in spite of the doubtful loyalty of some generals, the army could have nipped the Fascist revolution in the bud. Still we must remember that the king was given exaggerated reports of Fascist numbers and was extremely fearful of civil war. He also feared losing his throne to his rival, the duke of Aosta. Therefore, instead of having Mussolini arrested and shot, he called on him to form a new government. On October 28 the long-expected coup finally took place. Mussolini's Black Shirts marched on Rome as they had marched on and terrorized many a city over the past few years. At a window of the Villa Ruffo Scaletta, Sturzo watched as the Fascists marched by under the banners of the skull and crossbones. He turned his face to the wall and wept.

★ ★ ★

Others too had reasons to weep. The Fascists celebrated their victory in their usual way—pouring large doses of castor oil down the throats of their foes. Mobs of Black Shirts also ransacked the offices of many newspapers and pillaged shops and bookstores, heaping books in the streets and burning them. They broke into the houses of their political enemies and forced foreign embassies to fly the Italian flag. More than 2,000 murders were committed in the first year of their rule. The turning point in Fascism's takeover was the establishment of the Fascist militia by royal decree on January 14, 1923. It gave Mussolini his own private army.

Mussolini moved swiftly to co-opt the Church by granting a number of favors that didn't affect his hold on power: Within two weeks he had taken measures to rescue the Bank of Rome, which held large deposits of Vatican funds and was in danger of insolvency. He restored the crucifix to the schools and changed taxation policies that had been designed to do grave harm to the Church. He doffed his anticlerical and atheistic robes and proclaimed himself profoundly religious in spirit, paying homage to Catholicism as a great spiritual and moral power. Pius XI and his secretary of state, Cardinal Gasparri, may not have swallowed this entirely but it convinced them that it would be easier to work with Fascism than with liberalism.

Sturzo vs. Mussolini

With a good percentage of its members in the Parliament, the PPI could have stymied Mussolini by refusing to participate in his ministry or to support his government. In that case the ruffian would have had to dissolve the Parliament and call for new elections, or, frankly, do away altogether with the chamber. But the PPI decided to give him a chance. Sturzo absolutely opposed this policy, but he was unable to prevail over the party directorate and eventually acquiesced. Why he didn't resign there and then is a matter for speculation. It was probably a momentary failure of his clarity of vision together with his personal hesitancy as a loyal priest to take on the Vatican, which had expressed such high hopes for the new regime.

In his first speech in the Parliament, Mussolini insulted and blandished the legislature by turns. Buoyed by the general euphoria that swept the country, he promised to contain Fascist violence while professing his respect for all religions. For Sturzo, it was a bitter ordeal to watch the members of his own party berated, mocked, and deceived by a man for whom he felt only contempt. As the months went by some of his advisers urged him to conform and counseled patience until the new government could bring about internal order and peace. But he knew that the only peace the opponents of this regime would feel was the peace of the graveyard, or of exile.

At the same time, the billing and cooing between Mussolini and the pope went on. In addition to the conciliatory measures already mentioned, Mussolini indulged in such gestures as presenting Pius with a gift that was especially pleasing to a former librarian—the precious Chigi library. Then, in a secret meeting with Gasparri, Mussolini avowed his willingness to settle the Roman question. No wonder the pope's *L'Osservatore* continued to sing the praises of the man who a leading cardinal called the "reconstructor of the fate of the nation."[24]

Sturzo now embarked on his last and perhaps his most noble battle—the struggle to save the soul of the PPI and to keep it free of any compromise with Fascism. Against him, his clerico-Fascist opponents deployed formidable arguments drawn from the Catholic counterrevolutionary tradition of the nineteenth century. They argued that collaboration with the man they called "Il Duce," which means the leader, could mean the beginning of a new relation of the Church to the masses as the latter were reeducated in the spirit of obedience and submission to authority, attitudes long cherished by Catholic traditionalists as essential to the social order. Collaboration, they also said, would mean sharing in a great crusade to save the Church and the West from the expansionary forces of Bolshevism. Moreover, when Fascist outrages were cited, these clerical apologists countered by recalling persecutions of the Church by liberal governments. Finally, they had recourse to the classical distinction between the "thesis" and the "hypothesis" so beloved by Catholic political thinkers. Since the thesis (or the ideal)—a society permeated by Christian principles—is impossible to fulfill under modern conditions, why should the Fascist hypothesis (or the concrete possibility) be any less valid than the liberal hypothesis, that is, the democratic state?

Where did the PPI stand, many Catholics increasingly wondered. A party congress was planned for Turin in April 1923 to provide an answer. Little remains of Sturzo's correspondence at this point, and therefore one can only imagine his anguish as he prepared to lead his party into the most decisive congress of its brief history.

At the congress, Sturzo crafted a response to Fascism that was typically brilliant—unemotional, subtle, and worded with extreme care. He never even mentioned the word "Fascist" but his condemnation of the Fascist

[24]Ibid., p. 152.

ideology was clear to all who could read. He lashed out against a pantheistic concept of the state, against the centralizing perversion attempted in its name, and against the concept of the deified nation. The state, he said, is not the *source* of natural human rights; its task is to safeguard and coordinate them. In effect, Sturzo laid bare the insidious cancer of collaborationism that threatened his party's organism. Some blamed him for not denouncing Fascism by name. Mussolini, however, got the message. His *Il Popolo d'Italia* condemned Sturzo's speech. "Sturzo," it said, "disowned the Empire . . . the history of Catholicism . . . and [even] the Sacred Empire of Dante . . . Don Sturzo has not got a Roman soul. He has the mentality of a pastor and of a Protestant professor like [President] Wilson."

The Fascist campaign against Sturzo now escalated as Mussolini announced his plan for electoral reform necessitated by the increasing strength of the opposition. The plan would do away with the proportional system and guarantee Fascist control of the legislature by allotting two thirds of the seats to the party that gained a plurality of the vote. When the bill came up for discussion in July 1923, it was quickly apparent that a Popolare vote against it would mean the bill's defeat. Sturzo was an uncompromising opponent of the bill and had the rank and file behind him. However, as the debate went on, ominous sounds started to emanate from the Vatican hinting at the need for Sturzo to resign. The Fascist press hinted at the harsh fate the Church would suffer for allowing one of its priests to "provoke a revolutionary situation."[25] And the Fascists threatened to occupy all the churches of Rome if the Popolari voted against the bill. Nor did the American ambassador help Sturzo's cause by the praise he lavished on Il Duce, who was present at a dinner with him on June 29, 1923. The ambassador spoke of how Italy had, during the last eight months, raised on high the "ideals of human courage, discipline and responsibility."[26]

But the Black Shirts did not spend a lot of time on words: They cudgeled one opponent of the bill nearly to death, and throughout the debate they thronged the lobbies and galleries of the chamber, carrying ropes they threatened to use on any deputy who voted against the bill.

[25] Ibid., p. 167.
[26] Ibid.

Sturzo Undone by the Vatican

The day the debate on the bill began was the same day Sturzo walked into the meeting of the party directorate and, in obedience to orders from the Vatican, handed in his resignation. He still hoped to use his influence to prevent passage of the bill and keep the struggle for democracy alive but his hope proved futile. Only his presence in Parliament could have galvanized the party in face of the enormous pressure exerted by Mussolini: Il Duce knew that all depended on the PPI and so he relentlessly threatened and coaxed its deputies until he broke down their resistance. When the vote was taken on July 15, only eight members of the PPI voted against it, while most of them abstained. For all intents and purposes, Italian democracy was history.

The desire of the Vatican to stay on good terms with the regime at almost any cost was soon poignantly revealed. This involved the case of one Father Minzoni, a former military chaplain, a priest of Argenta, and a member of the PPI. His work among youth was so successful that it threatened to undermine Fascist influence in that quarter. Two thugs took care of the problem by bashing in his skull. Minzoni's archbishop sent a Fascist priest to say his funeral mass while the pope remained silent. But the Popolare carried on its lonely opposition. In the election of 1924 they were able to return forty deputies—proof that a sizable body of Catholics had not succumbed to the siren song of the beast. But darkness had descended on the people and night was about to fall.

Before all the lights went out, however, one man took up the torch of freedom and illuminated forever the full horror of the nightmare. Giacomo Matteotti was born in 1885 and was elected a socialist deputy in 1919. He became an ardent, absolute, and unrelenting enemy of Fascism. His weapon was the catalogue of Fascist crimes—a scrupulously accurate documentation of the terrorism that the Fascists had used to steal the election. When Matteotti on May 30, 1924, stood up in the legislature to proclaim the illegality of the regime, a roar from the Fascist bench drowned out his message. As he left the podium he remarked, "You can now prepare my funeral oration."[27] Ten days later he was jumped by five Fascist thugs, thrown into a car, stabbed to death, and buried in the Roman countryside. Though his body was not discovered until that August everyone knew he

[27] Ibid., p. 182.

was another victim of Fascism. The Popolari and the other opposition deputies left the chamber in protest and quartered themselves on the Aventine Hill. For some months the fate of Mussolini's regime hung in the balance. It would have taken only a courageous act of leadership to oust him. But the opposition was hopelessly divided and only temporized, hoping that the pressure of public opinion would drive Mussolini out of office. But time was on the side of the beast.

Tragically, the one voice that might still have rallied the moral forces of Italy was silent. The pope could see no salvation in the overthrow of Fascism. That could lead only to chaos and disorder, he believed, as well as the postponement of a settlement of the Roman question and a strengthening of socialism. Meanwhile, one last chance to save democracy in Italy remained. If the two largest groups who had fled to the Aventine, the PPI and the socialists, were to combine, there was a chance they could bring down the Fascist regime. Alcide De Gasperi, Sturzo's successor, and Sturzo himself argued forcefully for such a policy. But the Vatican press denounced it. Finally the pope himself intervened and resolved the issue by condemning any collaboration of Catholics with the socialists. The fundamental contradiction in the Popolare's position was finally revealed with stark clarity: the party claimed to be "a confessional body with the freedom to make its own decisions but it also claimed to be obedient to the papacy in moral matters, and the pope had taken care to make collaboration with the socialists a moral matter."[28] This was a blow the party could not and did not survive.

One question remained—the fate of Sturzo. He was still a thorn in the side of both the Vatican and the Fascist regime as he continued his impassioned pleas in defense of democracy. Determined to silence him completely, the Fascists made repeated attempts to eliminate him but his luck held and he escaped their traps. On one occasion, he went for a few days' rest to the monastery of Monte Cassino but had to flee when warned that local Fascist bullies were gunning for him. His apartment in Rome was broken into by Fascists set on his "material suppression," as Mussolini put it, but not before Sturzo had already sought safety in the home of Prince Ruffo della Scaletta.[29]

What the Fascists couldn't accomplish—the removal of Sturzo's accusing presence—the Vatican did. First, they ordered all priests to cease involve-

28 Ibid., p. 190.
29 Ibid., p. 191.

ment in politics. Then, a few weeks later, they issued Sturzo a Vatican passport and advised him to leave Italy forthwith.

Exile

Sturzo took up residence in London, expecting only a short stay in the foggy capital. However, twenty-two years were to pass before he saw the sunny skies of Italy again. It was a bitter ordeal. Uprooted from his native soil and stranded in the cold north at the age of fifty-four with virtually no knowledge of English and little of French, he could only write nostalgically of the sweet Italian church bells, the perfume of the citronella, the vivid colors and lovely blue sky of his dear Sicily, and the delightful religious feasts and processions of his homeland. In his absence, the PPI tried to carry on. He urged it to go down with dignity rather than compromise with the regime. He held before them the example of St. Athanasius who, when persecuted by the Arians, took flight and from his hiding place continued to speak out in defense of the faith. Actually the PPI had only a short time left under the worthy leadership of Alcide De Gasperi who, in Sturzo's absence, presided over its last congress in Rome in June 1925.

As the years passed Sturzo continued to pour out a stream of anti-Fascist writings which, however, had little effect on his coreligionists back in Italy: the Vatican, most of the clergy, and the masses of Catholics were not anti-Fascist before 1940. Like most Italians they accepted the regime and believed that it would last a long time. Sturzo was reduced to a lone voice crying in the wilderness and clinging to his faith in the Church, if not always in the political judgments of the Vatican. As he said: "If we believe in the Church it is not because of the merits of Pius XI or of any other pope, nor will we leave it because of their unworthiness; we believe in the Church because Jesus Christ himself founded it."[30]

Bereft of his old friends, dependent on the charity of new ones, and snubbed by Catholic officialdom, he lived out the long years of lonely exile. Not in silence, however: He poured out scholarly and insightful books and articles on history and sociology. With burning clarity he set forth the spiritual principles he believed formative of European civilization at a time when many Catholics were selling their birthrights for a mess of Fascist pottage. One would think the spectacle would have filled him with nausea

[30] Ibid., p. 194.

and bitterness but in his conversation and writings he displayed only charity, patience, candor, and an invincible optimism.[31]

A German refugee priest, H. A. Reinhold, told about a visit he paid to Sturzo in London in 1935. After entering one of a row of shabby apartment buildings, Reinhold found the priest sitting in a dark little room behind his desk, which was a small sewing table. The room was lined with bookcases and all around him were stacks of newspapers and magazines. As he looked at the small figure wrapped in blankets, he thought: "Benedict XV risen again! That was my first impression. The same noble head, aquiline nose, the wise and tired eyes, the grace of the priest's greeting and his beautiful, rich voice."[32]

Sturzo remained in bomb-ravaged London until 1941 when, broken in health and fearful of being imprisoned by the British as an alien of an enemy country, he took refuge in the United States. There he continued his anti-Fascist efforts, founding an association of democratic Catholics called the "American People and Freedom Group." The association challenged the benign view American Catholics tended to take of the Fascists in Italy and Spain, on account of the privileges they accorded the Church. His was an ungrateful task that bore fruit only during the Second World War when people began to appreciate Sturzo's prophetic wisdom.

Last Years

With the Allied victory in 1945, Sturzo had to deal with the prospect of returning to Italy. Certainly the Vatican would hardly welcome with joy a priest whose arrival would recall the whole unhappy history of the Church's relations with Mussolini. Nor would they welcome one so opposed to them over the future of Italy. Sturzo believed the Italian monarchy had, by its connivance with Fascism, forfeited its claims. He also called for a democratic progressive republic and the full exercise of modern freedoms, including

---

[31] In 1931 the pope forced Mussolini to back down when the dictator tried to eliminate Catholic Action, which had become a refuge for many leaders of Sturzo's outlawed Popolare. In his encyclical *Quadragesimo Anno* (1931), the pope expressed grave fears not only about Marxism and unbridled capitalism but also the "exclusively bureaucratic and political character of the new Fascist syndical and corporative organizations." His experience with Mussolini and Hitler eventually led the pope to recognize in modern dictatorships the most formidable danger to Christianity in our time.

[32] H. A. Reinhold, "Don Luigi Sturzo: A Memoir" *(The Commonweal,* November 30, 1951), p. 194.

total religious freedom. The next pope, Pius XII, was more open to such ideas than was his predecessor—but not as open as Sturzo. And there remained the difficult issue of the Vatican's continuing sympathy for the restoration of the Italian monarchy. The pope, on the other hand, still captive to the old model of Church–state relations and fearful of subversion by the communists, favored restoration of the monarchy.

Did the pope really want another union of throne and altar? Sturzo asked. The idea horrified him since he believed this "sacred union" was responsible for most of the disasters that had afflicted the Church from the French Revolution to the Spanish Civil War. If implemented, it would undoubtedly mean another fifty years of anticlericalism in Italy. In any case, Sturzo was *persona non grata* to the Vatican at this point and he was advised by Amleto Cicognani, the apostolic delegate to Washington, to postpone his departure from exile in the United States. Even if Sturzo did return, he did not expect to head the Popolare, now resurrected as the Christian Democrats: The party needed a lay person at the head, he insisted, lest it get caught in the same bind that had occurred under Mussolini when Sturzo, as a priest, had to resign in obedience to the Vatican. He would only return, he told De Gasperi—now the head of the Christian Democrats—if it would help the cause. In the meantime many touching letters arrived from old friends who begged him to come back. One wrote: "Sicily awaits you [for] in the hearts of the multitude you are the symbol of anti-Fascism and the struggle for freedom."[33]

The issue of whether Italy would be a monarchy or a republic was settled by referendum on June 2, 1946. The republic won by a margin of two million votes. The voting also confirmed the primacy of the Christian Democratic Party (35 percent of the votes) as well as the strength of the party's extreme left wing.

Sturzo returned to Italy three months later after twenty-two years in exile. At seventy-five, with a weak heart, he wanted only a couple of rooms in a convent where he might have "silence and peace." This was arranged by a friend who found him lodging with the Canossian sisters. There, in two sparsely furnished rooms, he lived until his death thirteen years later. He tended to his weak heart by an adherence to a simple regimen of work and prayer and a rigorous diet that allowed him neither meat nor vegetables. Visitors would find him behind his desk, which was loaded with books and newspapers, keeping abreast of all the bizarre twists and turns of Italian

[33]De Rosa, *Don Luigi Sturzo,* p. 436.

politics. With great regret, he had to refuse the invitations of his friends to visit once more his beloved Caltagirone—he knew that the emotion of seeing once more those lovely churches, and hearing the sound of those bells that had haunted him all during his long exile, would have been the death of him.

The Italy he returned to was a much different country than the one he had left. There were many trends that troubled him, especially the statist concentration of power in the government, the parties, and the giant corporations. He became the Cassandra of Italian politics as in numerous articles he warned of the danger these trends posed to individual freedom. Appointed a senator for life he was able to bring his concerns into the legislature where he vigorously advocated reforms to assure greater public scrutiny of the operations of Parliament and of the parties.

Always in precarious health, he left his residence only to attend the Senate. As he sensed the end approaching he lay his pen down at times and wondered what it all meant—those sixty or more years of constant political battles; long years in exile trying to warn the world and his fellow Catholics of the dangers of Fascism; and now his last crusade, the battle against a political and social climate he found increasingly amoral. At the same time a nagging scruple assailed him: whether the Church really understood what he had tried to do and whether his differences with the Church might have involved some sin of pride or disobedience on his part. As his final hour approached, he found his answer only in prayer. On July 23, 1959, looking as pale as a corpse, he vested and began his morning mass in spite of an aide's insistence that he go back to bed. "Don't you realize," he said, "the value of a single mass?" He managed to get to the final "Oremus" before collapsing. When the doctor arrived, he whispered to the sick man: "Don Luigi, the Lord is near." And Sturzo replied, "Let us thank the Lord." His agony was protracted and death did not come until August 8.

In his last testament, Sturzo declared his love for both his friends and his adversaries while he begged pardon from the latter. The long struggle he had fought for human freedom and democracy, he said, was not something he had entered upon to win glory or fame. It was not something he planned, but had occurred under the pressure of events he could not foresee. It brought him many tribulations and much sorrow, but he offered it all for the glory of God. He prayed that all his misery and all the guilt he had incurred in his long career would be taken away "by the merits of Jesus

Christ and the intercession of the Virgin Mary whom I invoke now and at the hour of my death."[34]

Sturzo's Legacy

1. Sturzo is remembered above all for his passionate committment to democracy at a time when the official Church looked askance at it and when it was losing ground in Europe. As the moving spirit behind the Popolare he gave Italy a mass democratic party of Catholic orientation. Though short-lived this effort to unleash the democratic forces among the Catholics of Italy bore fruit later on in Italy's postwar Christian Democratic movement. It also provided a model for other Christian Democratic parties in Europe and Latin America.

2. He labored to overcome the divisiveness of religion in political life by fashioning a policy located between the extremes of clericalism and anticlericalism.

3. He gave powerful witness to the freedom and autonomy of the human person. Point VIII of the inaugural platform of his party states: "Freedom and respect for the Christian conscience considered as the foundation and safeguard of the life of the nation, of the liberties of the people and of the increasing development of civilization in the world."

4. His ideas on social reform were based on *Rerum Novarum* but went beyond it by calling for such measures as land reform, votes for women, and other progressive social measures.

[34]Ibid., p. 482.

TEN

Two Catholic Revolutionaries: Michael Collins (1890–1922) and Eamon de Valera (1882–1975)

PEOPLE on Lower Mount Street in Dublin in the afternoon of the first Sunday after Easter 1916 saw a curious spectacle: a hatless figure in bedraggled uniform marching in front of a hundred shabby and dirty men. Before them walked a Red Cross worker carrying a white flag. Beside them stepped British soldiers with rifles at the ready. A look of disgust crossed the hatless figure's face when he saw people rushing outdoors to offer cups of tea to the British soldiers. Later he described the anguish of that moment as he realized how little his countrymen supported what he and his men had tried to do. "Ireland," he wanted to shout at them, "has a right to freedom . . . Our rebellion would not have failed had you come out even though armed with hay forks only."

He had empty hours in his cell during the ensuing week to reflect on the sad events of the Easter Sunday Rising, to listen to the firing squads outside, and to await his own imminent execution. In a letter to a nun at the college where he had taught mathematics he wrote:

Dear Sister Gonzaga,

I have just been told that I am about to be shot for my part in the rebellion. Just a parting line to thank you and all the sisters (especially

Mother Attracta) for your unvarying kindness to me in the past and to ask you to pray for my soul and for my poor wife and little children whom I leave unprovided-for behind. Ask the girls to remember me in their prayers.

Goodbye. I hope I'll be in heaven to meet you.

Yours faithfully

(Sgd) E. de Valera

A few days later an officer arrived and read to him the verdict of the court. De Valera had been convicted and sentenced to death. Then the officer read a second document changing the sentence to penal servitude for life.

At the same time on the Irish coast another insurgent, Michael Collins, was herded onto a cattle boat to be shipped to prison in England. He would have been waiting for execution like de Valera if one of the guards had not ripped off his staff-captain's insignia with a bayonet. With 289 untried Irish prisoners he arrived at Stafford Detention Barracks on April 31, 1916, as Irish Prisoner No. 48 F. Stripped of all his possessions, he was most upset by the loss of his handkerchief.

In the most passionate moment of modern Ireland—the Easter Rebellion—de Valera and Collins shared in the luck of the Irish: Both were spared

Eamon de Valera

death. But their reprieves bore these two men of cunning and faith in action into the "terrible beauty" of the next years: into the tragedy and triumph that created independent Ireland.

Early Years of de Valera

De Valera was born in New York City on October 14, 1882, at the New York Nursery and Child's Hospital on Lexington Avenue. He was christened Edward (in Irish, Eamon) after St. Edward the Confessor. His mother, Catherine Coll, had left Ireland nearly penniless when she was twenty-two. An attractive girl, intelligent, with a fine sense of humor, she worked for a time as a domestic. In 1881 she married Vivion de Valera, the son of a Spanish sugar trader. Vivion died within a few years and Kate put little Edward in the care of her grandmother, who lived in Bruree, Ireland, while she returned to work in America. There Edward shared a small cottage with his grandmother, his uncle Pat, and his aunt Hannie.

Uncle Pat had a keen interest in the Irish Nationalist movement and little Edward would often have heard the name of the heroic but defeated Parnell, the leading champion in the 1880s of Irish home rule. After Daniel O'Connell's failure to achieve home rule in the 1840s, Charles Stewart Parnell (1846–1891) was the next great hope. He was able to make effective use of obstructionist tactics, demonstrations, and threats of violence to further the cause. The Liberals in the English Parliament finally endorsed home rule and the prime minister, William Gladstone, introduced a bill in 1886. However, it split the Liberal Party and was defeated. Parnell retained his command of the Nationalist Party until 1890 when a divorce court revealed that he had been living with the wife of another politician, William Henry O'Shea. Repudiated by the Catholic bishops and the majority of the party and debilitated physically, he lost the battle to recover his position and died in 1891.

Eamon began at the National School in Bruree on May 7, 1888. As he made his way to school through the little village he would pass near the forge, the cooper's yard stacked with barrels, and the bootmakers' shops. Nearby stood a forbidding barracks where the police displayed their polished carbines and threatening bayonets as a salutary reminder to the populace. One of his earliest memories was people gathering in the village to the sound of a drum and brass band to begin the boycott of a local landowner and horse breeder, John Gubbins. The boycott, one of Parnell's ideas, was an important weapon in the agrarian revolution. De Valera also remembered the stirring sermons of Father Eugene Sheehy whose work with the organization of rural workers, the Land League, had landed him in prison. The priest's fervent nationalism deeply touched the heart of young de Valera. The need for land reform was obvious in a country where 750 of the 20,000 title-holders owned half of the land.

Uncle Pat was a demanding taskmaster and disapproved of wasting time with games. He kept Eddie busy around the farm and would thrash him if he malingered. Fifty years later, when accused in the Dail Eireann (the de facto Irish legislature) of knowing nothing about farming, de Valera declared that there was no farm work that he had not done. He had spanceled the goats, milked the cows, cleaned out the cowhouses, followed the tumbler rake, taken his place on the cart, taken milk to the creamery, and harnessed the donkey and the horse.[1]

He soon proved himself a diligent scholar also. I was able myself to see the high grades he received in an exhibit at the National School in Bruree. In 1896 he began studies with the Christian Brothers in Charleville, walking seven miles each way. The honors he gained enabled him at the age of sixteen to win a scholarship to Blackrock College, outside Dublin. Walking through the city on his first day he crossed O'Connell Bridge and caught sight of beautiful Merrion Square. Little did he realize that it would one day be for him a field of battle.

Blackrock College was not a place for the easygoing. The young scholars were busy at every hour going in silence from chapel to class, from class to meals, from meals to class; every day there was a period of recreation and four or five hours of study hall. De Valera continued to win honors, including a scholarship to University College, Blackrock. His political views as a debater gave little indication of the future revolutionary: At the time he thought constitutional monarchy preferable to republicanism.

For a while he contemplated becoming a priest but the lukewarm response he got from a priest when he broached the topic turned him away. However, he maintained a high level of religious observance and was active in the St. Vincent de Paul Society, which brought him face to face with what for him was unimaginable pain and suffering. At the age of twenty-one he left Blackrock to take up a teaching position at Rockwell College, near Cashel. After two years he moved back to Dublin. After a year there teaching at a Jesuit college he moved on to the Training College of Our Lady of Mercy, Carysfort, Here, and to other schools where he taught at

[1]M. J. MacManus, *Eamon de Valera* (Chicago: Ziff-Davis, 1946), p. 11.

intervals. He gained a solid reputation as an energetic, lucid, and patient teacher. He also found time for rugby, at which he excelled.

An interest in Gaelic dating back to 1896 became a passion. He studied diligently and in 1908 joined the Gaelic League—a decision with far-reaching consequences. To further improve his Gaelic he decided to spend his summer holidays at Tourmakeady, an Irish-speaking district in County Mayo. The choice of Tourmakeady was not an accident. His fiancée, Sinead Flanagan, was a devoted student of Gaelic herself and attended the Irish College there. In 1909 their romance blossomed and on January 8, 1910, they were married in St. Paul's Church, Dublin. The marriage was a good one. Although Sinead was a prominent member of the Gaelic League, she preferred to stay out of the limelight. She attended to the domestic chores and freed Eamon for the nationalist cause they passionately believed in.

The Making of Michael Collins

Eight years younger than de Valera, Michael Collins came from a line of tenant farmers whose history of dispossession was as long as that of any Irish Catholic family. His parents farmed an eighty-acre plot at Woodfield near Sam's Cross; the land had been in the Collins clan for seven generations. The world he grew up in was small and closed off; sheer survival was always a challenge. The memory of the terrible famine of 1848 hung over the farmers as an ever-present reminder of what a harvest failure might mean. Ruthless landlords constantly threatened eviction.

Michael was the youngest of eight children and a bright, cheerful, and fearless boy. He showed early the aggressiveness and quick temper that later would bring him his share of enemies. He was also tenderhearted and would hide birds in their nests from his closest companions lest they disturb or steal them. His father, Michael John Collins, already seventy-five at his birth, was the supreme influence on his life. Sitting in the kitchen or going about the farm, Michael would listen to the sturdy old man tell stories about the great nationalist heroes and recite the poetry of the cause.

Michael also began learning himself what it meant to be an Irish Catholic in a country under British rule. His brother John told him how a battering ram had been used to level the mud-walled home of an evicted tenant and how "the family stood there bewildered, the children shivering in the raw November afternoon, the man sullen and afraid to fight." The people had suffered from injustice for so long they had come to accept it as the will of God. But not Michael. Once, passing the home of an evicting landlord, he

Michael Collins

cried out to a companion: "When I'm a man we'll have him and his kind out of Ireland!"[2] As a teenager he already regarded Arthur Griffith (the founder of Sinn Fein) as the man who held the key to Ireland's future.

He was only fourteen when his mother decided it was time for him to think seriously about his own future and prepare himself for a job. She arranged to have him study for the British Civil Service examination. He passed it and left Sam's Cross for the first time at the age of sixteen to take a job in London with the Post Office Savings Bank. For the next nine and a half years he held a variety of jobs while living with his sister Hannie and waiting for his hour of destiny. Meanwhile he read widely, constantly jotting down facts and figures and biographical details of such Irishmen as O'Connell and Parnell. Under his sister's aegis he read widely—Hardy, Meredith, Wells, Bennett, Conrad, Swinburne, Wilde, Yeats, Colum, Stephens, and Shaw. Whitman's *Leaves of Grass* stirred him to the depths. He called it "a true transcript of a soul."

Collins saw that the weakness in Ireland's previous bids for freedom was

[2]Margery Forester, *Michael Collins—The Lost Leader* (London: Sidgwick & Jackson, 1971), p. 16.

the lack of unity of the people pressing the cause and he looked for groups seeking to strengthen that unity. Of all the parties, Sinn Fein seemed to hold the greatest promise for unity. Collins immersed himself in Sinn Fein's campaign to gain control of local government in Ireland as a means toward ultimate independence. But Sinn Fein's early successes in these elections were undermined by the steady flow of emigration from the poor country. This remorseless drain of Ireland's youth and labor force threatened her economy and hopes for independence. Sinn Fein's long-term view of gradual constitutional change began to seem unrealistic, and Collins soon joined the Irish Republican Brotherhood, a secret society inspired by Parnell's dictum: "I have long ceased to believe that anything but force of arms will ever bring about the redemption of Ireland." On a November night in 1909 in London Michael was sworn into the Brotherhood. "It may be said that in doing so he was taking the most eventful step in his whole life. Everything of consequence he did subsequently in the political or military spheres turned on the taking of that oath."[3]

The Rising

The lives of de Valera and Collins began to intersect as the movement for Irish freedom gained momentum. Within a few months of each other, they enlisted in the militant Irish Volunteers, de Valera in November 1913 and Collins in April 1914. The Volunteers were founded to meet the threat from Ulster Protestants. But an army without arms looked silly, so the Volunteers smuggled in weapons under the nose of the British police. On July 26, 1914, a yacht pulled in at Howth. Each of the Volunteer companies appeared out of the darkness, grabbed their rifles, and disappeared. De Valera's company was the last to receive their arms. He realized that after marching twenty miles his men were in no condition to march back to Dublin carrying heavy Mauser rifles. He dismissed two thirds of the men, who left their rifles with others who stayed behind. Then he went back to Dublin to fetch his motorbike. Returning to the shore he then ferried the men home one by one with the rifles hidden under the apron of his sidecar. By the time he finished, the first light of dawn was beginning to streak the horizon.

Collins had joined the Volunteers while still in London. But when in January 1916 Britain imposed compulsory military service on the Irish, he realized it was time to leave England and return home. He soon found a job

[3]Leon O'Broin, *Michael Collins* (Dublin: Gill and MacMillan, 1980), p. 6.

as financial adviser to the Plunkett family who lived near Dublin. Their home was one of the centers of revolutionary ferment and Michael was soon drawn into planning the touchstone event of Irish independence—the Easter Rising.

De Valera was also involved in the planning and was given charge of one of four battalions organized to keep British troops from reaching the center of Dublin once the rebellion began. To prepare himself he took frequent walks through the district, sizing up the terrain. He also took frequent trips on a train that ran through the district to figure out how to immobilize it, since it would be used to carry British troops into battle.

By January there were signs that Dublin Castle (British headquarters in Dublin) had wind of a coming rising and that the Volunteers' time was running out. The executive council of the Irish Republican Brotherhood set policy for the Volunteers even though the two organizations were technically separate. It fell to Patrick Pearse, the head of the Brotherhood, to set the date for the rebellion. He chose Easter Sunday, April 23, 1916. His faith told him it was the perfect day for the resurrection of the nation. However, Eoin MacNeill, the head of the Volunteers, had no such mystical faith; he thought that under the circumstances a rising was not only futile but immoral. This difference between Pearse and MacNeill pressed the issue of dual authority. For the moment, however, the executive council of the Brotherhood solved the dilemma by keeping MacNeill in the dark.

On Wednesday of Holy Week a courier handed de Valera a note with the password "Howth"; de Valera responded with his own prearranged signal: "Bruree." The cryptic exchange set the rising for Easter Sunday at midnight. On Good Friday evening de Valera said goodbye to his wife and four children and for the first time intimated to Sinead that serious business was afoot. A simple will provided very little for their future and the thought of the likely suffering ahead for them troubled him deeply. After making his last confession at the University Church, he spent the night at the home of one of his officers. On Holy Saturday night he stayed at headquarters and briefed his troops, going over in detail all aspects of the coming battle.

But Murphy's law intervened. A German ship, the *Aud,* while bringing arms to the rebels had reached port at Tralee Bay but was captured by the British. At the same time, Roger Casement, who was supposed to direct the operation, had landed on the Kerry coast but, ill and exhausted, was captured.

Aware of the disaster, Collins awakened Holy Saturday morning with no illusions about the outcome of the rising. He knew that the people of Ireland were not behind them and he was certain the rebellion would amount to no more than a gesture. But nevertheless he was bubbling over with anticipation.

Eoin MacNeill, the reluctant rebel, heard by chance of the imminent events and resigned himself to the folly until, hearing of the *Aud* disaster, he acted quickly. He issued orders to all Volunteers to demobilize. By Sunday morning, bewildered by orders and counterorders, most of the Volunteers dispersed. The glorious hope was beginning to fade.

De Valera awakened on Easter Sunday morning shocked at MacNeill's notice in a newspaper cancelling the mobilization. If they turned back now, how would they even be able to inspire the men again? But his spirits lifted with the news that a military council was to be held in Labor headquarters at Liberty Hall to determine the next move. It proved to be one of the most important meetings in Irish history. Those present—Pearse, Connolly, Clarke, MacDonagh, McDermott, Kent, and Plunkett—agreed that they had reached the point of no return. The British were certain to try to disarm them now that their intent was clear. And if they let the British take the initiative, they would be sitting ducks. The rising was set for noon the next day, Easter Monday. De Valera was told to be ready.

On Easter Monday morning, Collins met with Plunkett and his aide-de-camp Brennan-Whitmore at the Metropole Hotel. Armed with automatics, the three set out for the focal point of the rebellion—the takeover of the General Post Office (GPO). At Liberty Hall Plunkett, Pearse, and Connolly, the Labor leader, conferred in a small room while Collins stood by in silence. Shortly before noon, the four lined up with 150 or so men and started out for the post office. They were a motley crew: some in a dark green uniform, some in light green, some in the semblance of a uniform. Their weapons too were a mix: rifles, shotguns, pickaxes, pikes. They would have been laughable but for their determined order and discipline. They marched behind Connolly, his leggings polished, his head held high, wearing a look of triumph. Only a few people were outdoors at that early hour on the holiday. As the marchers came out of Abbey Street and headed toward the towering Nelson pillar, Connolly's voice suddenly rang out: "Left turn, the GPO—Charge!" The guards at the post office were easily overwhelmed.

Collins joined those who were shattering and barricading the windows, while panic-stricken holiday strollers, indignant old ladies, weeping girls, and outraged civil servants came pouring out of the building. The green, white, and orange flag of the Irish Republic soon waved proudly over the captured structure. Pearse began reading the proclamation:

> Irish men and Irish women: In the name of God and of the dead genera-
> tions from which she receives her old tradition of nationhood, Ireland
> through us summons her children to her flag and fights for her freedom!
> . . . In every generation the Irish people have asserted their right to
> national freedom and sovereignty; six times during the past three hundred
> years they have asserted it in arms. Standing on that fundamental right
> and again asserting it in arms in the face of the world, we hereby proclaim
> the Irish Republic as a Sovereign Independent State, and we pledge our
> lives and the lives of our comrades in arms to the cause of its freedom, of
> its welfare, and of its exaltation among the nations.[4]

Throughout the next days of battle, Collins plotted combatant positions on a map; at other times, the irrepressible clown sang and joked, getting even the careworn Pearse to smile. De Valera's battalion was to cover the southeastern part of a circle of defense around the city. However, it was soon evident that the confusion over MacNeill's order had had a disastrous effect. Only 200 of a thousand Volunteers had shown up. De Valera's battalion, originally numbering 500 men, could count only 130 when the action began. Hence he could not close the circle with the other battalions but had to concentrate his men in defense of three bridges and the railway that ran through the area. His command post at Boland's Bakery gave him a clear view of the battle. Incessantly busy, de Valera moved from one post to another, anxious about his poorly trained men facing fire for the first time. He ordered one sentry back to his post when he found him saying the rosary with other sentries—a sign of the mystical if ill-timed fervor so characteristic of the rising. When two of the sentries guarding a key outpost told him they had only single-shot rifles, he unbuckled his Mauser pistol and handed it over with four hundred rounds of ammunition. But the booming of artillery from a British gunboat coming down the Liffey made it clear that artillery, not rifles, would decide the outcome.

The British reinforcements, several thousand strong, landed at Dun Laoghaire not suspecting the ambush de Valera had in store for them. Young Englishmen who had never been under fire were mowed down, perfect

---

[4]Max Caulfield, *The Easter Rebellion* (Boulder, Colo.: Roberts Rhinehart Publishers, 1963), pp. 72–73.

targets for snipers behind the high iron palings and thick shrubs. Another British section was driven back when they neared the railway line; their main assault on the Mount Street Bridge met furious fire from fourteen Volunteers. It took nine hours for the British to capture the bridge. Their casualties were 234 killed and wounded while the Volunteers lost only four men. On the next day de Valera's men came under heavy sniper fire. De Valera realized that a distillery nearby with a tower on the roof would give snipers who captured it a great vantage point. He managed to climb an iron ladder, his silhouette making a perfect target, and hang a green flag from the tower—a brilliant ruse that kept the British from taking it. The ongoing boom of artillery and the spray of broken glass made the defenders believe an assault on the bakery was imminent. But Friday evening came and still no attack. Unaware that the rising was all but over, de Valera decided to rest after a week without sleep. A great pall of smoke lay over the city.

By Saturday morning it was obvious to some of the rebels that they would have to surrender. Pearse led his exhausted men down O'Connell Street past Nelson high on his pillar. Under the stares of rank upon rank of British troops, the little contingent lay down their weapons. They were marched to the Rotunda Hospital lawn nearby. One of the prisoners, Liam Tobin, later a close associate of Collins, described the scene:

> The whole area looked as if it had been struck by an earthquake. Fires were still smouldering. Tramway standards were buckled over, trailing their wires about the street. The blackened ruins, the gaping holes in the roadway, the stench of burning—all gave rise to the sense of defeat and despondency which seemed to sweep over us.

Meanwhile de Valera and his men still awaited the final assault. On Sunday morning, ready for a fight to the finish, de Valera was starting to shave when a woman from the auxiliary arrived with an order signed by Pearse: He and his men were to lay down their arms. Finally convinced that it was not a British trick, de Valera and his men lined up behind a Red Cross worker carrying a white flag. He gave the sad order "to ground arms" and long remembered the cracking sound as the weapons hit the street. Then with British soldiers at their side they marched across the bloodied Mount Street Bridge. The jeers they heard from the sidewalks made them painfully aware of their countrymen's indifference.

They finally arrived at Richmond Barracks where the grim-visaged general, Sir John Maxwell, had forced the first batch of prisoners to stand all Saturday night and all Sunday under a drenching cold rain and intense sun.

Collins never forgot seeing the stick struck from under crippled Sean MacDermott. Providentially Collins' own staff-captain's insignia was ripped off with a bayonet. Lynx-eyed officials yanked out those they believed to be ringleaders. They rarely missed their quarry, but some of them would live to regret one they had overlooked.

De Valera: from Prison to Politics

De Valera recorded the events in a few notes in his diary. Outside his cell the leaders were lined up and shot, one after another. After his court-martial on Monday, May 8, he wrote to a rugby-playing friend:

> Just a line to say I played my last match last week and lost. Tomorrow I am to be shot—so pray for me—an old sport who unselfishly played the game.

But as the number of those executed continued to grow, a change of feeling took place. Voices in the press, British and American as well as Irish, began to raise questions about the harsh reprisals. Many agreed with George Bernard Shaw, who said: "The men who were shot were prisoners of war . . . I cannot regard as a traitor any Irishman taken in a fight for Irish independence against the British government, which was a fair fight." Two still had to pay the price: the wounded Connolly—shot as he lay propped up in a chair; and Sean MacDermott, shot after limping to the wall. But de Valera, who was believed to have little chance because he had caused so many casualties, was sent to prison instead of to heaven.

Or one might say to hell. For Dartmoor Prison was at least a good replica of that more famous place. Determined not to be broken nor to go mad, de Valera found his biggest enemy was the deadly monotony. The "black and white walls, the damp, barely lighted cells, the drab figures of the convicts, the blue-coated warders, the meager prison dietary, the single-file 'ring' of morning exercise taken with measured paces and in dead silence . . . the little tent of blue that prisoners call the sky."[5] De Valera soon emerged as the leader of the prisoners. When the Irish Nation League proposed that the prisoners be treated as prisoners of war, he organized several actions to back the demand. After mass on Sunday, they were going to take over the prison and force the authorities to summon the military. But the plan was discovered and they ended up saying the rosary in their cells instead. The next step

[5] MacManus, *Eamon de Valera,* p. 36.

was to damage the prison by systematic destruction of windows and lamps while singing "God Save Ireland." The authorities in response dispersed the prisoners and sent de Valera to another jail. Arriving there, he continued his acts of defiance by cracking windows and refusing to obey orders.

When a huge protest meeting was held in Dublin, the British realized it was time to relent and released the prisoners. A year before, the rebels had left Dublin in chains, little noticed by the public. But a year under the British yoke and stories of their harsh treatment had wrought a great change. Now huge crowds in Dublin awaited the heroes of the Easter Rising. When news came that they had landed at Kingstown, people marched in military formation to the train terminal at Westland Row to give them a tumultuous welcome.

Though he had never intended to have a political career, de Valera could not refuse when the Volunteers asked him to contest the election at East Clare as a Sinn Fein candidate. It was a momentous decision. He proved to be a formidable campaigner. Not an orator in the grand Irish tradition of O'Connell and Parnell, he was still an effective, if sometimes long-winded speaker. Standing in his Volunteer uniform on a platform overlooking the square, he had to convince the hard-headed farmers of Clare that he was not some madcap romantic but a leader with a grand vision of Ireland's destiny. He insisted that Ireland's case be heard at the Versailles peace conference; that the Catholic majority in Ulster would not surrender their rights to the Protestant minority; and that he would never abandon the principles of the Easter Rising. "In the name of God and of the dead generations from which she receives her old tradition of nationhood, we declare the right of the people of Ireland to the ownership of Ireland . . . to be sovereign and indefeasible."[6] Was Clare ready for de Valera's position? The answer came back loud and clear: He received 5,010 votes, and Lynch, his Unionist opponent, 2,035.

Sinn Fein's Amazing Duo

While de Valera was gaining prominence in the Sinn Fein, Collins' star was also rising. Since his release from prison in late 1917, he had helped reorganize the Irish Republican Brotherhood and was elected secretary of its Supreme Council. He was also elected to the Provisional Executive of the Irish Volunteers and spent much time in gun-running expeditions and in-

[6]Ibid., p. 47.

formation gathering. He also took an active part in Sinn Fein while not sharing its belief that Irish freedom could be attained by nonviolent constitutional means. But he greatly admired Arthur Griffith, its indefatigible publicist and president.

One of Collins' defining moments came when Tom Ashe, a fellow Sinn Fein organizer, died in prison on September 25, 1917, from a hunger strike. The death of the handsome Easter Week commandant and Sinn Fein's most effective speaker caused a huge storm of anger to break out all over the land. Thousands flocked to his funeral, where he lay in state in his Volunteer uniform. Collins spoke his eulogy at the grave in Irish and English. It was the last time Collins himself wore the uniform, for he now realized he had to go underground.

As his contacts within the movement broadened, Collins became known as the man to get things done. In spite of a style described as "ruthless" by an unfriendly colleague, he was greatly appreciated for his forceful leadership, enormous capacity for work, and grasp of every essential detail: "The quickest intellect and nerve that Ireland bred," according to one well-informed observer. But it was de Valera, an unknown only eighteen months before, who was increasingly looked on as the leader of the independence movement. The boys and girls of the countryside would sing:

> Up de Valera! He's the champion of the right
> We'll follow him to battle 'neath the Orange, Green and White!

A number of qualities were combined in his formidable personality: integrity, transparent sincerity, courage, patience, unbounded self-confidence, and an inherent sense of dignity. He was also best able to draw together the differing factions in the independence movement.

A convention of Sinn Fein was held at the Mansion House in Dublin on October 25, 1917, to approve a new constitution and elect a president. It was a heated affair. Brugha, the extreme republican, was hardly willing to sit in the same room with the moderate Sinn Fein leader Arthur Griffith, who favored a monarchy. Michael Collins and Rory O'Connor walked out and had to be fetched back by de Valera. Finally they agreed on their objective: to secure international recognition of Ireland as an independent Irish Republic. Having achieved that status, the Irish people might by referendum choose their own form of government. Realizing the drawback in having a moderate as president, Collins took steps to have de Valera elected. Griffith graciously agreed to step down and de Valera assumed the presidency. The Sinn Feiners also drew up a constitution that provided for a constituent assembly to carry on the functions of a de facto Irish government. The legislature was called the Dail Eireann and its membership was opened to all adults of Irish birth or parentage, except those in some way linked with Great Britain.

Sinn Fein was given a tremendous boost when a successful German offensive on the Western front induced the British to impose compulsory military service on the Irish. The country reacted with fury, and de Valera in the name of Sinn Fein drafted a pledge stating their determination to resist conscription. The Catholic bishops, who had been silent during the rebellion, published a courageous manifesto that called the conscription "an oppressive and inhuman law which the Irish people have a right to resist by every means that are consonant with the law of God." The bishops also asked the people to subscribe to de Valera's anticonscription pledge, and called for a collection to fight conscription. The pledge was signed at every Catholic church door in the country.

A British campaign to arrest Irish political stalwarts also backfired when the executives of Sinn Fein and the Irish Volunteers met on May 17, 1918. Collins warned them that Dublin Castle was going to "round up" the leaders. De Valera ignored the warning, thinking that going into hiding would make work for independence too hard. The Royal Irish Constabulary followed him to Greystones and, when he stepped off the train, arrested him. He and others were charged with involvement in a German plot and put on board a cruiser for internment in England. But as the ship pulled out, a large crowd on the dock gave them a rousing sendoff—a sign of the popular groundswell now lifting Sinn Fein as a reaction to the mass arrests. The gradualist Irish Parliamentary Party was all but finished—its belief in gaining independence by constitutional action overwhelmed by a new radical politics. Sinn Fein won an overwhelming electoral victory in December 1918; most of its candidates were in prison.

Meanwhile de Valera hatched an ingenious plan to escape. He had been serving mass in prison since his arrival and had noticed that the chaplain left his key to the outside in the sacristy. One day, on the pretext of getting a cruet, de Valera returned to the sacristy and made wax impressions of the key in candle drippings. Then he sent his cohorts a drawing of the key incorporated into a supposedly humorous cartoon of a prisoner with a big key. They were instructed in Irish to make a key from the drawing, send it in a cake, and make arrangements to meet him outside the prison. There were a number of hitches. Several times a key was sent in that didn't work. After five cakes and much sweat, de Valera finally had one that fit. His cohorts waited for a night when the moon was on the wane. Then on a February evening de Valera saw the prearranged signal—a sharp beam of a flashlight. He answered with a flare made from four or five matches. Then he and two companions, opening and then locking a series of doors, made it to the outside wall where Collins and Boland were waiting. A key they had inserted had broken in the lock; de Valera put his own key in the lock and with a prayer pushed against the broken shank. It fell to the ground as de Valera opened the rusty gate with a thunderous noise. But their luck held and no one heard them. Meeting soldiers with their dates returning to a hospital nearby, Boland put his arms around de Valera, a friendly couple hastening on their way and calling out "Good night, chums" to the distracted soldiers.

With his wonted skills, Collins had organized the whole affair with perfection. De Valera reached Manchester at midnight only five minutes behind schedule. He remained there for a week in the home of a chaplain to the workhouse. All Ireland marveled at his wizardry and the world press looked on in wonder. When the house came under surveillance, de Valera, dressed in a colonial uniform, managed once again to elude the authorities. On February 18 he got word from Collins that it would be safe to come home. Hidden aboard the *Cambria,* he left Liverpool and arrived in Dublin on the morning of February 20.

De Valera Appeals to the U.S. Public

The meetings of the Dail in April 1919 were devoted to measures that would make it effective in governing Ireland. Cathal Brugha, the temporary president, resigned in favor of de Valera, who was unanimously chosen. Soon came the disheartening news that Ireland would not get a hearing at Versailles. President Wilson did not think the treaty should be applied to the domestic issues of the victors of the Great War but only to the vanquished. Still hoping to get international recognition, de Valera decided to go to the United States and plead at the bar of public opinion. America, he thought, would understand the Irish longing for independence from England.

Arrangements were made for de Valera's departure from Liverpool. Smuggled onto the *S.S. Lapland,* he spent eight days lying on his coffin-like bunk, wretched with seasickness. Landing on June 11, he was hustled off to a secret place so that the persons involved in smuggling him could not be traced. Word soon got out, however, and a huge crowd awaited him when he arrived at New York. He was met by the tricolor of the Irish Republic and the Stars and Stripes as well.

He had come to the country with a threefold mission: to secure recognition of the Irish Republic from the government of the United States; to raise money; and to get the widest possible publicity for Ireland's claim to independence. Unfortunately, he didn't get far with his first wish. President Wilson, a staunch Presbyterian of Scotch Irish heritage, had little sympathy for the Irish cause.

But the biggest thorn in de Valera's side during the trip was Judge Cohalan, the head of the Friends of Irish Freedom—the premier pro-Irish organization in America. Arrogant, ruthless, and devoutly American, he was as "accomplished a master of intrigue as ever American politics had produced."[7] Dedicated to bringing about the downfall of President Wilson, whom he hated, he fought tooth and nail to defeat the League of Nations which upheld principles of self-determination dear to de Valera's cause. Then a dispute arose over the question of floating an Irish bond in America. Cohalan opposed it and predicted a disastrous failure. His organization had established an Irish Victory Fund which had already raised over a million dollars. He wanted to leave well enough alone. But after consulting a lawyer named Franklin Delano Roosevelt, de Valera went ahead with what became a sensational success. The loan speedily topped the five million mark.

Then hostilities flared up again. At America's Republican Convention of 1920, Cohalan opposed de Valera's effort to get a plank inserted in the platform calling for the recognition of the Republic of Ireland. At the Democratic Convention, President Wilson engineered the defeat of a similar proposal. After the American elections were over de Valera set up a new organization, The American Association for the Recognition of the Irish Republic, that would work in unison with Ireland's hoped-for elected government. The new group's membership soon dwarfed Cohalan's Friends of Irish Freedom.

Collins' State of General Disorder

While de Valera was barnstorming in the United States, Michael Collins was busy at home creating what he called a "state of general disorder."

As director of organization he was in charge of integrating the work of the Volunteers. He had to construct a picture of the Volunteer movement

---

[7] Ibid., p. 68.

for every part of the country—the total number of men on the rolls and those he could rely on, and the amount of arms, ammunition, and equipment. A Volunteer officer, Ernie O'Malley, described Collins at work in his office:

He was pacing up and down. We shook hands. He jerked his head to a chair to indicate that I should sit; he took a chair which he tilted back against the wall. On shelves were green membership cards, heaps of *The Irish Volunteer Handbook,* and stacks of white copies of the organization scheme. Behind his desk was a large map of Ireland marked with broad red streaks radiating from Dublin. He was tall, his shoulders were broad; his energy showed through rapid movement. A curving bunch of hair fell on his forehead; he tossed it back with a vigorous head twist. "I'm sending you to Offaly," he said, "I want you to organize a brigade in the country . . ." He had a strong, singing Cork accent; his brown eyes studied me fixedly. He pointed out companies on a map and mentioned officers' names . . . He gave me . . . lists of equipment that could be made locally . . . notes on the destruction of railways, bridges and engines with and without explosives . . . He crossed to the window. "They're looking for me now . . . the G men." Collins laughed. "Good luck," he said and shook hands.[8]

His escapes from the police soon became legendary. As minister of finance in de Valera's government-in-waiting, Collins kept an office in the upper story of 6 Harcourt Street, the headquarters of Sinn Fein. On September 10, 1919, the building was raided by the military and police. At first he opened a window to climb down a drainpipe, but finding none he decided to bluff his way out. He handed his revolver to a typist to hide just as an inspector of the G Division entered. The inspector didn't recognize Collins—few of them knew what he looked like. As Collins snatched up some papers the inspector ordered him to hand them over. But Collins refused, telling him it was none of his business. "And what are you doing," Collins said, "spying on your fellow countrymen?" As the inspector paused, momentarily taken aback by the remark, Collins rushed past him and a policeman at the door and bounded upstairs. Grabbing onto a skylight, he hoisted himself onto the roof and dove into a building next door where he stayed until the raid was over.

As director of intelligence in Sinn Fein he constantly sought ways to

[8]O'Broin, *Michael Collins,* pp. 34–35.

infiltrate G Division of the Dublin Metropolitan Police and was in the end able to recruit several young detectives. One of these, Ned Broy, came from a family that had roots in the nationalist tradition. His job for the police was to type reports sent in daily on Sinn Fein movements. But he would simply put in an extra carbon and pass on the extra report to his Sinn Fein contacts. In time Collins had four men in key positions in the G Division. They would leave messages in various places—the public library, pubs—and would also meet with Collins over tea. One night Broy even let him into the G Division headquarters after locking in the sleeping constables. Collins spent hours going through the official files, even reading those about him-self. Eventually, Collins extended his network of inside contacts even into Scotland Yard and the British army. Strategically placed officers, typists, and secretaries supplied him with valuable information. His network included workers in hotels, on the railways, and on cross-channel boats. His spies in the post office would intercept government letters and telegrams and tap phones.

An important component of his system was what he called his Squad. It consisted of twelve or so extremely trustworthy men on whom he could call at any hour of the night or day. They were his executioners. Convinced that every previous Irish rebellion had failed because of spies who infiltrated the movement, he was determined to prevent this by a ruthless elimination of quislings and informers. One of the first to go was a man named Quinlisk, a former member of Casement's brigade who arranged with the Dublin Met-ropolitan Police to set up Collins. Quinlisk had arranged to have an inter-view with Collins in Cork where the police would be ready to nab the rebel. But the plan was discovered and passed on to Collins. Quinlisk was soon dead. A succession of spies met a similar fate. Collins also took his campaign of intimidation straight to the halls of British power. Assistant Commissioner W. C. Forbes Redmond was brought down from Belfast to reorganize the demoralized detective division. One of Collins' spies gave Collins a photo of him and Redmond was spotted and assassinated outside the Standard Hotel in Harcourt Street shortly afterward. Soon after his death the Metropolitan Police ceased to be an anti-insurgent force of any conse-quence.

A huge price was put on Collins' head. The police became obsessed with him. "Michael Collins is here. We know it!" they would shout as they raided a hotel or a pub or a house. But they weren't able to find even a good photo of the elusive Collins. While the hunt intensified, Collins calmly went about his business through the streets of Dublin, always well dressed, never with a weapon or paper that would identify him. When accosted by a suspicious policeman, he would bluff his way through. One night his luck almost ran out. He and his crew went to eat at a private room in Gresham's Hotel but, with none available, they took a table in the main dining area. Some policemen nearby took notice and one of them escorted Collins into a cloakroom, where he looked him over carefully while scrutinizing a photograph. In desperation Collins was about to grab for the policeman's gun when the man simply turned on his heel and let him go. For the first and last time in his life, Collins got drunk. Later, with his hair still wildly disheveled where the officer had run his fingers through it, Collins asked Rory O'Connor what he would have told the country lads if Collins had been captured. O'Connor drew a knife across his throat. "I wouldn't have been here to tell anything," he said.

Soon the British obsession with the revolutionaries became a flat-out shoot-to-kill policy in which undercover agents posing as republicans broke into the homes of members of Sinn Fein and shot them down in front of their families. To help the demoralized police, who were mostly Irish and ostracized by the populace, England's Prime Minister Lloyd George in March 1920 let loose the infamous Black and Tans, an official group of ill-disciplined misfits who specialized in murder, pillage, and arson. In the latter part of 1920, the terror reached a climax. On Bloody Sunday, November 21, Collins' squad in Dublin assassinated twelve undercover agents and two auxiliaries (members of a special police force). That afternoon the auxiliaries retaliated by invading a football game in Croke Park and firing indiscriminately into the crowd, leaving fourteen dead and sixty wounded.

Wrestling with Lloyd George

The Black and Tans had just burned Cork when on Christmas Eve, 1920, de Valera arrived back in Dublin. Collins had arranged to have him smuggled back and then arranged a hiding place. But at the same time no impression could be given of defeat. The result of these conflicting concerns was a policy of isolated, powerful actions. A decision was made to destroy the venerable Custom House. Within a few hours the monumental building was reduced to a huge pile of blackened stones and marble. As a result, many government records were destroyed. De Valera's luck ran out when a lorry full of Black and Tans stopped at his hiding place in Glenvar. He tried to slip out through a rear garden gate but it was locked. Taken into custody, he was thrown into a filthy cell at Bridewell. But after a few unpleasant hours, a high-ranking government official showed up and had him transferred to a nice room in Portobello Barracks and then had him released. Completely nonplussed, de Valera headed for his wife and family in Greystones. The mystery was soon resolved when a letter from Lloyd George was handed to him, inviting him to a meeting in London. The world was astonished. The constant message from London had been unyielding opposition to terrorism: Force would be met by force until the last embers of revolt were stamped out. "No British Government in modern times," said Sir Winston Churchill, "has ever appeared to make so sudden and complete a reversal."

De Valera's reply to George insisted that there could be no peace "if you deny Ireland's essential unity and set aside the principle of national self-determination." An intermediary of George met with de Valera in Ireland and tried to convince him that Ireland should accept dominion status as South Africa had. But he was astounded at de Valera's "continual harping on visionary aims." At a meeting with the unionists of Ulster, de Valera stressed that any settlement with George would have to include the whole of Ireland.

To accompany him to London, de Valera chose three members of his cabinet—Arthur Griffith, Austin Stack, and Robert Barton—plus several others. Michael Collins took his omission from the delegation as a slight and spent several hours walking up and down in a garden arguing heatedly with the president; but de Valera tried to explain to his chief enforcer that Collins would be photographed if he went, which would reduce his effectiveness if war were to resume.

Emotions ran high when de Valera arrived in London. The Irish were out in force and with shouts of support greeted him at Euston Station. Singing and praying the rosary, they were present again later when he arrived at 10 Downing Street for his first meeting with George. This great wizard of diplomacy, the star of the Versailles Conference, was so excited before de Valera arrived that he kept walking up and down as he planned strategy. To suitably impress the Irishman, he had a great map of the vast extent of the British Empire unfurled on the wall. An imperial conference had just been concluded and George pointed out to de Valera the chairs where the premier of each dominion had sat. One was kept vacant and Lloyd George paused, waiting for de Valera to ask the obvious question—For whom? But de Valera refused to play the game. Finally George supplied the answer—"For Ireland."

After three meetings, little progress was made. De Valera's insistence on Ireland's right to be an independent republic met with a totally negative response. Then, on July 20, Lloyd George's final proposals were delivered to de Valera. They offered Ireland dominion status. This involved, among other things, British naval control of the Irish seas and use of Irish soil for defense. When de Valera flatly rejected the terms, George threatened war and asked whether de Valera wanted responsibility for that. The Irish leader replied that any war would rest on George's shoulders. When George declared: "I can put a soldier in Ireland for every man, woman and child," de Valera responded: "Very well, but you would have to keep them there." After several more heated exchanges, de Valera departed, leaving the document containing the proposals on the table. Thinking he had left it there on purpose, Lloyd George was upset until de Valera, realizing his mistake, sent for it. "How very Irish," remarked the prime minister's secretary.

With the threat of war hanging over him, de Valera returned home and strove for a formula that would bridge the differences between the two sides. The word "association" came to his mind. Ireland, he said, might be associated as a republic with the British Commonwealth. The cabinet's reaction was ho-hum. But the next morning, as he was sitting on the side of his bed tying his bootlaces, the term "external" flashed into mind. As he put it in a draft accepted by the cabinet, "The Irish people would be ready to attach themselves as an external associate to that partial league known as the British Commonwealth of Nations."

After an exchange of correspondence that did little to move the discussion forward, George invited de Valera to a conference at Inverness to see if any way could be found to reconcile their opposing points of view. De Valera accepted but in his reply noted that his delegates would attend as representatives of an independent and sovereign state with only that authority granted to them by their people. The response was handed to George while he was on a fishing holiday and in good humor. The mood vanished when he read the letter. "It won't do," he said a couple of times. "We all have to give something but Mr. de Valera will give nothing." George insisted that he would not negotiate with de Valera as the representative of an "independent and sovereign state." It would mean official British recognition of the severance of Ireland from the empire. Then de Valera saved the process by proposing that delegates meet without any prior conditions. Finally, after another lengthy correspondence, George accepted and suggested they start again with a conference on October 11, 1921, in London. The outcome was a signal achievement for de Valera. The conference would be held without prior conditions. By standing firm, he had forced the prime minister to change his position.

Setting Bounds to the March of a Nation

The extremely complicated story of the negotiations has been told often and in great detail. Here we can only present the basic facts. At the outset the delegates (now including Collins) to the conference were given instructions to the effect that nothing final or binding was to be signed without referral back to Dublin. The British had seldom mounted a more formidable group of players: Lloyd George, the wiliest of diplomats; Austen Chamberlain, almost from boyhood steeped in the practice of statecraft; Lord Birkenhead, a brilliant lawyer and peerless debater; Winston Churchill, the "bulldog aristocrat" and dyed-in-the-wool imperialist. Moreover, these Englishmen were in the flush of victory in the Great War, representing a nation of unlimited resources and "sitting proud, arrogant and self-confident in the very hub of Empire." What chance did the sharp but novice Irish diplomats have against such a team? Unfortunately, the Irish delegation from the beginning bore within itself the seeds of disunity. Griffith was never totally committed to the republican ideal; Collins was reluctant to participate and from the beginning was skeptical about the chances of Britain accepting de Valera's formula of external association.

Ironically the first development that nearly scuttled the conference arose from a telegram from the "pope of peace"—Benedict XV. In response to the papal message of encouragement, George composed a reply for the Crown stating its hope for an end to the "troubles in Ireland." An incensed de Valera responded with a telegram to the pope asserting that the source of the Irish difficulties was the long history of Britain's brutal efforts to rob the people of their liberty. A furor erupted in the press. At the next meeting Lloyd George called de Valera's letter "defiant and ill-conditioned." But the conference proceeded.

Many sessions took place before the main issue emerged: England was determined to keep Ireland within the empire while the Irish delegation was equally determined to refuse even dominion status. De Valera hoped that his formula of external association would bridge the difference. George asked whether it meant that "if all other conditions are satisfied, you are prepared to come inside the Empire as New Zealand, Canada?" Arthur Griffith replied, "That is not quite our idea of association." What then about the Crown? "We are willing," said Griffith, "to accept the Crown as head of the association." In other words, the Irish were willing to associate with the British for certain common purposes. But they would do so not as members of the British Commonwealth but from outside it—thus preserving their independence and integrity. At the same time they would be willing to recognize the king as head of the association. But George was dead-set against two proposed aspects of the association—the exclusion of the Crown from purely Irish affairs and the omission of an oath of allegiance.

Griffith returned to Dublin on December 3 with the British proposals: dominion status, formally equivalent to that of Canada but with the concession of certain naval facilities to Britain as well as Britain's having the right to demand further military facilities in wartime; and the oath of allegiance to the British king as an organic part of the Irish Constitution. This would make the king chief executive of the Irish state and the source from which all authority in Ireland derived. The partitioned Ulster counties were to be permitted to "opt out" of an all-Ireland Parliament but, if they did, a boundary commission was to be established to set the frontier between the north and the rest of Ireland. The Ulster question also provided the Irish delegation with an attractive way out. If Ulster refused to join an all-Irish Parliament, then the Irish would be justified in breaking off the negotiations with George; Ulster could be blamed for the rift; and George would have no basis for going to war. The alternative—a breakdown in the talks over Ireland's refusal of dominion status—would sharply oppose Britain and Ireland and make war likely. But no such attractive way out presented itself. In fact, the Irish delegation became split—some, like Collins, favoring inclusion in the dominion over the possibility of war; others willing to take the British to the brink. But George divined the split and decided to work on Collins. He saw him in private and assured him that if a break in the talks occurred, the whole world would know that it was over the issue of dominion and not over Ulster.

Then George proposed half-measures to defuse the possibility of the Irish using the issue of Ulster as an escape. Finally he laid down his ultimatum: Sign the agreement accepting dominion or there will be war within three days. They had until ten o'clock that night to make their decision. Churchill remembered Collins departing the meeting "as if he was going to shoot someone, preferably himself. In all my life I have never seen so much suffering and passion in restraint."

All now depended on Collins, who was sure that George was not bluffing. Would it not be better to accept the treaty with the advantages it offered, rather than allow the continuance of a war that could not be won? He thought of his home at Sam's Cross and what people there would want: the practical advantages of the treaty or the symbols of the republic along with economic ruin. Moreover, any decision made would have to be ratified by the Dail and the people. He was not abandoning the republic, he thought, but postponing its ultimate recognition. But would others who had risked everything feel the same way? A dark curtain hung over the future and a deep gloom settled over his soul.

At the Irish delegation's quarters in London the tension was extreme. When Barton, the other principal in the Irish delegation, heard of Collins' decision to sign, he was thunderstruck: Collins, the soul of the resistance. The idea that Collins was contemplating dominion status had never entered his mind. Now Barton faced a fearful choice. How could he violate his oath to the republic? Perhaps George was bluffing. But without Collins to lean on he could not bear the terrible responsibility of bringing war. His ordeal of conscience lasted two hours. Finally he decided to sign. At 2:20 A.M. on Tuesday, December 6, 1921, the Anglo-Irish Treaty was signed. When one of the English delegates, Lord Birkenhead, appended his signature to the treaty, he turned to Michael Collins and said, "I may have signed my political death-warrant tonight." Collins replied, "I may have signed my actual death warrant."

Collins vs. de Valera

De Valera had gone on a tour of the troops and in Limerick on Monday night, December 5, he declared: "Nothing will be accepted that deprives the nation of the essentials of freedom . . . Contests like this go in the end to the spiritual forces, even though it takes a long time."[9] The next morning he heard that an agreement had been signed. It seemed too good to be true. The delegation must have gotten what we wanted, he thought, for surely they would not otherwise have signed. But a sense of foreboding was soon confirmed when he received an outline of the treaty provisions. As he read it his face turned white and his lips tightened. There was no other way of looking at it. Ireland had lost; he had lost.

That morning Collins rose at eight after only three hours sleep and went as usual to mass. "I don't know how things will go now," he wrote to his fiancée, Kitty Kiernan, "but with God's help, we have brought peace to this land of ours." Before he entered the cabinet meeting on December 8, Collins thought de Valera would approve the treaty. But he was quickly disabused of the notion. For while the vote was four to three in favor, de

[9] MacManus, *Eamon de Valera*, p. 127.

Valera was in adamant opposition. It was a crushing blow for Collins—even though his side had won, he had lost de Valera. "Poor Ireland," Collins said that night to a friend, "back to the back rooms again." Lost and demoralized, he broke down and wept.

It was soon apparent, however, that the public in general was, with Collins, happy to have peace after the terrible strife and bloodshed of revolution. "Most men cannot long stand the strain of prolonged effort to live in accordance with very high ideals."[10] The Roman Catholic hierarchy also supported the treaty. There were, in fact, many ready to accept Collins' view of the treaty as a stepping stone toward the republic. On the other hand, there were those who believed it meant the forfeiture of Ireland's national aspirations.

The historic Dail debate on the treaty—the greatest flood of oratory in Irish history—began on December 14 and lasted until the first week in January. Every deputy spoke, some interminably and some for only a few minutes. Day after day, the chamber resounded with the voices of men passionately pleading and arguing for and against the treaty. After Griffith's motion to approve was seconded, de Valera rose. "He was," wrote the special representative of the *Irish Independent,* "in magnificent form—mentally and physically. Unquestionably his speech electrified the Assembly. His blinding sincerity so impresses you that you find yourself listening dazzled and profoundly moved. Every word came with rugged clearness."[11]

Leaning over the table at the left of the Speaker, de Valera immediately struck at the heart of the problem: "Did the Irish people think we were liars?" Then, after a pause, rapping the table with his knuckles to emphasize every word, he said slowly: "I am against this treaty because it does not reconcile Irish national aspirations with association with the British Empire. I am against this treaty, not because I am a man of war, but because I am a man of peace . . . Does this assembly think the Irish people have changed so much within the past year or two that they now want to get into the British Empire after seven centuries of fighting? . . . that they want the British king as their monarch? It is not King George as a monarch they choose; it is Lloyd George."[12] The tension grew. Collins sat with chin thrust out, clenching papers in his hand. De Valera closed with the words

[10]Crane Briton, *The Anatomy of Revolution* (New York: Vintage Books, 1965), p. 224.
[11]MacManus, *Eamon de Valera,* p. 133.
[12]Ibid.

used by Parnell nearly forty years before: "Time will tell whether this is a final settlement; you are presuming to set bounds to the march of a nation."

Later Collins rose to his feet. In repose his eyes glimmered softly and with humor. One of the members described him in action:

> He spoke passionately, eagerly, pervadingly. He had his manuscript before him. He rarely consulted it. He preferred to rely on his intuition—on the unfailing native power of the Irishman to move, arouse and convince his hearers. Now and again he felt his smooth chin. He tossed his thick black hair with his hands. He rummaged among his documents. Like Mr. de Valera, he stands now upright, now bent, now calm, and now quivering with emotion. No responsibility was shirked. "I speak plainly," he said. He did.[13]

In his opinion the treaty gave freedom—not the ultimate freedom that all nations hope for and struggle for, but freedom to achieve that end. "They [the British] have admitted us as friends into the nations of their community."[14] He stood by his signature with absolute firmness. The next day he wrote to Kitty Kiernan: "Yesterday was the worst day I ever spent in my life."[15]

As the Dail debate entered its last days, Collins was worn to a frazzle and pained by the personal attacks he had to endure. At times he vented his frustrations in violent language and in bouts of weeping. But as the time came for the vote, he stood strong and confident in the cause to which he had pledged himself: "Let the Irish nation judge us now and for future years." The vote showed sixty-four in support of the treaty, fifty-seven against. Collins sprang up to assure everyone that there was to be no winning side in this result but that all should work together for unity. Stretching out his hand to de Valera, he restated all his old love for the president. As the crowd gathered outside began cheering de Valera broke down and wept while men and women in the room wept with him. "Henceforth, whatever the immediate outcome, there would be a bitter struggle between Collins and de Valera, both now fully alert to the incompatibility between their policies and personalities. Neither could reconcile himself for long to the role of second-in-command. Two ruthless men would inevitably be locked

---

[13] Forester, *Michael Collins—The Lost Leader,* p. 269.
[14] Ibid.
[15] Ibid., p. 271.

in a struggle for leadership, de Valera with the ruthlessness of righteousness, Collins with the ruthlessness of necessity."[16]

The Sheer Madness of It All

As chair of the provisional government taking over from direct British rule, Collins made a constant effort to reconcile the pro- and anti-treaty sides. But the split was too deep. What began as a profound political problem was now heading toward civil war.

Could the republic be, in effect, disestablished—by putting itself under the authority of the Crown—if the majority in Ireland voted to do so? Even if the majority voted to do so? This was the terrible dilemma dividing the people. De Valera put it succinctly: "The conflict between the two principles, majority rule on the one hand and the inalienability of the national sovereignty on the other, that was the dilemma of the Treaty." An historian has noted: "Whatever the morality of armed resistance to an Irish government representing an actual or supposed majority, de Valera warned unceasingly that there were people who would rather die than acknowledge Britain's King as their king."[17]

Collins undertook an incredible balancing act to stave off civil war. A definite step toward such a war occurred when the Army of the Provisional Government was split by the anti-treaty forces calling themselves the Irish Republican Army (IRA). Collins for a time continued to cooperate with the IRA in order to assist the beleagured Catholics in the north. He also felt the tug of old loyalties toward men who were once his comrades in the struggle. However, the two sides inexorably moved toward war. Two of Collins' old friends, Rory O'Connor and Liam Mellowes, along with other IRA leaders on the night of April 13, 1922, seized the Four Courts in Dublin. This fine eighteenth-century building was one of the most imposing landmarks of the city, housing not only the law courts but the tax offices and records of the British administration. Its seizure was meant as a blow against the establishment, both the old and the new. In spite of pressure to take action, Collins held firm; he still hoped to find unity by negotiation, and he thought of force against the anti-treaty side as only a last resort.

---

[16]J. J. Lee, *Ireland, 1912–1985: Politics and Society* (New York: Cambridge University Press, 1989), pp. 53–54.

[17]The Earl of Longford and T. P. O'Neill, *Eamon de Valera* (London: Hutchinson, 1970), p. 186.

In these circumstances it was a great relief for the Dail and the country when Collins and de Valera signed a pact that would provide for a coalition government including pro- and anti-treaty representatives. In the coming elections, voters would be able to elect a panel of candidates from both sides. This ensured that elections would be held giving whatever side came out on top a legitimacy that might forestall fratricide. And Collins could argue that the pact gave the opposition a last chance to assume a responsible and constitutional part in restoring the country without losing face by having to accept the treaty. With economic chaos in full swing, unity was a supreme consideration.

However, the Constitution for the Free State—the charter imposed by the British on a new Ireland inside the dominion—ruled out any hope of a working coalition government. Published on June 16, the morning of the elections, the charter's provisions for the oath to the authority of the Crown and for the role of the governor-general were totally unacceptable to the republicans. British rigidity had destroyed the possibility of unity. The elections further ruined the chances of a coalition government as the anti-treaty candidates went down to defeat. Only a government pledged to uphold the treaty was now possible. Collins had reached the tragic point where compromise for the sake of unity had to be subordinated to the people's desire to proceed in accordance with the treaty. Collins the enforcer of the revolution had become the enforcer of the Crown.

When Field Marshal Sir Henry Wilson was shot dead on his doorstep by Irish republicans, civil war became a certainty. Wilson was hated as the evil mind behind the murderous activities of Orange gangs. His death represented a new level of battle. The British Parliament was used to members of the Dail being assassinated; they weren't used to political killing so close to home. The colonial secretary, Winston Churchill, lost all patience. An ultimatum was dispatched to Collins: There was to be no more dillydallying with the rebels in the Four Courts.

When Collins heard of the ultimatum he was beside himself. He had already decided to move against the Four Courts but now it would look as though he were doing it under British orders. "Let Churchill come over and do his own dirty work," he snarled.[18] But he could no longer delay and on Tuesday, June 27, the provisional government issued an ultimatum to the Four Courts rebels to surrender by 4 A.M. the next day. Two eighteen-pound field guns were brought up and aimed across the Liffey River at the

---

[18] Forester, *Michael Collins—The Lost Leader,* p. 320.

Four Courts building. But the rebels remained unmoved. At 4:07 A.M. on Wednesday, Dublin was awakened by the sound of crashing shells announcing the beginning of civil war.

Two days later the rebel garrison surrendered unconditionally. It took longer to pacify the other republicans, including de Valera, who had holed up in the buildings and hotels nearby. De Valera managed to escape but Cathal Brugha remained in the Hammam Hotel with a small garrison. Under heavy gunfire the building was set ablaze and those inside marched out to surrender—all but Brugha. When he finally emerged he tried to escape by running down a smoke-filled lane between the flaming buildings. Both friend and enemy shouted for him to stop. As he continued in flight, the troops fired and he fell, mortally wounded. When Collins got the news he wept uncontrollably: "I would forgive him anything . . . because of his sincerity." Less than a month later, the same fate befell Harry Boland who was sleeping in a hotel when it was raided by troops. He bolted down a corridor, was shot through the abdomen, and fell mortally wounded. Collins was twisted in a paroxysm of grief. He wrote to Kitty Kiernan: "I passed by Vincent's Hospital . . . and thought of the times together . . . I only thought of him with the friendship of the days of 1918 & 1919 . . . I'd send a wreath but I suppose they'd return it torn up." When de Valera heard the news of Boland's death, he was crushed. He had lost his most faithful friend.

The provisional government would not accept a truce until the anti-treaty forces handed over their arms, while the republicans had little stomach for fighting their ex-comrades. Moreover, the republicans lacked cannons and were ill-equipped in general compared with their British-supplied opponents. As commander-in-chief of the nationalist army, Collins' strategy was to strike at the republicans from the sea. Government troops pushed across Kerry and West Cork taking the republican strongholds as they went. Finally, on August 11, the last republican stronghold of Cork fell and the republicans retreated to the countryside to carry on guerrilla warfare. On August 12, Arthur Griffith—worn out by a life of constant stress—died. Collins led the funeral march in Dublin. At the grave a priest said: "Michael, you should be prepared—you may be next." Collins turned. "I know," he said.

With the republicans in the countryside, de Valera heard the news of Arthur Griffith's death. "He was, I believe, unselfishly patriotic . . . if only he had not stooped to the methods he employed to win." At this time, one of de Valera's American friends, Peter Golden, found him in a neat, whitewashed kitchen of a house in the hills, near Gougane Barra. The household was saying the rosary in Irish while de Valera knelt against the back of a chair with his face buried in his hands. When the prayers were over, de Valera greeted him courteously. Golden noted how "not a word of bitterness escapes this man against any of those now so bitterly opposed to him—not even against those who certainly have not in any way spared him . . . He speaks with great kindness of Arthur Griffith and of his fine pioneer work for Ireland."

Collins' tour of the southwest made him aware of the sheer chaos and madness of the war. He decided to go to Cork, the center of rebel resistance, where he hoped to establish contact with the rebels and end the senseless slaughter. On Sunday, August 20, after saying goodbye to Kitty, he took off in an open touring car followed by a Crossley tender with a few troops and an armored car. He had shrugged off a warning. "No one's going to shoot me in my own county." After spending two nights in Cork, he took off early Tuesday morning in an optimistic mood after getting a sense of the popular feeling. On the way to Bandon, they had to ask directions from a stranger who, fatefully, had just spent the night guarding a house where some republican officers were meeting. The stranger reported seeing Collins to the republican officers. They decided to lay an ambush at the Beal na mBlath crossroad in case Collins were to return that way. In the meantime Collins traveled on to Clonakilty, a little town near Woodfield, his birthplace. Gathering his family and friends together in the Five Alls, a pub where he had downed many a pint, he told them he had come to seek an end to the hostilities. He had come home again to all the things that had been dear to him, and now it was time to end his journey.

The light was waning as the convoy made its way along a deserted ribbon of road that ran between hills toward Beal na mBlath. The republicans, who had waited all day in ambush, decided Collins had taken another route and were already on the way back to their base. A few had remained and were removing a barricade they had placed across the road when Collins' escort roared into sight. Before diving for cover, the republicans fired at the approaching vehicles. Collins ordered the driver to stop and leapt out, taking shelter behind the armored car while firing away. The main body of the attackers heard the shots and hurried back across the hills. Both sides pumped volley after volley at targets they could barely see in the near darkness. The engagement lasted for almost half an hour when a cry went up: "The C. 'n C. is hit." A bullet had penetrated the back of Collins' head above the right ear. Two aides knelt by their chief while another intoned the words of the Act of Contrition. Collins died as he would have wished—in the Cork hills and under the Cork sky.

The news of Michael Collins' death plunged Ireland into unimaginable grief. Men and women who had never met him stopped in the streets and wept. In the Ilmainham Jail one of the inmates told of seeing "about a thousand kneeling republican prisoners spontaneously reciting the Rosary for the repose of the soul of Michael Collins." His body lay all day in St. Vincent's Hospital where, only three weeks before, the corpse of Harry Boland had lain. Kitty, totally broken by grief, somehow managed to make it to the chapel where he lay, splendid in his uniform with a crucifix on his breast. She bent over and kissed his lips. On Sunday evening they bore him to the Pro-Cathedral from which, after Requiem High Mass next morning, the cortege set out for the cemetery. Placed on a gun carriage drawn by six black horses, his body was brought to its final resting place as hundreds of thousands of people jammed together along the funeral route on the pavement while others watched from roofs, windows, and monuments.

De Valera did not share the elation of the man who brought him the news of Collins' death. "It's come to a very bad pass when Irish men congratulate themselves on the shooting of a man like Michael Collins."

The provisional parliament met on September 9. Its proceedings finally convinced de Valera of its illegitimacy. Its only authority, he realized, derived from the British Acts and not from the Dail. But it still took time for him to consent to the formation of a rival government-in-waiting, as he questioned whether the republicans had the military and physical ability to maintain such a government. However, with himself as president, it was finally proclaimed by the republican army in November. But the Catholic bishops of Ireland denied the republicans' claim to legitimate authority, accused them of carrying on a system of murder and assassination, and imposed on them the penalty of excommunication. To his old friend, Archbishop Mannix, de Valera expressed his dismay at the bishops' lack of charity and foresight. He castigated those who sold their national birthright for an ignoble mess of pottage and declared that there would always be Irish men and women who would die for the cause of Irish freedom. He concluded with a request for the archbishop's blessing. A short time later the pope himself attempted a futile try for peace.

The provisional government escalated its repressive measures as the war continued on. It executed Erskine Childers, the British civil servant who had joined the Irish independence movement and smuggled in arms at Howth in 1914. His crime was the possession of a small pistol, hardly more than a toy. Childers, de Valera said, was "of all men I ever met the noblest." Reprisals and counter-reprisals continued. As a response to the shooting of two deputies of the provisional government, the four leading republican prisoners were shot without trial. The republicans responded by burning down the houses and offices of government officials. Ireland was spiraling down into its own hell.

A Remarkable Political Comeback

Instead of surrendering, the republicans decided simply to quit. De Valera thanked them for saving "the nation's honor." The struggle, he told them, now had to be transferred to the political plane. A convention of Sinn Fein delegates asked him to represent Ennis in the Free State legislature. He immediately accepted but knew that a public campaign appearance would be risky. A "murder gang," believing he was personally responsible for Collins' death, was gunning for him. But he would not be deterred. Knowing that he would be arrested, he wanted to make it as public as possible in order to prove to all that the election was not a free one. After a hazardous journey down the north side of the Dublin–Limerick road, he managed to reach Ennis the night before the election. Free State troops were alerted to grab him before he could reach the platform that stood in the center of the square. But riding in an open car, he got to the platform before the troops could nab him and as he climbed the steps a roar went up from the crowd. He had only managed to say a few words when he felt a sharp pain in his left leg. As dizziness overcame him, he fell into the arms of the crowd around him. The pain soon eased and he was able to stand and walk down the steps where the soldiers took him into custody. An examination later revealed a slight wound from a piece of bullet that had pierced his leg.

While de Valera was held in prison he won the election, polling more than twice the number of votes of his rival. His incarceration, however, was to last for almost a year. At first the conditions were severe. Not even his wife was allowed to see him although she was able to leave parcels and messages at the gate. But gradually the rules were relaxed. In the meantime, his mother in the United States joined the clamor for his release, badgering members of Congress and appearing at large public gatherings. On July 16, 1924, the prison door finally opened for him. He left to begin the most remarkable comeback in modern democratic politics.

One of his first acts was to reconstitute the Second Dail with himself as president. But without any financial resources it was able to do little if anything. For his first public meeting since his release, he chose to appear at Ennis on the anniversary of his arrest. He opened his address with these words: "I am afraid I would disappoint a number here if I were not to start by saying, 'Well, as I was saying to you when we were interrupted.'" He went on to make it clear that he had not changed his fundamental principles. "We can never give allegiance to any foreign power," he insisted. The aim of Sinn Fein, he pointed out, still held good—to secure international recognition of an Irish Republic. He maintained that only when the people were really free—that is, under no pressure from England or from any outside power—could their choice of a form of government be the expression of their own free will.

De Valera's party, Sinn Fein, continued to make progress with forty-eight deputies elected to the Free State Dail by March 1925. But their continued protest policy of abstention from occupying their seats in the Dail diminished their impact on public affairs, and itself became an unresolvable issue within the party. De Valera decided it was time to form a new party. Fianna Fail (derived from a term meaning "island of destiny") was born at a large meeting in April 1926 in the La Scala Theater in Dublin. Fianna Fail's aim, de Valera said, was "to remove the oath and to advance the national cause by cutting the bonds of foreign interference one by one until the full internal sovereignty of the twenty-six counties was established beyond question." He recognized that entering the Free State Dail meant de facto recognition of continued British control. But recognition did not mean acquiescence. The new party also called for the construction of a socially just society where opportunity would be afforded every Irish citizen to live a "noble and useful Christian life"; a fair distribution of land; and a self-sufficient economy.

In the election of June 1927, Fianna Fail garnered forty-four seats to the forty-six won by the ruling party (Cumann na nGaedheal). But when de Valera and the Fianna Fail deputies approached the legislative seat at Leinster House on the opening day of the session, June 23, they faced their old excruciating dilemma: to sign or not to sign the oath to the Crown. But the crafty de Valera created a sleight-of-hand way out that won acceptance among his Fianna Fail colleagues. One could take the oath if it were publicly made clear that the oath was a mere formality and that the only allegiance of the deputies was to the Irish nation. When de Valera presented himself to the clerk of the Dail, he refused to swear on the Bible, and before pledging allegiance to the Crown he declared, "I am taking no oath." On leaving he declared that he would one day burn the registry on the streets of Dublin. The episode was a turning point in the history of Ireland.

Over the next years de Valera's deft leadership paved the way for the elections of 1932, when Fianna Fail emerged as the largest party. On the afternoon of Wednesday, March 9 of that year, a huge enthusiastic crowd gathered at Leinster House to be present when de Valera took over the reins of government. In the morning he attended mass at the cathedral and at 2:30 P.M. made his way toward Leinster House. For most of the next twenty-seven years de Valera was president of Ireland.

His tenure was marked by triumph and tragedy. He successfully revised the Anglo-Irish Treaty out of existence in April 1938, securing from England recognition of total independence for the twenty-six southern counties. This ironically vindicated Michael Collins, who had argued that the treaty was only a stepping stone to freedom. De Valera also healed the wounds of the civil war. "Ireland reaped handsome dividends from this policy in the rapid subsidence of Civil War bitterness and the steadfastness of the people, army and civil service in the testing days of the 1930s and 1940s."[19] But he tragically made no progress toward unity with Northern Ireland, although he was stymied in the matter by an economic war with England and by Ulster's strengthening ties to the Crown.

De Valera's vision of Ireland has been called utopian but it testifies to a man of imaginative political passion—and one heavily influenced by the concerns of the social encyclicals of the Catholic Church:

> The Ireland which we have dreamed of would be the home of a people who valued material wealth only as a basis of right living, of a people who were satisfied with frugal comfort and devoted their leisure to things of the spirit; a land whose countryside would be bright with cosy home-steads, whose fields and villages would be joyous with the sounds of industry, with the romping of sturdy children, the contests of athletic youths, the laughter of comely maidens; whose firesides would be forums for the wisdom of serene old age. It would, in a word, be the home of a people living the life that God desires that men should live."[20]

[19] Longford and O'Neill, *Eamon de Valera*, pp. 464–465.

[20] M. Moynihan, *Speeches and Statements by Eamon de Valera, 1917–1973* (Dublin: Gill and Macmillan, 1980), p. 466.

The Collins and de Valera Legacy

We must not think of the Irish struggle for independence as an "unfortunate aberration engineered by a band of fanatics. Ireland's demand for freedom was part of a worldwide chorus inspired by the [First World] war; indeed, Irish aspirations were quite modest compared with those of other nationalities."[21] The revolutionaries did not aim at fundamental changes in Ireland's economic and social structure. Their overriding goal was the expulsion of Great Britain. And their overwhelming tragedy was the civil war.

Collins, it seems, shares blame for the fratricide especially because of his attempt to placate both the British and the republicans. This left him open to the charge of duplicity which in turn undermined his authority and created a false sense of possibility, the closing off of which only intensified passions. The death of Collins, as the Irish historian J. J. Lee has noted, was the great public tragedy of the civil war. He was irreplaceable.[22] A leader of rare perceptiveness, he anticipated the evolution of the Irish state more accurately than de Valera. He also showed great moral courage in pragmatically signing the Anglo-Irish Treaty, a courage rarely found in men disposed to uncompromising revolutionary ideals. Moreover he was de Valera's equal as a political tactician, and de Valera himself could hardly rival Collins' popular electoral appeal.

Estimates of great historical figures are notoriously diverse. Certainly in the case of de Valera there is no consensus. Some biographers, in sheer admiration of his incredible tenacity and integrity, tend to gloss over his errors and mistakes—his share of responsibility for the civil war, or the demagoguery with which he exploited the Ulster issue for political gain. One who doesn't gloss over his shortcomings is a recent biographer, Tim Pat Coogan, who attributes to de Valera a lust for power that caused him to thwart Collins at every turn and helped to precipitate the civil war. Coogan also insists on de Valera's disastrous ignorance of economics, his rigid Catholicism, and his inability to take a creative approach to the problem of partition. "What then was de Valera?" Coogan queries. "A hero or a fraud? A patriot and a statesman or a ward-heeling politician? A scholar or an obscurantist? A charlatan or a seer? He had elements of all these things in

---

[21]Joseph M. Curran, *The Birth of the Irish Free State—1923* (University of Alabama: University of Alabama Press, 1980), p. 279.

[22]Lee, *Ireland, 1912–1985*, p. 64.

him."[23] Most observers, however, would agree that de Valera was one of the outstanding political leaders of the twentieth century. He was a revolutionary with a difference. As he said, "Ours was not a revolution in the ordinary sense—it was not an internal revolt. It was a revolt against external domination." Less pragmatic than Collins, he was nevertheless both a great revolutionary and a great constitutionalist. "He assumed power," says Professor Desmond Williams, "as an apparent revolutionary, in a potentially revolutionary situation and, having gained most of his political objectives by constitutional means, was to become outside a lasting symbol of representative democracy."[24] His devotion to democracy was intense; he was "a democrat in the bone," as one observer said. In this respect he reminds us of his two great Christian democratic contemporaries, de Gasperi and Schumann.

Perhaps more than any other figures discussed in this book, Michael Collins and Eamon de Valera testify to the historical limits within which the Catholic faith is always lived out—historical limits understood in light of the Vatican's position and in light of the longed-for unity in love of the heavenly kingdom. At a time when the Vatican was suspicious of democracy and political independence, Collins and de Valera were men whose faith rightfully inspired them to embrace both. In the face of the obligation of Christian love, Collins and de Valera were men whose faith led them to reasonable political positions that nevertheless generated a civil war—a war in which they were enemies. Their Catholic belief was rooted in the struggles of history.

---

[23] Tim Pat Coogan, *Eamon de Valera* (New York: HarperCollins, 1995), p. 703.
[24] Quoted in Longford and O'Neill, *Eamon de Valera,* p. 464.

ELEVEN

Maritain (1882–1973) and Mounier I (1905–1950)

The social revolution will be a moral revolution or none at all.
—Péguy

O N A SUMMER AFTERNOON in Paris a couple strolled together through the lovely Jardin des Plantes on the Left Bank of
the Seine. It housed a natural history museum and the two often
walked this way after their classes at the Sorbonne. They would feed the
bears in their pits and the lions in their cages as they discussed the day's
events. But on this day, as one of them later recounted, they were terribly
despondent. Three years of intensive study had filled their minds with facts
but offered no answers to the questions that tormented them: questions
about the meaning, if any, of words such as truth, justice, goodness, and
pity. Their professors seemed quite at ease in their own absurd, meaningless
universe where positivism reigned supreme by the power of its sole
dogma—namely, that the scientific method of strict quantification revealed
reality. They worshiped facts and never tired of accumulating them. Questions of meaning and value were dismissed as literally nonsensical.

That summer day the two had reached the point where they could no
longer live in the Sorbonne's universe. Without some light being shed on
the meaning of existence, their lives were not worth living. If it were only
the suffering of one single child, even if animals alone were left to suffer on
the earth, some explanation would still be demanded. Before leaving the

Jardin des Plantes that day, they decided on their course of action. If they could find no one, nothing, to deliver them from the nightmare of a sinister and useless world, Jacques Maritain and Raissa Oumansoff would end their lives.

It was at this point that they discovered Henri Bergson, a lecturer at the rival College de France. In two important books, *Essay on the Immediate Data of Consciousness* and *Matter and Memory,* he had already mounted a sustained critique of positivism. For the two seekers, his lectures had the effect of a revelation. As Raissa Maritain, who had been Raissa Oumansoff, later said, he moved them "away from the empty and colorless world of universal mechanism and toward the universe of qualities, toward spiritual certainty, toward personal liberty."[1] Under Bergson's guidance they found their true vocation. Raissa's young companion and future spouse was Jacques Maritain, who would become a great Catholic philosopher and one of the architects of the Catholic intellectual renewal that culminated in the Second Vatican Council.

Seeking and Finding

Jacques Maritain was born November 18, 1882, the son of Paul Maritain and Geneviève Favre-Maritain. His mother was the daughter of Jules Favre, a founder of the Third Republic and a diplomat involved in negotiating the end of the Franco-Prussian War. Geneviève raised Jacques in her own brand of undogmatic and very liberal Protestantism, while Jacques' father was a nonpracticing Catholic who had little influence on his upbringing.

In reminiscences of his childhood Jacques later noted that by the age of thirteen or fourteen he was already considerably troubled by the thought that children his age were toiling as much as eleven hours a day to provide him with his bread and wine, his roof, his bed, his books, and the time to read. He became a socialist although he wondered whether, with his bourgeois privileges, he had the right to call himself one. In any case he swore that "everything he would be able to think and to know he would consecrate to the proletariat and to humanity and to prepare the revolution."[2] But Jacques' most defining characteristic was the tremendous hunger for philosophical or metaphysical truth he felt from his earliest years. He remembered

[1] Raissa Maritain, *We Have Been Friends Together* (Garden City, N.Y.: Doubleday Image Books, 1961), p. 80.

[2] Jacques Maritain, *Notebooks* (Albany, N.Y.: Magi Books), p. 8.

at the age of sixteen flinging himself down on the floor of his room in despair because he could find no answer to his questions.[3] On entering the University of Paris, he found, as Raissa would put it, that history had replaced metaphysics as the queen of the sciences there. All problems were treated as questions of mere fact to be resolved by methods appropriate to the physical sciences. The academic culture promoted an aggressive spirit of intellectual nihilism.

Despite such a depressing atmosphere, Jacques nevertheless discovered kindred spirits, fellow seekers who became lifelong friends. One of these was Ernest Psichari, a grandson of the historian and critic Ernest Renan. The young Psichari, like the young Maritain, sought after meaning passionately in a turbulent world. He fell in love with Jacques' sister only to discover that she was already pledged to someone else. He first attempted suicide and then plunged into a life of debauchery. At last, determined to pull himself together, he joined the army where, during long journeys over the immense expanses of the African desert, he experienced an almost mystical sense of liberation. Eventually he found faith in God and Christianity. His book *Le Voyage du Centurion* recounted his spiritual pilgrimage.

Another extraordinary friend was Charles Péguy, publisher and editor of the *Cahiers de la Quinzaine* housed on the rue de la Sorbonne. A writer of genius and a crusader for social justice, Péguy was a great Catholic poet and at the same time a man of action; he was a socialist, a defender of Dreyfus, a scorching critic of the vulgar democracy of the republic, a peasant who saw through the smug self-satisfaction of the bourgeoisie. A devoted husband and father, he suffered much from financial worry and also from frequent misunderstandings with his freethinking wife. His work bespoke his peasant origins, marked as it was by a deep love of the soil, a religious sense, and a deep patriotism. His devotion to St. Jeanne d'Arc as a patriot whose heroic death symbolized a "unity of person, faith, and nation" synthesized his own ideals. "Péguy mirrored the tensions in the souls, ideals, and lives of the young Catholics who wished to find a mission for themselves in the modern world and a place for the Church in structuring their times . . . he offered a way around, or perhaps, beyond the political choice of allegiance or dissent to the Republic."[4]

[3] Peter Redpath in Deal Hudson and Matthew Mancini, eds., *Understanding Maritain* (Macon, Ga.: Mercer University Press, 1987), p. 93.

[4] Joseph Amato, *Mounier and Maritain* (University of Alabama: University of Alabama Press, 1975), p. 101.

But Jacques' greatest friend, and the love of his life, was to be Raïssa Oumansoff, a Russian emigré Jew and fellow student whom he met collecting signatures for a letter protesting the treatment of Russian socialist students by tsarist police. Over the petition these two started a conversation that would continue uninterrupted for the next sixty years.

Jacques immediately introduced Raïssa to Psichari and Péguy, among his other good friends, and in their later joint despair it was Péguy who rescued them. In 1901 Péguy took Jacques and Raïssa to hear Henri Bergson's lectures at the Collège de France. These lectures marked a crucial turning point in their spiritual development. An access to ontology now opened up for them and they decided to pursue their natural bent toward philosophy.

The most influential French philosopher of the day, Bergson hoped to heal what had become an acrimonious strife between science and religion. The dominant view among intellectuals and scientists was that of positivism, a strictly rationalist and materialist approach that maintained that only what can be empirically verified can be known. Bergson, on the other hand, stressed the role of intuition, which offered privileged access to aspects of reality inaccessible to the rational processes of our mind. He cited such instances of intuition as our experience of the human self and its transcendence of nature; the difference between mechanically measurable time and our experience of duration; the mystery of human freedom in a material world; the inadequacy of the intellect in trying to explain invention, creation, life. He believed one could acknowledge all the findings of science and at the same time allow for another dimension of reality outside its ken. Though a Jew with no explicit belief in God, Bergson articulated a way of thought that could support belief in the spiritual.

Bergson inspired hope in Jacques and Raïssa but they continued to feel a spiritual void. It led them to make the acquaintance of Léon Bloy, a brilliant writer whose book, *La Femme Pauvre,* they happened to read. Bloy was a kind of John the Baptist who lived a hand-to-mouth existence in the moral desert of Paris with his wife and children while writing books filled with furious denunciations of the vices of his age. Most despicable in his eyes were the mediocre Christians whom he accused of tarnishing the name of Christ. Jacques and Raïssa accepted—with much trepidation—an invitation to visit him but immediately felt at ease in the presence of this "impressive man past middle years with white hair, low voice, and deep-set dark eyes with their mingled look of melancholy and kindness." As Jacques wrote: "Once the threshold of this house was crossed, all values were dislocated, as though by an invisible switch. One knew, or one guessed, that only one sorrow existed there—not to be a saint. And all the rest receded into the twilight."

Bloy did not try to convert them but, as Raissa said, only brought them face to face with the question of God in all its power and urgency. They were deeply impressed by his profound knowledge of the Bible and his belief that Christ formed in his person the union between the Old and New Testaments. But they were far from Bloy's belief in God and still considered themselves agnostics, if not atheists. Even after overcoming doubts about God's existence they continued to shrink from joining a church whose members, in spite of their religion, seemed to do so little for the temporal salvation of people.

Jacques also feared losing the intellectual independence he had always prized so dearly. Then Raissa, whose health was always precarious, became ill and during her illness was greatly consoled by prayer. Finally on April 6, 1906, they told Léon Bloy of their decision to seek baptism. Jacques, Raissa, and Raissa's sister, Vera, were received into the Church in June with Bloy as their godfather. Jacques' mother was horrified that her son, the grandson of Jules Favre, arch anticlericalist and a founder of the Third Republic, would do such a thing. It was a catastrophe and the ruin of all her hopes. She told him how she herself had left the Church when quite young because she was scandalized by the remarks of a priest in the confessional, and then later met another bad priest. She dreaded his conformity to a Church she regarded as authoritarian and reactionary. Later Jacques told of how some idiot wrote to his mother that he had just read a book written by Bloy in which there was a reference to Jacques Maritain. "Tell me that it is not your son, the grandson of Jules Favre!" he exclaimed. Mme Favre-Maritain hoped to get Charles Péguy to dissuade Jacques, but when Péguy met with Jacques he announced that he too had decided to become a Catholic. "Christ's body is larger than we think," he told Jacques. But Péguy's wife refused to be married in the Church or have the children baptized, which kept Péguy from receiving the sacraments.

Apostle of Thomism

Jacques passed his *agrégation de philosophie* at the Sorbonne, and then, after completing a course in biology there, he and Raissa went to Germany so he could study under Hans Driesch. The latter was a noted biologist and theorist of dynamic vitalism—a philosophy based on the view that life could not be explained mechanically or chemically. Jacques was happy to find that

Driesch was interested in Bergson's *Creative Evolution.* On returning to Paris, Jacques got a job with the publisher Hachette compiling reference books. In the meantime Raissa read and fell in love with the *Summa* of Thomas Aquinas. Overwhelmed with "joy, with light and with love,"[5] she urged Jacques to read it. Also enormously impressed he plunged into the task of familiarizing himself with the vast theological and philosophical system of Aquinas and realized that he was already a Thomist without knowing it. He found in Aquinas the solution to problems he was wrestling with: nature and grace, faith and reason, science and wisdom. It confirmed him in his belief that reason could be trusted and religion reconciled with science. Jacques, Raissa, and Vera together began the long novitiate in which "our little community took shape on a kind of monastic base—as not being of the world, in the world." To advance toward the perfection of charity they also put themselves under the guidance of Father Humbert Clerissac, a Dominican priest, whom Jacques described as a great master in the illuminative life. All the while they devoured books on the lives of the saints and on spirituality, and the works of the mystics. Father Clerissac also monitored Jacques' progress in Thomism. On one occasion Jacques tells how the good priest pulverized an essay he had written on intelligence and reason with "my half-Kantian, half-Bergsonian vocabulary."[6]

Jacques now sought ways to apply Thomas's principles to modern life. Having secured an appointment to teach philosophy at Collège Stanislas, a prestigious boys' school, he also started at the same time a series of lectures at the Institut Catholique. His lectures "On the Philosophy of Bergson and Christian Philosophy" marked his first open break with Bergsonism. Some have considered these lectures the origin of the "Neo-Thomist" movement. Jacques himself rejected that label, considering himself simply a Thomist. This was part of a Catholic intellectual revival that had significant influence on youth, many of whom were drawn to the writings of a number of brilliant Catholic novelists and poets such as Claudel, Francis Jammes, Péguy, and Léon Bloy. Ernest Psichari himself became a Catholic in 1913, shortly before his tragic death at the outset of the First World War. Péguy also died leading a charge against the Germans in the battle of the Marne.

Jacques was given a medical exemption from military service, and after a visit to Rome and a private audience with Pope Benedict XV he continued his teaching. But in 1918 he received a large legacy from a friend, Pierre

[5] Maritain, *Notebooks,* p. 51.
[6] Ibid., p. 62.

Villard, who had come to him for spiritual guidance. Villard was killed in the last days of the war, leaving half of his estate to Jacques who was henceforth free to devote himself entirely to writing and study while continuing his and Raissa's very modest lifestyle. With part of the money he was also able to start a center for Thomistic studies. According to his idea, the center would gather together people familiar with Thomistic principles and their application to discoveries in different fields, as well as desirous of disseminating them to the general public. Members would be required to make a definite commitment to Thomistic principles, to read the *Summa* daily for at least a half hour and give another half hour to prayer and meditation. In 1923 they moved the center to Meudon, a small town near Paris. For the next sixteen years this house became the center of the Thomist revival and welcomed a stream of philosophers, scientists, physicians, writers, poets, musicians—Catholics for the most part but also Orthodox, Jews, and Protestants, a veritable Who's Who of French Letters.

Jacques' book *Art and Scholasticism* inspired discussions on such themes as the relationship between art and morality and artistic treatment of the problem of evil. Those involved in these discussions included leading artists such as Marc Chagall and such writers as Max Jacob, Paul Claudel, and Julien Green. The composer Igor Stravinsky was present at times, as were the philosophers Gabriel Marcel and Nicholas Berdyaev. The meetings and retreats at Meudon were decisive in many lives. In addition to the Sunday afternoon gatherings there were also yearly week-long retreats at which, for many years, the Dominican theologian Garrigou-Lagrange preached. The first was attended by some thirty persons and in the last years two or three hundred, many of them from various countries. A number of baptisms and professions of faith took place in the little chapel of the Maritains' home, as well as vocations to the priesthood. One of these involved Jean Cocteau, the avant-garde poet, essayist, novelist, film-maker, and playwright. In despair over the death of his young friend Raymond Radiguet, Cocteau tried every means to overcome grief, including opium, until he finally turned to Maritain. On the advice of Jacques and some other friends, Cocteau entered a sanitarium and was apparently cured. Later, while visiting Meudon, he met Jacques' friend Father Charles Henrion who lived a life of contemplation in the African desert. At the first sight of the priest's gaunt face and white form Cocteau was hypnotized. As he said, "A priest gave me the same shock as Stravinsky and Picasso." He made his confession to Father Henrion and received Communion. Though the conversion did not last, Cocteau always kept a warm spot in his heart for Jacques and regularly sent him tickets to his plays. Later, in his reminiscences, he mentioned Maritain as one of those who had influenced him the most.

Maritain and André Gide were the two leading lights on the French literary scene at the time, and Maritain's relations with Gide form an interesting chapter in his life. There was some hope entertained by Maritain and his friends that Gide might be converted but Gide rejected their overtures, which he called mere flirtations. On one occasion Maritain and Gide had an encounter that Gide compared to two duelers, each searching the other for a weakness, as Maritain tried to dissuade Gide from publishing *Corydon,* a passionate defense of homosexuality. Maritain's effort was unsuccessful. When Gide later expressed his allegiance to communism, Maritain called his conversion an attempt to realize values that were essentially evangelical. He predicted (accurately), however, that Gide would not remain a communist since communism compromised the freedom of the artist.

Action Française

The "peace and equilibrium" that Jacques enjoyed after his conversion was rudely disturbed by the crisis in 1926 that involved his connection with Action Française, a right-wing movement headed by Charles Maurras. Maurras' strong advocacy of Catholicism in spite of his own agnosticism attracted to his side many Catholics who were grateful for his vigorous defense of the Church against the anticlericals. Completely immersed in philosophy at the time, Maritain had little interest in politics and was not aware of the danger of getting mixed up with Maurras' crowd. But Maritain's spiritual director Father Clerissac was a great admirer of Maurras and was largely responsible for associating Jacques with the movement. Jacques even collaborated with Maurras in setting up an important new periodical, the *Revue Universelle,* for which he contributed articles on metaphysical subjects. But when Pope Pius XI condemned Action in 1926, Maritain severed all connections with the movement and published a book pointing out the errors of Maurras and Action, including exaggerated nationalism. Looking back later he blamed his political naiveté for his involvement with the movement. He had closed his eyes, he said, to Maurras' profound atheism, his cult of violence, his intellectual tyranny, and his odious way of conducting his polemics—"all in the absurd hope of bringing about doctrinal corrections and installing a Christian philosophy in the very heart of a school whose political principles I did not realize . . . at that time . . . suffered from incurable errors."[7]

The puzzle has always been how Maritain could ever have gotten involved with such an anti-Semitic, antirepublican movement. He was after all the grandson of a founder of the Third Republic, a close friend of Péguy, a defender of the Jews, an intimate of Bloy, married to the Jewish Raïssa, and since his youth dedicated to social justice and the cause of the laboring classes. No doubt there were a variety of factors. Clerissac was one of those numerous clergy at the time—including Pius X himself as well as cardinals, abbots, and bishops—who saw in democracy and the republican form of government the diabolical incarnation of the errors condemned in Pius IX's Syllabus. They could not imagine a democracy untainted by "modernism" and anticlericalism. The advent of another liberal pope like Leo XIII appeared unthinkable, and they linked the future of the Church as well as of civilization with the far right. Maritain was at this stage easily persuaded of the virtue of blind obedience to a spiritual director, and he could not but take seriously the Dominican's scoffing at his democratic leanings and socialist tendencies as "the remains of the old man which had to be put off." He learned the hard way to distinguish between a teaching of the supreme authority of the Church and the merely personal opinion of an individual clergyman, but it was a lesson that would stand him in good stead. Henceforth he never took a stand on an issue without a painstaking examination of it in the light of his philosophical principles and the voice of his own conscience.

The Action Française affair also marked a decisive shift in his philosophical orientation as it turned his attention to social questions. He saw how Aquinas's principles could be applied to the field of social and political action. It was in this area that he was to make his most significant contributions to Catholic philosophy. Maritain knew that, since *Rerum Novarum,* there existed a Catholic social movement based on the encyclicals of the popes but there were in his opinion too few Catholics who were really committed to improving the conditions of the working class. In 1931 Pius XI's *Quadragesimo Anno* appeared and gave a new impetus to the promotion of Christian social justice. Jacques now identified himself with the leaders of this growing Social Catholic movement.

His life project, he understood now, was to apply Thomism to political

[7]Bernard Doering, *Jacques Maritain and the French Catholic Intellectuals* (Notre Dame: University of Notre Dame Press, 1983), p. 30.

and social philosophy. Maritain's single most important text on political and social questions was *Humanisme Intégral* (True Humanism), which originated as a series of lectures given in Santander, Spain, in 1934. It was his most important political work to date. These lectures show him indeed as the true grandson of Jules Favre; they also manifest the spirit of cooperation and tolerance that would later characterize the documents of Second Vatican Council and justify calling Maritain one of the architects of the council.

The immediate context of *True Humanism* was a general European sense of crisis, a feeling that civilization itself was on trial. The First World War, the Russian Revolution, the rise of Fascism, and the Great Depression were all seen as more than temporary detours from the path of historical progress. And as another war loomed, anxiety grew about the fate of the West. A number of writers explored themes relating to man, culture, and civilization often in the most pessimistic vein. The philosophers Edmund Husserl, Martin Heidegger, Karl Jaspers, Karl Barth, Gabriel Marcel, Nicholas Berdyaev, and others agonized over the sick soul of Western man and spoke of the need for a new civilization.

Maritain traced the crisis to what he called the prevailing anthropocentric humanism. He envisaged a new civilization that would be based on a true humanism, not a Rousseauian humanism in which divine grace disappears into nature. It would be an *integral* humanism, which would meet the whole range of human needs—physical, emotional, mental, and spiritual. In this light the crises of Western culture were viewed as the outcome of several historical shifts that moved Western culture away from the humanism of medieval Christendom. Maritain called these shifts or turning points the classical moment, the bourgeois moment, and the revolutionary moment.

Whereas medieval culture was God-centered, in his view, the modern period saw a radical shift away from the search for divine grace to a humanism centered on the search for human liberty. Thus an increasing naturalism in art, a new sense of adventure, and a fascination with profits marked the beginning of the age of humanism. This was an anthropocentric humanism, eventually a bourgeois humanism that abandoned economic and political life to dehumanizing forces that finally and justly engendered the nemesis, Marxist socialist humanism. The materialist view implicit in bourgeois humanism was replaced, in socialism, with a dialectical materialism whereby all values were seen as mere reflections of economic conditions. The atheism it entailed was the outcome of that bourgeois decadence which held industrial production to be the supreme means of human happiness.

"Catholicism," Maritain held, "alone could respond to Marxism and the emerging totalitarianisms by furnishing Western man with a new historical ideal."[8] He also saw Thomism as a humanism that could provide the framework for a new culture. It was a living and progressive system that respected nature and reason and reconciled grace and liberty.

In the Thick of Controversy

But Maritain did not just sit in his study and ponder the rise and fall of civilizations. He was heavily involved in all the controversies that ripped France apart during the thirties. When the extreme right almost succeeded in pulling off a coup d'état during the riots of February 6, 1934, the Socialists and Communists joined hands in the Popular Front. Maritain felt Catholic intellectuals should take a stand. He and four friends published a manifesto signed by fifty-two prominent Catholic writers, artists, and scientists who deplored the injustices of both Right and Left and called for a pluralist, humanist political order. The individual Christian, they said, must apply Christian principles to social problems, especially the principles of justice and charity.

This manifesto *Pour le Bien Commun* made a strong impression on public opinion. It was the first time that "the concerted voice of Christian humanists had made itself heard."[9] It also marked the beginning of an era of manifestos launched by Maritain and his friends against the conservative and nationalist right wing. Quite a few attacks were made on Maritain personally both from within and without his Church. Talk of "red Christians" could be heard from those shocked to hear Maritain call for prayers for the Communists who had fallen in the riots.

When Mussolini invaded Ethiopia in 1935, Maritain and his colleagues published another manifesto—*Pour la Justice et pour la Paix*—which denounced the idea that the so-called superior races had the right to impose their civilization and culture on the lesser ones. It was signed also by a number of non-Catholic leftists including André Gide and Julian Benda. The Ethiopian War and later the Spanish Civil War were to break the French Catholic alliance with the Right.

Another vehicle Maritain used to convey his social and political views was the journal *Sept* which he helped direct until its suppression in 1937. During its short career (three years), *Sept* was probably the most influential

[8] Amato, *Mounier and Maritain*, p. 143.
[9] Doering, *Jacques Maritain and the French Catholic Intellectuals*, p. 72.

Catholic periodical in France.[10] "It represented, in general, the new tendency in the Church to put heavy emphasis on social reform, in line with social justice, and to show favor to the democratic and pluralistic forms of social organization";[11] it also sealed Maritain's reputation as a political liberal.

Sept refused to be identified with any particular political party; it aimed to find above the parties a "position which will be the meeting place of all men of good will."[12] This was in accord with Maritain's belief that the Church should not be identified with any political party. Catholics who shared a particular historical ideal, he believed, might band together in a party but this party should not limit its members to Catholics or even Christians.

The stands that *Sept* took were risky for Catholics because they were often at variance with the official Catholic line. However, it was the stand that *Sept* took on the Spanish Civil War that pitted it against virtually the whole bloc of Catholic opinion and brought about the journal's demise.

The plight of the Spanish Church was grievous indeed, and the resulting pressures on *Sept* and on Maritain as a Catholic to support Franco and the nationalists were incredible. The atrocities were indescribable: Thousands of churches were pillaged and burned, and thousands of nuns and priests were slain often in the most gruesome ways. Many read this as a forecast of the fate of the whole European Church and looked on General Franco, who led the revolt, as the savior of Christendom. But Maritain and some of his fellow Catholic writers, like Mauriac and Bernanos, didn't agree. They saw the Church's bloodbath as retribution for its long and stubborn resistance to the demands of social justice and for its blindness to the needs of the miserable workers. They also pointed to the atrocities perpetrated by Franco's forces against the workers and the poor, and they noted that even Catholic Basques were massacred by Franco's forces.

Bernanos had witnessed the first skirmishes at Majorca and initially thought he was seeing *gesta Dei per Hispania*. But within a few months, when he saw the gruesome purges instigated and encouraged by the clergy and bands of brutal Italian Fascists, he changed his mind. He found this "paradoxical mixture of cynicism and hypocrisy"[13] disgusting. It was another example of the Church's tendency to join its interests with those of

[10]Ibid., p. 75.
[11]Ibid.
[12]Ibid., p. 78.
[13]Ibid., p. 92.

the propertied classes and identify its causes with the politics of the right wing that Maritain had decried for years—a sentiment that Bernanos expressed in his book *Les Grands Cimetières sous la Lune.* Maritain did not publish his own views until the early months of 1937, when Franco permitted Hitler to experiment in Spain with new tactics of war such as the intense bombing of cities. The bombing of Guernica, and the machine-gunning of its people from airplanes as they tried to flee, moved Maritain and his friends in May to draw up a manifesto for *The Basque People.* It was signed also by Mauriac and Bernanos.

But the renowned Catholic poet Paul Claudel publicly took the other side in this furious dispute when he published his poem "To the Spanish Martyrs" in June 1937. It was a glowing tribute to the eleven bishops and 16,000 priests slain at the outbreak of the war, whom Pope Pius XI had just added to the church's official list of martyrs. "In a single burst of flame," Claudel said, they "had colonized heaven." Maritain's response, "On the Holy War," was not slow to appear. "It is a horrible sacrilege," wrote Maritain, "to massacre priests, even if they are 'fascists' (they are the ministers of Christ), out of hatred for religion; and it is another sacrilege, just as horrible, to massacre the poor, even though they are 'Marxists' (they are the people of Christ), in the name of religion." He went on to reject Claudel's idea of a holy war in an age when the temporal order had become autonomous. "Let people kill, if they think they have a duty to kill, in the name of the social order or of the nation; that is already horrible enough; let them not kill in the name of Christ the King, who is not a military leader, but a King of grace and charity who died for all."[14]

Maritain's article fell like a bomb on the right-wing camp for he was the first Catholic philosopher to question the theological arguments its members used in defense of Franco's cause. (At the same time the Spanish bishops issued a paper arguing that Franco's revolt could be justified as legitimate self-defense in view of the violent acts perpetrated against the Church by the anticlericals.) Then Paul Claudel unleashed a tirade against Maritain, numbering him among the ideologues putting forth extravagant projects of mediation. The two henceforth were regarded as the leaders and symbols of the conflicting points of view.

To help bring the war to an end Maritain took part in establishing the Committee for Civil and Religious Peace in Spain. His efforts were not appreciated in the Vatican's Holy Office, dominated as it was by conserva-

[14]Ibid., p. 107.

tive clerics. Nor was his mentor, Garrigou-Lagrange, happy with Maritain's activities. In a testy mood he came to Meudon in 1937 to preach during the annual retreat and advised Jacques to keep his opinions on current events private, confining himself instead to metaphysics. Jacques was enraged, contrary to his usually placid and gentle nature. "I find myself in a black fit of anger, which I cannot hide," he noted in his diary. It was not the last time he would find himself crossing swords with the reactionary Dominican who had played such a key role in his spiritual journey.

The dispute between Claudel and Maritain over Spain broadened to include Jacques' critique of capitalism and his idea that Christians must "be in a constant state of mobilization to radically transform the temporal order on the basis of social justice." Claudel totally opposed such ideas. A Christian, he maintained, had no obligation to work for a new social order. What he should do is take care of the duties of his state as the father of a family or the head of a business; or as a civil servant, diplomat, priest, or the like—and then, if he had the inclination and time to work on social problems such as alcoholism, prostitution, or housing, he might do so out of charity but not out of justice. Maritain's kind of radical ideas, he warned, produce only Robespierres and their reigns of terror.

In reply to this criticism Maritain quoted Pius XI in *Quadragesimo Anno,* severely criticizing capitalism and asserting the need to regulate—according to the norms of social justice—the distribution of the resources of this world. Predictably, Claudel would have none of it. Instead he complained about having encyclicals thrown at his head and continued to accuse Maritain of calling for revolution, although Maritain had insisted that by mobilization he did not mean revolution. Since the "dialogue" was going nowhere Maritain signed off by saying, Well, let's just ignore the cries of the poor and go back to sleep as the Apostles did during the agony of the Father of the poor.

Another forceful stand Maritain took was in opposition to anti-Semitism. He gave a public lecture in Paris on the subject in February 1938, a time when racist articles were beginning to appear in the press. He reminded his compatriots and fellow Catholics that the Christian religion was descended from Judaism. Anti-Semitism, he proved, was inadmissible on any grounds, religious, historical, or metaphysical.

Exile in America

As war approached, Jacques continued his lectures and writing and on February 8, 1939, gave a lecture on the "Twilight of Civilization." After reviewing the intellectual and spiritual causes of Europe's decay he saw hope in signs foretelling a new humanism. It would be one based on Christian principles of justice and brotherly love. It would also, he felt, be imbued with the spirit of American democracy, which embodied basic Christian values.

War broke out on September 9, 1939, while Raissa and Jacques were staying at the Abbey of Fontgombault. When an uneasy calm descended after Hitler's initial conquest of the lowlands, Jacques decided to carry out his planned schedule of lectures in the United States. When he and Raissa embarked at Marseille on January 5, 1940, they never realized how long it would be before they could return. On June 14 in New York they heard the news over the radio of the German entry into Paris and knew that returning to France was out of the question. As one of the leaders of the anti-Fascist movement, Jacques was a marked man; and shortly after Paris fell, the Gestapo came looking for him at the Institut Catholique.

Jacques looked on in anguish as France wrestled with the agonizing decision of whether to resist and risk complete destruction or to cooperate with the Nazi conquerors and survive until eventual Allied victory. Fully appreciative of the painful dilemma Pétain faced as the head of the Vichy government, Maritain prayed that he might maintain a morally responsible position. But when Pétain betrayed his hopes by an active collaboration with Hitler's criminal policies, Maritain felt compelled to speak out against the Vichy government.

The Maritains' apartment in Greenwich Village became, like the house in Meudon, a center for French intellectuals and artists in exile in the New York area. Gatherings at their apartment were always lively, according to Julie Kernan, their friend and biographer. Jacques and Raissa, she says, kept the conversation going while tea and cakes were served or peanuts and ginger ale for Jacques. Ms. Kernan was present the time that Marc Chagall burst in—gray hair tumbling to his shoulders and merry face aglow—carrying a large bouquet of red roses for Raissa, the same bouquet that later appeared dreamlike in one of his paintings.

Many of the exiles who frequented Jacques' apartment had been brought into the United States with his help. So numerous, in fact, were his efforts in this regard that he became known as the man to see when someone had to be brought across the Atlantic to safety. One of these was Gustave Cohen, a professor at the Sorbonne who was able to find a position at Yale thanks to Jacques. He collaborated with Jacques in setting up a unique wartime creation, the École Libre des Hautes Études. As the only free French university in existence at the time, it was enthusiastically approved of by General Charles de Gaulle. Its many emigré French and Belgian professors kept alive in the New World the glorious tradition of French scholarship.

After the death in 1943 of Henri Focillon, the school's first president and a close friend, Jacques succeeded him. It was probably the busiest time of his life. While presiding over an institution that embraced over 1,000 students he also lectured widely around the country and continued to pour out a stream of articles and books. *A Travers le Désastre* (France My Country) was hurriedly composed right after France's fall, containing his reflections on the tragedy. Published clandestinely and circulated widely in France by the underground, it had a profound influence. As soon as America entered the war, Jacques began a series of regular broadcasts to France. Shortly after the Allied landing in Normandy he made an address to his fellow Frenchmen that was broadcast in France by the Office of War Information. It was above all a plea for unity as the country began its reconstruction.

Emmanuel Mounier

While Jacques waited out the war years in America, a young protegé of his named Emmanuel Mounier was coming to national prominence in France as the editor of a lively Catholic journal of opinion, *Esprit*. The upbringing and education of Mounier, the son of a humble pharmacist in Grenoble, stands in some contrast to that of Maritain. Jacques, a Parisian by birth and the grandson of a founder of the Third Republic, was from his teens conversant with all the intellectual fashions of the time and alert to the twists and turns of the political world. Mounier arrived in Paris in 1923 at the age of eighteen—a serious, timid, and diligent lad from a stable household, interested in science and medicine, but essentially a provincial with much to learn about the broader culture of the day.

Mounier's studies in the Faculty of Sciences did not go well. By the spring of 1924 he was in deep despair, even to the point of considering suicide. Upon his return to Grenoble his affectionate and doting father introduced him to a young professor of philosophy, Jacques Chevalier. The latter was at first unimpressed by the "large blond boy with blue eyes and a

Emmanuel Mounier

pale complexion . . . [who] seems very intimidated and says practically nothing. When he speaks it is in a precipitous rush."[15] In time, however, he came to appreciate the rare qualities of young Mounier and took him under his wing. The relationship that blossomed was of the utmost importance for Mounier's education. Eventually he became Chevalier's unofficial secretary, editing the proofs of his work on Bergson and transcribing the discussions that followed Chevalier's lectures. He idolized Chevalier, whose lectures he described in glowing terms:

> The vast hall of fifteen hundred seats grows silent . . . This dissimilar crowd, freed for an hour from its distractions seems to form a unity of fervent souls in a prayer devoted to the truth . . . Below, the lecturer. His face still suffused by the glow of youth . . . all his diverse themes converge . . . as if a cathedral of ideas were being constructed before us . . . At the end the spontaneous applause of the crowd.

Chevalier was a devoted student of Bergson, whose profoundly evolutionary view he believed to be the answer to the Catholic Church's most pressing problem: how to adapt to the advances of modern culture. This was

---

[15]John Hellman, *Mounier and the New Catholic Left,* 1930–1950 (Toronto: University of Toronto Press, 1981), p. 13.

especially true, he felt, in regard to the three main intellectual revolutions of modern times—the democratic, the scientific, and the historicist movements. Bergson, he believed, was the first philosopher to improve on Descartes and Pascal who were, he felt, "the Aristotle and Plato of modern times."[16] Chevalier called Bergson the Plato of his own time whose work prepared a person for faith in God—a view that was confirmed when, at the point of death, Bergson announced his moral adhesion to Catholicism.

Like Jacques and Raissa Maritain before him, Chevalier felt that Bergson offered a means of escaping the dreary materialist and positivist smog permeating the halls of academia. He especially appreciated Bergson's insistence on the dimension of time as the essential constituent of reality; his emphasis on intuition; his acceptance of the limits of philosophy in grasping reality; and his acceptance of the mysterious character of existence. Building on these insights, Chevalier endeavored to construct a science of the individual. He hoped thereby to reverse the entire history of Western philosophy with its focus on the abstract and the general. He wanted to reintroduce the concepts of individuality and personality that were absent from contemporary thought, to show the primacy of the spiritual realms of freedom, faith, and God, and to elucidate the nature of reality as a free act of God, Creator and Father.[17]

Chevalier's Bergsonian approach pitted him against Maritain, who believed in a revitalized Thomism as the key to spiritual renewal. Though Maritain was much indebted to Bergson for his religious conversion, he felt, as we have seen, that Bergson's thought was anticonceptual and therefore ultimately incompatible with Catholic doctrine and its clearly defined concepts. Chevalier, on the other hand, believed the revolution in modern thought too radical to allow for the synthesis with Thomism called for by Maritain. In any case it was through Chevalier that Mounier came to know and appreciate Bergson, who with Chevalier greatly influenced Mounier's distinctive philosophy of personalism.

After his stay in Grenoble, Mounier returned to Paris in 1927 full of confidence in the future. The atmosphere of the Sorbonne with its stench of intellectual pride repelled him but he was enthusiastic about philosophy and buoyed up by the signs of Catholic renewal he saw around him. A Catholic literary renaissance was in progress and included a number of brilliant thinkers and writers, some of them converts, whom Mounier was soon to know

[16] Amato, *Mounier and Maritain,* p. 86.
[17] Ibid., p. 85.

personally: Jacques Maritain, the Jesuit theologian Jean Danielou, the lay philosopher Jean Guitton, the historian and philosopher Étienne Gilson, and the Jesuit historian Henri Bremond. He himself was involved in the dynamic Association Catholique de la Jeunesse Française, a middle-class student organization aimed to encourage social and civic awareness among its members. Mounier's first two published articles appeared in the Christian Democratic paper *La Vie Catholique,* which had close ties with the ACJF. But the articles were not political in intention; his concerns at the time were mainly in the realm of philosophy. Mounier was also active in the Society of St. Vincent de Paul, whose members carried out charitable activities among the poor; but he shared the complacent attitude of the typical middle-class Catholic at the time and his contacts with the poor did not seem to cause him much concern.

The young Mounier found the emotional support he needed in Chevalier's friends, in particular Jean Guitton and especially Père Guillaume Pouget, a gifted intellectual priest and a disciple of Bergson. He spent two afternoons a week for five years at the feet of Pouget, covering a great amount of material on topics related to the faith. The grounding he received in the faith, as well as the example of the scholarly ascetic and humble priest, would later serve him well as he maintained his loyalty to the Church under very trying circumstances.

At these seminars conducted by Pouget, Mounier met the Jesuit priest Père Jean Danielou, who brought him into one of the most sophisticated grand-bourgeois Catholic circles in Paris. Danielou's family was somewhat unusual: His father was a prominent anticlerical radical socialist and a friend of Prime Minister Aristide Briand, while Jean and his mother were at the center of French Catholic intellectual life.

Just at this time, the death of Mounier's closest friend Georges Barthélemy plunged him into a severe emotional crisis. The sudden loss of his oldest friend marked the end of his youth, he said, and forced him to undergo an intellectual and religious reconversion. It involved him "in grasping the mysterious unity of all men in time and eternity—sensing what it means to participate in life with other men and what it means to give oneself for them."[18] These thoughts and sentiments would later figure prominently in his philosophy of personalism.

Barthélemy's death also reinforced Mounier's natural aversion to the Sorbonne and its ethos. Nevertheless he went ahead with his final examina-

[18]Ibid., p. 94.

tions in 1928 for the *agrégé* and astonished everyone by his performance. While such fellow students as Jean-Paul Sartre and Simone de Beauvoir failed on their first try, Mounier not only passed but came in second only to Raymond Aron, later a prominent right-wing political philosopher and sociologist. Mounier's dazzling success did not shake his abiding distrust of mere intellectual achievement, however. Like a contemplative monk he could see no point in intellectual effort that did not deepen one's spiritual life and awareness of God's presence. He set to work on his thesis, an extremely ambitious study of personality that would involve research in biology, law, psychology, theology, and Christology. It would also consider individualism in the historical forms it had taken in the Reformation, in theories of natural law, in Rousseau, Kant, modern liberalism, and aestheticism, as well as in religion and mysticism.

New Guides—Maritain and Péguy

Mounier had been invited to join the Sunday afternoon gatherings in the Maritains' bungalow in Meudon. Jacques Maritain no doubt saw in Mounier a young man of promise, someone who could serve well in the search for a new relationship of the Church to the modern world. Eventually, Maritain would replace Chevalier as the major influence in Mounier's life. But at this point the more important event was Mounier's discovery of the work of Charles Péguy. He began to study Péguy in earnest around 1928 and was soon totally absorbed in the man, his writings and his life. Thanks to Péguy, Mounier abandoned his plan for an academic career, put aside his thesis, and began looking for a way to carry on the "revolution" that Péguy had called for. Like many French Catholic youths at the time Mounier found in Péguy some of the answers for which he was desperately searching. There seemed to be only two options open to a Catholic, neither of them satisfactory: to reject the republic and democracy in line with the Church's historic stand on these issues (but this was called into question by the Church's recent condemnation of Action Française, the right-wing monarchist movement); or to accept the republic and bourgeois democracy (but this was unpalatable in the light of its crude materialistic and individualistic tendencies). In short, young Catholics had no adequate political and social philosophy as a guide.

Mounier regarded Péguy as Bergson's greatest disciple, but his attraction to Péguy was deeply personal as well as intellectual. Like Bergson, Péguy denounced the whole antispiritual character of the Third Republic: "its bourgeois man, its overriding reduction of life to habits, ideals to interest, the present to money and the past to lifeless facts."[19] Péguy also, like Bergson, saw as characteristic of bourgeois society the way it split Body from Spirit. Mounier also found in Péguy the same disgust that he felt with the Sorbonne and its nauseating pretenses. Most important, Péguy insisted that life and thought were inseparable, like two hands clasped in prayer. It was this unity of thought and person that enabled Péguy, in Mounier's view, to transcend the dichotomies of individualism versus collectivism, materialism versus idealism, romanticism versus classicism.

Péguy was the crucial factor in the passage of Mounier from philosophy to life, from faith to action. Bergson had taught Péguy that it was through the point of action that spirit enters matter and that therefore action must constantly be revivified at its source; otherwise it sinks into mere politics. This insight helped to explain why history shows such a constant tendency to deterioration, and also why there is reason for hope in spite of this constant deterioration. "To push action out of fidelity to its end, and then let God decide, herein we find Péguy's code of the good battle."[20] This was to be Mounier's code, as well as the reason that he carried his training in philosophy and theology to the public square with the special commitment to make the revolution moral or not at all.

Esprit

In 1931 Mounier felt the time was ripe for a new Catholic journal. The world was in the throes of the Great Depression. For many intellectuals the reigning ideology of liberal individualism appeared useless to deal with the unprecedented economic and social crisis. Some turned to Marxist collectivism, which had already made great headway among the working class. But Mounier saw that after several false starts in the early decades of the century, Social Catholicism was gathering its momentum. Special impetus came from Pius XI's encyclical *Quadragesimo Anno* (1931), which was hailed around the world for its daring call for a radical restructuring of the capitalist system. At the same time the French Church was beginning to move away from the antirepublican nationalist right wing. Mounier was able to persuade two friends, Georges Izard and André Deleage, to join him in the

[19] Ibid., p. 102.
[20] Ibid., p. 103.

venture. Izard was a polished and dynamic adept while Deleage was himself a strong personality and a convert to the Church.

Maritain lent his full support to the project. He lined up potential contributors, secured office space in the Desclée de Brouwer publishing house, and played a crucial role in determining the character of the review. Maritain believed that the economic depression beginning to harrow France was only a warning sign of a deeper crisis in civilization, and he wanted the journal to be a source of Christian understanding of this crisis. He hoped the journal might be a starting point for a broad inquiry into the Church in his lifetime.[21] Madame Danielou suggested *Esprit* as its name, in allusion to the Communist review *Matter*. (She also warned Mounier to be careful of Maritain. "He is a delicious soul, but he often has bad judgment."[22]) For his part, Mounier begged Maritain: "Promise never to hide your opinion, on whatever subject. It would be a security for me to feel that transparency of our friendship, that nakedness of your affection."[23] Among others associated with the journal were such luminaries as Daniel Halévy, Henri Daniel-Rops, Robert Aron, the Thomist Étienne Borne, and the Christian trade unionist and medieval scholar Paul Vignaux.

Among the most distinguished and original collaborators was the Russian Nicholas Berdyaev, whose family belonged to the military aristocracy but whose liberal ideas caused him to be exiled by the czar to the north of Russia. Eventually given permission to study in Heidelberg, he returned to Russia a convinced and devout Christian committed to social reform but critical of Marxism. In trouble for his criticism of the Orthodox hierarchy, he had welcomed the Bolshevik revolution; nonetheless in 1922 he was expelled with a number of other intellectuals and settled in Paris, where his house, like Maritain's, became a meeting place for Christian thinkers.

Characteristic of the French intellectual spectrum, the diversity of views among the contributors to *Esprit* was very broad. Maritain and Izard in particular were almost diametrically opposed. Maritain's emphasis on spiritual renewal collided with Izard's desire for *Esprit* to serve as the launching pad for a leftist political coalition that would offer an alternative to capitalism and communism. Still, the July prospectus bugled a hopeful note of unity in its proclamation: "We feel ourselves united . . . by a fundamental

[21] Ibid., p. 107.
[22] Hellman, *Mounier and the New Catholic Left,* p. 41.
[23] Ibid., p. 42.

concern for the . . . spirit . . . against the usurpations of matter and the dissolution of the person."

Certain immediate skeptics advised the group to hold a séance and chant in unison: *"Esprit,* are you there? If so, knock once."[24] Nor was the Catholic establishment overjoyed to read in the prospectus: "Our hostility is as vivid against capitalism, in its present practice . . . as against Marxism or Bolshevism. Capitalism reduces the person to a state of servitude irreconcilable with the dignity of man; it orients all classes and the whole personality toward the possession of money; the single desire of which chokes the modern soul. Marxism is a rebel son of capitalism."

Mounier's Personalism

"Personalism" was a very popular catchword at the time. It stood for belief in the dignity and spiritual grandeur of the individual person. It opposed all systems that would diminish the individual, either by confining him to the atomistic society of liberal capitalism or enslaving him to an economic system, a party or a state. Nietzscheans, disciples of Husserl and Heidegger, and many Christians all shared similar concerns about certain antiperson trends found in the liberal, capitalist bourgeois world as well as in the communist. Mounier discerned the roots of atomistic capitalism in the egotism of the Renaissance, the subjectivism of the Reformers, and the secularizing liberalism of the French Revolution.

Interest in the concept of the person was also fostered in the 1920s and 1930s by the revival of Thomism. Basing himself on Aquinas's definition of the person as an individual rational substance, a definition taken from Boethius, Jacques Maritain distinguished between the individual and the person. For Jacques, "person" stood for reason and wholeness whereas "individual" stood for matter and incompleteness. "In his view, the individual, that is man considered in his material aspect, was at the service of the community, which was in turn at the service of the person, man considered in his spiritual aspect, who was in turn at the service of God."[25] A proper understanding of person therefore involved awareness of the person as primarily spiritual and also awareness of the person's complexity as the most perfect thing in nature.

In view of the diversity of personalisms Mounier felt it necessary to

[24] Ibid.
[25] Michael Kelly, *Pioneer of the Catholic Revival* (London: Sheed and Ward, 1979), p. 46.

define the Christian personalism heralded by *Esprit*. With this in mind he gathered thirty persons together on May 11, 1934, at a little café in the Parisian Latin Quarter. A philosophy group that included Maritain, Nicholas Berdyaev, Gabriel Marcel, Jean Wahl, and Georges Gurvitch was set up and it proved to be the most influential in carrying out the task. "Ironically," as John Hellman says, "the effort to create a personalism proper to *Esprit* was spearheaded by foreigners with German philosophical formations, who were respectively Orthodox and Jewish—despite Personalism's decisive influence on a generation of French Catholics."[26]

Looking for a coherent theory of man as the basis of his spiritual revolution, Mounier found the concept of person most meaningful. It seemed to have the broadest potential for reflection and exploration. To speak of a "person," he said, was to designate a spiritual presence in a man beyond time, space, or consciousness; in other words, a moral absolute.

He distinguished three essential dimensions of the person: incarnation, communion, and vocation. "Incarnation" designates the dimension which binds man inseparably to this material environment through his body: Mounier emphasized that man should not seek to deny this condition of his existence, but should use it to fulfill and transcend himself. "Communion" designates his situation as a part of one or several human societies. "Vocation" designates the aspiration which leads man to discover what will most fulfill his deep spiritual nature. To each of these dimensions Mounier allocated a fundamental exercise which would allow a man to realize his person more completely. To incarnation corresponded commitment, the recognition of one's materiality and the effort to spiritualize it. To communion corresponded self-denial, the determination to live in and for others. To vocation corresponded meditation, the persevering quest for a greater knowledge of oneself and of the spiritual reality beyond oneself.[27]

Mounier's existentialist tendencies were revealed in his call for man to accept his insecurity and the need to risk all in bearing witness to the truth; to accept life "as adventurous and compromised, impoverished and isolated."[28] But Mounier was likewise moved by his deep sense of friendship and morality; his desire to serve God and his fellow man; his belief that man

---

[26]Hellman, *Mounier and the New Catholic Left*, p. 81.
[27]Kelly, *Pioneer of the Catholic Revival*, p. 48.
[28]Amato, *Mounier and Maritain*, p. 118.

only becomes himself by becoming more than himself. Existentialism could not offer a total explanation to us because it is God alone who establishes, gives, and measures meaning.

Mounier's personalism called for an openness to the richness of experience and a willingness to change one's ideas constantly through the interplay of reflection and action. But for Mounier the person was not only a metaphysical entity; the person was a normative model of ethical values. The ethical, social, and political policies of a community were to be judged by how well they promoted the development of each individual person within it. People, he maintained, were starved for true community. Persons living in true communities were still few and far between; a great number pass their lives without any experience of true communion. True communities reconcile a man to himself, exalt him, transfigure him.[29] True communities, however, could be founded only on "solidly constituted persons" who, as in the case of the religious orders, were able to inspire and lead by example. The rise of fascism and communism, he thought, were in their own way manifestations of the age's desire for community.

In his *Personalist Manifesto* (1936), Mounier set forth a programmatic statement of the cultural and political aims of both himself and *Esprit,* with a view to playing a role in planning the progressive reforms promised by the new government. The communitarian personalism he advocated was a profoundly anticapitalist philosophy that he hoped would inspire the formation of communities rooted in the mystical body of the divine Christ. There communities would espouse a lifestyle of simplicity and poverty. They would also have, he said, a new approach to art that would once more be "mixed in with the day-to-day life of everyone, as it was in the Church, in dances and popular holidays, as it ought to be in the factory, the countryside, the home, in public buildings."[30] His authentic "person" would not be the Nietzschean hero but the Christian saint who goes to the limit in abandoning himself.

Michael Kelly notes the lack of originality and of coherence in Mounier's personalism, which in fact was a grab-bag of ideas drawn from many sources. But the point is that it spoke of values shared by French Catholics and at the same time was general enough to appeal to other Christians and even nonbelievers. It could therefore act as a unifying and energizing synthesis of currents of thought that could move people to concerted action.

[29]Hellman, *Mounier and the New Catholic Left,* p. 84.
[30]Ibid., p. 82.

Moreover, Mounier's philosophy of personalism was based on values that Catholics easily shared and recognized. By working them into a rough synthesis he hoped to draw Catholics together into a more conscious solidarity and lead them toward concerted activity. Finally, personalism was open to a wider range of human activities than those associated with the Church, and therefore it could draw support from those outside the Church. Hence "Mounier could rightly claim to be carrying forward the Church's work of understanding and responding to the modern world, particularly in the area of social problems."[31]

Esprit's Early Career

Though *Esprit* was generally regarded as a Catholic undertaking and its early subscribers were Catholic for the most part, from the beginning its "Catholic" character was soft-pedaled. It appeared to be international and nonconfessional. Mounier kept the Catholic connection deliberately vague in order to strengthen its appeal to all those with a spiritual view of the world. He therefore steered clear of issues involving Catholic dogma. This proved to be an effective strategy for several reasons. It enabled him to avoid conflicts with the Catholic hierarchy over doctrine, while its broad approach served to open Catholics to the currents of contemporary thought.

No doubt remembering his own misadventure with Action Française, Maritain strictly warned Mounier against "goose-stepping philosophy" with its "self-styled revolutionaries" and insisted that the journal make clear that it held to "Christianity" more than to "revolution." As time went on, Maritain was increasingly disturbed not only by the vague spiritualism found in some of *Esprit*'s articles but also its leaning toward German left-wing national socialism.

To counter Maritain's charge that there was nothing particularly Christian about *Esprit,* Mounier put out an issue dedicated to Christianity. He distinguished sharply between bourgeois Christianity as found in the Christian Democrats, which he deemed a sell-out, and true Christianity which had not lost its "sense of Being," its commitment to love and to the meaning of the Cross. A number of Catholic writers answered his fire with fire. The novelist François Mauriac accused Mounier of playing into the hands of the communists with unfounded attacks on the Christian bourgeoisie. The French middle class, Mauriac said, was the crucible in which the genius of

---

[31] Kelly, *Pioneer of the Catholic Revival*, p. 52.

our people has come to fruition. The Jesuit editor of *Études* charged Mounier with intellectual Bolshevism and another commentator thought his harping on "revolution" was irresponsible.[32]

When a 1933 edition of *Esprit* spoke of the need for a communist revolution to precede the personalist revolution, Maritain was really incensed. It was absolutely imperative, he told Mounier, to clarify what he meant by his "spiritual revolution"; otherwise he would merely be taken in tow by the violent revolutionaries. Finally, he told Mounier he was tired of having to send him these continual remonstrances. The problem, he said, was that Mounier lacked collaborators who were seeking true sanctity.

In the meantime the official Church had taken none too kindly to Mounier's "ecumenism." To ward off a rumored condemnation, Mounier drew up a paper pointing out some of the *Esprit*'s achievements. First, it competed with the Communists on their own ground. Second, it brought Catholics out of their intellectual and political ghetto and allayed some of the suspicions about Catholicism among nonbelievers. Finally, it promoted contacts with progressive movements and, in particular, the working class. The archbishop of Paris, Cardinal Verdier, had advisers who were friendly to *Esprit* and they were able to convince the cardinal that Mounier was orthodox. No doubt Verdier was not too hard to persuade, being himself called the "Red Archbishop" because of his support of audacious youth movements. Indeed, Verdier hoped that *Esprit* might become the "avant-garde" of the Christian apostolate. It was certainly one of the few Catholic-dominated reviews that was read outside of Catholic circles. The three other leading cultural reviews—*Commune, Europe,* and *Nouvelle Revue Française*—were dominated by Communists or their fellow travelers.[33] A condemnation of *Esprit* would have been a great blow to progressive Catholics similar to the Sillon debacle in 1910.[34] A condemnation would have made it very difficult for all those who, like Mounier, were trying to lead Catholics out of their right-wing ghetto.

By the summer of 1935 it was clear that "communitarian personalism" was catching on. A number of talented writers and thinkers were drawn to this "most lively vehicle for Christian thought," in the opinion of such scholars as Maurice Merleau-Ponty, Jacques Ellul, and Jean Danielou. At the same time the old guard—Maritain, François Mauriac, Jacques Chevalier,

---

[32]Hellman, *Mounier and the New Catholic Left,* pp. 66–67.
[33]Kelly, *Pioneer of the Catholic Revival,* p. 63.
[34]See chapter on de Mun.

Maurice Blondel, and Jean Guitton—could no longer identify with its positions and moved on. Maritain, for instance, switched over to the Dominican review *Sept,* whose informed and pluralistic Catholicism he found more to his taste. Still *Esprit* numbered correspondents from some of the major cities of France, Italy, and Spain, who brought considerable talent and academic standing to the review. It was a satisfying moment in Mounier's life and he augmented his joy by marrying Paulette Leclercq, an *Esprit* enthusiast despite her upper-middle-class "liberal" (that is, non-Catholic) Belgian family.

Dialogue with Communists

One of the sharpest challenges faced by the personalists of *Esprit* was how to relate to communism. How could *Esprit* say anything positive about a movement that aimed at liquidating the entire spiritual heritage of the West? In the first *Esprit,* nevertheless, Berdyaev gave some credit to the movement for its critique of capitalism, its rejection of exploitation, and its efforts at economic planning—although, as he said, none of this could make up for its godless materialism.

Berdyaev's spiritualist critique remained the basic position of *Esprit,* but the journal maintained such a fair-minded and objective approach toward the Communists that Mounier was invited to speak at some of their rallies despite his admission that he was not well versed in Marxism. But Marcel More published important articles on Marx in *Esprit* and was the only prominent French Catholic intellectual (besides the Jesuit Fessard) to make a serious study of Marx at the time. More emphasized the humanistic aspect of Marx's writings and rejected the usual equation of Marxism and Stalinism.

Mounier disagreed, seeing the roots of Stalinism in Marx's derivation of man's spirituality from the economic—or, as he put it in his *Personalist Manifesto,* "in Marx's fundamental negation of the spiritual as a primary, creative and autonomous reality."[35] What was needed, Mounier said, was a balanced revolutionary ideology that was not vitiated by Marx's myopic concentration on the economic aspects of human history.

A much more radical Catholic journal at the time, *Terre Nouvelle,* took umbrage at this and accused *Esprit* of being unable to stand the sight of blood. Social Catholicism, it declared, needed a good dose of Marxism to

[35]Hellman, *Mounier and the New Catholic Left,* p. 104.

bring it down to earth. *Terre Nouvelle*'s cover flaunted a white cross embla-zoned on a red hammer and sickle—a symbol that Mounier found wrong, but appropriate in communicating the journal's confusion of two distinct faiths, political and religious. *Terre*'s message calling for collaboration with the Communists met with swift condemnation from the Vatican.

Dalliance with the Fascists

As the international scene heated up in the mid-thirties, *Esprit* took a rather benign (naive, its critics said) view of developments in Nazi Germany and Fascist Italy. As Hitler began to flex his muscles, one of *Esprit*'s team, Maurice de Gandillac, called his actions reasonable. Then in May 1935 Mounier himself attended a rally of Fascist youth in Rome and praised the radically anticapitalist speeches. His friend de Rougement later described the scene:

> A choir spoke: "We were wallowing in the mud, held to the ground and humiliated" . . . (Some mournful and muted rolls of drums) . . . "The people were divided, led astray" . . . (the sounds of civil war, cries, a machine gun) . . . "But the old Germanic legend told us that the Liberator would descend from the snowy mountains" . . . (popular singing, then fanfares) . . . "The old legend has become reality! He has come to reawaken his people."

Remaining faithful to his concept of the "third way," Mounier criticized the Nazis for their identification of the state with the *Volk*. He blamed both Nazis and the Communists for subordinating the person to the community, making the community an end in itself; whereas for the personalist the only raison d'être of the community is to enable the person to fulfill himself.

Mounier's approach to the Nazis and Fascists was in line with his view of the evolution of spiritual forces in the twentieth century and his refusal to follow the knee-jerk type of reaction typical of the French Right and Left. *Esprit*'s attitude toward the Fascists was therefore never as clearcut as it was toward the Communists. It maintained a generally neutral attitude toward Mussolini's regime; and when Hitler reoccupied the Rhineland in 1936 it praised him as vigorous, decisive, and tough in contrast to flabby, indecisive French politicians. Mounier had no love for Hitler's bloody totalitarian regime but he did not believe that National Socialism, a momentous histori-cal movement, would be stopped by the liberal democratic forces. Only a "communitarian personalist revolution" was equal to the challenge.

When Spain erupted into civil war, *Esprit* leaned toward a pro-republic position and the position of the Spanish POUM, a party of dissident ex-communists. Mounier's attitude toward the Spanish Civil War, the defining international affair of this period, was complex. He deplored the polarization the war caused in France but he placed himself firmly on the side of the working class and the noncommunist Left. As with other major issues he constantly shaded his opinions with a full range of reservations to ensure their compatibility with the teachings of the Church; hence the difficulty with a straightforward reading of his writings.

When his old mentor Chevalier condemned *Esprit*'s complacency toward the Spanish communists in view of the recent papal encyclical *Divini Redemptoris,* Mounier countered that the encyclical actually encouraged him to persevere with his "third way." It defended the legality of the republic "against perjuring generals and the threat of a fascist state under Germano-Italian influence."[36] Eventually, however, *Esprit* took a position of neutrality, as did Maritain.

As Hitler continued to draw his noose around Europe's neck, Mounier continued his refusal to believe that war was inevitable. And he continued to look kindly on certain aspects of Nazism which he compared favorably with the corrupt democratic regimes of the West. France, he felt, needed a similar authoritarian transformation, a personalist democracy that would restore the function of leadership. And he praised the communitarian feeling of the Nazis and their analysis of the solitude of modern man; their vision of the world, he said, was an exciting one. In fact he insisted that the essential difference between personalism and Nazism, was over the understanding of the person's relation to the collective. Or, as he put it: Is the person the primacy of man over matter, or indeed only a lien which would attach the individual to the collective spirit?[37]

Pope Pius XI's 1937 encyclical *Mit Brennender Sorge* denounced the Nazi myths of blood and race. Its denunciation of the Nazi atrocities apparently helped to moderate Mounier's tendency to take a sanguine view of Hitlerism. As Fascism spread in France, both in the tradition of the French extreme Right and in imitation of the German and Italian models, Mounier finally took a strong and lucid stand against it, arguing that it must be countered by a resolute and forceful affirmation of true values.

He was sure that the only solution to Europe's plight was a total spiritual

---

[36]Ibid., p. 120.
[37]Ibid., p. 134.

renewal. Cardinal Innitzer's welcome to Hitler's troops marching into Vienna was, for Mounier, just one more sign of the spiritual entropy of the West. "Defeats, blood and despair . . . will be necessary before a new Christendom can regain its heritage from the ruins of nineteen centuries of effort." France and England's capitulation at Munich was another sign of the condition, a spiritual malady that has infected "the petit bourgeois, [with] their indifference to the misfortunes of others, their morose perfidy, their deference to force, their generalized I-don't-give-a-damnism."[38] Even after the dismemberment of Czechoslovakia, the brutality against the Jews, the invasion of Poland, and the outbreak of war itself, Mounier refused to "recognize an absolute Christian imperative to fight the Nazis."[39] He tried to maintain a line that was both firmly "anti-Fascist" and yet basically "pacifist."

How to understand this strange complacency as Europe trembled with fear at the sight of Hitler's legions on the march? We must keep in mind that for Mounier, war was not the main issue. A war, whether won or lost, would not solve the main problem—the spiritual bankruptcy of the West. The only hope was a spiritual revolution, not a military solution. Moreover, as a student of Bergson and now Teilhard de Chardin, the Jesuit paleologue, Mounier held an evolutionist view that saw history moving man toward a supernatural destiny. The "spirit of God," he believed, "moved history with a long-term wisdom."[40] Or in Teilhard's phrase, "What rises must converge."

Esprit *Carries On*

On August 23, 1939, Joachim von Ribbentrop signed the Nazi–Soviet nonaggression pact. On September 1, German and Soviet troops marched into Poland. On September 2, France and Great Britain declared war on Germany. Mounier was inducted into the army (the *chasseurs alpins*) but was still able to keep *Esprit* going. As war began, *Esprit* maintained an attitude of serene objectivity, eschewing bellicosity and acknowledging that all parties were guilty. It did not take a pacifist line but tried to focus attention on the problems France would face when the war was over. Mounier spoke of the need to rebuild France and spark a spiritual reawakening. As the blitzkrieg

[38] Ibid., pp. 137–140.
[39] Ibid., p. 142.
[40] Ibid., p. 143.

rained fire and destruction down on the army and the country, he maintained his lofty metahistorical perspective. The disaster, he said, would at least "bring us out of the blind alleys of the past."[41]

Mounier and his personalist confreres had foreseen and foretold the coming calamity and they had a point of view, a philosophy that enabled them to make sense of it. They also belonged to a network of like-minded individuals in positions of influence around France and Belgium with definite plans for reorganizing labor, renewing the educational system, and moving Europe beyond the old concepts of liberal democracy. No wonder that, in the few weeks following the collapse of France under the Nazi onslaught, some of them were called to high office and power in the new order. The time had come to lay aside the rhetoric and meet the sobering tests of power. "The children of the new Renaissance would face the new dark ages."[42]

In September of 1940 Marshall Pétain outlined the principles of his social policy, and the rhetoric resembled personalist ideas. "The new social organization would not be 'liberalism' nor 'socialism' or 'capitalism' since his regime would put an end to the reign of economics." It would "subordinate the money factor to the human factor." Pétain argued that Christianity had conferred a "spiritual value on the most humble labour" and declared: "We aspire with all our soul to restore that value which ultimately reposes on respect for the human person." And he echoed the old personalist call for good men in key places: "So will arise the true elites which the former regime spent years destroying . . . the cadres needed for the well-being and dignity of all." The "economy had to be 'organized and controlled' to 'break the influence of the trusts.' "[43]

The similarity here with personalism was not coincidental. Pétain's statements were written, in fact, by men closely associated with *Esprit* or imbued with personalist ideas. In short there was no lack of personalists as well as pious Catholics at Vichy in 1940 and 1941. Mounier might be forgiven for believing, at that point, that personalism was an idea whose time had come.

Many of his associates at *Esprit* were totally opposed to working with Pétain's Vichy regime. Paul Vignaux declared "one can only hope for the victory of England, all other hypotheses are meaningless."[44] But Mounier was convinced that the Reich was there to stay and that France would have

[41] Ibid., p. 156.
[42] Ibid., p. 157.
[43] Ibid., p. 168.
[44] Ibid., p. 173.

to find a place within an authoritarian Europe. After all, with Russia in league with Hitler, America uncommitted, France humiliated, and continental Europe overrun, few people expected England to hold out. Mounier alluded to the fall of the Roman Empire when elite Romans, who were Christians, set about converting the savage invaders. With his friends, the Dominicans Paul and Maurice Montuclard, he saw an opportunity to replace the stale bourgeois Church with a new "manly" Christianity based on the working classes that would revive the Church's communitarian tradition.

In his decision to continue with *Esprit,* Mounier felt it would be better to keep the channels of communication open and to make every effort to exert a moderating influence on the regime. There was still some recognition of true values within the Vichy regime, he thought, and still some degree of independence allowed in some of its intellectual circles. Some compromises would be necessary, but he took the half-loaf approach as the best under the circumstances.

In spite of the refusal of many of his old associates to join him in such a risky endeavor, he was able to pull together a team including Jean Danielou, Gabriel Marcel, and the journalist Hubert Beuve-Méry. After the war his defenders noted that in spite of the appearance of collaboration, *Esprit* artfully carried on a subtle campaign of opposition by the use of allusive and ambiguous language. Ridiculous or outrageous statements made by the regime would be noted without comment under the label *"Pour servir à une histoire de notre temps."* Barbs would be hidden in book reviews. The censors were even induced to allow articles by Jews, and quotations from banned books.

Esprit gained a wide readership by reason of its calm and intelligent discussion of events when such calm and intelligence was otherwise noticeably absent. Moreover it occupied probably the furthest point of opposition a publication could reach in Nazi-occupied Europe without risking suppression and worse. Thus its appeal to dissenters. Action Française, the true mentor of Vichy, recognized *Esprit*'s dissident tone very early and began attacking it as early as December 1940.

A curious episode at this time was Mounier's involvement in the École Nationale des Cadres d'Uriage, a training camp for French youth located near Grenoble. In setting up the camp, the Vichy government wanted to create a new type of French youth by restoring "the sense of authority and of collective discipline," and intended "to substitute for indifference, skepti-

cism and dilettantism a love of the committed life."[45] They were to be
weaned away from their worn-out individualism and imbued with the spirit
of socialism. Invited to participate, Mounier and his friends were excited by
the possibility of "spiritualizing" French youth in accord with the personalist philosophy. However, suspicions of Nazi influence on the camp were
confirmed when Vichy was forced into tighter collaboration with the Nazis
and their anti-Semitic policies. When Mounier began to highlight the differences between the Nazi ideology and personalism, the enemies of personalism at Vichy were able to get *Esprit* suppressed and Mounier removed
from his post in the youth movement. Mounier was jailed for a brief time,
and his role as a major intellectual force in Vichy collapsed. His elimination
was part of a general effort to remove Catholic influence over French youth.

Until its suppression, *Esprit* was the most dissident of the nonclandestine
reviews. Its large following of supporters that had been built up before the
war, and its popularity with many young intellectuals with no other means
of expression, enabled it to wield great influence. Can *Esprit* therefore claim
any credit for slowing down the creeping Fascism that Vichy stood for? One
has to agree with Hellman that Mounier was certainly not clear-cut in his
attitude toward the Vichy regime and the Nazi domination of Europe. But
still it is true that Mounier maintained his integrity under great pressures,
and at a time of low morale was able to provide youth especially with a
symbol of idealism and courage.[46]

Militant resistance was just beginning at this point, and though not actively involved Mounier did keep in contact with the leaders of *Combat,* one
of the groups that was coming to the fore in the early months of 1941. In
any case, on January 15, 1942, Mounier was arrested and jailed when his
name was found on a document with the names of known resisters. Moreover, at this point the *Esprit* group was also suspected of forming a network
of resisters. Though Mounier pleaded innocence and total incapacity for
political action, the months dragged on with no resolution of the case.
Finally he began a hunger strike to draw attention to his plight and was
transferred to a hospital when he appeared in danger of death. In spite of his
later claim that the resistance leaders were supposed to meet at his house on
the day of his arrest, the authorities failed to turn up any evidence against
him. He was freed and took up residence in the mountain village of
Dieulefit.

[45]Ibid., p. 175.
[46]Kelly, *Pioneer of the Catholic Revival,* p. 97.

Mounier's imprisonment, dramatic hunger strike, and trial focused national attention on him as numerous prominent French patriots used the occasion to indirectly register opposition to the regime by protesting his arrest. Consequently his name would henceforth be indelibly linked with the resistance cause. The prestige he thus accrued helped to make his thinking a serious competitor in the postwar contest of ideologies. In fact, the two years following the end of the war marked in many ways the pinnacle of achievement for Mounier and *Esprit*. Personalism became widely accepted as the most dynamic and fertile current of Christian thought. Its insistence on the value of the human person as the keystone of Catholic social thought reflected the best in contemporary Church thinking. *Esprit*'s socialist humanism synthesized much of the political theory that had emerged from the resistance.

TWELVE

The Personalist Revolution:
Maritain and Mounier II

WHILE MOUNIER carried on with difficulty his anti-Vichy efforts in occupied France, Maritain from his exile in America did what he could to stiffen the spirit of French resistance. When he returned to France in the fall of 1944 he found few signs of unity. Divisions were deep. Communists especially, as he said, were creating problems in every direction while "there is a very real fifth column which continued to cherish Pétain and create a milieu favorable to acts of violence."[1] The Church too was deeply divided, as a good number of the bishops had collaborated with the Vichy regime to an extent that many Catholics felt was treasonous. They urged the dismissal of at least thirty-three of the French bishops as well as the papal nuncio himself, Monsignor Valerio Valeri.

It was a delicate situation, and de Gaulle wanted an ambassador to the Vatican of whose consummate finesse he could be sure. He asked Maritain to take the position. It was not a job Maritain felt suited for and it would gravely interfere with the philosophical work he felt was primary. But de Gaulle would take no refusal and Jacques finally submitted. With Raïssa and

---

[1]Doering, *Jacques Maritain and the French Catholic Intellectuals*, p. 204.

Vera he took up residence in Rome amid the faded grandeur of the Palazzo Taverna in the ancient Renaissance sector. He and Angelo Roncalli, the new papal nuncio in Paris, were able to work out a solution to the problem of the traitorous bishops. Only three were forced to resign.

The two dealt with other pressing problems facing the French Church. They saw eye to eye on the French worker-priest movement, for instance, and helped to ward off its suppression although this did occur after both left their posts. Another common concern was with the direction of a new French political party, the Mouvement Républican Populaire (MRP), which was composed chiefly of liberal Catholics who had worked on social reform before the war. No doubt they found much agreement here too, for later, as Pope John XXIII, Roncalli issued several social encyclicals that show a definite resemblance with Maritain's social views.

Jacques' relations with high-ranking churchmen were not always cordial. He had enemies in the Vatican who had never forgiven him for his stands on the Action Française, the Spanish Civil War, and his opposition to the Vichy regime. He had been warned by his friend Yves Simon that "the muck of their mudslinging would fall on him like rain."[2] When Garrigou-Lagrange himself cast suspicion on Maritain's orthodoxy, the indignant Maritain took the opportunity in a letter to the "sacred monster of Thomism" (in the words of François Mauriac) to get some things off his chest:

> Whatever our political differences may be, you had no right whatsoever in this regard to cast the slightest suspicion on my doctrine. When you took the side of Marshal Pétain, to the point of declaring that to support de Gaulle was a mortal sin, I felt that your political prejudices blinded you in a matter that was very serious for our country, but it did not even cross my mind to suspect your theology or to accuse you of deviation in matters of doctrine.
>
> I might add that I was very sorry about the way you compromised Thomism through your political positions that were justifiably odious to those who were struggling for the liberation of our country.[3]

He went on to say that the behavior of the Thomists was one of the reasons why so many young minds were deserting Thomism. Garrigou-Lagrange and his ilk often set up roadblocks to the acceptance of the social

[2] Ibid., p. 209.
[3] Ibid., p. 223.

teachings of Leo XIII and were taken in by "outrageous illusions in the domain of national politics."

The Roman churchman he found most congenial in spirit was Monsignor Giovanni Battista Montini, the Vatican undersecretary of state and future Pope Paul VI. As a young priest Montini had translated Maritain's *Three Reformers* (a book Maritain later took little relish in), and the two became fast friends. As archbishop of Milan, Montini put Maritain's social teachings into practice as he devoted much time and energy to the problems of workers and the poor. As pope he called Maritain "my teacher" and used Maritain's social and political thought as the basis of his social encyclicals, in which he quoted Maritain directly.

In spite of his many duties as ambassador, Maritain was able to carry on his writing and lecturing. At St. Louis des Français he established a center where young men from the various seminaries in Rome could hear lectures by outstanding authorities in cultural and social fields. He also resumed lectures at the Angelicum and published several works including *Existence and the Existent,* his contribution to the current debate about existentialism. It was occasioned by the popularity of Heidegger and Sartre, whose bleak view of man Maritain countered with a Thomistic version of existentialism based on the human being as participant in the *ipsum esse subsistens,* the subsistent being, God.

Princeton

In 1948 Maritain accepted an invitation to teach at Princeton University, where he remained for the next twelve years. His graduate courses embraced such problems as the relation of the person to the common good, the meaning of the natural moral law, and the nature of the rights of man. He presented a critical version of Thomistic morality. His students appreciated this slight, white-haired figure with his wry humor and delicate intellectual courtesy; in turn, Maritain's book *Reflections on America* paid tribute to the generous spirit of Americans who were always ready to support anyone who might add to the common treasury of the mind.

The Princeton years were richly fruitful ones. While lecturing extensively around the United States and abroad, Maritain was able to publish a number of his most significant philosophical works. *Man and the State* was based on the Walgreen lectures he delivered at the University of Chicago in 1950. Along with *True Humanism,* it is considered his most significant contribution to political philosophy.

An Odd Friendship

While in America Jacques made many friendships with people from a wide variety of backgrounds. Included among them were such well-known social activists as Dorothy Day, John Howard Griffin, and Thomas Merton. One of the oddest friendships was with the radical community organizer Saul Alinsky. How did an agnostic Jewish "troublemaker," happiest when leading a noisy march against City Hall, seal a deep personal friendship with a Catholic philosopher who was uneasy with crowds and preferred quiet little gatherings with a few chosen friends? The courteous scion of the French grande bourgeoisie and the gruff offspring of poor Russian Orthodox Jewish immigrants met during Maritain's wartime exile in America and soon found they had much in common. Both were passionately committed to the democratic idea and delighted to share their insights: the practical ideas of the one dovetailing with the speculative ideas of the other—Alinsky's gut feelings with Maritain's philosophy of personal dignity. Both had profound trust in the common man.

One can imagine Maritain chuckling over Alinsky's proposal to the clergy who were trying to prevent a riot in the Oakland community.

> "The problem in Oakland is that the power structure doesn't know there are any Negroes. We'd show them some Negroes." He would stage a "Watermelon March," and a "Sunday Walk." Several hundred of the blackest Negroes would be dressed in coveralls, handed watermelons and marched from City Hall to the *Oakland Tribune.* Equally dark-skinned Negroes, elegantly attired, would take a Sunday stroll through the best white neighborhoods.[4]

Their friendship spanned thirty years and ended only with the death of Alinsky in 1972. In one of his first letters to Jacques, Alinsky asked him for a photo of himself that he could keep near his desk as a cherished possession. It would help him cope with the cynicism and materialism that was so thick around him. After receiving the picture he thanked Jacques and asked him to always look upon him as a devoted friend. "Jacques Maritain," he wrote, not yet feeling ready to call him simply Jacques, "you are so filled with love, humility and compassion for your fellowmen that you annihilate my defenses of skepticism and cynicism." In contact with Jacques, he said, he had

---

[4]Hudson and Mancini, eds., *Understanding Maritain,* pp. 40–41.

the same feeling that he had had at his Bar Mitzvah, "that there is a good and great spirit close to me . . ."[5] Henceforth he said his inner voice would ask: "Would Jacques Maritain think this right or would he think it wrong?"

The two men encouraged each other in their work. Maritain sent Alinsky copies of his books and articles while Alinsky sent Jacques copies of his speeches and accounts of his latest activities. Monsignor John Egan noted that Maritain was always pushing and encouraging Alinsky in his work with the downtrodden, always inquiring about his undertakings and what he was planning. At Jacques' behest Giovanni Montini, the new archbishop of Milan, brought Alinsky to Milan as a consultant. Montini was concerned about the Church losing the workers to the Communists and wanted advice on methods of community organization and the training of leaders.

Once again at the urging of Maritain, Alinsky wrote his famous *Reveille for Radicals,* a kind of handbook for urban radicals. Before it was even bound he sent Jacques two sewn copies, and in the bound copy he finally sent he wrote: "To know Jacques Maritain is to know a richness and spiritual experience that makes life even more glorious."[6] Jacques in turn praised the author as a "truly great man, a real son of the pioneers [who] . . . has discovered in his people's organizations the creative sap of American life, and I believe in them can be found the germ of an authentic renewal of democracy."[7]

The real depth of Maritain and Alinsky's friendship, however, is most evident in the way they opened their hearts to each other at times of great personal loss. After Saul's wife, Helene, drowned in Lake Michigan in 1947, Saul thanked Jacques for a letter of condolence that was so touching, he said, that he wept over it and placed it in a special folder where he could always look at it. Then he poured out his feelings:

People . . . think that I am doing well. What they do not know is that my heart is completely broken and life seems utterly empty and horrible. The agony of the loneliness becomes at times unbearable. Every morning my pillow is wet from my tears and I can't tell you how many times I have prayed for death. The sight of my children forlornly inquiring for their Mommy . . . this smashes those pieces of my heart that still remain.[8]

[5] Ibid., p. 44.
[6] Ibid., p. 46.
[7] Ibid., p. 47.
[8] Ibid., p. 48.

In 1962 Alinsky traveled from Chicago to New York to visit with Jacques, and in 1966 he volunteered to accompany his old friend to Mansfield, Texas, where Jacques was to meet John Howard Griffin. But Alinsky was not able to make the trip and his visit with Maritain at the time was the last time they saw each other. When Jacques returned to France he went to live in a tiny hermitage with the Little Brothers of Jesus. Alinsky found this hard to understand, and in several letters Jacques tried to explain his move. He insisted that he was not giving up the struggle for justice and human dignity but would now pursue it on the level of prayer. With his lifelong task now ended, he felt he had been given a new job by his "Boss."

Maritain's friendship with Alinsky was one of the most noteworthy of the many friendships he made in the United States, but all these friendships helped to change radically his conception of democracy and the political process. He became an important advocate of democracy. He told Alinsky how much he loved America and how he was intoxicated by her soul and hopes, "that great human dream which is permeated with the Gospel infinitely more than the Americans themselves believe."[9]

Tragedy did not spare the Maritains. He suffered a heart attack in 1954, making him thereafter a partial invalid. A year later Raissa was hit by a motorcyclist in Paris and badly bruised. Her sister Vera, who was at the scene, was terribly unnerved and a year later suffered a heart attack and several months later was stricken by cancer. The next three years were extremely trying ones for Jacques and Raissa as Vera battled the disease while they expended every possible effort in her care. Her last days were extremely painful and left Raissa herself shattered in health and virtually prostrate. She recovered enough to travel to Paris with Jacques the following year but on arrival suffered a cerebral thrombosis. Until her death four months later, in November 1960, Jacques spent most of his time at her bedside. At last the doctor had to limit his visits; when Jacques was there, Raissa was so agitated by her efforts to speak that she was totally exhausted. Jacques now had to remain in an adjoining room and listen for the sounds that either alarmed or reassured him, and he rarely went out except for mass. To be cut off from someone with whom he had passed his entire adult life in a close and total communion of thoughts and sentiments was almost more than he could bear. During these weeks Saul Alinsky did not forget his friend. He wrote to say that he was "heartsick with what is happening to you and only wish I could be with you to be able to do something, anything

[9] Ibid., p. 55.

which might make it more consolable."[10] Jacques' only relief was to take up his work, writing as hard as he could. Raissa's condition steadily worsened and by November 2 it was clear the end was near. She received the last sacraments while totally conscious and thanked the priest with a smile. Two days later she passed into eternity.

To friends who feared for the totally exhausted man's own life, Jacques said he had survived even himself. However, as his strength returned he set about making decisions about his future. One of the tasks he dreaded was returning to the house in Princeton where Vera, Raissa, and he had spent so many happy years. As he wrote to his friend, the novelist Julien Green:

> I was very much afraid of entering our empty house . . . at any rate in the very heart of my sorrow I had the impression that Raissa was waiting for me in the living room . . . her atmosphere and her spirit were there with that grace, that gay yet grave sweetness . . . I firmly believe, as you do, that Raissa is happy and that she wants me to be courageous . . . I have lost the presence of her whom I loved more than myself . . . [but] it is true that she is with me ceaselessly and that she watches over me.[11]

While at Princeton Jacques had made his first contact with a religious community that would now play a significant role in his life. The meeting occurred when the Little Brothers of Jesus' founder Fr. René Voillaume visited Jacques seeking help for a course in philosophy he was trying to organize. In founding the order in 1933, Fr. Voillaume had sought to carry out the idea of Charles de Foucauld, a French army officer who had become a priest. After ordination he returned to the Sahara to lead a life of prayer and contemplation and serve the desert nomads, the most forsaken of peoples. The Little Brothers, faithful to the spirit of Fr. Charles, live in the slums among the poorest of the poor, sharing their lives and engaging in works of humble service on their behalf. They welcome all who come to them offering them friendship, food, and help in sickness. Jacques had known Fr. Voillaume since the foundation of the community and took a deep interest in its progress, seeing it as a needed spiritual challenge to a materialistic world.

His "sixty sons," as he called the Little Brothers, were a great joy to him. He seemed to regain his health in the atmosphere of peace and trust he found in the tiny hermitage at Toulouse they fixed for him. They were men

[10] Ibid., p. 51.
[11] Doering, *Jacques Maritain and the French Catholic Intellectuals,* p. 216.

from a great variety of backgrounds, and to accommodate their different levels of education Jacques lectured in an informal style, constantly updating his lessons as he dealt with the great philosophical questions that people have always faced.

His lectures on the problem of "God and the Permission of Evil" were later published in book form. Together with his *Existence and the Existent,* he considered it his most important contribution to Thomistic thought. Like his other writings they show that his Thomism was in no way a closed, static system. He always insisted on the realism of true Thomism and its openness to every advance of human rationality and experimental knowledge. He was also committed to a Thomism that was fully cognizant of the history of thought.

Honors came to him in his little cell in Toulouse. Thanks to the intervention of his friend Étienne Gilson he was nominated for and received the Grand Prize of Literature from the French Academy in 1961. A yet more momentous honor came to him in connection with the Second Vatican Council, which opened at Rome in 1962. Some of its major pronouncements reflected ideas that he had long stood for and that were considered radical when he first advocated them: ecumenism, religious liberty, the dignity and rights of the human person, the condemnation of anti-Semitism within the Church, the enhanced role of the laity, and recognition of the values of science, art, and democracy. As we have noted, Pope Paul VI was a personal friend of Jacques' and not only cited him in his encyclical *Populorum Progressio* but also kept some of his books alongside his bed. In the pope's address at the last session of the Council, Paul referred to him as "the great Christian philosopher Maritain." And it was Jacques who was chosen to receive the council's "Message to Intellectuals" from the pope in the solemn ceremony that closed Vatican II. Clad in the humble gray habit of the Little Brothers, amid princes of the Church in resplendent garments, he took the document from the hands of the visibly moved pontiff. It was a profoundly symbolic gesture that expressed very poignantly the role of Maritain in the twentieth-century Church.

The Peasant of the Garonne

But even this was not the final act of his drama. As the first shock waves from the Second Vatican Council began to hit the Church, François Mauriac wondered in distress what Maritain thought about it all. He soon got his answer when Maritain's *The Peasant of the Garonne* appeared in November

1966. "I gulped it down like milk," Mauriac told his well-known philosopher friend Jean Guitton, who was also ecstatic about the book.

What was milk to some was sour milk to others. The book, which was above all an attack on the "neo-modernists and their pseudo-scientific and pseudo-philosophical claptrap," became an immediate bestseller. The prime targets of Maritain's wrath were the liberal theologians, the phenomenologists, the existentialists, the Freudians, the extreme ecumenists, and especially the Teilhardians, whom he accused of trying to desupernaturalize the Church. They would reduce its message to a purely natural one and create a church no different in essence from all those organizations that aim at world betterment. Instead of seeking to convert the world, these new theologians were genuflecting before it. They avoided such unpopular topics as the next world, the cross, and sanctity, while enraptured with the discoveries of modern culture—discoveries not indeed worthless, in Maritain's view, for he too believed in the struggle to overcome the age-old evils of injustice, war, and poverty. A Christian, however, could only ransom the time by dying to the world, like the saints—holding the world in contempt for the love of Christ in order to love the world with the redeeming love of Christ.

The new theologians, Maritain asserted, wanted to create a new Church while jettisoning the old with all its outdated baggage and alienating ways. The high priest of this new Church, he claimed, was Teilhard de Chardin. While paying due respect to the Jesuit's zeal for truth and painful trials with authority, Maritain dismissed his "Christology of the cosmic Christ" as a poetic intuition and called his theology a new form of Gnosticism in which the main dogmas of the Church—original sin, resurrection of the body, distinction between nature and grace, and finally redemption—were radically transformed.

With these pronouncements, a storm broke over the old philosopher's head and he was pilloried from both the Right and the Left. At first the Right was delighted with the idea of Maritain's lashing out at the liberals. But they soon realized that he had not really come over to their camp; his commitment to the basic achievements of the council was too obvious. So they decided instead to attack his credibility and show that the old radical firebrand was unable to face the fires he himself had helped to ignite.

The dismay of the Left was, if anything, even more intense, for they felt betrayed: Maritain seemed to disavow his own liberal legacy. Forgetting perhaps that Maritain had always combined political liberalism with theological conservatism they accused him of "returning to his vomit," of betraying a "profound and culpable ignorance of the contemporary problems facing the Church such as penance, sexuality, and the role of the priest in the modern world."[12] His supposed inability to deal with the aftermath of the council was attributed to his myopic Thomism which had ill-prepared him to understand those living in the real world that was shaped by positive science, evolution, psychology, and existential philosophy. Still other critics, such as the Jesuit Bruno Ribes, focused on the book's pervasive negativism which they saw as unfortunately preventing many from appreciating the valuable insights it in fact offered. Yves Congar felt this negativism was most noticeable in Maritain's unwillingness to give any credit to the theologians who had prepared the breakthroughs at the council, breakthroughs that Maritain himself professed to admire. Finally, some found it paradoxical that Maritain refused to attribute good will to so many of his contemporaries when he himself had often spoken so eloquently of the need, in a divided world, to cooperate with all of good will.

Maritain was shaken and hurt by the barrage, and though he had intended *Le Paysan* to be his last work he continued to write, partly it seems to modify the impression of harshness and intransigence it had caused. His next work, *On the Church of Christ,* had none of the mordant satire of the previous work. Among his many reflections on the Church he noted here, as one of the great accomplishments of the Vatican Council, its call to lay persons to assume responsibility for tackling social evils and injustices. It is no longer necessary or appropriate, he said, for priests to organize and lead the laity in the temporal sphere, and he foresaw a new form of clericalism were this change to occur. He felt there was a good chance that the world could move beyond capitalism and communist totalitarianism, given full lay commitment to the search for social justice.

In 1970, at eighty-eight, Jacques decided to enter the society of the Little Brothers and began a year of novitiate. Though his health was beginning to fail he was still able to make annual visits to his beloved Alsatian village of Kolbsheim, where Raïssa was buried and where there were so many mementos of their life together. He would walk in the forest they had both loved so much, and he spent long hours sitting alongside her grave. In spite of extreme debility he was still able to get there in January 1973, lying on a mattress in the back of a station wagon. Three months later on the morning of April 28 he rose as usual with the help of one of the Little Brothers, but shortly afterward collapsed from heart failure. A few moments later death came peacefully in the presence of four of the brothers. His body was later

[12]Ibid., p. 230.

taken to Kolbsheim where the funeral was held in the Lutheran church, there being no Catholic parish in Kolbsheim. It was attended by many friends and dignitaries including Pope Paul's personal representative. Afterward, in a silent cortège, they accompanied the Little Brothers who carried the simple wooden coffin to the quiet cemetery and laid him to rest beside Raissa. On the small unpretentious tombstone underneath the name RAISSA MARITAIN were inscribed—as he had wished, in much smaller letters—the words "et Jacques."

His Political Philosophy

Jacques Maritain's spiritual and intellectual journey epitomizes, perhaps better than that of any other Catholic, the distance the Church traveled intellectually during the first part of the twentieth century. He saw as one of his main tasks "the reconciliation of the vision of Joseph de Maistre, the arch Catholic reactionary, with that of Lamennais in the higher unity of the supreme wisdom of which St. Thomas Aquinas is the herald to our time."[13] To this effort he dedicated a number of his more than seventy books.

His thought moved from a rightist position in the twenties to a critique of capitalism and communism in the thirties. He then moved from his stance of natural-rights liberalism in the forties to a close identification in the fifties with the American version of liberal democracy. Finally, in the sixties, he took up an increasingly critical attitude toward the radical tendencies in Catholic theology and political thought.

The papal condemnation of Action Française in 1926 and the crisis this caused in Maritain's own personal life turned his attention away from philosophical to political and social issues. Thomism, he realized, could be effectively applied to political and social issues. His most important writings in this endeavor include *The Things That Are Not Caesar's* (1927)—connected with the papal censure of Action Française. The others are *Integral Humanism* (1936), *Man and the State* (1951), *The Person and the Common Good* (1947), *The Rights of Man and Natural Law* (1942), *Du Regime Temporel et de la Liberté* or *Freedom in the Modern World* (1933), and *Christianity and Democracy* (1943).

[13]Jacques Maritain, *Freedom in the Modern World* (New York: Charles Scribner's Sons, 1936), p. 126.

Integral Humanism—the Key

The basic key to Maritain's political philosophy is found in *Integral Humanism,* which explores the concept of humanism, the view that man is (or should be) the measure of all things and that civilizations should render man more truly human. Of course one's understanding of the human being is the crucial matter in judging what is a truly humanist system. For Maritain the human being lives at the same time on two levels—or, as he puts it, "man is at once a natural and a supernatural being."[14] Hence he calls his philosophy *integral* humanism inasmuch as it attempts to meet the needs of man on both levels. "This 'humanism of the Incarnation' would serve the needs of the masses and their right to a temporal condition worthy of man and to a spiritual life. It would be a movement that would carry labor toward the social responsibility of its coming of age. It would be a 'Christian-personalistic' democracy."[15]

One of the gravest threats to integral humanism, Maritain thought, was the growing menace of Fascism in the 1930s as it captured Spain, Italy, and Germany. Its success, he believed, was due to the lamentable decay of political philosophy during the classical, bourgeois, and revolutionary moments of history. The key to this decay was the adulteration of the concept of sovereignty, which he defined as "supreme power separate and transcendent . . . and ruling the entire body politic from above"—obviously the prerogative of God alone. But modern thinkers identified sovereignty with, successively, the monarchy, the state, and finally the body politic or Rousseau's abstract General Will. "And since this General Will supposedly possessed unconditional autonomy, it excluded any smaller groups of citizens from the right to autonomy, thus creating a tyranny of enforced conformity that was a prototype for the fascist political order."[16]

From his early manhood Maritain had been in the thick of many of the battles of French intellectual life. He fought against positivism and materialism, clericalism and the bourgeois spirit. After his conversion he led the charge against Bergsonism and modernism. Then in the crisis over the condemnation of Action Française there was his painful struggle to rethink

[14] Quoted in John M. Dunaway, *Jacques Maritain* (Boston: Twayne Publishers, 1978), p. 66.

[15] Joseph Evans and Leo Ward, eds., *The Social and Political Philosophy of Jacques Maritain* (New York: Doubleday Image Books, 1965), p. 165.

[16] Dunaway, *Jacques Maritain,* p. 67.

his political and social philosophy. This opened up a new chapter which saw him take part in establishing the new radical Catholic journals *Esprit* and *Sept,* followed by his having charges leveled against him for being a Communist. Above all there was his involvement in the passions and agitation over the aggressive moves of Italy and Germany, and the issuance of manifestos by the Catholic "Left." Finally he witnessed the eruption of the Spanish Civil War, that savage prelude to the impending conflagration.

When the world war came in 1939, it confirmed his premonitions about the direction of the modern world. He called it "not a simple national war, nor a policing action, nor a holy war, nor an ideological war, it is a war of civilization . . . What was collapsing was the long-tottering structure of the French bourgeoisie." What was dying was what Péguy "called the modern world, roughly speaking a four-century block of history." What was emerging might be the civilization he had sketched in *True Humanism*.[17]

During the Second World War Maritain was even more active in political problems than in the previous decade. As Hitler's troops overran the Lowlands and Norway, and as France braced itself for the coming invasion, Maritain contemplated the new order that would follow German defeat. To assure a lasting peace, he insisted, Europe and Germany must be rebuilt along federal lines. Whatever diminution of national sovereignties might be required, the sacrifice must be made if there was to be any hope for Europe. Above all, he insisted, Germany must not be subjected to the kind of reprisals and humiliations imposed on her by Versailles.

Maritain also envisaged the new world order as a pluralist one built on a consensus about basic human values. While Christianity, he was certain, could provide the best defense of these values, he recognized the fact that many people who would be most active on their behalf would not be Christians. As he said, history shows that it was the rationalists in France who proclaimed the Rights of Man, and it was atheistic communists who abolished the absolutism of private property in Russia.

That the world has entered on a revolutionary period, he said, is now a matter not of controversy but of record. One is accordingly entitled to declare oneself a revolutionary in order to mark one's intention to rise to the height of the occasion; and to mark as well one's understanding of the necessity for radical reform that will change, in their distinctive "humanist-inhuman" character, the essential principles of our existing regime of civilization.

---

[17] Also translated as *Integral Humanism* (New York: Charles Scribner's Sons, 1968).

Maritain pointed out the danger of thinking of revolution primarily in terms of visible transformation; rather, as Péguy has said, the social revolution will be a moral revolution or none at all. If omnipotent love would transform our hearts, half the work of reform would already be accomplished. The transformation we need is much more radical than the revolution of the revolutionaries. The communist revolution, for instance, only accentuated the radical principles at the base of capitalist disorder. For the Christian it is these radical principles that have to be changed in order to change the whole orientation of our cultural life.

A New Christendom

Maritain often spoke of a new Christendom that he felt would emerge from the total breakdown of the order that had held sway in Europe for four hundred years. The goal would be to build a new Christendom on a religious basis. However, unlike the old order it would not be a sacred order but a secular one, more pluralistic than the old and with full political freedom and economic justice. Though composed of a variety of spiritual groups it could be appropriately labeled "Christian" to the extent that its values reflected those of the Gospel.

Maritain had a strongly positive view of medieval Christendom as a laudable attempt to incarnate the Gospel in a temporal system. But unlike many Catholics at that time he was not nostalgic about it. Medieval Christendom was not a model for later times. It had its own serious flaws. He felt that the task of the Christian in our time was to structure a new Christendom that would respond to the current needs of human beings. The central need, as he saw it, was for a system that would foster true spiritual freedom, "the holy freedom of the creature whom grace unites to God."[18]

Maritain envisaged a Christendom that would be pluralist, a Christianly inspired humanist democracy, not a society dominated by the Church as in medieval Christendom. He remained firm in calling for the elimination of the capitalist economic system, believing that the measure of all things in the capitalist economy is bound to antihumanist preoccupations: productivity, technology, money.[19] He felt it would be a serious error to tie Christendom to the capitalist economic system. "The temporal task of the Christian world is to work on earth for a socio-temporal realization of the Gospel

---

[18] From Maritain, *Integral Humanism,* as quoted in Dunaway, *Jacques Maritain,* p. 71.
[19] Dunaway, *Jacques Maritain,* p. 74.

truths."[20] And he underscored the failure of the Christian world in this regard.

In calling for pluralism Maritain completely abandoned the classic Catholic position that distinguished the ideal situation from the actual situation. The ideal situation was supposed to be a society where the Catholic Church, with all the rights and prerogatives of an established church, would act as a limit on religious freedom; the actual situation was supposed to be a recognition on the part of the Church that seeking such establishment, at the present moment of history, would be counterproductive. Together with the writings of others, such as the American Jesuit John Courtney Murray, Maritain prepared the way for the reversal of Catholic teaching on religious freedom at the Second Vatican Council, which laid to rest the classic position. But he defended the Syllabus of Errors (1864) and the nineteenth-century Church's condemnations of liberalism. They were a necessary response to "the false metaphysics from which the opponents of the old order drew their energy and their passion . . . These acts of condemnation were for Catholics a definitive statement of truths of capital importance. Not that the Church had condemned the modern world or the new age, for such words have no meaning. She made a beginning by purifying the domain of thought and by eliminating error."[21]

The conservatism of the nineteenth-century Church Maritain saw as motivated by the "duty of protection she owed to a multitude of souls and also out of loyalty to temporal forms that in spite of many acts of resistance and sometimes of oppression had served her in her spiritual ministry through long centuries of time. The Church, while struggling against the existing abuses, attempted to support as long as they had any life in them [the] types of social structure that have been inherited from the Christian past and that had endured the test of time."[22]

The Church's relation to the world was a topic of much concern to Maritain. He saw the Church as the kingdom of God in an embryonic form, and warned against confusing the world with the kingdom. The role of the world is to prepare for the coming of the kingdom of God inasmuch as the world becomes more fully human in realizing greater justice, freedom, and respect for the dignity of each person. The Christian must participate in this movement of the world toward the kingdom. The Christian is

---

[20]Maritain, *Integral Humanism*, p. 42.
[21]Maritain, *Freedom in the Modern World*, pp. 100–101.
[22]Ibid., p. 101.

preeminently a social being as well as a spiritual one, and must be involved in the task of social reconstruction. It is a task that calls for "secular saintliness."

Maritain paid tribute to the work of the popes who had formulated the principles and essential truths governing the whole field of economic affairs. These doctrinal declarations of Pope Leo XIII and Pope Pius XI, he said, had a profound effect on legislation and public opinion.

Human Rights

Maritain based his concept of human rights on the idea of natural law and of God as the prime source of natural law. For Maritain, natural law is based on the assumption of a human nature common to all people. His theory of human rights assumed a universe ordered in Thomistic teleological fashion by God in a hierarchy of ends. Our rights and duties flow therefore from our natural orientation to these ends. His summary of the rights of the person includes religious rights, property rights, rights to freedom of expression and association, and rights to a job and to a salary.

He condemned so-called "freedom of choice" wherein freedom is seen as an end in itself. This is a liberal or individualist conception whereby "all possible acts of free choice may be available [so that] men may appear like so many little gods, with no other restriction on their freedom save that they are not to hinder a similar freedom on the part of their neighbor. Such an outlook ignores the heavy and severe burdens that lie on man in real life. Only a limited number can enjoy this kind of freedom and only by oppression of the remainder of their fellows. The essential values of social justice and the common good are forgotten. What remains are only a multitude of bourgeois ends in themselves with unlimited freedom to own and trade and enjoy."[23]

True freedom, on the other hand, is freedom that is ordained toward the realization and progress of the spiritual freedom of individual persons. It holds justice and friendship to be the true foundations of social life. According to this philosophy, civil society is ordered not to the freedom of choice of each citizen but to a common good of the temporal order, which includes not only material but also moral well-being. In other words, the common good in the temporal order is an intermediate end—not a final one.

In Maritain's view, true freedom does not exalt itself to the level of an

[23] Ibid., p. 41.

absolute good. It is essentially directed to the establishment of social conditions that will secure for the masses of men a standard of material, intellectual, and moral life that will be conducive to the well-being of the whole
community. Thus every citizen may find in this standard a positive help to
the progressive achievement of his freedom of autonomy. Such a political
philosophy is at one and the same time both communal and personal.

On Democracy

Maritain was a firm believer in democracy and the modern freedoms. He
pointed out how much democracy owes to Christianity, insofar as many of
its features were either derived from Christianity or were defended and
supported by Christianity. These would include the sacredness and dignity
of the human person, equality in the rights of each person, the distinction
between the rights of God and the rights of Caesar, the brotherhood of
man, and the concern with improving and emancipating the condition of
human beings.

Maritain emphasized the importance of "right instincts" for a successful
democracy and insisted that these can be developed only on the basis of
religious values. He saw a general Christian education for the nation as a
condition for the political success of democracy. He believed that without
the "leavening" of Christian values, democracy is in danger of falling into
either the extremes of individualism or the extremes of collectivism. It is the
task of the individual Christian to leaven society with those values that
undergird and strengthen democracy. Chief among these values Maritain
lists personalism, communitarianism, and pluralism.

Personalism is founded on the understanding of the human being as, in
Maritain's words, "a reality which, subsisting spiritually, constitutes a universe unto itself, relatively independent within the great whole of the universe and facing the transcendent Whole which is God."[24] As a person,
then, the man or woman is free, social, and spiritual, and possesses the rights
that Maritain lists in *The Rights of Man and Natural Law*. This closely antici-
pates a similar list in the United Nations Universal Declaration (1948) which
Maritain helped to plan.

Communitarianism denotes an attitude of concern for the good of the
whole community as opposed to an excessive individualism. Communitarianism has found expression in a wide range of social welfare laws promoted

---

[24] Quoted in Hudson and Mancini, eds., *Understanding Maritain*, p. 158.

by Maritain's followers. What distinguishes it from *collectivism* is the belief—articulated by Aquinas in his *Summa*—that man is not ordained to the political community but to God.

As to *pluralism,* Maritain called specifically for "an organic heterogeneity in the very structure of civil society." This would include autonomy for regional and minority groups, decentralization, and diversification of public functions. He quotes Pius XI on subsidiarity, which the pope defined as "an injustice, a grave evil, and a disturbance of right organization for a larger and higher organization to arrogate to itself functions which can be performed efficiently by smaller and lower bodies."[25]

Looking at the history of the struggle for freedom, Maritain noted how medieval society did justice to the spiritual side of man but was unable to develop the institutions necessary for full expression of human freedom. Modern times, on the other hand, saw a great expansion of human freedom but tragically this was accompanied by the rejection of God, the only guarantor of human freedom. Here Rousseau's anthropocentric views had enormous influence. The result has been an excessive individualism, materialism, and egalitarianism that opened the door to totalitarian solutions such as communism.

In examining the origins of modern democracy, Maritain found that it had gotten off on the wrong track and he traced the cause of modern democracy's parlous state to its beginnings. He was convinced that bad ideas have bad consequences, and he believed that two bad ideas had poisoned the spiritual wellsprings of modern democracy: One was Descartes' dualistic view of human nature, and the other was Rousseau's atomistic view. Descartes held that human beings consist of two distinct and separate substances, the mind and the body; this means that "knowers are sundered from the world of objects; all they can grasp of that world are its appearances. If it were not for their faith in God, human beings would despair of there being any congruence between what they think they know and the nature of the world of extended bodies outside of them."[26] He thus split man into a natural creature and a "believing double" who could pursue his material self-interests while confining to a separate sphere whatever spiritual concerns he might have. Behold the source of untrammeled individualism, the creed of the emergent bourgeois! Democracy developed to the extent that it coincided with the interests of this social class.

---

[25] *Quadragesimo Anno* (1931).
[26] Hudson and Mancini, eds., *Understanding Maritain,* pp. 133–134.

Rousseau completed the damage wrought by Descartes. He imagined the individual in nature as self-sufficient but transformed, through the social contract, into a fragment of the whole. Individuals were merely the atoms of a society that is ruled by the general will.

In the darkest hours of the Second World War, Maritain spoke of the tragedy of the modern democracies that had not yet realized democracy. He saw two main reasons for this failure. First, the modern states had evolved a political democracy but not a social democracy. Second, they failed to secure the proper foundation for democracy in the values of the Gospel—primarily, belief in the person's infinite worth and the unity of mankind. The Christian origins of the democratic impulse, in sum, had been lost. But the other extreme—the modern freedom-destroying totalitarian societies—were if anything even more bereft of spiritual life, spiritually empty cities swept by the acrid winds of materialism. There was at least a chance, he felt, for the democracies to recover their roots in Christian and natural law and a belief in the person's dignity, whereas restoration to spiritual health seemed most unlikely in the case of communism.

Democracy, in other words, was for him basically a moral enterprise and he warned that it would perish when people lost belief in the moral values that undergird it. Belief in the dignity of the human person and in human rights, human equality, freedom, law, mutual respect and tolerance, the unity of mankind and the ideal of peace, was essential for the survival of democracy.

Maritain's reading of Thomas on democracy shows how he was able to penetrate beyond the letter to the spirit of Aquinas's work. Most of his Thomist contemporaries opposed democracy as Thomas had favored a mixed form of government made up of aristocratic, oligarchic, and democratic components. But Maritain realized that Thomas could hardly have opposed democracy as we know it since it hadn't yet developed. What was of abiding importance was his claim that the legitimacy of a government resided in the people.[27]

During the Second World War Maritain's thoughts about democracy came to maturity. As we've seen, some of his earlier writings show a certain diffidence in regard to democracy. But his time in America both before and during the war had a profound influence on his attitude toward democracy. As he said: "In actual fact, it is in America that I have had a real experience of concrete existential democracy . . . Here I met democracy as a living

[27] Ibid., p. 151.

reality."[28] Maritain undertook an intense study of democracy which led to the writing of a number of books, from *Christianity and Democracy* (1943) to *Man and the State* (1951).

As the war developed, Maritain became increasingly generous in his appreciation of the United States. His book *Integral Humanism* betrayed an outlook that was thoroughly European, but as his experience of the United States broadened he realized that in many respects it was closer than old Europe to his ideal of a new Christendom. Like any concrete historical ideal, his new Christendom was far distant from any present reality, but many of its characteristics were perceptible in the United States. It was, for instance, a classless society in the social sense. It was also, he insisted, a religious society that he believed would remain resistant to the forces of secularization that were elsewhere so powerful. He also saw it moving beyond capitalism to becoming a society of communities and persons. In its separation of state and society, and in its guarantees of separate juridical and political bodies, the United States approximated his pluralist ideal. Finally, as the focus of all the really progressive energies since the breakup of the Middle Ages, it embodied the hope of mankind for the future and for the possibilities of a new Christendom. It was this wholehearted appreciation of American liberal democracy that "baptized him as a liberal and made him indisputably an adherent to the tenets of freedom, brotherhood and social justice."[29]

Legacy

As for Maritain's influence on the Church in general, we must keep in mind that many of the ideas he fought for have become part of conventional wisdom in the Church. Two of the most important documents of the 1960s, the Vatican Council's *Declaration on Religious Freedom* and Pope Paul VI's encyclical *Populorum Progressio,* bear the imprint of Maritain's thought, and the latter even cites him.

Some features of his political thought might be questioned. For instance, his straining for the middle ground sometimes gives the impression of artificiality. Moreover, one might also question his contention that integral humanism and a sound democracy demand a citizenry with strong religious convictions. After all, it was the rationalists and skeptics of the Enlighten-

---

[28]Doering, *Jacques Maritain and the French Catholic Intellectuals,* p. 179.
[29]Amato, *Mounier and Maritain,* pp. 156–157.

ment who paved the way for modern democracy. Moreover, history shows the potential for civil strife that religion can have.

But it seems likely that a hundred years from now Maritain's political writings will still be read. His specific achievements are as follows: 1) He established a Thomistic basis for democracy, religious pluralism, and human rights, and thus played a major role in reconciling the Church with democracy. 2) He moved the Church's traditional critique of liberalism in a more positive direction. His philosophy of personalism actually incorporated most of liberalism's principles within a more socially oriented perspective. 3) He thus provided a theoretical justification for the welfare state and for agrarian reform and worker participation. 4) Finally, he helped to open a ghettoized Catholicism to other religions and philosophical traditions while maintaining a strong Thomistic outlook seasoned by a more socially oriented alternative—personalism. 5) At the same time he provided a solid philosophical foundation for the Christian democratic parties that flourished in Europe and Latin America after the Second World War. All in all, in his efforts to bring about a more positive relationship of the Church with contemporary culture he carried on the work of such pioneers as Lamennais and Sturzo.

Nietzsche to the Rescue

While Maritain during the postwar period continued to pursue his Thomistic speculations on matters of social and political morality, Mounier moved in a totally different direction. He saw a great crisis ahead for the Church, and the need for a profound renewal if it was to survive. It must begin, he felt, by facing the brutal fact that it had almost completely lost its way. It had become just a façade for the bourgeoisie who used it to shore up its own mediocre and conservative values. To arouse it from its slumbers, Mounier turned to Nietzsche, whose critique of the Church and Christianity he thought was the most trenchant and the closest to the truth. He made this point in his book on the future of Christianity *L'Affrontement Chrétien,* and in another work on the formation of character. These writings reflected his own deeply personal experience of the Church, which he now saw as a major source of spiritual and psychological problems going all the way back to his youth.

Mounier used Nietzsche only as a means of provoking the Church to self-scrutiny. For he felt that Nietzsche's critique was valid only as regards certain perversions of Christianity. He therefore warned Christians against those perversions and he pointed out ways in which the perversions could be overcome.[30] One sees here one of the signs of the widespread movement of renewal and reappraisal that was beginning to surface in the Church and culminated in Vatican II.

Mounier chose Nietzsche as the acid test because he thought Nietzsche's analysis of the Christian character amazingly on target. He agreed with Nietzsche that Christianity was indeed a religion of the weak, of cowards afraid of the future, of colorless virgins who had lost the fire in their bellies. Mounier noted that he was often nauseated by the stupid sad look on the faces of people entering and leaving a church. By its obsession with sex the Church had emasculated the souls who were its captives, while the Christian family had conspired with the Church to turn its children into spiritual eunuchs. Nietzsche blamed puritanical sex education for "that awkwardness before life, that puerile timidity and sense of constraint" that characterized many Christians.[31]

The stress on humility, authoritarian methods of teaching, and moral intimidation, Mounier agreed, which in their medieval formulation were intended to temper the brutal manners of a violent age, now produced browbeaten individuals without strength or joy. The exaltation of obedience in and out of season robbed the young Christian of his rightful spiritual autonomy, and a morbid obsession with suffering for its own sake maimed sensitive temperaments. He added that even the Christian virtue of charity could be perverted into a lukewarm sentimentality, a spineless refusal to stand up for the truth, and a neurotic retreat into childishness.

Among the other ills of Christianity that Mounier singled out was its tendency to hyperintellectualism. Maritain's metaphysical speculations had never greatly interested Mounier and now he began to see them in Jungian terms, as a way of avoiding life. Again, the spirituality encouraged by the Church, he came to realize, was often a form of self-deception or vanity or psychosis. Psychiatry had revealed much about the way the "undisciplined imaginings of feeble souls" had invaded Christian spirituality.

In other words, he maintained, the Christianity we know is not the Christianity of Jesus Christ; it is the corrupted bourgeois version, which in effect isn't Christianity at all. The so-called "Christian" has been unmasked as just another bourgeois *gentilhomme,* no longer motivated by faith, hope, and charity but by "security, economy, social immobility and measured

[30]Kelly, *Pioneer of the Catholic Revival,* p. 122.
[31]Hellman, *Mounier and the New Catholic Left,* pp. 191–192.

ambitions."[32] If a real test of faith were to come we might not find a single Christian left in the world. "We might [then] have to search in the byways and thickets for that heroic Christianity which shall remake, in boldness of life, a new vision of the eternal tradition."[33]

Other Catholics at the time looked for renewal of the Church in the recovery of its dynamic intellectual tradition. Maritain and others believed the battle had to be fought in the realm of philosophy, where the spirit of radical subjectivism and skepticism had corroded the faith of modern man. Mounier himself had entered into the effort to recover the dynamic intellectual tradition of Christianity. He had pursued the interior life with Chevalier, philosophy with the Maritains and Berdyaev, scripture with Father Pouget (the friend of the modernist Alfred Loisy), plus study of the fathers, the saints, and the mystics on his own. But now he did a 180-degree turn. It was not a weak intellectual basis that had caused the modern apostasy, he was now convinced; it was the image of the Christian that was projected by the Church. For example, he asked, why has the Church lost the working man? Not because of his intellectual doubts but because the typical bourgeois Christian style of life was so repulsive. To become a Christian, in that sense, would make the worker feel he had lost some of his humanity.

Nevertheless Mounier was convinced that in spite of all its faults and failures, Christianity was inherently a dynamic and aggressive faith that was capable of creativity and adventure. It was able to overcome both life and death and held the key to self-transcendence. These virile qualities gave Mounier confidence in Christianity's power to survive the coming upheaval, which he expected would be all-encompassing. He thus turned his back on the static Catholicism he had long identified with in favor of a Christianity that was open to change, a dynamic, vital, and forward-looking faith. The stable fixed universe of Thomism he traded in for an evolving universe. Aquinas's ontological insights were not as meaningful for him as Pascal's gropings for "faith is a wager." He called his new version of the faith a Christian agnosticism and reveled in the paradox. He agreed with Nietzsche's rejection of abstract philosophy, and he was sure there was no future for the kind of intellectual system-making so beloved of Maritain. What would draw people to Christianity would be true communities of committed persons. The Catholicism of the majority was no longer distinguishable in his mind from the bourgeois culture he loathed.

[32] Ibid., p. 194.
[33] Ibid., p. 195.

No doubt this spiritual revolution of Mounier was a significant moment in the history of French Catholicism. His Nietzschean personalist Christianity seemed to offer real possibilities for the reform of Christianity.

Esprit *Faces a Changed World*

A new chapter in *Esprit* history opened up with the end of the war. In post-liberation France, Mounier and *Esprit* occupied a unique position of influence and prestige. No other ideology within Catholicism could match personalism in comprehensiveness and appeal. Its insistence on the central value of the human person was generally acknowledged as the keystone of Catholic social thought. Personalism thus occupied a vanguard position in the French Church's spiritual and intellectual struggles with its ideological rivals. Its analysis of existentialism provided a solid alternative to the better-known version of Jean-Paul Sartre.

But *Esprit* itself was no longer the review of the young nor *the* voice of an intellectual generation, as before the war. Nor could it any longer count on a closely knit, intensely committed network of supporters who were dedicated to personalist principles and spread across Europe. Finally, its mission had changed: It now had to deal with a total recasting of the political forces in France. Two parties that before the war had little influence emerged in 1944 as the two strongest—the Communists and the Christian Democrats (MRP).

Very important for *Esprit*'s future was the changed situation of the Catholic Church. The hierarchy had suffered a loss of moral authority because of its ambiguous role and, to some extent, identification with Pétain and the Vichy regime. Likewise the conservative and traditionalist wing was scarred. The initiative therefore fell into the hands of the progressives who were able to project a new image of the Church as a partner in the rebuilding of France. A number of the most prominent leaders of the postwar reconstruction were in fact Catholics, including General de Gaulle, the president of the national council; Georges Bidault, head of the Christian Democratic MRP; and Maurice Schumann, the prime minister. In general, Catholics were much more visible in the public life of France than before the war. Moreover, the failure of the Pétain regime to resurrect a "Catholic France" had laid this myth to rest for good and the Church was no longer considered a threat. Finally, many young Catholics involved in the resistance, like Mounier, had broken out of the ghetto of the Catholic Right. They were anxious to continue the dialogue with the Socialists and Communists already begun in wartime.

Anxious to take a leading role in the dialogue, Mounier rushed back to Paris as soon as it was possible and managed to publish the first edition of the new *Esprit* in December 1944, the first review to appear in liberated France. He was able to clear up some ambiguities in *Esprit*'s wartime role by cleverly rewriting its history, touching up the shadows in its relations with Vichy and highlighting its stance of opposition to Pétain's regime that had ultimately caused its suppression. As a result *Esprit* was looked on as one of France's major cultural and political reviews.

In the mood of national euphoria, many, like Mounier, hoped that the three major political forces—the Communists, the Socialists, and the Christian Democrats—would be able to find common ground in bringing about a total renewal of the nation. However, he realized that the Socialists and Christian Democrats would be at a disadvantage in such a dialogue since they lacked the kind of solid doctrinal base that gave the Communists their strength. Hence he hoped to make personalism that base although he had some grave reservations about the Christian Democratic Party, the MRP. He felt it was loaded down with a dead weight of conservative supporters, though the progressives in the MRP gave him some hope.

Postwar Dialogue with the Communists

Various factors conspired to encourage the effort toward dialogue with the Communists. There was an anti-Americanism that was fostered by intellectuals like Mounier who regarded the United States as a bastion of unregenerate capitalism and the G.I.s as barbarians who played with life and war. He sarcastically alluded to the "luxurious American armies" and those American troops who didn't think Italian women beautiful because they were not neat and hygienic. All in all, he saw Americans as potential fascists who in perfect good conscience might someday unload the full weight of their technology on Europe in an effort to dominate the world.

As Hellman says, if Mounier's anti-Americanism was unusual for a French Catholic his attitude toward Christian Democracy was even more so.[34] But we must keep in mind Mounier's constant belief that history was moving toward a radical upheaval. If the historical opportunity was rightly seized it could lead to a moral and spiritual renewal. He called on Christians

---

[34]Ibid., p. 209.

not to fear the transformation of their traditional values. They should be bold and strong in destroying the former bourgeois capitalist structures and replacing them with socialist ones. But he thought the Christian Democratic Party lacked a true Christian spirit and feared that it might abort this revolution by giving shelter to the forces of reaction. The Communists on the other hand he regarded as the most likely agents of revolutionary change.

By May 1947 the good ship "tripartism" (the alliance of Christian Democrats, Communists, and Socialists) had foundered on the rocks of cold-war realities and the exclusion of the Communists from the government following their protest against its economic policy. At the same time the Communists were ousted from the governing coalitions of other Western European countries. Then, as the economy in France deteriorated, strikes and demonstrations occurred and were met with government repression. The response of the working class was divided, weakening them and isolating the Communist Party. France fell into the American orbit. But Mounier would have no part of the cold-war anticommunism that swept the West. He hoped instead for a fusion of the three main forces then vying with each other in France: the Socialists, the Communists, and the Christian Democrats. Personalism, he hoped, might serve as the ideological expression of their fundamental aspirations.

Moreover he now saw the possibility of a fruitful relationship between Marxism and Christianity. Previously he had spoken of going beyond Marxism, but he had now come to believe in the superiority of Marxism's economic and social analysis and its insights into alienation. Its most severe shortcoming was its failure to recognize the spiritual as an "autonomous primary creative reality." He believed therefore that Christian personalism could supply what Marxism lacked: *intériorité* (inwardness) and the sense of transcendence. He looked forward to a mutual surpassing of each other as together the two movements—Christian personalism and Marxism—"undertook the great and total exploration of the new man, in which all the lasting values of eternal man could be saved and transfigured."[35] As to the Communist hatred of religion, it was important to realize, Mounier insisted, that the Christianity hated by the Communists was not authentic Christianity but the bourgeois version that he had come to despise.

In opening up a dialogue he was determined to make a great effort to avoid the kind of polemics that might confuse the issues and harm the cause

[35] Ibid., p. 212.

of truth. It was a task of great difficulty, he admitted, but worth trying. He hoped such a dialogue might encourage the Communists to take a critical look at the limitations of Marxism. And he felt hopeful that Christian personalism could overcome some of these because of the dynamic principles that were built into it. His eventual aim was to get the Communists to temper their rigid economic determinism and admit that spiritual forces could also play a decisive role in events.

He noted his agreement with the Communist unmasking of liberalism as a "historical corruption tied to particular economic and social structures . . . a rootless liberty . . . while the essence of true liberty was to give oneself to something greater than oneself."[36] Communists and Christians, he claimed, were almost alone in the postwar epoch in "sharing faith in man and history." By a selective version of the Christian tradition he showed how much the Marxist and Christian views of history had in common. Citing Genesis and a variety of Christian sources he argued that Christians too believed in the potential of humanity to transform the earth into a realm of peace, joy, and freedom. As a recent example he cited the Jesuit Teilhard de Chardin's vision of humanity rendering nature divine through its own divinization. The static, pessimistic world-hating philosophy found among many Christians was actually, he tried to show, a misreading of the great Christian tradition. Sin he saw more as a social condition, and he downplayed the struggle between vice and virtue in the heart of the individual.

By 1949, however, his hopes for a fruitful dialogue with the Communists had considerably weakened. The coup d'état in Prague in early 1948 convinced Mounier that Stalinist Communists would use noncommunist groups to reach power but would dump them afterward. At the same time, the French Communists proved increasingly rigid and intolerant of criticism. Moreover, he was alarmed at the uncritical, naive pro-Communism of the *Chrétiens Progressistes* movement, some of whose members were his erstwhile disciples. They wanted to use Marx for their political analyses but the Christian faith in dealing with spiritual problems. Mounier, however, had begun to shy away from this approach for he believed that one's political philosophy was conditioned by one's understanding of man, and Marx was wrong about man.

Nevertheless Mounier remained convinced that the Left, including a reformed Communist party, was the best hope for the future. He redoubled his efforts to build bridges between the Left and the Communists and often

[36]Ibid., p. 214.

stood with the Stalinists on controversial issues, as in the case of the Atlantic pact, the Marshall Plan, and the trial of Cardinal Mindszenty. His efforts to promote dialogue with the Communist Party were blocked by the suspicions of the Communists that his real aim was to undermine them. But the Communists' charge of insincerity cannot be sustained. Mounier's diary and personal papers showed that Mounier hoped for a "personalization" of Communism that would have allowed him and his following to join a reformed Communist party. He lamented the fact that he had run into an "iron curtain of ideas, of feelings," and that while the enemies of Communism had done much to close off dialogue, the Communist Party "had hardened and installed itself . . . in an airtight system."[37]

As time passed, his hopes for revolutionary change faded. The Americanization of Europe proceeded apace and Europe faced gloomy prospects "with a democracy ruined by money and a socialism ruined by statism."[38] Amid all this intellectual *Sturm und Drang,* Mounier never wavered in his Catholic faith which was "lodged firmly, like a block of granite, at the centre of his life."[39] When the Vatican issued a decree in 1949 that forbade Catholics to join the Communist Party or collaborate with them in setting up a Communist state, he thought it a great mistake but he kept his feelings private.

Dialogue with Sartre

As he wrestled with this turn of events, Mounier increased his attention to the existentialist movement that had attained great popularity at the end of the war. He believed it could be most helpful in the dialogue with the Marxists. Its stress on the need of the person for *intériorité* could supply a needed corrective to Marxism's neglect of this aspect. Moreover, its concept of the person as free and yet called to decision also resonated with the personalist perspective.

To throw light on the movement as it then was, Mounier had already published his *Introduction aux Existentialismes* (Paris, 1947), which began with a history of existentialism tracing it back to Pascal as its chief precursor. One of Mounier's major aims was to highlight the Christian alternative to the atheistic existentialism of Nietzsche, Heidegger, and Jean-Paul Sartre. He

[37] Ibid., p. 239.
[38] Ibid., p. 237.
[39] Ibid., p. 240.

argued that, taken historically, existentialism was linked to a religious view of life, Kierkegaard being the most obvious example. The real challenge presented by existentialism, Mounier believed, was how to reconcile Kierkegaard and Marx.

In grappling with Sartre's opus he found much to agree with but rejected his key definition of man as totally free, totally indeterminate. Mounier argued rather that man was conditioned by a network of forces. Moreover, Sartre's idea of man as a nothingness *(le néant)* he characterized as a negative, impoverished, and humiliating view, an ontology of despair in place of the Christian ontology of hope. He also tried to show how Sartre's atheism logically removed the grounds of all morality. With no external point of reference to go by, any atrocity could be permitted on the basis of the agent's subjective intensity (Sartre's criterion of morality)—just as Marx's view of historical determinism could justify and did justify the basest atrocities.

Devotees of Sartre, of course, would not admit that Mounier had gotten the best of the argument, especially since he failed to give a coherent account of existentialism as a social and cultural movement and also failed to explain the great popularity of Sartre's version. But this established Mounier's reputation as an expert on existentialism and he was much in demand for public presentations on the topic. As far as Catholics were concerned, Mounier helped to make them aware of Christian existentialism and helped the progressives among them to entertain ideas of change and rethinking previously considered off-limits.

Mounier was often linked with Teilhard de Chardin as a Christian progressive and a believer in the future of a humanity transformed by the Christian religion. But in fact, near the end of his life, Mounier adopted an agnostic approach to future developments or what he called a "tragic optimism." No one could say, he argued, whether "a socialistic type of economic structure is better suited to the progress of the kingdom of God than a capitalist economy."[40]

His capacity for work remained enormous. He had to prepare a series of broadcasts for French and British audiences while also preparing conferences for *Esprit* and papers for UNESCO gatherings and other international meetings. At the same time he continued editing his journal as well as authoring many new publications. He drove himself unmercifully until his physical stamina could no longer support his mental powers. Warning signs

---

[40] Ibid., p. 245.

were given by several heart attacks he suffered, the first one in the fall of 1949. However, he kept going at the same pace, driven by his belief in the importance of generosity and self-donation. In the middle of the night of March 21–22, 1950, his wife heard him groan and then heard no further sound. He died of a heart attack.

Legacy: A Beacon for Progressive Catholics

In his effort to reassess the Church's place in the modern world, Mounier stood as a beacon for progressive Catholics who prepared the way for Pope John's great council. As Étienne Borne says, Mounier saw with astonishing clarity the coming storm that would shake Christianity to its foundations,[41] a crisis that would extend in fact to all forms of contemporary civilization. In particular he saw in both Catholicism and Communism an attempt to reinforce authoritarian structures, an attempt he believed would ultimately have a disintegrating effect on both. And, as Borne says, Mounier was that most unusual of philosophers, one totally involved in the battles of his time and therefore able to aliment his thought with his own experience of combat. He was ruthless in exposing the fallacies of those who were mere upholders of the status quo. But he was totally open to ideas from whatever source, provided they were cogent and sincerely held. They might seem mutually antagonistic but he would try to reconcile them on a deeper level. "Marx and Pascal," he might say.

Mounier's impact on the political and social thought of French Catholics was considerable. No longer confined to their extreme right-wing ghetto, they were now spread across the political spectrum with increasing numbers located in the left and progressive forces of the nation. Mounier definitely helped to bring this about by his insistence on questioning old habits of thought and on the need to adapt to the realities of a fast-changing world.

In seeking an alternative to both individualism and collectivism, Mounier, like Maritain, addressed a problem facing the Church since the French Revolution—namely, to find a political doctrine that would enable it to answer the challenge of liberalism and socialism.

In their defense of the person, the family and pluralism and in their aspiration to serve the worker and destroy the greatest abuses of capitalism, Mounier's and Maritain's social and political thought can be read as

[41]Étienne Borne, *Mounier* (Paris: Éditions Seghers, 1972), p. 138.

supporting commentaries on the social encyclicals of Pius IX, Leo XIII, Pius X and Pius XI. In this perspective the mixture of apocalyptical and eschatological tones of Mounier's and Maritain's considerations of the modern world reflect the Church's painful uncertainty about its security in the modern world and equally strong certainty that it has and will again be able to win the hearts of men and help them build their civilizations. Like Bloy and Péguy their views were a projection of their hopes for a world wherein the sacral and religious would infuse and enlighten the material, the political and the social; a world wherein men in all their thoughts and activities would measure themselves against the eternal verities of faith. Beyond what seemed to them the crumbling of one civilization, there appeared the possibility, the hope for a "New Middle Ages."[42]

Mounier's writings are today largely ignored by those who owe much to his ideas. The avant-garde in the Catholic student movements, the Catholic Action movements, the trade unions, industrial chaplaincies, peace and other social reform movements, and the like now look to other sources of inspiration—the documents of Vatican II and papal encyclicals as well as the scholarly tomes of economists, sociologists, and political scientists.[43]

Hellman cautions against a too simplistic view of Mounier as a bold, stolid, isolated left-wing Catholic before the war, a resistance hero during the war, a postwar pioneer in Christian–Marxist dialogue who helped transform French Catholicism from a reactionary pro-Pétain Church to the open Church of the worker priests and Teilhard de Chardin. Actually, Hellman maintains, the historical image is much more confused. Mounier was a "peculiar mixture of violent language and private timidity,"[44] a morass of hesitations and contradictions and unfortunately given to rewriting his own history at every turn. Nevertheless in the final analysis he stands as a herald of the open Church of Pope John, a Catholic who assumed the nearly impossible task of uniting left-wing political activists and devout religious believers.

"Thus Mounier could be committed to revolution and indifferent to politics, an enthusiastic admirer of the Marxists and an anti-Marxist, a communist sympathizer and an anti-communist, a purist democrat and an authoritarian. In his plethora of paradoxes he prefigured the new style of the

[42] Amato, *Mounier and Maritain,* pp. 145–146.
[43] Kelly, *Pioneer of the Catholic Revival,* p. 174.
[44] Hellman, *Mounier and the New Catholic Left,* p. 9.

Catholic Left after the Second Vatican Council. He had wanted, with his personalist formula, to restore perspective to the political passions of his day. Revolutions, he thought, should be made for people and not for abstractions and parties; when they were not made for people above all, they degenerated into destructive, fanatical aberrations."[45]

Mounier was the last of those who tried to form a synthesis and global vision of problems that pertain to different orders but are connected: religion, philosophy, politics. Or, as Étienne Borne points out, Mounier, Camus, and Sartre were the last ideologues who claimed to have ideas about "man." The epoch of attempts at broad comprehensive explanations of the world is long past.

Mounier called his vision of man a tragic optimism. Living through the nightmarish events of the 1930s and 1940s, he needed little reminder of the apparent absurdity of the human condition: the vain efforts expended in the cause of peace and justice, the anguish and pain on all sides, the anarchy, chaos, and corruption in political and social life, the deep sense of impending doom, the death, decay, and despair all around. But as a deeply committed Catholic, Mounier was able to sustain to the end a basic though tragic optimism, believing as he did that life was good and to be accepted as part of a loving God's creation, providence, and redemption. Above all, his belief in Christ's incarnation grounded his faith that man can transcend his own egotism and find in God his true self.

[45] Ibid., p. 252.

THIRTEEN

Dorothy Day (1897–1980): The Personalist Revolution, American Style

B Y ANY MEASURE, May 1, 1933 was not an ordinary day. In Moscow a million soldiers marched through Red Square as part of the vast Soviet May Day celebration. In Berlin a similarly huge number of Germans marched through the streets to honor their new chancellor, Adolf Hitler. And in Union Square, New York, 50,000 leftists gathered to hear speakers denounce Hitler and call for revolution. But for many American Catholics that May 1 is mainly remembered as the day that Dorothy Day walked into the rally on Union Square and began selling the *Catholic Worker* for a penny a copy. The small tabloid's statement of purpose was addressed to all those "sitting on park benches, or huddled in shelters or walking the streets in a vain search for work and . . . losing hope."[1] It wanted them to know that there were men of God working for their material as well as spiritual welfare in obedience to the popes who had called for a social order based on social justice.

---

[1] *Catholic Worker*, Vol. I, No. 1, 1933.

A Lot of Life

Dorothy Day was born November 8, 1897, in Brooklyn Heights, the third of five children of John and Grace Slaterlee Day. John was a newspaperman, a religious skeptic, fond of horse-racing and whiskey. "We children did not know him very well," Dorothy recounted in her autobiography, "so stood in awe of him, only learning to talk to him after we had left home and he began to treat us as friends—casual friends it is true, since he was always impatient with our ideas and hated the radical movement which both my sister and I were involved in later . . . But he was a good man and a happy man in his own circle and he enjoyed life greatly." Dorothy's mother "had a temperament which helped her through much hardship and uncertainty. She refused to worry when things were going badly and when the family had its periods of poverty . . . Whenever mother had extra troubles or a specially hard day's work behind her, she used to bathe and dress with particular care as though she were going to a dinner party. She reigned over

Ade Bethune, Dorothy Day, Dorothy Weston, Jacques Maritain, and Peter Maurin

the supper table as a queen and had as much interest in entertaining her . . . children as if we were all adult friends in for a party."[2]

Religious interests and influences began early in Dorothy's life. In 1904 John Day took a newspaper job in California, where the family eventually settled in Oakland. A devout Methodist family lived next door. Dorothy went to Sunday School and church with their young daughter. "Then I began to experience real piety, in the sense of the sweetness of faith. I believed, but I did not know in what I believed. I became disgustingly, proudly pious. I sang hymns with the family next door. I prayed on my knees beside my bed. I asked my mother why we did not pray and sing hymns and got no satisfactory answer. No one went to church but me. I was alternately lonely and smug."[3] Around this same time, though, Dorothy also began to feel "afraid of God, of death, of eternity."[4] Many nights she fell to sleep and dreamed of God as a "great noise that became louder and louder, and approached nearer to me until I woke up sweating with fear and shrieking for my mother."[5] Later in life, Dorothy wondered whether these nightmares happened before or after the San Francisco earthquake.

The great earthquake struck in 1906, devastating nearby San Francisco and badly damaging Oakland. The young Dorothy awakened from sleep to feel her bed rolling back and forth on the polished floor while from her window she could see water splashing out of a water tank nearby. John Day's place of work was destroyed in the earthquake and the family left Oakland as soon as possible, moving to Chicago where they lived in a dingy tenement flat.

Unable now to afford household help, and in poor health because of a series of miscarriages, Dorothy's mother needed the help of her daughters. Both Dorothy and her sister felt very important to be taking on the home responsibilities and knowing that their mother counted on them. The work grew tiresome after a while, but Dorothy had become accustomed to "doing her share." "Without knowing it," she later wrote, "I had imbibed 'a philosophy of work,' enjoying the creative aspect of it as well as getting satisfaction from a hard and necessary job well done."[6]

Dorothy's budding spiritual life took a formative turn, too. She made friends with her twelve-year-old Catholic neighbor, a girl named Mary.

---

[2] Dorothy Day, *The Long Loneliness* (New York: Harper and Row, 1952), p. 27.
[3] Ibid., p. 20.
[4] Ibid.
[5] Ibid.
[6] Ibid., p. 24.

One night as they lay out on the back porch, tired from their day's work, Mary recounted for Dorothy the life of one of the saints. The particulars were soon forgotten, but not Dorothy's "thrilling recognition of the possibilities of spiritual adventure."[7] One day, too, Dorothy happened upon another neighbor, Mrs. Barrett, taking a few minutes for prayer while her children were down at the corner store, "I felt a burst of love toward Mrs. Barrett that I have never forgotten, a feeling of gratitude and happiness that warmed my heart." Dorothy realized in retrospect that it was the kind Mrs. Barrett who through their encounters "gave me my first impulse toward Catholicism."[8]

By the age of ten, Dorothy's joy in the goodness of creation demanded an expression greater than she could shape. She found that expression in the Psalms: "Whenever I felt the beauty of the world in song or story, in the material universe around me, or glimpsed it in human love, I wanted to cry out with joy. The Psalms were an outlet for this enthusiasm of joy or grief . . . My idea of heaven became one of friends and meadows, sweet with flowers and songs and melodies unutterable, in which even the laughing gull and the waves on the shore would play their part."[9] Dorothy and her brothers attended the nearby Episcopal church, where the prayers and the anthems made an indelible mark on her.

John Day finally found a job as a sports editor and the family was able to move to a spacious house with a library where Dorothy could indulge her passion for books. During her last year of high school her reading took a sharp turn to the left. The writings of authors like the anarchist Peter Kropotkin made her aware of the plight of the poor, and on her daily strolls with her new baby brother, she explored the grim west side of Chicago where she saw for herself the ravages of social injustice. The poor and the workers whom she saw living in squalor were not, she felt, a shiftless lot deserving of their fate, as the smug middle-class morality would have it. They were victims of a heartless society. She sensed that "from then on my life was to be linked with theirs." To identify with the oppressed she deliberately sought out jobs that demanded hard physical labor and taxed her to the limit while she pursued a college education.

She also began earning small amounts by writing. Dorothy had a great love of words and the way they could conjure up the endless variety of

[7] Ibid.
[8] Ibid., p. 25.
[9] Ibid., p. 29.

human experience. She read the history of the labor movement and took a great interest in the careers of Big Bill Haywood, Mother Jones, Elizabeth Gurley Flynn, Eugene Debs, Carlo Tresca, and the Haymarket martyrs (labor organizers hanged in Chicago). "Her heart thrilled at those unknown women in New England who led the first strikes to liberate women and children from the cotton mills."[10] She formed a close friendship with Rayna Simons, a young Jewish girl who died a few years later in Moscow while preparing to become a revolutionist.

Once again the family moved, this time back to New York. Dorothy was eighteen and unable to stand her father's opinions so she decided to find a job and an apartment of her own. She rented a squalid little apartment in a neighborhood where mothers hung over fire escapes and crowds of children played in the gutters. No ordinary newspaper would hire a woman reporter but she was able to twist the arm of the editor of the Socialist daily *The Call,* and got hired. These were heady days. She covered a speech by Elizabeth Gurley Flynn—later a leader of the American Communist Party—and was so impressed by her description of the misery of the mineworkers in Minnesota that she emptied her purse when a collection was taken and had to skip lunch for some days afterward. She also interviewed Leon Trotsky who later helped launch the Russian Revolution. One of her closest friends and a coworker at the time was the socialist writer Mike Gold, who shared her radical opinions but not her bed, in spite of gossip to the contrary. Another friend more liberal in her sexual habits was Peggy Baird, an artist who managed to sketch Dorothy in the nude but was unable to get her to doff her stricter sexual ethic. (Fifty years later Peggy became a Catholic and ended up with Dorothy at the Catholic Worker.)

On March 21, 1917 at Madison Square Garden, in the words of William Miller, Dorothy joined with thousands in reliving the first days of the revolt in Russia. "I felt the exultation, the joyous sense of victory of the masses as they sang . . . the workers' hymn of Russia," described in *The Call* as a "mystic, gripping melody of struggle, a cry for world peace and human brotherhood."[11]

After a quarrel that erupted when a radical tried to kiss her at the Anarchist Ball, she moved on to the staff of *The Masses,* the premiere organ of the American Left. She rubbed elbows with its brilliant intellectual editor John Reed, who later founded the American Communist Party and wrote a

[10] Ibid., pp. 46–47.
[11] William Miller, *A Harsh and Dreadful Love* (New York: Liveright, 1973), p. 46.

famous eyewitness account of the Russian Revolution, *Ten Days That Shook the World*. That year *The Masses* took a stand against America's involvement in the First World War and was suppressed by the government, but not before Dorothy managed to get out its last issue in December 1917.

At the age of twenty Dorothy had already seen a lot of life: She had left college after one year, struck out on her own in a new city, faced all the craziness of New York as a reporter, and lost two jobs in quick succession. She had cradled in her arms a young man overdosed from heroin, been brutally jailed following a suffragist demonstration at the White House, and seen the world turned upside down by war. Now she struck up an acquaintance with a playwright whom she met in a saloon in Greenwich Village. His first play, *Bound East for Cardiff,* had just proved a resounding success but he was depressed and drinking heavily after the end of his affair with John Reed's wife, Louise Bryant. Eugene O'Neill and Dorothy became fast friends. They had much to share: Both worked as reporters, both were writers, both were drawn to outcasts, and both were haunted by a sense of God's presence. One of her most vivid memories of O'Neill was listening to him intone from memory Francis Thompson's *The Hound of Heaven*. Dorothy often found much comfort in dropping into St. Joseph's Church on Sixth Avenue where the people in silent adoration gave her a feeling of warmth and hope. O'Neill understood. The two friends often walked the streets in the late hours and sometimes Dorothy had to put O'Neill to bed, drunk and shaking with the terrors that tormented him. But they never became lovers. It wasn't what she wanted. She felt close to him because he seemed to have the same sense of loneliness and emptiness that drove her to visit those churches.

Beginning to feel the emptiness of the bohemian life, Dorothy sought a new way to serve the poor and the suffering. She took a job as a hospital orderly cleaning bedpans, giving baths and rubs, and changing bedsheets and dressings. The flu epidemic of 1919 was raging and the hospital was crowded with dying patients. An orderly named Lionel Moise worked with her, undressing longshoremen and helping to cart dead bodies down to the morgue. Moise was a macho, a drifter who had seen a lot of the world while working in all sorts of jobs—deckhand on a freighter, movie cameraman in Latin America. Currently he was working off a hospital bill he had incurred after being mugged and brought in unconscious. Dorothy fell insanely in love with him, moved into his apartment, and waited on him like a slave. When they quarreled and broke up she apparently tried suicide but survived and resumed the affair. Dorothy then discovered she was pregnant. Fearful that Moise would leave her if she had the child, she made the agonized decision to have an abortion. Moise took off anyway, leaving some money and a farewell note.

Her next move was "marriage on the rebound" to Barkeley Tobey, a wealthy man twenty years her senior. During a trip abroad she spent six months on the isle of Capri and forever after associated it with the smell of spaghetti and red wine. The marriage lasted only a year but it gave her the leisure to write a novel, *The Eleventh Virgin*. After leaving Tobey she headed for Chicago hoping to resume her affair with Moise. She ended up in jail after being arrested in the famous Palmer raids on the pretext that the rooming house she stayed at was in fact a brothel. It was a most terrifying experience. Made to undress before armed men, "we were given prison clothes and put in cells . . . a woman in the next cell beat her head against the bars and howled like a wild animal."[12] In the end Dorothy regarded the experience thankfully, for it made her more aware of all those thousands upon thousands of workers who had suffered much more—beatings, maimings, even murder while standing up for the rights of labor.

Upon release she once more got a job as a reporter and rented a room owned by three Catholic women. Seeing their daily life, their devotion, their high moral standards, she began to feel that Catholicism was something rich and fascinating and felt drawn again to the Church of the immigrants and the masses of poor.

Finally managing to disconnect from Moise, and after a stint down South as a reporter for the *New Orleans Item,* Dorothy's fortunes changed dramatically when she received a windfall from the sale of *The Eleventh Virgin* to Hollywood. Then it was back to Greenwich Village, where she hooked up with the literary crowd there including Allen Tate, Hart Crane, and John Dos Passos.

Realizing that she needed peace and quiet if she was to write, Dorothy bought a beach house on Staten Island. Thus began the four most joy-filled years of her life. Once again she fell in love, this time with a marine biologist, anarchist, and gifted fisherman, Forster Batterham. They agreed to live together on weekends and Dorothy had the rest of the time to herself to enjoy the sounds of the sea, the cries of the gulls, and the noise of children at play. She loved Forster madly "in every way, as a wife, as a mother even. I loved his lean and cold body as he got into bed smelling of the sea and I loved his integrity and stubborn pride." It pained her that he

[12]Day, *The Long Loneliness,* p. 104.

was so against marriage and had no desire to bring children into what he saw as a heartless and cruel world. Nor could she understand how he could deny God's existence when the world was so full of beauty. She found herself praying more frequently, the rosary especially, and took special delight in praying before a statue of Mary.

Having long assumed that she was unable to have a child because of her abortion, she was stupefied one day to find she was pregnant. It was bad news to Forster, but Dorothy was delirious with joy. Tamar Theresa was born on March 3, 1927. Dorothy had to record her experience on paper; her article "On Having a Baby" was printed in *The New Masses* and was highly praised in the radical press around the world.

The overwhelming joy she felt turned her even closer to God. "No human creature," she said, "could receive or contain so vast a flood of love and joy as I felt after the birth of my child. With this came the need to worship, to adore. I heard many say they did not need a Church to praise Him but my very experience as a radical, my whole make-up, led me to associate myself with others, with the masses, in praising and adoring God."[13] The only way Dorothy could really express the depth of her feeling at the birth of the child was to have Tamar baptized. She knew it would enrage Forster and his friends, who saw the Church as a tyrannical and oppressive institution condemned by its own history. But Dorothy refused to deal with the argument on those grounds. The Church she saw was the Church whose portals were crowded with people coming and going, the Church that had shepherded the masses throughout the centuries. She met a nun, Sister Aloysia, while out walking on the beach and asked her how she could get her child baptized.

Forster reacted predictably and tension began to build. In spite of his first reaction, however, Forster was delighted with his little daughter, and Dorothy began to hope that he might change his mind about marriage too. But it was not to be. At this time, too, the immigrant Italian anarchists Sacco and Vanzetti were executed for murder after a trial that riveted the attention of the nation and the world. Forster and Dorothy were both griefstricken at what they saw as a horrible miscarriage of justice. Forster saw it also as an indictment of the Church, which had stood by unprotesting. The differences between the two finally exploded and Forster left, slamming the door. For Dorothy, it was the moment of truth. She called the parish priest and made arrangements to be received into the Church. Later she recalled how

[13] Ibid., p. 139.

little joy she had felt on the day of her baptism and how divided were her thoughts. Was she betraying the victims of injustice and oppression by entering a Church whose priests so often ignored the poor and said nary a word about social justice? Why so much talk about charity and so little about social justice? As Dorothy later remembered, "I felt that charity was a word to choke over."

"Hello, I Am Peter Maurin"

The next five years were dark ones for Dorothy. She missed her old radical friends and felt alone in a Church that seemed so distant from her social concerns. It was a time of intense searching as she tried to find a way of making a living for herself and Tamar and also devote herself to social action. An offer of a job writing dialogue for the Pathe Motion Picture Company brought her and Tamar to Hollywood in the summer of 1929, but it proved to be a short sojourn as both the job and the atmosphere of the studio depressed her.

After a trip to Mexico where the lively faith of the people greatly impressed her, she returned to New York. On the advice of her confessor she began a practice that would become lifelong—attending daily mass and receiving Communion. But the Great Depression was now in its second year and her dismay at the lack of leadership by the Church was matched by the awareness of her own lack of involvement on behalf of the poor and unemployed. She decided to join the great Hunger March of winter 1932–1933. The marchers walked from New York to Washington, D.C., decrying their own desperate plights and calling for jobs, old-age pensions, relief for mothers and children. Largely ignored by the popular press, along the route the marchers were regularly harassed by police using tear-gas and clubs. When they reached Washington, Dorothy stood on the curb feeling pride in the marchers' courage and dedication to justice, and at the same time sorrow that it was the Communists and not the Christians who had organized the action. Thinking to herself, "How our dear Lord must love them," she walked to the Shrine of the Immaculate Conception where she knelt in the crypt and prayed tearfully that God would show her some way to use her talents for the poor.

Little did she realize that her prayer was to be answered by the poorly dressed gentleman who knocked on the door of her apartment after her return to New York. "I am Peter Maurin," he said. "George Shuster [editor of *Commonweal*] told me to look you up. Also, a red-headed Irish Communist in Union Square told me to see you. He says we think alike." Dorothy at the moment was tired from her trip to Washington and not in a receptive mood. But he returned again the next day and was able to get her full attention. Peter, it seems, had already decided on the basis of her articles, information he had picked up, and his own impressions that Dorothy was a woman of destiny, a twentieth-century Catherine of Siena, sent by God to renew the Church as Catherine had done in her day.

Peter Maurin: a Gentle Radical

Peter Maurin was born in 1877, the eldest of his father's twenty-three children. His mother's name was Marie Pages; she bore her husband five children and died in 1885. Peter's father remarried and eighteen more children followed. Peter's forebears had been peasants from time out of mind. The family lived in a small French village two hundred miles from Barcelona. Peter's parents did not speak French, but rather a Catalonian dialect. In 1882 public school education was made mandatory in every village and thus Peter and his brothers and sisters were afforded an education. Many of them later entered religious life.

Peter left home to work at the age of fourteen. In time he taught at a Christian Brothers' school in Paris, and always pursued his own voracious course of reading and study. While with the Brothers he was inducted into the military and served for a year. It was a bad year for he hated the whole business—the training to kill, the low moral standards, and the loss of individual dignity. His interest in politics and advanced ideas on pacifism and social organization stemmed from this experience. On January 1, 1903, when his annual vows expired, he left the Brothers and joined a study circle under the influence of Marc Sangnier's twice-weekly newspaper, *Le Sillon* (not to be confused with the socially progressive, Catholic decentralist *Sillon* movement). *Le Sillon* "understood the chaos of the times," Peter once explained to Dorothy, but he became disillusioned of finding a suitable response to the chaos in the events and ideas then surrounding him. "I did not like the idea of revolution. I did not like the French Revolution, nor the English Revolution. I did not wish to work to perpetuate the proletariat so I never became a member of a union. Besides I was an unskilled worker. I was always interested in the land and men's life on the land."[14]

"That is why I went homesteading to Canada in 1909, but after two

[14]Ibid., p. 177–178.

years, when my partner was killed, I moved about the country with work gangs and entered this country in 1911, where I have been ever since."[15]

"Peter," Dorothy later wrote, worked "on farms, in brickyards, in steel mills, at every kind of unskilled labor, from Chicago to New York . . . He settled in Chicago for awhile and made a successful living teaching French . . . He read constantly, he worked and he taught."[16]

One of the strongest convictions he had acquired in all his variegated experience was a Franciscan sense of the beauty of poverty. He lived totally at the mercy of circumstance, depending for food and lodging on whatever money he might happen to make at his odd jobs. His unencumbered life-style allowed him ample time for reading and study and he gradually shaped a very personal vision of the kind of social order he thought the Gospel called for. Always eager to talk about it with whomever, he loved to frequent the steps of the New York Public Library or the area around Union Square where he could buttonhole people.

Many humorous stories are told about the unkempt, seedy-looking Maurin as he made his speaking rounds. On one occasion he was supposed to speak at a women's club in Westchester but Dorothy received a frantic telephone call from the ladies who said he hadn't showed up. Since she had put him on the train herself, she told them he must be in the station. "But there's no one there but an old tramp sitting on the bench asleep," came the reply. "We knew it had to be Peter," Dorothy said.[17]

Peter found three contemporary groups of thinkers particularly sympathetic with his own concerns, and all of these became major influences within the Catholic Worker movement. These groups were the French personalists, the Russian anarchists, and the English distributists.

Emmanuel Mounier's journal *Esprit* was launched in 1932, and Peter Maurin instantly recognized a kindred spirit. Maurin subscribed wholeheartedly to the personalist belief in the absolute value of each person and he rejected any political system—fascism, communism, or capitalism—that denied it in practice. Mounier's early mentor Jacques Maritain became a personal friend of the Catholic Worker movement during the time of his American exile during the Second World War. And Mounier and Maurin both drew on such thinkers as Proudhon, Léon Bloy, and Charles Peguy. Maurin was particularly impressed by Bloy's view of voluntary poverty as a

[15] Ibid.
[16] Ibid.
[17] Miller, *A Harsh and Dreadful Love*, p. 19.

straight path to freedom and to God, while at the same time asserting the diabolical consequences of poverty for the poor who had no choice. The contrast between voluntary poverty and destitution would be a central theme in Catholic Worker thought.

Among the Russians, Peter was most influenced by Kropotkin and Berdyaev. The former's *Fields, Factories, and Workshops* offered a radical alternative to the social Darwinism so popular at the time. Contrary to the idea that human beings are destined by nature to be pitted against one another in a ruthless struggle, Kropotkin argued that people are naturally cooperative and that society can be organized around these positive tendencies.

Berdyaev's Christian vision found the meaning of history in the incarnation and redemption as achieving the fulfillment of human personality. For Berdyaev, Christ is freedom incarnate, and human history is the continual struggle of persons to become free, creative, and responsible. The human persona must always be a subject, not an object. But there is a constant tendency to objectify the other person by using him or her as a means to satisfy one's own lust, desire for power, or wish for comfort. Such objectification is depersonalizing. Only by going out to the other person in works of mercy, love, liberation, and justice does one achieve one's own freedom and perfection and foster the same in others.

The liberal systems (which foster "progress") and the Marxist system (aimed toward "material satisfaction") both work against human freedom because both manipulate the person through the use of social force, rather than freeing persons within society to live in accordance with their full human dignity. Peter found himself in agreement with the social thought of the so-called English distributists, Catholic thinkers such as Eric Gill, G. K. Chesterton, and Hilaire Belloc, who favored a broad distribution of land and capital rather than the concentration in the hands of an elite few. The distributist vision of a decentralized economy of land-owning farmers, artisans, and small business owners has been criticized as a nostalgic version of the Middle Ages as they never were; but as Mel Piehl notes, "the English movement was essential in pointing Day and others toward what became enduring concerns of the group: the spiritual nature of work, the oppressively large scale of modern society, the necessary connection of property and responsibility and the quality of everyday life."[18]

[18]Mel Piehl, *Breaking Bread: The Catholic Workers and the Origin of Catholic Radicalism in America* (Philadelphia: Temple University Press, 1982), p. xx.

"A Philosophy So Old It Looks Like New"

While Peter Maurin adopted the term "personalism" to describe his philosophy, his thinking was not founded on what Piehl calls "the visionary Gallic abstractions" of Mounier and *L'Esprit*.[19] Rather, Maurin's philosophy started with the teaching of St. Thomas Aquinas on the nature of the human person. As Maurin expressed it in one of his "Easy Essays":

> According to St. Thomas Aquinas
> man is more
> than an individual
> with individual rights;
> he is a person
> with personal duties
> toward God,
> and his fellow man.
> As a person
> man cannot
> serve God without serving the Common Good.[20]

Dorothy Day wrote about Maurin: "While decrying secularism, the separation of the material from the spiritual, his emphasis . . . was on man's material needs, his need for work, food, clothing, and shelter. Though Peter went weekly to confession and daily to Communion, and spent an hour a day in the presence of the Blessed Sacrament, his study was of the material order around him . . . Peter's idea of justice was that of St. Thomas—to give to each man what is his due."[21]

Aquinas understood the human person as being created in the image and likeness of God; because of this, every person embodies the mystery and dignity of the Creator. The createdness of human beings means that the material is founded on the spiritual, and this point became the hinge of both Maurin's philosophy and the Catholic Worker movement. It meant that human material and spiritual needs cannot be pitted against one another. To meet our neighbors' material needs is to meet their spiritual needs, provid-

[19] Ibid., p. 71.
[20] Peter Maurin, *Easy Essays* (Chicago: Franciscan Herald Press, 1977), p. 44.
[21] Dorothy Day, "Introduction" in Maurin, *Easy Essays,* p. ix.

ing that our help proceeds from love and that it recognizes God in the other person.

In her autobiography, Dorothy Day remembered how Peter Maurin's teachings all started with love: "He did not begin by tearing down, or by painting so intense a picture of misery and injustice that you burned to change the world. Instead, he aroused in you a sense of your own capacities for work, for accomplishment. He made you feel that you and all men had great and generous hearts with which to love God. If once you recognized this fact in yourself you would expect and find it in others . . . It was seeing Christ in others, loving the Christ you saw in others. Greater than this, it was having faith in the Christ in others without being able to see Him. Blessed is he who believes without seeing."[22]

Maurin's Christian understanding of the fundamental goodness of creation meant that, contrary to the view of other radical social philosophies, the present society does not need to be destroyed to make way for the new. Maurin called for reconstruction in the place of destruction:

> The Catholic Worker believes
> in creating a new society
> within the shell of the old
> with the philosophy of the new,
> which is not a new philosophy
> but a very old philosophy,
> a philosophy so old
> that it looks like new.[23]

Maurin's program for reconstruction comprised three points, each one aiming to correct a serious imbalance in the modern way of life. The first point of the program was the personal practice of the traditional corporal works of mercy—feeding the hungry, giving drink to the thirsty, clothing the naked, sheltering the homeless, visiting the sick and those in prison, and burying the dead. The Worker movement realized this point in the houses of hospitality that were set up first by Dorothy Day and then by inspired readers of their newspaper all over the country.

The second point of Maurin's program was a "green revolution." "There is no revolution," he told Dorothy, quoting Lenin, "without a theory of

---

[22] Quoted in Marc Ellis, *Peter Maurin: Prophet of the Twentieth Century* (New York: Paulist Press, 1981), p. 36.

[23] Maurin, *Easy Essays*, p. 77.

revolution. Only what is needed is not a bloody Red Revolution built on piles of corpses but a peaceful Green Revolution." This was his agrarian ideal of farming communes. It would rescue workers, he held, from the hopelessness of life in the cities and enslavement to wage labor. This was to prove the most problematic of the Catholic Worker's undertakings from its founding to the present day.

The third point as what Maurin called "the clarification of thought": regular discussions, meetings, and study groups that would bring together "the workers and the scholars" in an exchange that would benefit both. "We need," said Maurin, "to keep trained minds from being academic" and "to keep untrained minds from being superficial." Together, a way can be found from "things as they are to things as they should be."[24]

When Dorothy Day called the Catholic Worker an anarchist movement, she meant that the revolution would be made by means of direct action without the need for state involvement or direct Church sanction. The Worker movement was based on what Maurin called the "dynamite inherent in [the Church's] message." He wrote: "If the Catholic Church / is not today/ the dominant social force,/ it is because Catholic scholars / have failed to blow the dynamite / of the Church / have wrapped it up / in nice phraseology, / placed it in an hermetic container / and sat on the lid. / It is about time / to blow the lid off / so the Catholic Church / may again become / the dominant social dynamic force."[25] These radical teachings and their transformative implications were there, just waiting for Christians to take them seriously.

One of Maurin's most eloquent and inspiring essays sums up his philosophy beautifully:

1. To give and not to take
   That is what makes man human.
2. To serve and not to rule
   That is what makes man human.
3. To help and not to crush
   That is what makes man human.
4. To nourish and not to devour
   That is what makes man human.
5. And if need be

[24]Ibid., p. 36.
[25]Ibid., p. 3.

to die and not to live
> That is what makes man human.

6. Ideals and not deals
> That is what makes man human.

7. Creed and not greed
> That is what makes man human.[26]

Publishing a Penny Paper and Doling Out Soup

Peter was far readier to embrace Dorothy as a new St. Catherine of Siena—
"who would move mountains and have influence on governments, temporal and spiritual"—than Dorothy was to embrace Peter's program, however
compelling, as a workable plan for a movement. But Peter had a concrete
notion of how to begin that couldn't fail to grab Dorothy's attention: "We
were to popularize this program . . . by publishing a paper for the man in
the street."[27]

Peter peppered Dorothy with examples from the lives of the saints: "St.
Francis de Sales scattered leaflets like any radical. St. John of God sold
newspapers on the streets. We didn't have to do things on a big scale, Peter
made it clear." But printing even a small newspaper required money: Where
would the funding come from? Peter replied with confidence: "In the
history of the saints, capital was raised by prayer. God sends you what you
need when you need it. You will be able to pay the printer. Just read the
lives of the saints."[28]

Dorothy was persuaded. Using her kitchen for an office and the Paulist
Press as her printer, she dashed off articles on labor, strikes, and unemployment for the first issue. Peter contributed the first of his *Easy Essays*. The
Catholic Worker came out in time to hand out to the workers and radicals
celebrating May Day on Union Square. Most could afford the price: one
cent.

The growth of the paper was phenomenal. Within a few months the
circulation increased from 2,500 to 75,000 and by the mid-1930s it had
passed the 100,000 mark, exerting much influence on young and old alike
who yearned for a dynamic Catholicism. *Orate Fratres,* the progressive Cath-

[26]Peter Maurin, "Personal Essays," *Monthly Symposium on Personalist Democracy,* CW
Papers in W-10 Box 1, January 1938, 5.6.

[27]Day, *The Long Loneliness,* pp. 172–173.

[28]Ibid., p. 173.

olic journal, called it "a veritable godsend in our time of social disintegration and unrest."[29] Priests were putting stacks of it in the rear of their
churches and sisters were buying it for their schools.

But strangely, one person at least was not altogether happy with the
paper—Peter. After taking a look at the first issue, he left and wasn't seen
again for several weeks. He was disappointed because he felt it missed the
point. Just a lot of news about strikes, unemployment, lockouts, racism,
trials—just one more radical journal. A Catholic paper, he thought, should
be articulating a vision of a new society, not bemoaning the troubles of the
one that should be laid aside. Peter thought that all the efforts of the radicals
to organize strikes, push for better wages, and reform labor conditions were
a waste. Urban society, the factory, and the mass production assembly lines
were evils that no simple modification would cure. They brutalized people.
The only salvation lay in creating small, cooperative communities of artisans
and craftsmen with small, worker-owned factories that would be close to
the land. When Peter finally returned, Dorothy listened to him with an
open mind and tried to absorb his lesson. However, her natural bent was
more toward the here-and-now and practical solutions. So she continued to
fill the pages of the *Worker* with stories about striking workers or demonstrations by the unemployed and the homeless, while at the same time trying to
project the vision of a "future that had fewer smokestacks and smaller
cities."[30]

A description of Dorothy at the time by her friend Julia Porcelli noted
her likeness to Greta Garbo with her beautiful bone structure, jaw, and
handsome coloring. "But more than her looks was her presence. When she
enters a room, you are very much aware of her."[31]

Dorothy now rented a vacant barbershop below her apartment on Fifteenth Street and the Catholic Worker family began to grow. People who
had heard of the Catholic Worker program came to find out for themselves.
One of them was Steve Hergenham, a German carpenter who had lost the
home he built because of the Depression. A pregnant girl, Margaret, arrived
from the Pennsylvania mining region and became the cook. An old Arme-
nian in a long black coat, wearing a black hat over his white hair, came with
his cat named Social Justice. Distinguished visitors like Father John LaFarge

[29] Patrick G. Coy, ed., *A Revolution of the Heart* (Philadelphia: Temple University Press,
1988), p. 25.

[30] James H. Forest, *Love Is the Measure* (New York: Paulist Press, 1986), p. 85.

[31] Miller, *A Harsh and Dreadful Love*, p. 90.

and Jacques Maritain mingled with students, the aging, and street people at Peter Maurin's "Workers' School." Maritain asked Maurin to tell Dorothy how happy he had been to visit her, adding, "I wish I could have said all that was in my heart—never was I more vexed by inability to speak fluent English. It seemed as if I had found again in the Catholic Workers a little of the atmosphere of Peguy's office in the Rue de la Sorbonne. And so much good will, such courage, such generosity!"[32]

There were also more than a few troublemakers, cranks, and other eccentrics who gravitated to Fifteenth Street and then to the new location on Charles Street in Greenwich Village, as well as to the farm they opened on Staten Island in 1935. The other members of the "family" tried to persuade Dorothy to evict these "freeloaders," bums, and deadbeats but she adamantly refused. She believed that problems should be suffered, not solved by imposing order. "The more we suffer," she said, "the more we learn." One irascible old man, a blatant racist, railed constantly at "the kikes, the dingoes and the dagoes." When he was on his deathbed he told Dorothy she could have his cane if she would wrap it around the neck of those bastards. Then he smiled and died with the words, "God has been good to me." Another visitor who came to stay was a communist Jew from Central Europe who would recite the Psalms in Hebrew before sitting down to eat. He threw himself into gardening at the farm, working all day in the hot sun "for the sake of a Holy Communism." "Christ was in his heart," Dorothy said, and she loved him. But unfortunately he aroused the ire of a fellow eccentric when he took bread one day and said "I am Lenin . . . this is my body broken for you." The man he provoked scared him into taking off in a hurry. He was not seen again.

The breadline for the unemployed and the denizens of the Bowery became longer as the Depression dragged on. Feeding sometimes a thousand people a day and housing forty or fifty while turning out a penny newspaper demanded funds. When the funds ran out, as they regularly did, Dorothy and Peter would take turns going to Church praying and begging for money. However, with the help of Dorothy's simply written and direct appeals they were usually able to raise the money needed.

Inspired by Maurin's agrarian ideal and with a donation of a thousand dollars, the Worker was able to purchase a farm in Easton, Pennsylvania. They named it Maryfarm. Thus began an experiment that would bring troubles of its own. On Mott Street, one of their sites, the hospitality was

[32]Ibid., p. 71.

completely open and the place was soon overcrowded with would-be farm-ers. But Maurin was more interested in planting ideas than corn; on the first day everybody sat around the big dining-room table listening to Maurin, who was overjoyed to see his dream come true. But some did begin to plant and sow and soon cars were returning to Mott Street loaded with produce.

In the meantime Peter turned his attention to another concern of the Workers, the need for the Church to reach the blacks. While the revolution to alter their condition was still decades away, the Catholic Workers had already nailed their colors to the mast. Writing about the nine black Scotts-boro youths threatened with execution for a false allegation of rape, Doro-thy traced the antagonism between whites and blacks to the industrialists who fomented racism to divide them. While applauding Father John LaFarge's interracial councils, the *Worker* noted how deeply rooted segrega-tion was in Catholic institutions.

In May 1934, Maurin opened a storefront in Harlem where he could hold meetings and engage blacks in friendly conversation. One of his aims was to show them that the Church had a definite social program that was of interest to blacks as well as whites. Arts and crafts classes were offered and literature was displayed. It was tough sledding; a few Catholics handing out pamphlets and giving instructions, mainly to children, were hardly going to offset black people's deeply ingrained impression of Catholic racism. But Maurin was nothing if not dogged, and he tried parading a group of stu-dents through the streets with placards inscribed with pithy quotes from his *Easy Essays*. A rain of insults laced with garbage fell on them and quickly cooled their youthful ardor. Later Peter was set upon by thugs who battered his face into a mass of bruises. But during a riot the next year, spurred by the Depression, Peter's storefront was spared when someone shouted, "Hey, they're okay!" However, he was finally forced to leave when the owner heard of his pacifist stand and asked him to clear out.

Tackling the Tough Issues

At first Catholics saw the Catholic Worker movement as the front-line force against the Communist threat. But the *Worker* soon disabused people of this idea. As Dorothy wrote, "A Communist beaten and kicked reminds us of Jesus as He fell beneath the weight of His cross."[33] For American Catholics just beginning to move into the mainstream, the *Worker*'s personalism was a

[33] Ibid., p. 74.

strange world. They saw its manner and its sharp critique of bourgeois values as un-American. Even more unsettling, the Catholic Worker's neutral stance on the Spanish Civil War and its outspokenness against Catholic anti-Semitism had many critics charging the movement with enmity to the Church itself.

The outbreak of the Spanish Civil War in 1936 confronted the *Worker* with an excruciatingly difficult decision. The loyalists who supported the government were for the most part anti-Catholic and proceeded to massacre priests and nuns and burn down churches in a paroxysm of mindless violence. Thousands of priests, including bishops, and hundreds of nuns were killed. For many if not most Catholics these outrages were enough to guarantee their support of the fascist General Franco, head of the rebel forces. For these Catholics the war became a holy crusade against atheistic communism. But some Catholic intellectuals, led by Jacques Maritain in France, declared themselves neutral, unable to identify with either the fascist Franco and his Nazi supporters or with the communist loyalists. Identifying with Maritain's personalist view, the *Worker* too declared its neutrality and, as William Miller says, was probably the only U.S. Catholic paper that tried to present the views of the European Catholic intellectuals.

The mail began to sizzle. The *Worker* was accused of trying to be more Christian than Christ Himself. Patrick Scanlan, the editor of the Brooklyn *Tablet,* was quite disturbed and reported the strong reaction of Cardinal Hayes when he heard that after he had publicly prayed for Franco, a Catholic, Dorothy Day—in a Catholic hall—was doing just the opposite.[34] Another voice denouncing the *Worker*'s stand was *Social Justice,* a paper edited by Father Charles Coughlin, the "radio priest" of Royal Oak, Michigan. Coughlin was riding high at the time. With his booming voice and clever rhetoric he was able to convince millions of listeners that the Depression had been caused by a cabal of international bankers and communist Jews. Coughlin helped to foment the anti-Semitism that was spreading rapidly at the time, and not only in Germany. On August 18, 1938, his paper began to publish *The Protocols of the Elders of Zion,* a preposterous forgery that included a supposed plan by Jewish leaders to take over the world. For Jews in Germany especially it was a time of increasing terror as the Nazi campaign against them escalated. The episode called *Kristallnacht* (the "Night of Broken Glass") occurred on November 9–10, 1938, when hoodlums ran free to

[34]Ibid., p. 143.

pillage Jewish shops, destroy synagogues, beat and even kill any hapless Jews they could get their hands on.

When Jews saw the Coughlinites out selling *Social Justice* they could at least take comfort in seeing others selling the *Catholic Worker*. Dorothy was a faithful friend of the Jewish people while Maurin had a special love for the Jews as God's chosen people. He regularly wrote articles for the *Catholic Worker* denouncing the evil of anti-Semitism and reminding his readers that whenever they met a Jew they should be "reminded of Christ and love him for being of the race that Christ was part of."[35]

One reader incensed at the *Worker*'s criticism of Coughlin decided it was time to tell Dorothy off: "I think you are still a dirty Communist parading as a loyal Catholic . . . a two-faced hypocrite, a wolf in sheep's clothing, serving your Red master, Joseph Stalin, who guides you from his capital at Moscow."[36]

Absolutely No to War

The outbreak of World War II opened up a whole new chapter in Catholic Worker history. From the start the Worker espoused a pacifist position which it had already outlined in 1936 when it organized Pax, an association of Catholic conscientious objectors. Pax's declaration of principles included the following: the belief that no war was justifiable in modern times; the right to judge for oneself the morality of war; a refusal to bear arms or otherwise assist in the carrying on of a war; support for a strong international body to settle disputes between nations; determination to expose the acts of munitions-makers, warmongers, and military supporters; and finally a commitment to prefer love to the technique of class war.

After her conversion Dorothy had renounced the idea of class conflict. She still believed in the need to change social structures but only through nonviolent means such as prayer, fasting, picketing, noncooperation with evil. History taught her that force begets greater force and the cycle of violence constantly escalates. Moreover, as a person of faith she could accept the idea that a just cause might not triumph here on earth. Dorothy buttressed her pacifist position with arguments from the Fathers of the Church and citations from the pope, Pius XII. Many friends and supporters, how-

[35] Ibid., p. 147.
[36] Ibid., pp. 149–150.

ever, found it too much: "False, unpatriotic and dangerous," in the words of one.

Even within the ranks of the Workers there was discord, with some of the pacifists giving vent to feelings that were far from pacifistic. Dorothy herself cracked the whip when she found out that in some Worker houses the *Worker* was suppressed because of its excessive focus on pacifism. She suggested that dissidents should dissociate themselves from the movement, having particularly in mind the Workers' Seattle house headed by Father H. A. Reinhold. He protested vigorously and questioned whether she had the right to take the name of the whole movement and reduce it to this one issue. Another priest warned her against being lumped with Coughlin and his followers and the America Firsters, all of whom opposed entry into the war, albeit from motives profoundly different than Dorothy's. Did she not realize that civilization itself was at stake? Could she really contemplate the world prostrate under the Nazi Iron Heel?

At first the Workers saw the war was as just a repeat of the 1914–1918 war, which revisionist historians judged imperialist, unjustifiable, and absurd. But was the analogy convincing? By 1940 it had become clear even for Dorothy that it wasn't. However, she continued to adhere to her mystical vision of the need to show mankind that love was the answer, and to her mystical belief in overcoming evil with the weapons of the spirit.

For most Americans, Pearl Harbor was absolute proof that the Japanese were a perfidious race and had to be stopped. Would Dorothy now admit the error of her ways? people wondered. Her answer was not long in forthcoming. The headline of the January, 1942 issue of the *Worker* read, "We Continue Our Christian Pacifist Stand":

> We are still pacifist. Our manifesto is the Sermon on the Mount, which means we will try to be peacemakers. Speaking for many of our conscientious objectors, we will not participate in armed warfare or in making munitions, or by buying government bonds to prosecute the war, or in urging others in these efforts . . . But neither will we be carping in our criticism . . . We have been the only country in the world where men of all nations have taken refuge from oppression.

When told that the war was a battle for decent human values, Dorothy stated that the *Worker* had been fighting this battle for many years. How, she asked, can we talk about going abroad to fight for human values when right in our own backyard we let pass the most horrible assaults on human dignity? She reminded her readers of a recent incident when a white mob shot a black man and dragged him through the streets behind a car. While he was still alive they poured kerosene on him and burned him to death, then left his body lying in the street.

The *Worker* lost a hundred thousand in circulation as a direct result of Dorothy's staunch pacifistic stand, and the movement itself faltered as many of the members could not agree with *Worker* pacifism. Sixteen houses closed, one half the total. Among those who walked away was Father Charles Rice, who took his Catholic Radical Alliance with him. Another was John Cogley, later a prominent journalist. Dorothy nevertheless continued to build the case for a Catholic pacifism. In this she was greatly aided by Father John Hugo, a priest of the Pittsburgh diocese, whose scholarly articles filled page after page of the *Catholic Worker*. Father John A. O'Brien also gave her assistance with articles on the papal calls for peace at Christmas and Easter. Letters regularly arrived from Workers who were now scattered around the globe in the armed services and from the conscientious objectors detained in camps. Gordon Zahn wrote from his camp at Rosewood in Owings Mills; referring to the government's accounts of Japanese atrocities, he argued that Americans were equally brutal, equally affected by the organized hatred of war.

As the war dragged on, the wartime economy prospered and the numbers on the bread line on Mott Street dwindled. Dorothy made one of her periodic cross-country bus trips, staying with friends and at Worker houses along the way. The bus terminals were jammed with soldiers, their wives and children, and she was often bone weary. In Seattle the sight of barrage balloons strung out across the bay reminded her of "grotesque idols, deities of the state, served by a uniformed priesthood who put their trust in all these works of their hands, to save them from the wrath of the Lord."[37] Another trip the following year took her to the South. In Alabama she was appalled by the hideous condition of the black sharecroppers who were forced to live like animals, crowded into shacks with holes in the roofs. At Fort Benning she heard local people complaining of how the Northerners and the army were taking the black man "out of his place." She heard many stories of blacks lynched and mutilated. One boy at the age of twelve had both legs and arms broken because he had offended a white man and was left horribly crippled for life. Dorothy could not help crying out: "Oh the

[37] Ibid., p. 176.

suffering, the poverty of these poor of Christ, and the indifference of Christians."[38]

The Need to Let Go

Readers noticed a distinct change in emphasis in the *Catholic Worker* during these war years. It reflected a new stage in Dorothy's spiritual quest as she began to feel a strong pull toward the desert, toward a quieter and more contemplative life. The Worker movement itself, she felt, needed this change of direction. She was confirmed in her opinion by a retreat held at the Workers' Pennsylvania farm in August 1940 when seventy-five workers gathered for days of silence and prayer. Previous gatherings of workers from around the country had been largely filled with discussion and did little to build up the spirit of unity. But this retreat was different: It fostered "a sense of comradeship, and a sense of Christian solidarity" that would surely strengthen them all in their work.

The next year's retreat was given by Father Hugo. His retreats were no picnic. He prescribed fasting and complete silence besides prayer during the week-long exercise. On some occasions, continual days of rainfall added to the other mortifications to make it a most trying experience for the less spiritually inclined. But Dorothy exulted. "We were on a high hill overlooking a flowing river, but down below we could see the smoke and grime of Easton . . . God bless . . . [those] who have made such a retreat possible." Later she said that through the retreats "we began to see for the first time the incomparable heights to which man is called . . . We saw the basis of our dignity."[39]

Feeling the need to let go, Dorothy decided to take a year off and find a place where she could read, think, and pray. One of the Workers was opposed and reminded her that Christ hadn't taken a year off. But undaunted she set out for Cincinnati in September 1943 where she put up at the Grail, a community of lay women in Loveland, Ohio. A month later she and Tamar moved to Farmingdale, Long Island, where there was an agricultural school Tamar was interested in. Dorothy fixed her abode in an abandoned schoolroom previously used for domestic science courses and filled with stoves and sinks. It was a hard six months. She spoke of trying to keep her resolve to spend two hours every day praying and meditating. Often in

[38] Ibid., p. 180.
[39] Ibid., p. 189.

an agony of boredom she had to force the rosary beads through her hands while trying to move her numb lips. By March she had to admit that she was not cut out for such a solitary life: "Community, whether of the family, or convent or boarding house, is absolutely necessary."[40]

At the same time the seventeen-year-old Tamar decided she had waited long enough to get married. "Tamar," her mother wrote, "grew up knowing what she wanted, and that was to make things." Her interest was in arts and crafts, and like her father she was absorbed by biology and astronomy. Tamar "wanted to farm. She wanted to marry young and live on a farm. She was impatient with school for not offering the practical training she desired."[41] Now she had fallen in love with David Hennessy, a young man who had come to Maryfarm in 1941. She had wanted to marry him earlier but Dorothy insisted she wait. Soon after Tamar's eighteenth birthday, and with Dorothy's blessing, Tamar and David pronounced their vows on April 19, 1944, at Easton Church. It was a Worker wedding. Absolutely no frills. Tamar had to bathe in a pail and didn't even have a mirror to see how lovely she looked in her gown.

Returning to her beloved community, Dorothy celebrated the twelfth-anniversary issue of the *Worker* as Germany surrendered. One by one the fellows who had been called away by the war were returning from their outfits or their conscientious objector camps, and in some cases picking up life in the community where they had left off. And as the war with Japan reached its nuclear crescendo at Hiroshima, Dorothy thought of the vaporized victims of the bomb, the men, women, and babies. Will we "breathe their dust in our nostrils, feel them in the fog of New York on our faces, feel them in the rain on the hills of Easton?" she asked. How could anyone believe God approved of this outcome? One could speak of it only as according to his permissive will, the will that allows evil to happen.

Dorothy's commitment to nonviolence and to love of one's enemies would be given a good test. In September 1944, plans to transform Maryfarm into a center for prayer and formation were announced. Farming communes, Dorothy confessed, were simply not workable in the present circumstances. At first the response was enthusiastic. Father Pacifique Roy came to Maryfarm as chaplain and there was daily mass and a round of feasts and fasts and much exhilaration. But dark clouds hovered. One of the denizens of Maryfarm had elevated himself into a quasi-sacerdotal role and

[40]Ibid., p. 192.
[41]Day, *The Long Loneliness,* pp. 238–239.

with his band of adherents was now accusing her of perverting the original purpose of Maryfarm. He himself tyrannized his followers, compelling them to bow and scrape before him while restricting the women to silence and performance of the heavy work. These dissidents made life so miserable for Dorothy and the others that they finally despaired of the whole business and simply moved out, leaving most of Maryfarm to the dissidents.

A Time for Tears

Dorothy did not give up the idea of a retreat center and in the spring of 1947 a new farm was bought for $16,000 and christened Maryfarm Retreat House. Soon people were digging and planting, and in time a harvest of potatoes, rutabagas, corn, and tomatoes was on its way to Mott Street. Peter came to the farm to live, but he no longer waxed eloquent on the joys of the simple life. As the retreats and conferences went on, he sat quietly under his favorite pine tree, his mind and memory slowly fading away. At Mott Street he wandered away one day and could not be found in spite of the frantic efforts and anxious prayers of the community. Four days later he somehow managed to find his way home to a tearful welcome by the community. He was now only a shell of his old self. "The fact was," Dorothy wrote, "he had been stripped of all. He had stripped himself throughout life; he had put off the old man in order to put on the new . . . He had stripped himself, but there remained work for God to do. We are to be pruned as the vine is pruned so that it can bear fruit, and this we cannot do ourselves. God did it for him. He took from him his mind, the one thing he had left, the one thing perhaps he took delight in . . . He was sick for more than five years. It was as though he had had a stroke in his sleep. He dragged one leg after him, his face was slightly distorted, and he found it hard to speak. And he repeated, 'I can no longer think.' "[42]

Death came mercifully on a Sunday in May 1949. The funeral mass was a triumphant celebration attended by a great number of friends—as well as angels and saints, according to Dorothy. Peter was lovingly carried in castoff clothes to a donated grave. The *L'Osservatore Romano* reported his death on the front page, noting that perhaps a saint had died; *Time* magazine also paid tribute to him as a joyful Christian who had tried to build up the kind of society where, to use Peter's own words, "it would be easier for people to be

[42]Ibid., pp. 274–275.

good." For Dorothy the death of her teacher, spiritual guide, and mainstay was an almost unbearable loss.

"I Loved the Communists"

From September 1949 to June 1950 a series of events cast an ominous shadow over the world: The loss of China to the Communists, the Alger Hiss trial, the first Russian nuclear test, and the Korean invasion seemed to portend an apocalyptic showdown of America with the forces of world Communism. The country was a sitting duck for any unscrupulous politician who knew how to exploit the potential for public panic. One did appear, as everyone knows: Joe McCarthy, the junior senator from Wisconsin, burst onto television holding a sheaf of papers claiming he had the names of a hundred or more "card-carrying Communists" in the State Department.

Dorothy herself was often accused of being a Communist. While her friends knew this was a lie, they were unhappy with the way she lent credence to the charge by associating with prominent Communists like Mike Gold and Elizabeth Gurley Flynn. The anti-Communist hysteria mounted, and ten leading Communists including Flynn were jailed for "conspiring to overthrow the United States government," but Dorothy would not be cowed. She protested that those imprisoned should be allowed freedom on bail to prepare their defense. She referred to the jailed Communists as "brothers" and said, "I can say with warmth that I loved the Communists I worked with and learned much from them. They helped me to find God in His poor, in His abandoned ones, as I had not found Him in the Christian churches . . . My radical associates were the ones who were in the forefront of the struggle for a better social order where there would not be so many poor."[43] While she hoped, with Marx, that the state would wither away, she disagreed with the Communists (as well as the Republicans, the Democrats, and many Christians) on the need for violence.

"Although we disagree with our Marxist brothers on the question of the means to use to achieve social justice, rejecting atheism and materialism in Marxist thought and in bourgeois thought, we respect their freedom as a minority group in this country . . . and extend to them [the imprisoned Communists] our sympathy and admiration for having followed their con-

[43] Forest, *Love Is the Measure*, p. 128.

science."[44] On occasion she even attended rallies promoted by Communists. One Catholic journalist berated her for a lack of common sense. A priest critic challenged the Workers to "come out in the open, declare yourselves Bolshevik Communists and fight the Church like men."[45] When a Vatican decree in 1949 reproved Catholics who collaborated with Communists, a Father Broderick used the pulpit of St. Patrick's Cathedral to heap abuse on the "so-called idealist Christian Left." For Dorothy it was all a sad reminder of Jesus' words about one's enemies being of one's own family.

One of the mysteries of Dorothy's career was how she survived in a diocese headed by Cardinal Spellman. He stood worlds apart from her on most social issues and was especially irritated by her complacent (if not worse) attitude toward the "Red Menace." From time to time rumors would fly of a coming suppression but it never materialized. Many thought the hour had finally come in 1949 when she took on the cardinal over the strike of gravediggers at Calvary cemetery. Since the workers belonged to the CIO, Spellman apparently believed the strike was Communist-inspired and refused even to meet with the men. Dorothy joined the picket line in front of the cardinal's palatial office behind St. Patrick's Cathedral. She later remembered the shamefaced look of the seminarians who were hauled in to break the strike. Dorothy's plea to the cardinal to meet with the men met with no response.

This was undoubtedly the first picket line of lay Catholics in front of any bishop's office, and her part in it pushed the cardinal's patience to the limit. Dorothy was invited to the chancery, where she met with one of the cardinal's staff who told her she would have to either take the "Catholic" off the paper's name or cease publication. Since she had often spoke of her readiness to cease publication if ordered to do so by Church authority, her compliance was assumed. She responded instead with a masterpiece of a letter in which she spoke of her willingness personally to change the paper's name, but the unwillingness of all the others involved. She called for dialogue instead of the suppression of a paper with a circulation of 63,000. This would create an enormous scandal and put a formidable weapon in the hands of the Church's enemies. She also reminded the cardinal that the Church had never blessed capitalism, and that in advocating a society built on neither capitalist nor communist premises the *Worker* was in line with the

[44] Miller, *A Harsh and Dreadful Love,* p. 229.
[45] Ibid., p. 231.

thrust of papal teaching. Finally she promised in the future to make the paper "less dogmatic, more persuasive, less irritating, more winning."

The archdiocesan order was dropped. The cardinal won the strike, however, and the workers were compelled to join an American Federation of Labor union. In this as in other encounters, Dorothy said, the cardinal was always personally gracious and pleasant—and, as one of the Workers said, would even buy their paper when he saw it for sale.

As one might expect, the execution of the Rosenbergs in June 1953 for spying in the service of Russia was a most painful experience for Dorothy. How in justice, she asked, could we execute people for doing what we ourselves are doing in other countries? But she was glad that the Rosenbergs had gone to their death while firmly and quietly professing their innocence, and that Ethel's last gesture was one of love as she warmly kissed one of the matrons who accompanied her. "Let us have no part with the vindictive state," Dorothy said mournfully.[46] While acknowledging that both the United States and Russia were equally guilty of warmongering, most of the Workers' criticism was directed at the United States and its massive buildup of arms. Predictably they were accused again of being Communists or at least pro-communism.

This charge would be renewed a few years later following the Catholic Worker's positive response to Castro's victorious revolution in Cuba in January 1959. While most of the country saw it as a dangerous development, a number of writers in the *Catholic Worker* applauded the revolution as a good thing for the poor. Dorothy took this line also and even argued that the Church had brought on itself the persecution it now suffered. She pointed out how the Church in Latin America was often just a tool of the rich and powerful, and was indifferent to the extreme misery of the poor. The violence used by Castro, she argued, was less evil than the violence used by those who oppress the poor.

The *Worker's* acceptance of Castro's revolution outraged some of its readers. The editor of *The Register* said Dorothy was rotten with pride and called her movement "phony." On the other hand a Cuban intellectual felt that Dorothy was right on target and warned that if Catholics didn't accept Dorothy's type of "secular monasticism," the Church would collapse under the pressure of Marxist-Leninism or in the ashes of a nuclear disaster.

Thomas Merton commended Day for the stand she took and added that some readers "may get quite hot about the fact that you want to point out

---

[46]Ibid., p. 235.

that Castro may have had good intentions and in actual fact has been less wicked than our mass media want him to have been. People who are scared and upset use a very simple logic, and they think that if you defend Castro as a human being you are defending all the crimes that have ever been committed by Communism anywhere and they will feel that you are threatening them."[47]

In the midst of the furor Dorothy felt she needed to see Cuba for herself. She heard Castro speak and thought him a "great speaker." In fact she said: "Will it be shocking to our readers to learn that as I heard him speak . . . the sound of his voice, his manner of oratory, his constant repetitions reminded me of Peter Maurin?"[48] But she spent most of her time in Cuba visiting with the ordinary folk and was much impressed by the resourcefulness they displayed in their straitened circumstances. Everywhere she noticed schools and clinics being opened and she was impressed by what seemed a spirit of hope among the people.

Ammon Hennacy—a Radical's Radical

Day told long-time Catholic Worker Stanley Vishnewski that there "were three men who had a great influence on my life, and as a result, on the Catholic Worker: Reverend Pacifique Roy, Peter Maurin and Ammon Hennacy."[49]

Many persons of radical temperament passed through the portals of the Catholic Worker but none of them surpassed Ammon Hennacy in total, absolute, and undivided commitment to the pacifist cause. His impact on the Catholic Worker and vice versa was considerable. A devoted anarchist, he believed government a great beast and he fought a lifelong battle against it. He used to say that he had met two great men in his life, Alexander Berkman and Peter Maurin, but it is obvious from his autobiography that Berkman was the one who really shaped his thought. Dorothy once described him as "deep and narrow." Nevertheless, the perseverance and courage he displayed in remaining faithful to his vision until the end was truly inspiring.

Ammon was born in 1893 in Negley, Ohio, to Baptist parents. His

---

[47] Nancy Roberts, *Dorothy Day and the Catholic Worker* (Albany: State University of New York Press, 1984), p. 156.

[48] Ibid., p. 157.

[49] Coy, ed., *A Revolution of the Heart*, p. 163.

childhood was a happy one but he recollected consenting to be baptized at the age of twelve after having heard a hell-and-damnation sermon that terrified him. He soon began having doubts about the faith and was advised to go and hear Billy Sunday. He did and was confirmed in his skepticism and proceeded to unbaptize himself by announcing to the startled congregation that he did not believe in God or the Bible.

Among the crucial experiences in his youth were the trips he took in 1912 with Mother Bloor, a veteran socialist and radical organizer. She came to eastern Ohio to organize socialist locals and observe the labor situation. He drove her around in a horse and buggy while she instructed him in the "true faith," using illustrations from her long experience in organizing labor. She was especially active in the textile industry where she fought against the exploitation of children. Ammon found her marvelous and a great inspiration on the development of his radical ideas.

He then began a vagabond sort of life in the course of which he met a number of other leading socialists. He supported himself by selling cornflakes house to house and proved himself a born salesman. With the money earned he was able to enroll in Hiram College in 1913. The following year he moved on to Madison, Wisconsin, where he studied journalism at the university while again selling cornflakes. When Emma Goldman came to the campus to lecture on anarchism and free love, Ammon was the one who introduced her to the audience. In 1915 he moved to Milwaukee and sold aluminum ware while the war raged in Europe. He had decided to move next to Ohio State University but on the day before he was supposed to leave he attended a party of young socialists where a young lady named Selma Nelms caught his eye and captivated him by her radicalism. He knew he had found the love of his life, but would she have him? Considering his talents as a salesman the outcome was probably never in doubt. Within two weeks they were engaged.

His year at Ohio State turned out to be one of his most pleasant; he was happily involved as the president of the Socialist Club and all-purpose campus radical. But America's entry into the war brought a swift end to Ammon's apprentice days. Ammon immediately said NO to the draft. Keeping one step ahead of the police, he moved from town to town passing out antiwar and antidraft leaflets. The leaflets asked, "Young men, are you going to refuse to register for military service in a foreign country while the rich men who have brought on this war stay at home and get richer by gambling in food stuffs? We would rather die or be imprisoned for the sake of justice, than kill our fellow men in this unjust war." Finally, after an evening of postering downtown storefronts in Columbus, Ohio, he was arrested and placed in solitary confinement.

The next two years would put his anarchist convictions to a formidable test. After being sentenced to two years he was moved to the federal penitentiary at Atlanta. There, much to his delight, he was able to meet his hero Alexander Berkman, the anarchist who had stabbed Henry Clay Frick during the great Homestead strike. For a year Ammon managed to avoid trouble, but when he organized a strike of the prisoners to protest the rotten fish they were served he was thrown in the "hole." For ten days he was fed only a cup of water and a slice of bread each day. Then he was moved into the "light hole," a tiny cell lit with only a twenty-watt bulb, his food brought in a pail. Nearby a prisoner called "Popoff" was hung for eight hours at a time by his hands and Ammon had to sit there and listen to his groanings hour after hour. The warden was determined to break Ammon and would periodically bring the draft registration form for him to sign. Amid nightmares of people hiding in sewers and pigs dripping blood and gore, Ammon began to sink to the depths of despair.

Then when he was just about ready to cut his wrists with a sharpened spoon he happened to catch a glance of Berkman. He remembered how Berkman had spent years in a dark hole in the Allegheny federal penitentiary for trying to assassinate Frick. Reflecting on how much more Berkman had suffered than himself, he became once more determined that he must go on and try to work for a better world. While in prison, he began to study the Bible and meditate on Jesus and his Sermon on the Mount. His mind swiveled between choosing the way of hatred and revenge and heeding Jesus' call to love one's enemies and to overcome evil with good. Finally, with a tremendous leap of faith he committed himself to Jesus. Henceforth he would call himself a "non-Church Christian." Soon he would add the word "anarchist."

He was finally released from the penitentiary in March 1919. On Christmas Eve he and Selma kissed and vowed "to stay together as long as we loved each other—for the Revolution."[50] A happy period of his life began as he and Selma took off on a trip around the country which included traveling for three weeks on a leaky coal barge from Norfolk to Boston. In Chicago they placed a rose on the graves of the anarchists connected with the Haymarket riots.

They finally decided to settle down for a while and bought a piece of land

[50]Miller, *A Harsh and Dreadful Love,* p. 276.

near Waukesha, Wisconsin. A happy interlude began in Ammon's so often harried life. He got a job with a local dairy and built a small, comfortable house; meanwhile, two daughters arrived to complete their dream. But the peace and security they felt was soon disrupted in 1931 when Ammon led a strike at the dairy and lost his job and his house. Their next stop was Milwaukee and a job for Ammon as a social worker. In 1937 a copy of the *Catholic Worker* came into his hands and brought about another big change in his life. The next year he was able to meet Dorothy when she came to speak at the Catholic Social Action Congress, and he was soon out on the streets selling the *Catholic Worker*.

But Selma finally had enough. As war loomed she anticipated another showdown between Ammon and the Feds (which in fact the Feds decided they didn't need), and she decided for the sake of her daughters' future it was time to leave. Her own radical ardor had cooled and she could no longer stand the strain of being wife to America's number-one radical. It was a separation that broke his heart for he deeply loved Selma and the girls. Many nights he wept tears in his loneliness.

The thought behind his stance is found in his *Book of Ammon,* which has been called "one of the finest sources of anarchist philosophy."[51] Ammon focused all his hopes for social change on the individual, as social systems, he believed, merely reflect the ideas of their individual members. The only effective power for this purpose is spiritual power, which is found in the promptings of the individual's conscience. He saw no point in trying to reform government because by its nature government tries to coerce people into acting justly instead of working through the individual's conscience. He regarded meetings, resolutions, demonstrations, and all such means of social change as a waste of time. The political victories they might bring weren't worth two pennies, in his opinion, because they do not effect changes in people's hearts.

As he hawked the *Catholic Worker* or picketed, Ammon directed most of his considerable energy toward influencing the individuals with whom he came into contact.

Finally he believed that anarchism without a spiritual foundation was useless. True anarchism must be rooted in the ethical principles of Jesus and Gandhi, though he understood that what has traditionally kept anarchists away from religion is the way religion has so often been linked to capitalism and warmongering.

For all Ammon's deep foundation in faith, he was not very interested in

---

[51] Ibid., pp. 141–142.

theology. He had no need to study theological treatises in order to appreciate the wickedness of sin. For him sin was an overwhelming fact and was most evident in the constant refusal of people to take responsibility for their part in social injustice.

Ammon found deep meaning in the Catholic teaching about grace. He realized that his one-person revolution was not possible without grace, but he eschewed speculation on the topic. For him the important thing was to put one's body where one's mouth was. He had no sympathy with the school that says "There's truth on both sides." The evil-doers were evil and not to be excused as merely misguided. "I talked to Ammon about not judging others," Dorothy remembered. "He doesn't see it . . . black is black and white, white."[52] By his highly public fasts and civil disobedience he wanted to "waken up the timid pacifists who know better and don't do better. Someone has to raise the ante of what should be expected of a Christian and a Catholic."[53]

Ammon met Dorothy again in Phoenix in 1949, and feeling the full force of her God-centered personality he went on to visit Mott Street in New York and began work on his autobiography while staying at the Peter Maurin farm. But the lure of the road struck again and he took off to preach his gospel. Two years later he returned to the Catholic Worker's new Chrystie Street house, and under Dorothy's spell and the influence of a retreat decided to seek baptism in the Catholic Church—a move he later regarded as precipitous even though it was preceded by two years of study. In any case, for the next ten years or so he raised the ante for the Catholic Workers as he led them to a new level of pacifist activism and civil disobedience.

His first target was the air-raid drills conducted by the city of New York whose purpose he felt was to foment a war psychology. With his customary brashness he informed the FBI that the Catholic Workers intended to advise noncooperation with the drill. For J. Edgar Hoover's benefit he added, "We are, as you know, subversives, though no more than always."[54] On June 15, 1955, he and Dorothy and thirty or so other activists continued to sit on the benches of City Hall Park after the alarm sounded. When ordered by the police to take cover they refused and were hauled off to jail. The judge found them guilty but suspended the sentence. But each time they repeated

[52] Ibid., p. 146.
[53] Patrick G. Coy, "The One-Person Revolution of Ammon Hennacy," in Coy, ed., *A Revolution of the Heart* (Philadelphia: Temple University Press, 1988), pp. 148–149.
[54] Roberts, *Dorothy Day and the Catholic Worker,* pp. 149–150.

their protest in subsequent years they were sent to prison. By 1961 some 2,000 people came to join them. In 1962 the city called off its war games, a move due in some part to Dorothy Day and her supporters.

Commonweal was apparently the only Catholic publication that defended Day and the Workers on their air-raid protests. It found two major issues involved: freedom of conscience ("How far may the State go toward compelling an individual to cooperate in what he believes to be wrong?") and constitutional procedure ("To what extent may the Bill of Rights be suspended and the police power invoked against free speech and free assembly during a mock emergency?"). *Commonweal* concluded that if "a woman like Dorothy Day" could be imprisoned in America for "bearing witness to the Gospel as she believed it must be witnessed to, then a terrible thing has happened to our country."[55]

The FBI took a different view. They tried to prod the attorney general into prosecuting the demonstrators on the basis of their allegedly seditious leaflet "The Only Thing We Have to Fear," which had advocated nonregistration for the draft. But the attorney general's office argued that "advocacy" was protected by the First Amendment. This was the third time Hoover had tried to persuade the federal government to prosecute the Catholic Worker movement for sedition.[56]

In the course of the protests Dorothy and Ammon had gone to jail four times. On one occasion the judge accused them of not rendering to Caesar the things that are Caesar's and Ammon retorted, "Caesar has been getting too much around here and someone has to stand up for God." Dorothy noted how much she hated the whole business: the public spectacle, the tension on the faces of the police who feared the havoc some deranged person might create, the obscene and filthy talk of the "tormented women" she met in the prison. It made her think about who was responsible for their degradation: all those, she concluded, who are so preoccupied with their own pleasure they have little time to care about these poor creatures.

Ammon made a practice of picketing the local federal building every August 6 to commemorate the bombing of Hiroshima. He fasted as well— one day for every year that had elapsed since the dropping of the bomb. He also picketed and fasted at missile sites and at the sites of atom and hydrogen bomb tests. One year he gained illegal entry to the missile base in Omaha; he was arrested and given six months in the Sandstone penitentiary. On the

[55]Ibid., p. 151.
[56]Ibid.

1958 anniversary of Hiroshima he decided to picket and fast in the nation's capital for forty days. Every morning he arose, heard mass, read the *New York Times* until nine o'clock, and then stationed himself in front of the Atomic Energy Commission. The employees generally were courteous and even Lewis Strauss, the chairman, would give him a mock salute as he strode by. One employee who realized well the effects of radiation applauded Ammon's action. By the time it was over Ammon had lost thirty-one pounds.

Catholics were often the least tolerant observers. At Cape Canaveral Ammon passed out leaflets in front of the local Catholic church. The pastor came out and told him to take the word "Catholic" off his sign, which the ushers then seized and tore up. The chief of police arrived and told him he had better "get his ass out of town or else." Undeterred, Ammon took up his post again in time to catch those leaving the next mass. This time the ushers took a more emphatic tack with this herald of the Red Menace. They hustled him across the street and threatened to "take him over the hill." The police chief arrived again and took Ammon to the mayor's house. While the two pondered what charges to make, Ammon told them any charge would do; he wouldn't sue them for false arrest, he explained, because he didn't believe in the courts. Thoroughly consternated, the officer in charge repeated several times that if it weren't for his uniform he would beat the hell out of Ammon, and then he ordered him to get out of town. Having lost all his leaflets, Ammon decided he might as well comply.

People who did not know Ammon might picture him a self-obsessed, humorless fanatic and publicity hound. But his friends knew otherwise. Eccentric he was, but as one friend said, "You can't possibly conceive of what a humorous character he was."[57] Invited to speak at a Lions Club meeting in 1937, for instance, he began by noting how "the early Christians were thrown to the lions . . . while the modern ones join the Lions Club." He could also use his sharp wit to jolt scoffers. Take his reply to two youths who told him they read his column only as a source of amusement, but then invited him to visit them. He declined, explaining that "the duties of a Catholic revolutionist are very arduous in these days of devil worship," and he concluded, "Keep on with your studies, boys, and may your minds be enlightened, but not too quickly, for perhaps you could not stand the change."[58]

[57] Coy, ed., *A Revolution of the Heart*, p. 155.
[58] Miller, *A Harsh and Dreadful Love*, p. 291.

Ammon left the Church when, like Tolstoy, he could no longer stand the way it managed to shirk the social demands of the Sermon on the Mount. How could he stay in the same Church with Cardinal Spellman, who called for total victory in Indochina? On the arms race in general there was a vacuum in Church leadership, and yet this issue involved the very future of the human race. Considering the burning clarity of his own vision, forged in such a crucible of suffering, one can understand the frustrations that finally drove him out of the Church.

Ammon died too soon to see the bishops beginning to exert the kind of leadership he prayed for. One can only imagine the satisfaction he would have felt in hearing about Archbishop Raymond Hunthausen's 1981 decision to withhold 50 percent of his federal income taxes in protest of the ballooning military budget. Or again, for the first time in U.S. history, the arrest in 1987 of Catholic bishops who committed acts of civil disobedience at the Nevada nuclear test site—the locale of Ammon's own lonely vigil of picketing and fasting years before. Or in November of the same year at the same site, a demonstration by over 400 Catholic Workers and supporters and the arrest of 200 of them.

Ammon left New York and the Worker house in 1961 and moved to Salt Lake City where he set up the Joe Hill House, his own house of hospitality. It was there in 1970 that his days of picketing came to an end. He had always prayed that he might die on the picket line and even half expected someone to shoot him down. His prayer was granted when at the age of seventy-six he was felled by a fatal heart attack while picketing at the Utah state capitol to try to halt the execution of two condemned murderers. His last written words were: "All that I'm trying to do is to go a bit farther like Christ did."

Give Peace a Chance

The election of Pope John XXIII in 1959 and his call for renewal and updating was joyful news to the Catholic Workers. Dorothy made a trip to Rome to "present ourselves as . . . first fruits of his great encyclical *Pacem in Terris* and . . . to pledge ourselves to work for peace and to ask too, a more radical condemnation of the instruments of modern warfare."[59] The pacifist stance of the *Catholic Worker* took on a new relevance with the emphasis that Pope John, Vatican II, and Pope Paul VI put on the need for the Church to be involved in the quest for peace. Pope Paul VI's cry to the

[59] Ibid., p. 310.

United Nations—"War, never again"—was especially welcome to the peace activists of the Catholic Worker who understood it as a mandate for pacifism in the nuclear age. They also rejoiced at the Vatican II schema, "The Constitution of the Church in the Modern World," which called for clearer government recognition of the rights of conscientious objectors.

Thanks to these developments as well as to Pope Paul VI's criticism of United States involvement in Vietnam, the American Catholic Church was split over the war. On the side of Pope Paul were leading Catholic clergy such as Thomas Merton, the Rev. John McKenzie, the Rev. Robert Drinan, and Fathers Daniel and Philip Berrigan, along with the liberal Catholic press—*Commonweal, Jubilee,* the *Critic,* and the *National Catholic Reporter.* They denounced the war as one of the most immoral acts in American history. But on the other side were found most of the Catholic press and the bishops, including Cardinal Spellman of New York, and the majority of the parishioners. The bishops remained pro-war almost to the end. Nevertheless, in spite of its pacifism the circulation of *Catholic Worker* increased during the sixties, from 77,000 in 1965 to 89,000 in 1967. In contrast to the situation during the Second World War there was no division in the Worker ranks. When it came to the war in Vietnam, as Tom Cornell said, everyone in the Catholic Worker community was horrified.

Two Catholic peace organizations originated at this time, the American Pax Association and the Catholic Peace Fellowship. Pax was sponsored by the *Catholic Worker* and a number of prominent American Catholics including Dorothy Day, Thomas Merton, Karl Stern, and Gordon Zahn. Under the direction of Eileen Egan, it hoped to attract those who wanted peace but did not embrace total pacifism. In 1971 it reorganized to affiliate with Pax Christi, the international Catholic peace association. The Catholic Peace Fellowship was founded in 1964 by the Berrigans and three former *Catholic Worker* editors—Tom Cornell, Jim Forest (a Navy veteran), and Marty Corbin. Its activities included educating Catholics about their own peace traditions, participating in nonviolent antiwar protests, and counseling conscientious objectors.

In February 1965 the *Catholic Worker* published a statement signed by Day and other Catholic activists, scholars, and theologians giving as reasons for opposing the war that it "suppressed the aspirations of the people for political independence and economic freedom" and "increased the threat of nuclear catastrophe and death by chemical and biological warfare."[60] The

[60]Roberts, *Dorothy Day and the Catholic Worker,* p. 162.

signers undertook to encourage civil disobedience in order to stop the flow of American soldiers and munitions to Vietnam. The *Catholic Worker* was the first Catholic publication to advocate civil disobedience as a legitimate form of antiwar protest. "There is only one way to end this insane war," Dorothy later said: "Pack the jails with our men." And she repeated, "Pack the jails!"[61]

To give the peace movement further impetus Dorothy went to Rome again in September of 1965 with her friend Eileen Egan to take part in a ten-day fast. It proved a painful experience, as the hunger pangs pierced to "the very marrow of [her] bones," but she felt it a small sacrifice for one coming from a country where people have so much. And she could greatly rejoice at the statement of Vatican II (The Constitution of the Church in the Modern World) calling for legal provision for "those who, for reasons of conscience, refuse to bear arms, provided that they agree to serve the human community in some other way . . . We cannot fail to praise those who renounce the use of violence in vindication of their rights and who resort to methods of defense which are otherwise available to weaker parties too."

Meanwhile Cardinal Spellman gave aid and comfort to the hawks by his annual Christmas tour of American military bases overseas. On Christmas Day 1966 he told the troops, "This is a war for civilization . . . and [we] pray . . . we shall soon have the victory . . . for less than a victory is inconceivable."[62] The Catholic Peace Fellowship picketed and marched to show that Spellman did not speak for all American Catholics. Dorothy herself avoided direct criticism of the cardinal but expressed her "pain and grief at the pictures of all the women and children who have been burnt alive in Vietnam or the men who have been tortured and died . . . [while] we are supplying arms and money to the rest of the world where we are not ourselves fighting . . . What are all these Americans, so-called Christians doing all over the world?"[63]

On November 6, 1965, Tom Cornell and his group began burning their draft cards in Union Square before a crowd of two thousand after a moving talk by Dorothy. Counter-demonstrators broke in to douse the burning cards with water, but Cornell and his group ignited them again as their adversaries shouted, "Burn yourselves, not your cards!" and "Give us joy, bomb Hanoi." Two weeks later Roger LaPorte, one of the youths present

[61] Ibid., p. 160.
[62] Ibid., p. 164.
[63] Ibid.

that day, immolated himself in front of the United Nations. Before he died thirty hours later he said, "I am a Catholic Worker. I am antiwar, all wars. I did this as a religious action."[64]

The Workers were horrified and very perplexed. Many of them hardly knew the young man who had only recently moved into one of the apartments on Kenmare Street. They found out that he had attended a Catholic prep school and had spent two years in a Trappist seminary and was recently studying literature at Columbia. Those who did know him well described him as a warm, gentle, and affectionate person who loved to tease.

Eventually the Workers were able to work through the tragedy intellectually and spiritually. In a statement, the *Catholic Worker* commented:

> He was trying to say to the American people that we must turn away from violence in Vietnam, and he was trying to say something about the violence that is eroding our own society here in the United States and our city of New York. And so he made this sacrifice attempting to absorb this violence and hatred personally, deflecting it from others by taking it voluntarily to himself. At the same time, we strongly urge people committed to peace to employ other means in expressing their commitment . . . bearing witness . . . to build a . . . nonviolent society, a society of conscience.

Critics of the Worker movement saw a connection between the youth's death and what they called the "simplistic" type of thinking encouraged by Dorothy and the Workers. A priest writing in *Our Sunday Visitor* called her "an apostle of oversimplification" who distorted beyond recognition "the position of the Popes."[65]

A New Twist

By 1967 nearly 500,000 American troops were in Vietnam at a total monthly cost of about two billion dollars. The Catholic peace movement took a new turn in October 1968 in Catonsville, Pennsylvania. Nine activists including Fathers Daniel and Philip Berrigan stood and prayed together around a bonfire they had just made of files seized from a Selective Service office.

The Berrigan brothers were not born pacifists, by any means. Raised in a somewhat conventional Catholic family from the rugged Iron Range of

[64]Miller, *A Harsh and Dreadful Love*, p. 321.
[65]Roberts, *Dorothy Day and the Catholic Worker*, p. 161.

northern Minnesota, both had subscribed to the dogmas of the cold war until the 1960s when they were shaken out of their complacency by articles they read in the *Catholic Worker* by Thomas Merton and others. As a Josephite missionary ministering to blacks in the South, Phil Berrigan (a veteran of World War II) was convinced of the connection that Merton drew between domestic racism and the cold war. Daniel Berrigan was a Jesuit priest and a poet who was attracted by the spiritual values of the Worker movement. When transferred to New York he spent time with the Workers as an unofficial chaplain and soon joined in their protests against the Vietnam war.

After several years of organizing, picketing, marching, and being arrested with little or no impact on government policy, the Berrigans decided new tactics were called for. They would join the "ultraresistance" and engage in the destruction of war-related government property. Their aim: to force the average American to question the morality of the war in Vietnam. The Catonsville raid was certainly successful in this regard, judging by the great amount of publicity it generated and the number of books, articles, and plays that were devoted to the questions it raised. In addition, the Catonsville action inspired more than fifty similar acts of protest over the next five years.

Conservative Catholics, of course, abhorred this development, and wondered how long the Berrigans would manage to avoid suspension. (Actually Phil was shipped off to Latin America by his superiors.) But many admirers both in and outside the Church were happy to see priests who were trying to awaken the slumbering American social conscience, especially that of Catholics. The Catholic Workers themselves were obviously concerned, and in articles and letters in the *Worker* dwelt on the implications of Catonsville for the future of the peace movement. Up to this point they had limited their protests to actions that did include serving time in prison but did not involve any destruction of property other than their own draft cards. They wondered how to reconcile this violence toward property with their own Worker philosophy of nonviolence. There was concern that the restricted action of a thoughtful few could inspire more extreme actions on the part of less disciplined followers.

As a participant in the antiwar movement, Tom Cornell had seen the escalation of militant protest. In his analysis of the Catonsville raid he noted that the swelling antiwar protests reflected a general frustration with liberal politics. The assassinations of Martin Luther King and Robert F. Kennedy, the failure of Eugene McCarthy's crusade, and the massive intervention by police at the national Democratic Convention in Chicago, as well as Hubert Humphrey's political demise at the hands of the law-and-order candidates Nixon and Wallace, were events sufficient to discourage anyone who had previously believed rational debate would sway the American public from its disastrous course. Nevertheless Cornell took a fairly positive view of the new form of resistance.

Dorothy herself had great difficulty coming to terms with Catonsville. At first she expressed unreserved enthusiasm for the Berrigans and their friends and praised their "very strong and imaginative witness against conscription." In a later address to the Liturgical Conference she called their act an "act of prayer." She also traveled to Baltimore to lend them her support when their federal trial convened on October 7, 1968. She wondered if the government would get the message: Responsible, middle-class people were fed up with the war. She also noted its significance as a wake-up call for the Church, whose alliance with the state—along with its failings on other social issues—scandalized so many.

But as time passed she formed misgivings about the ultraresistance of the Berrigans and company. In view of their talent for publicity she was afraid lest they unintentionally create a mass movement attractive to large numbers of spiritually immature youths. The kind of demonstrations they favored might easily get out of control, causing injury to themselves and to others. Dorothy maintained (and Ammon backed her) that peaceful picketing combined with prayer and fasting was the surest form of protest inasmuch as it enabled one to meet people in a nonthreatening way and facilitated communication with them. It surely corresponded best to the model Christ had used to advocate nonviolent revolution. It also corresponded to the "little way" of one of her favorite saints, Thérèse of Lisieux—that is, making little daily acts of sacrifice without calling attention to oneself or having concern about their visible results.

Dorothy was also unable to sympathize later on with the way the Berrigans mounted a complex legal defense that required large amounts of money. In seeking justice they seemed to belie the basic position of the peace movement, namely, that one should not expect justice from a system that institutionalized injustice. Thus Dorothy preferred to continue her own style of resistance to the war while maintaining her other involvements as well.

Still in the Struggle—with Chavez

Peter Maurin had not favored Worker involvement in labor disputes because he was opposed to the whole system. There would be no justice, he kept saying, until a new order based on cooperation was installed. However, though Dorothy agreed with him in theory she still supported organized labor and often picketed with strikers. Dorothy often put her body on the line—whether it was for the Southern Tenant Farmers' Union trying to get justice for the poor sharecroppers or the UAW workers sitting down in the Fisher Body Plant in Flint. During the famous sitdown in Flint, Dorothy had managed to get into the building by standing on a box and crawling through a window. Later she was invited to visit Governor Frank Murphy, a regular reader of the *Catholic Worker,* who did much to resolve the Fisher Body strike.

As the 1970s opened, Dorothy did not let up in her zeal. One of the causes that evoked great sympathy on her part was Cesar Chavez's efforts to organize the farmworkers. Completely at the mercy of the often brutal labor contractors whom they relied on for work, they were the most downtrodden workers in the country. Efforts to organize them were a sad history of defeat after defeat, of strikes smashed with violence, and of government collusion with growers who used police to bring in strikebreakers. In addition there were other nearly insurmountable obstacles to organizing farmworkers. They were specifically excluded from the Wagner Act of 1935 which provided legal protection for workers wishing to organize. Moreover, by the nature of their work many of them were migrants who were dispersed and nearly invisible in the communities where they temporarily resided.

Then Cesar Chavez came along. At the time of Cesar's birth in 1927 the Chavez family owned its own farm in Yuma, Arizona. When his father lost the farm in 1937 during the great drought and the Depression, the family became migrant farmworkers. "All we could take with us," he said, "was what we could jam into our old Studebaker." In the following years they made their living picking grapes, lettuce, potatoes, and sugar beets, and experienced to the full the hardships and insecurity of migrant workers. In 1944, at the age of seventeen, Cesar joined the Navy, hoping to escape to a better life. Instead, the two years that followed were the worst of his life. He hated the heavy regimentation and found the racial discrimination intolerable. After his discharge he began working again in the fields. Then in 1952 he was signed up by a community service organizer, Fred Ross ("the best organizer I ever met"), to do voter registration. Eventually he decided to use the lessons Ross taught him to pursue his longtime dream of organizing the farmworkers. In 1962—with the agreement of his wife, Helen, the support of a few friends, and the sum of $1200—he founded the National Farmworkers Association.

Chavez had turned into a superb organizer and by 1964 he had signed up a thousand workers. It was a union built on plodding hard work and very personal relationships. With Delano, California, as his headquarters he drove around in an old Mercury station wagon, meeting workers and signing them up one at a time. In spite of their poverty he insisted they pay regular dues. The dues gave the worker a stake in the success of the union. He was determined to maintain the union's independence and refused to take monies offered by other unions and the AFL-CIO.

Thus began the big grape strike and boycott. In September 1965, 2,700 field workers meeting in the hall of Our Lady of Guadalupe Church in Delano voted to go out on strike. The first vineyards targeted covered about four hundred square miles. Eventually the strike would spread to cover wine grapes used by a whole host of wineries with such labels as Schenley, Almaden, Christian Brothers, and Gallo.

The threat and at times the fact of violence was always present. Growers pushed people around on the picket lines, ran tractors at them, and drove cars and pickups with guns and dogs at high speed around their lines. Some of the workers began to murmur about "burning these sons-of-bitches down," but Chavez was determined to hold to nonviolence. As a student of Gandhi he was tremendously impressed by Gandhi's success in breaking the iron grip of England over India. Like Gandhi he felt that there was no limit to what nonviolence could achieve in overcoming the age-old evils of oppression, hatred, and violence. Gandhi had taught him that nonviolence was not inaction and that, in fact, it demanded the highest degree of mental creativity and spiritual energy. Gandhi had described it as a form of moral jujitsu: One had to keep one's opponent off balance while adhering to one's principles. Cesar used nonviolent means to reach those within the movement, too. At one juncture, UFW (United Farm Workers) pickets did retaliate with violence against the provocations of the growers. Chavez responded with a fast that continued for twenty-five days, until the problem was resolved.

A creative use of symbols was apparent from the beginning. Chavez decided to call for a national boycott of grapes and wine in October 1965 and made Schenley the main target. The timing was right, for the latent moral fervor of Americans was ready to blaze out in one of its cyclical eruptions. Word of the boycott spread with amazing rapidity as people from all walks of life rallied to "La Huelga" (the cause). Volunteers from churches, civic groups, college campuses, and labor unions took up signs painted with the union's official emblem, the Black Aztec Eagle, and begged shoppers not to buy grapes.

The great battle raged for four years in the vineyards of the San Joaquin Valley. The grape growers and winemakers responded with every weapon at their command from media campaigns to lawsuits and court injunctions. However, Chavez was in tune with the mood of a large segment of Americans, and among other things was able to attract some top-flight talent to his staff. Like the rest of the staff and Chavez himself they were willing to work for a pittance—five dollars a week plus room and board while they put in countless hours and stretched themselves to the limit on behalf of the cause.

Chavez used to say "The growers have the money but we have the truth." In any case the union's organizers were able to present their version of the truth in the mass media by a clever use of street theatrics. One of the most successful of these was a march they organized from Delano to the state capital of Sacramento, a distance of three hundred miles. Walking single file, keeping good discipline, and preceded by the American flag, the Mexican flag, and the banner of Our Lady of Guadalupe, the people marched wearing red armbands with the black eagle and carrying the *huelga* flags. At night they celebrated with singing and speeches, mariachi bands, and dramatic readings and plays. People came out from the towns to offer them hospitality and join them for part of the way. Local labor unions came out to show solidarity. National attention was drawn to the march and by the time they reached Stockton, some fifty miles from Sacramento, the marchers numbered around five thousand. A phone call to Cesar informed him that Schenley wanted to sign a contract.

A devout Catholic, Cesar was not too scrupulous about the dubious tactic of using the sacred symbols of the Church to promote the farmworker cause. During the critical strike at the Di Giorgio ranch there was great difficulty in communicating with the workers since a court order restricted the number of pickets. Chavez then took his old station wagon and made it into a shrine to Our Lady of Guadalupe with her picture, candles, and flowers. He parked it across the street from the Di Giorgio gate and the workers began coming to say a prayer or just to take a look. It proved an ideal means of talking with and signing up workers who previously couldn't be reached.

Cesar often expressed his appreciation for the great support he got from the Catholic Church. Large numbers of priests and nuns were active on the picket lines. On one occasion more than forty of them were arrested on one afternoon in southeast Fresno County. In a rare intervention of this kind, the Conference of Catholic Bishops appointed a committee of three bishops to look into the boycott. They were Joseph Donnelly of Hartford, Connecticut; Humberto Medeiros of Brownsville, Texas; and Walter Curtis of Bridgeport, Connecticut. As staff they relied principally on Msgr. George Higgins of the Bishops' social action department. A portly, scholarly, and matter-of-fact type of priest, he was deeply committed to the Church's stand on the rights of labor. As a mediator he was respected for his sense of fair play and devotion to principle, all of which proved invaluable in the torturous negotiations of the farmworkers with the growers.

Higgins secured the American bishops' endorsement of the boycott, and together with Dorothy Day he helped to make possible Chavez's private audience with Pope Paul in 1974. The pope praised him for his "sustained effort to apply the principles of Christian social teaching" and for working with the American bishops' Ad Hoc Committee on Farm Labor. Cesar presented a UFW flag to the pope, who posed with Chavez and the unfurled flag for a photo. The next day Archbishop Benelli, the pope's top aide, lauded Chavez "for teaching us the lesson of the terrible responsibility we have as Christians, namely, the need to be of service to our brothers and sisters in the name of Christ." This message was given in the presence of some two hundred Catholic religious superiors and was communicated to some seventy American bishops. It was a sure sign that the American Catholic Church's support of the boycott was intensifying.[66]

Thanks to steadfast adherence to his principles and his deft practice of moral jujitsu, Chavez was able to forge a movement involving millions of Americans in one of the most extraordinary social and political movements in their history. In fact, Cesar was constantly amazed at the wide diversity of support he got from "a very good cross-section of Americana here. Some of the kids have pretty wealthy parents, and a lot are middle class, of course. Then there are people like the other organizers and me. And there are the

[66]Jacques Levy, *Cesar Chavez* (New York: W. W. Norton & Co, Inc.), pp. 522–525.

farm workers. We have labor people and church people. Protestants like Jim Drake and Chris Hartmire, participating Catholics who came from religious orders, Jewish kids and agnostics."[67]

The pressure of the boycott grew enormously as the cities of Boston, New York, Philadelphia, Chicago, Detroit, Montreal, and Toronto were practically emptied of table grapes. The five-year strike and boycott ended in July 1970. With Bishop Donnelly as mediator, grape growers representing 42 percent of California signed a contract with Cesar's union. At one point the growers broke off the negotiations and went home. But then Giumarra, the leading grower, heard that Acme, the giant supermarket chain, had taken all his produce off their shelves and that Kroger in Cincinnati and buyers in Detroit had canceled their grape orders. Giumarra wasted no time in resuming negotiations, which led to the contract. A month later George Meany, president of the AFL-CIO, announced the end of the grape boycott.

But there was still to be no peace in the orchards and fields of California. Lettuce would now take the place of grapes as a sign of contradiction. Knowing they would be Cesar's next target, the lettuce growers quickly signed a sweetheart contract with the renegade Teamsters Union. Ousted from the AFL-CIO because of their link with organized crime, the Teamsters with their chain-swinging, skull-cracking goons would more than live up to their unsavory reputation. Before the strife ended they would send many farmworker pickets and volunteers to the hospital.

Cesar called for a boycott of lettuce and once again his army of starry-eyed idealists hit the streets to make their pitch to lay off lettuce. But this time the struggle was even more uphill as they lost most of their hard-won contracts while the Teamsters played a deceptive game, making and breaking agreements with them. Moreover, agribusiness (large agricultural corporations) grew more determined than ever to break this "dangerous leftist movement." Richard Nixon, who was in the White House partly due to Teamster support, was more than willing to put the power of the federal government behind the Teamsters' schemes. On July 10, 1973, the nation's largest winery, Gallo Brothers, with a UFW contract for six years nonetheless signed a four-year Teamster contract.

When Dorothy Day heard what was going on and learned of Cesar's need for help, she said: "Let's go." She felt a close identification with the farmworker movement which, like the Workers, was dedicated to nonvi-

[67] Ibid., p. 197.

olence and also drew inspiration in part from the social encyclicals of the popes. She had already met Chavez when he visited New York in 1967 and 1969, and in 1971 she visited the Farmworkers' headquarters in Delano. "Remember the boycott and help the strikers," she wrote in the *Catholic Worker,* "[They are] . . . the poorest and most beloved of God's children."[68] She felt in Chavez a kindred soul whose dedication to nonviolence was sincere.

Now in July 1973 she came once more to lend Cesar support in his unequal battle with the Teamsters, the growers, and the government. A California judge had forbidden farmworker picketlines. But Dorothy said, "My path was clear. The UFW has everything that belongs to a new social order." She decided to join the forbidden farmworker picket lines. A small army of police descended on the pickets but she remained calmly seated on her little folding cane chair in their midst. A famous photo catches Dorothy through an oval frame made by the arms of two big troopers standing over her. She sits hands clasped to knees with broad-brimmed hat slightly tilted and a look of steely determination that might stop a grizzly bear. But the police arrested her along with ninety-nine others, including thirty nuns and two priests, and kept them in prison for nearly two weeks.

Their release was celebrated at a mass. Chavez later said, "It makes us very proud that Dorothy's last trip to jail took place . . . with the farmworkers."[69] They felt they had won a small victory but it would take two more years of struggle before a California Bill of Rights for Farmworkers was passed, making it possible for the farmworkers to vote for the union of their choice. The elections of that fall pitted the United Farm Workers against the Teamsters; the Farm Workers won an overwhelming victory.

However, the decades ahead saw more human drama, more sacrifice, more victories, and even more defeats as the enemies of the union were able to gut the farmworker bill and use the courts and police to block unionization. The UFW remains still stymied at the end of the 1990s, far from realizing its goals of humanizing farm labor. Cesar is sometimes blamed for the debacle, supposedly due to his rigidity and autocratic ways—unfairly, perhaps, since the main cause is the changed political climate in California as well as the country. If not yet successful in organizing the mass of farmworkers, the movement nevertheless has already achieved significance

---

[68] Forest, *Love Is the Measure,* pp. 168–169.
[69] Roberts, *Dorothy Day and the Catholic Worker,* p. 166.

by the way it demonstrated the great potential of nonviolence. When Chavez died in April 1993, Monsignor Higgins rightly paid tribute to the remarkable vision of this "great and good man."[70]

The Race Is Run

As the 1960s passed into the 1970s, a new breed came along, youths whose ideas and lifestyle jarred considerably with the traditional tone and temper of the Catholic Worker community. They were alienated from the Church whose traditions they scorned and whose moral constraints they felt infringed on their freedom. But their sexual revolution would find no friend in Dorothy. She was firmly committed to the teachings of the Church on sexuality, on marriage and its indissolubility.

"This whole crowd," she said, "goes to extremes in sex and drugs." It was "a complete rebellion against authority, natural and supernatural, even against the body and its needs, its natural functions of childbearing. It can only be a hatred of sex that leads them to talk as they do and be so explicit about the . . . sex organs." This was "not reverence for life . . . it is a great denial."[71] Finally Dorothy felt she had no choice but to turn some of them out because "people do not support the Catholic Worker to support a group of young ones who live from hand to mouth."

At the same time she well understood these young people's dismay and cynicism about the "bourgeoisity" of the Church and its lack of leadership in matters of social justice. She herself had suffered much from the compromises she had to make with the Church's glacial pace in moving toward a social conscience. But now as ever, the question and its answer were the same: "Where else shall we go except to the Bride of Christ, one flesh with Christ? Though she is a harlot at times, she is our Mother."[72]

As Dorothy passed into her middle seventies she was still going strong, traveling widely and speaking at numerous gatherings. Her last speaking trip was in August 1976 when she traveled to the Eucharistic Congress in Philadelphia where she and Mother Teresa were invited to speak. In her address Dorothy recalled the events that had led her to the Church and the Eucharist—how the material world "began to speak to my heart of the love of

---

[70] *Commonweal*, June 4, 1993, p. 4.
[71] Miller, *A Harsh and Dreadful Love*, p. 337.
[72] Ibid., p. 339.

God" and how she was attracted by the physical aspects of the Church, the bread and wine, the oil and water, the incense.[73]

Always ready to admit her own failings, she was much embarrassed by the increasing number of accolades that came her way in her later years. The Jesuit magazine *America* devoted a special issue to her as an individual who best symbolized "the aspiration and action of the American Church community during the past forty years." In bestowing on her the Laetare medal, Notre Dame University lauded her as one "who comforted the afflicted and afflicted the comfortable."[74] And when Cardinal Cooke came to visit her, bringing a message from the pope, she was "overwhelmed."

As she neared eighty she more and more felt captive to her frail body and "sick, weak heart" and was often confined to her room, where from her window she could see "a sycamore tree with a few little seed balls hanging from it, the pigeons flying and squirrels on the roof edge, the sky a cloudless blue." At Easter 1979 Cesar Chavez came for a visit, and in June, Mother Teresa.

Except for an occasional visitor, her day was broken up by recitation of the divine office and Psalms, times of silent prayer, reading, meals, radio and television. Watching Eugene O'Neill's plays on television brought back many memories of the saloon on Sixth Avenue where they had spent so many evenings together.

The column she continued to write for the Catholic Worker began to make only sporadic appearances and by 1980 was reduced to one- or two-sentence diary notes. She heard of the Workers' week-long vigil at the Pentagon and longed for one more time on the picket line. Her final written words spoke of the "beautiful statue of the Madonna behind the altar in the Maryhouse chapel" carved by her sister-in-law. On November 29 Tamar came to see her late in the afternoon. Dorothy asked her for a cup of tea. As she sipped the tea she remarked how good life can be at certain times and held Tamar's hand. At 5:30 P.M., with Tamar at her bedside, Dorothy's great heart simply stopped beating and death came gently and peacefully.

Her body was clothed in a simple blue-and-white checkered dress and placed in an unvarnished pine coffin in the little chapel at Maryhouse. People came by the thousands to say goodbye, from all walks of life and every political and religious stripe including atheists as well. Her grandchildren carried the coffin to the nearby Nativity Mission Church where she

---

[73] Forest, *Love Is the Measure,* p. 187.
[74] Ibid., pp. 180–181.

had worshiped so often. At the entrance Cardinal Cooke blessed the body before a huge crowd that included Forster Batterham, whom she had never ceased to call her husband. A simple stone marked the spot where she was buried on Staten Island near the beach house where her conversion had occurred. Engraved on it were the loaves-and-fishes symbol she had used so often, along with her name, dates, and the words "Deo Gratias."

At a Memorial Mass celebrated on January 26, 1981, Cardinal Cooke pointed out in his homily that "she had been called upon to make a voluntary and complete surrender of human love to divine love."[75]

Legacy

"The first hippie."
   —ABBIE HOFFMAN[76]

"The Catholic Worker is not just a journal but a revolution."
   —PETER MAURIN

"A spiritual revolution is upon us . . . It is a permanent revolution, this Catholic Worker movement."
   —DOROTHY DAY, *Catholic Worker,* December, 1933

Describing the sort of revolution she meant by "permanent revolution," Dorothy stated: "The greatest challenge of the day is how to bring about a revolution of the heart, a revolution which has to start with each one of us. When we begin to take the lowest place, to wash the feet of others, to love our brothers with that burning love, that passion, which led to the Cross, then we can truly say, 'Now I have begun.' "

"As a Catholic Worker she considered herself one of a community of revolutionaries who are encouraged in trying to build a new social order, marked by anarchism, pacifism and the works of mercy."[77]

"By their mission field approach to reform, the Catholic Workers furnished a sense of direction to the enlarging corps of Catholics anxious to crusade for social justice."

   —AARON ABELL, *American Catholicism and Social Action*

[75] Eileen Egan, *Cross Currents,* Winter 1980–1981, p. 377.
[76] Roberts, *Dorothy Day and the Catholic Worker,* p. 165.
[77] June O'Connor, *The Moral Vision of Dorothy Day* (New York: Crossroad, 1991), p. 67.

The influence of Dorothy and the Catholic Worker movement on the American Church, not to mention the country as a whole, has been remarkable. As one observer said, while few have adopted the positions of the Workers there are even fewer who have been untouched by them. The philosopher J. M. Cameron credited Dorothy and her associates with having "done more to preserve the balance and sanity of American Catholicism than anything else."[78] The mainstream monthly *St. Anthony Messenger* has written: "Part of coming to terms with being a Catholic in today's world is in fact coming to terms with Dorothy Day."[79] Such key concepts of the Catholic Worker movement as nonviolence, simplicity of life, indiscriminate love, and personal responsibility have left a deep impression on the American Catholic Church.

A prime example of Worker influence is the flourishing Catholic peace movement. Much of its present vitality is due to the Workers who for decades stood as lonely prophets within a Church that had long viewed war as, at times, a moral option. But the war in Vietnam and the nuclear arms race caused many Catholics to question their Church's traditional stand on war. Finally, in a historic shift, the American bishops themselves issued a rightly acclaimed pastoral that placed them at odds with the country's nuclear weapons strategy. They also endorsed pacifism as an acceptable moral choice for Catholics, and paid homage to Dorothy Day and Martin Luther King for the profound impact their nonviolent witness has had on the Church.[80]

It may surprise some to hear that the *Catholic Worker,* in spite of its unassuming format and quiet voice, ranks in the forefront of radical American journals. It has been compared favorably to other distinguished radical journals such as the *Guardian,* I. F. Stone's *Weekly* (1953–1971), and the *Nation.*[81] It has maintained an almost preternatural consistency as a voice of protest, a journal committed to social justice and peace activism.

[78] Roberts, *Dorothy Day and the Catholic Worker,* p. 174.

[79] Ibid., p. 174. Talk about Dorothy's canonization took on new life when John Cardinal O'Connor, the Archbishop of New York, recently said he would take steps toward proposing sainthood for Dorothy. Others thought that such an elevation to those lofty realms might diminish that earthy quality of her personality which is so much a part of her appeal. See the *New York Times,* Nov. 10, 1997.

[80] Ibid., pp. 172–173.

[81] Ibid., p. 174.

Postscript

What would become of the Worker movement when Dorothy died? This was a question often asked as her health declined. As of 1998 it is still flourishing, with St. Joseph's House and Maryhouse in New York and several dozen Catholic Worker Houses of Hospitality and farming communes around the country. Its journalistic organ, the *Catholic Worker,* has been cut down to eight issues a year but it is still a quality paper with the same design it has always had; it is sprinkled regularly with fond references to Dorothy and reprints of her articles. Of course no one expects another Dorothy Day to come along to keep both paper and movement at the same glorious level of interest and excitement, for after all, hers was a "unique constellation of talents." But the movement continues to attract dedicated and creative people who intend to carry on Dorothy's work.

FOURTEEN

Konrad Adenauer (1876–1967): The Resurrection of Germany

O N AUGUST 23, 1944, two men knocked on the door of a large, handsome house in the village of Rhöndorf outside of Cologne. The young woman who opened the door was visibly disturbed to recognize one of them as a local policeman. After entering, one of the men took Konrad Adenauer into his bedroom to interrogate him while the other sat down in the drawing room to speak with Frau Adenauer. Feeling sorry for the now terrified woman, the good-natured man tried to tell her what he knew. "Those up above [perhaps] are afraid these gentlemen might do something if the war goes wrong."[1] Konrad Adenauer emerged from the bedroom and was taken away as his grandchildren, crying and screaming, crowded around him. Later he was handed over to the state security service of the Gestapo at the headquarters near Bonn. During the next three months Konrad Adenauer would spend some of the worst hours of his life.

[1] Paul Weymar, *Adenauer* (New York: E. P. Dutton and Co., 1957), p. 121.

The Center Party and Its Vicissitudes

Konrad Adenauer was the "one great German statesman of the century" and the outstanding figure produced by German Social and Political Catholicism.[2] He started his political career as a member of the Center Party, the political home of German Catholics since the days of Otto von Bismarck (1815–1898). The Center Party was formed in 1871 to defend the interests of Catholics in the newly unified and Protestant-dominated Germany. The Center's aims were to preserve the protection of religious rights guaranteed by the Prussian Constitution and to prevent overcentralization of government.

The formation of the Center Party was most unwelcome to the dictatorial "Iron Chancellor" Bismarck, who determined to isolate and destroy the party. The definition of papal infallibility just passed at the Vatican Council

Konrad Adenauer

[2]Terence Prittie, *Konrad Adenauer* (Chicago: Cowles Book Company, 1971), p. 17.

(1870) provided him with a weapon. Ridiculing the definition as a product of superstition, he called for a *Kulturkampf* (struggle for civilization) against the Catholic Church.[3] The *Kulturkampf* eventually ended in a dismal failure for Bismarck. As the historian Hajo Holborn says, though Bismarck tried to blame the failure of his *Kulturkampf* on the Machiavellianism of the priests, it was actually the "firm faith of the German Catholics in their church that defeated the Prussian government . . . Bismarck was unable to [understand] . . . the religious foundation of the Roman Catholic Church."[4]

For the next sixty years the Center Party, as the second largest party in Germany, played a pivotal role in the federal parliament or Reichstag. One of the major issues that faced the Center during this period was its relation to the Catholic trade union movement, which burgeoned with the impressive growth of German Social Catholicism in the 1890s. Trade union leaders like Adam Stegerwald constantly insisted on the need for the Center to foster greater social consciousness among its largely middle-class constituents.

This debate was disrupted by the coming of World War I and the collapse of Germany after its defeat on the battlefield in 1918. Chaos took over with mutinies in the navy, rioting in the streets, and the threat of imminent starvation. Added to all this was the enormous psychological disarray caused by defeat, and the humiliation inflicted on Germany by the victors at Versailles who excoriated the Germans as warmongers and loaded them with impossibly heavy reparations. Kaiser Wilhelm abdicated and fled the coun-

---

[3]One of the most dramatic episodes of the Center's history during the *Kulturkampf* occurred in 1887. The pope felt the time had come for a religious settlement and dispatched two notes to the Center requesting them to vote for a military budget that Bismarck was having difficulty getting passed. When he got wind of the papal intervention, Bismarck exulted. The Center, he believed, was caught in an insoluble dilemma. If the Center acquiesced in the pope's request, it would be "unmasked" as a tool of a foreign power; if it defied the pope it risked losing the support of the pious among its members. Either way, Bismarck could reckon, the Center would suffer the crippling blow his *Kulturkampf* had failed to deliver. But the able leader of the Center, Ludwig Windthorst, rose magnificently to the occasion. In a famous speech at Gurzenich in Cologne, Windthorst was able to argue persuasively from certain passages in the papal letter that in political matters the Center had complete freedom. Without casting a slur on the pope's authority, Windthorst had extricated his party from the trap the pope had unwittingly set. As he climbed down from the rostrum amid enthusiastic cheers, Windthorst uttered a sigh of relief. He had "preserved his party and kept it united in the face of the most dangerous challenge it had ever faced." Margaret Lavinia Anderson, *Windthorst: A Political Biography* (Oxford: Clarendon Press, 1981), pp. 348–353.

[4]Hajo Holborn, *A History of Modern Germany* (Princeton, N.J.: Princeton University Press, 1969), p. 265.

try, leaving the government to reorganize under a new constitution at Weimar; Germany became known as the Weimar Republic. The decade and a half that followed was one of unremitting disaster for Germany. Crippled by the debt for reparations, the German economy fell into a tailspin. Hunger spread and unemployment reached incredible numbers, while inflation destroyed the middle class. In March 1920 the Kapp Putsch by paramilitary units aided by elements in the army and its chief of the general staff attempted to overthrow the republic. A general strike by the free trade unions saved the republic for the time being but total political and economic chaos still threatened. Monarchists yearned to return to the authoritarian order of the past while socialists looked to a classless utopian future. In the splintered middle stood the Center and the other parties committed to democracy but often too caught up in their own party interests to realize that time was running out.

Voices in the Center Party had been raised earlier calling for a new party that would draw together all Christian and national-feeling Germans into a new "Christian" and "democratic" party. Stegerwald wanted to reform the Center party and change its name in order to make the broadest possible appeal to the workers, to the already democratically minded element of the Center Party, and to other nonsocialist Germans. Father Heinrich Brauns, a Centrist leader, agreed. "The matter is urgent," he had declared, "so that the masses do not . . . swing over to social democracy." Stegerwald was determined to show that the socialists held no monopoly on social conscience. He saw that a solid social policy was the key to national integration and insisted that a nation without social justice would perish. But the leaders of the Center Party meeting at Duisberg in November 1918 had rejected Stegerwald's proposals. There would be no reform nor any change of name. The name was a "source of spiritual energy," a reminder of "history and tradition and of its great leaders." Stegerwald, however, continued to argue for the party's transformation, and at the party's Reich (the state) committee in October 1920 he insisted that a reformed party would ease Germany's passage through the "valley of misery." He claimed that the existence of four nonsocialist parties was absurd.[5] Joseph Wirth, leader of the Center's left wing, thought Stegerwald's proposal absurd. Pointing to the terrible ravages of hyperinflation and its consequence, the impoverishment of the

---

[5] Noel D. Cary, *The Path to Christian Democracy* (Cambridge, Mass.: Harvard University Press, 1966), p. 82.

middle class, he predicted increased social conflict. The task at hand was not to transform the party but simply to salvage it.[6, 7]

In a speech to the trade union delegates at Essen on November 21, 1920, Stegerwald painted a dark picture of the country's condition. The crisis of capitalism, he said, showed how humanity's moral development had lagged far behind its scientific and technological progress. Weimar's "formal democracy" was unequal to the task of social reconstruction. The fragmented party system was unable to face the challenge of socialism. Only a large moderate party pooling the patriotic, Christian, popular, and truly social-minded circles from all strata of the population could do so.[8]

On June 24, 1922, the assassination of Walter Rathenau of the German Democratic Party (DDP) by a right-winger alerted the other parties to the threat from the right. The majority Socialists and the moderate wing of the Independents completed their reunification while the three parties in the middle—the Center, the German People's Party (DVP), and the German Democratic Party (DDP)—agreed to make themselves available for coalitions. Father Heinrich Brauns called for "a coalition of just two strong parties, one socialist, one nonsocialist, that would distance themselves from the extreme right, commit themselves to the constitution, and govern together.[9] And to strengthen the role of the Center Party as the core of the proposed coalition, Brauns also proposed that the Center add a significant number of Protestants to its electoral lists for the next campaign. (In the light of Konrad Adenauer's later success in thus reforming the party system, it is worth noting that at the annual convocation of German Catholics *(Katholikentag)* in July 1922, he urged just such a step.) But once again the Center's leaders backed away from undertaking any true party-system reform.

By November 1923, inflation had reached its zenith—four trillion marks to the U.S. dollar. At the end of the year Centrist politician Wilhelm Marx formed a minority coalition government of the middle with Social Democratic toleration. His government negotiated a reparations payment scheme (the Dawes Plan) and brought inflation under control. During the next ten years, the Center took part in a series of coalition governments, four of them headed by Wilhelm Marx. Tensions mounted during this period over

[6] Ibid.
[7] Ibid., p. 83.
[8] Ibid., pp. 84–86.
[9] Ibid., p. 98.

the inclusion of the German National People's Party (DNVP) in a Centrist coalition. Also disturbing to many Centrists was the support given to the right wing by the Westphalian agrarian Centrists led by Franz von Papen in electing Field Marshall Paul von Hindenburg president of the Reich.

In view of the polarization of the Center, advocates appeared who favored dissolving the Center to facilitate the establishment of a two-party system. They insisted that parties based on distinct ideologies (in German, *Weltanschauungen*) were no longer useful, nor was the mediating role of the Center Party any longer realistic. The journalist Heinrich Teipel, a leading advocate of two-party reform, envisaged a "national-conservative" party against a "progressive-Europeanist" one. With workers in both camps the party would not be class-based; at the same time, given the present state of the world's development, both parties would have to be capitalist. The Center Party was no longer needed to defend Catholic interests, he pointed out; as a matter of fact, there were now more Catholics outside than within.

Teipel's proposal crashed when the year-long Centrist crisis was resolved with the withdrawal of the DNVP from the government. When Wilhelm Marx formed a new government once again including the DNVP, Joseph Wirth refused to give it his vote. Wirth went on the attack, appearing at rallies of the republican paramilitary Reichbanner group to call for a "higher unity" of all sincere adherents of the republic.

Wirth's view that confessional concerns should be subordinated to the common interests of the country was underscored by the controversy over denominational schools. The Catholic convocation in 1927 saw a wave of speeches assigning top priority to the need to give equal status to denominational schools. Father Ludwig Kaas called the demand "unrenounceable"; the Center's executive board agreed and demanded total compliance with this position by all Centrists. However, the school bill failed and the Centrist-headed government fell. Wirth saw it all as confirmation of his view that parties based on *Weltanschauungen* were no longer of value. As historian Noel Cary sums it up: "The Center had exacerbated subcultural tensions in an already deeply divided nation; it had diverted the nation's energy from higher priorities; it had endangered the development of the cooperative instinct in the DVP [German People's Party]; and it had failed to secure the bill's passage."[10]

By the time the world financial crisis struck in 1929, German democracy had all but expired. The last democratic chancellor, Center Party member

[10]Cary, *The Path to Christian Democracy*, p. 116.

Heinrich Brüning, bypassed democratic processes to rule by decree in an unsuccessful attempt to quell the mounting disorder in the streets, where Nazi stormtroopers now regularly brutalized their opponents.[11] Believing that his plan for economic revival was beginning to work, Brüning called elections in the hope of gaining support for the moderate democratic parties. They resulted instead in making Adolf Hitler and the Nazis the second-largest party. With President von Hindenburg virtually senile, his advisers, including Kurt Schleicher, plotted freely to set up an authoritarian government and destroy the Socialists and the trade unions. In May 1932 they made Franz von Papen, still nominally a Centrist, chancellor. The Centrist press denounced von Papen as a renegade and the party refused to participate in the new government. But the time of Centrist capitulation to the Nazi program was drawing near.

In the next election campaign of July 1933, the Nazis polled 37.4 percent. The Centrist Joseph Joos tried to negotiate a coalition with the Nazis in spite of previous Centrist claims that the Nazis were irresponsible, virulently anticlerical, and heathenistic. The Center Party's fear of the Communists, as well as their gullibility in believing that the Nazis could be educated in constitutionalism, played a part in the Centrist decision to seek cooperation with the Nazis. The Center was spared the ignominy of a coalition with the Nazis only because Hitler refused the offer. Kurt Schleicher assumed the chancellorship in the hope of setting up a military government. When this attempt failed, Hindenburg named Hitler chancellor and von Papen vice-chancellor. While not opposed to Hitler as chancellor, the Center held aloof this time from entering the government.

During the next campaign, the Nazis, with government backing, engaged in widespread terror. One of their victims was Adam Stegerwald, who was severely beaten as he tried to deliver a speech. Hitler gained an absolute majority and then asked for an enabling act that would allow him to rule by decree for four years. To attain the two-thirds majority needed, Hitler needed the Center's support. In voting unanimously for the act, the Center signed its own death warrant. Their decision to comply was fueled by many considerations: the Nazi use of terror, the fear of being labeled unpatriotic and of the likely decimation of Centrist civil servants with the economic hardships this would cause, and Hitler's pledges to respect the role

---

[11]The Nazi or National Socialist party originated after World War I. Under its leader Adolf Hitler, it espoused Aryan supremacy, anti-semitism, anti-communism, German expansionism, the cult of the führer and the annulment of the Versailles Treaty.

of the churches. But the noteworthy absence among these pledges of any guarantee of the civil rights of others gravely compromised the Center's venerable claim of defending not just the civil rights of Catholics but the general principle of minority rights. Inexplicably the Center overlooked the fact that Hitler had given nothing but his word that he would live up to his pledges.

As Noel Cary says: "Opposition to the Enabling Act would seem, prima facie, to have been the only position in accordance with the Center's self-image as a "constitution party," for it would have forced the Nazis to reveal the illegal nature of their dictatorship."[12] Instead, Centrist approval allowed the Nazis to hide behind the façade of constitutional compliance. Centrist ex-chancellor Wilhelm Marx justified the acquiescence of the Center in Hitler's tyrannical state by invoking the "Catholic" principle of recognizing any regime that had achieved dominance. The conscience of the Centrists was eased by the cooperation of the bishops, who rescinded their anti-Nazi prohibitions and urged Catholics to support the state.

It was soon clear that the Center's days were numbered. Father Kaas was spotted traveling to Rome at the same time that von Papen was on his way to the Vatican to negotiate a Reich concordat. Kaas eventually telephoned from the Vatican to ask Centrist leaders why the party had not yet dissolved. The dissolution of the party was announced simultaneously with the forthcoming signing of the concordat. As a face-saving measure, the concordat was hailed as a Centrist triumph and the culmination of its work. The concordat did preserve the denominational schools and the church subsidy but it banned the political action of priests and eliminated many of the Catholic Church's social and vocational organizations. Hitler soon showed how flimsy were guarantees not backed up by a vigilant Catholic party. As Noel Cary says: "What Bismarck and Leo XIII, in the face of Windthorst's resistance, could not arrange, Hitler and Pius XI, with Kaas's eager collaboration, did."[13]

The Mayor of Cologne

At the time of Hitler's accession, Konrad Adenauer was the very popular mayor of Cologne. Born in Rhineland, Cologne on January 5, 1876, he died April 19, 1967, in Rhöndorf, only a few miles away from his birthplace.

---

[12]Cary, *The Path to Christian Democracy*, p. 139.
[13]Ibid., p. 141.

Terence Prittie calls him "the one great German statesman of the century."[14]

His father, also named Konrad Adenauer, had served in the Prussian Army before leaving to marry and settle down as a clerk in the district court. He was a man of few words, strict with the children, whom he trained in the traditional German virtues of honesty, duty, industry, thrift, and self-control. The family, for instance, ate only potatoes on Sundays in order to save money for a Christmas tree.

The younger Konrad studied law at Freiburg University on a scholarship. For six years he was a full-time student. His contemporaries remembered him as a reticent, colorless, nose-to-the-grindstone type of fellow, though his poverty and a frail constitution may have had something to do with this impression. While he was a student he and a friend managed to travel around Italy and Switzerland on a few pennies—trips that must have instilled in the young Adenauer his first clear concept of "his" Europe, the "Western Europe for which the Rhinelanders felt a real sense of kinship, and to which they belonged much more than to Prussia."[15] Adenauer remained a Western European all his life. His lifelong distrust of Prussia stemmed from his childhood experience of the *Kulturkampf,* which for the German Catholics of the time was a defining experience.

After receiving his law degree at the age of twenty-three he obtained a position in a private law firm in Cologne, and in January 1904 married into the socially prominent Weyer family. In 1906 he ran successfully for the Cologne City Council with the help of the head of the law firm, who was chairman of the Cologne Center Party. Adenauer thus began a municipal career that was to last twenty-seven years, until the Nazi seizure of power. His personal life was marked by tragedy. His wife, Emma, who bore him three children, was stricken with an incurable illness. While carrying a heavy burden of work at the city hall, he would take his midday break with her, then spend hours at her bedside in the evening reading to her and seeing her safely to sleep. The care of the children also devolved on him and they remembered his strict discipline and the skinhead haircuts he insisted the boys have since they were "hygienic and cheap." These days of incessant anxiety and work he called "absolute hell," and it was at this time he began to sleep badly—an affliction that stayed with him for the rest of his life.

World War I came as an awful shock to the prosperous and proud nation

---

[14]Prittie, *Konrad Adenauer,* p. 17.
[15]Ibid., p. 27.

of 63 million people who were enjoying a constantly increasing level of comfort. Adenauer had little time to ponder the absurdity of the war or to indulge in the frenzy of patriotism that gripped his fellow citizens. As head of the Cologne Food Department he had to use the utmost ingenuity in finding ways to procure food for 600,000 people near the brink of starvation. His inventions, "Cologne soya-sausage" and "Cologne maize bread," helped to fill empty stomachs and reinforced his popularity. An automobile accident at the time left him so disfigured that his family could hardly recognize him the first time they saw him in the hospital because his cheekbones, nose, and jaw had been reset so poorly. During his convalescence, a delegation from the council came to see whether his mental reflexes had been affected. With the dry humor that was his trademark he told them that it was only the exterior of his cranium that had been damaged. The city agreed and elected him mayor. On October 18, 1917, at his installation the forty-one-year-old Adenauer, tall, slim, and clad in black, told the people:

> There is nothing better life can offer than to allow a man to expend himself fully with all the strength of his mind and soul, and to devote his entire being to creative ability. This field you have opened up for me by electing me Lord Mayor of the City of Cologne, and for this I thank you from the bottom of my heart.[16]

The Germans' enthusiasm for the war had by this time slowly ebbed away. The food shortage had become desperate and for long periods turnips were the only vegetable available. Children walked barefoot to the government-run soup kitchens. Finally, the great German spring offensive in 1918 collapsed and the hope of victory expired. In Cologne Adenauer had to deal with the revolutionary republic that was proclaimed by returning troops who set up a "Workers and Soldiers Council." He ordered police into action against looters and stopped the mutineers from hoisting the red flag over the Town Hall. Thanks in part to his steadiness and courage, Cologne was spared the violence that swept through Berlin and other German cities. In all the turmoil and chaos, Adenauer demonstrated that remarkable composure and common sense so characteristic of his whole career.

In September 1919, three years after the death of his wife, Adenauer married for a second time. At twenty-five his new wife Gussi was much younger than her forty-three-year-old husband. She was charming, fond of children and flowers, and cheerful with much zest for life. Tragedy struck

[16]Ibid., p. 36.

anew when their first child died three days after birth. In time four more children were added to the lively Adenauer household. Like his own father, Herr Adenauer was strict but the family he presided over was a happy one. He also presided over a lively city as the German economy began to recover. One of the projects he was most proud of was a handsome greenbelt of meadows and forests that was created in place of the old forts that had encircled the city. Many other improvements were added during his tenure: a large university, a sports stadium, the Rhein-Herne Canal, a suspension bridge over the Rhine.

Adenauer's talents and unbounded energy made him an obvious candidate for national office and he was approached several times to form a government during the hectic days of the Weimar Republic. But on each occasion, after reflecting on the constant see-saw of Reich governments, he demurred. Might he have saved the Weimar Republic? Some think his toughness, resilience, and staying power were just the qualities that were needed in a chancellor at the time. But others point out that he stood too far to the right in the Center Party to win its continued support.

In the election of 1929, held under the shadow of world depression, Adenauer barely managed to scrape by. The Nazis capitalized on voter uncertainty and distress to begin their advance to power. In the elections of 1930 they increased their numbers in the Reichstag from 12 to 107. The Communist Party representation rose from 54 to 77 at the same time. The Nazis also emerged victorious in the street battles with the Communists and Social Democrats. Some five million men organized to carry on this "civil war" faced only 10,000 police who were supposed to maintain order. In 1931, 182 people were killed and over 15,000 wounded.

Adenauer at first regarded the Communists as the greater threat but by the middle of 1932 he had recognized the real menace of Nazism. Adenauer had already incurred the wrath of the Nazis when, as a member of the Prussian Commission, he opposed the Nazis' plan to dissolve the Prussian Parliament, which the Nazis feared might become a focus of democracy in the new authoritarian Reich they were planning to establish. When Hitler, as the German chancellor, visited Cologne in February 1933, Adenauer failed to meet him at the airport but sent a member of the city council in his place. Adenauer had also refused permission for swastikas to be hung from the bridge over the Rhine, though he allowed them at the fairgrounds where Hitler was to speak. These and other moves made by Adenauer in opposition to the Nazis were to cost him dearly.

A Marked Man

Targeted now by the Nazis as an enemy, Adenauer began to feel the heat. Warned that he was about to be liquidated, he slipped away in a friend's car early in the morning of March 13, 1933, leaving his official car standing by. His destination was Berlin to meet with Hermann Goering, the Reich minister of the interior. Strangely Adenauer didn't seem to realize that the horribly cruel, vain, and utterly unprincipled Goering was the last man to ask for help. Goering reminded Adenauer coldly of the supposedly anti-Nazi stands Adenauer had taken and added that he was under official suspicion for embezzlement of city funds. It was a bleak moment for Adenauer. Without a friend in high places, and with the Center Party in the process of dissolution, he needed a refuge until the Nazi storm blew over. Fortunately he found Ildefons Herwegen, an old school friend who was now the abbot of the monastery of Maria Laach. Herwegen offered him a hiding place.

It turned out to be an ideal arrangement. Living in the beautiful monastery with its fine library, Adenauer had the opportunity to read widely, to pray, and to meditate on his experience. He read the great papal social encyclicals *Rerum Novarum* and *Quadragesimo Anno* for the first time and they made a decisive impression upon him. He discovered in them "a comprehensive and coherent program inspired by belief in an order willed by God which was perfectly practicable in terms of modern society."[17] Instead of the class struggle, they proposed a vision of the world where the worker could be released from the spiritual and material pressures of his seemingly hopeless situation. He was also deeply impressed by the encyclicals' emphasis on the tendency of the state to extend its power at the expense of personal liberty. As Paul Weymar says, Adenauer's subsequent political work could not be explained without reference to these months at Maria Laach.[18]

The interlude came to an end rather abruptly when the governor of the Rhineland ordered the abbot to tell Adenauer to leave. In spite of the abbot's refusal to comply, Adenauer left anyway so as not to cause problems for the monastery. His next move on the run took him to Neubabelsberg, a small place on the outskirts of Berlin where he found a house suitable for himself and his family. Located in a gloomy forest in the heartland of Protestant Prussia, near a city Adenauer hated and not far from the official

[17] Weymar, *Adenauer,* p. 100.
[18] Ibid.

headquarters of the Nazi government, it was a forbidding choice. Nevertheless the children later remembered this as a happy time and Adenauer kept his fears to himself. The doting father was able to spend much time with his children, taking them on picnics, teaching them to swim, and joining in their fun and games. Family solidarity was something he greatly valued and he made the most of this opportunity to strengthen it.

But the turbulent world outside soon intruded again when Hitler launched a massacre of his enemies in June 1934. It started with the murder of Ernst Roehm, the second most powerful Nazi, head of the three million member SA (Storm Troopers). Roehm had talked of moving the Nazi revolution into its second phase by installing a socialist order and totally unifying the country. After successfully disposing of his arch rival with minimum public outrage, Hitler took advantage of the moment to eliminate all his opponents, real and imagined. In the bloodbath that followed, many high-ranking politicos were gunned down including General von Schleicher and his wife; Edgar Jung, a personal assistant of von Papen; and Erich Klausener, head of Catholic Action. Many prominent Social Democrats were flung into the newly created concentration camps. The Centrist ex-chancellor Heinrich Brüning, however, was able to escape to the United States.

Adenauer was picked up by the Gestapo while he was with his family in the garden watering his flowers. Interrogated with the threat of torture, Adenauer steadfastly maintained his innocence of any involvement in a plot against the Nazi regime and was finally released. But he knew that it was not his last encounter with the Gestapo. As he told an old friend, "Hitler will never lose a single one of his former opponents from sight and if the regime blunders into mistakes we shall have to pay for them."[19] He was soon proven right. A warning came from Abbot Ildefons that he was in grave danger and he went again into hiding while his family waited in suspense for his return.

That scare lifted, and with the help of a government pension, Adenauer moved his family into a big old house in the village of Rhöndorf on the east bank of the Rhine. The Gestapo struck again in 1935. An order arrived expelling him from the district of Cologne. Leaving his family again he found refuge in a vacant building used at times as a convalescent home for priests. All alone in the large and cheerless dwelling in his sixtieth year, without work or purpose and facing a future that seemed dark and hopeless,

[19]Ibid., p. 110.

he felt his spirit broken and an overwhelming sense of frustration. In his words he was like "a tree which had been torn up by the roots and tossed into the river of life to drift aimlessly downstream."[20] But in 1936 the expulsion order was unexpectedly rescinded and he was able to return to his family at Rhöndorf.

When the war broke out in 1939 he was firmly convinced that the Nazis would not and should not win. Sure that the Nazis would make a new roundup of "suspects," Adenauer spent his time gardening and working on his house. He took no part in the 1944 conspiracy to assassinate Hitler. The extremely cautious Adenauer would not have put his family at risk of the terrible reprisals he knew the Nazis would take when the plot failed, as he was sure it would. The plot miscarried on July 20 when a bomb planted in Hitler's office exploded but only injured the Führer. Retribution against those conspirators who were discovered was swift and gruesomely fatal.

Caught in the Nazi Net

Adenauer's guarded behavior throughout the war was not sufficient to protect him against suspicion in the wake of the assassination attempt. On August 23, 1944, he was taken into custody as part of a comprehensive police sweep throughout the whole Reich. The detention center where he was interned with other political prisoners was a depressing sight. The prisoners' bunks were in three tiers, the air stale and stifling, and the place was infested with bugs. His wife and daughter caught a glimpse of him, pale and emaciated, before they were chased away from the barbed-wire fence. The sight spurred them to action and soon parcels of food arrived not only from the family but from friends and all sorts of people who had heard of his plight. He was glad to share his abundance with the other inmates, many of whom were doctors, lawyers, politicians, civil servants, and university teachers. At least there was plenty of intellectual stimulation in the dreadful camp and Adenauer later remembered discussing for hours problems of religion and politics, art and science. At the same time they were all continually reminded of the horrible fate that probably awaited them as fellow inmates would suddenly disappear into the extermination camps.

One day Adenauer's name appeared on the list of those being sent to Buchenwald—a virtual death warrant. With the help of a friendly doctor, Adenauer was able to feign illness and was transported to a hospital. From

[20]Prittie, *Konrad Adenauer*, p. 95.

there a friend of the family, Major Hans Schliebusch, arrived in an official Luftwaffe (German Air Force) car and secured his release with the help of a fake document. Schliebusch brought him to Nister Mühle, an old mill forty miles southeast of Cologne. The allies were already advancing into Germany and Adenauer planned to lie low until the end of the war.

But the Gestapo were immediately on his trail and arriving at Rhöndorf took his wife, Gussi, away for interrogation. Greatly distraught, their daughter Libet went to the commisar, Herr Bethge, to find out where they had taken Gussi. "He was a short stocky man," she remembered, "with black hair, fanatical eyes, and a skin like tanned leather. He remained seated behind his desk as I entered and for a long time scrutinized me in silence. Then he asked gruffly: 'What do you want?' 'Please, I should like to see my mother, Frau Gussi Adenauer,' I said. He shrugged his shoulders and didn't seem to think it necessary even to answer." After she began to cry he told her again to go home. Then narrowing his eyes he gave her a crafty look. " 'Do you happen to know, by any chance, where your father is hiding out?' I shook my head and said nothing. Impatiently Bethge repeated, 'Come on now, get out of here!' When I refused to leave, Bethge got furious and yelled at me, 'You impertinent little beast! Get out of here at once!' " When Libet still refused to leave, he slammed his fist down on his desk and shouted, "This is the biggest piece of insolence I've ever come across! Who do you think you are?" Staring at her fixedly his expression gradually changed as he seemed almost amused by her stubbornness. "All right . . . just to get rid of you. Your mother has been taken to Brauweiler prison."[21]

After getting a permit to enter the prison, Libet found her mother in a terrible state, her hair unkempt about her face, her eyes reddened and swollen, her voice toneless. Libet found out later what had happened. After refusing to disclose her husband's whereabouts, Gussi had been thrown into the basement of Brauweiler prison with a throng of prostitutes. She was nearly overcome by suffocating, nauseating odors from human excrement, cheap perfume, and perspiration. The women were dancing and singing and when Gussi failed to join in they reacted at first with hostility and then left her alone. She was brought out and interrogated by Herr Bethge, who focused a powerful electric lamp in her eyes. After several sessions and her repeated denials of knowledge of her husband's whereabouts, Bethge threatened to put her two daughters down in the basement until they found her

[21] Weymar, *Adenauer,* p. 135.

husband. The thought of her two young daughters kept in that hell-hole horrified her. How could her husband ever forgive her if she betrayed him? But would he want her to sacrifice her daughters for his sake? In a toneless voice she said: "He is in the Westerwald—at the Nister Mühle."

Flushed from a loft in the mill by three Gestapo officials, Adenauer was taken to Brauweiler where his wife was being kept in solitary confinement. She had fallen into a deep depression and had begun to hallucinate. After a few days it was decided to release her and she was escorted to the visitor's room. She was still there when Adenauer happened to enter. The two at first were speechless. Then he said tenderly, "Gussi." She began to cry and stammer, "They threatened . . . the children . . ." "I know it all," he interrupted as she flung herself into his arms. "Don't, Gussi. Don't torture yourself. We're all in the hands of God."

At Adenauer's suggestion, Libet got in touch with her brother Max, a lieutenant in the army, who came to visit his father. Adenauer's cell was directly below the interrogation room and Max later remembered his father talking about the screams and the slashing noise of the beatings, which went on sometimes for hours. "These Gestapo people," Adenauer told Max, "have no human feelings left at all. The other day one of these torturers said, 'Some of them scream with fear before I've touched them, and they always get a double dose.' "[22] Max left Brauweiler determined to secure his father's release. After a number of attempts, he finally went to the Gestapo headquarters itself in Berlin. He was at first rebuffed but finally he played his trump card, demanding to know from the Gestapo official how a soldier could maintain his morale on the front when his father has been arrested for no reason at all. Duly impressed, the official promised to do everything in his power to secure Adenauer's release.

On a Sunday in November an air raid occurred nearby and the Gestapo officials in Brauweiler joined the prisoners in the shelter. Spotting Herr Bethge among the officials, Adenauer asked him if his release had come. "Yes," Bethge said, "it came today." "In that case," Adenauer said, "I wish to be released today." "Suit yourself," Bethge said. Without collar or tie and without shoelaces or suspenders, Adenauer left the prison with a friendly prison official and trudged down the road to Weiden where a friend picked him up in his car. He arrived home at Rhöndorf, weak and undernourished, to await the arrival of the Americans.

The great American spring offensive opened up and by March it was

[22]Ibid., p. 148.

obvious that the Americans would cross the Rhine below and almost directly opposite Adenauer's house. Improvising an air-raid shelter out of a small storage cellar, the Adenauers watched and waited. On March 8, with the shells coming closer, the family crowded into the shelter. During the next week Adenauer periodically left the shelter to survey the scene of battle from his garden bench high above the Rhine. "The Americans have now crossed the Rhine to the north as well," he came back to report one day during the battle. On another day, two shells passed immediately over his head and exploded fifteen feet away as he threw himself on the ground; luckily, his only injury was a temporary loss of hearing. On the seventh day there was silence. Adenauer returned from his observation post and reported excitedly, "The Americans are here!" Down below, an endless chain of American tanks and armored vehicles clanked along the road above the river bank. Column after column of jeeps followed, the steel helmets of the soldiers glittering in the sun. With eyes blinking from the unaccustomed light, the inhabitants of the shelter silently watched the awesome spectacle unfolding below. The first one to find his voice was Adenauer's little son Schorsch. "The war is over!" he cried. The following morning a jeep pulled up in front of their house and two American officers stepped out with a request that Adenauer resume his position as mayor of Cologne.

No Time for Tears

The gay and beautiful ancient city he loved was now nothing but rubble and ashes. Nearly all its lovely Romanesque churches had been destroyed while its towering Gothic cathedral still stood but with huge gaping holes from several direct hits. The bridges over the Rhine were all gone. A population of three quarters of a million had been reduced to 32,000 living like cave dwellers in the basements of their ruined homes, cooking in the open on a few bricks set on the tops of mountainous heaps of rubble. The challenges facing the seventy-year-old mayor were mind-boggling: no water, no gas, no electricity, no streetcars or automobiles, and a nearly starving population.

The labor demanded was Herculean, compelling Adenauer regularly to spend eighteen hours a day in his office. Feeding the populace was the most pressing task and he turned to the American military commander for help. With his understanding and active support, Adenauer set up food depots and requisitioned all the available means of transport to scour the countryside and purchase from the peasants whatever could be obtained—potatoes, grain, vegetables, and cattle. He also organized convoys to bring home prisoners from the concentration camps, expedited rubble clearance, hired architects to plan a virtually new city. His relations with the American authorities were excellent; when the British took over in June 1945, however, things went from bad to worse. The British Labor government manifested a marked preference for the Social Democrats in Germany, and the British officials in Cologne found Adenauer's assertive style impertinent for a vanquished German. Matters came to a head when Adenauer gave an interview to the press suggesting that the military occupation be replaced with a system of international control, and asking the British to think of Germans as Western Europeans. Brigadier John Barraclough, the salty chief administrative officer for the North Rhine zone, summoned Adenauer to his office and dismissed him as mayor. What rankled Adenauer permanently, it seems, was not just the manner of his dismissal but Barraclough's assertion that Adenauer had been remiss in his duties as mayor.

The Birth of a New Party: Christian and Democratic

The dismissal actually was a blessing for Adenauer. It gave him the opportunity to participate in organizing the nascent Christian Democratic Union (CDU), one of whose chief centers was in Cologne. There, in fact, this broadly-based, interdenominational party was founded in April 1945.

Various factors conspired to make possible a reshaping of the party system in Germany after the Second World War. The old denominational, ideological, and class differences had been largely swept away. In particular, the old Protestant elitist conservatives were greatly weakened by the destruction of the Prussian Army and the Prussian state and the domination of East Prussia by the Soviets.[23] Catholics were now in the majority in some of the semiautonomous occupation zones. Moreover, some Protestants and Catholics had worked together in the non-Communist resistance. In this situation, a number of former Centrists such as Konrad Adenauer, Adam Stegerwald, and Jakob Kaiser saw the chance of overcoming the old rivalries that had debilitated German democracy: Catholics against Protestants, labor against the middle class, and Christians against socialists. They also hoped to build a

[23]Ibid., p. 149.

bridge to the other countries in Western Europe where democratic Catholic parties had emerged.

The Christian Democratic Union was formally constituted on September 2, 1945. A most important meeting of the executive council of the CDU took place at Herford in the British Zone on January 19 and 20, 1946. Noting that he was the senior member present, Adenauer with an easy grace simply took control of the meeting by taking the "chair," which was vacant. At the end of the meeting he was duly elected the party's president and permanent chairman.

The leaders Adenauer, Stegerwald, and Kaiser had somewhat contrasting views of the kind of party they wanted. Believing that democracy was rooted in Christianity, Adenauer wanted to emphasize the party's basic Christian outlook. The CDU, in his mind, should be coherent, democratic, moderate, and inclusive of all Christians. When some questioned the wisdom and propriety of calling a political party "Christian," thus mixing up politics and religion, Adenauer demurred. In his own hand he inserted into the party program these words: "A Christian view of life must once more take the place of materialist beliefs . . . Christian ethics . . . must become the determining factors in the reconstruction of the state and in the delimitation of its powers and authority; they must be the guiding principles for the definition of the rights and duties of the individual, for economic and social life, and for the relations of the nations among each other."[24]

Democracy, he insisted, was not to be understood as a process of leveling down toward a mediocre average. On the contrary, "true democracy is the soil in which a fully developed individual personality is rooted."[25]

Moreover, to avoid the splintering of parties that had bedeviled the Weimar Republic and to build a healthy democracy, Adenauer urged the adoption of a two-party system based on the Socialists (SPD) and the CDU. One of these would form the government while the other formed the loyal opposition. In this scheme of things the inclusion of Protestants in the CDU was vitally important, and to allay their fears Adenauer insisted that the CDU was an entirely new party with no connections to the old Center. The current attempt to revive the Center Party, he felt, frivolously divided the Christian camp.

Adam Stegerwald, the trade union leader, wanted a party that would emphasize the need for social justice. Industrialization, he said, had alienated

[24]Ibid., pp. 178–179.
[25]Ibid., pp. 171–172.

people from God and nature while producing only boom and bust. Nazism had offered its cure for this spiritual and material malaise but the cure had proven worse than the disease. Christian democracy, Stegerwald insisted, was the answer but it had to entail "community consciousness," without which democracy, he felt, was meaningless. Stegerwald looked hopefully to other socially conscious pro-Christian movements such as the Roosevelt coalition in the United States and the British Labor Party. Blaming the landowning conservative elites and the industrialists for turning Germany over to Hitler, he wanted to make sure that the economically powerful were kept at bay in the new party. But he died of pneumonia on December 3, 1945, not living to see an outcome he would have hated: the CDU formed as a democratic alliance of both popular and elite constituencies.

The head of the CDU in Berlin, Jakob Kaiser, a Christian socialist, wanted the CDU to form a bridge between East and West in order to save Germany from partition into hostile blocs. Kaiser also thought world trends were moving toward socialism as the bourgeois period came to a close. But Adenauer held that the bourgeois age would never end because people would always value personal freedom and property. Like Adenauer, however, Kaiser believed that "Christianity's 'highest law' was freedom of the individual [and] this law distinguished Christian socialism's pursuit of the common good from dogmatic Marxist collectivism."[26]

Karl Spiecker, the leader of those attempting to revive the old Center Party, controlled the party's only journal (the twice-weekly *Rhein-Ruhr-Zeitung*) and used it to propound his vision of a revived Center. A revived Center Party, he argued, should eschew all ideology, in particular the Christian, and instead welcome all who shared its political goals. He believed the Weimar Republic had collapsed not because of the excess of parties but because the parties let disagreements over ideology impede them from genuine political cooperation. Spiecker thought Adenauer and the CDU would fall into the same trap since the two-party system they proposed would be based on competing ideologies, the Christian versus the socialist. Moreover he felt that the CDU's attempt to unite Protestant and Catholic in a party was absurd since Catholicism, Protestantism, and Christianity were not political categories. Spiecker hoped that by freeing the Center from an attachment to the Christian or Catholic *Weltanschauung* it could become a moderate catch-all party along the lines of the British system, where the two parties, Conservative and Labor, did not embody ideological contrasts but

[26]Cary, *The Path to Christian Democracy*, p. 196.

set forth different political goals. British Labor contained Catholics and Protestants, Christians and Marxists. When the British voted they did so for political reasons.[27]

Actually Adenauer and Speicker were not as far apart as it might seem. The Christian *Weltanschauung* for Adenauer was always primarily "a matter of supporting individual dignity, combating totalitarianism, and advancing the integration of 'Christian' western Europe."[28] Spiecker eventually led an exodus of Centrists into the CDU, convinced that the CDU would overcome its emphasis on so-called ideology. He had come to see, however, that in the circumstances of the cold war the central issue was whether the Christian or non-Christian vision of Europe would prevail.

A Daunting Challenge

Adenauer's first journey after the war took him to Luxembourg in 1946 for a conference of parliamentarians from many European countries. One of the main questions on the agenda was: "What is to become of Germany?" Concerned that the future of Germany would be discussed in the absence of any Germans, Adenauer managed to inveigle an invitation from the reluctant president of the conference. He and a friend arrived in Luxembourg without any usable money since the reichsmark was not accepted outside Germany. With hunger pains gnawing, they sat at a restaurant table trying to appear nonchalant in front of the puzzled waiters while waiting for a friend who had failed to show up. Finally Adenauer declared, "Hang it, I'm going to eat now! Someone will pay for it." While Adenauer tackled his food with gusto, his friend, who was not that optimistic, was too nervous to eat much. But Adenauer's optimism was justified when the friend they were awaiting finally arrived.

The conference opened the following day with delegates from eighteen nations present. Allowed to attend only as an observer, Adenauer sat in the

---

[27] Another voice in the revived Center Party, Helene Wessel, a forty-eight-year-old former social worker and a gifted speaker, took a somewhat different tack. She wanted a party whose chief concern was social justice based on Christian precepts. The task ahead of society, she thought, was to build a moral and institutional framework that would further the solution of problems of divorce, broken homes, and illegitimacy whose spread she deemed a symptom of the social tensions of the industrial age. For her it was only common sense to cooperate with those who shared the same goals. "Accordingly Wessel called for a socially minded partnership of Center and SPD, but not for a unified, *Weltanschauung*-free party." Ibid., pp. 252–271.

[28] Ibid., p. 243.

very last row in a dark corner, "calm and immobile as a Tibetan monk,"[29] while the conferees—Frenchmen, Dutchmen, Luxembourgers, and others including even some Basque refugees—settled the issues facing Germany. At the end of the congress, Adenauer was invited to speak and gave a masterly performance. He made no attempt to conceal Germany's crimes, the responsibility of National Socialism for the Second World War, the atrocities of the Third Reich. He said: "During the years of National Socialism the German people behaved in such a manner that I despised them. But since 1945 I have learned to feel some renewed respect for my people . . . Despite all the misdeeds of National Socialism, the German people have a right to claim that they should not be judged solely by this one epoch in their history."[30] At the end he won over the meeting by an unqualified pledge to a united Christian Europe. "Today I regard myself primarily as a European, and only in the second place as a German," he declared as a wave of applause thanked him.

With no rival of equal stature and clarity of vision, Adenauer was able to move from his chairmanship of the zonal executive council to chairmanship of the whole CDU. It was to be his political base for the next twenty years. One of his objectives was to prevent the CDU from becoming a catch-all umbrella for a loosely associated group of parties with a variety of political persuasions—Weimar all over again. Hence his concern to give the CDU a leadership with strong authority and sense of purpose. His other objective was to defeat the Berlin CDU's plan to establish the headquarters of the national CDU in Berlin. The leaders of the Berlin CDU believed that the establishment of CDU's headquarters in Berlin would assist in reunifying east and west Germany. But the Prussian spirit of Berlin had always been obnoxious to Adenauer, and the danger of Soviet influence over the CDU there was now obvious, since Berlin was within the Soviet-controlled zone. At a meeting in February 1947 the CDU representatives from all four zones decided against Berlin as CDU party headquarters. They agreed with Adenauer that the consolidation of the three western zones was the right way to work for German unity and that the CDU should not expose itself to the forceful intervention of a totalitarian power. The hopes of the leaders of the Berlin CDU for reunification of Germany were destroyed in June 1947, when the Soviets rejected the Marshall Plan for large-scale economic aid to

---

[29]Words of a correspondent for a Belgian newspaper who was present. Ibid., p. 182.
[30]Ibid., p. 183.

Europe. The Soviet zone of Germany—the eastern zone—was to be economically amputated from the three western zones.

A description of Adenauer at this time noted that

[H]e appeared to be physically frail. Like his fellows he had too little to eat in those first three post-war years . . . He moved and spoke with a relaxed grace and restraint, while the mass of his fellow politicians were indulging in hysterics over dismantling, denazification and the lack of bread. In the midst of men who spent their time looking for extra rations or getting prematurely drunk at the first "mixed" Allied cocktail parties, Adenauer seemed an obvious choice for the Chancellorship. He preserved in the face of the occupiers of his country a dignity that was virtually unique, thus marking himself out as the best man to deal with them on behalf of his fellow Germans. In them he inspired confidence alike by his refusal to complain about material discomforts and by his steely insistence on getting on with the tasks of political organization. Work and responsibility were making him into a younger, healthier man.[31]

The German correspondent of the London *Daily Mail* later described Adenauer's "high, serene brow, the curious Mongoloid cheek-bones and the bright, intelligent eyes of this spare, reserved man, already in his seventies . . . He was quiet, dignified, clipped in speech and to the point. Adenauer . . . does not get his way by pounding the table; he uses men by flattering them, charming them with silky good humour or freezing them with quiet contempt."[32] Another observer noted his strange "power to stand outside the Germans, like a beloved father or even grandfather. He knew, none better, the weakness that had betrayed them."[33]

Patience and perseverance were Adenauer's trademarks and they stood him in great stead during these first postwar years. At their end he found himself the head of one of the two potentially most powerful political parties in the 'rump-Germany' west of the Elbe. After an impeccable performance as a German citizen in the dark days of his country's defeat, he was ready to move on to the next stage in his long political Indian summer. Ahead of him lay monumental tasks: framing a democratic constitution for a country with an ambivalent experience of democracy, running for office in the first

[31]Prittie, *Konrad Adenauer*, p. 121.
[32]Ibid.
[33]Ibid., pp. 122–123.

elections held under its terms, and forming a government that would be a model for the foreseeable future. "No man of 72, in the whole of history, has faced such a daunting challenge. No man, whether septuagenarian or not, faced it with such blithe awareness."[34]

Socialist vs. Christian Democrat

The first meeting of the British Zonal Advisory Council on March 6, 1946, brought together the two men who would dominate West German politics during this crucial period: Dr. Kurt Schumacher, the leader of the Social Democratic Party, and Konrad Adenauer. When Sir Sholto Douglas, the British commander-in-chief and military governor, appeared, he was introduced first to Schumacher, a favorite of the British Labor government. Sir Sholto gripped Schumacher's left hand (he had lost his right arm in the First World War) cordially and the two continued in good humor conversing privately for fifteen minutes or so while Adenauer waited. Glancing at his watch, Adenauer whispered to a friend, "You'll see, it won't take that long with us." Adenauer was finally introduced. "Well, Herr Oberburgermeister," Sir Sholto asked genially, "and what was your political career?" Adenauer answered: "Oh, in 1917 I became chief mayor of Cologne. In 1933 I was dismissed by the National Socialists because of political unreliability. In March 1945, I was reinstated by the Americans, and in October of the same year I was dismissed once more, by the English, because of incompetence. That's why I am now in the zonal advisory council." Sir Sholto stared at Adenauer, speechless. Then he walked on. "You see," Adenauer said. "With us it has taken exactly one minute and forty-five seconds!"[35]

Kurt Schumacher was then at the height of his influence. He was generally expected to be the future German chancellor. He was a forceful speaker, incisive and sharp, and his cutting remarks, which were edged with bitter irony, were often quoted. "The modern democracies seem to regard the Horsemen of the Apocalypse as their cavalry," was one of his best. Adenauer's style was in total contrast: dry, unemotional, terse. He aimed to convince his hearers solely by the inexorable logic of fact. The Protestant Schumacher and the Catholic Adenauer were a study in contrasts in other ways as well. Adenauer's only rival of real stature, Schumacher was a bache-

[34]Ibid, p. 123.
[35]Weymar, *Adenauer*, pp. 187–188.

lor, a Prussian, and a chain smoker; while Adenauer, the devoted husband and father, could not stand Prussians and hated the habit of smoking. Schumacher considered Adenauer a double-dealing and Jesuitical reactionary. A dedicated socialist, Schumacher despised capitalism and privilege of any kind. Though a decent, honest man, Schumacher invariably made a bad impression on strangers. He had lost an arm in the First World War, and his American biographer, Lewis Edinger, wrote of his "tortured body," his "fanatical eyes" and "jerky gestures."[36] His shortness of temper was no doubt due in part to his feeling that he had little time left to put Germany on a solid socialist basis and he was appalled by what he considered Adenauer's attempt at a "bourgeois restoration." It is interesting to speculate on what might have happened if Schumacher rather than Adenauer had taken the helm in Germany after the war. It seems unlikely that the temperamental Schumacher would have been able to restore foreign confidence in the trustworthiness and reliability of the Germans to the extent achieved by Adenauer.

Besides Adenauer, the other ace in the deck of the CDU was Professor Ludwig Erhard, head of the Bi-zonal Economic Council and the main force behind West Germany's gathering economic recovery. His theory, the Social Market Economy, combined freedom and state control of the national economy in a singularly successful synthesis. The main trouble with a planned economy, Erhard argued, was the mechanical interference by the state in the structure of the economy. The state, for example, fixed maximum prices, which destroyed the natural order of supply and demand. Lower prices, Erhard believed, were better achieved by allowing the free interplay of economic forces in the arena of open competition. State intervention was called for only when prices began to rise—a situation the state could regulate better by means of tariff, finance, and taxation policies. His theory had already borne fruit. By mid-1949 there was more food and a bigger supply of consumer goods in the shops, more jobs, and the start of a building boom. With his rosy cheeks, his ample girth and his confident predictions of better times on the way, Erhard was the man to appeal to the floating vote as well as to confirmed antisocialists.

As the electorate prepared to vote for the first time in the Federal Republic of Germany, three main issues faced them: unemployment, housing, and the destitution of the refugees from the east. In their approach to solutions, the CDU and the SPD were divided by diametrically opposed philosophies.

---

[36]Prittie, *Konrad Adenauer*, pp. 128–129.

Adenauer had boldly placed Erhard's social market economy in the forefront of the CDU program, while the Social Democratic Party adhered firmly to its belief in state ownership of heavy industry, socialization, and a planned economy.

With fundamental views thus clashing, the election campaign was marked by drama and suspense. The candidates had only three short weeks to educate a largely ignorant electorate, many of whom were young people unfamiliar with democratic processes. Adenauer spared no effort racing to and fro on the road from morning till night.[37] Most neutral observers, however, expected the SPD, a venerable party with a record of integrity, to triumph over the fledgling CDU. It had a vastly greater membership than any other party and the support of the trade unions. Schumacher indulged in personal attacks on Adenauer, whom he now hated, while Adenauer kept to the high road.

The election results were a grievous shock to Schumacher and the SPD. The final tally showed that the CDU had beaten the SDP by 7,360,000 votes to 6,930,000. The third strongest showing was made by the FDP (Free Democratic Party) with 2,790,000 votes. The Communists were left far behind. The high voter turnout—78.8 percent of the 32,000,000 in the Federal Republic—showed that democracy was alive and well in Germany.

"So Help Me God"

Seven days after the election, a meeting of the leaders of the CDU was held at Adenauer's house at Rhöndorf. Two questions on the agenda were crucial: Should there be a coalition with Social Democrats or not? And who should be chancellor? After a lively debate about the first question, Adenauer's argument prevailed: Their ideological difference with the Social Democrats was a gulf too wide to bridge and would make it impossible to get the government moving. The second question was settled in less than a minute. Adenauer accepted the nomination. "My doctor has no objections," he said with a smile. A month later, September, 15, 1949, the oath of office was administered to Adenauer before a crowded audience in the main chamber of the federal parliament building in Bonn. His voice rang clearly and distinctly through the house: "I swear, so help me God!"

His first address to the Bundestag as federal chancellor then followed. Noting the progress that had been made toward a free and united Germany,

---

[37] Ibid., p. 140.

he admitted that there was still much to be done. The German people were still divided and Germany was not yet accepted as an equal partner among the free nations of the world. He pointed to all the tasks that lay ahead and insisted on the need to bring about social justice and the relief of suffering and want. He stressed the importance of flexibility in applying the principles of the social market economy, and called for help especially for war widows and orphans and those incapacitated in the war. Denazification was important but had to be carried out in a fair and balanced way.

The Bundestag was a turbulent place in 1949. Observers were often appalled at the antics of the members, described by one British observer as "freaks and dullards." Was it going to be the Weimar Republic all over again? they wondered. There was little real debate; absorbed in their newspapers or private conversations, no one seemed to listen to anyone else. Speakers were often interrupted by heckling and catcalls. At times the building rocked with the noise of four hundred men stamping their feet, shouting and laughing. Angry at their pitiful showing in the elections (a consequence of the abysmal behavior of the Soviet occupation), the Communists were the rowdiest. Under Moscow's coaching they tried to disrupt the proceedings by continuous interruptions. Adenauer was a particular target of their jibes, which were often of the most primitive kind.

Through it all Adenauer maintained his wonted composure, his face a mask of inscrutability. One duel of wits with the Communists occurred when he touched on the danger from radicals either of the Right or the Left. When the Communists laughed at this Adenauer turned to them: "Never mind, you aren't half as radical as you make yourselves to be." The Communist deputy Renner responded: "And you aren't half as social as you would now have people believe!"[38] Adenauer had to let the laughter subside before he could continue.

Another such exchange with the Communists occurred when Adenauer referred to "some less good contacts" with neighboring nations:

Renner: ". . . you better not forget the Saar Territory."

Adenauer: "Let me, for a start, not forget the Soviet Union!"

Renner: "I can see this part of your speech has been drafted by an expert!"

Adenauer: "Herr Renner, you are an envious man!"

After the laughter died down Adenauer declared, "We are ready to live in peace . . . with the Soviet Union." He concluded by pledging to work

[38]Weymar, *Adenauer,* p. 281.

for a European Union in which one day Germany would march as a free nation side by side with the nations of the free world toward a better future.

Restoration of German National Sovereignty

One of Adenauer's main objectives was the restoration of full sovereignty to the Federal Republic. One step toward that goal was taken by the Petersberg Agreement, which brought German participation in the Ruhr Authority, the international board that controlled the great industries of the Ruhr. The idea of taking part in this hated reminder of Germany's subjugation was intolerable to the SPD and led to one of the wildest scenes in the Bundestag. Adenauer produced a statement from the Trade Union Congress that supported his position. Totally unable to believe that the trade unions would back Adenauer, Schumacher called it a forgery. But the trade unions' statement was confirmed by a phone call to Trade Union headquarters. As the noise in the chamber reached a crescendo at 3 A.M., Schumacher called Adenauer "the chancellor of the Allies." Pandemonium broke loose. The president tried in vain to make himself heard. Finally he shouted above the din: "Mr. Deputy Schumacher! . . . I herewith call you to order." But the agitation was such that there could be no question of continuing. A deputy moved to adjourn and the sitting was suspended until 6 A.M. Schumacher was suspended for a gross affront to the standing orders.[39] No doubt poor Schumacher, already near death from a long illness, had been driven nearly insane by the obvious success of Adenauer's negotiations with the Allies and by the total exclusion from them of himself and his party.

Rearmament of Germany and integration of the Federal Republic into the European Defense Community would be, Adenauer felt, the final step on the way to his country's achievement of full sovereignty. In view of its position on the front line facing the Soviet armed forces in Eastern Germany, it was essential for Western Germany to contribute its share to the defense of Western Europe. But sentiment in Germany against rearmament was deep. A strong pacifist movement had sprung up, and contrary to much thinking in the Allied countries, a career in the army had lost its luster for most German males. The incredible devastation of Germany in the Second World War was an object lesson not easily forgotten, and there were few German youths who were anxious to become cannon fodder. The Evangelical Churches were taking an increased interest in the subject of German

[39] Ibid., pp. 304–305.

reunification and saw in rearmament a barrier to its attainment. The SPD also was beginning to lean toward the pacifist principles it had so blithely laid aside in August 1914.

But Adenauer was ready to grasp the nettle. A study by an ex-general indicated that the Soviet preponderance in conventional arms was overwhelming while American nuclear supremacy was only temporary. Adenauer was ready to promise that Germany would join in the defense of Western Europe if the Allies would revise the Occupation Statute. The Allied High Commissioners would then become ambassadors, and the Federal Republic would enter into normal diplomatic relations with its Western partners. In effect, the reluctance of the German people to rearm would be overcome if the Federal Republic were given back its independence. The talks to end the occupation began on September 24, 1951, and were the most difficult that Adenauer had yet undertaken. They were to drag on far into 1952. After various twists and turns the European Defense Community treaty agreements were signed on May 26 in Bonn and on May 27 in Paris. The EDC treaty provided for a European Defense Community that would integrate German armed forces into a European army. This basic concept was essential to Adenauer's strategy for creating a European union. The EDC treaty, Adenauer believed, would achieve some of his major goals: the establishment of effective government, the restoration of German national sovereignty, and the integration of the Federal Republic in the "Europe of Charlemagne." An ominous fact, however, moderated Adenauer's joy: France had not yet signed the EDC treaty.

France's reluctance to accept Germany as a partner in the defense community was due not only to the longstanding enmity between the two nations but also to a continuing dispute over the Saar, the coal and steel mining center that had belonged to Germany before the Second World War. France—which wanted to "Europeanize" the Saar to keep it from reverting to West Germany—held a trump card: the power to block the implementation of the European Defense Committee. While negotiations over the Saar continued, France stalled on the issue of the EDC treaty. Finally the French premier, Pierre Mendès-France, agreed to put the EDC agreements before the French National Assembly, and in return Adenauer agreed to a referendum by the Saarlanders that might Europeanize the Saar. Mendès-France did bring the EDC treaty before the national assembly, but thanks in part to his negative assessment of its terms, the Assembly rejected it. In one fell swoop the EDC treaty between Great Britain and the six EDC states—a vast structure—had been thrown into the wastepaper basket.

It was the greatest and most shattering disappointment Adenauer had suffered in all his long political career. It was only a year since his party had won a stunning absolute majority in the national elections—a victory saluted as a verdict on his European policy in general and on his concept of the European Defense Community in particular. The *New York Times* had called it a "one-man triumph." Now everything he stood for and had worked for seemed reduced to nothing. According to one biographer, Adenauer was so incensed he didn't speak for two days. "The great plan whose prime object had been to bring about a final reconciliation between France and Germany had achieved the precise opposite: at no time since the end of the war had relations between the two been more tense than now." [40]

In the most controversial and sensational interview of his career, given to *The Times* of London, he vented his feelings: "If the European idea is now wrecked by the action of France, will not that mean a return . . . not to the Nazism of Hitler, but a return certainly to some form of nationalism? . . . I still hope that she [France] will recover her greatness, and that the European Defense Community will yet come into being . . . The conception of Europe cannot be killed by a procedural discussion in the French National Assembly with the help of a hundred Communists."[41]

In fact, all was not lost. At this most critical moment in his fortunes, his patient efforts for years to build up trust with the Allies bore sudden fruit. Sir Winston Churchill, in a renewed term as prime minister, sprang into action. He sent his foreign secretary, Anthony Eden, on a whirlwind tour of European capitals that culminated in the Brussels Pact (October 3, 1954), which restored West German sovereignty and provided for the Federal Republic's inclusion in NATO. The pact was not the equivalent of the EDC treaty. It did not create Adenauer's desired European Army with its political ramifications for European unity. But it did create a basis for practical cooperation between the European nations, which gave Adenauer some hope that it might generate trust and confidence to build on.

[40] Ibid., p. 480.
[41] Ibid., pp. 481–482.

Reconciliation with France

Adenauer never ceased to regret France's rejection of the EDC treaty. Nevertheless much had been accomplished by the European powers toward full Franco-German reconciliation: the restoration of West German sovereignty, German rearmament, and the resolution of the Saar question. Adenauer had played a crucial role in these developments, and for the rest of his time in office and up to his death he would make Franco-German reconciliation one of his main concerns.

When Charles de Gaulle came to power in France in June 1958, many deemed it a setback for Adenauer and his hopes for reconciliation with France. De Gaulle had been a prisoner-of-war in Germany during the First World War, and during the Second World War had determined with every fiber of his being to bring about Germany's defeat. Moreover, in Adenauer's eyes de Gaulle was not a "good European" for he had opposed the European Defense Community and had previously little good to say about the European Common Market. Adenauer also found his rhetoric about *la gloire de France* unsettling. Nevertheless he decided to pay a visit to de Gaulle at Colombey to see if he could find some common ground with *le grand général*. The two got along well and found they were in basic agreement on a number of issues including disarmament, support of the Common Market, and the Middle East. De Gaulle even showed interest in a united Europe though not as "a tool of America." Adenauer was charmed by de Gaulle's friendliness and informality and much impressed by the "aura of moral integrity" he projected. Their second encounter at Bad Kreuznach went so well that talk began of a Paris–Bonn axis. In spite of the promising start, however, Adenauer had much to worry about. Convinced that the Western powers had "absolutely no notion of what a dangerous situation" Europe faced from the Soviets, he found France's complacency shocking. During the course of 1960, France withdrew her Mediterranean fleet from NATO; closed France to U.S. aircraft equipped to carry nuclear weapons; and siphoned off troops to Algeria, leaving inadequate contingents in Germany. There were in fact many differences to be overcome before their relationship was finally crowned by the Franco-German Treaty of Friendship and Co-operation of January 22, 1963.

Social Reforms

Adenauer was accused by his critics of being interested only in foreign affairs. He did allow his ministers much leeway with domestic issues but he was definitely concerned with them. He was able to maintain good relations with the powerful German trade unions that were united in the Trade Union Congress (DGB) with a membership of over six million. Putting aside, for the time being, their goals of the socialization of heavy industry and the installation of a British-style welfare state, the unions followed a practical philosophy that accorded well with Adenauer's own. The head of the trade unions, Hans Böckler, happened to be a personal friend of Adenauer's and in 1951 the two men were able to get enacted a "Co-partnership Law" that gave workers a share in the decision-making of the corporations. The law brought industrial peace to Germany for several decades. Adenauer's efforts vis-à-vis other social reforms were less impressive and they were effected in patchwork fashion.

The Jewish Question

One of the issues that Adenauer felt presented a clear moral challenge had to do with the treatment of the Jews in Nazi Germany. He insisted on the need for Germany to make some effort to atone for the horrifying so-called "final solution" perpetrated by the Nazis. Their attempt to exterminate all Jews resulted in the death of six million innocent Jewish men, women, and children in Germany alone. Adenauer realized that no monetary sum could in any way make up for this terrible crime against humanity, but he was determined to show some sign of Germany's repentance through a concrete act of restitution. He was even ready to take upon himself a share of the guilt, as was evident on one occasion when a Jewish delegation reproached him personally with a long catalogue of German crimes. He might have taken offense, as one observer said, but did not. Instead he continued working out the details of the restitution agreement until finally it was signed in Luxembourg on September 10, 1952, and later ratified by the Bundestag. It designated 3,500 million marks (nearly $900 million) to settle Jewish claims. Adenauer personally intervened in the debate on the bill, which passed the Bundestag by 288 votes to 34 with 86 abstentions. The agreement was loyally carried out over the next twelve years. When the Arab League made threats to break off trading relations with Germany because of this agreement, Adenauer said, "There are higher things to think about than good business deals. And we want a different sort of Germany from the Germany of Hitler."[42] Adenauer's efforts to restore something approaching normal German–Israeli relations, undoubtedly owed something to this sentiment. Also, among his Jewish friends was one who was very close, Daniel Heinemann, who had come to his aid financially when he was being persecuted by the Nazis.

Years of Plenty

Adenauer traveled to the United States in April 1953 in recognition of the need to cultivate the best possible relations with the leader of the free world. The visit turned out to be a great success. One of the highlights was an emotional meeting with President Eisenhower who had prepared the ground by expressing a willingness to "forgive" the "new" Germany. At the same time Adenauer and U.S. Secretary of State John Foster Dulles basked in the warmth of a friendship built, no doubt, on the same belief in God and hatred of Communism. It was also a friendship based on the attraction of opposites, as Terence Prittie remarks: "Dulles impulsive, temperamental but at heart a down-to-earth, low-church New Englander; Adenauer calm, reserved, symbolic of a much older civilization than that of the United States, suspected—absurdly—of being the agent of the Vatican."[43]

Without doubt the years 1948 to 1953 were the most productive of Adenauer's life. "During those five years he took part, always in the key role, in organizing the Christian Democratic Party, framing a West German constitution, regaining sovereignty for the Federal Republic; earning for it a place in the Western Alliance, laying the foundations for lasting friendship with the traditional foe, France, and winning two Federal elections."[44] He reaped his political reward during the next five years, which saw him reach the pinnacle of his power and popularity. His control of the Federal Republic was so complete that Terence Prittie calls this period "Chancellor democracy." With no leader to equal the now deceased Schumacher, the Social Democrats were in total disarray and offered such feeble opposition that Adenauer complained about not having opponents worthy of his mettle.

[42]Prittie, *Konrad Adenauer,* p. 206.
[43]Ibid., p. 209.
[44]Ibid., p. 213.

By the time of the 1957 elections, West German stomachs were full, unemployment was down, and the cost-of-living index compared favorably with the rest of Europe. Adenauer could point to the recently signed Treaty of Rome which set up a European Economic Community with a common market to be fully integrated within fifteen years. The German people gratefully handed Adenauer his greatest electoral victory as the CDU won a majority of forty-three seats in the Bundestag. When some wondered about an eighty-two-year-old man taking on another four-year term, Adenauer liked to tell the story of Pope Leo XIII, hale and hearty at the celebration of his ninetieth birthday: When the dean of the diplomatic corps expressed the wish that the pope would still be as fit and strong when he reached one hundred, Leo had replied, "Why would you put such low limits on the compassion of God?"

The Russian Bear

Adenauer's tactics in dealing with the Russians could be summed up in the old saying, "When you sup with the devil, use a long spoon." He had absolutely no faith in the word of the Soviet Union. He was convinced that its ultimate aim was world domination, and the record showed that he had good reason. The Soviets had annexed the three Baltic states of Estonia, Latvia, and Lithuania; the eastern half of Poland, Rumanian Bessarabia and the Bukowina, half of the German province of East Prussia, and parts of Finland and Czechoslovakia. Added to this were its attempt to seize West Berlin and its brutal suppression of popular movements in East Germany and Hungary. Sometimes Adenauer was pilloried for a "monomanic" inflexible attitude toward the Soviets and he was called the ultimate "Cold War Warrior," but he was totally unmoved by such criticisms. He was convinced that Russia would never give up East Germany, its extremely useful security zone. He was equally convinced that it was vital for the Federal Republic to hold on to West Berlin.

Adenauer was therefore extremely cautious in handling a number of Soviet proposals aimed ostensibly at reunification of Germany but actually, as Adenauer believed, intended to sow disunity in the ranks of the Allied powers. His response to Soviet proposals was typically to call for free, universal, direct, and democratic elections in the whole of Germany, followed up by the election of a National Assembly and the drafting of an all-German constitution. Within the Federal Republic, opposition to Adenauer's intransigence came not only from the SPD but also from those espousing a neutralist position that would exclude any alignment of Germany with either side. The neutralists were unable to gain any large constituency and by 1955 were in decline.

The climax of Adenauer's relations with the Soviets came when he accepted their invitation to Moscow. The Russians wanted to restore diplomatic relations with the Federal Republic, while Adenauer hoped to secure the return of German prisoners-of-war and also, by personal contacts, to soften the Soviets' attitude toward the Federal Republic. The Russians were on their worst behavior. Nikita Khrushchev yelled and shook his fist at the impassive Adenauer when Adenauer made reference to the atrocious behavior of the Red Army in Germany. As it turned out, nothing came of the visit and the next years brought no progress toward German–Soviet understanding. In the meantime Adenauer had much to worry about: signs appeared that the United States might cut its military commitments abroad. When the Russians launched the first artificial satellite, Sputnik, on October 6, 1957, Adenauer was frankly delighted. "I regarded this Sputnik almost as a gift from Heaven, for otherwise the free world would have sunk even further into its twilight sleep."[45]

Those who criticize Adenauer for failure to make any progress toward German reunification do not realize what Adenauer was up against. As Terence Prittie says, "Confronted by the unique combination of Soviet distrust and cunning, brutality and doubt, no statesman in the history of the world would have reached an understanding."[46]

The Final Chapter

In 1958 Adenauer was nearing eighty-three and some in the CDU felt it was time for *Der Alte* (the old man), as he was called, to think about slowing down. When it was suggested that he run for the presidency he at first cottoned to the idea, provided that the powers of the president were enlarged—a presidency of the type de Gaulle had instituted in France, perhaps. When the public heard that Adenauer might step down, they were thunderstruck. Adenauer seemed such a permanent fixture it was hard to imagine anybody else as chancellor. However, some parliamentary members were thinking of nominating Erhard for the post. Adenauer was furious as he felt Erhard was totally unfit for the job. There were some stormy scenes in the

[45] Ibid., p. 255.
[46] Ibid., p. 260.

chambers of the CDU as Adenauer adamantly opposed the nomination of Erhard. Finally he let it be known that he would remain as chancellor. One member of the CDU, Eugen Gerstenmaier, confronted Adenauer at the entrance to one of the parliamentary chambers and stared at him angrily. Adenauer merely looked down at him calmly and remarked: "It's a curious thing that you can tell, just from a man's eyes, the hate in his heart." Gerstenmaier stomped out of the doorway as Adenauer continued on his way. The revolt had come to an end. Erhard later said the difference between him and Adenauer was structural: "He was Gothic, and I was Baroque."[47] Another member quipped, "Adenauer should also run for the papacy."

Adenauer was not overjoyed when John F. Kennedy succeeded Eisenhower in the 1960 U.S. presidential election. Adenauer had a high regard for Eisenhower but once called Kennedy a "cross between a junior naval officer and a Roman Catholic boy scout."[48] The young president's razzle-dazzle style irked Adenauer, who felt the exercise of high office demanded order, experience, and calmly reasoned reflection. He feared that Kennedy might make dangerous concessions to the Soviet Union in regard to the U.S. policy toward Germany. In this regard, of course, he was proven wrong, for Kennedy made it clear that no such changes would be made.

The coming Federal Republic election campaign of 1961, Adenauer's fourth, promised to be a great challenge to the aging chancellor. He now had a formidable opponent in the SPD's Willy Brandt, the successful governing mayor of Berlin. Moreover, the SPD had dropped its concept of class warfare and its leftist plan for nationalization of heavy industry, and had cozied up to the enlarged German bourgeoisie who were enjoying unprecedented prosperity.

With the campaign underway, an overnight Soviet move caught Adenauer and West Germany completely by surprise. As dawn broke on August 31, 1961, the people of West Berlin saw an ugly sight—an enormous wall many miles in length was beginning to rise on the perimeter sealing them off from East Berlin. Tons of brick and concrete slabs had been rushed in during the night by an endless row of trucks, and thousands of soldiers had worked all through the night to construct a wall that was already four to five feet high in places; it was to become a fifteen-foot-high barrier surmounted by barbed wire and protected on its eastern side by a no-man's-land of

[47] Ibid., p. 277.
[48] Ibid., p. 283.

trenches and obstacles. The wall was intended to stop the flow of refugees from the East German "workers' paradise," an exodus that numbered a thousand people per day. Its mastermind, Walter Ulbricht, the Soviet's East German satrap, had the gall to call it a "Wall of Peace" while confessing that its real purpose was to stabilize the East German economy.

Western intelligence had completely failed to foresee this event that would cement the division of Germany for decades to come. Western leaders seemed stunned, uncertain about their next move. Roused out of his bed in Rhöndorf and given the news at 4:30 A.M., Adenauer attended Sunday mass as usual and then did absolutely nothing for twenty-four hours. He then resumed electioneering as though nothing had happened. Meanwhile Brandt capitalized on the event, flying at once to Berlin to protest the action. When, a week later, Adenauer finally visited the beleaguered city he met with a chilly reception.

The building of the wall and Adenauer's lackadaisical reaction no doubt affected the election returns. The eighty-five-year-old Adenauer found himself in a battle for his political life. The election returns showed that the CDU had lost its absolute majority in the Bundestag and had to form a coalition with the Free Democrats. There was some chance that Adenauer would be ousted in the bargaining process with the Free Democrats. But once again Adenauer played his cards right and managed to get the support of Erich Mende, the head of the Free Democrats, by threatening to include the SPD in a coalition. Elected chancellor for the fourth time on November 7, 1962, Adenauer concentrated his energies on foreign affairs and signed his much sought Franco-German Treaty of Friendship and Co-operation in January 1963. It was, he believed, his crowning achievement and when de Gaulle stepped forward after the signing and kissed him on both cheeks, the "old man" could not hold back his tears. He resigned in October; almost his last action in office was to pay a visit to de Gaulle. In his last address to the Bundestag he praised the Germans for their courage and good sense, thanked God that the Germans once more had good friends, and called for continuity in Germany's foreign policies. Then in a fitting gesture he stepped down, leaving his seat on the cabinet bench, and took his place at his old desk.

Sunset and Evening Star

The old man now had too much time on his hands and tried to fill it with his roses, his collection of paintings, his devoted family, and his music. He also stayed heroically at a job he hated—writing his memoirs. But his frustration at being out of the picture sometimes burst forth in unfair criticism of his successor, Erhard, whom he still believed totally unsuited for the office. Looking at Europe he was depressed by the still virulent national rivalries that were wrecking his hopes for a truly united Europe. In his last notable speech, in Madrid on February 16, 1967, he appealed for a truly unified Europe that would be able to stand up against the weight of Soviet power.

Two months later he was forced to his bed by an illness that was mercifully brief. He worried not about himself, as his son Paul said, but about Europe, whose continuing disunity troubled him grievously as did the danger of nuclear war. But to the end he remained the man whose staunch faith had always been the rock-like foundation of his life. As he said one time when someone expressed surprise that he had never been to Rome: "And do you suppose, because I have never stood in St. Peter's, I might lose my Christian faith?"[49] He died on April 19, 1967, and his body lay in state in the Cathedral of Cologne where his old friend Cardinal Frings conducted the funeral mass. Then his body was brought back to Rhöndorf and buried in the Waldfriedhof cemetery. Among the world's great who came to pay him honor was David Ben-Gurion, who had helped him begin the process of healing one of Germany's most painful memories.

The Legacy

"The greatest German statesman since Bismarck," was Winston Churchill's verdict. Who would disagree? The magnitude of Adenauer's accomplishment must be measured against the pitiful state of Germany when he took the helm. One can hardly imagine how bleak the picture was. Besides facing a totally devastated country whose cities lay in ruins, he had to cope with a profoundly demoralized populace. Stripped of all honor and dignity after the instigation and loss of two wars and the degradation visited upon them by the Nazis, the Germans could see little reason for hope. It is an amazing fact that within a decade, Adenauer was able to instill in the German people a renewed sense of honor and dignity and to restore their reputation in the community of free nations. He was also able to lead a people with little experience of democracy into embracing a wholehearted commitment to democratic principles.

[49]Ibid., p. 310.

Adenauer's specific achievements indeed speak for themselves: restoration of the full sovereignty of the Federal Republic; integration of the Federal Republic into the fabric of the Western nations through participation in the Council of Europe, the Common Market, and NATO; the reconstruction of Germany's economy into the most prosperous in Europe; and finally the achievement he was most proud of—ending two centuries of Franco-German enmity by the Treaty of Friendship and Co-operation.

FIFTEEN

Oscar Romero (1917–1980) and Revolution in El Salvador

O
N MARCH 24, 1980, Oscar Romero, the archbishop of El Salvador, was assassinated as he was saying mass in a convent chapel; he was the latest victim in an ongoing conflict between a large sector of the Latin American clergy and the powerful elite that control many Latin American countries.

The conflict was rooted in a powerful new theology that had spread like wildfire in Latin America in the decade of the 1970s and had won over many of the clergy. It was called "liberation theology" because it called for the liberation of the poor from their age-old bondage to the forces that enslave them and keep them in misery, and it energized many of the clergy who resonated to its scriptural vision of a God who hears the cry of the poor and demands justice for them. By 1981 the spread of this theology was a cause of concern to conservative forces in the United States. In that year President Ronald Reagan met with a group of advisers to discuss the threat to the stability of Latin America posed by liberation theology. It had become a force to make dictators tremble.

Though taking final shape mainly in Latin America, there is no denying its European roots: Jacques Maritain's integral humanism, Emmanuel Mounier's committed personalism, Teilhard de Chardin's progressive evolu-

Oscar Romero

tionism, Henri de Lubac's social dogmatics, Yves Congar's theology of the laity, and Johann Metz's political theology.[1] It emerged in Latin America as a powerful alternative to Marxism, which for a long time was the only real alternative to capitalism. While not anti-Marxist, liberation theology incorporated two items missing in Marxism: it is non-elitist and it is linked with the grass roots through religion.

The real breakthrough for liberation theology occurred at Medellín in 1968 when the Latin American bishops embraced its basic point of view: the need for "liberation" rather than "development," the buzzword of progressives up to this time. Medellín was a startling event. The Church in Latin America had always functioned as a faithful ally of the rich and powerful. It served the regimes well by its works of charity that often alleviated at least the extremes of hunger and misery, and by the way it held before the eyes of the poor the crucified Christ as a model of resignation and submission. Now at Medellín the bishops were preaching the need for conscientization (raising the consciousness) of the masses, and liberation.

How explain such a change? For one thing, there was the obvious failure of the policy of economic development that had originally inspired great

[1] Frei Betto in Marc Ellis and Otto Maduro, eds., *The Future of Liberation Theology,* (Maryknoll, N.Y.: Orbis Books, 1989), p. 32.

hope when it was initiated by John F. Kennedy's Alliance for Progress. Instead of ameliorating the poverty and misery of the masses in Latin America, it had exacerbated it. For many sensitive folk the conditions of the poor were absolutely intolerable. There was also the tremendous change of climate in the Church inspired by the Second Vatican Council and its call for openness and dialogue. The conciliar document *Gaudium et Spes* urged Catholics to get involved in the struggle for social justice as the popes had been urging them to do since the encyclical *Rerum Novarum* of 1891. While *Gaudium* contained criticism of certain socialist and communist practices, it also pointed out the abuses of capitalism. It affirmed the right to form labor unions and to strike. It corrected traditional Catholic teaching on the right of private property by emphasizing the social obligations inherent in this right.

No doubt also influencing the bishops' extraordinary awakening was the impact of the worldwide stirrings of social conscience as marches, demonstrations, and even riots focused public attention on issues of social justice. The approach the bishops took was indeed revolutionary. Instead of indulging in stock platitudes about sin and human malice they focused on the actual social realities of Latin America. They described the situation common to their countries as "unjust" and "promoting tensions that conspire against peace." They traced class tensions to the radical disparity and inequality between rich and poor, and they accused the powerful of lacking sensitivity to the misery of the poor. They saw the poor as victims of "institutional violence" visited on them by the rich and powerful, and they declared that peace is impossible in such a situation.

Fr. Gutiérrez Hears the Cry of the Poor

The new theology of liberation that proved so influential at Medellín was especially associated with a Peruvian priest, Gustavo Gutiérrez, whose path-breaking book, *Teología de la Liberación*, appeared in 1971. It summed up a decade of reflection on his pastoral work in the slums of Lima and his dialogues with fellow priests who shared his concerns. Born in 1928 into a middle-class family of mixed Indian and Hispanic heritage, he began medical studies at the University of San Marcos with the idea of becoming a psychiatrist. In midstream, he decided to become a priest and entered the seminary where his intellectual gifts were soon recognized. In 1951 he was sent to study at the great Catholic academic centers of Europe, spending the next eight years at universities in Louvain, Lyons, and Rome, before being ordained in 1959.

On his return from Europe in 1960 he taught part-time at the Catholic University of Lima and was soon drawn into pastoral work with the poor of Lima. It was this first-hand experience of the misery of the poor that forced him to reassess much of his education. He was shocked to find that the theology he had learned in the centers of European learning was mere verbiage in regard to the poor. Profoundly shaken, he began to interrogate Scripture and the Catholic tradition with the viewpoint of the poor in mind.

A Brazilian Dominican, Frei Betto, describes Gutiérrez as a mystic who moves in the political realm of theology with all the finesse of a Jesuit. A small man of dark complexion, of part Hispanic and part Indian extraction, he wears, Betto says, the sad expression of one all too familiar with the thin line that separates life from death. His keen theological eye has focused above all on the suffering of the poor where he finds the Lord present in spite of his seeming absence. This suffering permeates Gutiérrez's own life, for his delicate health is a constant nagging concern. However, he can sit for hours on an airport bench, writing an article or listening to someone, all the time biting nervously on a toothpick with his strong, slightly separated teeth. In his lectures he displays a sense of humor that enables him to maintain a measure of critical distance from any fact. As Betto says, "He never lets himself be betrayed by emotion for he knows that nothing human deserves to be taken too seriously."[2]

Gutiérrez has never worked as a lone ranger. From the very outstart of his search for a new theology he was careful to share his concerns with like-minded priests whose experience and viewpoint resembled his. These soundings finally came to fruition in 1968 at Chimbote, Peru, when he presented the fundamental outline of what for the first time he called "liberation theology."

The ground was prepared for the success of Gutiérrez's book by the fact that liberation theology had already penetrated deeply into the Latin American Church. It is an extraordinary phenomenon that is documented very well by Father Raymond Muñoz in his work *Nueva Conciencia de la Iglesia en América Latina*. Covering the period from 1965 to 1970, Father Muñoz analyzed over 300 documents reflecting the views of church groups and representatives from Mexico to Chile, showing a basic consensus taking root

[2]Ellis and Maduro, eds., *The Future of Liberation Theology,* pp. 34–36.

within a large sector of the Church during this time. The documents join in calling attention to the inhuman social and economic situations existing in Latin American countries. They depict these conditions as a form of actual violence against the poor caused by local capitalist systems with the backing of the major capitalist powers (especially the United States). They find it strictly accurate to speak of a need for revolutionary change, and while the hope is for nonviolent change, they recognize that peaceful revolution may be precluded by extreme repression. Many of the documents state the belief that socialism, including socialization of the means of production, may offer the best hope. And finally there is a general agreement that the clergy fall into two groups—those on the side of the powerful and those on the side of the poor.

Gutiérrez gives an account of his reaction when he began work among the poor in the 1960s. He discovered three things:

> That poverty was a destructive thing, something to be fought against and destroyed . . . that poverty was not accidental . . . but the result of a structure . . . [and] that poor people were a social class. It became crystal clear that in order to serve the poor, one had to move into political action.[3]

Gutiérrez speaks often of creating not a new theology but a new way of *doing* theology which he calls "praxis." It has become one of the buzzwords identified with liberation theology and is defined succinctly by Paulo Freire as "reflection and action upon the world in order to transform it."[4] It presupposes a commitment to the poor and the determination to act on their behalf. According to its theorists, there is a constant dynamic in praxis—one's action for the poor inspires critical reflection while this reflection leads one to more effective action. Two important differences distinguish praxis from the traditional Christian belief in the importance of both faith and works. One difference is that in praxis, the action called for is meant to change the world; the second difference is that the action is intended to empower the poor to take charge of their own lives, to "become the artisans of their own liberation," as Gutiérrez put it.

[3] Quoted in Paul Sigmund, *Liberation Theology at the Crossroads* (New York: Oxford University Press, 1990), p. 32.

[4] *Pedagogy of the Oppressed*, p. 36, in R. McFee Brown, *Gustavo Gutiérrez* (Atlanta: John Knox Press, 1980), p. 68.

From Medellín to Puebla

Soon after Medellín, conservative bishops began to have second thoughts about the documents they had signed. They began to realize that the thrust of Medellín was toward radical change both within society and within the Church, and they were troubled by the specter of fire-eating priests and nuns quoting Medellín and mouthing the word "revolution." Reviews, articles, and interviews attacking Gutiérrez and liberation theology began to appear, orchestrated by those in high places. Gutiérrez was a prime target since he had played a central role in drafting some of the key documents of Medellín, and his book *A Theology of Liberation* (1971) was already being cited as the textbook of the movement.

The leader of the opposition was Archbishop López Trujillo who in 1972 became the secretary general of CELAM (the Latin American Conference of Bishops). In this post he was able to marshal the troops for an assault on liberation theology. In preparation for the next episcopal conference at Puebla (Mexico) in 1979, he and his staff issued a preliminary document insisting on a gradualist approach to the solution of social problems, emphasizing the importance of doctrinal orthodoxy, and calling for a deemphasis on the commitment to the poor. But the document was too conservative for the majority of the bishops and had to be revised.

Nevertheless, Trujillo was determined to avoid at Puebla what he considered to be the "catastrophe" of Medellín and he was able to exclude from participation a veritable *Who's Who in Latin American Theology*. No liberation theologians were invited. Among those excluded were Gutiérrez himself, Juan Luis Segundo, Hugo Assmann, Jon Sobrino, Ignacio Ellacuria, Raul Vidales, Enrique Dussel, Segundo Galilea, Pablo Richard, and José Comblín. The liberation theologians, however, were able to influence the outcome by the simple solution of coming to Puebla anyway and renting a house nearby. Though they could not enter the seminary grounds where the conference was held, they received the progressive bishops who left the enclosure to come to consult them, and they spoke daily with the press. As a result they had an active hand in drafting many of the conference documents: the revised texts were "smuggled" in by the sympathetic bishops and won endorsement by the conference as a whole.

Pope John Paul II, who opened the conference, had the unenviable task of trying to hold the bishops to a middle way, which consisted of condemning social injustice while banning close political involvement by priests. In fact, the final documents contain something for everyone and each side could quote passages in its own favor. Capitalism is stigmatized for its idolatrous worship of wealth, Marxism for its materialism, and liberation theology is simply ignored. However, the door opened by Medellín was not slammed shut, as witnessed by the bishops' affirmation of the Church's "preferential option for the poor." The term was a compromise, a watering down of the more straightforward "option for the poor," but its inclusion at all is a remarkable fact considering the much more conservative climate that had by then taken hold of both the world and the Church.

A Bishop on the Right

One of the bishops at Puebla whose destiny had been linked in a singular way with Medellín and liberation theology was Oscar Romero, archbishop of San Salvador. Romero was born in the remote Salvadoran village of Ciudad Barrios on August 15, 1917. His father, Santos Romero, was the village postmaster and owned a modest house that still stands at the corner of the main plaza. Santos was not a particularly religious man, but Oscar remembered how nevertheless he taught him to pray. Oscar's mother, Guadalupe, bore Santos eight children, one of whom died at birth. Her most striking feature was a square jaw that was even more pronounced in her son Oscar.

Oscar's father wanted him to be a carpenter, so at the age of thirteen Oscar was apprenticed and learned to make tables, chairs, and coffins. But his mind was set on the seminary, and after a few months he was able to enter a minor seminary run by the Claretians in San Miguel. It was like one big family, he said later, recalling the happy years he spent there. In 1937 he went on to the national seminary in San Salvador and a short time later was sent to Rome to study at the Gregorian University. A classmate in Rome described him as "of medium height, dark complexion, deliberate bearing, like one who is not hurried to arrive because he knows he will get there. With other persons he was peaceable, calm . . . a bit shy. . . . He was observant of the regulations, pious, concerned for his priestly training in every aspect . . . With others, he could make friends and was regarded by us who were his friends for his simplicity and desire to help."[5] Romero was deeply impressed by the man who was pope at the time, Pius XI. After Pius's death in 1939, Romero remembered approaching the catafalque and

[5]James R. Brockman, *Romero: A Life* (Maryknoll, N.Y.: Orbis Books, 1989), pp. 37–38.

putting his hand reverently on the dead pope's right arm. He called him the pope he most admired, the prelate who stood up against Mussolini and Hitler.

Ordained in Rome in 1942, Romero arrived back in El Salvador after a trip that, because of wartime conditions, took four months. In priest-scarce Latin America, bishops wasted little time in heaping responsibilities on energetic and talented young priests. Within a few months he was appointed secretary of the diocese and pastor of the cathedral in San Miguel, all the while serving two other churches as well. He helped edit the diocesan paper, and gained fame as a preacher through his Sunday sermons broadcast on five radio stations in the small city. He was also able to complete the construction of the cathedral while carrying on a ministry that included visiting the countryside and the jails and promoting a host of societies and organizations including Alcoholics Anonymous, the Legion of Mary, the Knights of the Holy Sepulcher, the Third Order of St. Francis, and Caritas, which distributed food to the poor. Raúl Romero (no relation) whom he took into his rectory as a foster son, remembered his zeal and cheerfulness and how in visiting the jails to say mass he also brought movies along to relieve the prisoners' boredom.[6]

As Romero was approaching his silver anniversary as a priest, his energy and zeal had earned him a near monopoly of power in San Miguel as rector of the seminary, editor of the diocesan newspaper, and secretary to the bishop. But when a new bishop was appointed who was less willing to delegate responsibility, Romero decided it was time for him to move on. In 1967 he was appointed secretary-general of the national bishops' conference with an office in San Salvador. He was subsequently also named executive secretary of the Central American Bishops' Secretariat. It was a natural stepping stone to the episcopate, and in 1970 he was named auxiliary bishop in San Salvador. His ordination was celebrated in the gymnasium of a local high school with a great abundance of civil and religious dignitaries and much fanfare. Critics, however, thought the ostentatious event most inappropriate in view of the widespread poverty in San Salvador.

Romero was, in fact, if anything lukewarm toward the new currents pulsing through the Latin American church. Though he took a basically positive view of the changes inaugurated by Vatican II, and often referred to Vatican II in his talks, he was unhappy with some of the subsequent devel-

[6] Ibid., p. 40.

opments and omitted mention of Medellín in his sermons and clergy meetings.

It was at this time also that he became noticeably friendly with the conservative Catholic organization Opus Dei, which he later praised as "a mine of wealth for our church."[7] In 1971 he was appointed editor of the diocesan newspaper *Orientación* to replace a priest who had paid inordinate attention to social issues. Romero was able to shift the paper's focus to safer issues like drugs, alcoholism, and pornography. But this did not mean that he avoided controversy; indeed, he sparked it, in particular with an editorial in which he blasted a Jesuit secondary school for teaching Marxism as part of a "liberating education." Headlines in the papers decried Marxist instruction in Catholic schools, while TV and the attorney general began an investigation of the charges.

While the Jesuits eventually won a vote of confidence from the parents at the school, Romero continued *Orientación*'s campaign against what the paper called the "mutilation of Medellín" by leftist Catholics. Progressive Catholic opinion found his ready defense of the established order quite disturbing.

Another fracas with the Jesuits occurred when the bishops appointed Romero rector of the major seminary in order to restore discipline, which they felt had deteriorated: The Jesuit rector had been guilty of such infractions as allowing the seminarians to engage in sport without wearing their cassocks and to leave the seminary grounds more freely than in the past. The bishops decided to start over with a new faculty and a new crop of seminarians, sending the others elsewhere or dismissing them. But the reorganization failed. The big, gray, nearly empty building proved too demoralizing and the costs prohibitive. Romero finally had to admit to defeat.

But his star continued to rise. In 1974 Romero was given a diocese of his own, Santiago de María, which embraced some 400,000 at least nominal Catholics. With characteristic energy and enthusiasm he hit the ground running, using every means to reach his people, mounting loudspeakers on a jeep and moving around even to remote settlements to preach, play sacred music, and administer the sacraments. He was typically responsive to the needy and usually found ways to supply poor parishes with equipment and building materials. As the homeless multiplied in Santiago during harvest time, he lodged them in the cathedral rectory and offices and in a clergy meeting hall.

[7] Ibid., p. 46.

Even though social unrest was mounting and wanton massacres of peasants by the National Guard became common knowledge, Romero remained loath to blame the government. In 1975 a series of such incidents occurred, culminating in an overnight invasion of Tres Calles, a hamlet in Romero's diocese, by government troops. They ransacked the houses and hacked to death five *campesinos* (peasants). The next day Romero went to console the grieving families but hesitated to make a public protest and felt uneasy with the protest songs at the mass he concelebrated with several priests.

His great concern at the time was that the priests were being politicized, but he was unaware how politicized he himself was in defending the status quo. He prepared a memorandum enumerating a number of factors influencing the clergy's politicization. First was the "liberating education" offered by the Jesuits in their schools and at the Central American University in El Salvador, in their publications, in their "new Christology," and in their pastoral work among the poor. Next he cited the work of the Salvadoran Justice and Peace Commission of Father Ramón Vega and its bulletin *Justicia y Paz* with its biting criticism of capitalism. Finally, he noted the spread of peasant development centers operated by priests, nuns, and other committed Christians making use of analysis. His own hope, he concluded, was in a spiritualizing of the clergy that would bear witness to the hope and transcendence of Christianity.[8]

One of the aforementioned development centers, Los Naranjos, was in his own diocese. His determination to make fundamental changes in its approach involved him in heated discussions with the priests in charge, who accused him of betraying Medellín. But the dialogue was fruitful for in the end he was able to persuade the priests to adopt a modified proposal while he himself was forced to make a more serious study of Medellín. Coincidentally, at the time there appeared Pope Paul's apostolic exhortation *Evangelii Nuntiandi,* which emphasized the Church's commitment to the temporal as well as the spiritual liberation of the oppressed. The message made a deep impression on Romero and no doubt was an important factor in his remarkable spiritual evolution.

Romero was still regarded, however, as a staunch conservative when he was chosen in 1977 by the Vatican to succeed the retiring archbishop of San Salvador, Luis Chávez y González. Chávez, who had served as archbishop

[8]Ibid., pp. 56–58.

since 1938, had been a forceful advocate of social justice. Under his leadership some 200 Salvadoran bishops, priests, sisters, and lay people had gathered in June 1970 for a pastoral week intended to explore new directions for their ministries in the light of the events of Vatican II and Medellín. They admitted that the Church had failed to advance liberation and yet that "people still look to the Church as the force that can liberate them." They resolved to establish base communities; to end clericalism; to form leaders dedicated to the integral development of the human person and the formation of communities; to work for conscientization of the people; and to struggle against obstacles to peasant unionization.

So the big question in the minds of the clergy when Romero was installed was whether he would try to dismantle Chávez's legacy of social justice and put the Church "back on the right path" as the outgoing president of El Salvador, Arturo Molina, urged him to do. The leading liberation theologian Jon Sobrino tells how he saw "bad times in store when he heard of Romero's appointment."[9]

Romero's installation came at a moment of heightened government violence. Using the unrest surrounding the fraudulent February elections as a pretext, the government had arrested and deported several priests. The National Guard had detained and tortured another. Attacks on the Church were rife in the national press, and the Jesuit university had been bombed six times in the last year. Then, only five days after Romero's installation as archbishop, the army undertook a massacre of civilians in San Salvador itself. Some 50,000 people gathered in the Plaza Libertad to protest massive fraud in the recent elections. Troops with armored cars cordoned off the square. They gave the remaining crowd of about 6,000 ten minutes to disperse and then opened fire, wounding and killing many. A large number of the demonstrators took refuge in the nearby Church of El Rosario and were rescued only when a truce was arranged with the help of the retired archbishop, Chávez.

At first it was not too clear where Romero stood. He joined with his fellow bishops in drafting a strong statement that expressed their concern for the violence against the peasants, the deaths and disappearances, the intimidation against the Church, and the expulsion of priests. But above all, the bishops deplored the lack of social justice and the state of suffering in which the large majority of the nation's people lived. They declared it the

[9] Ibid., p. 4.

Church's mission "to struggle for and to further justice, to know the truth, to achieve a political, social, and economic order conformed to God's plan . . . Even at the risk of being . . . persecuted, the church must lift up its voice when injustice possesses society . . ." Speaking in unmistakably concrete terms, the bishops asserted that while the Church's message of salvation is open to all, this same good news demands that it "cannot remain unmoved between those who have great tracts of land and those who have not even a minimum to farm for subsistence, between those who have access to culture, to recreation, to an opulent life, and those who must struggle day by day in order to survive, who live in habitual unemployment and with a hunger that debases them to the direst levels of undernourishment."[10]

But after a few days Romero was having second thoughts about the statement they had drafted, and wondered about the wisdom of proclaiming it. Bishop Arturo Rivera, the former archbishop's close colleague and the clergy's own preference to have succeeded him, prevailed on Romero to read the statement at the eight o'clock mass scheduled for March 13. But Romero decided he would not read it again at the Church of San José de la Montaña where the congregation would include many wealthy parishioners.

Putting the Church on the Side of the Poor

However, whatever reluctance he had to disturb the rich and powerful was soon overcome before March 13. On March 12, Rutilio Grande, a Jesuit priest working with the peasants at Aguilares, was murdered while driving to neighboring El Paisnal to say mass. An old man and a boy with him were also killed. Rutilio and his fellow Jesuits ministered to some thirty thousand peasants around Aguilares who barely scraped out a living in the sugar cane fields, where they could find work only at harvest time. The Jesuits had encouraged the peasants to organize, and Rutilio himself had minced no words in sermons denouncing injustice and encouraging the people to take charge of their lives. None of this brought joy to the small clique of landowners living luxuriously in their haciendas.

The murders happened around 5:30 in the afternoon. By 10 P.M. the archbishop had made his way to Aguilares to join the hundreds of *campesinos*

[10]Ibid., p. 7.

and the dozen priests who were present for an emotion-filled mass in the presence of the three bodies now covered with sheets.

The next day, March 13, Romero read the bishops' statement both at the cathedral and at the Church of San José de la Montaña. The day after that he read it once again in the cathedral, before the papal nuncio and a crowd that overflowed into the streets, Romero eulogized Rutilio. He was a priest, Romero said, who was a messenger of liberation, a liberation rightly based on faith. Because Rutilio was such a messenger, he was killed.

The word "liberation" in the mouth of a bishop known as an arch conservative: What was going on? Jon Sobrino, Romero's friend and counselor, believed the murder of Rutilio Grande had shaken him to the roots. Romero had always felt great personal respect for Grande and had even chosen him to be the master of ceremonies at his ordination to the episcopate. Nevertheless, he had felt Grande's social-activist view of the pastoral ministry ill-conceived. How a zealous, virtuous priest could be so misguided had remained an enigma for him. Then, over the dead body of Grande—who like Jesus had laid down his life for his sheep—he realized that Grande's view of the ministry must be right and his own wrong. Romero's "conversion" was strengthened by another fact—the reaction of Catholics he had deemed loyal, devout, and orthodox. He soon found out how loyal they were when he began to say things that threatened their selfish interests. Finally the warm, loving reception he received from the poor when he took the first steps toward them moved him enormously and consolidated the feelings he had had while standing over Grande's body.

The day after the funeral mass in the cathedral, Romero brought together the clergy, some female religious, and several lay people. All agreed that the murder of Rutilio was part of a general persecution of the Church. They saw arrayed against the Church the government, the military, and such organizations as the Eastern Region Farmers' Front (Faro) and the National Private Business Association (ANEP). These were people who were obviously frightened by the new image of a Church committed to proclaiming the program of Medellín and preaching the gospel of liberation to the *campesinos*. It was therefore necessary, those at the meeting felt, to show the Church's solidarity with the archbishop as well as the Church's determination to continue the struggle. They backed a proposal to close the Catholic schools for several days and to celebrate only one mass for the entire country the next Sunday—the archbishop's mass at the cathedral. Finally, they called for representatives of the Church to absent themselves from any public functions that might be interpreted as support for the elite.

One powerful church figure, however, was not happy with these decisions. Emanuele Gerada, the papal nuncio in San Salvador who many of the clergy considered too friendly with the rich and powerful, called Romero on the carpet and berated him as imprudent and irresponsible. He warned him of the potential consequences of defying the government ban on public gatherings by celebrating the single mass next Sunday. Fortified by the support of his clergy, however, Romero refused to back down and left the meeting much dismayed. It had been a humiliating encounter, all the more because he had previously enjoyed cordial relations with the nuncio. Sunday's mass went ahead as planned. The attendance was magnificent—a hundred thousand strong, many of them Catholics who had been estranged from the Church for years. The confrontation with the nuncio was Romero's first serious one with high officialdom in the Church. The consequences were lasting and the animosity he incurred would permanently color his relations with the curia and cause him much suffering.

To offset the negative reports that he knew the nuncio was, no doubt, sending to Rome, Romero felt it wise to go and present his case personally to the Holy Father. He departed for Rome on March 26. In spite of some unpleasant moments at the Congregation for the Bishops (where the secretary lectured him on etiquette and protocol), it was a surprisingly good experience. In a private audience, Paul VI warmly took his hand and told him to have courage: "You are the one in charge."[11] Romero also took the opportunity while in Rome to extend his relations with the Jesuits, who were a power in his diocese. Their Central American University educated many sons and daughters of the upper class and was a constant thorn in the side of the ruling oligarchy. The Jesuit provincial for Central America joined Romero in Rome, bringing with him an extensive dossier of the terrible human-rights abuses in El Salvador.

Romero's first task on arriving home was to publish his first pastoral letter, entitled "The Paschal Church," a poignant reflection on the link between the Church in El Salvador and the paschal mystery of Christ. In his passage from death to life, Romero said, Christ personified the true Passover. The Church "is born of the Passover and lives to be sign and instrument of the Passover in the midst of the world." The mission of the Church, therefore, is to lead the people through their own Passover, the passage from death to life by conversion to the Gospel. At Medellín, he said, the Latin American bishops had realized that in preaching conversion they could not

[11] Ibid., p. 20.

be indifferent to the silent cry from millions of people "begging their pastors for a liberation they find nowhere else."[12] In listening to their cry the bishops had been faithful to Vatican II, which proclaimed the Church's spiritual vocation to be primary but also insisted on the need to link preaching the Gospel with preaching liberation. Finally, he said, since the Church's unique service to humanity is not essentially political or socioeconomic, it sincerely seeks dialogue with those responsible for decisions in these areas. Unfortunately, Romero said, this dialogue had been hampered in El Salvador by a great amount of misunderstanding.

Persecution of the Church

On April 18, less than two months into Archbishop Romero's tenure, President Molina called the bishops and nuncio together to register complaints about supposed antigovernment actions by various priests. Again Romero stood his ground. Priests loyal to the mandates of Vatican II and Medellín would have his support, he said, and should not be taken for Marxist subversives. The government brought tensions with the Church on itself by such irresponsible accusations. The very day of the meeting with Molina, the government's foreign minister, Mauricio Borgonovo, had been taken hostage by a small guerrilla group, the Popular Liberation Forces (FPL). The price for his demanded safe return was the release of thirty-seven political prisoners, but the government refused to negotiate. The archbishop made two public appeals on behalf of the poor soul but to no avail. Borgonovo's body was found on the evening of May 10, and on May 11 Romero held the funeral mass at the Church of San José de la Montaña. There he reminded the assembled leaders and members of the oligarchy that the Church rejects violence. "It has said so a thousand times, and none of its ministers preaches violence."[13]

That very afternoon Father Alfonso Navarro, a young pastor, was shot down in his rectory along with a boy of fourteen. A group calling themselves the White Warriors claimed responsibility, calling the murders a retaliation for the death of the foreign minister. Two hundred priests from all over El Salvador attended the funeral mass the next day, and once again Romero denounced the use of violence and the campaign of slander against the Church. But anonymous handbills continued to appear. "Be a patriot,

[12]Ibid., p. 24.
[13]Ibid., p. 28.

kill a priest," they said. "This is only the beginning," the murderers of Father Navarro had said.

The next attack on the Church occurred May 17 at Aguilares when troops arrived to force the peasants off land they had tilled for years. Houses were ransacked, some fifty people were killed and many more abducted. The soldiers seized the church for a barracks and sprayed the tabernacle with bullets, scattering hosts all over the floor. They assaulted one of the priests, seized the remaining three Jesuits and expelled them.

One month later, Romero went to Aguilares to install the new pastoral team, a priest and three sisters. He was greeted by a huge crowd who had waited for him for hours in the hot sun. At the mass he celebrated there with ten priests he preached in his sure, firm manner, applying the reading of the day from Zechariah to the suffering village before him: "You are the image of the divine one who was pierced for our offenses," he said.[14] He continued to the repeated applause of the congregation, calling Aguilares a model of pastoral ministry for the Church of El Salvador. As a victim of persecution, it was also a witness to all the parishes. With members of the National Guard within earshot, the archbishop prayed for reconciliation with the persecutors. When he brought his sermon to a close, the five thousand present warmly applauded.

After mass, the people walked in a procession with the Eucharist through the town square. At the town hall, they were confronted by armed and sullen guardsmen who came out and threatened to bar the way. But Romero, who was in the rear holding the monstrance, called out, *"Adelante!"* ("Forward!") and the troops made way. As Jon Sobrino says, from this moment on Romero was the symbolic leader of El Salvador.[15]

In the following weeks, right-wing press attacks on the "radicals" escalated. A concerted campaign to divide the Church became apparent. One writer distinguished between the good bishops and good priests and those who had become "bearers of an ideology that threatened to enslave all humanity."[16] The Church was able to respond in the columns of *Orientación* and through its radio station, YSAX, which broadcast Romero's Sunday homilies. These were by now eagerly awaited by most of the nation, as were the archbishop's regular Wednesday interviews.

The Jesuits also entered the fray with a series of articles addressed to "the

---

[14]Ibid., p. 62.
[15]Jon Sobrino, *Archbishop Romero* (Maryknoll, N.Y.: Orbis Books, 1990), pp. 27–28.
[16]Brockman, *Romero: A Life,* p. 68.

Salvadoran People." The Church in El Salvador, they said, was properly identifying with the dispossessed and therefore its message would be found displeasing by those bent only on protecting privilege and power. In response, the White Warriors gave the Jesuits thirty days to leave the country or be exterminated—certainly not an idle threat in view of the murder of Father Grande and the numerous bombings at Central American University. But the Jesuits affirmed their intention of remaining.

The Jesuits and the archbishop were by this time receiving vigorous expressions of support from around the world. But one of Romero's greatest consolations was the outpouring of letters from those people who listened to his broadcasts and deeply appreciated the efforts of the Church on their behalf. Many of them came from the small communities that had multiplied as the Church began to champion the interests of the poor. With the paucity of priests, only occasional visits were possible and thus many of these new communities were led by trained catechists and delegates of the word who conducted the religious services and bible study programs. Like the priests, the catechists were harassed by the National Guard and tortured and some even killed. But as one letter stated:

> We committed Christians are not frightened by so many threats, the more we are threatened the braver we feel and therefore we write you not to feel alone, we are all ready to accept any sacrifice.[17]

Romero now devoted a second pastoral letter (August 6, 1977) to a clarification of his and the Church's public commitments. This letter offers a good insight into the theology behind his stand. His purpose, he said, was to help people understand the changes going on in the Church of El Salvador, changes that he admitted were disturbing to many Catholics. These changes must be seen, he said, in the light of a fundamental change that has occurred in the Church's view of its relation to the world. The Church now sees the world as the primary arena where God works out his plan of salvation. In other words, the struggles of humanity to build a more just and peaceful society are an essential part of God's plan of salvation. The Church's role is to serve the world as a sign and sacrament of God's love working in history—indeed of God's love as the driving force of history.

A key factor in precipitating this change in the purpose of the Church, Romero said, was the renewed awareness of what it means for the Church to be the body of Christ, who founded it to keep himself present in history.

[17]Ibid., p. 78.

While on earth, this same Christ showed a special preference for the outcasts of society and lavished on them especially his love and compassion. As his body, the Church cannot do otherwise. This means in the present circumstances that it must denounce the sinful structures that keep the poor and the humble in a state of utter destitution and despair. As the Church does this, it is of course accused of being Marxist, of fomenting violence, and of meddling in politics. But these charges are false. The Church has always condemned the atheistic materialism that is the basic principle of Marxism, and the record shows that, far from preaching violence, even while being persecuted the Church continues to preach love and forgiveness. Nor does it meddle in politics, though it cannot avoid the political effects that flow from its preaching.

A few days after the publication of the pastoral letter, the country's new president, General Carlos Humberto Romero (no relation), invited the archbishop to sit down with him and discuss their mutual concerns. Archbishop Romero laid his cards on the table. Cooperation between the Church and the government, he said, could only be achieved in three stages: First there must be an end to human rights abuses, to the harassment of and the assaults on priests, and to the general persecution of the Church. Second, there must be meetings between representatives of the Church and high-ranking military officials to promote better understanding of the social doctrines of the Church, especially as stated at Medellín. The third and final stage would be reached when permanent measures were taken to alleviate the lot of the poor and to assure greater social justice.

The new president promised Romero to do all in his power to meet these demands but noted how difficult it was to deal with the country's selfish capitalists. Events would soon show how hollow such promises were.

The Split in the Hierarchy

The division in the hierarchy—which had been pretty well hidden till now—surfaced at the inauguration of the new president on July 1. Traditionally all the bishops attended these occasions. But Archbishop Romero thought that to do so would be a mockery; it was no secret that the government was in complicity with the right-wing terrorist squads and had done virtually nothing, in spite of promises by the president-elect, to investigate the murder of the two priests and the other outrages at Aguilares. Romero consulted widely about this matter, and the priests' senate and other pastoral workers agreed he should not go. In the end, only the nuncio and Bishops Álvarez and Barrera attended.

Bishop Álvarez's defense of his attendance in the pages of his diocesan newspaper shows the beginning of the animosity he and some of his fellow bishops would harbor for Archbishop Romero: "I feel contented and happy at having performed a function of the church in attending personally the transfer of the presidency . . . There is no persecuted church. There are some sons of the church that, wanting to serve, lost their way and put themselves outside the law. Behind us there is a people, and we will be a bridge of goodness for all Salvadorans, as far as we can serve them."[18]

The public censure of Romero by his fellow bishops did not stop at the local level. On October 4, 1977, news arrived of a statement made by Bishop Revelo who was representing the Salvadoran bishops at the synod of bishops in Rome. He had told the international assembly how disturbed he was by the Marxist and even Maoist sympathies of some Salvadoran priests who were engaged in training the catechists. And he accused these priests of giving too much attention to the social and political problems of the people instead of making solid Christian formation their first concern. A storm broke loose at home. The priests' senate blasted his remarks as "limited, exaggerated and biased," while Romero accused Revelo of giving ammunition to the Church's persecutors. The irony of it all was that Romero had already asked the Holy See to make Revelo his auxiliary bishop. He now tried to block the appointment but was unable to do so and had to make the best of a bad bargain.

Nor were the archbishop's troubles limited to the actions of his opponents. Some of his supporters could be seriously imprudent as well: In the spring of 1978 more than two hundred priests and religious (out of the total 1,125 in El Salvador) sent an emotional letter to the papal nuncio accusing him of causing grave scandal. He was charged with supporting a "repressive and unjust government" in open disagreement with the "pastoral and prophetic policy" of the archbishop and archdiocese. They begged him to hear the cry of a whole people and not make more difficult "our communion with the Holy See." And they prayed in the name of the martyrs for him "not to keep struggling against the light and the truth in the service of Caiaphas, Herod and Pilate."[19]

Bishops Barrera, Álvarez, and Revelo called an emergency meeting on

[18] Ibid., pp. 68–69.
[19] Ibid., pp. 109–110.

April 3 to secure from the bishops a statement of support for the nuncio. The statement labeled the allegations made against the nuncio unjust, disrespectful, malicious, insolent, irreverent, antievangelical, and more. Romero did not defend either the wisdom or the tone of the letter criticizing the nuncio, but asked whether the proposed statement of the bishops was any less inopportune; he also noted its failure to acknowledge the truth in some of the allegations about the nuncio. At this, Bishop Aparicio turned on Romero himself, accusing him of meddling in other dioceses, ruining the bishops' conference, dividing the country, and confusing the nation through his broadcast sermons and his articles in *Orientación*. "We're on to you," he told Romero, and now accused Romero himself of being the author of the letter to the nuncio. Romero called the charge a "slander."[20] The bishops voted four to one in favor of a statement supporting the nuncio. Romero's only consolation was the strong show of support given him the next day by his clergy.

Could it be long before government officials joined in open criticism of the archbishop? Romero was now speaking out against government corruption in bolder terms than ever. In one of his homilies that same spring, he made a scathing denunciation of the criminal justice system; he referred to "judges who sell themselves," and he demanded greater integrity from the Supreme Court in administering the system. His term "judges who sell themselves" caught the attention of the Supreme Court, whose members challenged him to name these judges. They figured he would be unwilling to risk a trial for slander and would have to back down; he could then be targeted as a coward and a blowhard.

The whole nation waited for his reply. On Pentecost Sunday the mood was tense in the cathedral as he began to read his carefully worded statement. People wondered how he would extricate himself from the trap. Reading rapidly and somewhat nervously, he said the Supreme Court had taken out of context his words "judges who sell themselves" in order to distract people from his main complaint against the Supreme Court—its complicity in a wholesale violation of human rights. Because of its inaction, he charged, officers of the government regularly deprived people of rights guaranteed by the constitution. The right of habeas corpus, for instance, was made a mockery when "mothers, wives and children from one end of the country to the other, have walked a way of the cross searching for their dear ones without finding any answer whatever." This, he said, while the court paid

[20] Ibid., p. 113.

lip service to the rule, "No one can be arbitrarily arrested, imprisoned, or exiled."

The same kind of disregard for human rights occurred with regard to the right to form labor unions as guaranteed by the constitution. "It is impossible," stated the archbishop, "to understand all the detailed inconveniences, hindrances, and obstacles put in the way of the farmworker to achieve the practice of that fundamental right." Finally he noted that the press had often called for investigations of the judicial system without any response from the judicial authorities. He expressed his hope that the Supreme Court, by asking him to further detail his earlier charges, was at last acknowledging broad problems with the judicial system preparatory to doing something about it. Loud applause broke out as he ended. People realized that he had turned the tables on his accusers and exposed the fundamental corruption of the justice system. The Supreme Court made no reply.

Sparring with Rome

Throughout his episcopate, Romero had constant worries about how much support he could expect from Rome. Paul VI had strongly encouraged him at their first meeting, but Romero had little control over what information the pope did or did not receive and his first year had won him formidable opponents. Sebastian Cardinal Baggio, the powerful prefect of the Congregation of the Bishops in Rome, was not one of Romero's fans. On May 24, 1978, Romero received a letter from Baggio inviting him to Rome for "a brotherly and friendly conversation" about the worsening situation in El Salvador. Bishop Rivera, now Romero's closest confidant and most loyal supporter among the Salvadoran bishops, accompanied him, and they arrived in Rome on June 17. Before meeting with the prefect, Romero prayed before the tomb of Peter one day and the tomb of Paul the next. These were grace-filled moments for Romero, who relived "in my heart, in my love, all those emotions of my days as a student in Rome."[21]

He needed all the inspiration and strength he could get, for the next day his "brotherly and friendly conversation" with Baggio turned into an inquisition. At the outset Baggio noted how much Romero had disappointed a number of those who had originally favored his appointment. It was obvious, as Romero later said, that Baggio had bought entirely the negative opinions of Romero's enemies. Baggio "was horrified" to think of what

[21] Ibid., p. 127.

kind of vocations were coming out of Romero's seminary. He called the honorary doctorate Romero had received from Georgetown University in February "a political trick," and his attitude toward the nuncio "an almost irreparable scandal." Romero did his best during the meeting, and in a letter to Baggio a few days later, to correct the prefect's misimpressions and faulty information. He repeated in his letter one final point he had made in person: "With the same simplicity as in our talk, I put it in writing that, if it is for the good of the church, with the greatest pleasure I will turn over to other hands this difficult governance of the archdiocese. But while I have it under my responsibility, I will only try to please the Lord and serve his church and his people according to my conscience in the light of the gospel and the magisterium."[22]

Fortunately Romero's visit with the pope the next day revived his spirit. Paul VI took both his hands and spoke "words of encouragement and understanding." In a later visit with Archbishop Casaroli, secretary of the Council for the Church's Public Affairs, Romero and Rivera characterized Romero's three main enemies in the episcopate: Álvarez was so close to the military he was nicknamed "the Colonel"; Barrera was in his dotage; and Aparicio was said to "wag his tail" when receiving favors from the government.

All in all Romero felt good about his visit to Rome, especially thanks to the encouragement he had received from the pope. "I have felt him so near to me, I leave feeling so grateful to him, that my heart, my faith, my spirit continue to draw nourishment from that rock where the church's unity is so palpable."[23]

Romero by now had begun work on his third pastoral letter. One of his main concerns was to clarify the relationship of the Church to the country's popular organizations, especially the two peasant unions FECCAS and UTC, whose membership included a sizeable number of Catholics. Two issues especially needed treatment: Marxist influence on FECCAS and UTC, and the use of violence.

At the outset of the letter, Romero insisted on the basic human right to organize. In the case of workers, he noted, this right to organize has been fundamental to the social teaching of the Church since Pope Leo XIII; it has been explicitly reaffirmed in many documents since, including John XXIII's encyclical *Pacem in Terris* and the documents of Vatican II. Though the same

[22] Ibid., p. 130.
[23] Ibid., p. 133.

right was guaranteed in the Salvadoran constitution, the workers and *campesinos* were systematically deprived of this right both by legislation and by terrorist actions of the rich and powerful.

As for the Church's active role, he said, it must first be understood that while the mission of the Church is the spread of the Gospel, the Gospel awakens the hearts of the faithful to the need to build and improve their human communities. Thus political commitment may arise from faith. It is not the role of the institutional Church to found political organizations or to favor one over another. But the Church's necessary concern for justice and its responsibility to interpret human events according to divine law mean that "it can and must give a judgment on the overall intentions and mechanisms of parties and organizations."[24]

Regarding the actions of individual Christians and church workers, specific guidelines were laid down. One, the autonomy of faith must be safeguarded so that the faith itself does not get identified with a specific political cause. This would mean that those lay people active in both the Church and political organizations must be aware of a possible confusion of roles and be ready, after consultation with their pastors and their own consciences, to opt for one public commitment or the other. Second, the Church, its preaching and liturgy, should not be used as a vehicle for political causes. In those exceptional cases where a priest seemed called to take on a political role, he should discuss these concerns with his bishop so that they might reach a joint discernment of the problem. Finally, the Christian engaged in the political process should not use methods inconsonant with the faith. These include the use of violence—which Romero's letter, quoting Paul VI, calls "unchristian and unevangelical," as well as ineffective and contrary to human dignity.[25]

The letter distinguished between the different types of violence that were involved in the civil strife. First of all there was institutional violence, perpetrated on the majority of Salvadoran men, women, and especially children who were deprived of the basic means of living. Those responsible for this form of violence included the international economic structures that adversely affected the national economic structures. Also responsible were the privileged who were determined to maintain their status at any cost, as well as those who sinned by omission in failing to take action to remedy the injustice. Then there was repressive violence used by the security forces to

[24]Ibid., p. 140.
[25]Ibid., pp. 139–141.

stifle any protest against injustice. There was also terrorist violence used by some of those attempting to bring about change; this was judged counter-productive since it only exacerbated the tensions in society and impeded efforts toward dialogue. Another category—violence used in legitimate de-fense—was seen as justified under several conditions: that the amount of force was kept to the minimum necessary, that all other means were ex-hausted, and that the violence did not cause greater evils than those it sought to remedy. Insurrection as a form of legitimate defense was viewed, in the light of Pope Paul VI's teaching and that of Medellín, as justifiable only in the very exceptional case "of evident and prolonged tyranny that seriously attacks the fundamental rights of the person and dangerously harms the common good of the country." In short, violence must always be a last resort. Finally, nonviolence was considered an option that was coming more and more to the fore in the Church. As Medellín had before him, Romero underscored the great moral force of nonviolence, which leaves the aggres-sor morally overcome and humiliated.[26]

But his fellow bishops (except for Rivera) saw no point in constructive dialogue with the peasant organizations. Much to Romero's dismay, only two days after the publication of this latest pastoral letter, the bishops issued their own much shorter statement. Though they affirmed the general right to organize, the focus of this statement was a biting criticism of FECCAS and UTC, which they saw tainted with Marxism and therefore not accept-able. FECCAS and UTC responded bitterly, accusing the bishops of joining the class struggle against them. Romero, however, wanted to use his pastoral letter to promote a dialogue that would not a priori exclude any of the parties; he also wanted to lay down a set of broad principles that should guide the Church in its relations with the organizations.

Romero's pastoral letter took note of the sudden death of Pope Paul VI on August 6, shortly before the letter's publication. His successor, John Paul I, reigned only a month before his own sudden death, although in that short time he charmed the world with his unassuming manner and simple homi-lies sparkling with humor and good sense. He put an end to the more than millennial papal traditions of overwhelming majesty and grandeur. His suc-cessor, John Paul II, was able to continue the transition to a more human and realistic view of the pope.

The sparring match between Romero and the nuncio continued under the newly elected pope. Romero refused to attend the reception given by

---

[26]Ibid., pp. 142–143.

the nuncio in honor of John Paul II. He had no desire to be photographed smiling with generals and cabinet ministers while shaking their bloodstained hands. For his part, the nuncio continued to build up his dossier on Romero and (as Romero heard from a well-positioned informant) continued his plotting to have Romero removed.

Romero wasted no time in laying his own case before John Paul II. In a letter of several pages, he described for the new pope the situation in El Salvador, the institutional injustice, the persecution of the Church, the murders and expulsions of priests. He described also the fundamental change that had occurred in his outlook when he became archbishop—when he, previously a man of conservative instincts, had felt called by God to stand beside his oppressed and abused people. He told the pope that in all his actions he prayed for light from the Holy Spirit, and he expressed his confidence that the soundness of his pastoral policy was proven by the many signs of renewal in the diocese, including the conversion of many estranged from the Church.

But unfortunately, Romero wrote to the pope, this feeling was not shared by the nuncio nor most of the other bishops. Their systematic opposition seemed incomprehensible. Thanks to this division, Romero observed, there was an impression that two Churches existed—the church of the nuncio and the "political, communist, and subversive" church of the archbishop.

During these same months, the bishops of Latin America had been making final plans for their upcoming conference in Puebla, Mexico, in January 1979.[27] High on the agenda would be an assessment of Medellín, and no one was sure whether the result would be a reaffirmation of the direction that had been set there or, as a fair number of the conservative bishops hoped, a shift of course to the right. The pope had announced his plans to open the conference himself with an address to the bishops. When he arrived at Puebla on January 26, 1979, he was met by wildly enthusiastic crowds everywhere he went. After his opening remarks, the bishops settled down to draft the documents that would, they hoped, bridge over the growing chasm between conservatives and progressives.

Romero worked quietly with the commission on evangelization and development and kept out of the wrangling and debating that often went on into the night. But the presence of one so intimately involved in one of Latin America's most explosive situations could not be ignored. Reporters

[27]See pages 499–500 above.

often interviewed him and valued his forthright answers. One press conference he gave showed him at his candid and diplomatic best. Should the
Vatican divest itself of its wealth? Romero: The Church needs money for its
work but it should give what is superfluous to the poor. Should the system
of nuncios and military vicars be done away with? Romero: They are
needed but they too need to be converted to the Gospel. He also spoke of
the terrible plight of the poor and how his closeness to them had led him to
a growing sense of the need for God. And in reference to the mothers of
those who had disappeared and been imprisoned, he said, "The Church
must echo their anguish."[28]

The increasingly conservative mood of the bishops was shown in the
small number (30 out of 200) willing to sign a letter expressing solidarity
with Romero. Moreover, Aparicio continued his campaign against the
Jesuits and Romero, accusing Romero of allowing Marxist priests to influence him. Romero did not defend himself directly but noted that he agreed
with the Jesuit General Father Arrupe who recently spoke in defense of the
Jesuits.

Romero returned from Puebla to a large reception at the Ilopango airport in San Salvador; in his sermon the following Sunday, February 18, he
dwelt on Puebla's message to the people—an optimistic message offering
hope to all parties in the struggle. While he spoke of the preferential option
for the poor, he also spoke words of encouragement to the rich. He urged
them and all political leaders, business leaders, specialists, and professionals
to spare no effort in searching for a solution to the problems of the poor.
"You have the key to the solution. But the Church gives you what you
cannot have by yourselves: hope, the optimism to struggle, the joy of knowing that there is a solution, that God is our Father and keeps on urging us.
He needed men to take the paralytic up to the roof and lower him before
Christ . . . who is the only one who can say, 'I have seen your faith. Get
up and walk.' And I believe that our people will get up and will walk."[29]

In May 1979, four months after Puebla, Romero went to Rome again,
this time for his first face-to-face meeting with John Paul II. The split in the
Salvadoran hierarchy had been put on public display in Puebla, where
Bishop Aparicio had informed the press that the Jesuits were responsible for
the violence in El Salvador; that Archbishop Romero was under the sway of

[28]Brockman, *Romero: A Life,* pp. 100–101.
[29]Ibid., p. 164.

Marxist priests; that the "disappeared" were with the guerrillas in hiding; and that militant priests were training children as guerrilla fighters.

In a private audience, John Paul II told Romero that in view of his extremely delicate situation they were thinking about assigning an apostolic administrator to his diocese—that is, a de facto second archbishop with the power to monitor Romero's activities. This would leave Romero, for all practical purposes, archbishop only in name. After they exchanged views on the subject, Romero left, disturbed but content that at least the pope had listened to him.

Once arrived home he sent Cardinal Baggio a memo setting forth his arguments against the idea. He argued that it would aggravate rather than solve the problem, which was rooted in the deeply troubled condition of the country. He did not think a new man would be able to improve relations between the Church and the government, which were bad because the people were alienated from the government. Moreover, it would make things worse by destroying the unity of the Church's ministry, a unity vitally important to its progress. And it would undo what he had so far achieved in holding together those who wanted to go faster and those favoring a more measured pace. The only solution, he said, was to keep up efforts to promote dialogue between all parties concerned.

More Priests Murdered

In November 1978 Romero had been nominated by members of the British Parliament for the Nobel Peace Prize. Though the honor eventually was awarded to Mother Teresa of Calcutta, the recommendation by Parliament indicated the international renown Romero was beginning to enjoy. But the recognition did not bring any letup in the war against the Church. On January 20, 1979, at a retreat center in El Despertar, an armored car crashed through the sheet metal gate and soldiers emerged with guns blazing. The priest in temporary charge, Father Octavio Ortiz, was found later in the courtyard, his body riddled with bullet holes and his face and head crushed. Four youths also died of gunshot wounds. The survivors—some thirty or so—were arrested, including the young children of one of the cooks. Guns were placed in the hands of the dead youths to "prove" the government's contention that it was a shootout with guerrillas.

On Sunday, January 22, 1979, an altar was set up in front of the cathedral for the funeral of Father Ortiz and the young men. The five bodies were placed before the altar as a hundred priests and some fifteen thousand faithful looked on. Romero was loudly applauded as he emerged, vested with mitre and crozier. He delivered a homily that would long be remembered. In blunt words, passionately spoken, he excoriated the security forces, the government, the press, and the president. The security forces, he said, were destroying the credibility of the government and the press. To get the truth it was necessary to read the foreign papers. He eulogized Father Ortiz as a witness of the kingdom who had worked with the poor all his life. Then he turned his attention to President Humberto Romero, who had recently traveled to Mexico: "The president . . . said in Mexico that there isn't any persecution of the church. He compromises our newspapers, putting in front-page headlines something which the cathedral here makes evident is a lie . . . To the question of whether or not the fourteen families [a term for the country's ruling elite] actually do exist in El Salvador, the president said, no, none of that exists, just as he denied that there are disappeared persons and political prisoners."[30]

In the spring and summer of 1979, right-wing paramilitary groups and security forces continued to make their deadly rounds. The mutilated corpses of their victims—teachers, labor leaders, *campesinos,* and political leaders—were often left on the streets and byways of the country, while the leftist forces responded with bombs, knives, and guns. All told, some 123 were killed in June alone. One of the dead was Rafael Palacio, a priest who—in addition to his work in the town of Santa Tecla—had taken on the job of pastor at Father Ortiz's home parish in San Salvador. After receiving a threat from the White Warriors Union, he confided to Romero the fear that he would be killed in retribution for the slaying of an army major by leftist guerrillas in Santa Tecla. The next day he was gunned down in the street in Santa Tecla. Once again Romero, the clergy, and the people gathered to mourn the death of a priest, the fifth one to die since Romero took over. "Where is our democracy's honor if people are to die in this way like dogs, with their deaths left uninvestigated?" he cried. Once more Romero ordered only one mass to be held in the diocese, at the cathedral, to show the Church's unity and the loss of a priest. "It would be sad," he said, "in a country where murder is being committed so horribly, were we not to find priests also among the victims. They are the testimony of a church incarnated in the problems of its people."[31]

Romero's adversaries, however, took a different view of the situation. In

[30]Ibid., p. 157.
[31]Ibid., p. 177.

May, Bishops Aparicio, Barrera, Álvarez, and Revelo prepared a document for Rome that in effect blamed Romero for the confusion and chaos in the Church and the country. It was a lengthy and bitter attack that cast the worst possible light on Romero's ministry and closely reflected government propaganda. It accused him of deceiving the world media into believing the Church was persecuted, of using his radio homilies to foment class war, of smearing the president and the Supreme Court, of siding with the guerrilla organizations, of trying to undermine Puebla, of seeking international renown for himself, of distorting the dogmas of the Church, and of subverting the authority of the hierarchy. Romero's whole performance, they charged, had created a crisis of faith for Catholics who could not understand how an archbishop could collaborate with cold-blooded Marxist criminals.

In spite of the seriousness of the charges, Romero said he felt at peace and that "God will have the last word." He even refused to give up hope of healing the breach among the bishops; in a letter to each of the four bishops who had made the charges, he made a passionate plea for unity. "God's children," he said, "are being murdered with impunity, especially the poor, God's favored, for whom at Puebla we made a preferential option." Was not their disunity making the repression and violence worse?[32]

One of the most dangerous allegations of the four bishops was the incredible charge that the murdered priests were either guerrillas themselves or were killed by their leftists comrades for trying to break away from them. When another priest, Alirio Napoleón Macías, was slain in his church by the Guardia Nacional in full view of witnesses, Aparicio once more blamed this murder, as well as those of the other priests, on the leftists. Romero replied in his homily the next Sunday: "I want to recall with affection the priests who have been murdered and express my solidarity with them." He noted that investigations by the archdiocese and the Inter-American Human Rights Commission of the Organization of American States had made clear that the priests were not killed by leftist groups but by the White Warrior Union or by government agents. In the case of Alfonso Navarro, a priest murdered by the right wing, he said, even the government had blamed the White Warrior Union.

[32]Ibid., pp. 180–181.

The Strife Intensifies

In spite of the great tension, painful anxieties, and extremely arduous nature of his work, Romero told his psychologist, Dr. Rudolf Semsch, that he felt a deep sense of peace and he even referred to a kind of cosmic experience of oneness that he had with the universe. This sense of peace was no doubt sustained by his deep interior life. As he said, "We all have a church within ourselves, our own consciousness. There God is, God's Spirit . . . Blessed are those who enter often to speak alone with their God." It was a practice that Romero himself faithfully stuck to, and it undoubtedly, fueled the energy that so amazed his friends. He drove himself mercilessly, seldom taking a day off, saying mass and preaching sometimes at three different locations in one day; at the same time he attended as closely as always to the pastoral programs of the diocese, and to all the administrative affairs of a busy archbishop.

Romero issued his fourth pastoral letter in the fall of 1979, having drafted it in close collaboration with the clergy and the faithful and especially with the grass-roots communities. He drew a grim picture of the widespread social injustice, fraud, and violation of human rights; he reiterated charges he had previously made against the government and the judicial system: law prostituted at the whim of a government of force; security forces that committed crime after crime with impunity; the malefactors responsible kept in power by means of fraudulent elections. As James Brockman says, the fourth pastoral letter did not break as much new ground as the third and hence did not get as much attention. But on the eve of Romero's death it summed up his ideas on the kind of pastoral ministry needed by the post-Puebla Church.

The Church, he said in this letter, must pay closer attention to the mass of the people, to inculcate in all Christians a critical outlook and a sense of control of their own destiny. They must be helped to progress from being a mass to being a people, and from being a people to being God's people, he insisted. The popular, devotional Catholicism of the people must be purified, completed, and dynamized by the Gospel, while those helping to bring this about will need great creativity and respect for the people so as not to wound their sensitivities.

As the country lurched toward civil war in the latter part of 1979, the government began to tighten the screws on Romero himself. In his Sunday homilies, Romero related how on several occasions he was stopped by security forces as he made his rounds. For instance, on a visit to Arcatao to celebrate a local fiesta, he was stopped, forced to put his hands on the roof of a car, and searched "like a common suspect." Moreover, a crudely written death threat from the White Warriors was sent to him in an official Defense Ministry envelope. Undaunted, Romero continued to hold the government's feet to the fire. In his homily of October 14, 1979, he cited statistics to show that, as he put it, the government was emptying the prisons of political prisoners by filling the cemeteries. He noted that those murdered for political reasons had numbered 147 in 1978, but that already in 1979 there were 580. A similar increase was seen in the number of the disappeared.[33]

The next day, as rosy-fingered dawn broke on the capital, the radio blared out news of a coup. A group of military officers had taken over and put President Romero on a plane to Guatemala. Among the least surprised was the archbishop, who had been informed of the plans and had promised the leaders of the coup his prayers. In a radio address the next day he called on the populace to be calm, thanked God that the coup had been bloodless, and prayed that the new government would keep the promises it was making. In turn the two colonels in charge paid him a personal visit and thanked him for his prudence and restraint.

The coup leaders seemed off to a good start, with only one military official among the prominent citizens on its panel. One member of the junta with a promising background was Román Mayorga, the young president of the Jesuit Central American University, who accepted the position on the junta on the advice of Archbishop Romero. The junta also included another member of the faculty of the University, Guillermo Ungo, active in politics as a Christian Democrat.

Members of the junta spoke in glowing terms of building a "new and better nation," one where "human life will be respected."[34] But although an atmosphere of greater outspokenness and freedom was noticeable, bombings and shootings continued. The guerrillas were not persuaded that leaders of a military coup, however apparently reformist, should be given a chance, and they remained hostile to the junta. On the other side, the security forces maintained their autonomy and continued operations. Finally, the chances of reform, never bright, disappeared once the oligarchy recovered from its initial shock and marshaled all the tactics at its command to regain control of the country. Owners used production stoppages and affluent matrons took

[33] Ibid., p. 198.
[34] Ibid., p. 203.

to the streets in hope of weakening the confidence of the junta. In response, the unions engaged in strikes and sit-downs. In all the confusion and turmoil the archdiocesan offices and the seminary were occupied for three days by leftist forces, one of whose members accused Romero to his face of betraying the people by his support of the reformist junta. It was an all-time low for the archbishop in his relations with the popular organizations.

Opposition forces within the military pressed their advantage during the disorder. The junta fell victim to a smooth countercoup after the right-wing groups succeeded in maneuvering their people into the key military posts. The civilian members of the first junta handed in their resignations and a new junta was set up by the military. A few days later the Supreme Court and the heads of other government ministries sent a belated demand to the new junta for the reassertion of independent government control over the military. The demand was ignored. In spite of the darkness that now heralded in the new year, Romero told the people on the Feast of the Epiphany they must keep their eyes on their star. No one, he said, had the right to sink into despair: The guiding star is the movement toward liberation that every Christian must continue to believe in.

Romero now walked a precarious line in trying to mediate between the left-wing and right-wing factions. While severe in his criticisms of the right, he never hesitated to point to the problems he saw with the left in spite of his sympathy with some of their aims. Among the traits he continued to find disturbing were some antireligious tendencies within their ranks, their outright rejection of even well-meaning government reform efforts, their use of violence, and their definite pro-Soviet bias.

On January 22 more than a hundred thousand people from different popular organizations gathered in the capital to celebrate the anniversary of the infamous peasant massacre of 1932. It started out peacefully on a bright Tuesday morning as people lined up to march, waving their colorful banners. They jammed the streets for miles as the huge procession moved slowly past the National Palace and the cathedral. After nearly two hours, half of the marchers were still waiting to move when sniper fire burst out from the roof of the National Palace. People scattered in all directions, many of them taking refuge in the cathedral while the unlucky lay bleeding and dying in the street. When the firing stopped, twenty lay dead and 120 were wounded.

The government immediately took over the radio and press and issued its version of the events, blaming the carnage on the marchers who, it said, had fired on various buildings and the like. In his Sunday homily Romero, however, blasted the government for gagging the media, which were allowed to recount only the government's version of the affair. What had in fact occurred was a massacre of people whose only offense was to petition the government in an orderly fashion for justice and liberty. It was this intransigent violence of the right, he said, that was the real cause of the communism that they hypocritically denounced. At the same time, the archbishop praised the popular organizations for the maturity they showed in not letting the attack provoke them to greater violence.

A week after the massacre, Romero flew to Europe to receive an honorary degree from Louvain University. He was able to stop at Rome on the way, where he attended a general audience of John Paul II. Spotting him among the bishops, the pope asked him to stay afterward for a chat. The encounter proved to be a positive one for Romero, as the pope expressed his sympathy with him in his difficult situation and encouraged him to continue his efforts for social justice and the poor. Although he warned Romero against being seduced by ideologies that corrupt movements for human rights, when Romero left the pope he felt that he had received "God's confirmation."[35] There was a disquieting word, however, from Cardinal Casaroli, the papal secretary of state, who had received formal complaints against Romero from the United States ambassador. The United States, which backed the junta, was disturbed by the revolutionary line Romero was supposedly following. However, both Romero and the cardinal agreed that the Church was not put on earth in order to give aid and comfort to the powers that be.

Romero returned home to the same orgy of violence he had left. Hearing about the gas masks and bulletproof vests the United States had recently shipped to El Salvador, and the plans to send further military aid, he was furious. How could this happen in an administration like that of Jimmy Carter who professed concern about human rights? In a letter to President Carter that sent shock waves through the Vatican when it was learned that Romero had read it at mass, he said: "Your government's contribution instead of favoring greater justice and peace . . . will undoubtedly sharpen the injustice and the repression."[36] The issue, Romero insisted, was really the right of self-determination that had been recognized at Puebla. He also pointed out that the military was now moving to greater extremes, threaten-

[35] Ibid., pp. 224–225.
[36] Ibid., p. 227.

ing and abducting even the families of those who belonged to the popular organizations.

In the following weeks Romero made an all-out effort to talk with all the players as the crisis intensified: members of the junta and cabinet, leaders of the popular organizations, intellectuals, diplomats, bankers, and even the guerrilla forces. He still clung to the hope that a nonviolent solution could be found. His most remarkable interventions, however, were the Sunday homilies he delivered during Lent in the final weeks before his death. These were the last testament of a priest in total union with his oppressed people and with his Lord. A premonition of his violent end now haunted him and the death threats against him had multiplied. But he refused to be intimidated and rejected the advice of friends who urged him to seek safety in flight. Like his Lord, he was to drink the chalice of suffering to its bitter dregs; and like his Lord—who being rich made himself poor—he was to share the lot of the dispossessed whose broken bodies littered the land.

The Chalice of Suffering

On February 24, 1980, the first Sunday of Lent, Archbishop Romero preached on Christ in the desert being tempted by the devil to idolatry:

> What a tremendous and timely lesson for our days! Why do men fight in El Salvador? For power . . . Woe to the powerful when they do not take into account the power of God, the only powerful one—when they try to subjugate people to their power by torturing, by killing, by massacring! What terrible idolatry is being offered to the god of power, the god of money! So many victims, so much blood, for which God, the true God, the author of human life, will charge a high price from these idolaters of power![37]

During that first week of Lent, he made a retreat with six priests at a house in the hills high above San Salvador. As his notes show, he sensed that violent death was very near and he felt terror at the prospect; but he was consoled by the thought that God assisted the martyrs and would assist him in his last moments. The important thing, he felt, was to give God all of his life. He resolved in his diary "to become more identified with Jesus each day, accepting his Gospel more radically. Toward this interior knowledge and following of Jesus I will direct my devotion to the Blessed Virgin and

[37] Ibid., p. 232.

my specific moments of prayer: meditation, mass, breviary, rosary, reading, examination of conscience." According to Brockman, "he was still dealing with the basic problems of perfectionism, rigidity, timidity, and overwork" that he had written about in his retreat notes for the last fifteen years, "but now his writing revealed a much greater serenity and acceptance of himself, a greater maturity and inner freedom . . . he now seemed freer, more serene and accepting of himself."[38]

On Sunday, March 23, 1980, with YSAX back on the air after the government had shut it down, Romero mounted the pulpit of Sacred Heart Basilica in lieu of the once-again occupied cathedral. In a sermon that lasted almost two hours, he defended the right of the Church to render judgments "in the light of God's words [that] illuminate social, political and economic realities." This is not meddling in politics, he argued, but exercising the legitimate mission of the Church as lately defined at Vatican II, Medellín, and Puebla. The Church will measure any political program—from land reform to the management of money—by the standard of God's definitive plan for human liberation. No program will succeed, he declared, that is imposed at the cost of bloodshed and suffering. At last, he made a direct appeal to the soldiers of the Guardia Nacional to stop killing their brothers and sisters, to disobey any such command that violates the law of God, and to listen to the voice of their conscience and the command of God: "Thou shalt not kill." He concluded: "In the name of God, and in the name of this suffering people, whose laments rise to heaven each day more tumultuous, I beg you, I beseech you, I order you in the name of God: Stop the repression!"[39]

These words sealed his death warrant. It was nearly 1 P.M. by the time the mass ended and he spent the rest of the afternoon with his friends Salvador and Eugenia Barraza. Before dinner, he played with and teased the children and had a scotch to relax. Later he took a little rest before driving out to Calle Real with the couple to say mass. Afterward he stood chatting with the people, who offered him gifts: fruit, eggs, a hen and a rooster, and money for the seminary and the radio station. His friends noticed an acute sense of sadness about him earlier in the afternoon, but by evening he had shaken it off and returned to his lodgings, where he presented the sisters with the hen and the rooster.

The next day was a busy one as usual. He spent time with a group of

[38] Ibid., p. 234.
[39] Ibid., pp. 241–242.

priests at the seashore, kept an appointment with the doctor, then visited his confessor Father Azcue. "I want to feel clean in the Lord's presence," he told him. By 6:00 P.M. he was back at the hospital chapel for the anniversary mass he was scheduled to say for the deceased mother of a friend, Jorge Pinto, a publisher whose newspaper *El Independiente* had just been destroyed by a bomb. Romero was advised not to go ahead with the mass since it had been advertised, imprudently, that he would be the celebrant. But he had become inured to threats and vested for mass as usual. Only a small number were present when Romero read the apt Scripture lessons of the day: "God has put all his enemies under his feet and the last of the enemies is death . . . The Lord is my shepherd . . . Unless the grain of wheat falls to the earth and dies, it remains only a grain." Concluding his brief homily, he invited those gathered to pray: "May [we] give our body and blood to suffering and to pain, like Christ, not for self but to teach justice and peace to our people. So, let us join together intimately in faith and hope at this moment of prayer for Doña Sarita and ourselves." At that, the crack of a rifle was heard.[40]

Romero was facing the altar and fell backward unconscious, blood streaming out of his mouth. His friends rushed forward and saw the hole in his left breast where the bullet had entered before lodging in his back. They carried him out of the church and down to the emergency room of the hospital where a nurse tried to start transfusion. As she searched for a vein, he stopped gasping and died.

He was laid out in Sacred Heart Basilica the next day. All through the week, from early morning to late at night, long lines of people filed by, many of them with tear-stained eyes. But the sad division was proclaimed by a banner put up by a group of fasting mourners who refused to remove it, telling Bishops Aparicio, Revelo, and Álvarez (as well as the junta and the U.S. ambassador) to stay away. The funeral mass was held on Palm Sunday at an altar erected in front of the cathedral and attended by a huge crowd, including bishops from Latin America and around the world and many other international church people. Gustavo Gutiérrez was among the three hundred clergy there. Of all the Salvadoran bishops, only Bishop Rivera attended. Cardinal Ernesto Corripio of Mexico was there as the pope's representative.

The police and security forces were noticeably absent and the mass proceeded quietly until the middle of Cardinal Corripio's sermon, when a

[40]Ibid., pp. 242–244.

bomb exploded; sounds of gunfire followed. People ran, terrified, in all directions. Some tried to climb a fence placed in front of the coffin. The archbishop was quickly buried in the tomb that had been prepared in the east transept. So many were now crowded into the cathedral that it was barely possible to breathe. They remained for two hours, until it was deemed safe to leave.

All efforts to identify those involved in Romero's murder were frustrated at the start. None of those in the church at the time got a glimpse of the killer: They had rushed forward to help the stricken archbishop. Not long after, Atilio Ramírez, the judge appointed to investigate the killing, had to fight off intruders at his home with his shotgun; a few days later he departed for Venezuela and did not return. However, he was reported as saying that the assassin had been hired by Major Roberto D'Aubuisson and General José Alberto Medrano, former military officers. This view was corroborated by the U.S. Ambassador Robert White, who named D'Aubuisson as the brain behind the assassination. Later developments also pointed to D'Aubuisson and Medrano, both of whom were closely associated with the death squads. However, attempts to bring them to justice ran up against the bad faith of government officials who resorted to various delaying tactics to impede investigations. Years later, enough evidence was gathered pointing to Captain Álvaro Antonio Saravia as a key figure in the murder that U.S. authorities arrested him in Florida and prepared to extradite him. The Salvadoran attorney general's request for his extradition, however, was blocked by the Supreme Court now under control of D'Aubuisson's own political party, ARENA. The attorney general was then dismissed for "incompetence and immorality."[41]

The Romero chapter, however, is not over although many in the state and the Church would have liked it to be. A campaign of slander initiated immediately after his death attempted to picture him as a tool of the left-wing factions, a basically weak man who succumbed to the pressures of radical priests and leftists. Even the Salvadoran bishops' conference tried to relegate him to the archives of history by rarely if ever mentioning the man or his message. But Romero continued—and continues—to live in the hearts and minds of ordinary people. Posters and graffiti everywhere recall him. He lives, as Jon Sobrino has said, above all in the shelters and relocation camps, the remote regions of the country, the bowels of city slums.[42]

[41] Ibid., p. 255.
[42] Sobrino, *Archbishop Romero*, p. 56.

The people there know how Romero gave himself to them without reserve. Puebla's erudite phrase, "preferential option for the poor," conveys little sense of the full concrete reality of his effort to live out this option. He literally rushed to the poor, as Jon Sobrino has said, to receive from them, to learn from them, and to enable them to impart to him the good news. He believed in them and took great pains to solicit their opinions. He wanted to know what was going on in their minds. He loved them and he let himself be loved by them.

The great outpouring of popular feeling after his death recalls the memory of Thomas Becket, another bishop slain at the altar in testimony to the truth. As with Becket's tomb at Canterbury, pilgrims come from all over to kneel and pray and seek Romero's intercession. Canonization may not now be in the offing, but the people have already decided the issue. Nor is his influence confined to El Salvador. Traveling in Asia, Sobrino was deeply impressed by how much Archbishop Romero means to Christians there, as well as to Marxists, Buddhists, and Hindus. "I have some bad news for you," a Frenchman, as he recalls, told him one day. "Archbishop Romero does not belong just to Salvadorans any more. He belongs to the world now."

Meanwhile, in the decade after Romero's death, El Salvador's agony continued. The death toll continued to mount. The figures, however, show that the murderous repression by the government and its paramilitary allies was on a much greater scale than the violence carried out by the leftists. Clergy and religious were in constant jeopardy. Not quite a year after the death of Romero, the bodies of four American women who had been working with the poor were uncovered in a crude grave near San Salvador: Dorothy Kazel, an Ursuline nun from Cleveland; Jean Donovan, a volunteer lay worker from the same city; and two Maryknoll sisters, Ita Ford and Maura Clarke. They had been seized two days before while driving from the San Salvador airport; they were then raped and murdered.

More than 70,000 people died in the civil war that Romero had begged his countrymen to avert. The great majority of these people were killed by the government's campaign of terror and aerial bombardment in the countryside; thousands of others died at the hands of the death squads acting in collusion with the military. One of the single most brutal episodes occurred in the early morning of November 16, 1989, when six Jesuits working at Central American University in San Salvador were dragged from their beds by thirty armed men in uniform and machine-gunned to death. Their cook and her daughter were also slaughtered. The reaction of horror and outrage around the world was enormous. But the high officials ultimately responsible have never been brought to trial.

Postscript

In January 1992 the government of El Salvador and its guerrilla foes signed a comprehensive peace treaty formally ending the twelve-year civil war. On October 4, 1994, the government of El Salvador and the FMLN, the major coalition of guerrilla groups, signed a declaration expressing their determination to see the 1992 peace accords fully implemented for the benefit of all. The statement recognized that progress had been made in strengthening and modernizing the democratic institutions of El Salvador. At the same time it expressed serious concern over the limited progress of the key land-transfer program and over delays and distortions in other reintegration programs. Much depended, as Boutros Boutros Ghali, the United Nations Secretary General, observed, on the commitment of the majority party, the Alianza Republicana Nacionalista (ARENA), to govern wisely and with moderation so that plurality could become an "integral feature of Salvadoran politics."[43]

Studies have shown that land tenure and the overall agrarian structure were common elements in the upheavals in Cuba, Venezuela, Guatemala, Colombia, Peru, Nicaragua, and El Salvador. A classic study of development articulated the explanation for these agrarian insurrections. Revolution is unlikely, the study claims, when the conditions of land ownership are equitable and provide a viable living for the peasants. However, when these conditions are lacking, then the potential for revolution is greatly increased unless the government takes prompt measures to remedy the situation.

The civil war that began in El Salvador in the late 1970s is seen by many observers as a textbook case of agrarian insurrection. The magnitude and course of the insurrection have been explained by a variety of factors including the roles of Nicaragua, Cuba, and the United States, the particular characteristics of the Salvadoran military, and the composition and interests of the so-called "coffee elite." But even the U.S. Kissinger Commission, which emphasized the role of Communist infiltrators, admitted the absolutely central part played by the land issue.

To support their contention that land inequality was basic to the outbreak of the insurrection, analysts pointed out that the landless of El Salvador, as a

---

[43] *UN Chronicle*, December 1994, v. 31, p. 24f.

proportion of the total national population, was one of the highest of any country in Latin America. Moreover, El Salvador's tiny size, large rural population, and the concentration of land in the hands of a few families of coffee- and cotton-growers, left only tiny plots of land for peasants to own.

One study indicated that when the landless and the tenant populations of a country exceed one fourth of the total population, revolution becomes a distinct probability. In fact El Salvador's landless and tenant populations had reached 25.9 percent in 1971. Since the percentage of landless to the national population had diminished by 1991 to 17 percent, it seems that El Salvador may no longer be a likely candidate for a further agrarian-based revolution. But the problem of alleviating the extreme deprivation of the rural landless remains.

Romero's Legacy

1. His martyrdom in the cause of social justice will stand as an inspiration to all those seeking peace and justice in the world. He certainly made more credible the recent call of the Catholic bishops for a preferential option for the poor.
2. His remarkable series of pastorals in the 1970s represent a substantial contribution to the Church's effort to update its social doctrine to accord with recent developments.
3. His pastoral ministry threw much light on the implications of liberation theology when it is applied to concrete situations.

SIXTEEN

Lech Walesa's (1943–) Revolution

AT 8 A.M. ON AUGUST 14, 1980, a young out-of-work electrician with a huge moustache clambered up the twelve-foot wall of the Lenin shipyard in the Baltic port of Gdansk, Poland. Below him a mass of workers fed up with the endless shortages milled around, refusing to return to work. The nearly unthinkable had happened—a strike had broken out in a "workers' paradise"! As the short, stocky young man looked on, the director of the shipyard, speaking from his perch atop a bulldozer, tried to soothe the strikers with the same old promises. They even seemed half ready to believe him when suddenly a voice called out: "Remember me?" The director stared up at the man standing on the wall above him: "I was a worker in this shipyard for ten years," Lech Walesa shouted, "but you kicked me out four years ago . . . We don't believe your lies anymore, and we're not going to be cheated again. Until you give us firm guarantees, we're going to stay right here where we are." Lech Walesa had climbed into the forefront of his country's tragic history.

An Arena of Destiny

Geography has been destiny for Poland. Situated in the exact center of Europe on a vast plain between the Oder and the Vistula, it has formed a natural arena for contending armies from east and west, north and south. As Igor Stravinsky put it: "If you pitch your tent in the middle of Fifth Avenue, don't be surprised if you're hit by a bus."[1]

However, it was protected from the Roman legions by the Carpathian Mountains, and it later missed being evangelized by the great missionaries of the seventh to ninth centuries. The country was pulled into the Western orbit in 966 by Prince Mieszko I (922–992). This wily ruler married a Czech princess and accepted Roman Christianity as a stratagem for countering the inroads of his more powerful Germanic neighbors. This orientation to Rome was later strengthened when Boleslaw III sided with Pope

Lech Walesa

[1] Mary Craig, *Lech Walesa and His Poland* (New York: Continuum, 1987), p. 22.

Gregory VII in his conflict with the Holy Roman Empire. In return the pope gave Boleslaw the royal crown; henceforth alliance with the papacy was one of the methods Poland used to withstand the pressures from the Holy Roman Emperors. This Western alliance, however, provided little help to Poland when the Central Asian Mongols invaded from the east in 1241. The invaders failed to establish themselves in Poland as they had in Kievan Russia, but they wrought fearful destruction by fire and the sword. To replenish the population the Polish princes called in German settlers whom they valued for their superior methods of land cultivation and their superior legal system. Many of these settlers founded towns that flourished under a system of self-government.

By the middle of the fourteenth century Poland was involved in a life-and-death struggle with powerful German princes to the north, south, and west. The only hope was an alliance with the great Lithuanian empire to the east. This was realized with the marriage of Queen Jadwiga of Poland to the Lithuanian Grand Duke Jagiello, and the conversion of the pagan Lithuanians to Christianity—"the greatest missionary deed of the late Middle Ages."[2] Jagiello ruled Poland as Ladislaw II. The union of Poland and Lithuania was consolidated by their great victory over the Teutonic Order in 1410 at the battle of Grunwald and Tannenberg. Eventually western Prussia, with its cities of Gdansk and Elblag, was incorporated into Poland, which thereby gained its long-sought access to the Baltic. Eastern Prussia was left as a fief of Poland.

With its enemies at bay, the Jagiello dynasty extended its power over most of East-Central Europe from the Baltic to the Adriatic and from the Black Sea eastward to the gates of Moscow. This marked the beginning of Poland's golden age. An intellectual renewal occurred that was nurtured by currents flowing from the Italian Renaissance and the Protestant Reformation. The Polish Renaissance's most notable luminary was Nicolaus Copernicus, a student at the University of Krakow, who in his *De revolutionibus orbium coelestium* dared to imagine a world with the sun as the center. There was also political renewal and the establishment of such rights as freedom of speech, freedom of religion, and habeas corpus at a time when these were lacking in most of Europe. These political freedoms brought heretics and Jews streaming into Poland in quest of the tolerance denied them elsewhere. The population of the Jews in Poland increased from 50,000 in 1500 to half a million by 1650.

[2]Ibid., p. 9.

A Nation That Refused to Die

But the glory and the power could not last. Poland's decline began in the seventeenth century as it faced a formidable menace from the Swedes, the Muscovites, and the Cossacks of the Ukraine. Its ability to cope with these enemies was gravely compromised by the irresponsibility of the boisterous, anarchic nobility who had gained total dominance over the country during its years of plenty. They had undermined the once vigorous burgher class by acquiring a monopoly of foreign and domestic trade; they had expropriated the peasants' land and reduced them to serfdom. Above all they had paralyzed the country's administration by use of the *liberum veto* which allowed one noble to stop any legislative measure no matter how important. In this state of debility, Poland suffered a series of defeats in the wars of the seventeenth century. It would soon pay an even more terrible price for its disorganization.

Russia, emerging as a great power early in the eighteenth century under Peter the Great, began to interfere in Poland's internal affairs. Peter was able to foment almost total anarchy in Poland, demoralize the people, block all reforms, and keep the country weak and prostrate. The first partition of Poland (1772) handed over one third of the country's resources to Russia, Prussia, and Austria. But this shock at last galvanized the Poles into undertaking a sweeping series of progressive reforms aimed at saving its national sovereignty. It abolished the *liberum veto,* limited serfdom, and extended the scope of civil liberties. Unfortunately, these changes only unsettled the reactionary elements of the Polish nobility. The ensuing civil discord within Poland provided Catherine II of Russia with a pretext to intervene and abolish the reforms. A second partition of Poland by Russia and Prussia occurred in 1792, leaving Poland effectively despoiled of its resources. Two years later even the agony of partition was superseded by the final death blow: Thaddeus Kosciuszko's uprising for Polish independence failed. Russia and Prussia divided up the rest of the country and wiped Poland off the map.

"No other event in modern European history produced such lasting changes in the balance of power as the extinction of a country situated at the crossroad of East and West and larger than France or Germany.[3] Russia's

---

[3]M. K. Dziewanowski, *Poland in the Twentieth Century* (New York: Columbia University Press, 1977), p. 29.

borders were moved to within two hundred miles of Berlin and Vienna, while Prussia's gains enabled her to embark upon the course leading to Bismarck's Second Reich. The Poles, however, refused to acquiesce in their demise. As Stanislaw Staszyc, one of their leading scholars said, "Even a great nation can fall, but only a worthless one can perish."[4] The Polish patriots' cry for independence would echo and re-echo in three failed revolutions (1794, 1830–1831, and 1863–1864). But even these defeats could not remove the Polish question from the conscience of Europe.

A Republic Reborn

The First World War changed Poland's situation dramatically. In a scenario long dreamed of by Polish patriots, the empires that had swallowed her up were now fighting each other and competing for her loyalty. Two options lay open for the Poles: One was to side with Russia in exchange for autonomy under a tsarist regime that it was hoped would become more liberal; the other was to side with the Central Powers and assist in Russia's social disintegration. As the war progressed, Poland shifted its allegiance to the Allies in time to win a seat at the Versailles Peace Conference. There Poland was resurrected like Lazarus from the dead.

But the reborn republic was a precarious creation with ragged and unstable borders and with a large component of non-Poles including Germans, Ukrainians, and Byelorussians. At first it appeared likely that it would fall victim to a Communist revolution and a takeover by the newly established Soviet Union. However, Poland's spectacular victory over Soviet Russia in the battle of Warsaw (1920) set back for twenty years Russia's plan to sovietize Central and Eastern Europe. Elated by the first Polish victory in two and a half centuries, the nation gravely underestimated the enormous challenges ahead. It sat between two hostile powers, Germany and Soviet Russia. Moreover, as a result of the First World War it was impoverished and in ruins—farms, factories, railroads, bridges, and buildings had all suffered enormous damage; eleven million acres of farmland were put out of use and six million acres of forests destroyed. As a legacy of partition it had to cope with three different systems of currency, of law, and of transportation and trading. Political life was marked by bitter turbulence as the Right and the Left struggled for power. Finally, antidemocratic forces won out. Fed up with the liberal political constitution of 1921, Marshall Pilsudski in 1926

[4]Ibid., p. 32.

engineered a coup d'état and installed an authoritarian regime. At his death in 1935 he left a deeply divided country.

Between the Devil and the Deep Blue Sea

The Second World War would devastate Poland and determine its fate for decades afterward. As Hitler consolidated his control at home in the late 1930s, Pilsudski's right-wing government tried to get France to make a preemptive strike against the Germans. But the Poles faced the lethargic, almost suicidal reluctance of France and England to oppose the German rearmament.[5] The Nazi occupation of Prague on March 15, 1939, finally brought the British and French to their senses. They committed themselves to the defense of Poland, but by then it was too late.

In the summer of 1939, Hitler signed a nonaggression pact with the Soviets. No longer fearing a Russian reaction to a German attack on Poland, on September 1, 1939, he unleashed seventy-five divisions against the hapless, brave country. While the Allies dillydallied, Poland went down fighting. Hitler's orders were merciless: All the Jews and educated Poles in Poland were to be exterminated and the populace enslaved. "It is our aim that the very concept 'Polack' be erased for centuries to come," said Hans Frank, the German satrap in Krakow. The Nazis applied Nietzsche's words literally: "Blood and cruelty are the foundation of all things."[6] While the Germans carved up Poland to the west, the Soviets conquered areas of Poland to the east. Stalin's mercies were no more comforting than Hitler's. He too was determined to destroy the Polish state and to exterminate all potential opponents, whether they were Polish, Jewish, Ukrainian, or Byelorussian.

When on June 22, 1941, Hitler invaded Russia a new chapter began in Poland's relations with the Soviet Union. As the two countries grappled in uneasy negotiations, Sikorski, the head of the Polish government-in-exile in London, pressed Poland's claims to the eastern marshes—the oil, natural gas, potash, and timber there being essential for Poland's economy. But the Soviets rebuffed these Polish overtures and the Allies did nothing to help. All the while the Soviets took every opportunity to strengthen the hitherto weak Polish Communist Party—although communism was hardly popular in Poland.

[5] Ibid., p. 100.
[6] Ibid., pp. 114–115.

While remaining an agent of Soviet policy, the Polish party dropped the term "Communist" and called itself the Polish Workers Party, and together with Moscow established the Lublin Committee of National Liberation. This committee declared itself to be the sole Polish representative in charge of all activities toward Poland's liberation. Its real aim was to take over political power in the country with the help of the Red Army.

The failure of the Warsaw uprising in October 1944 played right into this strategy. As the outnumbered Polish insurgents fought the German Army within the city of Warsaw, the Red Army stood by for six weeks on the eastern bank of the Vistula while Stalin waited. Above all he didn't want a victory by a heroic Polish underground army that would have enabled them to form the nucleus of a government with a stronger claim to legitimacy than the Lublin Committee. Without assistance the inevitable happened: the Polish underground was crushed. As one historian says: "The struggle [against the Germans] cost Poland about 200,000 victims from among the most patriotic, politically active element, and destroyed not only some 70 percent of the city but also the brain center of the most widespread and determined of Europe's resistance movement. As a result of this, the previously weak pro-Communist forces were given a chance to reassert themselves and fill the vacuum."[7]

The Communist Takeover

Poland felt it had a right to count on help from the Allies in any postwar standoff with the predatory Soviet bear. The country had suffered more severely from the war than any other country occupied by Germany. It had lost almost 40 percent of its material wealth and over a fifth of its population. It was the primary scene of the Nazi murder of millions of Jews. At the same time, it had contributed far more than its share to the Allied cause, having placed nearly a million men in the field. But the ungrateful Allies at the Yalta and Potsdam Conferences were willing to sacrifice the interests of Poland to appease the Soviet Union. As a result, the Soviets were able to install a Communist regime in Poland.

The Communist task, nevertheless, was formidable. "Of all the places in the world Poland was among those least prepared to embark upon a Communist experiment: it was overwhelmingly Roman Catholic, essentially

[7]Ibid., p. 134.

agrarian, and had a relatively small working class."[8] The Communist collec-tivist doctrine had small appeal for the individualistic and traditionalist men-tality of the Polish people. However, several factors were in the Commu-nists' favor: The old social structure had been dismantled by the Nazis, many non-Communist political leaders had been killed or had fled, and the old intelligentsia was greatly reduced. Moreover, the Big Three had allotted Poland a sizeable portion of the Western lands held by Germany, which could be used by the regime to reward its friends.

By 1947 the shaky regime had made significant progress in communizing Poland. Some of its policies met with some favor, such as its land reform program, which expropriated large estates and divided them up among peasants. The regime also improved the lot of the peasants by liquidating prewar debts, extending education and training in technical skills, and bringing electricity to the farms. Its policy of nationalizing industry, trade, and banking did not provoke great resistance since a considerable number of industries and banks had already been state-owned in prewar Poland.

Era of Gomulka

It is useful to think of the Communist era in several phases: the installation of a Soviet-backed regime at the end of the war; the era of Communist leader Wladyslaw Gomulka from 1945 to 1970 with an interruption from 1949 to 1957; the era of Edward Gierek from Gomulka's demise in 1970 to the rise of Solidarity (1980) and Walesa when General Jaruzelski tried to stem the Solidarity tide.

The Polish Communist regime throughout its history was less brutal than Communist regimes elsewhere. Under Gomulka, the secretary general, it allowed freedom of religion, freedom of movement, freedom to choose one's work, and freedom to criticize the government—privately. Gomulka, in fact, favored a "mild" revolution with as little coercion as possible and very gradual collectivization. He spoke boldly and strongly about the need to follow the Polish way to socialism and the need to maintain its indepen-dence vis-à-vis the Soviet Union. These were dangerous ideas at a time when the cold war was heating up. The Muscovites in his party finally denounced Gomulka as a deviationist, had him tried in August 1951, and put him under house arrest. The party was simultaneously purged of all "deviationists"—a full one fourth of its members.

[8] Ibid., p. 148.

The years between Gomulka's first fall from grace and Stalin's death in March 1953 were especially depressing. Horrible gray Soviet-style apartment buildings began to scar the horizon—mirrors of the moral smog enveloping the culture as all the traditional values of religious faith and moral principles were denounced and ridiculed. A "Six-Year Plan" to expand heavy industry and produce such items as jet planes and spare parts for Russian tanks was put into operation. Workers were driven unmercifully to meet production goals while the resulting shortages of consumer goods caused much hardship.

At the same time the need to hold a hostile public in line caused a tightening of restrictions on personal freedom and an increase of terror by the dreaded security police. Eye-witness accounts tell of hundreds of thousands arrested—many for just a chance remark. In the prisons they suffered beatings, interrogations under blinding lights, and other tortures that could reduce the strongest person to jelly in twenty-four hours. People were caught in the streets and released later unfit to live. The pervasive atmosphere of fear created unbearable tension as neighbor began to distrust neighbor or friend and many tried to save their own skins by accusing someone else.

A campaign was launched to encourage atheism and people were forced to listen to lectures on "scientific Marxism" that aimed at proving the absurdity of religion. A ban was placed on pilgrimages; processions and Catholic newspapers were shut down. It was even forbidden for restaurants to serve fish on Friday. Priests were spied on and their sermons carefully monitored while radio and press propaganda accused them of every crime imaginable. In September 1953 Cardinal Wyszynski, the primate of Poland, was arrested. By this time nine bishops and several hundred priests were held in prison.

Then came the famous speech by Russia's Nikita Khrushchev to the Twentieth Congress of the Communist Party in February 1956. He attacked the cult of personality and recounted the sordid story of Stalin's crimes. In effect, he undermined the legitimacy of puppet governments like Poland's that had been established by Stalin. It had an earth-shaking effect on the Poles. Was Stalin alone responsible, they asked, for their brutal, dreary, and soulless society? The answer seemed clear after the workers of Poznan demonstrated, demanding "bread and freedom," and the government sent in tanks to mow them down like dogs. Other strikes, riots, and demonstrations occurred. On August 15, 1956, over a million and a half pilgrims converged on the hill-top monastery of Czestochowa to celebrate the 300th anniversary of victory over a huge invading army by a handful of resolute Poles. It was perhaps the greatest religious demonstration ever; some had walked hundreds of miles to get there. The cardinal's throne, empty but for a great bouquet of red and white roses, was carried over the heads of the crowd. The people prayed for a miracle like the one in 1656. In October they believed their prayer was answered.

Gomulka was resurrected by a government that realized it was the only way to defuse the public's fury. As a victim of Stalin's vengeance, Gomulka could count on a certain amount of popularity. This was enhanced when in his programmatic speech he outlined his concept of the Polish way to socialism. He promised democratization of the party, an end to forcible collectivization, and some use of the market forces of supply and demand.

This "Polish October" was the beginning of a new chapter in the story of communism in Poland. Cardinal Wyszynski and most imprisoned clerics were set free. Religious instruction was allowed in the schools, and government control over Church appointments was abolished. Crucifixes were taken out of hiding and worn openly to work. A cultural renewal flourished as theaters put on Western plays, and clubs featured Western music, including jazz. Polish scholars and writers were allowed to travel to the West. This new freedom, however, could not alleviate all the misery nor the unending daily struggle for survival. People still lived in damp basements or half-rotting buildings and stood in long lines for food.

Gomulka had to have a cool head, strong nerves, and immense diplomatic skill, for the cruel fate of Hungary and Czechoslovakia showed how dangerous it was to try to liberalize a Communist regime. But for a time he showed a fine sense of just how much internal autonomy he could get away with without threatening the Soviets, who, as Marshal Zhukov said on a trip to Poland, could "crush them (the Poles) like flies." But Gomulka could not maintain this balancing act forever. As always happens in controlled societies, a little freedom begets the taste for more. And in response, Gomulka began to crack down. In fact, as he aged he became a rigid despot who surrounded himself with sycophants.

Gomulka also renewed the offensive against the Catholic Church. A ban was placed on religious instruction in the schools and the church's exemption from taxation was taken away. But the regime failed miserably in a contest with the Church for popularity. Cardinal Wyszynski announced a nine-year period of special prayers and events to prepare for the millennium of Christianity in Poland in 1966. The regime countered with a call to celebrate "People's Poland" as the high point of the millennium. They corralled people into parades, though many forced marchers managed to scurry away and join the Church parades instead. Microphones would mysteriously malfunction as the cardinal addressed a crowd or his voice would be drowned out by low-flying aircraft. When a picture of the Madonna that he carried with him disappeared, the cardinal carried around the empty frame. Everyone got the point. As a Warsaw woman said, the cardinal "was a great opposition leader. And the Church was the only opposition party we had."[9]

By the late 1960s Gomulka was up to his fat ears in problems. In taking on the Church he had lost a lot of ground. And in March of 1968 the students of Warsaw hit the streets. In August, during Alexander Dubcek's "Prague's Spring," the attempt by the Czechs to liberalize their Communist government, Gomulka horrified public opinion by sending Polish troops to aid the Russian invasion of Prague. He wanted to show Russia that Poland was a reliable ally, for he believed that Polish independence could be ensured only by maintaining a close relationship with Moscow.

Finally Gomulka got caught up in intricate anti-Zionist maneuvers within his party. Jews had always constituted a large percentage of the Communist party in Poland (50% in the 1930s), and many of them during the war had migrated to Moscow and later played a large part in the Sovietization of Eastern Europe. In the early postwar period, for example, many of the secret police were Jews as were most of the higher police officials in Budapest, Bucharest, and Warsaw, many of them survivors of the Nazi camps. They were not inclined to let considerations of mercy stand in the way when dealing with the class enemies.[10] But "the emergence of Israel and its increasingly pro-Western orientation brought about a change in the pro-Soviet sentiments of many Jews and also in Stalin's policies toward them."[11]

Gomulka instituted an anti-Zionist purge whose victims included some of the leading economists and proponents of reform in the country. Their demise helped to forestall the possibility of economic reform, and soon a scarcity of consumer goods infuriated an already disgruntled public. Then near the end of 1970 the regime added one more blow: It announced an increase in the prices of basic staples without any increase in wages. The

[9]Craig, *Lech Walesa and His Poland*, p. 115.
[10]Dziewanowski, *Poland in the Twentieth Century*, p. 199.
[11]Ibid.

timing was incredibly inept—right before Christmas. The predictable explosion occurred.

Dramatic and bloody mass demonstrations occurred on December 16 and 17 in the Baltic coast cities of Gdansk, Gdynia, Sopot, and Szczecin. The injury and the pain of those days still throb in the hearts and minds of Poles. "It was enough to be there, to hear the shots, to clear away the corpses, to watch the terrible burials by night. It was enough—to make a man remember for the rest of his life,"[12] Walesa later remembered, "I was only twenty-seven. I was inexperienced and didn't know how to handle a situation like that." When the strike broke, he had just been elected to the strike committee.

The regime finally had to capitulate to the demands of the workers. Gomulka stepped down in disgrace. This humorless, puritanical man who had been held up as a national hero, people finally realized, was always more a Communist than a Pole.

Gierek's Regime

In 1970 Edward Gierek stepped into the mess, and as the new leader of the Communist Party in Poland began a reversal of Gomulka's policies. He outlined changes in Gomulka's Five-Year Plan to shift emphasis to the needs of consumers, including more housing, more small cars, and more jobs. He also lifted some of the restrictions on freedom of the press and dedicated more money to scholarly research. To foster better relations with the Roman Catholic Church he promised to relinquish the 7,000 Church buildings that had been turned to other uses. He also allowed the construction of new churches, though not the 1,000 desired by Cardinal Wyszynski. However, on the issue of Marxist and atheistic indoctrination of Polish youth, Gierek would not compromise.

The pragmatic Gierek faced the same daunting challenge as his predecessor—how to liberalize the regime in response to pressures from a hostile public without provoking reprisals from the Soviets. Thanks to Gierek's new policies, living standards began to rise as more housing was built and more imported consumer goods began to pour into the country. Shelves bulged with television sets and the latest electronic devices. Visitors remarked on the new spirit of the country and how well fed and well dressed the people looked. But the bubble would soon burst. The overmanned, overcentralized

[12]Craig, *Lech Walesa and His Poland*, p. 126.

system needed more than the cosmetic changes Gierek introduced. When the OPEC oil crisis occurred in 1973, its effect on Poland's frail economy was devastating. Since its main trading partner, the Soviet Union, paid in rubles, Poland could not buy the increasingly expensive spare parts needed to keep its factories going.

In the face of mounting shortages, Gierek's options ran out and in June 1976 he had to bite the bullet and announce price increases. He readied the security forces to wreak swift vengeance on those daring to protest. When the workers at the Ursus factory in Warsaw tore up the tracks of the Paris-to-Moscow railway line, the police ran amok. They arrested any worker they could get their hands on. At Radom, where seventeen workers were killed, they forced thousands of the arrested to run a gauntlet, cracking their bones and beating them senseless. Heavy fines and long prison sentences were handed out. But the protests, to an extent, had worked: The price rises were rescinded.

The protests also signaled the existence within Poland of an organized resistance without parallel in the Soviet bloc. A group called KOR (The Workers' Defense Committee) that had been established by fourteen dissidents in September 1976 constituted a milestone in the history of Communist Poland. It provided legal help and other forms of assistance to the arrested workers and their families and exposed the corruption of the courts. The government struck back, subjecting KOR members to every kind of intimidation. But for KOR the regime was an empty façade whose main weapon was fear. "Once you can rise above your fear," they said, "you are a free man."[13] KOR carried on its work of preparing the people for change and laying the groundwork for a pluralist society. One of its audacious initiatives was the Flying University—unofficial seminars on the run, dealing with taboo subjects in Polish life and history.

Perhaps the most crucial element in the opposition was the Catholic Church. A brilliant group of Catholic intellectuals associated with *Tygodnik Powszechny,* the most prestigious Polish weekly, took the lead. They worked out an updated Catholic social philosophy (personalism) that emphasized the basic human rights of every human being. In this they followed the lead of the Second Vatican Council and France's Emmanuel Mounier, whose writings were highly regarded in Eastern Europe and Latin America, where Catholics were faced with repressive and brutal regimes. Already in the 1930s Mounier's vision of an alternate Catholic approach to socialism had

[13] Ibid., p. 146.

attracted the attention of young Polish Catholic intellectuals. During the Nazi occupation of Poland, members of Mounier's *Esprit* circles were active in the resistance and issued a translation of his *Personalist Manifesto.* Most of them lost their lives in the Warsaw uprising. In later years, the Polish personalists' emphasis on common human values led to alliances with non-Catholic intellectuals like Adam Michnik.

One of the leading figures in this Polish reflection on personalism was a priest-professor at the Jagiellonian University in Krakow—Karol Wojtyla, later Pope John Paul II. His interest in personalism was stimulated by his stay at the French-speaking Belgian College in Rome. Moreover, he explored personalist themes in his doctoral thesis on Max Scheler in 1969 and in his work "Love and Responsibility," a study of marital ethics. Cardinal Wyszynski also played a key role in the opposition. He heroically spelled out the God-given human and civil rights that the state must respect: the right to freedom of religion, among many other rights; participation in public life; and the freedom of parents to bring up children as they saw fit. While cautioning workers to be calm, Cardinal Wyszynski also declared that "it is painful that workers should have to struggle for their basic rights under a workers' government."

Nothing so stirred the hopes of the Polish people as the election of Cardinal Karol Wojtyla of Krakow to the papacy in October 1978. The news came at a dark hour. People were steeling themselves to shiver through another winter with the basics—coal, food, medicine—in short or nonexistent supply. But now the winter of their discontent was made glorious summer by this incredible priest. Poles could lift their heads once more and look squarely in the eyes of their Communist masters. Their euphoria reached a crescendo when nine months later the pope came home to a nation that greeted him with frenzied enthusiasm everywhere he went. Enormous crowds applauded his vibrant words of hope as he urged all, and especially the youth, to be proud of their Polish inheritance. Crestfallen Communists had to listen as thousands of Silesian miners sang out "Christ has conquered, Christ is king, Christ commands our lives." It was nothing less than a Polish Pentecost, a moral renewal and an incomparable spiritual experience that restored to the Polish people a sense of their nationhood.[14]

---

[14]Ibid., p. 155.

Enter Lech Walesa

But man does not live by euphoria alone. The economy continued its downward slide, and the toll of misery mounted. Mothers had to forage for food like animals, sometimes rising at 2 A.M. to join the queues of shoppers. They were lucky to end up with something better than rubbish. Jokes were the only form of protest and they were in abundant supply. As one put it, "Before the war you could go into a butcher's shop and find meat. Today the sign outside the shop says 'Meat' but you go in and find only the butcher."

Making matters even more intolerable was the fact that, while the ordinary people were barely surviving, their masters were living high on the hog. One of the most notorious cases involved Macij Szczepanski, a TV and radio boss who cruised around Warsaw in a huge BMW and publicly reveled in other perks—including a fleet of cars, a private plane, a mountain retreat, a private cinema, a yacht, and a harem of high-priced call girls. The corruption of the regime could no longer be concealed and its most hideous aspect was its absolute and utter mendacity. "It lied in the morning and it lied at night, it lied at noon when the sun was bright . . ." Orwellian doublespeak was so pervasive that the public didn't even believe the bad news when the government reported it.

In August of 1980 another rash of strikes broke out—in Warsaw first. The government tried to keep it under wraps, but KOR was able to send the news abroad and the Poles then picked up the story on the BBC or Radio Free Europe. The strike that brought down Gierek and broke the back of the regime started at the shipyard in Gdansk. Lech Walesa's words spoken from the top of the wall—"I'm here to tell you we don't believe your lies anymore"—reflected the conscience of the country.

Who was Lech Walesa? He was born on September 29, 1943, in a two-room stone cottage in the tiny village of Popowo on land so poor that, as Lech's brother said, nobody even tried to confiscate it. The years of his early childhood, especially 1951 to 1956, were especially hard ones for Poland and for the Walesa family personally. With nine mouths to feed, his stepfather, Stanislaw, had little time for nonsense. As Lech says, "At the age of five we tended the geese, at seven we took the cows out to pasture, at ten we took care of the other animals and did a variety of manual jobs."[15] Like his

---

[15] Lech Walesa, *A Way of Hope* (New York: Henry Holt and Company, 1987), p. 29.

stepfather, his mother, Feliksa, was typical of the region's peasantry—tough, stubborn, and hot-tempered. But his mother was also tenderhearted and Walesa's bond with her was exceptionally close. A deeply religious person, she could not think of allowing her brood to miss mass on Sunday. As Walesa says, "My faith can be said almost to have flowed into me with my mother's milk."[16] In the evening she would read to the children from Polish classics. "We didn't have television or even radio but we had books, and the whole world of nature was open for us to read. We were rich in the things that mattered," Walesa says.[17]

The children went to school at Chalin in a confiscated mansion where students gathered daily under a huge portrait of Stalin. Walesa seems to have been only an average student, better at crafts and sport than at academic work. But from his earliest years he showed the traits that marked him as a natural leader. He was an acute observer of people, a child who could "swim faster and further than the rest," a hard-headed boy who could see through the lies his teacher fed him about the horrors of American capitalism. "It sometimes seemed," he said, "that if it rained for the May Day parade, the Americans were to blame."[18]

Like many of the young people of the village, Walesa hoped to move to the Baltic coast where the newly rebuilt towns offered job opportunities. But his plans to become a licensed engineer fizzled out when the family could not afford the expense. Instead, in September 1959, he entered a trade school at Lipno to take a course in mechanized agriculture. He was a "troublemaker and smoker," according to one evaluation. His weakest spot was history. He saw through the classic jargon of communism and eternal class struggle. As he put it, "I was all the more inclined to reject this picture of the world because it differed substantially from what I heard at home and at church."[19]

Graduating with a certificate, he was conscripted two years later into the army where he was judged good material for promotion. But he had no desire for that kind of life, and upon leaving found a job with an agricultural cooperative in Linie. The government encouraged the spread of these cooperatives by furnishing them with new agricultural machinery that was withheld from private farms. Walesa soon learned to repair anything from a

[16] Ibid.
[17] Craig, *Lech Walesa and His Poland*, p. 89.
[18] Ibid., p. 90.
[19] Walesa, *A Way of Hope*, p. 36.

harrow to a television set, from motorbikes to washing machines. His desire to help people made him wonder at times whether he ought to become a priest, but he decided against it because he feared losing touch with ordinary people. Girls adored him because he was witty. But the place he lived in was getting him down. It was, he said, "a dead end, suffocating . . . unbearable . . . and my reputation as the best mechanic in the area . . . ridiculous."[20]

With little ado, in 1966 he set out for the coast and Gdynia. As he looked back later, he realized that this impulsive act was actually a response to something deep within his soul: "There was the sea . . . something vast, stretching out endlessly—possibly freedom . . . I let myself drift toward the Baltic region, by the sea where I would find—or lose myself—at last."

The train stopped at Gdansk and he hopped off to get a beer. But he failed to watch his time and the train pulled out without him. Not wanting to wait for another train, he decided to stay. "I came to Gdansk and met my destiny," he says. "I spent far too long drinking that beer. And in a sense I'm still drinking it."[21] A chance meeting with a friend led him to sign up for a possible job at the Gdansk shipyard. Within a few days, he was employed as an electrician in Ship 4. His crew laid cables on large fishing boats.

In his autobiography, Walesa tells of the miserable working conditions in the shipyard. There was dirt, filth, and grime everywhere, and few lockers or decent lavatories. Workers had to work without breakfast for several hours before getting a fifteen-minute break to stand in long lines to get a sandwich. The living conditions of many workers were just as bad. They had to share tiny rooms in ugly box-like hostels set on vacant lots littered with broken bottles. The rooms were a dreary mess: four gray walls, a few pieces of broken-down furniture, and lumpy mattresses. Walesa missed the family atmosphere of the cooperative and the feeling of solidarity there. In the shipyard he felt like a tiny cog in a huge operation—one of thousands of faceless men in shabby attire working in an atmosphere of unrelieved tension and gloom. But at least he was lucky to find a small room with a landlord who treated him like family. To his great good and lasting fortune he happened to pass by a flower stand one day and caught sight of "a pair of mischievous brown eyes in a sweet face framed by long dark hair." He could not get the vision out of his mind, and he was back a few days later to arrange a date. Within a few months, on November 8, 1969, they were

[20] Ibid., p. 38.
[21] Craig, *Lech Walesa and His Poland*, p. 122.

married; a little attic they found to live in became their home. But not for long, as Lech and Danuta were set on having a large family.

On the Path of Destiny

When the students revolted in 1968, Walesa watched the party officials turn workers against students by cynical use of propaganda. As a result, workers showed little interest in the goals of the student movement—among others, freedom of expression and the fight against censorship. Walesa himself tried to make his fellow workers understand the linkage of all the oppositions; if students were now targets of repression, workers would inevitably be targets, too. But there was little solidarity at this point. Walesa recalls that time, March 1968, as his initiation into the absurd and sordid world of Communist politics. One example says it well: The director of the Gdansk shipyard fell out of favor with the party because of an interview he gave that offended Gomulka. None of the party hierarchs would attend any of his ship launchings. The director then announced that he was renaming the shipyard the "Lenin" shipyard. Party officials could not very well ignore a rechristening ceremony in honor of Lenin. So the director was back in favor.

In December 1970, Walesa was out shopping for a baby carriage for Bogdan, his first child, when a strike broke out in the shipyard. Upon returning to the shipyard he tried to ward off violence by suggesting that the men organize to elect delegates for a central committee that would negotiate with the party officials. He himself was elected as chief delegate. But he has said that at the age of twenty-seven, with no experience of managing a strike, he was unequal to the challenge. While negotiations stalled, the government cordoned off the shipyard with troops. What Walesa feared most—Poles firing upon Poles—was the result. Workers pressed forward against the line of troops and the soldiers opened fire. Four workers were killed and the cry "Murderers, murderers!" filled the air. The strike wore on and finally the decision was made by the leaders to abandon the yard. Many of the workers wept and most saw the decision as a betrayal, but they realized that it would probably prevent the loss of more lives. "Twenty thousand of us—not six, which was the official figure—left the yard through lines of soldiers and militiamen," Walesa remembered. The strike itself failed but Walesa called it an "incomparable experience" inasmuch as it helped the workers to understand what made them behave the way they did in a crisis. It also convinced them of the need to find other solutions.

The strike had, of course, intensified the bad feeling between the state security apparatus and the workers. Agents would raid bars, grabbing hapless victims whom they would take to a "sobering-up room" where they would beat them to a pulp. But agents would not dare venture into the workers' part of the city, especially after dusk, if they valued life and limb. Walesa remembered the period after the 1970 strikes as a time of "complete lack of solidarity between the different sections of the population, in Gdansk itself and even in many workers' homes. There was a crushing sense of loneliness, fear and uncertainty about the prospects of our movement, and, in spite of everything, only the forlorn hope that our revolt had been a necessary one . . . Ours was the type of cause that is lost in advance, where one can count on nothing and nobody . . . We were simply outside the sphere of Western interest. Thirty-two million . . . people were in a sense crossed off the map of Europe."[22]

Lech's job at the shipyard was in constant jeopardy because of his refusal to keep his mouth shut. He was given the worst work and never allowed any kind of promotion. Finally in 1976 he brought matters to a head when he denounced the state-sponsored union, blasted the government for its lack of economic planning, and decried the lack of punishment for those who had murdered the workers in 1970. Instead of speaking calmly in measured words as he wanted to do, he began shouting. The authorities took notice. Lech was soon out on the street looking for a job. For Walesa, the late 1970s were a time of defeat and failure on every level: political, social, and professional. But here and there people were uniting in groups that would eventually converge to force a showdown with the government. Groups like KOR began to call for participation of the workers in public affairs, and to demand democratic elections to all the top government jobs. The Church also began speaking out forcefully in favor of human rights and social justice. And the visit of the pope electrified the nation.

Walesa's personal life at the time was happy though he and Danuta and their family lived on a tight budget in two tiny rooms, the smallest only five feet wide. Every two years brought a new arrival to share their cramped space until there were five children. At night the bedding had to be dragged out and nearly filled the apartment. The only other furniture consisted of a few small pieces and a stencil machine for printing leaflets. Walesa would take his turn washing the babies' diapers and bathing and feeding the children, and he believes this physical contact brought him a closeness with them that has remained strong in spite of all the time he has had to spend

---

[22]Walesa, *A Way of Hope,* pp. 80–81.

away. He lavishes praise on his wife as the source of his strength and the chief adviser who has guided him in making many of his most important decisions. "She could penetrate intuitively," he said, "to the heart of things and suggest, in a word, the right tone to adopt, or the correct solution to most problems." She was also "a woman of surprising gentleness . . . [with] a kindliness . . . [that was] like an invitation to another sort of life, one that isn't all struggle."[23]

Lech next found a job overhauling vehicles, but this didn't last long either. Again he was fired for being a troublemaker. With three months of unemployment benefits coming to him, he delayed accepting another job and instead used the time organizing. He would set off every morning with his toolbox bulging with underground literature. On the pretext of seeking employment he would gain entry to a factory and distribute his leaflets. He and his friends also distributed leaflets at churches to people leaving mass. This had to be done quickly because people were afraid of being seen to linger.

When his benefits expired, he finally had to take a job with an engineering firm that produced electrical equipment. Described by a senior worker as "the best automobile electrician bar none," he was also very popular with his fellow workers. But he was a marked man and the police watched his every move. They would follow him to a job site and after he left would ask everybody what he had done, with whom he had talked, and about what. This approach, however, quickly backfired. Walesa gained the sympathy of many of the workers who saw the police harassing him, read his leaflets, and joined the discussions he held about free trade unions. The organizing was necessarily slow and Walesa didn't think there would be free trade unions in his lifetime.

Lech felt it was most important to keep alive the memory of his colleagues who were slain in 1970, and he was determined to attend the anniversary observance of their deaths. The police were on the lookout but he was smuggled into the shipyard and gave a rousing speech before seven thousand men and women gathered at the spot of the martyrdom. He spoke to them about his own experience of that terrible December and his own feelings of responsibility for what had happened. He urged them to form independent groups for their own defense, and to help one another. Many people took notice of him for the first time that day.

The stepped-up police surveillance around his apartment began to attract

23 Ibid., p. 90.

the notice of nearby residents who previously knew him only as the chap who put holy pictures in his window on feast days and led his family to church every Sunday. Neighbors began acting as sentinels to warn him when the police were coming. They also gave the police a hard time when they came to arrest him. On one occasion, when he was barricaded in his apartment with his family, the neighbors poured hot water from the windows on security agents and threw down slippers and anything else they could lay their hands on.

A Leader the Workers Could Trust

The rash of strikes that engulfed the country in the summer of 1980 began in response to food shortages. Soon, however, "routine rumblings about the high cost of food became something qualitatively different: a struggle for the nation's soul with a corrupt and discredited regime."[24] The focal point of the struggle quickly became the huge shipyards at Gdansk and a strike called by the Free Trades Union.

When the sirens blew announcing the strike on August 14, 1980, Walesa was on a streetcar going to work. As he watched the unmarked police car following him, he wondered if the whole thing wasn't a trick. Was the government plotting to entice the "troublemakers" into the open and then gun them down? Nevertheless he made his way to the shipyard, climbed the wall, and rallied the strikers with his famous cry, "We don't believe your lies anymore!"

Walesa was intent on not repeating the mistakes of 1970. There would be no marches or demonstrations, no chanting of anti-Soviet slogans, no attacks on Party buildings, nothing to provide a pretext for bloody reprisals. And he and the strike committee decided to hold off on their central demand—the right to organize autonomous trade unions—and stick at first only to limited issues: reinstatement of Walesa and Anna Walentynowicz, an organizer like Lech who had been fired; erection of a monument to the workers massacred by the police in 1970; and a pay raise of 2,000 zlotys per worker.

The strikers secured access to the shipyard radio station; this enabled them to keep workers in other parts of the shipyard fully informed about the negotiations. At the same time the authorities in Gdansk kept in close contact with the state radio and television stations. The high drama would

[24]Craig, *Lech Walesa and His Poland*, p. 168.

be played out before a large audience including a great crowd of towns-people gathered at the shipyard fence.

After only three days of negotiation, the strike committee, which had been enlarged by a contingent of less savvy workers, ran out of steam. The majority wisdom agreed to settle for the demands the authorities found easy to concede—reinstatement of the two dismissed workers, erection of the monument, and compromise on the pay raise. Disheartened, Lech left the room. Outside he faced an angry crowd of workers from all over who had joined the protest in support of the shipyard workers. The leader of the bus drivers cried out, "If you abandon us now, we are lost. Buses can't face tanks."[25] Lech did a quick about-face. "Of course we're still on strike," he asserted, and urged the workers to stay put. A new committee with more backbone was formed. They drew up twenty-one firm demands that cov-ered the major issues including the right to form an independent trade union, the right to strike, the rights to freedom of speech and of the press, the release of political prisoners, an overhaul of the economy, and the improvement of working conditions. The whole nation backed this bold-ness. The strikers bore the hopes and fears of all Poles.

Walesa would often say: "Religion is my peace and my strength." And the feeling was strong among the strikers that God was with them. Pictures of the Virgin Mary and the pope were everywhere visible on walls and on lapels. A cross stood prominently in the shipyard—a sign, Walesa said, that marked the cementing for many days of a communion of strikers involving several hundred different enterprises—shipyards, factories, offices, universi-ties, right down to the various unions, associations, and societies.[26] Within a week there were five hundred firms represented in the shipyard.

Walesa undauntedly pressed the struggle. "I fear nothing and nobody, only God," he declared, all the while communicating his sense of calm to the crowd. His charisma and intuitive sense of the people's feelings was nothing short of phenomenal. Each night as he summed up the day's nego-tiations, the crowd would chant LESZ-EK or WALESA. In response, he would smooth down his thick hair and unruly moustache and raise his fists clenched together. He was half-comedian, half-general, a man who mixed slightly off-color jokes with strategic talk—all with plenty of crude slang and broken grammar. Then at the end he would give the victory salute while the strikers roared with approval.

[25] Ibid., p. 171.
[26] Walesa, *A Way of Hope*, p. 126.

After some stalling, the government finally sent to Gdansk a top-flight negotiator, Mieczslaw Jagielski. His tactic at first was to try to beguile the strikers' committee with vague verbiage and promises. But by now Walesa had too much experience to fall for the trap and he insisted on a concrete response to each of the twenty-one demands. The biggest stumbling block was the first one—the right to have a totally independent union. It would mean repudiating the Party's favorite fiction, their claim to be the vanguard of the working class. A deadlock ensued and Jagielski flew back to Warsaw to confer with the Central Committee. The Russian bear was positively growling with alarm. In the meantime the bishops weighed in with an explicit statement spelling out "the inalienable rights of the nation: the right to freedom of worship, to a decent existence, to truth, to daily bread, to a true knowledge of the nation's history," and so on—a real litany of human rights. The Church had thrown down "a gauntlet . . . on behalf of the workers."[27]

Rumors flew that paratroopers were about to land in the shipyard. But the strikers stood fast, saying, "It is better to die standing than to live on our knees."[28] After the workers sang the national anthem, Walesa told them to sing a hymn to God too because now "we can't go any further without God." The Party finally yielded and the agreement was signed by Jagielski and Walesa; the two were flanked by the images of Lenin, the cross, and the Polish eagle. After coming outside, Walesa was hoisted onto the shoulders of the crowd and in celebration tossed again and again up into the air to the cry, "LESZ-EK, LESZ-EK!"

Writers were hard put to describe the exhilaration of the people at that point. Wordsworth's phrase might well have served: "It was bliss in that dawn to be alive, and to be young was very heaven." Feelings of pain and frustration so long dammed up now came pouring out and the sense of relief and joy exceeded all bounds. To be able to speak freely again after thirty-five years was an unimaginable delight. Everyone—farmers, workers, writers, students, journalists, teachers—seemed willing to build a new society based on honesty and freedom. Over 900,000 members of the Communist Party itself applied for membership in Solidarity, the name of the new, autonomous trade union, and the dingy Gdansk hotel that served as the new union's headquarters was swamped with visitors.

They all wanted to see Lech. He could solve any problem. He was the

---

[27]Craig, *Lech Walesa and His Poland,* p. 181.
[28]Ibid., p. 182.

uncrowned king of Poland. He was its long-awaited messiah, sitting at his desk under a crucifix. During that time, he especially needed daily mass, he said, "to defend myself against the power that corrupts, to remind myself to be careful . . . God may not need me but I need God as my support."[29] For the first time he was able to meet with the Polish primate, Cardinal Wyszynski, "who embraced me warmly, clasping me in his arms like a father." Walesa learned much from the cardinal, who had a strong sense of history and a profound notion of justice. In spite of his harsh treatment, Wyszynski, Walesa remembered, was magnanimous toward the leaders of the government who he thought were condemned by circumstances to be mere puppets. When Gierek fell from power, Wyszynski visited the deposed party leader to console him; he found him disoriented and in a state of collapse. On various occasions during the Polish revolution, it was Wyszynski who saved the day by his judicious interventions. At his death in May 1981, the quarter million people who attended his funeral in Warsaw's Victory Square heard him proclaimed, in a state-sponsored tribute unprecedented in the Communist world, a "man of great moral authority recognized by the nation."

Solidarity Flexes Its Muscles

Walesa needed all the wisdom he could muster for some nasty storms ahead. As any historian knows, the forces set in motion by any revolution—violent or nonviolent—are seldom those of pure reason. Poland's revolution was no exception. Once their chains were broken, workers all over the country found all sorts of reasons to go out on strike—for better wages, for better living conditions, to settle old scores with management, and so on. Lech was forced to travel around the country in his little white Fiat trying to put out the fires of malcontent. He firmly believed in the possibility of reconciliation and he constantly urged the workers "to forgive . . . We can't put all the corrupt officials in prison. After all, who would pay for their upkeep?" [30]

But the hardliners in the Party were no more attuned to his message of reconciliation than were many of the disgruntled workers. On November 19, 1980, the security police broke into Solidarity's office in Warsaw and arrested Jan Narozniak, a young helper. Zbigniew Bujak, the young Warsaw

[29] Ibid., p. 199.
[30] Ibid., p. 193.

Solidarity chairman, threatened a regional strike unless Narozniak was released immediately, and for good measure demanded a full investigation of police and security services. This frontal assault on the system itself shocked Polish officialdom; it also shocked Walesa and above all it shocked Leonid Brezhnev, the Soviet president. An invasion by the Red Army was staved off, it seems, only by the intervention of the pope himself, who assured Brezhnev of Poland's willingness to "help itself" and of the Church's willingness to continue as mediator.

Lech's hold over the rambunctious workers in Poland was limited. He pleaded with them to stop their wildcat strikes and give the government a chance to govern. "We must sit down at the same table with government representatives and talk with them," he insisted. But events were moving out of his control. Jan Rulewski, an aggressive and reckless local Solidarity leader, was not convinced of a strategy of reconciliation and called a strike to protest the refusal of authorities to sanction his Rural Solidarity Union. On March 19, 1981, while farmers discussed the matter at a meeting, a force of 200 policemen broke in, drove them out, and beat them severely. Solidarity's National Commission was outraged and wanted to call an all-out strike immediately. But Walesa was able to persuade them to call instead a four-hour warning strike. It turned out to be the largest labor disruption in the history of the Soviet empire. It also whetted the country's appetite for even more protest. Walesa was a high-risk gambler but he was not foolish. He took to heart Wyszynski's warning of the danger to Poland's freedom and territorial integrity, and managed to avert a prolonged general strike. In return the government made some gestures of good will including the relaxing of censorship. The response immediately showed how starved the people were for truth. They formed lines at the newsstands that were as long and as eager as those that had formed at butcher shops. Posters appeared everywhere with the words, "Freedom, Dignity, Equality."

Solidarity had given the people hope and a new sense of dignity. The spirit of renewal even touched the Communist Party, whose reformers were on the rise. An emergency Party congress was held in July to discuss radical reform. One of the ideas was to restructure the Party along horizontal lines rather than along the vertical lines established originally by Lenin. This would have transformed the Party along social democratic lines on the Western model, with control coming from the base. But Brezhnev's menacing noises soon put a stop to the would-be reformers. The congress trotted back into the Soviet fold, making it unmistakably obvious that the Party was impotent either to lead the nation or to prevent its economic downward slide.

In early September 1971, the First Solidarity Congress opened in the Oliwa sports stadium in Gdansk while Russian naval maneuvers took place in nearby waters. The delegates gathered with a strong sense of their responsibility before history as the country trembled on the brink of catastrophe. But they had little experience with democratic procedures and they also lacked Walesa's realistic sense of the possibilities and his political vision. They wasted enormous time in squabbles over procedure and then horrified Walesa by calling for a national referendum on the government's right to control the hiring and firing of workers. Walesa, knowing what chaos a referendum would cause, was barely able to get the referendum proposal rescinded. Many delegates resented what they regarded as Walesa's dictatorial ways, and in a heavily contested election for chairman he only squeaked by with 55 percent of the vote. In spite of the bickering and endless speechifying, the congress did succeed in drawing up a "masterly blueprint for the sort of society most people in Poland wanted."[31] It emphasized the need to restore respect for the spiritual values that had been so neglected. It called for a pluralist Poland with free elections and a truly representative parliament. It did not call for dismantling socialism or eliminating the Party, but it demanded a form of social ownership controlled by groups and individuals and not only by the state.

The Solidarity platform was a hot potato tossed at General Wojciech Jaruzelski, who now held all the reins of power as prime minister, party secretary, and military chief. (The wags wondered whether he wouldn't be named the new primate too.) A rather curious-looking person who wore horn-rimmed dark glasses, had immobile features, and carried himself with a stiff ramrod bearing, he claimed to be a man of peace. He called a "summit meeting" with Cardinal Jozef Glemp and Walesa and proposed a series of talks on a wide range of social issues.

But meanwhile the wildcat strikes continued to proliferate and the country was caught in a vicious circle. The deteriorating economy provoked workers to strike, while their strikes then caused a further deterioration of the economy. Influenced by a hysterical television campaign against Solidarity, people began to think that maybe only the army could save them. While he was being smeared in the media as a "great liar" and a "provocateur," leading a group of madmen, Walesa was actually trying to talk sense to the

[31] Ibid., p. 221.

workers and save the peace. But Solidarity's commission ignored his pleas and called for a national referendum on the legitimacy of the Communist Party. This of course handed Jaruzelski just the pretext he had been waiting for. At 12:30 A.M. on the night of December 12, 1981, as they ended their discussion, the Solidarity commission members found their telephones and telexes cut off. Jaruzelski had imposed martial law. Walesa rose and told the commission, "Now you've got what you've been looking for." He then went home to await events.

The Crow Against the Eagle

The government wasted no time in grabbing the leaders of Solidarity. The net was cast wide and soon 15,000 were seized—often in brutal fashion. Walesa himself was taken from his flat and flown by helicopter to Warsaw.

In a broadcast to the nation, Jaruzelski spoke of the country tottering on the edge of the abyss and the need to preserve the basic requisites of socialist renewal. Poland, he said, would be put under the control of a Military Council of National Salvation—WRON in Polish and henceforth referred to by the Poles as WRONA or "the crow." The crow will never defeat the eagle, they would say.

But for the time being the crow's power was supreme. A stringent curfew was imposed; trade unions were suspended; newspapers were proscribed, except those of the regime; and a ban was placed on almost all activities including meetings, demonstrations, sporting events, and even private motoring. Many industries and the media were placed under military rule with heavy punishments and even the death penalty for disobedience. There was a constant movement of troops and tanks in public spaces with police constantly checking identity cards and swooping down on any group of more than four. But the climate of repression did not deter half of the three million Party members from turning in their cards in disgust.

After interrogation, Lech was interned in a hunting lodge in a dense forest near the Soviet border. Kept in a small room under constant surveillance, he found solace in reading things like Cardinal Wyszynski's prison memoirs and books on the Church's social doctrine including *On Human Work,* the pope's 1981 encyclical on workers' rights. When he was not allowed to attend the christening of his seventh child, Brigid, in March, some 50,000 went in his stead. For Walesa the whole experience was just one more school of life. He said that life is a constant series of fresh starts and one should not get bogged down with regrets about the past. The important thing is to keep moving on. He firmly believed in the Gospel's insistence on forgiveness of one's enemies and could truly say he had no hatred in his heart. "I always see the cross of Christ . . . [who forgave His enemies]." [32]

In a bow to world opinion, the martial-law government released Walesa in November 1982 after eleven months of detention. He was greeted at his apartment by a large crowd of supporters. Carrying banners saying LECH WE WANT ONLY YOU AND SOLIDARITY, they saw a pasty-faced man considerably fatter than he was a year before and obviously not well. He tried to settle down, stay out of the limelight, and simply get to know his family again. But once more a smear campaign was mounted accusing him of various forms of misconduct, and pictures were circulated that supposedly showed him in compromising situations with women. To escape the sordidness, he and Danuta set off on a pilgrimage to Czestochowa where he prayed to the Blessed Mother for guidance.

In the meantime, Solidarity was officially outlawed as part of Jaruzelski's "normalization" program. Those who refused to be normalized and took to the streets in protest were made to pay, some dearly. Underground, Solidarity called for a boycott of the May Day parade and held an alternative demonstration in Warsaw's old city. The participants were attacked by the police with tear gas and missiles. Many were hurt and over a thousand arrested. In Lublin and Wroclaw, police fired on demonstrators, killing a number of them. Even people who were simply on their way to mass were attacked by the police and beaten. These outrages continued to widen the gulf between the government and the people, and as Walesa noted at the time, made a future reconciliation almost inconceivable. [33]

But Walesa held to his course. At a press conference held on his return home, he said, "I remain faithful to our cause, and he who is faithful remains so forever." [34] To carry on he set up an office in his small apartment. He kept up contact with members of Solidarity—those in the open and those in hiding. His flat was bugged and the police followed him wherever he went. Finally, to keep him under even tighter control, he was put back in his old job as an electrician in the Lenin Shipyard. As Mary Craig has observed, it says much about his character that a man who shortly before was recognized as the uncrowned king of Poland could return to his old job

---

[32] Ibid., p. 246.
[33] Walesa, *A Way of Hope*, p. 256.
[34] Ibid., p. 249.

of electrician without batting an eyelash. "I am a worker and that's all I ever want to be," he said.[35]

The Nation's Only Refuge

Once again as in the past the Church proved to be the nation's only refuge in times of trouble. As the voice of the voiceless, the bishops spoke out forcefully in defense of Solidarity and of the need to renew dialogue. They also set up centers of assistance—legal, material, medical, and spiritual—for victims of the crackdown. People crowded the churches—virtually the only places they could publicly gather—and vented their feelings in prayers and hymns whose words they sometimes changed. A congregation in Warsaw changed the last line of the hymn, "God who dost defend Poland," from the acceptable "Lord, keep our country free" to the defiant version that had been sung under czarist oppression, "Lord, return our homeland to us free." This rendition soon spread everywhere and, to the dismay of the authorities, was sung with great passion.[36] In some churches, Christmas cribs were used to get the message across. One priest was arrested for putting up a crib with the Blessed Mother weeping before a manger overturned by tanks and a baby Jesus wrapped in barbed wire. Instead of the shepherds, the priest had placed by the crèche eight figures representing miners murdered in the repression.

While the Church became increasingly the focal point of resistance, the authorities prepared for an even greater show of force. Moscow certainly wanted one, since they saw the Church as the main reason for the failure of socialism in Poland. A campaign to discredit the clergy was mounted. Scandals were magnified or invented altogether and efforts were made to set the clergy against each other by labeling some "loyalists" and others "extremists"—the whole bag of dirty tricks used by Stalinists in the late 1940s. But such attacks only increased the Church's credibility as people packed the churches day and night.

In June 1983 the pope again visited the demoralized country and was greeted by enormous crowds hungering for words of comfort. The authorities insisted he stay out of politics and stick to pious generalities. But he refused and denounced the misery inflicted by military rule on the people, or, as he put it, "the . . . humiliation, the loss of freedom, the injustice,

[35] Ibid., p. 257.
[36] Craig, *Lech Walesa and His Poland*, p. 241.

the trampling of human dignity underfoot." He also made many pointed references to his solidarity with the Polish church and his homeland.[37] It was not the kind of message that had galvanized Poland into action four years before. It was a message of comfort in its assurance that hatred and evil could be overcome by love. Lech Walesa, himself at a low point in his hopes, drew strength—"like an electric charge"—from his personal meeting with the pope, who insisted on it against the wishes of the authorities. Walesa remembered, "I watched him getting on the plane and saw his big shoes and giant clip-clopping stride. Each step seemed to express peace and faith."[38]

He needed this support, for the government had by now pulled out all the stops in its continual campaign of slander against him. The media tried to portray Lech as the "enemy of the people" and trumped up stories about gifts "the Yank from Gdansk" got from abroad and about a million dollars he had hidden in the Vatican Bank. A thirty-minute TV film, "Money," tried to expose him as a fraud and embezzler with tapes of a supposed conversation with his brother Stanislaw. The pressure was heavy and continual and there is little doubt that Walesa saved Solidarity during this period by his steadfast refusal to buckle. As one of his former critics said, "If it hadn't been for him we'd have had a pseudo–Solidarity . . . [we'd have gotten] what the government wanted, to destroy the movement by taking it over."

The riot police continued to terrorize the helpless populace, beating, kidnapping, torturing, and even killing, as was documented by the Polish Helsinki Committee on Violations of Human Rights. But Walesa continued to preach his philosophy of nonviolence and reconciliation. It was remarkable that, with all the provocation, no bombs were thrown, no police stations blown up, no officials kidnapped, and no violence used by demonstrators except for isolated instances. The Nobel Prize for Peace was awarded to Walesa in October 1983 to pay tribute to his strategy of peaceful negotiation. The Nobel Committee praised him in these terms:

> The electrician from Gdansk, the carpenter's son from the Vistula valley has managed to lift the banner of freedom and humanity so high that the whole world can once again see it.

Walesa received the award in absentia: The Communist authorities would not let him travel to Stockholm. In the acceptance speech that was read for him Walesa reflected that for forty years he had been surrounded by "vio-

---

[37] Ibid., p. 259.
[38] Ibid., p. 260.

lence, hatred and lies," but had learned the lesson that "we can effectively oppose violence only if we do not resort to it." As Timothy Garton Ash says: "It is hard to think of any previous revolution in which ethical categories and moral goals have played such a large part; not only in the theory but also in the practice of the revolutionaries, not only at the outset but throughout the Revolution . . . moreover, it is an indisputable fact that in sixteen months this revolution killed nobody . . . This extraordinary record of non-violence, this majestic self-restraint in the face of many provocations, distinguished the Polish revolution from previous revolutions."[39]

A Priest Without Fear

Next to Walesa, one of the most courageous voices in Poland and in the Church was that of Father Jerzy Popieluszko. Chaplain to the steelworkers, he began to say a weekly mass for Poland in January 1982 at his parish of St. Stanislaw Kostka in Warsaw. Popieluszko spoke openly to great crowds of "a nation terrorized by military force," and he recounted in detail the violations of human rights by the regime, the ill treatment of prisoners, and the attempts to incarcerate healthy people in psychiatric hospitals.

As a reporter for the *New York Times* wrote, nowhere else from East Berlin to Vladivostok did anyone stand before ten or fifteen thousand people and use a microphone to condemn the errors of state and party. Nowhere in that vast stretch encompassing some four hundred million people was anyone else openly telling a crowd that defiance of authority was an obligation of the heart, of religion, of manhood, and of nationhood.[40] He did not indulge in the hate-filled tirades his enemies alleged; he preached the need for love and forgiveness.

As one might expect, he was relentlessly harassed and spied upon, his car and his house were vandalized, and he was accused of holding rallies hostile to the state. Between January and June 1984 he was interrogated thirteen times and even his casual callers were intimidated. Agents of the government were planted in his congregation to heckle and to turn the service into a political brawl. The government media spokesman, Jerzy Urban, called him the "Savonarola of anti-Communism" and "a spreader of political rabies."[41]

[39]Timothy Garton Ash, *The Polish Revolution* (New York: Charles Scribner's and Sons, 1984), p. 282.

[40]George Weigel, *The Final Revolution* (New York: Oxford University Press, 1992), p. 149.

[41]Craig, *Lech Walesa and His Poland*, p. 280.

Finally some of the higher-ups decided that "one man should die for the sake of the people," and three employees of the interior ministry were chosen for the job. On the night of October 19, 1984, acting as traffic policemen, they stopped Popieluszko's Volkswagen as he and a friend, Waldemar Chrostowski, were returning from a workers' mass. The agents ordered Chrostowski out, handcuffed and gagged him, and put him in the police car. Then they returned to the Volkswagen and ordered Popieluszko out. After beating him unconscious and binding and gagging him, they threw him in the trunk of their Fiat and took off. However, when they slowed down to avoid hitting a motorcycle, Chrostowski was able to throw himself out of the car, roll down a hill, and get away as his handcuffs broke open. When Popieluszko came to and began pounding on the trunk, they stopped and opened the trunk to beat him again. Incredibly, he managed to get away and they gave chase. Catching him, they again beat him unconscious, tied him up again, and threw him back in the trunk. Then he came to again and started beating on the trunk. They stopped again and this time, after beating him unconscious, gagged him and tied him in such a way that he couldn't move without strangling himself. At a huge dam on the Vistula river they took his by then probably lifeless body and heaved it over the railing into the icy waters below.

Had Chrostowski not escaped, the crime would have been covered up and word put out that some accident had no doubt befallen the missing priest. But when the news of the priest's abduction broke, all of Poland reeled with the shock. Walesa issued a dire warning of the consequences if a hair of his head should be harmed, and thousands gathered at St. Stanislaw, Popieluszko's home parish, for prayer each evening. The agony of suspense lasted for ten days as the government issued appeals for public help and police using dogs and helicopters scoured the countryside. Finally, the horribly mutilated body of the priest was fished out of the river and, after the autopsy, was brought to the Church of St. Stanislaw for burial. The outpouring of grief at his funeral was unlike anything ever seen in Warsaw. Delegates from Solidarity came from all over the country. More than 350,000 people prayed before the catafalque. Cardinal Glemp, six bishops, and six priests performed the rites.

Three interior ministry security agents and their immediate superior in the ministry were found guilty of murder in a trial that lasted twenty-five days. Capital punishment was ruled out since they had acted not from "base motives," the judge said, but from "excessive zeal" for eliminating an "enemy of the State." The judge's statement, in fact, summed up the slant the regime tried to put on the crime: Popieluszko was no innocent victim but a man who had incited violence by his inflammatory and unjustified harangues against the state. The actions of the Church too were put in the darkest light and, as Chrostowski said, the trial was used to "spit on the Church."[42]

As the trial demonstrated, the regime had hardened substantially in its determination to stamp out all forms of dissent. Disappearances and unexplained accidents were rife, while arbitrary arrests, summary court procedures, and conviction of detainees on trumped-up criminal charges became commonplace. On May Day of 1985 the riot police, armed with their truncheons, flares, smoke bombs, and water cannon, were kept busy breaking up demonstrations throughout the country. Three prominent activists— Bogdan Lis, Adam Michnik, and Wladyslaw Frasyniuk—were arrested and found guilty of crimes against public order by a judge who displayed "breathtaking mendacity."

During this grim time, the Church more and more took on the form of an alternative society. It was only there that people could renew their faith in a better future and feel some sense of hearing the truth. As one priest put it, people came to their churches to find out "what the hell was going on in the rest of Poland."[43] Under the aegis of the Church, Polish culture flourished in a proliferation of exhibits, seminars, concerts, poetry readings, and films. At Lech Walesa's parish, St. Bridget's in Gdansk, for instance, the pastor, Father Jankowski, decorated the church with modern art works memorializing prisoners of conscience.

Walesa's Astounding Victory

Lech Walesa continued his remarkable performance as a rallying point for all the social forces leagued against the regime. He set up a new provisional council and brought Solidarity out into the daylight again. He continued to believe in the power of nonviolence. As he said: "People on our side are convinced that nothing will be achieved by raised voices and violent actions . . . When the moment comes for dialogue, we must be ready."[44] And indeed the record of nonviolence in the Polish struggle, as Mary Craig says, is impressive. Where else would one find an article entitled "How Can We

[42]Ibid., p. 287.
[43]Weigel, *The Final Revolution*, p. 153.
[44]Craig, *Lech Walesa and His Poland*, p. 300.

Love the Zomo [riot police]?" and expect it to be taken seriously?[45] "Ours are spiritual values which we can never lose," Walesa said, "they form us and explain us, which is why the West finds us difficult to understand."[46]

Several developments in 1987 augured well for the future of Solidarity. Soviet President Mikhail Gorbachev instituted his new policy of *glasnost,* which Jaruzelski supported. And at a meeting in Moscow in April, the two men signed an agreement to promote a more honest account of Soviet–Polish history including facing the truth about the Russian massacre of Polish officers at the Katyn Forest in 1940. On his visit in 1987, the pope also helped the cause of Solidarity by constant references to human rights, pluralism, and free association, and by granting Walesa an audience. But Cardinal Glemp now withheld support from the movement, regarding it as contaminated with leftists.

The economy continued its downward spiral and Jaruzelski, a career military officer, unsurprisingly proved to possess little sense of how to deal with issues of supply and demand. His worst mistake was to link Poland's economy more tightly with the Soviets and their slipshod market. In the meantime, Walesa continued to insist that political reform was the key to improving the economy. But the government continued to resist legalizing Solidarity and tried to rally the country behind its own reform plans by holding a referendum. When the referendum failed and a series of strikes broke out, Jaruzelski offered to negotiate a new deal with Walesa if he would call off the strikes. Once more the ball was in Walesa's court. Many of his advisers thought Walesa would undermine his authority if he called off the strikes for the sake of negotiating with Jaruzelski. But with his superb sense of timing, Walesa realized the moment for a deal had arrived. A series of round-table talks was held, involving more than 500 persons and the most important sectors of Polish society, including the Church.

Out of these talks came a new social contract. The accords announced on April 6, 1989, legalized Solidarity and gave it a minority representation in the Sejm, the lower house of parliament. The elections that were held two months later produced an astounding victory for Solidarity. Its candidates made a clear sweep of all the seats they contested for the Sejm and all but one of 100 seats available in the Senate, the higher house. Most of the Communist leadership was routed out of office by the electorate. For Walesa

---

[45] The article reported an interview with a prominent Polish priest, Father Józef Tischner, in 1984.

[46] Craig, *Lech Walesa and His Poland,* p. 303.

it was mind-boggling. "Too much grain has ripened for me," he said, "and I can't store it all in my granary."[47] It turned out that the Communist Party was unable to form a government because its satellite parties, the United Peasants and the Democratic Party, rebelled and joined with Solidarity in a majority coalition. The Communists themselves were now the opposition.

The burning question was whether the Soviet Union would permit a government in Eastern Europe not dominated by the Communists. At this point, Gorbachev "provided a last nudge" in a consultation by phone with Rakowski, the head of the Polish Communist Party.[48] This drove the final nail in the Communists' coffin. On August 24, 1989, Solidarity's Tadeusz Mazowiecki was installed as the first non-Communist prime minister of an East European state in almost forty years. It's no wonder Mazowiecki was so overwhelmed that he fainted dead away at the swearing-in ceremony.

The Post-Communist Blues

To revitalize Poland's moribund economy, the Mazowiecki government opted for "shock therapy"—a speedy conversion to a market economy that would free up prices and enable small businesses to get started. However, a huge cry of pain was soon heard from those hurt in the transition. Farmers lost their price supports and large industries employing thousands of workers lost their subsidies. In the meantime, Jaruzelski realized his day was done and resigned, and in the elections of 1990 Walesa was elected president. But the tally of votes showed that Walesa no longer had the commanding position in the public eye that he had held before the Communist wall came tumbling down. Solidarity also had lost some of its luster and splintered into a number of bickering parties. When the dust of the elections of 1991 settled, there were twenty-nine parties represented in the Sejm—six of the nine largest descended from Solidarity.

But the really bad news came with the parliamentary elections of September 1993 that returned two parties of ex-Communists to power. A reformist coalition that included Walesa's Solidarity trade union party failed to take into account the revised electoral law that disqualified any party that

---

[47] Gale Stokes, *The Walls Came Tumbling Down* (New York: Oxford University Press, 1993), p. 127.
[48] Ibid., p. 130.

got less than 5 percent. Hence, although cumulatively gaining 30 percent of the vote, the coalition failed to win any seats in parliament. But the much more realistic and pragmatic Communist bloc united, and, though they polled only 20 percent, took 35 percent of the seats and gained control of parliament.

As president, Walesa often blundered. He allied himself with unreconstructed elements in the army and security services; in a few years, he managed to wreck the movement that had brought him to power; he capped it all with a miserable performance in 1995 when he alienated many voters by his arrogant ranting and use of crude language in a debate with Kwasniewski, the ex-Communist who was elected president.

How explain the incredible way Walesa and the Solidarity activists threw away their political capital and allowed the ex-Communists to win the prize? As one observer wisely noted, the heroes of Solidarity were tough, uncompromising idealists, as they had to be to survive under the pressures inflicted on them by the Communist regime. But the very qualities that made them heroes ill prepared them for the arena of modern politics where pragmatism, the art of compromise, coalition-building, legal proficiency, administrative management, and media showmanship are all essential for success.[49]

The Catholic Church also contributed to the decline of the reformers. As a bulwark against totalitarianism, it had won nearly universal esteem. But it managed to squander much of this good will in the post-Communist era by its authoritarianism and its clumsy interventions in the political process. A prime example was the way it worked behind the scenes to secure an executive decree to reinstate religious education in the public schools, instead of trusting public debate to decide the issue. On another front, it twisted the arm of parliament to drive through the most restrictive anti-abortion law in Europe outside of Ireland.

Viva Walesa!

Whatever the future holds, Lech Walesa will always be honored as the indomitable leader in the great revolution of conscience that helped to overturn a totalitarian society. Wherever people are struggling against op-

---

[49]Radek Sikorski, "How we lost Poland: Heroes do not make good politicians," *Foreign Affairs* (Sept.–Oct. 1996): 15f.

pressive regimes, his courageous stand for justice and human rights will stand as a beacon, a singular example of the achievement of great social change inspired by faith and by a vision of social justice he imbibed from the Church.

Index

Page numbers appearing in italic type refer to pages that contain illustrations.